UNIVERSITY CASEBOOK SERIES®

SALES

CASES AND MATERIALS

EIGHTH EDITION

MARION W. BENFIELD, JR.
University Professor of Law Emeritus
Wake Forest University School of Law
and Albert E. Jenner Professor Emeritus
University of Illinois College of Law

MICHAEL M. GREENFIELD
George Alexander Madill Professor of Contracts and Commercial Law
Washington University in St. Louis School of Law

FOUNDATION
PRESS

University Casebook Series is a trademark registered in the U.S. Patent and Trademark Office.

© 1980, 1986, 1992, 2004 FOUNDATION PRESS
© 2007, 2011 THOMSON REUTERS/FOUNDATION PRESS
© 2015 LEG, Inc. d/b/a West Academic
© 2020 LEG, Inc. d/b/a West Academic
    444 Cedar Street, Suite 700
    St. Paul, MN 55101
    1-877-888-1330

Printed in the United States of America

ISBN: 978-0-314-29076-2

To Dalida and Claire

PREFACE

This book originated in 1936 as Bogert and Britton, *Sales*, and in 1962 became Bogert, Britton and Hawkland, *Sales and Security*. After widespread enactment of the Uniform Commercial Code, in 1980 the book became Benfield and Hawkland, *Sales*, and enjoyed four editions. The fifth edition, which became Benfield and Greenfield, continued the basic structure of its predecessors. The main difference, continued in this edition, is a shift to the heavier use of problems. Many principal cases have been dropped or converted into notes; they have been replaced by a smaller number of new principal cases, many new or revised textual passages, and numerous new or revised problems. This latest edition also substitutes several new cases for older ones and adds new notes and problems. The primary substantive focus is Article 2 of the Uniform Commercial Code, but the book also considers Article 2A and the Convention on Contracts for the International Sale of Goods. It also addresses UCC Articles 5, 6, 7, and 9 insofar as those Articles affect the rights of buyers and sellers of goods.

Early editions of the book were designed primarily for use in upper-level courses on Sales, but they also were used successfully in first-year Sales courses. With its emphasis on developing the skills of dealing with a comprehensive statute and its reliance on the use of problems, the book remains suitable for both first-year and upper-level courses.

The primary criterion for selection of materials to be included in the book is effectiveness as teaching materials. Some are included for their description of the underlying business transaction; some are included for their exposition of the law; but all are included for the platform they create for exploring the rules and, especially, the methodology of the Code.

In the course of editing the judicial opinions, I have omitted numerous citations and footnotes without any notation of the omissions. The footnotes that remain bear their original numbers, and footnotes designated by letters or asterisks are explanatory footnotes that I have added to the opinions. I have corrected obvious typographical and grammatical errors in reprinted materials without using the conventional "sic." All references to Articles 2 and 2A are to the current official versions. References to Article 1 are to the 2001 revised version, which has been enacted in every state.

In preparing this edition, I am extremely grateful for the broad shoulders of Professors Benfield and Hawkland, two of the preeminent commercial law scholars of the twentieth century. Their work has provided a most solid foundation for me to build on, and Professor Benfield has reviewed the copy for this edition.

MICHAEL M. GREENFIELD

St. Louis, Missouri
July 2020

v

SUMMARY OF CONTENTS

TABLE OF CONTENTS

TABLE OF CASES

The principal cases are in bold type.

UNIVERSITY CASEBOOK SERIES®

SALES

CASES AND MATERIALS

EIGHTH EDITION

CHAPTER 1

INTRODUCTION

A. ORGANIZATION OF THE BOOK AND GOALS OF THE COURSE

This book deals with the sale and leasing of goods, an area of the law that ranges from simple transactions that sometimes involve unsuspecting consumers to multi-million dollar deals between commercial giants; from face-to-face arrangements to complicated documentary agreements that bring together a seller, buyer, carrier, insurance company, bank, and perhaps others. One focus of this book is the substantive law governing these various contracts: a close and hard look at the substantive law set forth in Articles 2 and 2A of the Uniform Commercial Code ("UCC" or "Code") as clarified by Article 1 and augmented by Articles 5, 7, and 9 of the UCC.

The book has a second and equally important focus: to develop the skills of understanding and using the UCC, a sophisticated and far-ranging statute that governs a substantial portion of the matters commonly associated with private law. The methodological emphasis in the first-year Contracts course typically is primarily on case law, on developing the important skills of reading cases carefully for their full factual and legal meanings, of synthesizing them, of distinguishing them, and of seeing their total importance and impact in a social and economic setting. In that study you may have considered, incidentally, some of the provisions of Article 2 of the UCC, such as, for example, section 2–207 dealing with the "battle of the forms." These exercises were important studies of some aspects of substantive law but they seldom were aimed at developing your skill in handling the legislative materials that make up the UCC. That is a primary mission of this book.

The goals of this book—to impart the substantive law of sales and leasing, including knowledge of the commercial background necessary to a full understanding of the operation of that law, and to teach the methodology of the UCC—involve a curious paradox. The substantive law of sales and leasing probably best can be taught by concentrating on the rules of law announced by the UCC, its Official Comments, and the cases decided under it, supplemented by expository text to assure full coverage. Such a concentration, however, disserves the effort to help you to learn how to use the UCC specifically and handle a complicated statute generally, because this assignment is best carried out by wrestling with statutory language in the resolution of problems without the aid of cases or commentary. But, just as an excessive emphasis on substantive law and commercial background can defeat the goal of learning UCC methodology, a too-rigid concentration on methodology can leave one with insufficient knowledge of the substantive law and the basic facts underlying sales and leasing transactions to put that methodology to its most effective use. We have tried to resolve this paradox by selecting principal cases in which judges reveal the commercial background and articulate the competing interests underlying the rules of law used in the cases, supplemented by expository text to fill gaps, all toward the end of developing competence in the applicable substantive law, and by using these same cases, plus numerous problems and thought-provoking questions to develop skills in handling the UCC.

The organization of the book is based on a logical consideration of the applicable law broken down into its component parts. The law of sales and leasing must answer four basic contract questions and two property questions. The contract questions are, (1) How are contracts formed? (2) Once formed, what are their terms? (3) How are those terms performed—i.e. what things must the parties do in the proper performance of those terms? and (4) What happens if they are not properly performed—i.e. what remedies are available upon breach? The property questions are, (1) Who has title to the goods? and (2) What are the rights of bona fide purchasers and creditors? The book follows this structure, departing from it only by a special treatment of documentary sales in its concluding chapter.

In 1986 the United States ratified the Convention on Contracts for the International Sale of Goods, which had been promulgated by the United Nations in 1980. That Convention often will apply to sale of goods contracts entered into between a party in the United States and a party in one of the other countries (at present more than 70) that also have ratified the Convention. We will frequently refer to the Convention.

B. BACKGROUND AND HISTORY OF THE UCC

1. SPONSORS

The Uniform Commercial Code is the most successful product of the uniform state law movement, which began in the 1890s. The Code is the joint product of two organizations, the National Conference of Commissioners on Uniform State Laws and the American Law Institute. Following is a brief description of the two bodies.

a. THE NATIONAL CONFERENCE OF COMMISSIONERS ON UNIFORM STATE LAWS

In 1890 a committee of the American Bar Association proposed that the states set up a national organization to prepare legislation on matters as to which uniform laws would be desirable which could then be adopted by all states. By 1892 New York had adopted legislation authorizing the appointment of commissioners to work with commissioners from other states to prepare uniform laws to be offered for adoption in the various states. In that year the first meeting of the National Conference of Commissioners on Uniform State Laws (NCCUSL) was held in Saratoga, New York. Commissioners from seven states attended that meeting.

In 1896 the Commissioners offered their first act, the Uniform Negotiable Instruments Act, which was ultimately adopted in all jurisdictions. Other uniform acts followed, including the Uniform Sales Act and the Revised Uniform Sales Act, the Uniform Conditional Sales Act, the Uniform Trust Receipts Act, and many others in both commercial and non-commercial areas.

Today NCCUSL also is known as the Uniform Law Commission (ULC). It is a government-supported organization, and each state appoints Commissioners to represent it. The primary financial support for the Commission comes from assessments levied against the states based on population. Each act of the Commission is drafted by a committee of commissioners, often with the help of a law professor acting as reporter-drafter. The drafting committee seeks advice from persons and organizations knowledgeable and interested in the area and invites the American Bar Association to send advisors to committee meetings. The entire Commission, composed now of more than 300 commissioners representing all states, the District of Columbia, Puerto Rico, and the Virgin Islands, meets annually for seven or eight days to discuss drafts of proposed acts. Under ULC rules each act must be read line by line at two annual meetings before promulgation. Often acts are before the Commission for four or five years, and sometimes longer, before they finally are approved. After approval, the Commission submits them to the House of Delegates of the American Bar Association for approval. Occasionally, concerns expressed by the ABA lead to redrafting of an act.

b.   THE AMERICAN LAW INSTITUTE

The American Law Institute (ALI) was created in 1923 as the result of a proposal by a committee of the Association of American Law Schools that a "juristic center" be set up to "promote the clarification and simplification of the law and its better adaption to social needs, to secure the better administration of justice, and to encourage and carry on scholarly and scientific work." The first work of ALI was preparation of restatements of the law in such areas as contracts, torts, property, trusts, and so on. As you already know from your other law school courses, the Restatements have been very influential. ALI also proposes Principles to govern emerging areas of the law (e.g., Principles of Software Contracts) and Model Acts (e.g., Model Penal Code).

ALI is a private, non-profit, self-perpetuating body composed of lawyers, judges, and law professors from all over the country. New members are nominated by present members of ALI and then approved by a membership committee and by the Council of ALI. There are about 3,000 elected members of ALI and a number of ex officio members such as the deans of all law schools approved by the American Bar Association, the chief justices of all state supreme courts, the presidents of the state bar associations, and many others.

ALI does its drafting work through reporters who work with a group of advisors and members of ALI who join consultative groups. It, like ULC, meets annually to discuss proposed drafts of Restatements and other projects. In addition to the drafting activities of ALI, it provides organizational and staff support for a substantial continuing legal education program in cooperation with the American Bar Association.

———

2. THE INITIAL DRAFTING HISTORY

The following excerpt describes the initial drafting of the Code in the 1940s and 50s.

Malcolm, The Uniform Commercial Code in the United States*
BACKGROUND AND HISTORY OF THE UNIFORM COMMERCIAL CODE—PERIOD 1938–52

In 1938, a proposal was sponsored by the Merchants Association of New York City for a federal sales Act to govern all interstate sales transactions. In response to this indication of the inadequacies in the Uniform Sales Act, the National Conference of Commissioners on Uniform State Laws undertook revision of the Uniform Sales Act which it had prepared in 1906. . . . In 1940, the National Conference adopted a proposal to prepare a uniform commercial code embracing a modernisation and co-ordination of the Uniform Sales Act . . . and all other Uniform Acts in the field of commercial law, with new provisions where no uniform Acts existed on important and closely related commercial problems. The American Law Institute joined in the undertaking the following year. . . .

Between 1945 and 1952 a great number of drafts and re-drafts of parts of the proposed code were prepared by a reportorial staff supervised by an Editorial Board.[8] They were considered successively by advisory groups of judges, lawyers and law teachers; by the Council of the American Law Institute and special Sections of the National Conference of Commissioners on Uniform State Laws; and then by the general membership of the two organisations. In preparing the several drafts and re-drafts, the reporting and advisory groups also consulted with individuals and organisations in business and banking circles in many parts of the country who had come forward with criticisms. . . .

---

  * 12 Inter. & Comp.L.Q. 226 (1963).

  [8] The Chief Reporter for the Code was the late Professor Karl N. Llewellyn of the University of Chicago Law School and the Associate Chief Reporter was Professor Soia Mentschikoff of the same Law School.

A final text of the proposed Code was completed in September 1951 and at that time was approved by the two Sponsoring Organisations and was also approved by the House of Delegates of the American Bar Association. During the next year a limited number of further amendments were made and in October 1952 an official edition of the Code with explanatory comments was published as the *1952 Official Text and Comments Editions.*

————

Pennsylvania adopted the Code in 1953 and by 1967 the District of Columbia and all the states except Louisiana had adopted the Code. Louisiana lawyers felt that the Code was incompatible with Louisiana's civil law system, but ultimately the state adopted all Articles of the Code except Articles 2 and 2A.

3. SCOPE OF THE UNIFORM COMMERCIAL CODE

The Code as originally adopted contained nine Articles, which are briefly summarized below.

Article 1. General Provisions. The other Articles of the Code each applies to a particular type of transaction. Article 1, on the other hand, has no specific transactional coverage, but rather states definitions and general rules applicable to any transaction covered by any of the other Articles. Article 1 was revised in 2001, and every state has enacted it.

Article 2. Sales. This Article covers sales of goods and is the primary focus of this course. ALI and NCCUSL approved extensive amendments to Article 2 in 2003, but no state enacted them, and they have been withdrawn.

Article 3. Commercial Paper. Article 3 covers negotiable instruments, including negotiable notes and checks. Amendments in 1990 and 1991 were widely enacted, but additional amendments in 2002 have been adopted in only about a dozen jurisdictions.

Article 4. Bank Deposits and Collections. Article 4 covers bank handling of checks and other items. The emphasis in the Article is on the rights and duties of banks between themselves and as against their customers as they take checks for collection and pay checks drawn on the account of their customers. Article 4 was amended in 1990.

Article 5. Letters of Credit. This brief Article covers some of the rules applicable to letters of credit. Letters of credit guaranteeing sellers that the price of goods will be paid are used often in international sales transactions. Article 5 was amended in 1995 and has been adopted by every state. The last chapter of this casebook addresses some aspects of letters of credit.

Article 6. Bulk Transfers. This Article imposes an obligation on buyers of a major part of the inventory of certain types of business to notify creditors of the seller so that the creditors can take steps to see that the seller pays its debts. On the recommendation of NCCUSL and ALI in 1989, all jurisdictions but Alaska and Maryland have repealed Article 6. Chapter 11 briefly addresses bulk sales.

Article 7. Documents of Title. Article 7 states rules applicable to the issuance and transfer of warehouse receipts and bills of lading. A revised Article 7 was promulgated in 2003 and has been adopted by all states.

Article 8. Investment Securities. Article 8 covers the issuance and transfer of stocks, bonds, and other investment securities. It was amended in 1994, and all states have enacted the amendments.

Article 9. Secured Transactions. Article 9 covers security interests in personal property. A security interest is an interest in property which secures performance of an obligation. The Article states rules on creation of the interest and the rights of the creditor to foreclose on the property if the debtor defaults on the secured obligation. It also states priority rules as between secured parties and as between a secured party and buyers or lien creditors. Article 9 was substantially revised in 1999, and all states have enacted the revision.

Two additional articles have been added to the original nine: Articles 2A and 4A.

Article 2A. Personal Property Leases. In 1989 the Code sponsors promulgated Article 2A covering leases of personal property. Modeled on Article 2, many of its provisions are identical to the provisions in Article 2. This book covers many provisions of Article 2A. The 2003 revision of Article 2 also included corresponding changes in Article 2A. No state enacted them, and they, too, have been withdrawn.

Article 4A. Funds Transfers. Also promulgated in 1989, Article 4A deals with systems for the transfer of funds in which the transferor directs its bank to transfer the funds to a third party (as opposed to transferring funds by sending a check to the third party). These systems usually involve transfers between banks by rapid electronic means. If the transferor is a consumer, a federal statute (the Electronic Funds Transfer Act) governs.

4. PERMANENT EDITORIAL BOARD

When the Code was originally promulgated, ALI and NCCUSL decided that a permanent body should be created and charged with the duty of oversight over the Code. In 1962 they organized the Permanent Editorial Board (PEB) for the Uniform Commercial Code, and each appointed five members to serve on it. The Board's first function was to secure uniform adoption of the Code. In its early years, therefore, it spent much of its time fending off proposed amendments to the Code. But as the Code became widely adopted, the PEB was able to turn its attention to needed improvements in the Code. Today the PEB, now composed of six members each from the two sponsoring organizations, meets periodically to discuss Code issues and make recommendations to ALI and NCCUSL as to possible drafting projects. The PEB itself does not engage in drafting, but from time to time it issues Commentaries on matters as to which the Code seems unclear or as to which some courts have taken positions that the Board believes to be inconsistent with the language or policy of the Code.

C. THE CODE AS "CODE"

A basic issue relative to interpretation of the Uniform Commercial Code is whether the Code is just another statute, bigger than most, but basically like all other statutes in a common-law jurisdiction, or whether, on the other hand, it is a code in the manner of civil-law systems. Following are short excerpts on the point from two of the era's foremost authorities on commercial law.

Hawkland, Uniform Commercial Code Methodology[*]

THE CODE CONCEPT

Although American lawyers tend to treat them as synonyms, there is a vast difference between a "code" and a "statute." This terminological confusion did not exist in earlier times, because then the word "code" had no legal meaning. The leading legal dictionary failed to list it as a term as late as the year 1797. This omission, it is believed, was not due to the fact that the word was completely missing from our legal nomenclature, but to the absence of the concept from our legal system. "The word was at hand, ready for use," reports Charles Hepburn, "but at this time, the beginnings of the nineteenth century, there was no one thing, actual or clearly designed, in the legal system of either England or the United States, to which 'code' was naturally and specifically applicable."

Several events occurred around 1800 to bring the term into general legal usage. The French substantially codified their law between the years 1804 and 1810, the same period during which Bentham was announcing a new jurisprudence proclaiming the merits of a "complete Code of Laws." Bentham's views were dramatically brought to the attention of the American bar when he offered to prepare for President Madison a complete code of laws for use by the American states. During this period, Edward Livingston was actually drafting Codes for Louisiana, and this too undoubtedly served to make lawyers aware of the new term.

While these developments brought the ancient word "code" into common legal usage, its meaning was rendered ambiguous by virtue of the fact that no American State, save Louisiana, had adopted the code concept as part of its jurisprudence. Thus the term was employed in different ways to mean "statute," "jurisprudence of a single subject,"

---

[*]   1962 U.Ill.L.Forum 291. The author's citations of authority are omitted.

"commissioner's manuscript," "all the statutes of the state," and "large part of the general laws of the state." Lawyers still use the term loosely, but presently it seems to be employed most frequently to connote a statute which regulates an area previously left to decisional law.

There is a wide difference between such a statute and a true code. A "code" is a pre-emptive, systematic, and comprehensive enactment of a whole field of law. It is pre-emptive in that it displaces all other law in its subject area save only that which the code excepts. It is systematic in that all of its parts, arranged in an orderly fashion and stated with a consistent terminology, form an interlocking, integrated body, revealing its own plan and containing its own methodology. It is comprehensive in that it is sufficiently inclusive and independent to enable it to be administered in accordance with its own basic policies.

A mere statute, on the other hand, is neither pre-emptive, systematic, nor comprehensive, and, therefore, its methodology is different from that of a code.

SYSTEMATIC CONSIDERATIONS

Since a true code pre-empts a large body of law and comprehensively deals with all of its parts, it obviously must be constructed systematically. This requires: (1) That its provisions be logically presented and coordinated and stated in language employing a chosen and consistent terminology; (2) that means be made available to handle competing and conflicting rules; (3) that means be provided to fill the gaps; and (4) that supereminent provisions be present to mitigate harshness which might otherwise flow from rigid rules.

The Uniform Commercial Code meets these requirements. Its provisions, following the organizational plan of most European codes, are logically divided into interlocking "articles," each handling one major subdivision of the entire subject. The first and last articles do not cover any traditional field of law. Article 1, instead, sets forth principles and definitions of general application, and article 10 provides rules relating to uniform construction, saving clauses, repealers, and the effective date. Subject to these general provisions, all the rules on sales are collected in article 2; commercial paper in article 3; bank deposits and collections in article 4; letters of credit in article 5; bulk transfers in article 6; documents of title in article 7; investment securities in article 8; and secured transactions in article 9.

A chosen and consistent terminology runs through the Code, a matter made possible by the forty-six generally-applicable definitions presented in article 1. These definitions, by and large, are both "conventional" and "real" in the jurisprudential sense. That is, they communicate to others conventional meanings and state real or essential attributes of the things defined.

METHODOLOGICAL IMPLICATIONS

Because the Uniform Commercial Code is a true code and states its own aims, courts construing it should make three changes in their standard legal method. They should: (1) use analogy, rather than "outside" law, to fill code gaps; (2) rely somewhat more heavily on the decisions of other code states in making their own decisions; and (3) give their own decisions somewhat less permanent precedential value.

———————

Kripke, Principles Underlying the Drafting of the Uniform Commercial Code*

Whatever may have been in the academicians' desire for more thorough-going changes in the law, it was recognized that, in order to be promulgated by the sponsor organizations as their product, the Code had to be conceived as a fundamentally conservative piece of amendatory legislation. The Code was prepared as a joint enterprise of its sponsors, the American Law Institute (whose prior work had been in the field of restatement of the law) and the National Conference of Commissioners on Uniform State Laws (the principal thrust of whose labors had been toward *uniformity*, not radical revamping). The drafts had to be approved by the Joint Editorial Board, by a Section of the National Conference, and by the joint membership meetings of the two organizations. The final product then had to be approved by the House of Delegates of the American Bar Association. While these institutions contain a sprinkling of judges and law school professors, fundamentally their membership is drawn from lawyers who have the interest and the ability to devote time to legal matters beyond the making of a living, i.e., principally the successful partners of established law firms with a corporate or other monied practice. Needless to say, the overall social, economic, and legal bent of such persons is conservative. As was proved with issue after issue on the floor of the joint meetings and in the work of the committees or sections, these lawyers instinctively react in opposition to any fundamental reshaping of the relative strengths of debtor and creditor, of secured creditor and unsecured creditor, of buyer and seller, of warehouseman and depositor, of carrier and bailor, or of bank and depositor. While they are willing to rectify matters where the law had developed lack of uniformity, their natural bent was opposed to change where the existing law presented a clear pattern.

It is fair to say that the draftsmen of the Code had an anticodification or antistatute predilection. They did not want to codify the law, in the continental sense of codification. They wanted to correct some false starts, to point the law in the indicated directions, and to restore the law merchant as an institution for growth only lightly kept in bounds by

———————

*   1962 U.Ill.L.Forum 321.

statute. To the present writer, the express statutory injunctions to give effect to all of the nonstatutory influences for growth are so strong that continental codification is a misleading analogy. The drafters did not intend that the solution to problems within the ambit of the Code must be found in the confines of the statute. Indeed, the drafters found themselves able in the official comments to extrapolate additional rules from the statutory text by repeated reference to the nonstatutory principles of decision.[56]

————

The debate as to whether the UCC is a true code or a mere statute has proved to be mainly important in determining the scope and meaning of 1–103(b), which provides:

> Unless displaced by the particular provisions of [the Uniform Commercial Code], the principles of law and equity, including the law merchant and the law relative to capacity to contract, principal and agent, estoppel, fraud, misrepresentation, duress, coercion, mistake, bankruptcy, and other validating or invalidating cause supplement its provisions.

Statutes (including the UCC), like cases, often fail to meet precise questions with precise answers. Many commercial disputes, of course, fit more or less easily under one or more sections of the UCC, and the courts have resolved them, by and large, by reference to these sections, with no need to go outside the Code for answers. This process seems to be employed instinctively in most situations and not as the result of any explicit jurisprudential pondering. On the other hand, there are some commercial law situations for which the UCC intentionally provides no answer, and in these cases the courts resort to the common law for solution or supplementation, justifying their approach by pointing to 1–103. In between these extremes a number of situations can be found in which a case obviously falls within the scope of a Code article (e.g., it clearly involves the sale of goods and thus falls under Article 2 of the UCC) but does not fit easily under any particular Code section. An ultimate question of great importance is whether such a case is to be resolved by the Code or by the common law, and the courts are divided on this matter. Those desiring to stay within the Code frequently utilize the technique of analogy in these cases, whereas other courts find justification in 1–103 to apply outside law. This division of opinion is not along any jurisdictional lines but tends to occur within each jurisdiction depending on the kind of case that is before the court and how it is

---

[56] For examples of instances where the comments seem to state rules going beyond anything found in the text, see § 2–305, comment 4; the comments to §§ 2–306, 2–604, 2–607, and § 2–716, comment 2. So strongly did some of the participants in the drafting process feel about the breadth of the comments that the final Code omitted an earlier provision referring to the official comments as legislative history available for interpretation. ALI & Nat'l Conference of Comm'rs on Uniform State Laws, Uniform Commercial Code 1952 Text and Comments § 1–102(3)(f), comment 2.

argued. There are valuable lessons to be learned from these cases, not the least of which is that philosophical ideas *do* play a role at least on the fringes.

CHAPTER 2

Scope of Article 2

Like most of the other Articles making up the UCC, Article 2 has a "scope" section (2–102) that, to a considerable extent, prescribes its coverage. This chapter examines the factors that courts consider in determining whether Article 2 is applicable.

A. The Sales-Service Hybrid

Section 2–102 provides that Article 2 "applies to transactions in goods." Sometimes it is easy to determine whether a transaction is within the scope of Article 2, e.g., a contract for the sale of a new or used ambulance (yes) or a contract for a haircut at a styling salon (no). But often a transaction concerns both goods and services. For example, in National Historic Shrines Foundation, Inc. v. Dali, 4 UCC Rep.Serv. 71 (N.Y.Sup.Ct.1967), a charitable organization sued the well-known artist, Salvador Dali, for breach of an alleged oral contract to appear on a television program designed to raise funds for the organization. As part of the program Dali was to paint before the cameras a picture of the Statue of Liberty and at the end of the program present the completed painting to the plaintiff, to be sold for its charitable purposes. Plaintiff estimated that the value of the painting would be $25,000. Dali denied making the contract, set up the statute of frauds of 2–201 of the UCC, and moved for summary judgment. Is this a transaction in goods, and therefore within the scope of Article 2? The court held not, that 2–201 was not applicable because the alleged transaction between plaintiff and Dali was for the rendition of services and not the sale of goods. Therefore, summary judgment was denied, and plaintiff was given the opportunity to prove that it had made the alleged agreement with Dali.

Did the court reach the right result in *Dali*? Didn't the alleged contract call for Dali to hand over a painting? Isn't the painting "goods"?

If an attorney contracts to prepare a will for a client, does Article 2 apply? No doubt your instinctive reaction is, no. But what reasoning leads you to this conclusion?

Problem. Tanner contracted with Poolco for the installation of an in-ground swimming pool in her back yard. Tanner agreed to pay $27,000, and Poolco agreed do the complete job, including excavation, supplying and pouring concrete for the pool and deck, installation of a ladder and diving board, and restoration of the lawn when the work was done. Poolco performed, and Tanner paid the agreed price. A month later Tanner slipped on the diving board and hit her head on the edge of the pool. She sues alleging that the diving board was poorly designed and was not fit for its ordinary purpose, thereby breaching the implied warranty of merchantability mandated by 2–314. Poolco defends by arguing that the contract was not a transaction in goods and therefore the rules of Article 2, including 2–314, do not apply. Which party is right: does Article 2 apply to this transaction? (In addition to 2–102, be sure to consult 2–103.)

BMC Industries, Inc. v. Barth Industries, Inc.

United States Court of Appeals, Eleventh Circuit, 1998.
160 F.3d 1322.

[Plaintiff, BMC Industries, manufactured eyeglass lenses. It decided to become the first company to automate production of the lenses and entered into a contract with defendant under which for $515,200 defendant would develop an automated production line and then produce, deliver, and install four of them. The contract required all modifications to be in writing. The original delivery date under the contract was June 1987. Subsequent written modifications extended the delivery date to October. However, the defendant encountered a number of difficulties and notified plaintiff that delivery would be delayed. First, defendant said it would deliver in December. Then, experiencing further problems, defendant moved the delivery date to April 1988, but also failed to meet that date. In August 1988 plaintiff was concerned that defendant would not perform and asked for assurances. It received a promise from Nesco, the parent company of defendant, that defendant would perform. Defendant finally tendered the production line in May or June of 1989, but plaintiff rejected delivery and brought suit.]

■ TJOFLAT, CIRCUIT JUDGE.

. . .

BMC's breach of contract count alleged that the second written amendment to the Contract established October 1987 as the deadline for Barth's performance. Because Barth failed to deliver the automated equipment by that date, Barth was in default of its contractual obligations. . . .

As an affirmative defense to BMC's breach of contract claim, Barth asserted that BMC's conduct after the October 1987 delivery date had passed amounted to a waiver of the delivery date under Article 2 of the Uniform Commercial Code ("UCC"). Although Barth failed to deliver the machines by October 1987, Barth argued, BMC executives urged Barth to keep working, BMC engineers continued to assist Barth in overcoming technical problems, and BMC executives agreed to increase the purchase price. Therefore, Barth claimed, BMC waived its entitlement to delivery of the machines in October 1987.

. . .

Additionally, Barth counterclaimed against BMC for breach of contract. Barth repeated its argument that BMC's conduct amounted to a waiver of the October 1987 delivery date, and asserted that the delivery deadline therefore became indefinite. Because Barth tendered the machines within a reasonable amount of time, Barth substantially performed its contractual obligations. Consequently, Barth claimed, BMC's refusal to accept delivery of the machines in May 1989 constituted breach of the Contract. . . .

[The trial court held that the transaction was not governed by Article 2 and that under Florida common law a waiver is not effective unless there is consideration or detrimental reliance. The court gave judgment for plaintiff on the jury verdict of three million dollars against Barth and two million dollars against Nesco, and it rejected defendant's counterclaim. Defendant appealed.]

On appeal, Barth contends that the district court erred when it concluded that the UCC did not apply to the Contract, and thus did not govern the waiver issue. Had the court applied the UCC, Barth argues, it would have concluded that BMC waived the October 1987 delivery date, and therefore breached the Contract by refusing to accept delivery in May 1989. . . .

[First] we consider whether the Contract was predominantly a transaction in goods (and thus governed by the UCC) or in services (and thus governed by the common law), and . . . [then] we examine whether BMC waived the October 1987 delivery date through its conduct after the delivery date had passed. . . .

The district court held that the Contract was predominantly for services rather than goods, and that the UCC was therefore inapplicable. We disagree.

The UCC's Article 2 only applies to "transactions in goods." Fla. Stat. Ch. 672.102 (1997). Goods are defined as "all things (including specially manufactured goods) which are movable at the time of identification to the contract for sale other than the money in which the price is to be paid, investment securities (chapter 678) and things in action." Fla. Stat. Ch. 672.105(1) (1997). A contract that is exclusively for services, therefore, is not governed by Article 2. Courts are frequently faced, however, with contracts involving both goods and services—so-called "hybrid" contracts. Most courts follow the "predominant factor" test to determine whether such hybrid contracts are transactions in goods, and therefore covered by the UCC, or transactions in services, and therefore excluded.[13] *See* Bonebrake v. Cox, 499 F.2d 951, 960 (8th Cir.1974). Under this test, the court determines "whether their predominant factor, their thrust, their purpose, reasonably stated, is the rendition of service, with goods incidentally involved (e.g., contract with artist for painting) or is a transaction of sale, with labor incidentally involved (e.g., installation of

---

[13] A few courts do not categorize hybrid contracts as either transactions in goods or services, but rather apply the UCC only to the sale of goods elements of the contract. *See, e.g.,* Foster v. Colorado Radio Corp., 381 F.2d 222, 226 (10th Cir.1967).

a water heater in a bathroom)." *Id.* (footnotes omitted). At least one Florida court has implicitly adopted the predominant factor test. *See* United States Fidelity & Guar. Co. v. North Am. Steel Corp., 335 So. 2d 18, 21 (Fla. 2d DCA 1976) ("Since the predominate nature of the transaction was the furnishing of a product rather than services, we believe that the fabricated pipe could properly be characterized as goods.").

Although courts generally have not found any single factor determinative in classifying a hybrid contract as one for goods or services, courts find several aspects of a contract particularly significant. First, the language of the contract itself provides insight into whether the parties believed the goods or services were the more important element of their agreement. Contractual language that refers to the transaction as a "purchase," for example, or identifies the parties as the "buyer" and "seller," indicates that the transaction is for goods rather than services. *See* Bonebrake, 499 F.2d at 958 (stating that language referring to "equipment" is peculiar to goods rather than services); Bailey v. Montgomery Ward & Co., 690 P.2d 1280, 1282 (Colo.Ct.App.1984) (holding that a contract that identifies the transaction as a "purchase" and one of the parties as the "customer" signals a transaction in goods); Meeker v. Hamilton Grain Elevator Co., 110 Ill. App. 3d 668, 442 N.E.2d 921, 923, 66 Ill. Dec. 360 (Ill. App. Ct. 1982) (stating that a contract that calls the parties "seller" and "purchaser" indicates a contract for goods).

Courts also examine the manner in which the transaction was billed; when the contract price does not include the cost of services, or the charge for goods exceeds that for services, the contract is more likely to be for goods. *See* Triangle Underwriters, Inc. v. Honeywell, Inc., 604 F.2d 737, 743 (2d Cir.1979) (stating that a bill that does not include services indicates a contract for goods); Lincoln Pulp & Paper Co. v. Dravo Corp., 436 F. Supp. 262, 275 & n. 15 (D.Me.1977) (holding that the contract at issue was for services after noting that the bill did not allocate costs between services and goods, and the evidence showed that the cost of the goods was less than half of the contract price).

Movable goods is another hallmark of a contract for goods rather than services. The UCC's definition of goods makes clear the importance of mobility in determining whether a contract is for goods; the UCC states that goods are "all things (including specially manufactured goods) which are movable at the time of identification to the contract for sale." Fla. Stat. Ch. 672.105(1) (1997). Noting the importance of mobility, one Florida court held that a contract to edit and publish printed materials was a contract for goods after stating that "the items allegedly furnished by the appellant were specially produced or manufactured and were movable."[15] Lake Wales Publ'g Co. v. Florida Visitor, Inc., 335 So. 2d 335,

---

[15] Mobility is measured as of the time the goods are identified to the contract rather than after the contract is completed. Consequently, equipment or materials that were movable, but were installed and became immobile fixtures as part of the contract, are still "movable" within

336 (Fla. 2d DCA 1976); *see also* Smith v. Union Supply Co., 675 P.2d 333, 334 (Colo.Ct.App.1983) (holding that a contract to provide the materials and labor for installation of a new roof was a contract for goods because "the materials to be installed . . . were 'movable at the time of identification to the contract for sale' " (quoting Colorado's version of the UCC)).

In this case, the district court relied primarily on *Lincoln Pulp & Paper* for its conclusion that the contract was for services rather than goods. The contract at issue in *Lincoln Pulp & Paper* involved the design and construction of a heat and chemical recovery unit in a pulp mill. The district court noted that, similar to *Lincoln Pulp & Paper,* the Contract obligated Barth to design, manufacture, test, and construct equipment, and also that the Contract's price did not allocate expenses between services and materials. The district court concluded that this case was sufficiently analogous to *Lincoln Pulp & Paper* to warrant the same result: a determination that the Contract was for services rather than goods.

The question whether a contract is predominantly for goods or services is generally one of fact. When there is no genuine issue of material fact concerning the contract's provisions, however, a court may determine the issue as a matter of law. Concluding that there are no material issues of fact as to the terms of the contract, the district court decided as a matter of law that the contract was for services. We review questions of law *de novo.*

Applying the "predominant factor" test to the Contract, we conclude that it was predominantly a transaction in goods. We reach this conclusion based on the contractual language, the circumstances surrounding the Contract, and the nature of the goods at issue.

Our starting point is the language of the Contract itself, which provides a number of indicia that the parties intended a contract for goods rather than services. First, the Contract is titled "PURCHASE ORDER," a reference that is used repeatedly throughout the document. This title is most instructive, as the parties have chosen to identify their agreement with a name that is almost exclusively used for transactions in goods. Second, the parties refer to themselves in the Contract as the "Buyer" and "Seller." Third, the Contract states that it is a purchase order "for the fabrication and installation of automated *equipment.*" (emphasis added). All of this contractual language is "peculiar to goods, not services," Bonebrake, 499 F.2d at 958, and indicates that the parties had a contract for goods in mind.

---

the UCC's meaning. Thus, for example, contracts for the sale and installation of equipment are frequently (but not always) held to be transactions in goods. Construction contracts, however, such as those for construction of a swimming pool or house, are usually held to be transactions in services. Although construction contracts typically involve materials that qualify as goods (such as concrete or roofing tiles, for example), the services element of such contracts is usually held to be dominant. *See* 1 James J. White & Robert S. Summers, Uniform Commercial Code § 9–2 (4th ed.1995).

Additionally, the Contract involves movable goods. Barth designed and fabricated the automated equipment in its own facilities, and planned to move the equipment to BMC's plant only once it was completed. Barth's original offer, which was incorporated into the Contract, included the term "F.O.B. Barth dock," meaning that the equipment was tendered to BMC once it was delivered to Barth's loading dock. Consequently, although Barth was still obligated to install and debug the equipment, it was clearly movable at the time it was identified to the Contract.[16]

Lincoln Pulp & Paper is distinguishable from this case. The district court stated that the Contract price, similar to *Lincoln Pulp & Paper,* does not allocate costs between services and goods. The district court failed to note, however, that the Contract allocates payments according to delivery of automated equipment; the Contract's payment schedule calls for the delivery and acceptance of each automated equipment line to be met by a $70,050 payment from BMC. If the Contract price were being paid predominantly for Barth's design and engineering services as BMC claims, then the parties would have pegged payments to completion of the engineering and design services, not to the delivery of equipment. Furthermore, while the cost of services made up over half of the contract price in *Lincoln Pulp & Paper,* the opposite appears to be true in this case. A total of $280,200, which is over half of the contract price, is pegged to the delivery of equipment.

Finally, we note that the court in *Lincoln Pulp & Paper* stated that "[a] sale of equipment is not removed from the scope of Article 2 merely because the equipment was specially designed and manufactured before delivery or installed by the supplier." 436 F. Supp. at 276 n. 16. In fact, it is not surprising that the Barth-BMC Contract included such a significant services element (i.e., design and manufacturing). Because no other company had successfully automated its eyeglass lens production, Barth had to spend considerable time designing this first-of-its-kind machinery. This necessary services element, however, does not remove the Contract from the category of agreements for specially designed and manufactured equipment to which Article 2 applies.

. . .

Having determined that the UCC governs this case, we must next apply Article 2's waiver provision to the Contract. [This portion of the court's opinion is reproduced infra at page 124.]

---

[16] BMC correctly points out that the mere involvement of movable goods in a contract does not mean it is a transaction in goods rather than services. *See* Whitmer v. Bell Telephone Co., 361 Pa. Super. 282, 522 A.2d 584, 587 (1987). In fact some movable goods must be involved in order for the contract to be labeled a "hybrid"; otherwise, the contract would clearly be a transaction in services, and the UCC would not apply. What is significant, however, is that the goods at issue here were movable when completed, unlike some contracts that only involve movable materials, which are subsequently used to construct an immovable fixture (such as a house or swimming pool). While the mobility of the completed goods is not dispositive, it is one factor to be considered.

QUESTIONS AND NOTES

1. The court applies what it calls the predominant purpose test to determine if Article 2 applies. What is the rationale for this test? (Hint: see the questions preceding the case.)

2. NewSpin Sports developed a product that would attach to a golf club and analyze the user's swing. To produce this product, NewSpin needed someone that could provide the electronic components to make it work. After providing specifications for the product and conducting extensive discussions with Arrow Electronics, NewSpin formed a contract with Arrow. This contract was titled, "Materials and Manufacturing Management Agreement Board Assembly," and it called for Arrow to use reasonable commercial efforts . . . to procure components . . . and to engage a subassembly house for the manufacture and assembly of Products . . . through a subcontractor on [NewSpin's] behalf pursuant to detailed, written specifications." The reference to a subassembly house meant that a third party would assemble the parts of the component that Arrow would supply to NewSpin and which NewSpin would incorporate into the product it was creating. The agreement provided that after Arrow developed and assembled the component, NewSpin would submit purchase orders to Arrow, and it specified several provisions to be contained in those purchase orders. Pursuant to the contract, Arrow supplied 7,500 components that NewSpin used to produce its product. More than forty percent were defective, and four-and-a-half years later NewSpin sued. The applicable statute of limitations for breach of a written contract was ten years, but for breach of a contract to sell goods it was four years (2–725)(1). Hence, to determine if the suit was timely, the court in NewSpin Sports, LLC v. Arrow Electronics, Inc., 910 F.3d 293 (7th Cir. 2018), had to decide whether the dispute was governed by Article 2 or by the common law. The court stated:

> According to NewSpin's reading of these provisions, Arrow would create a prototype of the component it needed using the provided specifications and, if satisfied with Arrow's work, NewSpin would issue purchase orders for the component Arrow created. The Agreement clarifies, though, that Arrow was not obligated to perform any work until NewSpin issued a purchase order for the components it sought. In other words, any "procur[ing]," "engag[ing]," or "assembl[ing]" services by Arrow would only be incidental to its provision and delivery of a finished good to NewSpin.

> Numerous other Agreement provisions confirm that the parties contracted primarily for a sale of goods. For instance, there is no separate payment from NewSpin to Arrow for its work: instead, the price would be "as agreed upon by Arrow and [NewSpin] from time to time as set forth in purchase orders issued by [NewSpin] and accepted by Arrow." In other words, NewSpin would pay for the finished products requested in purchase orders and would not pay separately for Arrow's services; this lack of a

price breakdown strongly indicates the predominant purpose of the Agreement is the sale of goods.

Arrow also provided a warranty in the Agreement that the products it would deliver "are manufactured or assembled pursuant to [NewSpin's] Specifications" and they "shall be free from defects in workmanship." There is no warranty running to the services Arrow would provide, further indicating the Agreement primarily concerns goods. Additionally, the Agreement makes NewSpin responsible for payment of sales tax, which "is found in the sale of goods, but not services." Next, Arrow would ship products to NewSpin "F.O.B.," which means " 'free on board,' a term used in transactions in tangible goods." Finally, title of delivered goods passes to NewSpin upon shipment, and "the passing of title" is another hallmark of sales contracts. 2–106(1) ("A 'sale' consists in the passing of title from the seller to the buyer for a price.").

The allegations in NewSpin's complaint further confirm this interpretation. NewSpin alleges "Arrow agreed to provide fully functioning components that met NewSpin['s] . . . specifications, and agreed to provide fully functioning components in conformance with the Agreement." NewSpin also alleges "Arrow agreed to engage a sub-assembly house for the manufacture and assembly of components." However, NewSpin does not claim Arrow breached the Agreement by failing to make this engagement or by engaging a substandard assembly house for this purpose. Instead, NewSpin alleges "the components sent by Arrow were defective and not in conformance with the specifications [NewSpin] had provided to Arrow, the representations Arrow had made, or the Agreement," and Arrow breached the Agreement "by providing [NewSpin] with defective components which failed to perform." NewSpin sought damages for the amount it paid to Arrow for defective components, the amount it was billed for components it did not receive, and the amount it incurred in shipping and replacing defective units. In other words, NewSpin only claims it suffered damages relating to faulty goods, not to any faulty services. This further confirms the predominant purpose of the Agreement is to provide NewSpin with physical goods rather than with assembly services.

NewSpin nevertheless points to . . . characteristics of the Agreement it contends demonstrate the parties bargained for services only: (1) the Agreement states no quantity, price, or delivery date of goods to be produced, ordered, or sold; (2) the Agreement's title demonstrates the parties contracted for management services . . . . NewSpin's arguments [cannot] overcome the plain language of the Agreement itself.

First, although the Agreement does not set out exact quantities, prices, or delivery dates for the goods at issue, the Agreement does address these terms. Per the Agreement, NewSpin's purchase orders must "set[ ] forth the quantities, descriptions, prices, and requested delivery dates for the Products to be supplied and Work to be performed." There is no need to include this provision in a pure services contract.

. . .

Second, NewSpin points out the Agreement's title ("Materials and Manufacturing Management Agreement Board Assembly") refers to manufacturing "management" but does not reference any "sale" of products. True, courts look to the labels parties use in order to determine contracts' predominant purposes. However, the Agreement's title is only one aspect of its terms; this is not enough to overcome the overwhelming focus of the rest of the contract on the completed products Arrow was to deliver to NewSpin.

. . .

In sum, the contractual provisions the parties agreed to, along with the allegations in NewSpin's complaint, demonstrate the Agreement's predominant purpose is the sale of goods to NewSpin. Any breach-of-contract claims relating to the Agreement are accordingly subject to the UCC's four-year statute of limitations.

3.   The court states that most courts use the predominant purpose test. But its use is not universal. In Anthony Pools v. Sheehan, 295 Md. 285, 455 A.2d 434 (Md.Ct.App.1983), the case from which the Poolco problem preceding *BMC* is drawn, the court acknowledged that under the predominant purpose test, the swimming pool transaction before it would not be governed by Article 2. It stated:

> Were the predominant purpose test mechanically to be applied to the facts of this case, there would be no quality warranty implied as to the diving board. But here the contract expressly states that Anthony agrees not only to construct the swimming pool, but also to sell the related equipment selected by the Sheehans. The Sheehans are described as "Buyer." The diving board itself is not structurally integrated into the swimming pool. Anthony offered the board as an optional accessory, just as Anthony offered the options of purchasing a pool ladder or a sliding board. When identified to the contract, the diving board was movable. See § 2–105. The board itself remains detachable from its support, as reflected by a photograph in evidence. The diving board, considered alone, is goods. Had it been purchased by the Sheehans in a transaction distinct from the pool construction agreement with Anthony, there would have been an implied warranty of merchantability.

> A number of commentators have advocated a more policy oriented approach to determining whether warranties of quality and fitness are implied with respect to goods sold as part of a hybrid transaction in which service predominates. See Farnsworth, Implied Warranties of Quality in Non-Sales Cases, 57 Colum.L.Rev. 653 (1957); Comment, Sale of Goods in Service-Predominated Transactions, 37 Fordham L.Rev. 115 (1968). To support their position, these commentators in general emphasize

loss shifting, risk distribution, consumer reliance and difficulties in
the proof of negligence. These concepts underlie strict liability in
tort. See Phipps v. General Motors Corp., 278 Md. 337, 363 A.2d
955 (1976).

A leading case applying a policy approach in this problem area
is Newmark v. Gimbel's Incorporated, 54 N.J. 585, 258 A.2d 697
(1969). There the patron of a beauty parlor sued for injury to her
hair and scalp allegedly resulting from a lotion used in giving her
a permanent wave. Because the transaction was viewed as the
rendering of a service, the trial court had ruled that there could be
no warranty liability. The intermediate appellate court's reversal
was affirmed by the Supreme Court of New Jersey which reasoned
in part as follows (id. at 593, 258 A.2d at 701):

> The transaction, in our judgment, is a hybrid partaking of
> incidents of a sale and a service. It is really partly the
> rendering of service, and partly the supplying of goods for a
> consideration. Accordingly, we agree with the Appellate
> Division that an implied warranty of fitness of the products
> used in giving the permanent wave exists with no less force
> than it would have in the case of a simple sale. Obviously in
> permanent wave operations the product is taken into
> consideration in fixing the price of the service. The no-
> separate-charge argument puts excessive emphasis on form
> and downgrades the overall substance of the transaction. If the
> beauty parlor operator bought and applied the permanent
> wave solution to her own hair and suffered injury thereby, her
> action in warranty or strict liability in tort against the
> manufacturer-seller of the product clearly would be
> maintainable because the basic transaction would have arisen
> from a conventional type of sale. It does not accord with logic
> to deny a similar right to a patron against the beauty parlor
> operator or the manufacturer when the purchase and sale
> were made in anticipation of and for the purpose of use of the
> product on the patron who would be charged for its use.
> Common sense demands that such patron be deemed a
> customer as to both manufacturer and beauty parlor operator.
> [Citations omitted.]

The court was careful to limit its holding to commercial
transactions, as opposed to those predominantly involving
professional services. Id. at 596–97, 258 A.2d at 702–703.

1 R. Anderson, Uniform Commercial Code (1970), § 2–102:5 at
209 refers to *Newmark* as illustrative of a possible trend in the law
and states:

> It is probable that a goods-services transaction will come to be
> subjected to Article 2 of the Code insofar as the contractor's
> obligations with respect to the goods themselves are involved,

at least where the goods involved could have been purchased in the general market and used by the plaintiff-customer.

. . .

1 W. Hawkland, Uniform Commercial Code Series (1982), § 2–102:04, at Art. 2, p. 12 has suggested what might be called a "gravamen" test . . . :

> Unless uniformity would be impaired thereby, it might be more sensible and facilitate administration, at least in this gray area, to abandon the "predominant factor" test and focus instead on whether the gravamen of the action involves goods or services.

The court in *Sheehan* held that the implied warranty of merchantability provided by 2–314 applied to the diving board.

4. Another alternative to the predominant purpose test is the divisible contract approach. In this alternative the court views the transaction as consisting of two contracts, one for goods and one for services. For example, if the contract in *BMC* had called for payment of $280,000 when Barth completed design of the production system, and the balance upon delivery of the equipment, the court might have concluded that in essence there were two contracts. The result would have been the same, but the analysis would have been different.

5. Do you agree with the results in *Sheehan* and in the permanent wave case (*Newmark v. Gimbel's*)? Is the gravamen-of-the-action test preferable to the predominant purpose test?

Assume that the general statute of limitations for lawsuits to recover for breach of contract is three years. Under 2–725 the statute of limitations for actions to assert rights under Article 2 is four years. Under the gravamen test, if plaintiffs in *Sheehan* sued three-and-a-half years after the pool had been installed, would the lawsuit be timely? Now assume that the plaintiffs sued not only for the injuries sustained because of the defective diving board but also for loss caused by the fact that the pool is only five feet deep instead of the eight feet that Anthony Pools had promised. Is the lawsuit still timely?

6. What characteristics of the transaction in *BMC* lead the court to conclude that it is within the scope of Article 2?

Is the problem of classification avoided where the contract contains a separate price for its service aspect? Some courts have so held. See H. Hirschfield Sons Co. v. Colt Industries, 107 Mich.App. 720, 309 N.W.2d 714 (1981), in which plaintiff bought a large scale for $16,525 and the contract called for the defendant to install it for an additional price of $12,242. Plaintiff complained that the installation was defective. The court held that Article 2 was not applicable. Accord, Dixie Lime & Stone Co. v. Wiggins Scale Co., 144 Ga.App. 145, 240 S.E.2d 323 (1977). How did the court in *BMC* make use of the price?

7. The court in *BMC* states that "[t]he question whether a contract is predominantly for goods or services is generally one of fact." Another court agreed, putting it this way:

Courts have split over whether the predominant purpose of a mixed contract presents an issue of law for the court or a question of fact for the jury. . . .

[One court] suggested the issue should be treated as a matter of law because contract interpretation commonly presents legal rather than factual determinations. That is true when the language of a written contract is unambiguous. But determining whether goods or services predominate in a mixed contract necessarily looks beyond the contractual language. It includes the reasons the buyer purchases the goods and the nature and extent of the integration of those goods with the related services. It likely requires detailed information about the goods and the services over and above what may be described in the contract. Given the case-specific inquiry and the factually driven nature of the determination, essentially considering all of the circumstances bearing on the transaction, we conclude the issue of predominance of goods or services in a mixed contract is fundamentally one of fact. As such, it typically should be left for the trier of fact rather than resolved on summary judgment.

But, of course, a court may decide an issue of fact if the material circumstances are undisputed in a given case. Absent a factual dispute, the question presented effectively becomes one of law.

Golden v. Den-Mat Corp., 276 P.3d 773 (Kan.App.2012).

8.   Problems.

a.   Hawley had a medical device surgically implanted to monitor her heart, glucose level, and white-blood-cell count. She was billed $20,000, which included $9,000 for the device and $4,000 for the other "movable things" used in the course of the surgery. Shortly thereafter the manufacturer of the device withdrew it from the market because it had serious adverse side effects in a large percentage of patients. Within a few months the woman experienced these side effects and had the device surgically removed. She sued the hospital for breach of warranty. Does Article 2 apply?

b.   The Nelsons wanted to refurbish their home, and they contacted Interiors, Inc., to help them with this project. The Nelsons and Interiors agreed that Interiors would suggest and, with the Nelsons' approval, would supply new furnishings, including a coordinated color scheme for the walls, floors, and fabrics. Upon completion of the project, the first floor of the Nelsons' home was completely refurbished, with new wallpaper, new furniture, and new carpets. Interiors billed them $67,000, which they paid. Six months later imperfections in the fabric of the furniture became manifest. The Nelsons sued for damages for the cost of reupholstering the furniture. Under the predominant purpose test, does Article 2 govern the outcome of this dispute?

9.   Dispensation of food in restaurants and blood in hospitals.
Under the Uniform Sales Act some courts held that the dispensation of food

in restaurants was not a "sale of goods" but an "utterance" or a service. Since there was no sale of goods, these courts concluded that no warranty could be implied. See e.g., Nisky v. Childs Co., 103 N.J.L. 464, 135 A. 805, 50 A.L.R. 227 (1927). The UCC reverses this result by providing in 2–314(1) that "Under this section the serving for value of food or drink to be consumed either on the premises or elsewhere is a sale."

Under the Uniform Sales Act some courts held that a blood transfusion was not a sale by a hospital or doctor to a patient, but rather a service, and hence no warranty protection was available under the statute. See, e.g., Perlmutter v. Beth David Hospital, 308 N.Y. 100, 123 N.E.2d 792 (1954). Article 2 does not address this matter specifically. Do the warranty provisions of Article 2 apply to blood transfusions? How would you argue this question on behalf of the hospital? On behalf of the patient?

Chances are good that your arguments on behalf of the hospital and patient were based to some considerable extent on analogy. Analogies underlie much judicial thinking, and this fact is both good and bad. An analogy is always logically fallacious. It can be expressed as the argument that because X has the properties A and B which also belong to Y, it must also have the property C, which also belongs to Y. On the other hand, it should be remembered that scientific thinking to a great extent is based on analogy, a technique that has proved (by subsequent empirical evidence) to be a valuable guide to the discovery of truth. Similarly, jurisprudence has been advanced immeasurably by the use of analogy.

A statute as extensive in its coverage as Article 2 of necessity must be drafted in rather general terms, because it would be impossible to list all the specific situations that might come to be decided under it. In this connection the experience of the Prussians in the 19th Century is edifying. The Prussians were convinced that they could cover every single situation in their code, and they drafted one that had more than 28,000 sections. But there still were gaps, and ultimately Germany resorted to commercial and civil codes drafted in very general language.

The UCC is generally drafted in broad language and should not be read the way one reads a conveyance of real property (i.e., if a matter is not specifically included, it is deemed to be excluded); still, some of the UCC sections are rather specific, and this fact solves some problems but creates others. No court would now find that the dispensation of food in a restaurant did not carry with it warranty protection under section 2–314, but it might find the inclusion of such a transaction under that section to have special (and confusing?) meaning in blood transfusion cases. Even though most states now have statutes specifically addressing the liability of persons who provide blood transfusions, it still is valuable to think about what arguments based on the language of Article 2 can be made for and against applying Article 2 to blood transfusions. The techniques you will use in thinking about that question are similar to the techniques often used in arguing whether as statute covers a situation similar to, but not the same, as a situation specifically covered by the statute.

———

B. COMPUTER SOFTWARE

A major issue in recent years has been whether Article 2 of the Code applies to the sale or licensing of computer software. When a customer pays for software on a disk for installation on the customer's computer, that transaction usually is a license that gives the customer the right to use the software under the terms of the license. The document embodying the license sometimes is inside the shrink-wrapped package containing the disk and cannot be read by the customer until the package is opened. Often the license appears only on the computer screen after the user has begun loading the software. Some have questioned whether these methods of calling the user's attention to the license document is sufficient to make the terms of the document binding under Article 2. Others (specifically, software suppliers) have questioned whether Article 2 applies at all.

Advent Systems Ltd. v. Unisys Corp.
United States Court of Appeals, Third Circuit, 1991.
925 F.2d 670.

[Plaintiff contracted with defendant to supply certain computer-related items, the major part of which was software that it had developed. When a dispute arose, the court had to decide whether the contract was for the sale of goods, so that the Article 2 statute of frauds applied. The trial court held that the contract was not for the sale of goods.]

■ WEIS, CIRCUIT JUDGE. . . .

In support of the district court's ruling that the U.C.C. did not apply, Advent contends that the agreement's requirement of furnishing services did not come within the Code. Moreover, the argument continues, the "software" referred to in the agreement as a "product" was not a "good" but intellectual property outside the ambit of the Uniform Commercial Code.

. . .

The increasing frequency of computer products as subjects of commercial litigation has led to controversy over whether software is a "good" or intellectual property. The Code does not specifically mention software.

In the absence of express legislative guidance, courts interpret the Code in light of commercial and technological developments. The Code is designed "[t]o simplify, clarify and modernize the law governing commercial transactions" and "[t]o permit the continued expansion of commercial practices." 13 Pa.Cons.Stat.Ann. § 1102(b)(1) (Purdon 1984). As the Official Commentary makes clear:

"This Act is drawn to provide flexibility so that, since it is intended to be a semi-permanent piece of legislation, it will provide its own machinery for expansion of commercial practices. It is intended to make it possible for the law embodied in this Act to be developed by the courts in the light of unforeseen and new circumstances and practices."

Id. comment 1.

The Code "applies to transactions in goods." 13 Pa.Cons.Stat.Ann. § 2102 (Purdon 1984). Goods are defined as "all things (including specially manufactured goods) which are moveable at the time of the identification for sale." Id. at § 2105. The Pennsylvania courts have recognized that " 'goods' has a very extensive meaning" under the U.C.C. . . .

Computer programs are the product of an intellectual process, but once implanted in a medium are widely distributed to computer owners. An analogy can be drawn to a compact disc recording of an orchestral rendition. The music is produced by the artistry of musicians and in itself is not a "good," but when transferred to a laser-readable disc becomes a readily merchantable commodity. Similarly, when a professor delivers a lecture, it is not a good, but, when transcribed as a book, it becomes a good.

That a computer program may be copyrightable as intellectual property does not alter the fact that once in the form of a floppy disc or other medium, the program is tangible, moveable and available in the marketplace. The fact that some programs may be tailored for specific purposes need not alter their status as "goods" because the Code definition includes "specially manufactured goods."

The topic has stimulated academic commentary with the majority espousing the view that software fits within the definition of a "good" in the U.C.C.

Applying the U.C.C. to computer software transactions offers substantial benefits to litigants and the courts. The Code offers a uniform body of law on a wide range of questions likely to arise in computer software disputes: implied warranties, consequential damages, disclaimers of liability, the statute of limitations, to name a few.

The importance of software to the commercial world and the advantages to be gained by the uniformity inherent in the U.C.C. are strong policy arguments favoring inclusion. The contrary arguments are not persuasive, and we hold that software is a "good" within the definition in the Code.

The relationship at issue here is a typical mixed goods and services arrangement. The services are not substantially different from those generally accompanying package sales of computer systems consisting of hardware and software. . . .

Although determining the applicability of the U.C.C. to a contract by examining the predominance of goods or services has been criticized, we see no reason to depart from that practice here. As we pointed out in De

Filippo v. Ford Motor Co., 516 F.2d 1313, 1323 (3d Cir.), cert. denied, 423 U.S. 912 (1975), segregating goods from non-goods and insisting "that the Statute of Frauds apply only to a portion of the contract, would be to make the contract divisible and impossible of performance within the intention of the parties."

. . .

In this case the contract's main objective was to transfer "products." The specific provisions for training of Unisys personnel by Advent were but a small part of the parties' contemplated relationship.

. . .

We are persuaded that the transaction at issue here was within the scope of the Uniform Commercial Code and, therefore, the judgment in favor of the plaintiff must be reversed.

QUESTIONS

1. In the last paragraph on the preceding page, the court refers to the policy arguments favoring inclusion of software contracts in Article 2. What are they, and how strong are they? The court asserts that the contrary arguments are not persuasive, but it does not identify those arguments. Can you identify any?

2. To support its conclusion, the court refers to musical recordings and books, sales of which it says are within the scope of Article 2. If Barnes & Noble sells a book that contains instructions for building a swing set, is Barnes & Noble liable under Article 2 when the binding fails and numerous pages fall out? Is it liable when the swing set collapses because the instructions omitted a crucial step? Cardozo v. True, 342 So.2d 1053 (Fla.App.1977).

3. If an attorney drafts a contract for a client but fails to include one of the terms that the parties to the contract agreed should be included, is the attorney's liability determined by the provisions of Article 2?

Architectronics, Inc. v. Control Systems, Inc.

United States District Court, Southern District of New York, 1996.
935 F.Supp. 425.

[Plaintiff (Architectronics) and defendant (CSI) entered into licensing agreements under which defendant had the right to use plaintiff's software as one component of a computer-aided-design (CAD) system that defendant would develop and which plaintiff and another entity (CADSource) would market. Under the agreement plaintiff would pay CSI a royalty on any of the systems that plaintiff and CADSource sold. Claiming that defendant breached the contract, plaintiff sued. The suit would have been barred by the four-year statute of limitations of UCC Article 2 (2–725), but not barred under New York's six-year general contract statute of limitations.]

■ MUKASEY, DISTRICT JUDGE.

. . .

Under the UCC as adopted in New York, a "transaction" need not involve a sale; "[t]he use of the term 'transaction' rather than sale in UCC § 2–102 makes it clear that Article 2 is not to be confined merely to those transactions in which there is . . . a transfer of title." 1 Ronald A. Anderson, *Uniform Commercial Code* § 2–102:4 (3d ed.1981) (citing Hertz Commercial Leasing Corp. v. Transportation Credit Clearing House, Inc., 59 Misc.2d 226, 298 N.Y.S.2d 392, 395 (N.Y. City Civ.Ct.1969), *rev'd on other grounds,* 64 Misc.2d 910, 316 N.Y.S.2d 585 (1st Dep't 1970)). The applicability of Article Two to a transaction is not defeated by the use of a license in lieu of a sale if the license provides for transfer of some of the incidents of goods ownership.

Under the UCC, '[g]oods' means all things (including specially manufactured goods) which are movable at the time of identification to the contract for sale other than the money in which the price is to be paid, investment securities . . . and things in action." *Id.* § 2–105. Generally, software is considered a "good," even though a finished software product may reflect a substantial investment of programming services. Schroders, Inc. v. Hogan Sys., Inc., 137 Misc.2d 738, 522 N.Y.S.2d 404, 406 (Sup.Ct. New York County 1987). However, copyrights, patents, and trademarks are classified as "general intangibles" under the UCC and are distinguished from goods. N.Y. U.C.C. Law § 9–106 & New York Annotations (McKinney 1990).

The [Software Development and Licensing Agreement (SDLA)] provided for two licenses. Under the first license, Architectronics granted CSI the right to use its DynaMenu software prototypes for joint venture-related purposes only. That license gave CSI a tool necessary for the development of the "Derivative Work," a new display driver. Under the second license, CSI granted Architectronics and CADSource the right to use, copy, and distribute the "Derivative Work." That license was the centerpiece of the transaction, because it provided Architectronics and CADSource with the valuable right to manufacture the new display driver and sell it to the public. Architectronics and CADSource bargained primarily for the right to mass-market the product, not for the right to install single copies of the display driver onto their own PCs. *See generally* Andrew Rodau, Computer Software: Does Article 2 of the Uniform Commercial Code Apply?, 35 Emory L.J. 853, 874–883 (1986) (distinguishing tangible software use rights from intangible intellectual property rights). CSI's upside in the deal also was linked to the rights to reproduce and distribute: the parties anticipated thousands of sales of the new product, and Architectronics and CADSource promised to pay CSI a $20-per-copy royalty on those sales. CSI stood to gain in royalties a sum that would dwarf the $2,000 development fee. Because the predominant feature of the SDLA was a transfer of intellectual property rights, the agreement is not subject to Article Two of the UCC.[5] Plaintiff's second contract claim therefore is timely because plaintiff filed suit within six years of CSI's first attempt to repudiate the SDLA.

QUESTIONS AND NOTES

1. What is the relevance of the book analogy in footnote 5?

2. Problem. General Motors wanted to produce a car to compete with the $98,000 Mercedes SL550. To that end, GM contracted with a famous European auto designer for the designer to create and deliver a prototype, which GM then will put into production. Is the contract between GM and the designer within the scope of Article 2?

3. What does the book analogy have to say about the applicability of Article 2 to the situation in which a shrink-wrapped disk is acquired in a store?

Use of a disk is no longer the predominant method of distribution. Instead, a user may acquire the software on-line from the supplier's web site. Or the supplier may design a program specifically for a particular user and deliver it to the user, either on a disk or electronically to the hard drive on the user's computer. Or a supplier may permit a user to access the supplier's mainframe computer to use the program, which remains on the supplier's mainframe. Are these transactions within the scope of Article 2?

If the contract is for off-the-shelf software, the courts are likely to conclude that the transaction is within the scope of Article 2. If, on the other hand, the contract calls for the supplier to design software specifically for the user, the courts are not likely to reach that conclusion. But what if the contract calls for the transfer of off-the-shelf software plus the provision of services? Then we have a case analogous to the hybrid goods-services transaction.

In Pain Center v. Origin Healthcare Solutions LLC, 893 F.3d 454 (7th Cir. 2018), SSIMED provided Pain Center with the software, Practice Manager, a billing program by which Pain Center would submit claims to SSIMED for subsequent transmission to insurers. It also provided Pain Center with EMRge, a records-management software that worked in conjunction with Practice Manager. The agreements called for SSIMED to supply the software and related services, including ongoing billing services, IT support, electronic claim-submission services, and five days of initial training in how to use the software. The system failed to transmit claims to insurers, causing Pain Center to lose large sums of revenue. Pain Center sued SSIMED alleging that its Practice Manager and EMRge software and

---

[5] This conclusion may follow more obviously from the following hypothetical analogous set of facts: Suppose that the parties here are book publishers, that Architectronics gives CSI a written outline for a new novel, and that CSI agrees to write the novel. An agreement provides that CSI will own the copyright to the novel, but will grant Architectronics the exclusive right to reproduce and distribute the novel. When Architectronics sells copies of the book to consumers, the sale will be a "transaction in goods" under the UCC. But in the agreement between Architectronics and CSI, Architectronics is contracting for intangible intellectual property rights, even though it will receive a "hard" copy of the novel when CSI finishes the project. The agreement to write the novel would not be a "transaction in goods" under the UCC.

related billing services caused these losses. Among other claims, Pain Center asserted breach of contract and breach of warranty. The court stated:

> The timeliness of Pain Center's claims for breach of contract depends on whether the contracts fall within the UCC. If the contracts are for the sale of goods and the UCC applies, then the claims are subject to a four-year limitations period, which expired long before Pain Center filed suit. If the UCC does not apply, then the claims are subject to Indiana's ten-year statute of limitations for written contracts and are timely.

> The judge held that the UCC's four-year limitations period applies, reasoning that the agreements in question are mixed contracts for goods and services in which goods predominate. The judge correctly identified the test used in Indiana for resolving a question like this but erred in its application.

> Where a contract involves the purchase of a "preexisting, standardized software," Indiana courts treat it as a contract for the sale of goods governed by the UCC. On the other hand, where a contract calls for the design of software to meet the buyer's specific needs, Indiana treats it as a services contract. For example, in Conway v. Gray Loon Outdoor Marketing Group, Inc., 906 N.E.2d 805 (Ind. 2009), the court held that the UCC does not apply where one party hires the other to design a custom website and provide webhost services.

> Here it's clear that Pain Center licensed SSIMED's preexisting, standardized software. SSIMED's sales representative . . . testified in deposition that the licensing agreements involved "standardized," "out-of-the-box-type software." She also explained that SSIMED does not design custom software to meet the needs of individual healthcare providers. She acknowledged that a healthcare provider could make minor changes to the standardized software, but she did not elaborate on the precise extent of this capability.

> In response Pain Center points to evidence that it asked for (and obtained) minor modifications within the confines of the standardized software. Dr. Alexander testified that he asked SSIMED to add a question to a patient survey and SSIMED did so. Pain Center's billing specialist testified that at her request SSIMED arranged for the payment amounts associated with certain billing codes to automatically populate in the software. Setting up field auto-population and adding a single survey question to a preexisting, standardized software program does not convert it into custom software designed specifically for a particular purchaser.

> . . . SSIMED used its preexisting, standardized software to serve Pain Center's objectives; it did not design a new, customized software program for its client.

Finally, Pain Center relies on contract language contemplating the possibility of purchasing custom programming services. But there's no evidence that Pain Center ever purchased these services or that SSIMED ever offered them. In sum, because the Practice Manager and EMRge programs were preexisting and standardized, we agree with the district judge that the software should be treated as a good. And because the two software programs are properly classified as goods, the contracts between SSIMED and Pain Center are appropriately characterized as mixed contracts for both goods and services.

To determine whether the UCC applies to a mixed contract for both goods and services, . . . Indiana courts ask whether the predominant thrust of the transaction is the performance of services with goods incidentally involved or the sale of goods with services incidentally involved. To determine whether services or goods predominate, the test considers (1) the language of the contract; (2) the circumstances of the parties and the primary reason they entered into the contract; and (3) the relative costs of the goods and services.

Here the language of the contracts is largely a neutral factor, though in some limited respects it points toward a conclusion that services predominate. Each agreement is a single double-sided sheet of paper: the front is a simple order form; the back supplies the terms and conditions of the agreement. The front also identifies services (e.g., "Monthly Services & Support," "On-site training") as well as software ("SSIMED EMRge" and "SSIMED Practice Manager Suite"). Pain Center paid for monthly billing services and IT support for the life of the contracts; the services are described on the back page as including "telephone support," "on-line support," and "electronic claim submission." The back of the Practice Manager contract also lists the various software modules incorporated in the Practice Manager software, including modules for collections, appointment scheduling, and electronic-claim submission, among others. In short, the language of the contract provides slight support for a conclusion that the predominant focus of these agreements was ongoing billing and IT services and that the software was a tool that allowed SSIMED to perform those services.

The next step in the predominant-thrust test asks us to examine the parties' circumstances to determine whether their primary reason for entering the contract was the goods or the services component. Pain Center argues that its primary reason for executing these agreements was to obtain SSIMED's billing services and that the software was merely a conduit to transfer claims data to SSIMED to allow it to perform those services. SSIMED counters that the parties' focus was software—not services—because Pain Center used the software day in and day out; it points out that the initial training on the programs lasted a total of only ten days.

Pain Center has the better of this debate. SSIMED overlooks that Pain Center received monthly billing and IT services for the life of both contracts. In fact, [SSIMED's sales rep] testified that SSIMED licensed its software *only* when purchased in conjunction with billing and support services. Pain Center used the software to input its daily insurance claims and transmit the data via zip file to SSIMED's billing system. After receiving a zip file from Pain Center, SSIMED generated claims files and submitted them to insurers. If the insurer refused to pay a claim due to an error, SSIMED placed them in the Client Center to be corrected. The software was merely the vehicle through which Pain Center communicated its claims information to SSIMED in order to access its billing and collection services. This second factor weighs heavily in favor of a conclusion that services predominate and that the goods were incidental.

The third and final factor—the relative cost of the goods and services—also points toward that conclusion. As the Indiana Supreme Court has explained, "[i]f the cost of the goods is but a small portion of the overall contract price, such fact would increase the likelihood that the services portion predominates." Under the Practice Manager agreement, Pain Center paid a one-time licensing fee of $8,000 for software; a one-time training fee of $2,000; and $224.95 each month for services and support for about nine years. Thus, for the life of the Practice Manager agreement, the services totaled approximately $26,294—more than three times the $8,000 licensing fee for the software. Under the EMRge agreement, Pain Center paid a one-time licensing fee of $23,275 for the software; a one-time training fee of $4,000; and $284 per month for services and support for about six years. Thus, the services totaled about $24,448—slightly more than the $23,275 software licensing fee. The relative-cost factor reinforces the conclusion that services predominate.

On balance, then, the predominant thrust of the two agreements is medical billing and IT services, not the sale of goods. So the UCC and its four-year limitations period do not apply. Instead, the breach-of-contract claims are subject to Indiana's ten-year statute of limitations for written contracts and are timely.

4. UCITA. In 1999 NCCUSL promulgated the Uniform Computer Information Transactions Act (UCITA) to govern transactions in computer information, including sales (licensing) of computer programs on disks. UCITA had a difficult gestation and has not fared well since its birth. It began as a proposal for addition to the UCC, to be known as Article 2B. When ALI, a co-sponsor of the UCC, became displeased with the direction in which the drafting of Article 2B was heading, it withdrew from participation in further development of the proposal. The withdrawal of ALI meant that the project could not continue as a part of the Uniform Commercial Code, so NCCUSL renamed the Act and continued with its development.

UCITA is a difficult statute technically. It has long, complex definitions and intricate substantive provisions. It has been criticized for its complexity, and there has been sharp disagreement about the wisdom of its substantive provisions. Software developers have generally been strong supporters of UCITA; many purchasers of software have opposed it. UCITA has been adopted in only two states (Virginia and Maryland), and at least four states (Iowa, North Carolina, Vermont, and West Virginia) have adopted "UCITA-shield" statutes providing that choice-of-law provisions applying UCITA to residents of those states are not effective. In August 2003 NCCUSL announced that it would not seek additional adoptions of UCITA.

Though widespread adoption of UCITA is unlikely, its scope provisions may be relevant to determining the proper scope of Article 2. As its title indicates, UCITA "applies to computer information transactions." (§ 103(a)). Section 102(a)(11) defines "computer information transaction" as "an agreement or the performance of it to create, modify, transfer, or license computer information or informational rights in computer information." Section 102(a)(10) defines "computer information" as "information in electronic form which is obtained from or through the use of a computer or which is in a form capable of being processed by a computer. The term includes a copy of the information and any documentation or packaging associated with the copy."

As you see from the last sentence quoted, UCITA covers the purchase or license of a computer program, including one contained on a disk, along with its licensing agreement and liability disclaimers. Therefore, in the two states that have adopted UCITA, these transactions would be removed from Article 2. This would seem to be the case also in Oklahoma, where the legislature revised the definition of "goods" to state that the term "does not include information." Okla. Stat. tit. 12A, § 2–105(1).

5.   In states that do not adopt UCITA, difficult problems of scope remain. An increasing number of goods contain software (sometimes called "smart goods"). For example, many of the systems in an automobile are controlled by software, with different programs for each system. Is the sale of an automobile beyond the scope of Article 2? If the software controlling the engine has a flaw that causes the engine to die when the car is traveling at highway speeds, will the buyer's rights be governed by the warranty provisions of Article 2?

What if the seller calls the buyer six months after she has purchased the car and says, "The manufacturer has just issued an improved software program to control the engine in your new car. It's only $50. Bring the car in, and we'll install the new software." If a flaw in this program causes the engine to malfunction, are the purchaser's rights governed by Article 2?

6.   **Distributorship and franchise agreements.** In a franchise relationship the franchisee acquires goods and intellectual property from the franchisor and sells goods and services under the franchisor's trademark. To what extent is the relationship governed by Article 2? In Zapatha v. Dairy

Mart, Inc., 381 Mass. 284, 408 N.E.2d 1370 (1980), the franchisee, Zapatha, claimed that the franchisor, Dairy Mart, wrongfully terminated the franchise under which Zapatha operated a Dairy Mart store. Zapatha argued that the franchise agreement was subject to Article 2 and that the provision allowing termination was unconscionable and its exercise was in bad faith under the relevant provisions of Article 2. In the course of upholding Dairy Mart's termination of the franchise, the court stated:

> We need not pause long over the question whether the franchise agreement and the relationship of the parties involved a transaction in goods. Certainly, the agreement required the plaintiffs to purchase goods from Dairy Mart. . . . However, the franchise agreement dealt with many subjects unrelated to the sale of goods by Dairy Mart. About 70% of the goods the plaintiffs sold were not purchased from Dairy Mart. Dairy Mart's profit was intended to come from the franchise fee and not from the sale of items to its franchisees. Thus, the sale of goods by Dairy Mart to the Zapathas was, in a commercial sense, a minor aspect of the entire relationship. We would be disinclined to import automatically all the provisions of the sales article into a relationship involving a variety of subjects other than the sale of goods, merely because the contract dealt in part with the sale of goods. Similarly, we would not be inclined to apply the sales article only to aspects of the agreement that concerned goods. Different principles of law might then govern separate portions of the same agreement with possibly inconsistent and unsatisfactory consequences.

> We view the legislative statements of policy concerning good faith and unconscionability as fairly applicable to all aspects of the franchise agreement, not by subjecting the franchise relationship to the provisions of the sales article but rather by applying the stated principles by analogy. . . . This basic common law approach, applied to statutory statements of policy, permits a selective application of those principles expressed in a statute that reasonably should govern situations to which the statute does not apply explicitly.

7.   **Contracts involving the sale of both goods and real estate.** In Dehahn v. Innes, 356 A.2d 711 (Me.1976), Dehahn orally agreed to sell and Innes orally agreed to buy for a price of $35,000 a 52-acre gravel pit, a backhoe, a bulldozer, a loader, a dump truck with plow, and a second truck and trailer. It was found that Dehahn had agreed to deliver the equipment in "ready-to-go condition." After numerous complaints about Dehahn's failure to put the equipment in this kind of condition, Innes notified him that he was canceling the contract. No payments were ever made pursuant to the contract. Dehahn sued for breach of contract, basing his cause of action on Article 2. Innes denied the applicability of Article 2. How would you decide the case? Do you need more facts than are given above to make your decision? If so, what are they and why do you need them? See 2–107.

8. "Unless the context otherwise requires." While 2–101 gives Article 2 the official title "Uniform Commercial Code—Sales," 2–102 provides that "Unless the context otherwise requires, this Article applies to transactions in goods. . . ." See also 2–106(1). Is there any inconsistency between these sections?

In *Architectronics* the court stated that since Article 2 applies to *transactions* in goods, its coverage is not limited to sales, and that, therefore, a licensing transaction could fall within Article 2.

Problem. Floyd, a rock star, misplaced his laptop, which contained the only copy of a recent recording session. To regain possession of the laptop, during an appearance on a late-night TV show, Floyd offered $100,000 for the return of the laptop with the session files intact. While rummaging through a trash bin in a city park, Augie found a laptop. Wondering whether it might be the one lost by Floyd, he turned it in to the police, who determined that it was indeed the one lost by Floyd. The police returned it to Floyd, but Floyd failed to pay the reward to Augie. When Augie sued, Floyd claimed that the lawsuit was not timely because it was filed more than four years after Augie returned the laptop. Does 2–725 bar recovery: is this a transaction in goods, within the scope of Article 2?

9. Leases: the scope of Article 2A. Article 2 applies to "transactions" in goods, and leases are transactions. Consequently, as originally enacted, Article 2 applied to leases. But leases have become a huge part of our economy—amounting annually to more than a trillion dollars—and several aspects of lease transactions merit different treatment than is appropriate for sales transactions (viz., some aspects of the parties' obligations as well as the remedies available in the event of breach by the lessee). Hence, in 1989 Article 2A was added to the UCC, providing that Article 2A applies to "any transaction, regardless of form, that creates a lease" (2A–102). If it is a lease, then Article 2A, not Article 2, applies. This means that it is necessary to decide whether a transaction is either a sale or a lease. Before exploring the criteria for making that decision, an explanation of why the parties might prefer a lease to a sale is in order. The reasons for preferring a lease to a sale include business, accounting, and taxation considerations.

- *Business considerations.* If a business can afford to pay cash for the equipment it needs, the choice is between a purchase and a lease. But the business may expect its equipment to become obsolescent for the business' particular purposes long before the equipment becomes useless for all purposes. If the equipment is leased, upon expiration of the lease the lessee returns it to the lessor, who may be in a better position than the lessee to dispose of it, whether by re-leasing it or by selling it. Since the lessee returns the goods, the total amount paid by the lessee does not cover the full value of the goods, but only the value corresponding to the lessee's use.

    If the business cannot afford to pay cash, the main alternative to a lease is a sale on credit with the seller retaining a security interest in the goods. To protect itself against other creditors of a buyer (or a buyer from the buyer), a credit seller must file a financing statement. Not so with a lease. Because a lessor retains title to the leased goods, the lessor does not need to file any financing statement. If the lessee defaults, the lessor may simply retake the goods. If the transaction were a sale, on the other hand, the secured seller would have to pursue the foreclosure proceedings that Article 9 specifies for enforcement of a security interest. This may make the supplier more willing to lease goods than to sell them on credit, thereby making it easier for a business to acquire goods by leasing than by purchasing.

Another business consideration is the ability of the parties to structure a lease so as to require the lessor to pay for insurance, maintenance, or repair of the leased goods. In a sales transaction, all those expenses would fall on the purchaser.

- Accounting considerations. When a business purchases an item on credit, its balance sheet lists the item as an asset and the amount owed for the item as a liability. This typically adversely affects the business' debt-to-equity ratio, which is a figure monitored by the business' other creditors (and investors). Leasing, on the other hand, does not affect the financial ratios. When a business purchases equipment or other capital goods, it may depreciate the goods over their useful life. It may not do this with respect to goods it leases.

- Tax considerations. The Internal Revenue Code permits businesses to depreciate capital goods on an accelerated basis, permitting greater deductions from income in the early years of a credit purchase than are permitted by accounting standards. If the business is losing money—and therefore does not need the benefit of the oversized deduction for depreciation—this tax factor may not be important, and leasing is more attractive.

The entire calculus of which form of transaction is preferable is quite involved, and this description barely scratches the surface. From a planning standpoint, much further study is required to determine whether a user or supplier should structure a transaction as a sale (on credit) or a lease. The concern at this stage of the book is whether a given transaction must comply with the Article 2 rules for sales or with the Article 2A rules for leases. For example, 2–316(2) and (3) apparently permit oral disclaimers of implied warranties, while 2A–214 requires that these disclaimers be in writing.

Section 2–106(1) defines "sale" as the passage of title for a price. Section 2A–103(1)(j) defines "lease" as "a transfer of the right to possession and use of goods for a term in return for consideration, but a sale . . . or retention or creation of a security interest is not a lease." Under this structure, if a transaction is a sale, it cannot be a lease. But 2A–103 adds that a retention or creation of a security interest is not a lease either. Section 1–201(b)(35) defines "security interest" as

> an interest in personal property . . . which secures payment or performance of an obligation. . . . Whether a transaction in the form of a lease creates a "security interest" is determined pursuant to Section 1–203.

Section 1–203 sets out standards for determining whether a transaction is a lease or a security agreement. Please examine that section in connection with the following two problems.

a.   Problem. Apex and Bestway entered into a transaction under which Apex leased to Bestway a new IBM computer at a rental of $1,000 per month for five years, at the end of which Bestway had the option to acquire the computer for an additional payment of $100. Apex claimed that it orally disclaimed all warranties of merchantability. Is the transaction a lease or a sale?

b.   Problem. Acme and Buildit entered into a transaction under which Acme leased to Buildit a used road-paving machine for three years at a rental of $2,000 per month, with an option to purchase the machine at the end of the three-year period for $10,000. Acme claimed that it orally agreed with Buildit that the transaction was "as is." Is the transaction a sale or a lease? Is it relevant that the reasonably expectable value of the machine at the end of the term was $30,000?

10. International transactions: the scope of CISG. There are three aspects to the scope of the Convention on Contracts for the International Sale of Goods: (1) whether the transaction is international; (2) whether the transaction is a type excluded from coverage of the Convention; and (3) whether the preponderant part of the transaction consists in the supply of labor or other services. Also, of course, it is necessary that the country whose law would apply has ratified the Convention.* As of July 1, 2015, more than 70 countries, including the United States, have ratified it.

First, the Convention applies only to sales of goods between parties whose places of business are in different countries (Article 1). Further, the Convention does not apply even though the parties have their places of business in different countries if that "fact does not appear from the contract or from dealings between, or from information disclosed by, the parties at any time before or at the conclusion, of the contract." (Article 1). The reason for the second limitation is that a seller or buyer who at the time of contracting has no reason to know that the Convention is applicable should not be bound by it. An example is a buyer who is buying for an undisclosed foreign principal. See J. Honnold, Uniform Law for International Sales § 41 (4th ed.2009).

---

*   Article 1(1) of the Convention provides that the Convention applies to contracts of sale between parties whose places of business are in different countries if (1) the countries have ratified the Convention, or (2) if the rules of international private law would lead to the application of the law of a country that has ratified the Convention. As permitted by Article 95, the United States has declared that it is not bound by the second ground for application of the Convention.

Second, Article 2 of the Convention provides that it does not apply to sales of electricity, ships, vessels, hovercraft, or aircraft. Nor does it apply to sales by auction or sales on execution or otherwise by authority of law. Further, it does not apply to goods bought for personal, family, or household use unless the seller neither knew nor had reason to know that the goods were bought for that use. The exclusion for consumer goods preserves the consumer-protection laws of the various countries.

Third, Article 3 provides that the Convention applies to contracts for the manufacture or production of goods unless the buyer is to supply "a substantial part of the materials necessary for such manufacture or production" (Paragraph 1), but "does not apply to contracts in which the preponderant part of the obligations of the party who furnishes the goods consists in the supply of labour or other services" (Paragraph 2). Since the manufacture of goods entails the use of "labour or other services," do the two rules of Article 3 contradict each other? Would the Salvador Dali contract (page 13 supra) be covered by the Convention?

In the sales-services hybrid transaction, what test does the Convention adopt? If the parties to the contract in *BMC v. Barth* were a Canadian tool-and-die maker and a United States optician, would the transaction be governed by the Convention?

In Problem 8(a), page 24, if the parties were a German seller and an American auto manufacturer, and the contract called for the seller to design and incorporate into the buyer's plant several pieces of robotic equipment, for $2 million, would the Convention apply? Would it be relevant that the cost of the movable things incorporated into the equipment is $1.1 million? $800,000?

C. RELATIONSHIP OF ARTICLE 2 TO OTHER LAW

1. APPLICATION OF ARTICLE 2 RULES IN NON-GOODS TRANSACTIONS

In Zapatha v. Dairy Mart, Note 6 on page 34, the court held that even though a franchise agreement established a relationship in which the franchisee regularly purchased goods from the franchisor, the franchise agreement was not governed by Article 2. The purchase of goods from the franchisor "was, in a commercial sense, a minor aspect of the entire relationship." Nevertheless, the court thought that the principles of good faith and unconscionability, found in Article 2, should apply to a franchise relationship. In Wille v. Southwestern Bell Tel. Co., 219 Kan. 755, 549 P.2d 903 (1976), the court invoked the unconscionability doctrine in a dispute over a provision in a contract to place an advertisement in the Yellow Pages telephone directory. It stated, "Although the UCC's application is primarily limited to contracts for the present or future sale of goods, many courts have extended the statute by analogy into other areas of the law or have used the doctrine as an alternative basis for their holdings."

This application of Article 2 principles by analogy to transactions clearly not within the scope of Article 2 is common. For another example, see Hoffman v. Horton, 212 Va. 565, 186 S.E.2d 79 (1972), which concerned an auction to foreclose a real estate deed of trust. Following a pause in the bidding, the auctioneer stated, "Going once, going twice, sold for $177,000," and struck the palm of one hand with the fist of the other. Immediately he was informed that he had missed a higher bid. The auctioneer proceeded to reopen the bidding. The litigation concerned the bidder's claim that he had purchased the property for the $177,000 initially announced by the auctioneer.

The trial court relied on Article 2, which in 2–328 states that an auctioneer has discretion to reopen the bidding if a bid is made "while the hammer is falling." The court stated:

> We disagree with the trial court that the transaction in this case, involving the sale of land, is controlled by [2–328, which] applies only to transactions relating to "goods."

> However, while the Uniform Commercial Code is not controlling here, we think it appropriate to borrow from it to establish the rule applicable to the transaction at hand. To vest the auctioneer crying a sale of land with the same discretion to reopen bidding that he has in the sale of goods is to achieve uniformity and, of more importance, to recognize a rule which is both necessary and fair.

Courts have turned to the UCC in cases beyond its scope because they believe it is superior law. In Appeals of Reeves Soundcraft Corp., 2 UCC Rep.Serv. 210 (ASB-CA 1964), the armed services Board of Contract Appeals considered a dispute involving the warranty obligation of a seller of magnetic tape to the federal government. Although the transaction concerned a sale of goods, the government claimed that the matter should be controlled by federal common law, not the state UCC. The Board agreed, but then held that the federal common law should be deemed to include relevant portions of the UCC, because there was little, if any, federal case law on the point involved, and, anyway, the UCC reflects "the best in modern decisions and discussion."

2. DISTINGUISHING REAL ESTATE FROM PERSONAL PROPERTY FOR PURPOSES OF THE APPLICATION OF THE UCC

In the *Hoffman* case it is clear that the contract involved the sale of real estate. Sometimes, however, it is not so clear whether real or personal property is involved. The distinction has been particularly important for purposes of the statute of frauds since, typically, it is much easier to satisfy the statute of frauds relating to personal property than real property. The problem has arisen most frequently in the context of contracts to sell crops, timber, and structures that are to be severed from land and delivered to the buyer for relocation.

With respect to crops, the common-law distinction did not turn on whether the sale involved growing crops or harvested crops. Instead, the distinction usually turned on the difference between *fructus naturales* and *fructus industriales*. *Fructus naturales* consisted of those things which grow without cultivation, such as grass and trees. *Fructus industriales* consisted of crops that must be planted and cultivated. The courts held that *fructus industriales* was "goods" for purposes of the sales statute of frauds, even though it was not severed from the land or matured at the time of the sale. See, for example, Green v. Armstrong, 1 Denio (N.Y.) 550 (1845). On the other hand, *fructus naturales* was often treated as land, even though the contract contemplated immediate severance. Smith v. Thomas, 224 Ala. 41, 138 So. 542 (1931); Baird v. Elliott, 63 N.D. 738, 249 N.W. 894, 91 A.L.R. 1274 (1933); Beckman v. Brickley, 144 Wash. 558, 258 P. 488 (1927); contra, Patton v. Lucy, 285 Ky. 694, 148 S.W.2d 1039 (1940); Hurricane Lumber Co. v. Lowe, 110 Va. 380, 66 S.E. 66 (1909). In Robbins v. Farwell, 193 Pa. 37, 44, 44 A. 260, 261, 262 (1899), the court stated, "If the agreement does not contemplate the immediate severance of the timber, it is a contract for the sale or reservation of an interest in land. . . . But when the agreement is made with a view to the immediate severance of the timber from the soil it is regarded as personal property."

With respect to the sale of buildings and fixtures that were to be severed and removed immediately, at common law the courts were inclined to permit the parties to treat the contract as involving "goods" for purposes of the statute of frauds. E.g., Wetopsky v. New Haven Gas Light Co., 88 Conn. 1, 90 A. 30 (1914); Cleveland Wrecking Co. v. Federal Deposit Ins. Corp., 66 F.Supp. 921 (E.D.Pa.1946); Cervadoro v. First Nat. Bank and Trust Co., 267 App.Div. 314, 45 N.Y.S.2d 738 (1944).

Consider the converse situation in which one sells goods that are to be affixed to real estate, with the property interest passing from the seller to the buyer after the affixture. In Frederick Raff Co. v. Murphy, 110 Conn. 234, 147 A. 709 (1929), the court held that a contract to do plumbing work and add fixtures was not for the sale of "goods," since under the agreement "title to the articles was not to pass to the [buyer] as in articles of personal property but in articles which, by the very terms of the contract, were to be affixed to and become part of the realty.

In what respects does the UCC change this common law?

3. PRIMACY OF OTHER STATUTES

Note that 2–102 not only states that Article 2 applies to transactions in goods, it also states that the Article does not "impair or repeal any statute regulating sales to consumers, farmers or other specified classes of buyers." There are numerous such statutes in every state. How do those statutes interact with Article 2?

Pet Dealers Association of New Jersey, Inc. v. Division of Consumer Affairs, Dept. of Law and Public Safety, State of New Jersey

New Jersey Superior Court, Appellate Division, 1977.
149 N.J.Super. 235, 373 A.2d 688.

■ Per Curiam. By this appeal Pet Dealers Association of New Jersey, Inc. challenges the validity of the Attorney General's regulations governing the sale of pet cats and dogs adopted pursuant to the Consumer Fraud Act, N.J.S.A. 56:8–4.

Pet Dealers first contends that the regulations in question conflict with Article 2 of the Uniform Commercial Code (N.J.S.A. 12A:2–101 et seq.) in that the regulations provide the consumer with broader remedies than are available under the Code. It is argued that since the regulations conflict with applicable statutory provisions, the regulations are invalid. A similar argument was recently made to and rejected by the Supreme Court in Jeselsohn, Inc. v. Atlantic City, 70 N.J. 238, 358 A.2d 797 (1976). There, auctioneers doing business in Atlantic City attacked a local ordinance which regulated auction sales. The ordinance required an auctioneer to refund, in full, the purchase price of an article when a demand for such is made within 72 hours after purchase. The basic contention as to the invalidity of the ordinance was that it conflicted with provisions of the Uniform Commercial Code regulating auction sales. In rejecting that argument the court said that the provisions of the Code dealing with sales, rescission and revocation of acceptance "are intended to give certainty and stability to the law of commercial transactions. In this sense they do not purport to limit the proper exercise of police power in the public interest." 70 N.J. at 244, 358 A.2d at 800. So here. The fact that the regulations are part of a statewide plan to combat consumer fraud rather than a local ordinance does not alter their legitimacy as a valid exercise of police power. In any event the Code expressly provides that it does not "impair or repeal any statute regulating sales to consumers * * *." N.J.S.A. 12A:2–102. Thus, there is no conflict between the Code and the Consumer Fraud Act, nor with the regulations adopted thereunder. . . .

For the foregoing reasons we conclude that the regulations challenged by "Pet Dealers" (N.J.A.C. 13:45A–12.1 et seq.) are valid.

Questions and Notes

1. In most civil law countries there is both a civil and a commercial code. The latter is usually made applicable only when one (or both) of the parties is a merchant, and the civil code applies when this condition is not met. Lawyers from civil law countries often assume that this dichotomy exists in

the United States, too, since we have a "Commercial Code." They are surprised to learn that most of the UCC covers transactions involving both consumers and merchants and all combinations thereof.

In a sense, however, the United States has been moving toward the distinction between merchant and consumer transactions observed in civil law countries, first, by setting forth some nineteen special rules for merchant sellers in Article 2 of the UCC, and, second, by the enactment of special legislation designed to give particular protection to consumers and others, such as farmers. With regard to this kind of special legislation, the lawyer must be careful in his or her statutory research, for local pressure groups (e.g., the dog and cat lovers of New Jersey) may be successful in securing legislation dealing with subject matter that may not seem particularly appropriate for special treatment. Transactions involving automobiles, home improvement products (or the installation thereof), and agricultural products (e.g., pesticides, seed, livestock, etc.) should be scrutinized carefully in terms of special legislation, since the bulk of special legislation involves consumers and farmers. For some interesting cases involving the interaction of special legislation on these matters and the UCC see, Morris Plan Co. of California v. Moody, 266 Cal.App.2d 28, 72 Cal.Rptr. 123 (1968) (interaction between Article 2 and the California Motor Vehicle Code); Feary v. Aaron Burglar Alarm, Inc., 32 Cal.App.3d 553, 108 Cal.Rptr. 242 (1973) (interaction between Article 2 and a California statute governing damages for breach of a contract for installation of a burglar alarm system); Potter v. Tyndall, 22 N.C.App. 129, 205 S.E.2d 808 (1974) (interaction between Article 2 and a North Carolina statute relating to the sale of agricultural fertilizer); Olson v. Molacek Bros., 341 N.W.2d 375 (N.D.1983) (impact of Article 2 on a North Dakota statute providing civil and criminal penalties for the sale of diseased cattle); Hoffman Motors, Inc. v. Enockson, 240 N.W.2d 353 (N.D.1976) (interaction between Article 2 and a North Dakota statute governing warranties on the sale of tractors to farmers). For a sense of the extent to which the states have enacted legislation regulating various kinds of consumer transactions, see the table of contents to Oregon Revised Statutes, tit. 50, ch. 646a (regulating the sale of manufactured homes, used goods, precious metals, telephone equipment, dogs, farm implements, motor vehicles, hazardous substances, infant cribs, children's products, portable electronics, and warranties on new motor vehicles and assistive devices.

2. A lawyer handling sales problems will soon learn of some of the statutes giving consumers special protection. Every state, for example, has one or more statutes protecting consumers against deceptive or unfair conduct by merchants or creditors. These are modeled on similar federal laws, such as the Federal Trade Commission Act, which prohibits unfair or deceptive acts or practices. These state laws often are referred to by their acronym, UDAP statutes. States also have enacted legislation that focuses on the credit aspects of sales transactions, often known as retail installment sales acts (RISAs). In addition, NCCUSL proposed a Uniform Consumer Credit Code (UCCC), which approximately a dozen states enacted.

In spite of the promulgation of the UCCC and other local statutes aimed at giving consumers special protection, Congress has been impatient with the efforts of the states and has made incursions of its own in the sales area, a significant example of which is the Magnuson-Moss Warranty Act, to be considered in Chapter 5.

3. It should be noted that there is a great difference between impairment and displacement. The UCC does not impair most regulatory statutes, but most regulatory statutes, in turn, do not completely displace the UCC. Thus, the sale of a cat in New Jersey may carry with it special remedies governed by the special legislation, but routine matters such as the price term and delivery requirements are governed by the UCC.

Finally, it should be observed that the time may come when it will be advisable to enact a "Uniform Consumer Code" to parallel the UCC, which, of course, would have to be appropriately amended to delete any coverage of consumer transactions. It may surprise you to know that the impetus for this change has been more from the commercial sector than from the consumer sector. What do you think commercial giants or small merchants have to gain by separating the statutory law of commercial and consumer transactions? Are their interests identical with regard to such a proposal?

D. Territorial and Temporal Limitations and Choice of Law

1. Choice of Law

The choice-of-law rules deal with two related questions: (1) To what extent can the parties choose the jurisdiction whose law will govern their transaction? and (2) Which jurisdiction's law applies if the parties do not choose a jurisdiction or if their choice is ineffective? Before turning to the Code rules on these issues, we should note that the court in which litigation is brought, called the forum, does not, and constitutionally cannot, apply its own substantive law to every matter that is brought before it. See Hay, Borchers, Symeonides & Whytock, Conflict of Laws ch. 3, sec. III (6th ed. 2018). An entire body of law has developed to determine what substantive law applies when a transaction has contacts in more than one state or country. For example, suppose a New York seller makes a contract to sell goods to a California buyer. Suppose, additionally, that the contract is valid under the laws of New York but invalid under the laws of California. If the law of the forum were applied automatically, the plaintiff (either buyer or seller) could control the result of any dispute by bringing the action in California or New York, depending on the outcome the plaintiff desired. The prevention of this phenomenon, called forum-shopping, is one of the main purposes of conflict-of-laws rules.

A related issue is whether the parties in the New York-California hypothetical can choose the law of either California or New York. Similarly suppose the contract is between two New York parties; can they choose the law of California as the law governing their transactions?

Section 1–105 of the 1962 version of the UCC mandated the application of the law of a particular state for a handful of transactions and gave the parties the competence to choose their own law for all others. This competence, however, was not absolute. The law chosen had to bear a "reasonable" relation to the transaction. Chapter 3 considers the meaning of this limitation.

The 1962 version also provided that if the parties failed to specify the law of a state that bears a reasonable relation to the transaction, or if they made no choice of law at all, then the law of the forum would apply, assuming that it bore an "appropriate" relation to the transaction.

In 2001 NCCUSL and ALI promulgated revised Article 1, which contained a choice of law provision that greatly expanded the parties' ability to choose their law. With exceptions for consumer transactions, in domestic transactions (i.e. those that do not bear a reasonable relationship to a foreign country) the parties were empowered to choose the law of any state, whether or not the state chosen has a reasonable relationship to the transaction. Similarly, in an international transaction, the parties could choose the law of any state or country whether or not the state or country had a reasonable relationship with the transaction.

This new choice-of-law provision was the subject of substantial attack, and as of 2008 none of the states adopting revised Article 1 had adopted the revised choice-of-law section. Instead, they all substituted the text of original 1–105 in place of the revised version. In 2008 NCCUSL and ALI relented and restored the original version, which now is 1–301.

2. TRANSITIONAL PROVISIONS

When a new statute governing private contracting is adopted, the statute, if well drafted, will state the extent to which transactions entered into before the effective date of the new statute are subject to the new statute. Those transitional provisions applicable to original Articles 2 and 2A, appear in Articles 10 and 11. Today it is unlikely that any of those pre-existing contracts exist or would call the transitional provisions into play.

CHAPTER 3

FORMATION OF THE SALES CONTRACT

A. INTRODUCTION

Prior to the enactment of the UCC, the formation of a sales contract with few exceptions was governed by the same rules as the formation of any other contract. Initially, the drafters strongly suspected that sales contracts needed different formation rules from those employed in, for example, contracts for construction, employment, or the sale of real estate. As a result of this suspicion, the drafters of the Code made a thorough investigation of how the formation rules were operating in the sales area. To their surprise, they found that in the main the common-law rules were working quite well. Their investigation revealed, however, a few situations that needed to be corrected by special rules applicable to sales transactions. These rules appear in Part 2 of Article 2, specifically, in the ten sections beginning with 2–201, and they are the principal focus of this chapter. In reading this chapter, please remember that unless Article 2 specifically provides otherwise, the contract formation rules of the common law continue to operate with full vigor in the commercial arena of sales law. See 1–103(b) and Official Comment 2.

B. OFFER AND ACCEPTANCE

The most important changes to the common-law rules of contract formation appear in sections 2–204, 2–206, and 2–207. Please read 2–204 now. When the parties have come to an agreement, that section seeks to make the agreement binding and to eschew the technicalities developed under the common law in some states that prevented formation of a contract. These technicalities often were expressed in terms of indefiniteness or lack of mutuality. They were used, for example, to invalidate contracts that contained on open-price term, those that were more or less indefinite as to the respective obligations of the parties as to the particulars of performance, and those that were vague as to the precise moment that the agreement had been struck. Subsection (2) makes it clear that it is unnecessary to identify the precise time at which the parties' interactions result in a contract. And subsection (3) loosens considerably the pre-Code requirements for definiteness. The following case provides a good example.

In Jannusch v. Noffziger, 379 Ill.App.3d 381, 318 Ill.Dec. 480, 883 N.E.2d 711 (2008), defendants were interested in purchasing plaintiffs' business, a food concession that traveled to various public events. The assets included a truck, trailer, cooking equipment, tables and chairs, and more. In August the parties agreed on a price of $150,000, defendants paid $10,000, took possession of the assets, and operated the business for the remainder of the season. When defendants refused to pay the balance of the price, plaintiffs sued, alleging that the parties had formed a contract. In response, defendants alleged they were operating the business as part of their attempt to determine if they wanted to purchase the business, emphasizing the indefiniteness and incompleteness of the agreement:

> . . . nothing was said in the contract about allocating a price for good will, a covenant not to compete, allocating a price for the equipment, how to release liens, what would happen if there was no loan approval, and other issues. Defendants argue these are essential terms for the sale of a business and the Internal Revenue Service requires that parties allocate the sales price [between the physical assets and good will]. "None of these items were even discussed much less agreed to. There is not an enforceable agreement when there are so many essential terms missing."

The court rejected defendants' argument:

> The essential terms were agreed upon in this case. The purchase price was $150,000, and the items to be transferred were specified. No essential terms remained to be agreed upon; the only action remaining was the performance of the contract. Defendants took possession of the items to be transferred and used them as their own. . . .
>
> The trial court noted that "the parties have very different views about what transpired in the course of the contract-formation discussions." It is not necessary that the parties share a subjective understanding as to the terms of the contract; the parties' conduct may indicate an agreement to the terms. The conduct in this case is clear. Parties discussing the sale of goods do not transfer those goods and allow them to be retained for a substantial period before reaching agreement. Defendants replaced equipment, reported income, paid taxes, and paid [plaintiff] for his time and expenses, all of which is inconsistent with the idea that defendants were only "pursuing buying the business." An agreement to make an agreement is not an agreement, but there was clearly more than that here.
>
> . . . The parties' agreement could have been fleshed out with additional terms, but the essential terms were agreed upon. . . . Returning the goods at the end of the season was not a rejection of plaintiffs' offer to sell, it was a breach of contract."

As with non-code transactions, litigants may have very different versions of the facts. Before applying the Article 2 rules governing formation, the court must determine the facts. For another good example, see ReMapp

Int'l Corp. v. Comfort Keyboard Co., 560 F.3d 628 (7th Cir.2009). The "intent to contract" required by 2–204(3) also is a question of fact for the trier of fact. The trial judge's finding of fact cannot be disturbed on appeal if supported by competent evidence in the record. Bethlehem Steel Corp. v. Litton Industries, Inc., 321 Pa.Super. 357, 468 A.2d 748 (1983).

QUESTIONS AND NOTES

1.   Granting the desirability of the liberalization of the law embodied in 2–204(3), is it not still important to find that the parties did, in fact, come to an agreement before a contract between them is found to exist? In other words, it is possible to work out rules of law that determine the details of performance once the parties have agreed on a deal, albeit vaguely as to some terms and details, but, is it not another matter to conclude that a vague interaction between them amounts to an agreement?

Problem. Dobbs, the owner of Dobbs Mfg. Co., desired to replace a large, expensive piece of equipment. He told Quipco's sales rep, Peterson, that he intended to purchase the replacement from Quipco and enlisted her aid to find a buyer for the item to be replaced. After finding a buyer for Dobbs' old equipment, Peterson met with Dobbs to discuss purchase of the replacement. They agreed on the precise piece of equipment, its price, and the time frame for delivery. They ended the conversation with Peterson saying that she would stop by Dobbs' factory the next day with a written version for the parties to sign. When Peterson showed up, Dobbs saw that the document called for payment on delivery, and the following colloquy occurred:

> Dobbs: "Oh, no, I can't sign that. We need to have 90 days credit."

> Peterson: "Sorry, we don't do that, but we could give you 30 days."

> Dobbs: "That's not enough. Look, you helped us with the sale of our old equipment, without charging any commission, so we didn't haggle as much on the price as we normally would. But we can't pay top dollar and also pay on delivery. We need some leeway on credit terms."

Quipco refused to extend the credit period, Dobbs refused to sign the document, and Quipco sued. Is there a contract?

2.   Since 2–204(1) states that a contract may be made "in any manner sufficient to show agreement," parties may form a contract by an exchange of e-mail communications. But this does not mean that every exchange of e-mails in which each party assents to an exchange necessarily results in a contract. (The same may be said of face-to-face and written communications.) An example is Alliance Laundry Systems, LLC v. Thyssenkrupp Materials, N.A., 570 F.Supp.2d 1061 (E.D.Wis.2008), in which the parties had a written contract for defendant to supply plaintiff with steel for 18 months. Pursuant to this agreement, plaintiff submitted written purchase orders, which defendant signed and returned. When the contract expired, plaintiff had not paid for all the steel that had been delivered, and defendant still had on hand a supply of steel that it had anticipated selling to plaintiff. Defendant sent several e-mails to plaintiff inquiring whether plaintiff was interested in buying this steel. In response, plaintiff sent an e-mail offering to buy the steel. Defendant replied by e-mail instructing plaintiff to send its purchase order. Meanwhile, defendant's credit department halted the transaction until plaintiff paid the balance still due for steel delivered during the 18-month contract. Ultimately, defendant refused to deliver to plaintiff, which sued and moved for summary judgment. Denying the motion, the court stated:

> I first consider the issue as one of contract formation: did defendant agree to sell the inventory to plaintiff? The Uniform Commercial Code ("UCC") governs this issue because the case involves the sale of goods. Article 2 of the UCC provides that "[a] contract for the sale of goods may be made in any manner sufficient to show agreement, including conduct by both parties which recognizes the existence of such a contract." In the present case, defendant invited plaintiff to submit an offer to purchase steel. On March 20, 2007, plaintiff did so by e-mailing defendant a spreadsheet detailing the items of defendant's inventory that it wished to purchase and the price it would pay. Later that day, defendant e-mailed a response directing plaintiff to supply a purchase order number so that defendant could "start shipping this metal to [plaintiff]." A reasonable jury could find that these e-mail communications formed a contract in which defendant promised to ship steel, and plaintiff promised to pay for it.

> However, in the parties' previous dealings, when defendant received a purchase order from plaintiff, defendant typically signed and returned it, and in the present case, defendant did not do so. Thus, a reasonable jury could conceivably conclude that the parties understood that until defendant signed and returned plaintiff's purchase order, their e-mail agreement was tentative. *Cf.* Francis H. Leggett Co. v. W. Salem Canning Co., 155 Wis. 462, 144 N.W. 969, 972 (1914) ("It is equally well settled, however, that letters or telegraphic communications between the parties will not be construed as a contract when it is plain that they were intended only as preliminary negotiations to be followed by a formal contract containing material provisions not contained in or to be inferred from the preliminary letters or communications.").

> The "conduct by both parties" after the initial exchange of e-mails is also relevant in determining whether the parties recognized the existence of a contract. Wis. Stat. § 402.204(1). Although plaintiff contends that on March 20, 2007, the parties formed a binding contract calling for the immediate shipment of steel, it did not object when defendant advised it that it would not ship steel until plaintiff paid its outstanding bill. If plaintiff believed that it had entered into a contract that required defendant to ship steel immediately, it is reasonable to infer that it would have demanded shipment by the end of March. Indeed, on past occasions when defendant did not ship metal on time, plaintiff

immediately inquired as to the status of the shipment. A jury might (but need not) infer from plaintiff's failure to complain that it did not recognize that the parties had entered into a contract. Thus, whether the parties formed a contract before defendant sold its inventory to someone other than plaintiff is a question of fact to be resolved by the jury after it considers all of the facts and circumstances surrounding the transaction and the parties' prior history.

3.   The law of contracts provides that an offer operates to create a power of acceptance in the offeree. Because the offeror is "the master of the offer," as many common law cases have stated, it is for the offeror to determine the nature and extent of the resultant power of acceptance, including the mode or form that the acceptance must take. As a consequence of these rules, it has generally been held at common law that an attempted acceptance made in a manner other than that prescribed by the offer is ineffective to form a contract. Does 2–206(1) of the UCC modify that position?

Problem. Suppose an offer is unclear as to the mode of acceptance, leaving the offeree in doubt as to how to bring a contract into being. This situation has happened with some frequency in commercial sales cases when telegrams and cablegrams were commonplace and economy of language was prevalent because the sender's cost of transmission was based on the number of words in the communication. Today communication by e-mail may be similarly terse. For example, a buyer, Vintage Discs, might send an e-mail, "Want 200 Elvis Presley CD sets. Ship Tuesday." Suppose the seller, Music Warehouse, e-mails back: "Will ship Tuesday, price $45." On Monday morning, before Music Warehouse has started performance, it receives from Vintage Discs an e-mail revoking the offer. If Vintage Discs can prove that it had written "Ship Tuesday" because it did not intend to be bound until Music Warehouse actually shipped the goods, is there a contract? Carefully read 2–206. Also look again at 2–204, and consult 2–305.

Instead of sending a revocation on Monday, what if Vintage Discs sent an e-mail, "Your price is too high, I don't want them at that price." Do the parties have a contract?

4.   Since Article 2 was drafted by the country's leading scholars and practitioners, it is not surprising that Article 2 has influenced judges resolving disputes not governed by Article 2. We have seen that already in the last chapter, at pages 39 and 40. Similarly, Article 2 influenced the drafting of the Restatement (Second) of Contracts, which was adopted in 1979. Thus, section 33 of the Restatement bears a striking resemblance to 2–204:

§ 33.   Certainty

(1)   Even though a manifestation of intention is intended to be understood as an offer, it cannot be accepted so as to form a contract unless the terms of the contract are reasonably certain.

(2)   The terms of a contract are reasonably certain if they provide a basis for determining the existence of a breach and for giving an appropriate remedy.

(3) The fact that one or more terms of a proposed bargain are left open or uncertain may show that a manifestation of intention is not intended to be understood as an offer or as an acceptance.

To what extent is this different from 2–204(3)?

C. STATUTE OF FRAUDS

Parliament enacted the Statute of Frauds in 1677 to avoid unfair results that seemed to flow from allowing courts to hear cases based on allegations of oral contracts. It was thought that where significant amounts of money were involved, the temptation to allege fraudulently the existence of contracts or terms that had not been made ought to be resisted by requiring some strong evidence that the allegations were true. Hence, the Statute of Frauds required a written agreement or other writing proving the existence of the contract and its essential terms. Unfortunately, rigid enforcement of the Statute of Frauds by some courts provided a shield for a bad-faith party by allowing that party to avoid a fairly made contract because of a failure to satisfy the formal requisites of the Statute. This led some other courts to avoid unjust results by ignoring or narrowly construing the Statute of Frauds.

In 1954 Parliament repealed the Statute of Frauds for sales cases governed by English law. Individuals studying and drafting the UCC were divided on the question whether the Statute of Frauds had done more harm than good, and a substantial number of them wanted to follow the English approach by eliminating it entirely. They were defeated in their efforts when the drafters promised to write a statute of frauds that would eliminate the potential for injustice by those who might be tempted to assert non-existent oral contracts, on the one hand, and those who would try to defeat, on technical grounds, contracts that in fact had been made, on the other hand. The result is 2–201, which generally requires a writing for contracts for more than $500. Consider whether the drafters made good on their promise.

————

Southwest Engineering Co., Inc. v. Martin Tractor Co., Inc.

Kansas Supreme Court, 1970.
205 Kan. 684, 473 P.2d 18.

■ FONTRON, JUSTICE. This is an action to recover damages for breach of contract. Trial was had to the court which entered judgment in favor of the plaintiff. The defendant has appealed.

Southwest Engineering Company, Inc., the plaintiff, is a Missouri corporation engaged in general contracting work, while the defendant, Martin Tractor Company, Inc., is a Kansas corporation. The two parties will be referred to hereafter either as plaintiff, or Southwest, on the one hand and defendant, or Martin, on the other.

We glean from the record that in April, 1966, the plaintiff was interested in submitting a bid to the United States Corps of Engineers for the construction of certain runway lighting facilities at McConnell Air Force Base at Wichita. However, before submitting a bid, and on April 11, 1966, the plaintiff's construction superintendent, Mr. R.E. Cloepfil, called the manager of Martin's engine department, Mr. Ken Hurt, who at the time was at Colby, asking for a price on a standby generator and accessory equipment. Mr. Hurt replied that he would phone him back from Topeka, which he did the next day, quoting a price of $18,500. This quotation was re-confirmed by Hurt over the phone on April 13.

Southwest submitted its bid on April 14, 1966, using Hurt's figure of $18,500 for the generator equipment, and its bid was accepted. On April 20, Southwest notified Martin that its bid had been accepted. Hurt and Cloepfil thereafter agreed over the phone to meet in Springfield on April 28. On that date Hurt flew to Springfield, where the two men conferred at the airfield restaurant for about an hour. Hurt took to the meeting a copy of the job specifications which the government had supplied Martin prior to the letting.

At the Springfield meeting it developed that Martin had upped its price for the generator and accessory equipment from $18,500 to $21,500. Despite this change of position by Martin, concerning which Cloepfil was understandably amazed, the two men continued their conversation and, according to Cloepfil, they arrived at an agreement for the sale of a D353 generator and accessories for the sum of $21,500. In addition it was agreed that if the Corps of Engineers would accept a less expensive generator, a D343, the aggregate price to Southwest would be $15,000. The possibility of providing alternative equipment, the D343, was suggested by Mr. Hurt, apparently in an attempt to mollify Mr. Cloepfil when the latter learned that Martin had reneged on its price quotation of April 12. It later developed that the Corps of Engineers would not approve the cheaper generator and that Southwest eventually had to supply the more expensive D353 generator.

At the conference, Mr. Hurt separately listed the component parts of each of the two generators on the top half of a sheet of paper and set out the price after each item. The prices were then totaled. On the bottom half of the sheet Hurt set down the accessories common to both generators and their cost. This handwritten memorandum, as it was referred to during the trial, noted a 10 per cent discount on the aggregate cost of each generator, while the accessories were listed at Martin's cost. The price of the D353 was rounded off at $21,500 and D343 at $15,000. The memorandum was handed to Cloepfil while the two men were still at the airport. We will refer to this memorandum further during the course of this opinion.

On May 2, 1966, Cloepfil addressed a letter to the Martin Tractor Company, directing Martin to proceed with shop drawings and submittal documents for the McConnell lighting job and calling attention to the fact that applicable government regulations were required to be followed. Further reference to this communication will be made when necessary.

Some three weeks thereafter, on May 24, 1966, Hurt wrote Cloepfil, . . . "Due to restrictions placed on Caterpillar products, accessory suppliers, and other stipulations by the district governing agency, we cannot accept your letter to proceed dated May 2, 1966, and hereby withdraw all verbal quotations."

On receipt of this unwelcome missive, Cloepfil telephoned Mr. Hurt who stated they had some work underway for the Corps of Engineers in both the Kansas City and Tulsa districts and did not want to take on any other work for the Corps at that time. Hurt assured Cloepfil he could buy the equipment from anybody at the price Martin could sell it for. Later investigation showed, however, that such was not the case.

. . .

Southwest eventually secured the generator equipment from Foley Tractor Co. of Wichita, a company which Mr. Hurt had one time suggested, at a price of $27,541. The present action was then filed, seeking damages of $6,041 for breach of the contract and $9,000 for loss resulting from the delay caused by the breach. The trial court awarded damages of $6,041 for the breach but rejected damages allegedly due to delay. The defendant only, has appealed; there is no cross-appeal by plaintiff.

The basic disagreement centers on whether the meeting between Hurt and Cloepfil at Springfield resulted in an agreement which was enforceable under the provisions of the Uniform Commercial Code. . . .

Southwest takes the position that the memorandum prepared by Hurt at Springfield supplies the essential elements of a contract required by the foregoing statute, i.e., that it is (1) a writing signed by the party sought to be charged, (2) that it is for the sale of goods and (3) that quantity is shown. In addition, the reader will have noted that the memorandum sets forth the prices of the several items listed.

It cannot be gainsaid that the Uniform Commercial Code has effected a somewhat radical change in the law relating to the formation of enforceable contracts as such has been expounded by this and other courts. In the Kansas Comment to 84–2–201, which closely parallels the Official UCC Comment, the following explanation is given:

> "Subsection (1) relaxes the interpretations of many courts in providing that the required writing need not contain all the material terms and that they need not be stated precisely. All that is required is that the writing afford a basis for believing that the offered oral evidence rests on a real transaction. Only three definite and invariable requirements as to the writing are

made by this subsection. First, it must evidence a contract for the sale of goods; second, it must be 'signed,' a word which includes any authentication which identifies the party to be charged; and third, it must specify quantity. Terms relating to price, time, and place of payment or delivery, the general quality of goods, or any particular warranties may all be omitted."

From legal treatises, as well, we learn that the three invariable requirements of an enforceable written memorandum under 84–2–201 are that it evidence a sale of goods, that it be signed or authenticated and that it specify quantity. In Vernon's Kansas Statutes Annotated, Uniform Commercial Code, Howe and Navin, the writers make this clear:

"Under the Code the writing does not need to incorporate all the terms of the transaction, nor do the terms need to be stated precisely. The Code does require that the writing be broad enough to indicate a contract of sale between the parties; that the party against whom enforcement is sought, or his agent, must have signed the writing; and that the quantity dealt with must be stated. Any error concerning the quantity stated in the memorandum prevents enforcement of the agreement beyond the precise quantity stated." (p. 116.)

The defendant does not seriously question the interpretation accorded the statute by eminent scriveners and scholars, but maintains, nonetheless, that the writing in question does not measure up to the statute of a signed memorandum within the purview of the Code; that the instrument simply sets forth verbal quotations for future consideration in continuing negotiations.

But on this point the trial court found there *was* an agreement reached between Hurt and Cloepfil at Springfield; that the formal requirements of K.S.A. 84–2–201 *were* satisfied; and that the memorandum prepared by Hurt contains the three essentials of the statute in that it evidences a sale of goods, was authenticated by Hurt and specifies quantity. Beyond that, the court specifically found that Hurt had apparent authority to make the agreement; that both Southwest and Martin were "merchants" as defined in K.S.A. 84–2–104; that the agreement reached at Springfield included additional terms not noted in the writing: (1) Southwest was to install the equipment; (2) Martin was to deliver the equipment to Wichita and (3) Martin was to assemble and supply submittal documents within three weeks; and that Martin's letter of May 24, 1966, constituted an anticipatory breach of the contract.

We believe the record supports all the above findings. With particular reference to the preparation and sufficiency of the written memorandum, the following evidence is pertinent:

Mr. Cloepfil testified that he and Hurt sat down at a restaurant table and spread out the plans which Hurt had brought with him; that they went through the specifications item by item and Hurt wrote each item down, together with the price thereof; that while the specifications called for a D353 generator, Hurt thought the D343 model might be an acceptable substitute, so he gave prices on both of them and Southwest could take either one of the two which the Corps of Engineers would approve; that Hurt gave him (Cloepfil) the memorandum "as a record of what we had done, the agreement we had arrived at our meeting in the restaurant at the airport."

We digress at this point to note Martin's contention that the memorandum is not signed within the meaning of 84–2–201. The sole authentication appears in hand-printed form at the top left-hand corner in these words: "Ken Hurt, Martin Tractor, Topeka, Caterpillar." The court found this sufficient, and we believe correctly so. K.S.A. 84–1–201(39) provides as follows:

"'Signed' includes any symbol executed or adopted by a party with present intention to authenticate a writing."

The official U.C.C. Comment states in part:

"The inclusion of authentication in the definition of 'signed' is to make clear that as the term is used in this Act a complete signature is not necessary. Authentication may be printed, stamped or written; * * * It may be on any part of the document and in appropriate cases may be found in a billhead or letterhead. * * * The question always is whether the symbol was executed or adopted by the party with present intention to authenticate the writing."

Hurt admittedly prepared the memorandum and has not denied affixing his name thereto. We believe the authentication sufficiently complies with the statute.

The evidence already cited would be ample to sustain the trial court's finding that an agreement was reached between Hurt and Cloepfil in Springfield. However, Cloepfil's testimony is not the only evidence in support of that finding. In a pretrial deposition, Mr. Hurt, himself, deposed that "we agreed on the section that I would be quoting on, and we came to some over-all general agreement on the major items." At the trial Hurt testified he did not wish to change that statement in any way.

Hurt further testified that in his opinion the thing which stood in the way of a firm deal was Martin's terms of payment—that had Southwest agreed with those terms of payment, so far as he was concerned, he would have considered a firm deal was made. Mr. Hurt acknowledged while on the stand that he penned the memorandum and that as disclosed therein a 10 per cent discount was given Southwest on the price of either of the generators listed (depending on which was approved by the Corps of Engineers), and that the accessories common to both generators were to be net—that is, sold without profit.

It is quite true, as the trial court found, that terms of payment were not agreed upon at the Springfield meeting. Hurt testified that as the memorandum was being made out, he said they wanted 10 per cent with the order, 50 per cent on delivery and the balance on acceptance, but he did not recall Cloepfil's response. Cloepfil's version was somewhat different. He stated that after the two had shaken hands in the lobby preparing to leave, Hurt said their terms usually were 20 per cent down and the balance on delivery; while he (Cloepfil) said the way they generally paid was 90 per cent on the tenth of the month following delivery and the balance on final acceptance. It is obvious the parties reached no agreement on this point.

However, a failure on the part of Messrs. Hurt and Cloepfil to agree on terms of payment would not, of itself, defeat an otherwise valid agreement reached by them. K.S.A. 84–2–204(3) reads:

> "Even though one or more terms are left open a contract for sale does not fail for indefiniteness if the parties have intended to make a contract and there is a reasonably certain basis for giving an appropriate remedy."

The official U.C.C. Comment is enlightening:

> "Subsection (3) states the principle as to 'open terms' underlying later sections of the Article. If the parties intend to enter into a binding agreement, this subsection recognizes that agreement as valid in law, despite missing terms, if there is any reasonably certain basis for granting a remedy. The test is not certainty as to what the parties were to do nor as to the exact amount of damages due the plaintiff. Nor is the fact that one or more terms are left to be agreed upon enough of itself to defeat an otherwise adequate agreement. Rather, commercial standards on the point of 'indefiniteness' are intended to be applied, this Act making provision elsewhere for missing terms needed for performance, open price, remedies and the like.

> "The more terms the parties leave open, the less likely it is that they have intended to conclude a binding agreement, but their actions may be frequently conclusive on the matter despite the omissions."

. . .

So far as the present case is concerned, K.S.A. 84–2–310 supplies the omitted term. This statute provides in pertinent part:

"Unless otherwise agreed

> "(a) payment is due at the time and place at which the buyer is to receive the goods even though the place of shipment is the place of delivery";

In our view, the language of the two Code provisions is clear and positive. Considered together, we take the two sections to mean that where parties have reached an enforceable agreement for the sale of goods, but omit therefrom the terms of payment, the law will imply, as part of the agreement, that payment is to be made at time of delivery. . . .

We do not mean to infer that terms of payment are not of importance under many circumstances, or that parties may not condition an agreement on their being included. However, the facts before us hardly indicate that Hurt and Cloepfil considered the terms of payment to be significant, or of more than passing interest. Hurt testified that while he stated his terms he did not recall Cloepfil's response, while Cloepfil stated that as the two were on the point of leaving, each stated their usual terms and that was as far as it went. The trial court found that only a brief and casual conversation ensued as to payment, and we think that is a valid summation of what took place.

Moreover, it is worthy of note that Martin first mentioned the omission of the terms of payment, as justifying its breach, in a letter written by counsel on September 15, 1966, more than four months after the memorandum was prepared by Hurt. On prior occasions Martin attributed its cancellation of the Springfield understanding to other causes. In its May 24 letter, Martin ascribed its withdrawal of "all verbal quotations" to "restrictions placed on Caterpillar products, accessory suppliers, and other stipulations by the district governing agency." In explaining the meaning of the letter to Cloepfil, Hurt said that Martin was doing work for the Corps of Engineers in the Kansas City and Tulsa districts and did not want to take on additional work with them at this time.

The entire circumstances may well give rise to a suspicion that Martin's present insistence that future negotiations were contemplated concerning terms of payment, is primarily an afterthought, for use as an escape hatch. Doubtless the trial court so considered the excuse in arriving at its findings.

We are aware of Martin's argument that Southwest's letter of May 2, 1966, referring to the sale is evidence that no firm contract had been concluded. Granted that some of the language employed might be subject to that interpretation, the trial court found, on what we deem to be substantial, competent evidence, that an agreement of sale *was* concluded at Springfield. Under our invariable rule those findings are binding upon this court on appeal even though there may have been evidence to the contrary.

. . .

We find no error in this case and the judgment of the trial court is affirmed.

QUESTIONS AND NOTES

1. In light of the language of 2–204(3) that the omission of terms is not fatal to the existence of a contract, how could defendant argue that the

absence of a payment term precluded the existence of a contract? Why does the court reject this argument?

2.   One asserting an enforceable sales contract has two hurdles to clear: (1) to show that the statute of frauds is inapplicable or has been satisfied; and (2) to show that the formation-of-contract rules have been fulfilled. These two matters often become blurred in a practical situation, and thus tend to be confused, because the kinds of concrete factual matters that are deemed to satisfy the statute of frauds or make it inapplicable also are likely to convince the trier of fact that a contract, in fact, was formed, just as concrete factual evidence of the formation of the contract is apt to satisfy the statute of frauds. But the careful analyst always recognizes that the two matters are separate and that both hurdles must be jumped. Did the court in *Southwest Engineering* address both issues?

3.   What does it take for a writing to evidence that a contract for sale has been made? Why does the court conclude that the standard was met? In another case, a seller claimed that the following writing satisfied the statute of frauds:

> "Confirming our telephone conversation, we are pleased to offer the 3500 shirts at $4.00 each and the trousers at $3.00 each with delivery approximately ninety days after receipt of order. We will try to cut this to sixty days if at all possible.

> "This is, of course, quoted f. o. b. Atlanta, and the order will not be subject to cancellation, domestic pack only.

> "Thanking you for the opportunity to offer these garments, ..."

The court held that the writing did not satisfy the statute of frauds. "It does not evidence a contract for the sale of goods, but very clearly is only an offer." Alice v. Robett Mfg. Co., 328 F.Supp. 1377 (N.D.Ga.1970), aff'd 445 F.2d 316 (5th Cir.1971).

In Howard Construction Co. v. Jeff-Cole Quarries, Inc., 669 S.W.2d 221, 228 (Mo.App.1983), the buyer relied on a writing of the seller, entitled "Proposal," that listed six items and the price for each. The parties met and, according to the buyer, agreed on the purchase and sale of the six items at modified prices, as marked by the buyer on the Proposal. The court criticized and rejected the reasoning of *Southwest Engineering*:

> The court's finding that the writing evidenced a contract has been severely criticized. That criticism stems from the fact that "[t]he memorandum before the court—on its face nothing more than a price list—was proof not of agreement, but, at most, only of negotiations." Finding such writing sufficient plants the seeds for allowing the statute of frauds to be satisfied by any evidence of mere negotiations.

> While U.C.C. § 2–201 was indeed designed to eliminate much of the rigidity produced by prior interpretations of the statute of frauds, it retained some safeguards against fraudulent commercial practices. The requirement that the writing indicate that a contract

for sale has been made is one of those safeguards. The words "as per our agreement," "in confirmation of," or "sold to buyer," would indicate that the parties had reached an agreement. Even the terms of the writing itself might be so specific and favorable to the party against whom the writing is offered that the court at least could draw the inference that an agreement had been reached. Such writings would deter fraudulent assertions that a contract had been agreed upon where in fact only negotiations had taken place. The price list which the Kansas Supreme Court found sufficient to indicate that a contract had been made, however, contained no such words or terms. . . .

Although the typewritten proposal was signed by an agent of Jeff-Cole (prior to the handwritten alterations made thereon by plaintiff's agent) and states specific quantity terms, no words on the writing allow for the inference that any agreement was reached between the parties and therefore it does not by itself meet the primary requirement of either § 2–201(1) or (2). Viewed in the light most favorable to the plaintiff, the unaltered proposal could be no more than an offer by Jeff-Cole.

In Veik v. Tilden Bank, 200 Neb. 705, 265 N.W.2d 214 (1978), however, a written offer was held to satisfy the statute ("all that is required is that the writing afford a basis for believing that the offered oral evidence rests on a real transaction"). Which of these cases best implements the policy underlying 2–201?

4.   **Problem.** A sales representative called on a business owner to discuss the sale of a generator. They talked about components, accessories, prices, warranty, delivery date, and payment terms. The business owner was not sure that she wanted to buy the generator. So the sales rep filled out and signed the seller's standard sales form, saying, "Think it over for a day or two. If you decide you want the generator, just sign this and send it in."

The sales form stated, "Seller agrees to sell and Buyer agrees to buy and pay for the following equipment pursuant to the following terms . . . ," and all the appropriate blanks were filled in. The business owner looked it over and said, "OK, I'll make a decision tomorrow." The sales rep left.

The business owner never called, wrote, signed, or returned the sales form. Not surprisingly, the seller never delivered the equipment. Meanwhile, the market price rose, and the business owner demanded delivery. The seller of course refused, and the business owner sued. Pointing to 2–201(1), she argues that she is entitled to damages. Is she right?

5.   **Problem.** Bayside Boats, a dealer attending a trade show, discussed a potential purchase with YachtCo, a manufacturer. YachtCo gave Bayside some product literature along with YachtCo's standard sales form for Bayside to use if it decided to purchase YachtCo's boats. YachtCo's name and address appeared in large letters at the top of the sales form. A week later the owner of Bayside Boats filled in the blanks on the form, specifying the models and the price of each, as listed in the product literature that he was given at the boat show. He mailed this form to YachtCo, which received it

but did not act on it in any way. When YachtCo later refused to deliver the boats specified in the form, Bayside sued. YachtCo defends in part on grounds that the requirements of subsection (1) of 2–201 have not been satisfied. What result? (For now, ignore subsection (2).)

6.   Can an e-mail message satisfy the Statute of Frauds? Presumably the answer is "yes" if the sender keys in her name at the end of the message or has an automatic signature block. But what if the sender does neither? Does a message from an e-mail account of the sender suffice, even if there is no authentication at the end of the message? In JSO Associates, Inc. v. Price, 2008 WL 904703 (Sup.Ct. Naussau Cty.2008) (a non-UCC case), the court held, "where there is no question as to the source and authenticity of an email, the email is 'signed' for purposes of the statute of frauds if defendant's name clearly appears in the email as the sender."

Further treatment of electronic contracting appears in Section F, page 104 infra.

Brooks Cotton Company, Inc. v. Williams

Tennessee Court of Appeals, 2012.
381 S.W.3d 414.

■ J. STEVEN STAFFORD, J.

. . .

I.   Background

Defendant . . . Williams is a cotton and soybean farmer with a high school education. According to [Brooks Cotton, the plaintiff], on or about August 5, 2010, Mr. Williams entered into an oral contract to sell his 2010 cotton production to Brooks Cotton. The alleged contract was recorded in the Brooks Cotton purchase book on August 6, 2010 and provided that Mr. Williams would sell his entire 1000 acre cotton production to Brooks Cotton. The price allegedly agreed upon was . . . $0.742 per pound of cotton. At the time of the alleged agreement, Mr. Williams had not yet harvested his cotton.[2] According to the record, Mr. Williams ultimately produced approximately 1206 bales of cotton in 2010. If the contract had been performed as allegedly agreed, the total contract price for Mr. Williams' cotton would have been approximately $446,000. Brooks Cotton sent written confirmation of the alleged agreement to Mr. Williams on or about September 4, 2010 . . . . Mr. Williams asserts that he never entered into an oral contract with Brooks Cotton, although he did not call or write Brooks Cotton to object to the written terms sent to him.

. . .

On or about November 18, 2010, Brooks Cotton filed a Complaint for Specific Performance, Injunctive Relief, and Damages against Mr.

---

[2]   This type of contract, wherein the farmer agrees to sell his crops prior to the harvest, is referred to as a "forward crop contract."

Williams. An injunction hearing was held on November 30, 2010. Mr. Williams testified at the hearing regarding his experience and skills in marketing cotton, stating that he had been a cotton farmer for approximately twenty-five years. Mr. Williams testified that, in the majority of the years prior to 2010, he had entered into a contract with Brooks Cotton to sell his cotton crop. In most of those years, however, Mr. Williams agreed to the contract in person at Brooks Cotton's office after the cotton had been harvested, rather than over the telephone prior to the harvest. Mr. Williams did testify that he was familiar with the practice of "booking" cotton over the phone, as he had previously "booked" his cotton with Brooks Cotton in 2003. Mr. Williams testified, however, that he did not "book" his cotton with Brooks Cotton in August 2010, but that he merely called to discuss cotton prices. In addition, Mr. Williams explained his process for determining the price at which he will sell his cotton, wherein he reviews the selling price of his cotton crop in the previous three years. Although Mr. Williams testified that he receives daily texts regarding the price of cotton, he explained that he was not familiar with the common practice of "hedging"[3] engaged in by many cotton merchants. David Brooks of Brooks Cotton explained that hedging is a common practice in the cotton trade. . . . Based on the testimony, the court issued a preliminary injunction on the sale of Mr. Williams' 2010 production of cotton. [In due course each party filed a motion for summary judgment. The trial court ruled that Williams was a merchant under the U.C.C. and granted partial summary judgment in favor of Brooks Cotton. Williams appealed.]

II. Standard of Review

Because this case was adjudicated by summary judgment, we first note that a trial court's decision on a motion for summary judgment presents a question of law. Our review is, therefore, *de novo* with no presumption of correctness afforded to the trial court's determination

When a motion for summary judgment is made, the moving party has the burden of showing that "there is no genuine issue as to any material fact and the moving party is entitled to judgment as a matter of law." Tenn. R. Civ. P. 56.04. . . .

III. Analysis

The central issue presented in this interlocutory appeal is whether a farmer, such as Mr. Williams, may be considered a merchant under the U.C.C. In this case, Mr. Williams' designation as a merchant is critical to the outcome of the lawsuit. If Mr. Williams is considered a merchant, then the merchant exception to the Statute of Frauds applies and the case can proceed; if Mr. Williams cannot be considered a merchant,

---

[3] "Hedging" refers to a practice by merchants, wherein the merchant protects his financial interests by "offsetting his purchases with a sale of futures contracts on the cotton exchange." According to the U.S. Supreme Court, hedging "drastically reduces the risk to both merchants and lenders."

regardless of whether he entered into an oral contract with Brooks Cotton, an oral contract will not be sufficient to bind him.

Generally contracts need not be in writing to be enforceable, unless they are of the kind that the Statute of Frauds or other law requires to be written. One type of contract that must be in writing is a contract for the sale of goods priced over $500. . . . It is undisputed that the alleged contract for the sale of Mr. Williams' 2010 cotton production far exceeded $500. Accordingly, unless an exception applies, the Statute of Frauds requires that the contract be in writing to be enforceable. However, the U.C.C. provides an exception to this rule in situations where both parties are merchants:

> Between merchants if within a reasonable time a writing or record in confirmation of the contract and sufficient against the sender is received and the party receiving it has reason to know its contents, it satisfies the requirements of subsection (1) against such party unless written notice of objection to its contents is given within ten (10) days after it is received.

Tenn.Code Ann. § 47–2–201(b). Accordingly, for Mr. Williams to be bound by any oral contract, this Court must first determine whether he is a "merchant" for purposes of the U.C.C. Statute of Frauds. The question of what is required to be considered a merchant for purposes of the Statute of Frauds is a question of first impression in this State. To resolve this issue, we must interpret the meaning of the word "merchant" in Tennessee Code Annotated Section 47–2–201(b). The Tennessee Supreme Court recently outlined the applicable principles when faced with a question of statutory interpretation:

> When dealing with statutory interpretation, well-defined precepts apply. Our primary objective is to carry out legislative intent without broadening or restricting the statute beyond its intended scope. In construing legislative enactments, we presume that every word in a statute has meaning and purpose and should be given full effect if the obvious intention of the General Assembly is not violated by so doing. When a statute is clear, we apply the plain meaning without complicating the task. Our obligation is simply to enforce the written language. When a statute is ambiguous, however, we may refer to the broader statutory scheme, the history of the legislation, or other sources to discern its meaning. Courts must presume that a legislative body was aware of its prior enactments and knew the state of the law at the time it passed the legislation.

Estate of French v. Stratford House, 333 S.W.3d 546, 554 (Tenn.2011). Accordingly, we will first consider the plain language of the statute. The term "merchant" is defined by Tennessee law:

> "Merchant" means a person who deals in goods of the kind or otherwise by his occupation holds himself out as having

knowledge or skill peculiar to the practices or goods involved in the transaction or to whom such knowledge or skill may be attributed by his employment of an agent or broker or other intermediary who by his occupation holds himself out as having such knowledge or skill.

Tenn.Code Ann. § 47–2–104(1). Accordingly, a contract " '[b]etween merchants' means [ ] any transaction with respect to which both parties are chargeable with the knowledge or skill of merchants." *Id.* at—104(3). The comments to this section elaborate on who is considered a merchant for purposes of the Statute of Frauds:

> The term "merchant" as defined here roots in the "law merchant" concept of a professional in business. The professional status under the definition may be based upon specialized knowledge as to the goods, specialized knowledge as to business practices, or specialized knowledge as to both and which kind of specialized knowledge may be sufficient to establish the merchant status is indicated by the nature of the provisions.

> The special provisions as to merchants appear only in this Article and they are of three kinds. Sections 2–201(2), 2–205, 2–207 and 2–209 dealing with the statute of frauds, firm offers, confirmatory memoranda and modification rest on normal business practices which are or ought to be typical of and familiar to any person in business. **For purposes of these sections almost every person in business would, therefore, be deemed to be a "merchant" under the language "who . . . by his occupation holds himself out as having knowledge or skill peculiar to the practices . . . involved in the transaction . . ."** since the practices involved in the transaction are non-specialized business practices such as answering mail. In this type of provision, banks or even universities, for example, well may be "merchants." But even these sections only apply to a merchant in his mercantile capacity; a lawyer or bank president buying fishing tackle for his own use is not a merchant.

Tenn.Code Ann. § 47–2–104, cmt. 2 (emphasis added). As such, the definition of merchant for purposes of the Statute of Frauds encompasses "almost every person in business." *Id.*

   . . . While [the] definition [in 2–104(1)] is instructive, it does not end the inquiry into whether a farmer is one who "deals in goods" or who "by his occupation holds himself out as having knowledge or skill peculiar to the practices or goods involved in the transaction." Accordingly, we must look beyond the plain language of the statute in order to determine whether a farmer is a merchant under the U.C.C. Statute of Frauds.

. . . According to *Williston on Contracts,* the question of whether a farmer can be a merchant for purposes of the Statute of Frauds has led to different applications among the states. First, courts have differing views as to whether the determination of who is a merchant is considered a factual question or a question of law:

> The majority of courts maintain that the question whether one is a merchant in a particular case, and for purposes of being bound by a confirmatory writing, is one of fact, although there are cases holding or suggesting that whether an entity can qualify as a merchant is a question of law for the courts to decide by applying the U.C.C. definition of merchant to the facts of the particular case, and it has been said that the question presents a mixed question of law and fact that whether there are circumstances in existence that would make one a merchant is a question of fact, but that once those facts are determined, whether they make a person a merchant is a question of law.

10 *Williston on Contracts* § 29:25 (4th ed.) (footnotes omitted). In addition, the question of whether a farmer is a merchant for purposes of the Statute of Frauds constitutes one of the more difficult and controversial issues with regard to the U.C.C. and, as such, has led to considerable disagreement among the states . . . .

Because there is no clear weight of authority regarding this issue, we find it instructive to consider cases from our sister states.

Mr. Williams cites various cases that have applied the above rule and found that a farmer cannot be considered a merchant for purposes of the Statute of Frauds. For example in *Loeb & Co., Inc. v. Schreiner,* 294 Ala. 722, 321 So.2d 199 (1975), the Alabama Supreme Court stated:

> . . .

> It is not sufficient . . . that one hold himself out as having knowledge or skill peculiar to the practices or goods involved, he must [b]y his occupation so hold himself out. Accordingly, a person cannot be considered a 'merchant' simply because he is a braggart or has a high opinion of his knowledge in a particular area. We conclude that a farmer does not solely [b]y his occupation hold himself out as being a professional cotton merchant.

> The remaining thing which a farmer might do to be considered a merchant is to become a dealer in goods. Although there was evidence which indicated that the appellee here had a good deal of knowledge, this is not the test. There is not one shred of evidence that appellee ever sold anyone's cotton but his own. He was nothing more than an astute farmer selling his own product. We do not think this was sufficient to make him a dealer in goods.

> . . .

Id. at 201–02.

The reasoning espoused in *Loeb* was followed in a number of jurisdictions [citing cases from seven states]. . . .

However, many of the courts cited by Mr. Williams note that a farmer could be considered a merchant, but that the facts simply were insufficient to conclude that the farmer was a merchant in that particular case. Accordingly, in many jurisdictions where the courts have held that farmers were not merchants with regard to the Statute of Frauds, the courts have not foreclosed the possibility that a farmer could meet that standard.

In contrast, Brooks Cotton cites a number of jurisdictions where the courts have found that a farmer may qualify as a merchant for purposes of the Statute of Frauds [citing cases from nineteen states, including three states cited by Mr. Williams].

We find the Colorado case of *Colorado-Kansas Grain Co. v. Reifschneider,* 817 P.2d 637 (Colo.Ct.App.1991), to be particularly instructive. In determining that a farmer may be considered a merchant with regard to the Statute of Frauds, the Colorado Court of Appeals stated:

> In considering the question at issue, we note that the cases which hold that farmers may be merchants reflect on the fact that today's farmer is involved in far more than simply planting and harvesting crops. Indeed, many farmers possess an extensive knowledge and sophistication regarding the purchase and sale of crops on the various agricultural markets. Often, they are more aptly described as agri-businessmen.

Id. at 640. . . .

In another case, *Rush Johnson Farms, Inc. v. Mo. Farmers Ass'n,* 555 S.W.2d 61 (Mo.Ct.App.1977), the Missouri Court of Appeals held that the farmer at issue was a merchant for purposes of the Statute of Frauds when, for "many, many years," the farmer kept abreast of market prices in order to annually sell his crops. The court relied on the ordinary dictionary definition of the term "deals" to mean "to buy or sell." Based on that definition, the court held that the farmer's practice of selling his annual crop for "many, many years" proved that the farmer "deals in goods of the kind." In addition, the court stated:

> This court does not believe that anyone in this day and age looks upon any person or corporation who conducts a farming operation as a simple tiller of the soil. It is well known that the marketing of a crop is certainly as important as the raising of it. [The farmer] fully revealed in this case his knowledge of the market and his thorough familiarity with marketing practices and procedures in trying to obtain the best price possible for his product. Under the definition of merchant, as contained in the UCC, Johnson fully qualified as such so that the oral contract in this case was not barred under the statute of frauds. . . .

Id. . . . However, the court cautioned that not every farmer may meet the definition of a merchant, but that the determination of whether a farmer should be considered a merchant for purposes of the Statute of Frauds "would depend on the individual experience and activities of the person involved."

. . .

We conclude that the framers of the U.C.C. did not intend to exclude all farmers from the category of merchants, simply because a farmer's primary occupation is the cultivation, rather than the sale, of crops. The sale of crops is as integral to the business of commercial farming as the cultivation. The framers included crops in their definition of goods. Tenn.Code Ann. § 47–2–105. Therefore, the framers clearly intended to include those that sell crops commercially in the definition of merchant, so long as that person either "deals in goods of the kind" or who "by his occupation holds himself out as having knowledge or skill peculiar to the practices or goods involved in the transaction." In addition, the definition of merchant is broadly construed for purposes of the Statute of Frauds, encompassing "almost every person in business," including an experienced commercial farmer. Tenn.Code. Ann. § 47–2–104, cmt. 2.

Based on the foregoing, we cannot conclude that the framers intentionally intended to omit experienced commercial farmers from the category of merchants. Accordingly, we adopt the rule that a farmer may be considered a merchant for the purposes of the merchant exception to the Statute of Frauds, when the farmer possesses sufficient expertise in not only the cultivation, but also the sale of crops. However, the determination of whether a particular farmer is a merchant is a mixed question of fact and law, which must be determined on a case-by-case basis, taking into account "the individual experience and activities of the person involved." *Rush Johnson Farms,* 555 S.W.2d at 65. Accordingly, we reverse the trial court's determination that "Tennessee's farmer[s]," as a whole, are considered merchants for purposes of the Statute of Frauds. Instead, trial courts should consider the following, nonexhaustive, criteria in determining whether a particular farmer is a merchant for purposes of the Statute of Frauds:

> the length of time the farmer has been engaged in the practice of selling his product to the marketers of his product; (2) the degree of business acumen shown by the farmer in his dealings with other parties; (3) the farmer's awareness of the operation and existence of farm markets; and (4) the farmer's past experience with or knowledge of the customs and practices which are unique to the particular marketing of the product which he sells.

Colorado-Kansas Grain, 817 P.2d at 640 (citations omitted).

Applying the above factors to Mr. Williams, we note that several factors weigh in favor of a determination that Mr. Williams was a merchant for purposes of the Statute of Frauds. First, Mr. Williams testified that he had been a cotton farmer for approximately twenty-five years and that throughout the years, he sold both his and his landlord's cotton production. Next, Mr. Williams testified that he had previously engaged in oral crop "booking," a practice that other farmers testified was common in the cotton trade. Mr. Williams also testified that he determined when to sell his cotton, and at what price, by using a three-year history of his cotton sales, as well as daily notifications about the price of cotton on the cotton market. Mr. Williams also testified that he receives periodicals about cotton farming, such as *Cotton Grower.*

However, some factors weigh against a determination that Mr. Williams is a merchant for purposes of the Statute of Frauds. First, Mr. Williams testified that he does not engage in the practice of hedging; indeed, Mr. Williams testified that he was unaware of what the term "hedging" meant. However, the testimony . . . [and] depositions of several other area farmers, established that hedging is a practice that is unique and integral to the marketing of cotton. In addition, though Mr. Williams testified that he had previously orally booked his cotton with Brooks Cotton, his testimony shows that he had only engaged in this practice once over the last several years. Further, the record is unclear whether the periodicals Mr. Williams receives deal with the cotton trade, or solely with cotton farming.

From our review of the pertinent factors, it is clear that . . . there are facts in this case both supporting and undermining a conclusion that Mr. Williams is a merchant for purposes of the U.C.C. Statute of Frauds. Therefore, we conclude that the existence of genuine issues involving the inferences to be drawn from the facts in this case should have prevented the trial court from granting summary judgment to either party. Accordingly, we affirm the denial of Mr. Williams' motion for summary judgment, reverse the grant of Brooks Cotton's motion for partial summary judgment, and remand to the trial court for a trial on the merits to determine if Mr. Williams should be considered a merchant for purposes of the U.C.C. Statute of Frauds.

QUESTIONS AND NOTES

1. Note the rationale for subsection (2): a party who sends a confirmation of an oral agreement cannot assert 2–201 as a reason for not performing, but in the absence of subsection (2), the party who receives that confirmation could await the time for performance and then perform only if at that time it is to his or her advantage, with no liability for failing to perform if non-performance is the advantageous course of action.

2. The court in *Brooks Cotton* believes that characterization of a farmer as a "merchant" depends on the precise characteristics of the farmer. This seems to make sense. But, given the definition of merchant, does it really? As to "deals in goods of the kind," the answer is yes, and the court has to decide how many transactions over what period of time constitutes "dealing."

But if that test is not met, the classification depends on whether the farmer "by his occupation holds himself out as having knowledge or skill peculiar to the practices or goods involved in the transaction."

In Frix v. Integrity Medical Systems, 2017 WL 4171987, at *9–*11 (W.D.Tenn. 2017), a physician agreed to purchase a CT scanner to replace his existing, less advanced scanner. When a dispute arose and the physician sued, it became necessary to determine whether he was a "merchant." He did not regularly buy or sell CT scanners, so the outcome turned on the meaning of the "by his occupation" language. Referring to *Brooks Cotton*, the court stated:

> An individualized approach stands in stark contrast to the occupation-based approach that the language of the statute plainly calls for. The court seems to ultimately distinguish between a regular farmer and an "experienced commercial farmer[ ]." . . . [But the] novice that manages to make his living from the smallest patch of earth may call himself a farmer as much as any agricultural corporate giant. Any distinction is therefore immaterial to this Court's analysis of section 47–2–104(1). What changes from case to case are the goods or practices involved in the transaction. Thus, the issue then becomes whether a physician inherently holds himself out as having knowledge or skills peculiar to medical equipment or the installation thereof.

> This is of course a much narrower reading of "merchant" than Defendant argues for. But Defendant's apparent assertion that the UCC envisions merchants as encompassing all professionals is inconsistent with the statutory language, which significantly restricts the knowledge or skill that would trigger the merchant provisions to such "knowledge or skill *peculiar to the practices or goods involved in the transaction.* Tenn. Code Ann. § 47–2–104(1) (emphasis added).

> . . . But the reason that physicians are not merchants under the UCC is that physicians are not experts in the equipment itself. There is nothing peculiar about being able to use a machine for its intended purpose. And there is no indication that physicians generally know how to take apart, put back together, install, or repair complicated pieces of machinery. . . . The Court finds that a physician, by mere virtue of being a physician, does not hold himself out as having skills or knowledge peculiar to the sale or installation of medical equipment. Accordingly, the Court must conclude that Plaintiff is not a merchant under the UCC . . . .

Are you persuaded that a physician is not a merchant under the "by his occupation" language? Would it be consistent with *Frix* for a court to conclude that under that language a farmer is a merchant?

3.   Problems.

   a.   Reconsider Problem 5, page 60: does YachtCo's sales form suffice under subsection (2) of 2–201?

b.   Co-op phoned Powerco, offering to buy a generator system pursuant to Powerco's posted prices and terms. Powerco's employee said, "Let me see if we can meet your deadline, and I'll get back to you." Powerco then sent a letter, "As you requested, we agree to sell you the following items at the following prices. . . ." In due course, Powerco tendered the goods, Co-op refused to accept delivery, and Powerco now sues. Does 2–201(2) make the agreement enforceable against Co-op?

4.   Promissory estoppel. In *Brooks Cotton* the buyer alleged a purchase on August 5, which it recorded in its purchase book the next day. If Brooks Cotton not only had recorded this transaction but also had resold the cotton to a mill, it might have asserted that it relied on the contract and that Williams was estopped to assert the statute of frauds as a bar to enforcement of the oral contract. That is what happened in Decatur Cooperative Assn. v. Urban, 547 P.2d 323 (Kan.1976). The court wrote:

> Courts have taken differing positions as to whether a party may be equitably estopped to assert the statute of frauds as a defense. One line of cases holds that to allow the concept of estoppel to preclude assertion of the statute of frauds as a defense to an oral contract would defeat the purpose of the statute. These decisions take the position that promissory estoppel may not be used to defeat the statute of frauds in any case, or at least in any situation where the policy of the statute would be frustrated.

> A substantial number of courts, however, hold that the doctrine of promissory estoppel may render enforceable any promise upon which the promisor intended, or should have known, that the promisee would act to his detriment, and which is indeed acted upon in such a manner by the promisee, where application of the statute of frauds to that promise would thus work a fraud or a gross injustice upon the promisee. Courts in this line of cases bottom their reasoning on the general equity principle that the statute of frauds was enacted to prevent fraud and injustice, not to foster or encourage it, and a court of equity will not ordinarily permit its use as a shield to protect fraud or to enable one to take advantage of his own wrong. This court has long been committed to the principles enunciated in the last sentence and on that basis has applied the doctrine of estoppel to cases wherein the statute of frauds would otherwise be applicable as a defense.

> . . .

> Recapitulating, appellant's theory is it changed its position in reliance upon appellee's conduct; that appellee was or reasonably should have been aware [that appellant would immediately resell the goods]; that appellant bound itself in the transaction and it would be unjust and a fraud upon appellant to permit appellee to speculate and profit on a risen market at appellant's expense. From the facts pleaded and placed before the trial court by stipulation it is clear appellant was entitled to invoke the doctrine of promissory estoppel so as to bar application of the statute of frauds and to have

an evidentiary hearing upon disputed matters in connection with that issue.

The Restatement (2d) of Contracts, adopted three years later, embraced this view:

> § 139.   Enforcement by Virtue of Action in Reliance
>
> (1)   A promise which the promisor should reasonably expect to induce action or forbearance on the part of the promisee or a third person and which does induce the action or forbearance is enforceable notwithstanding the Statute of Frauds if injustice can be avoided only by enforcement of the promise. The remedy granted for breach is to be limited as justice requires.
>
> (2)   In determining whether injustice can be avoided only by enforcement of the promise, the following circumstances are significant:
>
>> (a)   the availability and adequacy of other remedies, particularly cancellation and restitution;
>>
>> (b)   the definite and substantial character of the action or forbearance in relation to the remedy sought;
>>
>> (c)   the extent to which the action or forbearance corroborates evidence of the making and terms of the promise, or the making and terms are otherwise established by clear and convincing evidence;
>>
>> (d)   the reasonableness of the action or forbearance;
>>
>> (e)   the extent to which the action or forbearance was foreseeable by the promisor.

What statutory basis in the UCC is there for invoking estoppel? What statutory impediment is there to invoking estoppel? Not all courts agree with the position of the court in *Decatur Coop*. The Supreme Court of Washington wrote:

> If we were to adopt [Restatement (Second) of Contracts § 139] as applicable in the context of the sale of goods, we would allow parties to circumvent the UCC. For example, to prove justifiable reliance (an element of promissory estoppel), the promisee may offer evidence of course of dealing between the parties, as plaintiff did in this case. The Official Comments to RCWA 62A.1–205(4) [revised 1–303(d)] state that the statute of frauds
>
>> "restrict[s] the actions of the parties, and ... cannot be abrogated by agreement, or by a *usage of trade* ..." (Italics ours.) RCWA 62A.1–205, at 71.
>
> Notwithstanding our appreciation of plaintiff's dilemma, we cannot help but foresee increased litigation and confusion as being the necessary result of the eroding of the UCC if [§ 139] is adopted in this case. We join the other courts which limit the doctrine of promissory estoppel from overcoming a valid defense based on the

statute of frauds contained within the Uniform Commercial Code. . . .

Lige Dickson Co. v. Union Oil Co., 635 P.2d 103 (Wash.1981). The courts remain divided.

5. The court in *Decatur Coop* held that promissory estoppel may obviate the need for a writing. If the purpose of the statute of frauds is to keep oral evidence from the finder of fact because of fear that

> (1) the person claiming contract will either lie about or misremember the contract, and

> (2) the finder of fact will believe the mistaken evidence,

what justifies admitting the evidence if the party who claims that a contract exists also alleges its detrimental reliance on the oral contract? Will not that party lie in the same way about its reliance? Or do you think that the fact of reliance is more subject to proof by objective facts that are less likely to be manufactured or misremembered?

6. **Part performance.** Section 2–201(3)(c) provides that performance may make an oral agreement enforceable even if there is no writing. Please read that and consider the following.

Problems.

   a. Winston Winery claims that it entered into an oral contract with Vista Vines under which Vista would deliver 100 tons of grapes. Vista delivered 15 tons of grapes but denies that there was a contract for more than 15 tons. Does the partial delivery satisfy 2–201 so that Winston can offer proof that there was a contract for 100 tons? What result if Vista's pleading claims that the contract was for only 25 tons?

   b. Walton approached Franklin Ford about the purchase of a new car. After negotiations Franklin Ford prepared a purchase order for the sale of a specified model, to be ordered from the factory, for $16,500, and Walton signed it. Franklin Ford, however, did not. As stated in the purchase order, Walton gave $100 as a cash down payment. Six weeks later Franklin Ford notified Walton that the automobile had arrived but that they had made a mistake as to the price and that the car would cost $17,000 rather than the $16,500 stated on the purchase order. Does the down payment satisfy 2–201 so that Walton can offer evidence that the sales manager orally accepted the order when Walton signed it?

7. **Admissions.** If a party to an agreement admits in the context of judicial proceedings that a contract was made, 2–201(3)(b) makes that agreement enforceable even if there is no writing. In *Lewis v. Hughes*, 276 Md. 247, 346 A.2d 231 (Md.App.1975), plaintiff offered to sell her mobile home to defendant for $5,000. No other terms were stated. Defendant accepted the offer. On trial, he stated that he did not intend to pay $5,000, except over a period of time, and that he thought that the contract was still being negotiated. That is, he denied that a contract existed. The court stated:

> ". . . [I]t is apparent from . . . [Dr. Hughes'] testimony . . . that at the trial [he] admitted he told Mr. Baer [for communication to the plaintiff], without mention of any terms of payment, that he

would purchase the mobile home for $5,000. Of course, it is legally irrelevant, in the face of Dr. Hughes' objective manifestation of unconditional assent to the offer, that [he] thought the contract was still being negotiated and had a subjective desire to impose certain conditions on the manner of payment. Consequently, when on May 9 the lawyer, in accordance with his agency authority, informed [plaintiff] of Dr. Hughes' assent, there was an acceptance of the offer and a contract, as a matter of law, came into existence.

"We come then to the basic issue in this case, which is whether the Statute of Frauds is satisfied pursuant to § 2–201(3)(b) when the party denying the existence of the contract and relying on the statute takes the stand and, without admitting explicitly that a contract was made, testifies to facts which as a matter of law establish that a contract was formed. While we have found no case specifically deciding this question, numerous cases dealing with § 2–201(3)(b) seem to say that in such a situation the requirements of the statute have been fulfilled. . . . We hold that the Statute of Frauds does not bar enforcement of the contract involved in this case."

8. The possibility always exists, of course, that a defendant might inadvertently admit an oral contract during the course of a trial. Does this possibility mean that a court should never dismiss a case for failure to state a cause of action where the defendant has pleaded the statute of frauds? Compare Simmons Oil Corp. v. Bulk Sales Corp., 498 F.Supp. 457 (D.N.J.1980) ("Plaintiff argues, in addition, that the defendant should be required to file an answer, before raising the statute of frauds as a defense, on the chance it will admit the existence of the alleged contract. . . . This contention is without merit,") with M & W Farm Service Co. v. Callison, 285 N.W.2d 271 (Iowa 1979) (the defense of the statute of frauds should not ordinarily be adjudicated on a motion to dismiss because, under the statute, the party asserting the claim is entitled to an opportunity to elicit an admission from the opposing party of the existence of a contract.) Which of these views does Lewis v. Hughes support? Which of these views makes the most sense to you?

9.   Specially manufactured goods. Suppose a printer having a slack season prints calendars bearing the name and logo of a large department store. When the printer calls for delivery instructions, the department store denies that it had ever made a contract for the calendars. The printer, claiming that the department store had phoned in the order, sues for breach of contract. Can the department store rely on 2–201? See subsection (3)(a). If not, how can it protect itself against nonexistent deals?

Possibly because of an alleged buyer's vulnerability, at least one court has said the specially-manufactured-goods exception must be strictly construed. See Epprecht v. IBM Corp., 36 U.C.C. Rep. 391 (E.D.Pa.1983). This may be accomplished by finding the goods not to be specially manufactured after all. What is meant by "specially manufactured goods"? For an excellent case dealing with this question see Impossible Electronic Techniques, Inc. v. Wackenhut Protective Systems, Inc., 669 F.2d 1026 (5th

Cir.1982) ("The crucial inquiry is whether the manufacturer could sell the goods in the ordinary course of his business to someone other than the original buyer. If with slight alterations the goods could be so sold, then they are not specially manufactured; if, however, essential changes are necessary to render the goods marketable by the seller to others, then the exception does apply.") Note, however that this test does not eliminate the vulnerability of a person in the position of the department store above. But the alleged seller must persuade the fact finder that the parties actually formed a contract.

10. Noncompliance. Section 2–201 declares that contracts that fail to comply with its provisions are "unenforceable." This does not mean that they are "void" but only "voidable." Thus, failure to meet the requirements of 2–201 does not nullify a contract, but gives one of the parties an option to avoid it. As a result, a defense based 2–201 must be pleaded by the party seeking to use it, and only a party to the contract or a successor in interest can take advantage of it. In the absence of special pleading statutes or rules to the contrary, some courts have held that a defendant must plead 2–201 affirmatively and cannot raise it by a general denial.

11. Article 2A. Article 2A–201 is modeled on 2–201, though it raises the $500 of 2–201 to $1,000.

Problem. Construction Rentals (CR) delivered a large trenching machine to Utilico. Utilico used the machine for one month and then demanded that CR pick it up and refund $7,500 of the $10,000 that Utilico had paid. CR picked up the machine (see 2A–529(1)(a)) and now sues Utilico for damages claiming that Utilico had accepted the machine under a two-year lease at a rental of $2,500 per month, with the first two months rental plus a security deposit of $5,000 to be paid in advance. Utilico denies that there was a two-year lease, but says that the lease was for one month at a rental of $2,500, with a $7,500 security deposit. Can CR prove a term longer than a month under 2A–201(4)(c)?

12. CISG and the statute of frauds. Article 11 of the Convention on Contracts for the International Sale of Goods rejects the Article 2 approach. It provides: "A contract of sale need not be concluded in or evidenced by writing and is not subject to any other requirement as to form. It may be proved by any means, including witnesses."

D. THE BATTLE OF THE FORMS

Section 2–207, to which you were introduced in your Contracts course, is perhaps the most criticized section in Article 2. It is the subject of more law review articles than any other section, and it poses many difficult interpretive issues. As an introduction to the section, please consider the following, mostly easy hypotheticals.

1. ShirtShop sends an e-mail to Logo: "I offer to buy 100 polo shirts, assorted sizes, at $20 per shirt, I'd like delivery by February 1."

Logo responds: "I accept, we'll deliver on February 15."

At common law is there a contract?

2. ShirtShop: "I offer buy 100 polo shirts, assorted sizes, at $20 per shirt, delivery by February 1."

Logo: "I accept, payment is due on delivery."

At common law is there a contract?

3. Logo: "I offer to sell you 100 polo shirts, assorted sizes, at $20 per shirt."

ShirtShop: "I accept, please send all solid colors."

At common law is there a contract? Under 2–207 is there a contract?

4. Kiley's Kiosk: "I offer to buy 200 SR80 headphones at $70 each, shipment by February 1."

Grado: "I accept, but the price is $100 each."

At common law is there a contract? under 2–207(1)?

5. Kiley's Kiosk: "I offer to buy 200 SR80 headphones at $100 each, shipment by February 1."

Grado responds with a lengthy sales acknowledgment form, with the blanks filled in as follows: "This acknowledges receipt of your order for 200 Grado SR80 headphones at a price of $100 per unit. We will ship these goods by February 1." The form contains numerous other terms including an exclusion of consequential damages for breach of warranty.

Is there a contract under 2–207(1)?

Belden Inc. v. American Electronic Components, Inc.

Indiana Court of Appeals, 2008.
885 N.E.2d 751.

■ BARNES, JUDGE.

. . .

Belden manufactures wire, and AEC (American Electronic Components) manufactures automobile sensors. Since 1989, AEC, in repeated transactions, has purchased wire from Belden to use in its sensors.

In 1996 and 1997, Belden sought to comply with AEC's quality control program and provided detailed information to AEC regarding the materials it used to manufacture its wire. In its assurances, Belden indicated that it would use insulation from Quantum Chemical Corp. ("Quantum"). In June 2003, however, Belden began using insulation supplied by Dow Chemical Company ("Dow"). The Dow insulation had different physical properties than the insulation provided by Quantum.

In October 2003, Belden sold AEC wire manufactured with the Dow insulation. AEC used this wire to make its sensors, and the insulation ultimately cracked. Chrysler had installed AEC's sensors containing the faulty wire in approximately 18,000 vehicles. Chrysler recalled 14,000 vehicles and repaired the remaining 4,000 prior to sale. Pursuant to an agreement with Chrysler, AEC is required to reimburse Chrysler for expenses associated with the recall.

In 2004, AEC filed a complaint against Belden seeking consequential damages for the changes in the insulation that resulted in the recall. . . . [T]he trial court entered an order granting AEC's motion for partial summary judgment and denying Belden's cross-motion [for partial summary judgment]. Belden now appeals.

. . .

Belden first argues that the boilerplate language on the back of its "customer order acknowledgement" limited the damages available to AEC. The parties were involved in repeated transactions over many years. Prior to 1998, AEC sent all purchase orders by mail on a form that contained AEC's terms and conditions on the back. Beginning in 1998, AEC sent its purchase orders to Belden via fax. The faxed purchase orders only included the front of the form and omitted the terms and conditions printed on the back of the form.

On October 17, 2003, AEC sent Belden a purchase order containing the quantity, price, shipment date, and product specifications. Belden responded on October 22, 2003, with its order acknowledgement. The order acknowledgment referenced AEC's specific requests and contained boilerplate language on the back. At issue here is the language purporting to limit Belden's liability for special, indirect, incidental, or consequential damages. The back of order acknowledgment also stated:

> 1.2 Where this Agreement is found to be an acknowledgment, if such acknowledgment constitutes an acceptance of an offer such acceptance is expressly made conditional upon Buyer's assent solely to the terms of such acknowledgment, and acceptance of any part of Product(s) delivered by Company shall be deemed to constitute such assent by Buyer. . . .

Based on these exchanges, the parties dispute whether the limitation on damages is a term of their agreement. . . .

The parties disagree as to whether Section 2–207(2) or Section 2–207(3) applies. In Uniroyal, Inc., v. Chambers Gasket and Manufacturing Co., 177 Ind. App. 508, 380 N.E.2d 571 (1978), we addressed a strikingly similar issue. . . .

[W]e discussed the common law rules of contract formation and the UCC's modification of those rules:

> At common-law, for an offer and an acceptance to constitute a contract, the acceptance must meet and correspond with the offer in every respect, neither falling within nor going beyond

the terms proposed, but exactly meeting (those terms) at all points and closing with them just as they stand. An acceptance which varies the terms of the offer is considered a rejection and operates as a counter-offer, which may be accepted by the original offeror by performing without objection under the terms contained in the counter-offer.

§ 2–207 was specifically designed to alter the common-law "mirror-image" rule. The drafters recognized that in commercial practice, especially with the advent of printed forms, the terms of the "offer" and "acceptance" were seldom the same. They further recognized that the parties to a commercial transaction seldom were aware of the conflicting terms and conditions contained in the printed forms they exchanged. § 2–207 was therefore designed to allow enforcement of an agreement despite discrepancies between offer and acceptance, if enforcement could be required without either party being bound to a material term to which he has not agreed.

Id. at 512, 380 N.E.2d at 575 (quotations and citations omitted).

Pursuant to Section 2–207, if a contract is formed under Section 2–207(1), the additional terms in the acceptance are considered proposals and become part of the contract unless Section 2–207(2) renders the proposed terms inoperative. "However, if an acceptance is expressly conditioned on the offerer's assent to the new terms, and no assent is forthcoming, the 'entire transaction aborts.' " In other words, if an acceptance contains a clause conditioning the acceptance on assent to the additional or different terms, the writings do not form a contract. "Yet if the parties' conduct recognizes the existence of a contract by performance it is sufficient to establish a contract for sale." The terms of such a contract are those on which the writings of the parties agree, "together with any supplementary terms incorporated under any other provisions of this act." § 2–207(3).

We applied this framework in *Uniroyal* and rejected a line of cases suggesting Uniroyal's order acknowledgement was a counter-offer that Chambers accepted by taking the delivery of the goods and failing to object to the new terms. We reasoned that such an application revives the "last-shot" doctrine under the common law "mirror-image" rule, the very rule that Section 2–207 was intended to avoid, by binding the offeror to additional terms upon the mere acceptance of goods. Further, we observed that the purpose of Section 2–207 would not be well-served by allowing an offeree's responsive document to state additional or different terms, and provide that the terms will be deemed accepted by the offeror's inaction, because Section 2–207 presumes that business people do not read exchanged preprinted forms and assumes that the offeror would not learn of such terms. . . .

As in *Uniroyal*, we agree here that Belden could not unilaterally include terms that were expressly conditional on AEC's assent. Thus, the parties' writings did not create a contract. Nevertheless, we conclude that the parties' actions were in recognition of the existence of a contract and were sufficient to establish a contract for the sale of wire. The terms of the contract are the written terms on which the parties agreed and the "supplementary terms incorporated under any other provisions of [the UCC]." § 2–207(3).

The parties dispute, however, what supplementary terms are incorporated into their contract. The first question we must address is Belden's argument that the terms called for in Section 2–207(2) are included in the parties contract based on Comment 6, which provides:

> If no answer is received within a reasonable time after additional terms are proposed, it is both fair and commercially sound to assume that their inclusion has been assented to. Where clauses on confirming forms sent by both parties conflict each party must be assumed to object to a clause of the other conflicting with one on the confirmation sent by himself. As a result the requirement that there be notice of objection which is found in subsection (2) is satisfied and the conflicting terms do not become a part of the contract. *The contract then consists of the terms originally expressly agreed to, terms on which the confirmations agree, and terms supplied by this Act, including subsection (2).* The written confirmation is also subject to Section 2–201. Under that section a failure to respond permits enforcement of a prior oral agreement; under this section a failure to respond permits additional terms to become part of the agreement.

§ 2–207 cmt. 6 (emphasis added).

Belden urges that, based on the emphasized language, we look to Section 2–207(2) to determine whether the terms in the order acknowledgement are included in the contract. Pursuant to Section 2–207(2), Belden contends that its additional terms became part of the contract unless they materially altered the contract—the only exclusionary provision of Section 2–207(2) that is relevant under these facts. Belden claims that the limitation on damages does not materially alter the contract.

We need not determine whether the limitation on damages is a material alteration because we believe that Belden's reading of Comment 6 is overbroad. As the Supreme Judicial Court of Massachusetts has observed, . . . Commerce & Industry Ins. Co. v. Bayer Corp., 433 Mass. 388, 742 N.E.2d 567, 573 (Mass.2001) . . . :

> the criteria in [§ 2–207(2)] determine what "additional or different terms" will or will not be part of a contract that is formed by the exchange of writings. Where the writings do not form a contract, [§ 2–207(3)] states its own criteria—"those terms on which the writings agree" plus any terms that would

be provided by other Code sections. One cannot turn to subsection (2) as another Code section that would supply a term when, by its express provisions, subsection (2) simply does not apply to the transaction.

We agree with this reasoning. If we turned to Section 2–207(2) to determine the terms where the parties' writings did not create a contract, then Section 2–207(3) would be rendered meaningless. We will not do this. See City of Carmel v. Steele, 865 N.E.2d 612, 618 (Ind.2007) ("To effectuate legislative intent, we read the sections of an act together in order that no part is rendered meaningless if it can be harmonized with the remainder of the statute."). Thus, we rely solely on Section 2–207(3) to determine what terms are included in the contract.

Belden also argues that the parties' course of dealing is a "supplementary term" to be included by Section 2–207(3). Belden contends that the parties' course of dealing acknowledges the limitation on damages and that it is therefore included as a term of the contract.

There is a split in authorities as to whether Section 2–207(3)'s reference to "supplementary terms" includes course of performance, course of dealing, and usage of trade as defined in Section 1–205 [revised 1–303] or just the standard "gap fillers" contained in the Article 2 of the UCC. Compare Dresser Industries, Inc., Waukesha Engine Div. v. Gradall Co., 965 F.2d 1442, 1451 (7th Cir.1992) (concluding that under the Wisconsin UCC, a court is not limited to the standardized gap-fillers of Article 2, but may utilize any terms arising under the entire UCC, including course of performance, course of dealing, and usage of trade), with C. Itoh & Co. (America) Inc. v. Jordan Int'l Co., 552 F.2d 1228, 1237 (7th Cir.1977) ("Accordingly, we find that the 'supplementary terms' contemplated by Section 2–207(3) are limited to those supplied by the standardized 'gap-filler' provisions of Article Two"). For the sake of argument, we assume, without deciding, that the parties' course of dealing is in fact a supplementary term for purposes of Section 2–207(3).

[The court held that Belden had failed to prove that the parties' course of dealing established a limitation on Belden's liability for consequential damages. Since Belden breached an express warranty that its wire would conform to AEC's published standards, the trial court properly granted AES' motion for partial summary judgment and denied Belden's motion for partial summary judgment.]

QUESTIONS AND NOTES

1.   Some of the difficulty in applying 2–207 results from confusion about the role of each subsection. A careful reading reveals that each subsection has a distinct role. Subsection (1) answers a single question, viz., do the writings of the parties form a contract? That is its only role, and subsections (2) and (3) have nothing to contribute to answering that question. Subsection (2) addresses the single question, if the writings do form a contract, what are the terms of that contract? Subsections (1) and (3) have nothing to contribute

to answering that question. Finally, subsection (3) addresses two questions: if the writings do not form a contract, does the conduct of the parties form a contract? If so, what are the terms of that contract?

Which of these questions are involved in *Belden*?

2.   Please consider this variation of Problem 5, page 75: immediately after the quoted language, Grado's acknowledgment states, "Our acceptance of your order is conditional on the following terms . . . ," one of which is the exclusion of liability for consequential damages. Under 2–207 is there a contract?

3.   The court holds that Belden's acknowledgment form did not operate as an acceptance because it stated that "acceptance is expressly conditional on Buyer's assent solely to the terms of [this] acknowledgment." Instead, it amounted to a counteroffer. The court then proceeded to apply subsection (3) of 2–207. Should the court instead have looked to 2–206(1)(b)?

4.   Problem. Pipeco sent Davis Drilling a written offer offering to sell used steel pipe, delivery date to be October 15th. Davis responded with a written acceptance that changed the delivery date to December 15th. The December 15th date was clearly typed in on the front of the acceptance form. If this was a material change from Pipeco's offer, did that prevent Davis' response from operating as an acceptance?

If a contract was formed by this exchange of correspondence, what is the delivery term?

5.   Problem. Utilico sent Vestas a purchase order for a wind turbine. Vestas responded with its standard acknowledgement form, which had 16 clauses on the reverse side, one of which stated, "This acceptance is expressly made conditional upon offeror's assent to all the terms of this acceptance." Do the parties have a contract?

6.   What is the relationship between 2–201 and 2–207: 2–201(2), which operates when both parties are merchants, does not depend on whether the terms in the form are material or non-material. Under 2–201(2), then, may an additional term in an offeree's form become part of the contract if the offeror does not object within ten days, even if the alteration is material and would not become part of the contract under 2–207(2)?

7.   If the offeree adds a term on a matter on which the offer is silent, then the dispute typically centers on subsection (2)(b): is the offeree's term a material alteration of the offer?

Problem. Portals sends Coatings, Inc., a purchase order for a preservative to be used in the wood doors and windows that Portals manufactures. Coatings responds with its Acknowledgement, which directs the buyer to sign and return it, and which states, "In no event shall Coatings, Inc.'s liability for damages in respect to products sold hereunder exceed the purchase price of the products as to which a claim is made." Portals does not sign or return the Acknowledgment. The preservative proves to be defective, causing Portals' doors and windows to rot. Portals' customers complain and seek compensation, which Portals pays. Now Portals sues Coatings, Inc., seeking recovery under 2–714, including the amounts it paid to its customers. As we will see later, 2–714 authorizes recovery of these damages, but another section (2–719) permits the parties to agree to limitations on damages. Do the parties have a contract? Which subsection of 2–207 governs the answer to this question?

If the limitation in Coatings' Acknowledgment is part of that contract, Portals loses. Is the limitation part of the contract?

Official Comments 4 and 5 address the question whether a term is a "material alteration," but they do not define that term. Nor does any other section. Comment 4 refers to "clauses which would normally 'materially alter' the contract and so result in surprise or hardship if incorporated without express awareness by the other party." Comment 5 refers to "clauses which involve no element of unreasonable surprise and which therefore are to be incorporated in the contract."

In the case on which this problem is based, the court stated:

> [Buyer] contends that the damages limitation was a material alteration to the contract for purchase and sale. [Seller] disagrees, relying on U.C.C. commentary that says "a clause . . . limiting remedy in a reasonable manner" . . . involves "no element of unreasonable surprise" and will become a part of the contract unless an objection is raised. 2–207 U.C.C. cmt. 5. The "unreasonable surprise" is a reference to a previous comment wherein the drafters gave examples of clauses that "would normally 'materially alter' the contract and so result in surprise or hardship if incorporated without express awareness." *Id.* cmt. 4. Quoting this Circuit and Comment 4, the Minnesota Court of Appeals has said, "An agreement is materially altered if an addition would 'result in surprise or hardship if incorporated without express awareness by the other party.'" Likewise, in applying § 2–207, we have said, "Considerations of surprise and hardship must remain a part of the [material alteration] analysis." *See Johnson v. Murray,* 648 N.W.2d 664, 670 (Minn.2002) ("Uniform laws are interpreted to effect their general purpose to make uniform the laws of those states that enact them. Accordingly, we give great weight to other states' interpretations of a uniform law."[6]

. . .

The facts of this case concerning material alteration, that is, those which go to prove hardship or surprise, are really without

[6] Although the Minnesota courts and this Court are not among them, there are courts that have read U.C.C. § 2–207 Comments 4 and 5 together to exclude hardship as a factor to be considered in the analysis: that is, material alteration is not defined by hardship (it does not appear in Comment 5); hardship is a consequence of a material alteration (it does appear in Comment 4). The Seventh Circuit, for example, has said that "[h]ardship is a consequence, not a criterion. (Surprise can be either.)" *Union Carbide Corp. v. Oscar Mayer Foods Corp.,* 947 F.2d 1333, 1336 (7th Cir.1991). At first blush, that seems a fair reading of the comments, given the way they are worded. On the other hand, why would the drafters even mention "hardship" if it were not a factor to be considered in determining materiality? In any event, the comments do not have the force of law, and courts applying Minnesota law have declared that a finding of either surprise or hardship will result in a material alteration. . . .

dispute. After considering them, we conclude that enforcement of the damages limitation provision would result in both hardship and surprise to [Buyer].

Economically, the hardship to [Buyer] is clear—the $1.6 million [contract price that Seller] says it owes under the terms of the acknowledgment is a fraction of the [$53 million] out-of-pocket costs to [Buyer] resulting from [the product's] failure, not even considering [the $52 million] consequential damages. Under the terms of the boilerplate limitation, the distribution . . . of risk of the product's failure is dramatically altered, with [Buyer] bearing the brunt of it. The warranty that the jury found was for future performance. The failure of the product in the future—after it was applied to the wood and the wood was made into a window and installed in a building—would be, and was, catastrophic in terms of damages. Given that the warranty was for [the product's] future performance, the damages should remedy a failure of that future performance, not just refund the money spent for the product. Reimbursing the cost of the product—essentially "replacing" the product—would not enforce the warranty that [Seller] gave to [Buyer]. Moreover, most of the damages at issue were unquestionably foreseeable.

As for surprise, the provision was not negotiated by [Seller] and [Buyer]. While it appeared in all the acknowledgments, it was boilerplate language, in small print, on the back side of a form that was dense with other small print. . . . [Buyer] proffered evidence that [Seller] and other coatings manufacturers had always made things right when a product of theirs failed with consequences, not just refunding the purchase price of the product sold but replacing the [Buyer] product that was damaged as a result of the failure. Granted, the catastrophic nature of [the product's] failure was new to the relationship between [Seller] and [Buyer], but that would be all the more reason that [Seller's] refusal to pay consequential damages would be both a surprise and a hardship.

. . . It is true that Comment 5 to U.C.C. § 2–207 lists "a clause . . . limiting remedy in a reasonable manner" as one that will "involve no element of unreasonable surprise" and therefore will "be incorporated in the contract." Apart from the fact that the commentary does not have the force of law, we conclude on the facts of this case that the provision in reality did involve "an element of unreasonable surprise" to [Buyer]. The damages limitation language from the [Seller's] acknowledgment forms therefore did not become a part of the contract between [Seller] and [Buyer] and is not enforceable.

Marvin Lumber & Cedar Co. v. PPG Industries, Inc., 401 F.3d 901 (8th Cir.2005).

As stated above, the UCC does not contain a definition of "material alteration." Nor do the Restatements, though they do define "material." For example, in connection with articulating the standard for liability for misrepresentation, the Restatement (Second) of Torts § 538(2) provides that a "matter is material if (a) a reasonable man would attach importance to [it] . . . or (b) the maker of the representation knows or has reason to know that its recipient regards or is likely to regard the matter as important . . . although a reasonable man would not so regard it." And the Restatement (Second) of Contracts § 162(2) states that "a misrepresentation is material if it would be likely to induce a reasonable person to manifest his assent." Perhaps these non-UCC authorities are relevant to understanding when an alteration is material.

————

Northrop Corporation v. Litronic Industries

United States Court of Appeals, Seventh Circuit, 1994.
29 F.3d 1173.

■ POSNER, CHIEF JUDGE.*

. . .

The battle of the forms in this case takes the form of something very like a badminton game, but we can simplify it a bit without distorting the issues. The players are Northrop, the giant defense firm, and Litronic, which manufactures electronic components, including "printed wire boards" that are incorporated into defense weapon systems. In 1987 Northrop sent several manufacturers, including Litronic, a request to submit offers to sell Northrop customized printed wire board designated by Northrop as a "1714 Board." The request stated that any purchase would be made by means of a purchase order that would set forth terms and conditions that would override any inconsistent terms in the offer. In response, Litronic mailed an offer to sell Northrop four boards for $19,000 apiece, to be delivered within six weeks. The offer contained a 90-day warranty stated to be in lieu of any other warranties, and provided that the terms of the offer would take precedence over any terms proposed by the buyer. Lynch, a purchasing officer of Northrop, responded to the offer in a phone conversation in which he told Litronic's man, Lair, that he was accepting the offer up to the limit of his authority, which was $24,999, and that a formal purchase order for all four boards would follow. Litronic was familiar with Northrop's purchase order form, having previously done business with Northrop, which had been using the same form for some time. Had Lair referred to any of the previous orders, he would have discovered that Northrop's order form provided for a warranty that contained no time limit.

Lynch followed up the phone conversation a month later with a "turn on" letter, authorizing Litronic to begin production of all four boards (it had done so already) and repeating that a purchase order would follow.

———

* Some paragraphs of the opinion have been reordered to locate the statement of facts at the beginning of the excerpt.—Eds.

The record is unclear when the actual purchase order was mailed; it may have been as much as four months after the phone conversation and three months after the turn-on letter. The purchase order required the seller to send a written acknowledgment to Northrop. Litronic never did so, however, and Northrop did not complain; it does not bother to follow up on its requirement of a signed acknowledgment.

Although Litronic had begun manufacturing the boards immediately after the telephone call from Lynch, for reasons that are unknown but that Northrop does not contend are culpable, Litronic did not deliver the first three boards until more than a year later, in July of 1988. Northrop tested the boards for conformity to its specifications. The testing was protracted, either because the boards were highly complex or because Northrop's inspectors were busy, or perhaps for both reasons. At all events it was not until December and January, five or six months after delivery, that Northrop returned the three boards (the fourth had not been delivered), claiming that they were defective. Litronic refused to accept the return of the boards, on the ground that its 90-day warranty had lapsed. Northrop's position of course is that it had an unlimited warranty, as stated in the purchase order.

As an original matter one might suppose that this dispute is not over the terms of the warranty but over whether Northrop waited more than the "reasonable time" that the Uniform Commercial Code allows the buyer of nonconforming goods to reject them. UCC § 2–602(1). That in fact is how the magistrate judge framed the issue, as we shall see. But the parties continue to treat it as a "warranty" case. Their implicit view is that Litronic's 90-day warranty, if a term of the contract, not only barred Northrop from complaining about defects that showed up more than 90 days after the delivery of the boards but also limited to 90 days the time within which Northrop was permitted to reject the boards because of defects that rendered them nonconforming. We accept this view for purposes of deciding these appeals.

. . . The magistrate judge gave judgment for Northrop in the amount of $58,000, representing the money it had paid for the three No. 1714 boards that it had taken delivery of. Both parties appeal.

. . .

Litronic's appeal concerns the breach of its warranty on the No. 1714 boards. It wins if the warranty really did expire after only 90 days. The parties agree that Litronic's offer to sell the No. 1714 boards to Northrop, the offer made in response to Northrop's request for bids, was the offer. So far, so good. If Northrop's Mr. Lynch accepted the offer over the phone, the parties had a contract then and there, but the question would still be on what terms. Regarding the first question, whether there was a contract, we may assume to begin with that the acceptance was sufficiently "definite" to satisfy the requirement of definiteness in section 2–207(1); after all, it impelled Litronic to begin production immediately, and there is no suggestion that it acted precipitately in doing so. We do not know whether Lynch in his conversation with Lair made acceptance of the complete contract expressly conditional on approval by Lynch's superiors at Northrop. We know that he had authority to contract only up to $24,999, but we do not know whether he told Lair what the exact limitation on his authority was or whether Litronic knew it without being told. It does not matter. The condition, if it was a condition, was satisfied and so drops out.

We do not think that Northrop's acceptance, via Lynch, of Litronic's offer could be thought conditional on Litronic's yielding to Northrop's demand for an open-ended warranty. For while Lynch's reference to the purchase order might have alerted Litronic to Northrop's desire for a warranty not limited to 90 days, Lynch did not purport to make the more extensive warranty a condition of acceptance. So the condition, if there was one, was not an express condition, as the cases insist it be.

There was a contract, therefore; further, and, as we shall note, decisive, evidence being that the parties acted as if they had a contract— the boards were shipped and paid for. The question is then what the terms of the warranty in the contract were. Lynch's reference in the phone conversation to the forthcoming purchase order shows that Northrop's acceptance contained different terms from the offer, namely the discrepant terms in the purchase order, in particular the warranty— for it is plain that the Northrop warranty was intended to be indefinite in length, so that, at least in the absence of some industry custom setting a limit on warranties that do not specify a duration (cf. UCC Sec. 2–207, comments 4 and 5), a point not raised, any limitation on the length of the warranty in the offer would be a materially different term. Of course the fact that Northrop preferred a longer warranty than Litronic was offering does not by itself establish that Northrop's acceptance contained different terms. But Lynch did not accept Litronic's offer and leave it at that. He said that he would issue a Northrop purchase order, and both he and Lair knew (or at least should have known) that the Northrop purchase order form contained a different warranty from Litronic's sale order form. And we have already said that Lynch did not, by his oral reference to the purchase order, condition Northrop's purchase on Litronic's agreeing to comply with all the terms in the purchase order form, given the courts' insistence that any such condition be explicit. (Judges are skeptical that even businesspeople read boilerplate, so they are reluctant, rightly or wrongly, to make a contract fail on the basis of a printed condition in a form contract.) But Lynch said enough to make clear to Lair that the acceptance contained different terms from the offer.

Mischief lurks in the words "additional to or different from" [as they appear in 2–207]. The next subsection of 2–207 provides that if additional terms in the acceptance are not materially different from those in the offer, then, subject to certain other qualifications, they become part of the contract, § 2–207(2), while if the additional terms are materially different they operate as proposals and so have no effect unless the offeror agrees to them, UCC § 2–207, comment 3; if the offeror does not agree to them, therefore, the terms of the contract are those in the offer. A clause providing for interest at normal rates on overdue invoices, or limiting the right to reject goods because of defects falling within customary trade tolerances for acceptance with adjustment, would be the sort of additional term that is not deemed material, and hence it would become a part of the contract even if the offeror never signified acceptance of it. *Id.,* comment 5.

The Code does not explain, however, what happens if the offeree's response contains *different* terms (rather than additional ones) within the meaning of section 2–207(1). There is no consensus on that question. See James J. White & Robert S. Summers, *Uniform Commercial Code* 33–36 (3d ed. 1988); John E. Murray, Jr., "The Chaos of the 'Battle of the Forms': Solutions," 39 Vand.L.Rev. 1307, 1354–65 (1986). We know there is a contract because an acceptance is effective even though it contains different terms; but what are the terms of the contract that is brought into being by the offer and acceptance? One view is that the discrepant terms in both the nonidentical offer and the acceptance drop out, and default terms found elsewhere in the Code fill the resulting gap. Another view is that the offeree's discrepant terms drop out and the offeror's become part of the contract. A third view, possibly the most sensible, equates "different" with "additional" and makes the outcome turn on whether the new terms in the acceptance are materially different from the terms in the offer—in which event they operate as proposals, so that the offeror's terms prevail unless he agrees to the variant terms in the acceptance—or not materially different from the terms in the offer, in which event they become part of the contract. This interpretation equating "different" to "additional," bolstered by drafting history which shows that the omission of "or different" from section 2–207(2) was a drafting error,* substitutes a manageable inquiry into materiality for a hair-splitting inquiry into the difference between "different" and "additional." It is hair-splitting ("metaphysical," "casuistic," "semantic," in the pejorative senses of these words) because all different terms are additional and all additional terms are different.

Unfortunately, the Illinois courts—whose understanding of Article 2 of the UCC is binding on us because this is a diversity suit governed, all agree, by Illinois law—have had no occasion to choose among the different positions on the consequences of an acceptance that contains "different" terms from the offer. We shall have to choose.

The Uniform Commercial Code, as we have said, does not say what the terms of the contract are if the offer and acceptance contain different terms, as distinct from cases in which the acceptance merely contains additional terms to those in the offer. The majority view is that the discrepant terms fall out and are replaced by a suitable UCC gap-filler.

---

*   See John L. Utz, "More on the Battle of the Forms: The Treatment of 'Different' Terms Under the Uniform Commercial Code," 16 *U.C.C.L.J.* 103, 110–12 (1983).—Eds.

The magistrate judge followed this approach and proceeded to section 2–309, which provides that nonconforming goods may be rejected within a "reasonable" time (see also § 2–601(1)), and she held that the six months that Northrop took to reject Litronic's boards was a reasonable time because of the complexity of the required testing. The leading minority view is that the discrepant terms *in the acceptance* are to be ignored, and that would give the palm to Litronic. Our own preferred view—the view that assimilates "different" to "additional," so that the terms in the offer prevail over the different terms in the acceptance only if the latter are materially different, has as yet been adopted by only one state, California. Steiner v. Mobil Oil Corp., 20 Cal.3d 90, 141 Cal.Rptr. 157, 569 P.2d 751, 759 n. 5 (1977). Under that view, as under what we are calling the "leading" minority view, the warranty in Litronic's offer, the 90-day warranty, was the contractual warranty, because the unlimited warranty contained in Northrop's acceptance was materially different.

Because Illinois in other UCC cases has tended to adopt majority rules, e.g., Rebaque v. Forsythe Racing, Inc., 134 Ill.App.3d 778, 89 Ill.Dec. 595, 598, 480 N.E.2d 1338, 1341 (1985), and because the interest in the uniform nationwide application of the Code—an interest asserted in the Code itself (see § 1–102) [revised 1–103(a)(3)]—argues for nudging majority views, even if imperfect (but not downright bad), toward unanimity, we start with a presumption that Illinois, whose position we are trying to predict, would adopt the majority view. We do not find the presumption rebutted. The idea behind the majority view is that the presence of different terms in the acceptance suggests that the offeree didn't *really* accede to the offeror's terms, yet both parties wanted to contract, so why not find a neutral term to govern the dispute that has arisen between them? Of course the offeree may not have had any serious objection to the terms in the offer at the time of contracting; he may have mailed a boiler plated form without giving any thought to its contents or to its suitability for the particular contract in question. But it is just as likely that the discrepant terms *in the offer* itself were the product of a thoughtless use of a boilerplate form rather than a considered condition of contracting. And if the offeror doesn't want to do business other than on the terms in the offer, he can protect himself by specifying that the offeree must accept all those terms for the parties to have a contract. UCC Sec. 2–207(2)(a); Tecumseh International Corp. v. City of Springfield, 70 Ill.App.3d 101, 26 Ill.Dec. 745, 748, 388 N.E.2d 460, 463 (1979). Now as it happens Litronic did state in its offer that the terms in the offer "take precedence over terms and conditions of the buyer, unless specifically negotiated otherwise." But, for reasons that we do not and need not fathom, Litronic does not argue that this language conditioned the existence of the contract on Northrop's acceding to the 90-day warranty in the offer; any such argument is therefore waived.

It is true that the offeree likewise can protect himself by making his acceptance of the offer conditional on the offeror's acceding to any different terms in the acceptance. But so many acceptances are made over the phone by relatively junior employees, as in this case, that it may be unrealistic to expect offerees to protect themselves in this way. The offeror goes first and therefore has a little more time for careful specification of the terms on which he is willing to make a contract. What we are calling the leading minority view may tempt the offeror to spring a surprise on the offeree, hoping the latter won't read the fine print. Under the majority view, if the offeree tries to spring a surprise (the offeror can't, since his terms won't prevail if the acceptance contains different terms), the parties move to neutral ground; and the offeror can, we have suggested, more easily protect himself against being surprised than the offeree can protect *himself* against being surprised. The California rule dissolves all these problems, but has too little support to make it a plausible candidate for Illinois, or at least a plausible candidate for our guess as to Illinois's position.

There is a further wrinkle, however. The third subsection of section 2–207 provides that even if no contract is established under either of the first two subsections, it may be established by the "conduct of the parties," and in that event (as subsection (3) expressly provides) the discrepant terms vanish and are replaced by UCC gap fillers. This may seem to make it impossible for the offeror to protect himself from being contractually bound by specifying that the acceptance must mirror his offer. But subsection (3) comes into play only when the parties have by their conduct manifested the existence of a contract, as where the offeror, having specified that the acceptance must mirror the offer yet having received an acceptance that deviates from the offer, nonetheless goes ahead and performs as if there were a contract. That is one way to interpret what happened here but it leads to the same result as applying subsection (2) interpreted as the majority of states do, so we need not consider it separately.

Given the intricacy of the No. 1714 boards, it is unlikely that Northrop would have acceded to a 90-day limitation on its warranty protection. Litronic at argument stressed that it is a much smaller firm, hence presumably unwilling to assume burdensome warranty obligations; but it is a curious suggestion that little fellows are more likely than big ones to get their way in negotiations between firms of disparate size. And Northrop actually got only half its way, though enough for victory here; for by virtue of accepting Litronic's offer without expressly conditioning its acceptance on Litronic's acceding to Northrop's terms, Northrop got not a warranty unlimited in duration, as its purchase order provides, but (pursuant to the majority understanding of UCC § 2–207(2)) a warranty of "reasonable" duration, courtesy the court. If special circumstances made a 90-day warranty reasonable, Litronic was free to argue for it in the district court.

On the view we take, the purchase order has no significance beyond showing that Northrop's acceptance contained (albeit by reference) different terms. The fact that Litronic never signed the order, and the fact that Northrop never called this omission to Litronic's attention, also drop out of the case, along with Northrop's argument that to enforce the 90-day limitation in Litronic's warranty would be unconscionable. But for future reference we remind Northrop and companies like it that the defense of unconscionability was not invented to protect multi-billion dollar corporations against mistakes committed by their employees, and indeed has rarely succeeded outside the area of consumer contracts.

Affirmed.

QUESTIONS AND NOTES

1. *Northrup* concerns the application of subsection (2), which determines the terms of the contract when it is clear that the writings (or the oral interactions of the parties) form a contract. Its apparent "first-shot" rule making the terms of the offer binding, rather than the terms of the "acceptance" is seen as being only marginally better, if at all, than the traditional "last-shot" rule of the common law under which an "acceptance" that states additional or different terms becomes a counter-offer, which is accepted if the original offeror then accepts performance by the counter-offeror. Therefore, when the offeree's acceptance contains a term that conflicts with a term in the offer, most courts have adopted the so-called "knockout" rule under subsection (2). Under this approach neither party gets its way by virtue of including the disputed term in its form, and the court looks elsewhere to supply the term.

What language in 2–207 authorizes use of the knockout rule?

2.   Problem. Following a telephone conversation discussing a potential transaction in general terms, Logo sent ShirtShop a letter, "We will be pleased to sell you 1,000 polo shirts, assortment of stripes and solid colors, at \$20/shirt, transportation prepaid, payment due on delivery."

ShirtShop responded by sending a purchase order that repeated the quantity, price, payment, and shipping terms, but described the goods as "1,000 polo shirts, assorted solid colors."

Logo shipped 1,000 shirts, half solid colors and half striped. ShirtShop opened the shipping cartons, saw that half the shirts were striped, and sent all 1,000 back to Logo. Logo sued, alleging that ShirtShop breached the contract by refusing to accept the shirts. ShirtShop counterclaimed, alleging that Logo breached the contract by not delivering all solid colors. Which party prevails?

3.   Problem. Following a telephone conversation, Bender sent Samuels a purchase order for certain equipment, at prices and other terms discussed on the phone. Bender's purchase order contained the provision, "Payment will be made 90 days after delivery of the goods."

Samuels received the purchase order, and, after glancing just at the provisions dealing with quantity, description, and price, sent Bender its standard sales acknowledgment form. This form contained several boilerplate provisions, including, (1) "Our assent to this transaction is expressly conditional on your assent to the terms on this acknowledgment form, including any terms that are additional to or different from the terms on any purchase order you may have sent us," and (2) "Payment is due in full on delivery of the goods." Neither party communicated further.

In due course, Samuels' truck driver showed up at Bender's dock and left the goods without demanding payment. Upon learning what the driver had done, Samuels fired him and phoned Bender to inform Bender that payment is due on delivery and to request immediate payment. Bender refused, but said that Samuels would receive payment in 90 days. Bender paid 90 days after delivery, and ultimately, for other reasons, the parties wound up in litigation. Samuels asserted a claim for interest on the purchase price for 90 days. If the contract includes the term on Samuels' acknowledgment, Samuels is entitled to the interest.

    a.   Is Samuels' payment term part of the contract?

    b.   If not, when is payment due?

    c.   Assume there is a custom in this branch of the equipment industry that buyers are entitled to ten days credit. Would this affect your answer: is Bender liable for any interest?

4.   CISG and varying acceptances. The Convention on Contracts for the International Sale of Goods adopted only a part of UCC 2–207. Article 19 states:

> (1) A reply to an offer which purports to be an acceptance but contains additions, limitations or other modifications is a rejection of the offer and constitutes a counter-offer.

> (2) However, a reply to an offer which purports to be an acceptance but contains additional or different terms which do not materially alter the terms of the offer constitutes an acceptance, unless the offeror, without undue delay, objects orally to the discrepancy or dispatches a notice to that effect. If he does not so object, the terms of the contract are the terms of the offer with the modifications contained in the acceptance.

> (3) Additional or different terms relating, among other things, to the price, payment, quality and quantity of the goods, place and time of delivery, extent of one party's liability to the other or the settlement of disputes are considered to alter the terms of the offer materially.

Article 18(1) of CISG provides that "A statement made by or other conduct of the offeree indicating assent to an offer is an acceptance. . . ."

Problem. Sprint sends HTC a purchase order for 10,000 cell phones, which includes the term, "goods must be warranted to be merchantable." HTC sends Sprint an acknowledgement, which contains a disclaimer of all warranties. Neither party signs or returns the other party's form. In due course, HTC ships the cell phones, and Sprint pays for them. After distributing the phones to its customers, Sprint learns that many of the phones are defective. Sprint sues HTC. What result under CISG?

Professor Honnold has argued that under CISG sections 18(1) and 19, in cases where buyer and seller exchange order and acknowledgement forms with conflicting terms and then both perform, it would be permissible for a court to conclude that neither had accepted the "offer" of the other and that the contract was formed only by acceptance of performance. In that case, it would be appropriate to find that the contract consists of those terms on which the exchanged writings agree with supplementary terms filled in from CISG. J. Honnold, Uniform Law for International Sales § 170.4 (4th ed.2009). That, of course, sounds very much like 2–207(3). Do Articles 18–19 support this analysis?

5. **Leases.** Article 2A was drafted and adopted decades after Article 2. Because of the difficulty in applying 2–207 and because leases usually are not formed by an exchange of purchase order and acknowledgement forms, Article 2A does not contain any provision like 2–207.

E. LAYERED CONTRACTING

A layered contract, also known as a rolling contract, describes a relationship in which one party (typically the seller) drafts the contract document and encloses that document in the packaging that contains the goods, so that the terms are not available to the other until after he or she opens the package. The buyer knows the subject matter of the contract and the price, but the many other terms in the document are unknown at the initial stage of the transaction. This situation presents two questions: is there a contract? if so, are the terms enclosed in the package part of that contract?

Hill v. Gateway 2000, Inc.
United States Court of Appeals, Seventh Circuit, 1997.
105 F.3d 1147.

■ EASTERBROOK, CIRCUIT JUDGE.

A customer picks up the phone, orders a computer, and gives a credit card number. Presently a box arrives, containing the computer and a list of terms, said to govern unless the customer returns the computer within 30 days. Are these terms effective as the parties' contract, or is the contract term-free because the order-taker did not read any terms over the phone and elicit the customer's assent?

One of the terms in the box containing a Gateway 2000 system was an arbitration clause. Rich and Enza Hill, the customers, kept the computer more than 30 days before complaining about its components and performance. They filed suit in federal court arguing, among other things, that the product's shortcomings make Gateway a racketeer (mail and wire fraud are said to be the predicate offenses), leading to treble damages under RICO for the Hills and a class of all other purchasers. Gateway asked the district court to enforce the arbitration clause; the judge refused, writing that "[t]he present record is insufficient to support a finding of a valid arbitration agreement between the parties or that the plaintiffs were given adequate notice of the arbitration clause." Gateway took an immediate appeal, as is its right. 9 USC. § 16(a)(1)(A).

The Hills say that the arbitration clause did not stand out: they concede noticing the statement of terms but deny reading it closely enough to discover the agreement to arbitrate, and they ask us to conclude that they therefore may go to court. Yet an agreement to arbitrate must be enforced "save upon such grounds as exist at law or in equity for the revocation of any contract." 9 U.S.C. § 2. Doctor's Associates, Inc. v. Casarotto, 517 U.S. 681, 116 S.Ct. 1652, 134 L.Ed.2d 902 (1996), holds that this provision of the Federal Arbitration Act is inconsistent with any requirement that an arbitration clause be prominent. A contract need not be read to be effective; people who accept take the risk that the unread terms may in retrospect prove unwelcome. Terms inside Gateway's box stand or fall together. If they constitute the parties' contract because the Hills had an opportunity to return the computer after reading them, then all must be enforced.

ProCD, Inc. v. Zeidenberg, 86 F.3d 1447 (7th Cir.1996), holds that terms inside a box of software bind consumers who use the software after an opportunity to read the terms and to reject them by returning the product. Likewise, Carnival Cruise Lines, Inc. v. Shute, 499 U.S. 585, 111 S.Ct. 1522, 113 L.Ed.2d 622 (1991), enforces a forum-selection clause that was included among three pages of terms attached to a cruise ship ticket. *ProCD* and *Carnival Cruise Lines* exemplify the many commercial transactions in which people pay for products with terms to follow; ProCD discusses others. 86 F.3d at 1451–52. The district court concluded in *ProCD* that the contract is formed when the consumer pays for the software; as a result, the court held, only terms known to the consumer at that moment are part of the contract, and provisos inside the box do not count. Although this is one way a contract could be formed, it is not the only way: "A vendor, as master of the offer, may invite acceptance by conduct, and may propose limitations on the kind of conduct that constitutes acceptance. A buyer may accept by performing the acts the vendor proposes to treat as acceptance." Id. at 1452. Gateway shipped computers with the same sort of accept-or-return offer ProCD made to users of its software. *ProCD* relied on the Uniform Commercial Code rather than any peculiarities of Wisconsin law; both Illinois and South Dakota, the two states whose law might govern relations between Gateway and the Hills, have adopted the UCC; neither side has pointed us to any atypical doctrines in those states that might be pertinent; *ProCD* therefore applies to this dispute.

Plaintiffs ask us to limit *ProCD* to software, but where's the sense in that? *ProCD* is about the law of contract, not the law of software. Payment preceding the revelation of full terms is common for air transportation, insurance, and many other endeavors. Practical considerations support allowing vendors to enclose the full legal terms with their products. Cashiers cannot be expected to read legal documents to customers before ringing up sales. If the staff at the other end of the phone for direct-sales operations such as Gateway's had to read the four-page statement of terms before taking the buyer's credit card number, the droning voice would anesthetize rather than enlighten many potential buyers. Others would hang up in a rage over the waste of their time. And oral recitation would not avoid customers' assertions (whether true or feigned) that the clerk did not read term X to them, or that they did not remember or understand it. Writing provides benefits for both sides of commercial transactions. Customers as a group are better off when vendors skip costly and ineffectual steps such as telephonic recitation, and use instead a simple approve-or-return device. Competent adults are bound by such documents, read or unread. For what little it is worth, we add that the box from Gateway was crammed with software. The computer came with an operating system, without which it was useful only as a boat anchor. Gateway also included many application programs. So the Hills' effort to limit *ProCD* to software would not avail them factually, even if it were sound legally—which it is not.

For their second sally, the Hills contend that ProCD should be limited to executory contracts (to licenses in particular), and therefore does not apply because both parties' performance of this contract was complete when the box arrived at their home. This is legally and factually wrong: legally because the question at hand concerns the *formation* of the contract rather than its *performance*, and factually because both contracts were incompletely performed. *ProCD* did not depend on the fact that the seller characterized the transaction as a license rather than as a contract; we treated it as a contract for the sale of goods and reserved the question whether for other purposes a "license" characterization might be preferable. 86 F.3d at 1450. All debates about characterization to one side, the transaction in *ProCD* was no more executory than the one here: Zeidenberg paid for the software and walked out of the store with a box under his arm, so if arrival of the box with the product ends the time for revelation of contractual terms, then the time ended in *ProCD* before Zeidenberg opened the box. But of course ProCD had not completed performance with delivery of the box, and neither had Gateway. One element of the transaction was the warranty, which obliges sellers to fix defects in their products. The Hills have invoked Gateway's warranty and are not satisfied with its response, so they are not well positioned to say that Gateway's obligations were fulfilled when the motor carrier unloaded the box. What is more, both ProCD and Gateway promised to help customers to use their products. Long-term service and information obligations are common in the computer business, on both hardware and software sides. Gateway offers "lifetime service" and has a round-the-clock telephone hotline to fulfill this promise. Some vendors spend more money helping customers use their products than on developing and manufacturing them. The document in Gateway's box includes promises of future performance that some consumers value highly; these promises bind Gateway just as the arbitration clause binds the Hills.

Next the Hills insist that *ProCD* is irrelevant because Zeidenberg was a "merchant" and they are not. Section 2–207(2) of the UCC, the infamous battle-of-the-forms section, states that "additional terms [following acceptance of an offer] are to be construed as proposals for addition to a contract. Between merchants such terms become part of the contract unless. . . ." Plaintiffs tell us that *ProCD* came out as it did only because Zeidenberg was a "merchant" and the terms inside ProCD's box were not excluded by the "unless" clause. This argument pays scant attention to the opinion in *ProCD,* which concluded that, when there is only one form, "sec. 2–207 is irrelevant." 86 F.3d at 1452. The question in *ProCD* was not whether terms were added to a contract after its formation, but how and when the contract was formed—in particular, whether a vendor may propose that a contract of sale be formed, not in the store (or over the phone) with the payment of money or a general "send me the product," but after the customer has had a chance to inspect both the item and the terms. *ProCD* answers "yes," for merchants and consumers alike. Yet again, for what little it is worth we observe that the Hills misunderstand the setting of *ProCD.* A "merchant" under the UCC "means a person who deals in goods of the kind or otherwise by his occupation holds himself out as having knowledge or skill peculiar to the practices or goods involved in the transaction," § 2–104(1). Zeidenberg bought the product at a retail store, an uncommon place for merchants to acquire inventory. His corporation put ProCD's database on the Internet for anyone to browse, which led to the litigation but did not make Zeidenberg a software merchant.

At oral argument the Hills propounded still another distinction: the box containing ProCD's software displayed a notice that additional terms were within, while the box containing Gateway's computer did not. The difference is functional, not legal. Consumers browsing the aisles of a store can look at the box, and if they are unwilling to deal with the prospect of additional terms can leave the box alone, avoiding the transactions costs of returning the package after reviewing its contents. Gateway's box, by contrast, is just a shipping carton; it is not on display anywhere. Its function is to protect the product during transit, and the information on its sides is for the use of handlers rather than would be purchasers.

. . .

Perhaps the Hills would have had a better argument if they were first alerted to the bundling of hardware and legal-ware after opening the box and wanted to return the computer in order to avoid disagreeable terms, but were dissuaded by the expense of shipping. What the remedy would be in such a case—could it exceed the shipping charges?—is an interesting question, but one that need not detain us because the Hills knew before they ordered the computer that the carton would include *some* important terms, and they did not seek to discover these in advance. Gateway's ads state that their products come with limited warranties and lifetime support. How limited was the warranty—30 days, with service contingent on shipping the computer back, or five years, with free onsite service? What sort of support was offered? Shoppers have three principal ways to discover these things. First, they can ask the vendor to send a copy before deciding whether to buy. The Magnuson-Moss Warranty Act requires firms to distribute their warranty terms on request, 15 U.S.C. § 2302(b)(1)(A); the Hills do not contend that Gateway would have refused to enclose the remaining terms too. Concealment would be bad for business, scaring some customers away and leading to excess returns from others. Second, shoppers can consult public sources (computer magazines, the Web sites of vendors) that may contain this information. Third, they may inspect the documents after the product's delivery. Like Zeidenberg, the Hills took the third option. By keeping the computer beyond 30 days, the Hills accepted Gateway's offer, including the arbitration clause.

The Hills' remaining arguments, including a contention that the arbitration clause is unenforceable as part of a scheme to defraud, do not require more than a citation to Prima Paint Corp. v. Flood & Conklin Mfg. Co., 388 U.S. 395, 87 S.Ct. 1801, 18 L.Ed.2d 1270 (1967). Whatever may be said pro and con about the cost and efficacy of arbitration (which the Hills disparage) is for Congress and the contracting parties to consider. Claims based on RICO are no less arbitrable than those founded on the contract or the law of torts. The decision of the district court is vacated, and this case is remanded with instructions to compel the Hills to submit their dispute to arbitration.

Klocek v. Gateway, Inc.

United States District Court, District of Kansas, 2000.
104 F.Supp.2d 1332.

[Plaintiff purchased a computer and scanner from defendant. The parties disagree about the way in which plaintiff secured the computer from Gateway. He either purchased it in a store and took it home in the box, or Gateway shipped it to him in a box. Either way, in the box with the computer was a statement of terms of the sale, including an arbitration clause. This statement provided that by keeping the computer for five days, the buyer accepted the terms. Plaintiff set up the equipment, but the scanner would not work. Plaintiff sued for breach of warranty and breach of an agreement that the computer would work with certain peripherals. Defendant moved for dismissal of the suit on the ground that the in-the-box arbitration clause was binding. Only the portion of the opinion rejecting Gateway's claim is set out below.]

■ VRATIL, DISTRICT JUDGE.

Gateway asserts that plaintiff must arbitrate his claims under Gateway's Standard Terms and Conditions Agreement ("Standard Terms.") Whenever it sells a computer, Gateway includes a copy of the Standard Terms in the box which contains the computer battery power cables and instruction manuals. At the top of the first page, the Standard Terms include the following notice:

NOTE TO THE CUSTOMER

This document contains Gateway 2000's Standard Terms and Conditions. By retaining your Gateway 2000 computer system beyond five (5) days after the date of delivery, you accept these Terms and Conditions.

The notice is in emphasized type and is located inside a printed box which sets it apart from other provisions of the document. The Standard Terms are four pages long and contain 16 numbered paragraphs. Paragraph 10 provides

DISPUTE RESOLUTION. Any dispute or controversy arising out of or relating to this Agreement or its interpretation shall be settled exclusively and finally by arbitration. The arbitration shall be conducted in accordance with the Rules of Conciliation and Arbitration of the International Chamber of Commerce. The arbitration shall be conducted in Chicago, Illinois, U.S.A. before a sole arbitrator. Any award rendered in any such arbitration proceeding shall be final and binding on each of the parties, and judgment may be entered thereon in a court of competent jurisdiction.[1]

Gateway urges the Court to dismiss plaintiff's claims under the Federal Arbitration Act ("FAA,") 9 U.S.C. Sec. 1 *et seq.* . . .

When deciding whether the parties have agreed to arbitrate, the Court applies ordinary state law principles that govern the formation of contracts. First Options of Chicago, Inc. v. Kaplan, 514 U.S. 938, 944, 115 S.Ct. 1920, 131 L.Ed.2d 985 (1995). The existence of an arbitration agreement "is simply a matter of contract between the parties; [arbitration] is a way to resolve those disputes—but only those disputes—that the parties have agreed to submit to arbitration."

. . .

---

[1] Gateway states that after it sold plaintiff's computer, it mailed all existing customers in the United States a copy of its quarterly magazine, which contained notice of a change in the arbitration policy set forth in the Standard Terms. The new arbitration policy afforded customers the option of arbitrating before the International Chamber of Commerce ("ICC,") the American Arbitration Association ("AAA,") or the National Arbitration Forum ("NAF") in Chicago, Illinois, or any other location agreed upon by the parties. Plaintiff denies receiving notice of the amended arbitration policy. Neither party explains why—if the arbitration agreement was an enforceable contract—Gateway was entitled to unilaterally amend it by sending a magazine to computer customers.

[In an omitted part of the opinion, the court concludes that it is not sure whether the law of Kansas or Missouri applies to the transaction, but] [t]he Uniform Commercial Code ("UCC") governs the parties' transaction under both Kansas and Missouri law. *See* K.S.A. § 84–2–102; V.A.M.S. § 400.2–102 (UCC applies to "transactions in goods."); Kansas Comment 1 (main thrust of Article 2 is limited to sales); K.S.A. § 84–2–105(1) V.A.M.S. § 400.2–105(1) (" 'Goods' means all things . . . which are movable at the time of identification to the contract for sale. . . .") Regardless whether plaintiff purchased the computer in person or placed an order and received shipment of the computer, the parties agree that plaintiff paid for and received a computer from Gateway.

This conduct clearly demonstrates a contract for the sale of a computer. *See, e.g.,* Step-Saver Data Sys., Inc. v. Wyse Techn., 939 F.2d 91, 98 (3d Cir.1991). Thus the issue is whether the contract of sale includes the Standard Terms as part of the agreement.

State courts in Kansas and Missouri apparently have not decided whether terms received with a product become part of the parties' agreement. Authority from other courts is split. *Compare* Step-Saver, 939 F.2d 91 (printed terms on computer software package not part of agreement); Arizona Retail Sys., Inc. v. Software Link, Inc., 831 F.Supp. 759 (D.Ariz.1993) (license agreement shipped with computer software not part of agreement); *and* U.S. Surgical Corp. v. Orris, Inc., 5 F.Supp.2d 1201 (D.Kan.1998) (single-use restriction on product package not binding agreement); *with* Hill v. Gateway 2000, Inc., 105 F.3d 1147 (7th Cir.), *cert. denied,* 522 U.S. 808, 118 S.Ct. 47, 139 L.Ed.2d 13 (1997) (arbitration provision shipped with computer binding on buyer); ProCD, Inc. v. Zeidenberg, 86 F.3d 1447 (7th Cir.1996) (shrinkwrap license binding on buyer); *and* M.A. Mortenson Co., Inc. v. Timberline Software Corp., 140 Wash.2d 568, 998 P.2d 305 (2000) (following *Hill* and *ProCD* on license agreement supplied with software). It appears that at least in part, the cases turn on whether the court finds that the parties formed their contract *before* or *after* the vendor communicated its terms to the purchaser. *Compare* Step-Saver, 939 F.2d at 98 (parties' conduct in shipping, receiving and paying for product demonstrates existence of contract; box top license constitutes proposal for additional terms under § 2–207 which requires express agreement by purchaser); Arizona Retail, 831 F.Supp. at 765 (vendor entered into contract by agreeing to ship goods, or at latest by shipping goods to buyer; license agreement constitutes proposal to modify agreement under § 2–209 which requires express assent by buyer); *and* Orris, 5 F.Supp.2d at 1206 (sales contract concluded when vendor received consumer orders; single-use language on product's label was proposed modification under § 2–209 which requires express assent by purchaser); *with* ProCD, 86 F.3d at 1452 (under § 2–204 vendor, as master of offer, may propose limitations on kind of conduct that constitutes acceptance; § 2–207 does not apply in case with only one form); Hill, 105 F.3d at 1148–49 (same); *and*

Mortenson, 998 P.2d at 311–314 (where vendor and purchaser utilized license agreement in prior course of dealing, shrinkwrap license agreement constituted issue of contract formation under § 2–204, not contract alteration under § 2–207).

Gateway urges the Court to follow the Seventh Circuit decision in *Hill*. That case involved the shipment of a Gateway computer with terms similar to the Standard Terms in this case, except that Gateway gave the customer 30 days—instead of 5 days—to return the computer. In enforcing the arbitration clause, the Seventh Circuit relied on its decision in *ProCD,* where it enforced a software license which was contained inside a product box. *See* Hill, 105 F.3d at 1148–50. In *ProCD,* the Seventh Circuit noted that the exchange of money frequently precedes the communication of detailed terms in a commercial transaction. *See* ProCD, 86 F.3d at 1451. Citing UCC § 2–204, the court reasoned that by including the license with the software, the vendor proposed a contract that the buyer could accept by using the software after having an opportunity to read the license. ProCD, 86 F.3d at 1452. Specifically, the court stated:

> A vendor, as master of the offer, may invite acceptance by conduct, and may propose limitations on the kind of conduct that constitutes acceptance. A buyer may accept by performing the acts the vendor proposes to treat as acceptance.

ProCD, 86 F.3d at 1452. The *Hill* court followed the *ProCD* analysis, noting that "[p]ractical considerations support allowing vendors to enclose the full legal terms with their products." Hill, 105 F.3d at 1149.

The Court is not persuaded that Kansas or Missouri courts would follow the Seventh Circuit reasoning in *Hill* and *ProCD*. In each case the Seventh Circuit concluded without support that UCC § 2–207 was irrelevant because the cases involved only one written form. *See* ProCD, 86 F.3d at 1452 (citing no authority); Hill, 105 F.3d at 1150 (citing ProCD). This conclusion is not supported by the statute or by Kansas or Missouri law. Disputes under § 2–207 often arise in the context of a "battle of forms," *see, e.g.,* Diatom, Inc. v. Pennwalt Corp., 741 F.2d 1569, 1574 (10th Cir.1984), but nothing in its language precludes application in a case which involves only one form. . . . By its terms, § 2–207 applies to an acceptance or written confirmation. It states nothing which requires another form before the provision becomes effective. In fact, the official comment to the section specifically provides that §§ 2–207(1) and (2) apply "where an agreement has been reached orally . . . and is followed by one or both of the parties sending formal memoranda embodying the terms so far agreed and adding terms not discussed." Official Comment 1 of UCC § 2–207. . . .

In addition, the Seventh Circuit provided no explanation for its conclusion that "the vendor is the master of the offer." *See* ProCD, 86 F.3d at 1452 (citing nothing in support of proposition); Hill, 105 F.3d at 1149 (citing ProCD). In typical consumer transactions, the purchaser is the offeror, and the vendor is the offeree. *See* Brown Mach., Div. of John Brown, Inc. v. Hercules, Inc., 770 S.W.2d 416, 419 (Mo.App.1989) (as general rule orders are considered offers to purchase); Rich Prods. Corp. v. Kemutec, Inc., 66 F.Supp.2d 937, 956 (E.D.Wis.1999) (generally price quotation is invitation to make offer and purchase order is offer). While it is possible for the vendor to be the offeror, *see* Brown Machine, 770 S.W.2d at 419 (price quote can amount to offer if it reasonably appears from quote that assent to quote is all that is needed to ripen offer into contract), Gateway provides no factual evidence which would support such a finding in this case. The Court therefore assumes for purposes of the motion to dismiss that plaintiff offered to purchase the computer (either in person or through catalog order) and that Gateway accepted plaintiff's offer (either by completing the sales transaction in person or by agreeing to ship and/or shipping the computer to plaintiff).

Under § 2–207, the Standard Terms constitute either an expression of acceptance or written confirmation. As an expression of acceptance, the Standard Terms would constitute a counter-offer only if Gateway expressly made its acceptance conditional on plaintiff's assent to the additional or different terms. K.S.A. § 84–2–207(1); V.A.M.S. § 400.2–207(1). "[T]he conditional nature of the acceptance must be clearly expressed in a manner sufficient to notify the offeror that the offeree is unwilling to proceed with the transaction unless the additional or different terms are included in the contract." Brown Machine, 770 S.W.2d at 420. Gateway provides no evidence that at the time of the sales transaction, it informed plaintiff that the transaction was conditioned on plaintiff's acceptance of the Standard Terms. Moreover, the mere fact that Gateway shipped the goods with the terms attached did not communicate to plaintiff any unwillingness to proceed without plaintiff's agreement to the Standard Terms.

Because plaintiff is not a merchant, additional or different terms contained in the Standard Terms did not become part of the parties' agreement unless plaintiff expressly agreed to them. *See* K.S.A. § 84–2–207, Kansas Comment 2 (if either party is not a merchant, additional terms are proposals for addition to the contract that do not become part of the contract unless the original offeror expressly agrees). Gateway argues that plaintiff demonstrated acceptance of the arbitration provision by keeping the computer more than five days after the date of delivery. Although the Standard Terms purport to work that result, Gateway has not presented evidence that plaintiff expressly agreed to those Standard Terms. Gateway states only that it enclosed the Standard Terms inside the computer box for plaintiff to read afterwards. It provides no evidence that it informed plaintiff of the five-day review-and-return period as a condition of the sales transaction, or that the parties contemplated additional terms to the agreement. *See* Step-Saver, 939 F.2d at 99 (during negotiations leading to purchase, vendor never mentioned box-top license or obtained buyer's express assent thereto).

The Court finds that the act of keeping the computer past five days was not sufficient to demonstrate that plaintiff expressly agreed to the Standard Terms. *Accord* Brown Machine, 770 S.W.2d at 421 (express assent cannot be presumed by silence or mere failure to object). Thus, because Gateway has not provided evidence sufficient to support a finding under Kansas or Missouri law that plaintiff agreed to the arbitration provision contained in Gateway's Standard Terms, the Court overrules Gateway's motion to dismiss.

. . .

QUESTIONS AND NOTES

1.   What legal significance does the court in *Hill* give the phone call? Why does the court conclude that no contract was formed during that phone call? What significance does the court in *Klocek* give the initial interaction between the parties? Which court is right?

2.   The court in *Hill* does not apply 2–204 or 2–206. Are those sections applicable? If so, how? The court also does not apply 2–207. *Klocek* criticizes *Hill* for this. Which court is right?

3.   With respect to terms delivered with the goods only after a contract is formed, is there any basis in common sense for treating an express warranty differently from a disclaimer of warranties, an exclusion of damages, a forum-selection clause, or an arbitration clause?

Is there any basis in the law for treating them differently?

4.   **Problem.** Baker walks into Frank's Appliance Store and purchases a Cool-Aid window air conditioner. The entire transaction consists of Baker's saying, "I'll take one of those 13,000 BTU models that are on sale at $199.95," and the saleswoman's taking Baker's check and helping him load the unit into his automobile. When Baker arrives home and opens the box in which the unit is packed, he discovers a warranty card that conspicuously disclaims the warranties of merchantability and fitness. Is the disclaimer effective? See Admiral Oasis Hotel Corp. v. Home Gas Industries, Inc., 68 Ill.App.2d 297, 216 N.E.2d 282 (1965). Should it be? What is the substantive difference between the facts in the problem and the facts in the two preceding cases in the casebook?

5.   With which opinion do you agree, *Hill* or *Klocek*? Do you think that the Hills and Mr. Klocek knew when they ordered from Gateway that there would be some additional written material in the boxes in which the computers were packaged? If so, do you think that they knew that some of that material would contain limitations on their legal rights? Should they have known that written material in the boxes would contain limitations on their legal rights?

6.   What if the Standard Terms document in *Klocek* stated, "This contract is expressly conditional on your assent to the additional terms herein." Would the arbitration term be part of the contract?

7.   The issue in *Hill* and *Klocek* has arisen in many cases, and the courts continue to struggle with the issue. In DeFontes v. Dell, Inc., 984 A.2d 1061

(R.I.2009), plaintiffs purchased computers by mail order and over the Internet. Included in the box with each computer was Dell's "Terms and Conditions Agreement," which contained an arbitration clause. It stated that if the purchaser accepted delivery of the computer system, the purchaser would be bound by the terms and conditions. It also stated that if for any reason the purchaser were not satisfied with the computer system, he or she could return it "under the terms and conditions of Dell's Total Satisfaction Return Policy." The trial court held that the arbitration clause was not binding. The Supreme Court of Rhode Island endorsed the position of *Hill*, but nevertheless affirmed:

> . . . Under U.C.C. § 2–204, contracts for the sale of goods may be formed "in any manner sufficient to show agreement, including conduct by both parties which recognizes the existence of such a contract." The U.C.C. creates the assumption that, unless circumstances unambiguously demonstrate otherwise, the buyer is the offeror and the seller is the offeree. *See* Klocek v. Gateway, Inc., 104 F.Supp.2d 1332, 1340 (D.Kan.2000). Moreover, U.C.C. § 2–206 provides in relevant part,

> > "(a) Unless otherwise unambiguously indicated by the language or circumstances,

> > "(1) an offer to make a contract shall be construed as inviting acceptance in any manner and by any medium reasonable in the circumstances;

> > "(2) an order or other offer to buy goods for prompt or current shipment shall be construed as inviting acceptance either by a prompt promise to ship or by the prompt or current shipment of conforming or nonconforming goods * * *."

> If contract formation occurred at the moment Dell's sales agents processed the customer's credit card payment and agreed to ship the goods, as plaintiffs argue, then any additional terms would necessarily be treated as "[a]dditional [t]erms in [a]cceptance or [c]onfirmation" under U.C.C. § 2–207 or offers to modify the existing contract under U.C.C. § 2–209. Yet, the modern trend seems to favor placing the power of acceptance in the hands of the buyer after he or she receives goods containing a standard form statement of additional terms and conditions, provided the buyer retains the power to "accept or return" the product.

>   . . .

> The defendants argue that *ProCD* represents the majority view and we have found considerable support for their contention [citing numerous cases].

> Courts have not been universal in embracing the reasoning of *ProCD* and its progeny, however [citing *Klocek* and other decisions].

> After reviewing the case law pertaining to so-called "shrinkwrap" agreements, we are satisfied that the *ProCD* line of cases is better reasoned and more consistent with contemporary

consumer transactions. It is simply unreasonable to expect a seller to apprise a consumer of every term and condition at the moment he or she makes a purchase. A modern consumer neither expects nor desires to wade through such minutia, particularly when making a purchase over the phone, where full disclosure of the terms would border on the sadistic. Nor do we believe that, after placing a telephone order for a computer, a reasonable consumer would believe that he or she has entered into a fully consummated agreement. Rather, he or she is aware that with delivery comes a multitude of standard terms attendant to nearly every consumer transaction.

We therefore decline to adopt the minority view, as urged by plaintiffs, that a contract is fully formed when a buyer orders a product and the seller accepts payment and either ships or promises to ship. Instead, formation occurs when the consumer accepts the full terms after receiving a reasonable opportunity to refuse them. Yet in adopting the so-called "layered contracting" theory of formation, we reiterate that the burden falls squarely on the seller to show that the buyer has accepted the seller's terms after delivery. Thus, the crucial question in this case is whether defendants reasonably invited acceptance by making clear in the terms and conditions agreement that (1) by accepting defendants' product the consumer was accepting the terms and conditions contained within and (2) the consumer could reject the terms and conditions by returning the product.

On the first question, defendants notified plaintiffs that "[b]y accepting delivery of the computer systems, related products, and/or services and support, and/or other products described on that invoice[,] You ('Customer') agrees to be bound by and accepts those terms and conditions." This language certainly informed plaintiffs that defendants intended to bind them to heretofore undisclosed terms and conditions, but it did not advise them of the period beyond which they will have indicated their assent to those terms. The defendants argue that the meaning of the term "accepting delivery" is apparent to a reasonable consumer. We are not so sure. . . . "Acceptance of goods" has a technical meaning not easily discernable to the average consumer. A consumer may believe that simply by opening the package he or she has agreed to be bound by the terms and conditions contained therein. Indeed, many of the courts that have enforced so-called "approve-or-return" agreements cite language informing the consumer of a specific period after which he or she will have accepted the terms. *See, e.g., Hill* (terms govern if consumer retains beyond thirty days). The more problematic issue, however, is whether plaintiffs were aware of their power to reject by returning the goods.

Significantly, the agreement sent to Ms. DeFontes . . . contained additional language advising her of the method of rejection. The introductory provision of the terms and conditions agreement that defendants sent to her stated, "[i]f for any reason Customer is not satisfied with a Dell-branded hardware system, Customer may return the system under the terms and conditions of Dell's Total Satisfaction Return Policy * * *." In doing so, defendants explicitly contrasted acceptance of the terms with rejection of the goods, albeit while retaining some ambiguity whether rejection of defendants' proposed terms could reasonably be construed as dissatisfaction with "Dell-branded hardware." Many of the cases upholding shrinkwrap agreements cite explicit disclaimers advising consumers of their right to reject the terms. *See, e.g., ProCD* ("If you do not agree to the terms of this License, promptly return all copies of the software . . . to the place where you obtained it."). Although the [*ProCD*] language is significantly clearer, the terms and conditions agreement sent to Ms. DeFontes nevertheless made the important connection between acceptance of the terms by accepting delivery and rejection by returning the goods.

That this language is absent in the documents sent to . . . plaintiffs Mr. Long and Ms. Ricci is troubling and raises the specter that they were unaware of both their power to reject and the method with which to do so. The introductory provision that purportedly bound plaintiffs does not mention either the "Total Satisfaction Return Policy" or the thirty-day period in which a consumer may exercise his or her right to return the product. Rather, this policy is explained, if at all, in a distinct section of the terms and conditions agreement, which confusingly informed plaintiffs that "Dell Branded Hardware systems and parts that are purchased directly from Dell by an end-user Customer may be returned by Customer in accordance with Dell's 'Total Satisfaction Return Policy' in effect on the date of the invoice." Thus, the consumer is left to construe these provisions together and infer that his or her right to reject the terms extends beyond what would commonly be understood as the moment of delivery. This separate provision not only fails to establish a clear relationship between the consumer's acceptance of the terms by retaining the goods and his or her right to reject the terms by returning the product, but it further obscures the matter by forcing the consumer to refer to a separate document if he or she wants to discover the full terms and conditions of the "Total Satisfaction Return Policy." Even if the consumer reviews the total satisfaction return policy, we are not convinced that the policy clearly explains to a reasonable consumer that his or her right to return the product includes rejection of the terms and conditions agreement. We believe the [trial court] rightly concluded that although "Dell does provide a 'total satisfaction policy' whereby a customer may return the computer, this return policy does not mention the customer's ability to return based on their unwillingness to comply with the terms."

In reviewing the language of the terms and conditions agreement it cannot be said that it was reasonably apparent to the plaintiffs that they could reject the terms simply by returning the goods. We believe that too many inferential steps were required of the plaintiffs and too many of the relevant provisions were left ambiguous. We are not persuaded that a reasonably prudent offeree would understand that by keeping the Dell computer he or she was agreeing to be bound by the terms and conditions agreement and retained, for a specified time, the power to reject the terms by returning the product. [Therefore,] the hearing justice properly denied the defendants' motion to compel arbitration on the ground that the plaintiffs did not agree to be bound by the terms and conditions agreement. . . .

8.   For contrasting views of the courts' analysis in these cases, see Murray, The Dubious Status of the Rolling Contract Formation Theory, 50 Duq.L.Rev. 35, 80 (2012) ("There is no need to continue the deliberate misconstructions of statutes or precedents that the theory [of rolling contract formation] requires"); Posner, ProCD v. Zeidenberg and Cognitive Overload in Contractual Bargaining, 77 U.Chi.L.Rev. 1181, 1189, 1193 (2010) ("Easterbrook is the latest in a long line of celebrated judges who shape the common law to the needs of commercial actors. . . . Easterbrook is Cardozo's heir.").

F. ELECTRONIC CONTRACTING

1. FORMATION

Enza Hill sits down at a computer, goes to the web site of an Internet seller, and finds the computer she has been looking for. Enza decides to purchase it. She clicks on the "order now" icon appearing adjacent to the picture of the PC on the computer screen. The price and shipping costs then appear on buyer's screen. At the bottom of the screen there is a "continue" button. Enza clicks on that button and another screen appears on which she enters shipping-address information. At the bottom of that screen there is another "continue" button. She clicks that button and another screen appears asking for credit-card information. The requested information will include at least Enza's name as it appears on the card, the card number, and its expiration date. Enza enters that information and clicks a button that says, "Submit order." A screen then appears which says, "Credit card accepted. Thank you for your order."

Transactions similar to the one above occur thousands of times a day. Do they present any special legal issues?

One possible answer might be, no, there is no statute of frauds problem, and there is no formation problem.

As to the statute of frauds issue, nothing in Article 2 requires that the signature be by pen on paper, and nothing in Article 1 requires that the writing be on a piece of paper. The buyer's name appears on the order, at least in connection with the credit card information, and by submitting the order, she has shown an intent to authenticate the order. Therefore, the buyer has signed since under 1–201(b)(37) "signed" includes "any symbol executed or adopted by a party with present intention to adopt or accept a writing." Further, 1–201(b)(43) defines a writing as including any "intentional reduction to tangible form." If an intentional recording on tape of a spoken agreement satisfies the requirement that there be an intentional reduction to tangible form, as held in Ellis Canning v. Bernstein, 348 F.Supp. 1212 (D.Colo.1972), then the information on the hard-drives in the buyer's and seller's computers should also be tangible. Even if the image on a computer screen is not tangible, it is tangible once it is printed out.

As to the formation issue, it seems obvious that both seller and buyer intend to contract through the on-line process.

But a careful lawyer might question both of these assertions. As to the statute of frauds: "Hold on. Are you really sure that a click on a computer screen is a 'signing'? When Article 2 was being drafted in the 1940s and '50s no one was thinking of computer screens. If neither the buyer nor the seller ever prints out the information that appears on their respective computer screens, does the mere image on the screen satisfy 2–201 any more so than a skywriter in an airplane"? Are the zeros and ones on a disk or hard drive "tangible" and therefore a writing under the Article 1 definition?

As to formation: "How can a contract be formed if no human being at the seller's place of business knows that a contract has been made? If the seller's operation is highly automated, this may not occur for days. And if the seller is not bound until some human knows of and assents to the transaction, the buyer is not bound until that indefinite later time either." Can a contract exist if the seller is unaware of the interaction?

Other questions abound. For example, is the buyer bound by terms that he or she has not seen? If the buyer must click through screens that contain the terms desired by the seller, there is some basis for saying that those terms are part of the contract, even if the buyer has not actually read them. But what if the terms are accessible to the buyer only by clicking on a button labeled, "Terms and Conditions of Sale," and the buyer is not required to click on that button in order to complete the purchase: if the buyer does not click on it, are the terms and conditions part of the contract?

Further, is a computer printout admissible evidence of the existence of the agreement that it appears to show? Does a record kept only in electronic form satisfy record retention requirements applicable to some types of contracts?

Congress and the National Conference of Commissioners on Uniform State Laws both were concerned that the legal status of electronic transactions like the one described above be made clear. Hence, in 1999

NCCUSL promulgated the Uniform Electronic Transactions Act (UETA), and in 2000 Congress adopted the Electronic Signatures in Global and National Commerce Act, 15 U.S.C.A. 7001ff (popularly known as "E-Sign.")

E-Sign and UETA cover the same issues in very similar language, and E-Sign provides that it does not apply in states that have adopted UETA. More than 45 states and the District of Columbia have adopted UETA and thus are exempted from the federal law.

Please read UETA sections 3, 5(b), 6, 7, 9, and 14, and consider the following questions.

1.   **Problem.** Beth goes to Camera Castle's website to purchase a digital camera. The website invites prospective buyers to place orders and indicates that an order will be shipped to the address provided by the buyer within five business days after the order is placed. Beth provides credit-card and shipping information and clicks through the screens necessary to place the order.

   a.   If there is nothing on the website to indicate when a contract is formed, is the contract formed as soon as Beth has clicked on the button showing that the order has been submitted?

   b.   If Beth types on an otherwise blank address line, "offer contingent on shipment by noon tomorrow," will that provision bind the seller or prevent the formation of a contract?

   c.   If Camera Castle charges $2,000 to Beth's credit card, asserting that the price of the camera was $2,000, how can Beth prove that the price stated on the website was $1,000? See also UETA § 13.

   d.   If the order actually is placed by Beth's 14-year-old son, who took the credit card from Beth's purse without her knowledge or permission, is Beth bound by a contract?

2.   In Problem 1(c) above, does 2–201 prevent enforcement of the (alleged) contract? What if Camera Castle follows up the web site transaction with an e-mail to Beth which provides a confirmation number and states the price as $2,000? If Beth fails to respond to this e-mail until two weeks later, how does 2–201(2) affect Beth's claim that the price is $1,000?

3.   **Problem.** Steelco's installment contract empowers it to terminate the contract if Fritz's Frames fails to pay for an installment within 30 days after delivery. To do so, the contract specifies "notice in writing delivered to the buyer's principal office." May Steelco terminate by giving notice by e-mail?

4.   Another issue arising in contracts formed by electronic communication appears in the next chapter.

2. Terms

Nothing in Article 2 specifically addresses the process of forming contracts by the use of electronic communication, so common-law principles apply. Section 1–103(b) provides, "Unless displaced by the particular provisions of the Uniform Commercial Code, the principles of law and equity . . . supplement its provisions." Therefore, the rule that a party is bound by what he or she signs is still applicable, and in this context "signs" means "manifests assent" by sending an e-mail or clicking a button on a web page. But the terms of the contract prepared by the designer of the web page may not appear on the same web page or screen where the assent button appears. If the buyer cannot access the terms before manifesting assent, the terms will not be part of the contract; just as in the world of written contracts, terms that are not available to a party before he or she signs the document are not part of the contract. In the context of on-line contracts, courts insist that the non-drafting party have reasonable access to the terms before manifesting assent.

Nguyen v. Barnes & Noble, Inc.

United States Court of Appeals, Ninth Circuit, 2014.
763 F.3d 1171.

■ NOONAN, CIRCUIT JUDGE: . . . .

I.   Background

A.

The underlying facts are not in dispute. Barnes & Noble is a national bookseller that owns and operates hundreds of bookstores as well as the website www.barnesandnoble.com. In August 2011, Barnes & Noble, along with other retailers across the country, liquidated its inventory of discontinued Hewlett-Packard Touchpads ("Touchpads"), an unsuccessful competitor to Apple's iPad, by advertising a "fire sale" of Touchpads at a heavily discounted price. Acting quickly on the nationwide liquidation of Touchpads, Nguyen purchased two units on Barnes & Noble's website on August 21, 2011, and received an email confirming the transaction. The following day, Nguyen received another email informing him that his order had been cancelled due to unexpectedly high demand. Nguyen alleges that, as a result of "Barnes & Noble's representations, as well as the delay in informing him it would not honor the sale," he was "unable to obtain an HP Tablet during the liquidation period for the discounted price," and was "forced to rely on substitute tablet technology, which he subsequently purchased . . . [at] considerable expense."

B.

In April 2012, Nguyen filed this lawsuit in California Superior Court on behalf of himself and a putative class of consumers whose Touchpad orders had been cancelled, alleging that Barnes & Noble had engaged in

deceptive business practices and false advertising in violation of both
California and New York law. Barnes & Noble removed the action to
federal court and moved to compel arbitration under the Federal
Arbitration Act ("FAA"), arguing that Nguyen was bound by the
arbitration agreement in the website's Terms of Use.

The website's Terms of Use are available via a "Terms of Use"
hyperlink located in the bottom left-hand corner of every page on the
Barnes & Noble website, which appears alongside other hyperlinks
labeled "NOOK Store Terms," "Copyright," and "Privacy Policy." These
hyperlinks also appear underlined and set in green typeface in the lower
lefthand corner of every page in the online checkout process.

Nguyen neither clicked on the "Terms of Use" hyperlink nor actually
read the Terms of Use. Had he clicked on the hyperlink, he would have
been taken to a page containing the full text of Barnes & Noble's Terms
of Use, which state, in relevant part: "By visiting any area in the Barnes
& Noble.com Site, creating an account, [or] making a purchase via the
Barnes & Noble.com Site . . . a User is deemed to have accepted the
Terms of Use." Nguyen also would have come across an arbitration
provision, which states: . . .

III. Discussion

. . .

B.

"While new commerce on the Internet has exposed courts to many
new situations, it has not fundamentally changed the principles of
contract." *Register.com, Inc. v. Verio, Inc.,* 356 F.3d 393, 403 (2d
Cir.2004). One such principle is the requirement that "[m]utual
manifestation of assent, whether by written or spoken word or by
conduct, is the touchstone of contract." *Specht v. Netscape Commc'ns
Corp.,* 306 F.3d 17, 29 (2d Cir.2002) (applying California law).

Contracts formed on the Internet come primarily in two flavors:
"clickwrap" (or "click-through") agreements, in which website users are
required to click on an "I agree" box after being presented with a list of
terms and conditions of use; and "browsewrap" agreements, where a
website's terms and conditions of use are generally posted on the website
via a hyperlink at the bottom of the screen. Barnes & Noble's Terms of
Use fall in the latter category.

"Unlike a clickwrap agreement, a browsewrap agreement does not
require the user to manifest assent to the terms and conditions expressly
. . . [a] party instead gives his assent simply by using the website." *Hines
v. Overstock.com, Inc.,* 668 F.Supp.2d 362, 366–67 (E.D.N.Y.2009). . . .
Indeed, "in a pure-form browsewrap agreement, 'the website will contain
a notice that—by merely using the services of, obtaining information
from, or initiating applications within the website—the user is agreeing
to and is bound by the site's terms of service.'" *Fteja v. Facebook, Inc.,*
841 F.Supp.2d 829, 837 (S.D.N.Y.2012). . . . Thus, "by visiting the

website—something that the user has already done—the user agrees to the Terms of Use not listed on the site itself but available only by clicking a hyperlink." *Id.* "The defining feature of browsewrap agreements is that the user can continue to use the website or its services without visiting the page hosting the browsewrap agreement or even knowing that such a webpage exists." *Be In, Inc. v. Google Inc.,* No. 12–CV–03373–LHK, 2013 WL 5568706, at *6 (N.D.Cal. Oct. 9, 2013). "Because no affirmative action is required by the website user to agree to the terms of a contract other than his or her use of the website, the determination of the validity of the browsewrap contract depends on whether the user has actual or constructive knowledge of a website's terms and conditions." *Van Tassell v. United Mktg. Grp., LLC,* 795 F.Supp.2d 770, 790 (N.D.Ill.2011) (citing *Sw. Airlines Co. v. BoardFirst, LLC,* No. 06–CV–0891–B, 2007 WL 4823761, at *4 (N.D.Tex. Sept. 12, 2007)); *see also* Mark A. Lemley, *Terms of Use,* 91 Minn. L.Rev. 459, 477 (2006) ("Courts may be willing to overlook the utter absence of assent only when there are reasons to believe that the [website user] is aware of the [website owner's] terms.").

Were there any evidence in the record that Nguyen had actual notice of the Terms of Use or was required to affirmatively acknowledge the Terms of Use before completing his online purchase, the outcome of this case might be different. Indeed, courts have consistently enforced browsewrap agreements where the user had actual notice of the agreement. . . . Courts have also been more willing to find the requisite notice for constructive assent where the browsewrap agreement resembles a clickwrap agreement—that is, where the user is required to affirmatively acknowledge the agreement before proceeding with use of the website. *See, e.g., Fteja,* 841 F.Supp.2d at 838–40 (enforcing forum selection clause in website's terms of service where a notice below the "Sign Up" button stated, "By clicking Sign Up, you are indicating that you have read and agree to the Terms of Service," and user had clicked "Sign Up").

But where, as here, there is no evidence that the website user had actual knowledge of the agreement, the validity of the browsewrap agreement turns on whether the website puts a reasonably prudent user on inquiry notice of the terms of the contract. Whether a user has inquiry notice of a browsewrap agreement, in turn, depends on the design and content of the website and the agreement's webpage. Where the link to a website's terms of use is buried at the bottom of the page or tucked away in obscure corners of the website where users are unlikely to see it, courts have refused to enforce the browsewrap agreement. On the other hand, where the website contains an explicit textual notice that continued use will act as a manifestation of the user's intent to be bound, courts have been more amenable to enforcing browsewrap agreements. *See, e.g., Cairo, Inc. v. Crossmedia Servs., Inc.,* No. 04–04825, 2005 WL 756610, at *2, *4–5 (N.D.Cal. Apr. 1, 2005) (enforcing forum selection clause in website's terms of use where every page on the website had a textual notice that read: "By continuing past this page and/or using this site, you agree to abide by the Terms of Use for this site, which prohibit commercial use of any information on this site"). *But see Pollstar v. Gigmania, Ltd.,* 170 F.Supp.2d 974, 981 (E.D.Cal.2000) (refusing to enforce browsewrap agreement where textual notice appeared in small gray print against a gray background). In short, the conspicuousness and placement of the "Terms of Use" hyperlink, other notices given to users of the terms of use, and the website's general design all contribute to whether a reasonably prudent user would have inquiry notice of a browsewrap agreement.

Barnes & Noble argues that the placement of the "Terms of Use" hyperlink in the bottom left-hand corner of every page on the Barnes & Noble website, and its close proximity to the buttons a user must click on to complete an online purchase, is enough to place a reasonably prudent user on constructive notice. It is true that the location of the hyperlink on Barnes & Noble's website distinguishes this case from *Specht,* the leading authority on the enforceability of browsewrap terms under New York law. There, the Second Circuit refused to enforce an arbitration provision in a website's licensing terms where the hyperlink to the terms was located at the bottom of the page, hidden below the "Download" button that users had to click to initiate the software download. *See Specht,* 306 F.3d at 30. Then-Second Circuit Judge Sotomayor, writing for the panel, held that "a reference to the existence of license terms on a submerged screen is not sufficient to place consumers on inquiry or constructive notice of those terms." *Id.* at 32. By contrast, here the "Terms of Use" link appears either directly below the relevant button a user must click on to proceed in the checkout process or just a few inches away. On some pages, the content of the webpage is compact enough that a user can view the link without scrolling. On the remaining pages, the hyperlink is close enough to the "Proceed with Checkout" button that a user would have to bring the link within his field of vision in order to complete his order.

But the proximity or conspicuousness of the hyperlink alone is not enough to give rise to constructive notice . . . .

In light of the lack of controlling authority on point, and in keeping with courts' traditional reluctance to enforce browsewrap agreements against individual consumers,[2] we therefore hold that where a website makes its terms of use available via a conspicuous hyperlink on every page of the website but otherwise provides no notice to users nor prompts them to take any affirmative action to demonstrate assent, even close proximity of the hyperlink to relevant buttons users must click on—

---

[2] *See* Woodrow Hartzog, *Website Design as Contract,* 60 Am. U.L.Rev. 1635, 1644 (2011) (observing that courts "tend to shy away from enforcing browsewrap agreements that require no outward manifestation of assent"); Mark Lemley, *Terms of Use,* 91 Minn. L.Rev. 459, 472–77 ("An examination of the cases that have considered browsewraps in the last five years demonstrates that the courts have been willing to enforce terms of use against corporations, but have not been willing to do so against individuals.").

without more—is insufficient to give rise to constructive notice. While failure to read a contract before agreeing to its terms does not relieve a party of its obligations under the contract, *Gillman v. Chase Manhattan Bank, N.A.,* 73 N.Y.2d 1, 11, 537 N.Y.S.2d 787, 534 N.E.2d 824 (1988), the onus must be on website owners to put users on notice of the terms to which they wish to bind consumers. Given the breadth of the range of technological savvy of online purchasers, consumers cannot be expected to ferret out hyperlinks to terms and conditions to which they have no reason to suspect they will be bound.

QUESTIONS AND NOTES

1. What more could Barnes & Noble have done to ensure that its Terms of Use would be enforceable against users like Nguyen?

2. Similar issues of enforceability of terms arise in clickwrap contracts, where courts examine web site design to determine whether users have sufficient notice of where the terms are to be found. They look to the location of a hyperlink, the color and contrast of the link in comparison with other matter on the page, including other hyperlinks, and the number of steps (i.e. clicks) that the use must take in order to access the terms. See Moringiello & Reynolds, From Lord Coke to Internet Privacy: The Past, Present and Future of the Law of Electronic Contracting, 72 Md. L.Rev. 452, 466 (2013) ("In the world of electronic contracts . . . clickwrap is a meaningless term. Click-to-agree transactions come in many flavors. Sometimes the click is at the end of the terms so that a reader must at least scroll through to reach the 'I agree' icon, while [at] other times the click is next to a hyperlink that leads to the terms, either in one click or in several. Whether the terms are classified as clickwrap says little about whether the offeree had notice of them.")

G. CONTRACT MODIFICATION

Parties to a contract may decide during the course of performance that a modification of the contract is desirable. This may occur because the needs of one or both parties have changed, or because one of them has encountered difficulty performing the contract as originally agreed. They may, for example, agree to extend the date for the seller to complete its performance. Section 2–209 addresses modifications, and subsection (1) reverses the common-law rule that a modification must be supported by consideration. Once a contract is modified, the new term governs, and neither party may withdraw its assent to the change and insist on the original term.

A modification may be oral or in writing. But it is common for sales contracts to include a provision that any modification of the contract must be in a writing signed by both parties, or at least by the party that drafted the document. Subsection (2) validates this provision, and subsection (3) imposes some additional limit on oral modifications. Even if the contract contains such a provision, however, it is common for the parties to communicate orally during the course of performance and agree to adjustments in their performance. Are those agreements to be entirely disregarded? Please read 2–209, especially subsections (4) and (5), and consider the following cases.

Wisconsin Knife Works v. National Metal Crafters

United States Court of Appeals, Seventh Circuit, 1986.
781 F.2d 1280.

■ P<small>OSNER</small>, C<small>IRCUIT</small> J<small>UDGE</small>.

. . . Wisconsin Knife Works, having some unused manufacturing capacity, decided to try to manufacture spade bits* for sale to its parent, Black & Decker, a large producer of tools, including drills. A spade bit is made out of a chunk of metal called a spade bit blank; and Wisconsin Knife Works had to find a source of supply for these blanks. National Metal Crafters was eager to be that source. After some negotiating, Wisconsin Knife Works sent National Metal Crafters a series of purchase orders on the back of each of which was printed, "Acceptance of this Order, either by acknowledgment or performance, constitutes an unqualified agreement to the following." A list of "Conditions of Purchase" follows, of which the first is, "No modification of this contract, shall be binding upon Buyer [Wisconsin Knife Works] unless made in writing and signed by Buyer's authorized representative. Buyer shall have the right to make changes in the Order by a notice, in writing, to Seller." There were six purchase orders in all, each with the identical conditions. National Metal Crafters acknowledged the first two orders (which had been placed on August 21, 1981) by letters that said, "Please accept this as our acknowledgment covering the above subject order," followed by a list of delivery dates. The purchase orders had left those dates blank. Wisconsin Knife Works filled them in, after receiving the acknowledgments, with the dates that National Metal Crafters had supplied in the acknowledgments. There were no written acknowledgments of the last four orders (placed several weeks later, on September 10, 1981). Wisconsin Knife Works wrote in the delivery dates that National Metal Crafters orally supplied after receiving purchase orders in which the space for the date of delivery had again been left blank.

Delivery was due in October and November 1981. National Metal Crafters missed the deadlines. But Wisconsin Knife Works did not immediately declare a breach, cancel the contract, or seek damages for late delivery. Indeed, on July 1, 1982, it issued a new batch of purchase orders (later rescinded). By December 1982 National Metal Crafters was producing spade bit blanks for Wisconsin Knife Works under the original set of purchase orders in adequate quantities, though this was more than

---

* A spade bit is a drill bit used for drilling holes in wood. One end of the shaft fits into an electric drill, and the other end looks like flat paddle with a triangular point.—Eds.

a year after the delivery dates in the orders. But on January 13, 1983, Wisconsin Knife Works notified National Metal Crafters that the contract was terminated. By that date only 144,000 of the more than 281,000 spade bit blanks that Wisconsin Knife Works had ordered in the six purchase orders had been delivered.

Wisconsin Knife Works brought this breach of contract suit, charging that National Metal Crafters had violated the terms of delivery in the contract that was formed by the acceptance of the six purchase orders. National Metal Crafters replied that the delivery dates had not been intended as firm dates. It also counterclaimed for damages for (among other things) the breach of an alleged oral agreement by Wisconsin Knife Works to pay the expenses of maintaining machinery used by National Metal Crafters to fulfill the contract. The parties later stipulated that the amount of these damages was $30,000.

The judge ruled that there had been a contract but left to the jury to decide whether the contract had been modified and, if so, whether the modified contract had been broken. The jury found that the contract had been modified and not broken. Judgment was entered dismissing Wisconsin Knife Works' suit and awarding National Metal Crafters $30,000 on its counterclaim. Wisconsin Knife Works has appealed from the dismissal of its suit. . . .

The principal issue is the effect of the provision in the purchase orders that forbids the contract to be modified other than by a writing signed by an authorized representative of the buyer. The theory on which the judge sent the issue of modification to the jury was that the contract could be modified orally or by conduct as well as by a signed writing. National Metal Crafters had presented evidence that Wisconsin Knife Works had accepted late delivery of the spade bit blanks and had cancelled the contract not because of the delays in delivery but because it could not produce spade bits at a price acceptable to Black & Decker.

Section 2–209(2) of the Uniform Commercial Code provides that "a signed agreement which excludes modification or rescission except by a signed writing cannot be otherwise modified or rescinded, but except as between merchants such a requirement on a form supplied by the merchant must be separately signed by the other party." . . . The meaning of this provision and its proviso is not crystalline and there is little pertinent case law.

. . .

We conclude that the clause forbidding modifications other than in writing was valid and applicable and that the jury should not have been allowed to consider whether the contract had been modified in some other way. This may, however, have been a harmless error. Section 2–209(4) of the Uniform Commercial Code provides that an "attempt at modification" which does not satisfy a contractual requirement that modifications be in writing nevertheless "can operate as a waiver." Although in instructing the jury on modification the judge did not use the word "waiver," maybe he gave the substance of a waiver instruction and maybe therefore the jury found waiver but called it modification. Here is the relevant instruction:

> Did the parties modify the contract? The defendant bears the burden of proof on this one. You shall answer this question yes only if you are convinced to a reasonable certainty that the parties modified the contract.

> If you determine that the defendant had performed in a manner different from the strict obligations imposed on it by the contract, and the plaintiff by conduct or other means of expression induced a reasonable belief by the defendant that strict enforcement was not insisted upon, but that the modified performance was satisfactory and acceptable as equivalent, then you may conclude that the parties have assented to a modification of the original terms of the contract and that the parties have agreed that the different mode of performance will satisfy the obligations imposed on the parties by the contract.

To determine whether this was in substance an instruction on waiver we shall have to consider the background of section 2–209, the Code provision on modification and waiver.

Because the performance of the parties to a contract is typically not simultaneous, one party may find himself at the mercy of the other unless the law of contracts protects him. Indeed, the most important thing which that law does is to facilitate exchanges that are not simultaneous by preventing either party from taking advantage of the vulnerabilities to which sequential performance may give rise. If A contracts to build a highly idiosyncratic gazebo for B, payment due on completion, and when A completes the gazebo B refuses to pay, A may be in a bind—since the resale value of the gazebo may be much less than A's cost—except for his right to sue B for the price. Even then, a right to sue for breach of contract, being costly to enforce, is not a completely adequate remedy. B might therefore go to A and say, "If you don't reduce your price I'll refuse to pay and put you to the expense of suit"; and A might knuckle under. If such modifications are allowed, people in B's position will find it harder to make such contracts in the future, and everyone will be worse off.

The common law dealt with this problem by refusing to enforce modifications unsupported by fresh consideration. Thus in the hypothetical case just put B could not have enforced A's promise to accept a lower price. But this solution is at once overinclusive and underinclusive—the former because most modifications are not coercive and should be enforceable whether or not there is fresh consideration, the latter because, since common law courts inquire only into the existence and not the adequacy of consideration, a requirement of fresh consideration has little bite. B might give A a peppercorn, a kitten, or a robe in exchange for A's agreeing to reduce the contract price, and then the modification would be enforceable and A could no longer sue for the original price.

The drafters of the Uniform Commercial Code took a fresh approach, by making modifications enforceable even if not supported by consideration (see section 2–209(1)) and looking to the doctrines of duress and bad faith for the main protection against exploitive or opportunistic attempts at modification, as in our hypothetical case. See UCC 2–209, official comment 2. But they did another thing as well. In section 2–209(2) they allowed the parties to exclude oral modifications. National Metal Crafters argues that two subsections later they took back this grant of power by allowing an unwritten modification to operate as a waiver.

The common law did not enforce agreements such as section 2–209(2) authorizes. The "reasoning" was that the parties were always free to agree orally to cancel their contract and the clause forbidding modifications not in writing would disappear with the rest of the contract when it was cancelled. . . . But the framers of the Uniform Commercial Code, as part and parcel of rejecting the requirement of consideration for modifications, must have rejected the traditional view; must have believed that the protection which the doctrines of duress and bad faith give against extortionate modifications might need reinforcement not from a requirement of consideration, which had proved ineffective, then from a grant of power to include a clause requiring modifications to be in writing and signed. An equally important point is that with consideration no longer required for modification, it was natural to give the parties some means of providing a substitute for the cautionary and evidentiary function that the requirement of consideration provides; and the means chosen was to allow them to exclude oral modifications.

If section 2–209(4), which as we said provides that an attempted modification which does not comply with subsection (2) can nevertheless operate as a "waiver," is interpreted so broadly that any oral modification is effective as a waiver notwithstanding section 2–209(2), both provisions become superfluous and we are back in the common law—only with not even a requirement of consideration to reduce the likelihood of fabricated or unintended oral modifications. . . . National Metal Crafters, while claiming that Wisconsin Knife Works broke their contract as orally modified to extend the delivery date, is not seeking damages for that breach. But this is small comfort to Wisconsin Knife Works, which thought it had a binding contract with fixed delivery dates. Whether called modification or waiver, what National Metal Crafters is seeking to do is to nullify a key term other than by a signed writing. If it can get away with this merely by testimony about an oral modification, section 2–209(2) becomes very nearly a dead letter.

The path of reconciliation with subsection (4) is found by attending to the precise wording of (4). It does not say that an attempted modification "is" a waiver; it says that "it can operate as a waiver." It does not say in what circumstances it can operate as a waiver; but if an attempted modification is effective as a waiver only if there is reliance, then both sections 2–209(2) and 2–209(4) can be given effect. Reliance, if reasonably induced and reasonable in extent, is a common substitute for consideration in making a promise legally enforceable, in part because it adds something in the way of credibility to the mere say-so of one party. The main purpose of forbidding oral modifications is to prevent the promisor from fabricating a modification that will let him escape his obligations under the contract; and the danger of successful fabrication is less if the promisor has actually incurred a cost, has relied. There is of course a danger of bootstrapping—of incurring a cost in order to make the case for a modification. But it is a risky course and is therefore less likely to be attempted than merely testifying to a conversation; it makes one put one's money where one's mouth is.

We find support for our proposed reconciliation of subsections (2) and (4) in the secondary literature. . . . 2 Hawkland, Uniform Commercial Code Series § 2–209:05, at p. 138 (1985), remarks, "if clear factual evidence other than mere parol points to that conclusion [that an oral agreement was made altering a term of the contract], a waiver may be found. In the normal case, however, courts should be careful not to allow the protective features of sections 2–209(2) and (3) to be nullified by contested parol evidence." (Footnote omitted.) The instruction given by the judge in this case did not comply with this test, but in any event we think a requirement of reliance is clearer than a requirement of "clear factual evidence other than mere parol."

Our approach is not inconsistent with section 2–209(5), which allows a waiver to be withdrawn while the contract is executory, provided there is no "material change of position in reliance on the waiver." Granted, in (5) there can be no tincture of reliance; the whole point of the section is that a waiver may be withdrawn unless there is reliance. But the section has a different domain from section 2–209(4). It is not limited to attempted modifications invalid under subsections (2) or (3); it applies, for example, to an express written and signed waiver, provided only that the contract is still executory. Suppose that while the contract is still executory the buyer writes the seller a signed letter waiving some term in the contract and then, the next day, before the seller has relied, retracts it in writing; we have no reason to think that such a retraction would not satisfy section 2–209(5), though this is not an issue we need definitively resolve today. In any event we are not suggesting that "waiver" means different things in (4) and (5); it means the same thing; but the effect of an attempted modification as a waiver under (4) depends in part on (2), which (4) (but not 5) qualifies. Waiver and estoppel (which requires reliance to be effective) are frequently bracketed. . . .

We know that the drafters of section 2–209 wanted to make it possible for parties to exclude oral modifications. They did not just want to give "modification" another name "waiver." Our interpretation gives effect to this purpose. It is also consistent with though not compelled by the case law. There are no Wisconsin cases on point. Cases from other jurisdictions are diverse in outlook. Some take a very hard line against allowing an oral waiver to undo a clause forbidding oral modification. See, e.g., South Hampton Co. v. Stinnes Corp., 733 F.2d 1108, 1117–18 (5th Cir.1984) (Texas law); U.S. Fibres, Inc. v. Proctor & Schwartz, Inc., 358 F.Supp. 449, 460 (E.D.Mich.1972), aff'd, 509 F.2d 1043 (6th Cir.1975) (Pennsylvania law). Others allow oral waivers to override such clauses, but in most of these cases it is clear that the party claiming waiver had relied to his detriment. See, e.g., Gold Kist, Inc. v. Pillow, 582 S.W.2d 77, 79–80 (Tenn.App.1979) (where this feature of the case is emphasized); Linear Corp. v. Standard Hardware Co., 423 So.2d 966 (Fla.App.1982). . . .

Missing from the jury instruction on "modification" in this case is any reference to reliance, that is, to the incurring of costs by National Metal Crafters in reasonable reliance on assurances by Wisconsin Knife Works that late delivery would be acceptable. And although there is evidence of such reliance, it naturally was not a focus of the case, since the issue was cast as one of completed (not attempted) modification, which does not require reliance to be enforceable. National Metal Crafters must have incurred expenses in producing spade bit blanks after the original delivery dates, but whether these were reliance expenses is a separate question. Maybe National Metal Crafters would have continued to manufacture spade bit blanks anyway, in the hope of selling them to someone else. It may be significant that the stipulated counterclaim damages seem limited to the damages from the breach of a separate oral agreement regarding the maintenance of equipment used by National Metal Crafters in fulfilling the contract. The question of reliance cannot be considered so open and shut as to justify our concluding that the judge would have had to direct a verdict for National Metal Crafters, the party with the burden of proof on the issue. Nor, indeed, does National Metal Crafters argue that reliance was shown as a matter of law.

. . .

When a jury instruction is erroneous there must be a new trial unless the error is harmless. On the basis of the record before us we cannot say that the error in allowing the jury to find that the contract had been modified was harmless; but we do not want to exclude the possibility that it might be found to be so, on motion for summary judgment or otherwise, without the need for a new trial. Obviously National Metal Crafters has a strong case both that it relied on the waiver of the delivery deadlines and that there was no causal relationship between its late deliveries and the cancellation of the contract. We just are not prepared to say on the record before us that it is such a strong case as not to require submission to a jury.

Reversed and remanded.

■ EASTERBROOK, CIRCUIT JUDGE, dissenting.

The majority demonstrates that the clause of the contract requiring all modifications to be in writing is enforceable against National Metal Crafters. There was no modification by a "signed writing." Yet § 2–209(4) of the Uniform Commercial Code, which Wisconsin has adopted, provides that "an attempt at modification" that is ineffective because of a modification-only-in-writing clause "can operate as a waiver." The majority holds that no "attempt at modification" may be a "waiver" within the meaning of § 2–209(4) unless the party seeking to enforce the waiver has relied to its detriment. I do not think that detrimental reliance is an essential element of waiver under § 2–209(4).

"Waiver" is not a term the UCC defines. At common law "waiver" means an intentional relinquishment of a known right. A person may relinquish a right by engaging in conduct inconsistent with the right or by a verbal or written declaration. I do not know of any branch of the law—common, statutory, or constitutional—in which a renunciation of a legal entitlement is effective only if the other party relies to his detriment. True, the law of "consideration" imposed something like a reliance rule; payment of a pine nut (the peppercorn of nouvelle cuisine) is a tiny bit of detriment, and often the law of consideration is expressed in terms of detriment. But § 2–209(1) of the UCC provides that consideration is unnecessary to make a modification effective. The introduction of a reliance requirement into a body of law from which the doctrine of consideration has been excised is novel.

Neither party suggested that reliance is essential to waiver. The parties did not even mention the question in their briefs, which concentrated on the meaning of "signed agreement." So far as I can tell, no court has held that reliance is an essential element of waiver under § 2–209(4). One has intimated that reliance is not essential. Double-E Sportswear Corp. v. Girard Trust Bank, 488 F.2d 292, 295, 296 (3d Cir.1973), citing 1 Anderson, Uniform Commercial Code § 2–209:8 (2d ed.). The third edition of Anderson, like the second, states that reliance is unnecessary. Id. at § 2–209:42 (3d ed. 1982). See also Hawkland, Uniform Commercial Code Series § 2–209:05 (suggesting that reliance on a waiver by course of performance is unnecessary).*

Not all novel things are wrong, although legal novelties, like biological mutations, usually die out quickly. This novelty encounters an obstacle within § 2–209. Section 2–209(5) states that a person who "has made a waiver affecting an executory portion of the contract may retract the waiver" on reasonable notice "unless the retraction would be unjust

---

*   The sources the majority cites for the contrary position do not offer much support. Corbin's treatise on contracts views § 2–209(2) as a regrettable inroad on the flexible construction of contracts. 6 Corbin, Contracts § 1295 at 211–12 (1962). The word "reliance" does appear in Corbin's discussion, but I read it as a reference to § 2–209(5). Corbin's position is that § 2–209(4) and (5) should prevent § 2–209(2) from doing "serious damage"; the majority inserts a reliance requirement in § 2–209(4) to prevent what it sees as potentially serious damage to § 2–209(2). . . .

in view of a material change of position in reliance on the waiver." Section 2–209 therefore treats "waiver" and "reliance" as different. Under § 2–209(4) a waiver may be effective; under § 2–209(5) a waiver may be effective prospectively only if there was also detrimental reliance.

The majority tries to reconcile the two subsections by stating that they have different domains. Section 2–209(4) deals with oral waivers, while § 2–209(5) "is not limited to attempted modifications invalid under subsections (2) or (3); it applies, for example, to express written waivers, provided only that the contract is executory." This distinction implies that subsection (4) applies to a subset of the subjects of subsection (5). Things are the other way around. Subsection (4) says that an attempt at modification may be a "waiver," and subsection (5) qualifies the effectiveness of "waivers" in the absence of reliance. See comment 4 to § 2–209. The two have the same domain—all attempts at modification, be they oral, written, or implied from conduct, that do not satisfy the Statute of Frauds, § 2–209(3), or a "signed writing" requirement of a clause permitted under § 2–209(2). The majority suggests that § 2–209(5) also applies to signed waivers, but this gets things backward. A "signed writing" is binding as a modification under § 2–209(2) without the need for "waiver." Section 2–209(1) lifts the requirement of consideration, so a signed pledge not to enforce a term of a contract may not be revoked under § 2–209(5) unless the pledge reserves the power of revocation. Because "waiver" is some subset of failed efforts to modify, it cannot be a right to treat a successful effort to modify (a signed writing) as a "waiver" governed by subsection (5).

"Waiver" therefore ought to mean the same in subsections (4) and (5). Unsuccessful attempts at modification may be waivers under § 2–209(4). Then § 2–209(5) deals with a subset of these "waivers," the subset that affects the executory portion of the contract. Waivers affecting executory provisions are enforceable or not depending on reliance. We know from the language and structure of § 2–209 that there is a difference between waivers that affect the executory portions of contracts and waivers that do not. Under the majority's reading, however, there is no difference. No waiver is effective without detrimental reliance. It is as if the majority has eliminated § 2–209(4) from the UCC and rewritten § 2–209(5) to begin: "A party who has made [an ineffectual attempt at modification] affecting [any] portion of the contract may retract. . . ."

Repair work of this kind sometimes is necessary. A legislature has many minds, and as years pass these different people may use the same word in different ways; so, too, the shifting coalitions that create a complex statute may contribute to it multiple meanings of a single word, the more so because amendments may be added to a statute after other portions have been bargained out. Section 2–209 of the UCC is not a slapdash production or the work of competing committees unaware of each other's words, however. The UCC is one of the most carefully assembled statutes in American history. It was written under the guidance of a few people, all careful drafters, debated for a decade by the American Law Institute and committees of commercial practitioners, and adopted en bloc by the states. Vague and uncertain in places the Code is; no one could see all of the problems that would come within its terms, and in some cases foreseen problems were finessed rather than solved. But "waiver" did not call for finesses, and § 2–209 was drafted and discussed as a single unit. "Waiver" in § 2–209(4) and "waiver" in § 2–209(5) are six words apart, which is not so great a gap that the mind loses track of meaning.

The subsections read well together if waiver means "intentional relinquishment of a known right" in both. Section 2–209(4) says that a failed attempt at modification may be a waiver and so relinquish a legal entitlement (such as the entitlement to timely delivery); § 2–209(5) adds that a waiver cannot affect the executory portion of the contract (the time of future deliveries, for example) if the waiving party retracts, unless there is also detrimental reliance. But for § 2–209(2) the oral waiver could affect the executory portion of the contract even without reliance. It is not necessary to vary the meaning of the word to make sense of each portion of the statute.

The majority makes reliance an ingredient of waiver not because the structure of the UCC demands this reading, but because it believes that otherwise the UCC would not deal adequately with the threat of opportunistic conduct. The drafters of the UCC chose to deal with opportunism not through a strict reading of waiver, however, but through a statutory requirement of commercial good faith. See § 1–203 [revised 1–304] and comment 2 to § 2–209. The modification-only-in-writing clause has nothing to do with opportunism. A person who has his contracting partner over a barrel, and therefore is able to obtain a concession, can get the concession in writing. The writing will be the least of his worries. In almost all of the famous cases of modification the parties reduced the new agreement to writing.

A modification-only-in-writing clause may permit the parties to strengthen the requirement of commercial good faith against the careless opportunist, but its principal function is to make it easier for business to protect their agreement against casual subsequent remarks and manufactured assertions of alteration. It strengthens the Statute of Frauds. Even so, the Code does not allow the clause to be airtight. Comment 4 to § 2–209 states: "Subsection (4) is intended, despite the provisions of subsections (2) and (3), to prevent contractual provisions excluding modification except by a signed writing from limiting in other respects the legal effect of the parties' actual later conduct. The effect of such conduct as a waiver is further regulated in subsection (5)." In other words, the UCC made modification-only-in-writing clauses effective for the first time, but the drafters meant to leave loopholes. The majority's observation that waiver under § 2–209(4) could nullify some benefits of clauses permitted under § 2–209(2) is true, but it is not a reason for adding novel elements to "waiver." It might be sensible to treat claims of oral waiver with suspicion and insist on waiver by course of performance—for example, accepting belated deliveries without protest, or issuing new orders (or changing the specifications of old orders) while existing ones are in default. Waiver implied from performance is less prone to manipulation. This method of protecting modification-only-in-writing clauses gives waiver the same meaning throughout the statute, but it does not help Wisconsin Knife, for the claim of waiver here is largely based on the course of performance.

The reading I give to waiver also affords substantial effect to modification-only-in-writing clauses. To see this, consider three characterizations of the dealings between Wisconsin Knife Works and National Metal Crafters. The first, which Wisconsin Knife Works presses on us, is that there was no modification and no "attempt at modification" within the meaning of § 2–209(4). National Metal Crafters promised to deliver the blanks in the fall of 1981. When it fell behind, Wisconsin Knife Works had to decide whether to give up on National Metal Crafters (and collect any damages to which it may have been entitled) or ask National Metal Crafters to keep trying. National Metal Crafters may have been slow, but it had a head start on anyone else Wisconsin Knife Works might have asked to make the blanks. Wisconsin Knife Works wanted both to preserve its rights and to minimize its damages, and it did not surrender its legal remedies by trying to mitigate. It was entitled to throw up its hands in January 1983 and collect damages from National Metal Crafters for nonperformance.

The second characterization is that when National Metal Crafters ran into trouble producing on schedule, National Metal Crafters and Wisconsin Knife Works discussed the problem and agreed that National Metal Crafters could have more time in order to get the job done right. On this story, Wisconsin Knife Works valued a high quality product and a successful business relation more than it valued its legal right to prompt performance. Perhaps Wisconsin Knife Works did not even want performance so soon, for it was not ready to turn the blanks into spade bits and did not want blanks piling up in warehouses. So Wisconsin Knife Works told National Metal Crafters to take the time to do it right. On my view this would be a waiver under § 2–209(4). When National Metal Crafters took more time than Wisconsin Knife Works could stomach, Wisconsin Knife Works announced that too much is enough, and it retracted the waiver. Section 2–209(5) allowed it to do just this unless National Metal Crafters had relied to its detriment on Wisconsin Knife Work's words and conduct. Having retracted the waiver, Wisconsin Knife Works could declare National Metal Crafters in breach—but because the waiver excused National Metal Crafter's performance until January 1983, Wisconsin Knife Works could not collect damages for delay. The parties would simply walk away from the contract. See Dangerfield v. Markel, 252 N.W.2d 184, 191–93 (N.D.1977).

The third characterization is the one National Metal Crafters presses here. National Metal Crafters tells us that the purchase orders never were the "real" contract. Instead Wisconsin Knife Works and National Metal Crafters embarked on joint operations to find a new way to make spade bits. The purchase orders were parts of a larger joint venture, which did not have formal terms. As the parties went along they modified their understandings and accommodated each other's needs. The latest modification occurred when National Metal Crafters gave Wisconsin Knife Works a "pert chart" indicating realistic dates for quantity shipments, and people at Wisconsin Knife Works said that these dates and quantities were acceptable. The dates ran into April 1983. This implies that when Wisconsin Knife Works declared the relationship at an end in January 1983, it breached the contract (as modified), and National Metal Crafters is entitled to damages—at a minimum profits lost on blanks scheduled for delivery through April 1983, perhaps even profits National Metal Crafters anticipated through continuation of this relationship for a longer run.

Section 2–209(2) puts this third position out of court. The third story would be a thoroughgoing reshaping of the obligations, which could not occur unless reflected in a "signed writing." The "pert chart" is not such a writing because Wisconsin Knife Works, the party sought to be bound, did not sign it. The discussions could be at most "an attempt at modification" under § 2–209(4), and therefore could be a waiver. Under § 2–209(5) Wisconsin Knife Works could rescind its waiver prospectively unless that "would be unjust in view of a material change of position in reliance on the waiver"—here, for example, proof that National Metal Crafters had already manufactured the blanks scheduled for delivery in April 1983, or had bought equipment with no alternative use. National Metal Crafters has not argued that it had the sort of reliance that would enable it to enforce the executory portion of any modification, and therefore Wisconsin Knife Works was entitled to cancel the contract and walk away in January 1983 free from liability save for goods furnished or expenses incurred in reliance before January 1983. This treatment of § 2–209(5) solves, for the most part, the problem of fabricated claims of modification. "Attempts at modification" generally are not enforceable prospectively—and if there is commercial bad faith (that is, opportunistic conduct), they are not enforceable at all. There is no serious remaining problem to which a reliance element in the definition of waiver is a solution.

Because § 2–209(2) and (5) eliminate National Metal Crafters' principal position, we are left with the first two—either Wisconsin Knife Works stood on its entitlement to timely delivery but stuck with National Metal Crafters to mitigate damages, or Wisconsin Knife Works waived the requirement of timely delivery but in January 1983 rescinded the waiver. The jury's finding that Wisconsin Knife Works and National Metal Crafters "modified" their contract, though an answer to a legally erroneous question, resolves this dispute. Wisconsin Knife Works vigorously argued at trial that at all times it stood on its rights but went along with delayed delivery as a second-best solution. The jury's finding that Wisconsin Knife Works and National Metal Crafters modified their contract—in the words of the instruction, that Wisconsin Knife Works "by conduct or other means of expression induced a reasonable belief by [National Metal Crafters] that strict enforcement was not insisted upon, but that the modified performance was satisfactory and acceptable as equivalent"—necessarily rejects Wisconsin Knife Works's version of events. The evidence was sufficient to permit the jury to reject this version. We are left with "an attempt at modification" that may operate as a waiver, which Wisconsin Knife Works may and did revoke. See also Chemetron Corp. v. McLouth Steel Corp., 522 F.2d 469, 472 (7th Cir.1975), which defines the elements of waiver much as the district court's instruction defined modification.

If National Metal Crafters were claiming damages for lost profits, it would be necessary to determine whether National Metal Crafters detrimentally relied on Wisconsin Knife Works's waiver. But National Metal Crafters does not want damages for work to be performed after January 1983. It simply wants to defeat Wisconsin Knife Works's claim for damages for belated delivery. (It also sought and received $30,000 for reliance expenditures before January 1983, which is not problematic under my construction of § 2–209.) The jury, although improperly instructed, has found enough to support a judgment discharging National Metal Crafters from liability to Wisconsin Knife Works. This requires us to affirm the judgment.

A requirement of reliance will not make a difference very often—certainly not in this case. Any waiver that is more than a condonation of an existing default will induce some reliance. The buyer who asks a seller of fungible goods to defer delivery induces reliance even though the waiver of timely delivery will not affect the production of the goods. When the goods have a custom design, as the spade bit blanks do, some reliance is close to a certainty. I doubt that National Metal Crafters would have produced the same goods in the same quantity but for a belief that Wisconsin Knife Works wanted to have them. A change of position in reliance on the frequent discussions is all the majority requires. Summary judgment cannot be far away. Still, it is better not to ask unnecessary questions even when the questions have ready answers.

———

In Chapter 2 *BMC v. Barth* presented the issue whether a hybrid goods-services transaction is within the scope of Article 2. That case also contains an issue of contract modification. The following portion of the report repeats the description of the facts and presents the court's analysis of contract modification under Article 2.

BMC Industries, Inc. v. Barth Industries, Inc.

United States Court of Appeals, Eleventh Circuit, 1998.
160 F.3d 1322.

[Plaintiff, BMC Industries, manufactured eyeglass lenses. It decided to become the first company to automate production of the lenses and entered into a contract with defendant under which defendant would develop and install an automated production line. The contract required all modifications to be in writing. The original delivery date under the contract was June 1987. Subsequent written modifications extended the delivery date to October. However, the defendant encountered a number of difficulties and notified plaintiff that delivery would be delayed. First, defendant said it would deliver in December. Then, experiencing further problems, defendant moved the delivery date to April 1988, but failed to meet that date, too. In August 1988 plaintiff was concerned that defendant would not perform and asked for assurances. It received a promise from Nesco, the parent company of defendant, that defendant would perform. Defendant finally tendered the production line in May or June of 1989, but plaintiff rejected delivery and brought suit.]

■ TJOFLAT, CIRCUIT JUDGE.

. . .

BMC's breach of contract count alleged that the second written amendment to the Contract established October 1987 as the deadline for Barth's performance. Because Barth failed to deliver the automated equipment by that date, Barth was in default of its contractual obligations. . . .

As an affirmative defense to BMC's breach of contract claim, Barth asserted that BMC's conduct after the October 1987 delivery date had passed amounted to a waiver of the delivery date under Article 2 of the Uniform Commercial Code ("UCC"). Although Barth failed to deliver the machines by October 1987, Barth argued, BMC executives urged Barth to keep working, BMC engineers continued to assist Barth in overcoming technical problems, and BMC executives agreed to increase the purchase price. Therefore, Barth claimed, BMC waived its entitlement to delivery of the machines in October 1987.

. . .

Additionally, Barth counterclaimed against BMC for breach of contract. Barth repeated its argument that BMC's conduct amounted to a waiver of the October 1987 delivery date, and asserted that the delivery deadline therefore became indefinite. Because Barth tendered the machines within a reasonable amount of time, Barth substantially performed its contractual obligations. Consequently, Barth claimed, BMC's refusal to accept delivery of the machines in May 1989 constituted breach of the Contract. . . .

[After concluding that Article 2 applies to this transaction, the court turned to the question whether BMC waived the contract requirement that Barth deliver the goods in October 1987.]

1.

Although the UCC does not specifically lay out the elements of waiver, we have stated that waiver requires "(1) the existence at the time of the waiver a right, privilege, advantage, or benefit which may be waived; (2) the actual [or] constructive knowledge thereof; and (3) an intention to relinquish such right, privilege, advantage, or benefit." Dooley v. Weil (In re Garfinkle), 672 F.2d 1340, 1347 (11th Cir.1982). Conduct may constitute waiver of a contract term, but such an implied waiver must be demonstrated by clear evidence. Waiver may be implied when a party's actions are inconsistent with continued retention of the right.

As an initial matter, we must determine whether, under the UCC, waiver must be accompanied by detrimental reliance. Although it is settled that waiver under Florida common law must be supported by . . . consideration or detrimental reliance, courts disagree on whether the UCC retains this requirement. We conclude, however, that the UCC does not require consideration or detrimental reliance for waiver of a contract term.

Our conclusion follows from the plain language of subsections 672.209(4) and (5). While subsection (4) states that an attempted modification that fails may still constitute a waiver, subsection (5) provides that the waiver may be retracted *unless* the non-waiving party relies on the waiver. Consequently, the statute recognizes that waivers may exist in the absence of detrimental reliance—these are the retractable waivers referred to in subsection (5). Only this interpretation renders meaning to subsection (5), because reading subsection (4) to require detrimental reliance for all waivers means that waivers would *never* be retractable. *See* Wisconsin Knife Works v. National Metal Crafters, 781 F.2d 1280, 1291 (7th Cir.1986) (Easterbrook, J., dissenting) (noting that reading a detrimental reliance requirement into the UCC would eliminate the distinction between subsections (4) and (5)). Subsection (5) would therefore be meaningless.

. . .

Although other courts have held that waiver requires reliance under the UCC, those courts have ignored the UCC's plain language. The leading case espousing this view of waiver is Wisconsin Knife Works v. National Metal Crafters, 781 F.2d 1280 (7th Cir.1986). . . . Writing for the majority, Judge Posner concluded that the UCC's subsection (2), which gives effect to "no oral modification" provisions, would become superfluous if contract terms could be waived without detrimental reliance. Judge Posner reasoned that if attempted oral modifications that were unenforceable because of subsection (2) were nevertheless enforced as waivers under subsection (4), then subsection (2) is "very nearly a dead letter." According to Judge Posner, there must be some difference between modification and waiver in order for both subsections (2) and (4) to have meaning. This difference is waiver's detrimental reliance requirement.

Judge Posner, however, ignores a fundamental difference between modifications and waivers: while a party that has agreed to a contract modification cannot cancel the modification without giving consideration for the cancellation, a party may unilaterally retract its waiver of a contract term provided it gives reasonable notice. The fact that waivers may unilaterally be retracted provides the difference between subsections (2) and (4) that allows both to have meaning. We therefore conclude that waiver under the UCC does not require detrimental reliance. Consequently, without reaching the issue of detrimental reliance, we consider whether BMC waived the Contract's October 1987 delivery date.

2.

Applying the elements of waiver to the facts before us, we hold as a matter of law that BMC waived the October 1987 delivery date. The October 1987 delivery date was a waivable contract right, of which BMC had actual knowledge. We also conclude that BMC's conduct impliedly demonstrated an intent to relinquish that right.

The most cogent evidence of this waiver is BMC's own representation of its relationship with Nesco. Throughout this litigation, BMC has maintained that Nesco, beginning in August 1988, "stepped in and promised to complete the project. In doing so, Nesco expressly represented that all of its resources were committed to the project, and instructed BMC to deal solely with Nesco." According to BMC, therefore, Nesco voluntarily became liable, in the fall of 1988, for Barth's completion of the project. By that time, however, the October 1987 delivery date had already passed. If, as BMC claims, the contract was already breached, then Nesco could never have performed its obligations; Nesco was in breach of its promise as soon as that promise was made, and could have been sued by BMC the next day. For Nesco's promise to have meaning, BMC must have given Barth and Nesco additional time to perform—in other words, BMC must have waived the October 1987 delivery date.

. . .

Furthermore, BMC's course of dealing with Barth evidenced BMC's waiver of the October 1987 delivery date, because BMC failed timely to demand compliance with that contract term or terminate the Contract and file suit. When a delivery date passes without the seller's delivery, the buyer must object within a reasonable time and warn the seller that it is in breach.

. . .

Until 1989 . . . BMC continued to act as though both parties were bound by the Contract and that Barth was not in default of its obligations: the October 1987 delivery date passed without comment from BMC; engineers from BMC frequently provided advice or assistance to help Barth personnel overcome technical problems; BMC executives frequently visited Barth's production facilities and encouraged Barth to continue working to complete the equipment; BMC even continued to spend money on the project—in December 1987, over one month after the October 1987 delivery date had passed, BMC purchased an additional $71,075 worth of springs and tooling for the machines. In sum, rather than terminating the Contract, or at least warning Barth that it was in breach after the October 1987 delivery date had passed, BMC continued to act as though the Contract remained in effect.

This is not to say that BMC never complained that Barth had missed deadlines; BMC executives frequently expressed their concern and disappointment that the project was so far behind schedule. On April 5, 1988, for example, the Chairman, President, and CEO of BMC sent a letter to Barth in which he stated: "[T]he project is well behind schedule, and each day of delay represents lost savings for Vision-Ease. I hope that Barth will exert every effort to ensure the speedy completion and installation of the equipment and avoid any further delay." But while BMC complained of delays, it never declared Barth in default or terminated the contract—instead, BMC told Barth to keep working. After Barth had spent an additional eighteen months of time and money and, according to Barth, was prepared to deliver the machines, however, BMC suddenly decided to terminate the Contract. This BMC could not do.

The UCC states that when a contractual delivery date is waived, delivery must be made within a reasonable time. *See* Fla. Stat. ch. 672.309(1) (1997). Consequently, because BMC waived the October 1987 delivery date, Barth was only obligated to deliver the machines within a reasonable time period. We remand this case to the district court for a new trial on the question of whether Barth tendered the machines within a reasonable time period.

. . .

QUESTIONS AND NOTES

1.   Section 2–209(4) provides that if the contract contains a no-oral-modification clause, an oral attempt at modification may operate as a waiver. It does not, however, specify what is waived. There are two possibilities:

- it may operate to waive the contract term that the parties have attempted to modify, or

- it may operate to waive the provision requiring modifications to be in writing.

Which is it?

Assume that ShirtShop has a contract to purchase 500 polo shirts of assorted solid colors from Logo, delivery on April 1 and payment due 10 days after delivery. On March 15 ShirtShop phones Logo and asks for a longer period of credit, saying that it would be willing to pay a portion of the price on delivery and the balance in 45 days. During this phone call, they agree that ShirtShop will pay 30% of the price on delivery and the balance 45 days later. Logo tenders delivery of the goods on April 1, and ShirtShop says it can pay only 25% of the price at that time. Fearing that it may never receive the balance of the price, Logo refuses to complete delivery. Who breached?

If the attempted modification waives the payment term of the contract, then that term disappears from the contract. But what term replaces it? When is ShirtShop obligated to pay? On the other hand, if the attempted modification operates to waive the no-oral-modification clause, then the telephone conversation effectively replaces the original term of the contract with the new term, even though the contract states that any such modification must be writing.

This difficulty is present in many of the cases, but the courts often do not address it expressly.

2.   Waiver of a contract right may occur by oral or written communication. More frequently, at least in litigated cases, waiver occurs by conduct. For example, a contract may require a party to give written notice, but the party instead gives oral notice. If the other party acts upon receiving that oral notice, the conduct of that other party in acting upon the oral notice operates to waive the requirement that the notice be in writing.

In cases like *Wisconsin Knife Works* and *BMC v. Barth*, an attempt to modify the contract, which does not comply with 2–209(2), nevertheless may operate to waive the delivery date specified in the contract. Delivery then would be due at a reasonable time, per 2–309(1).

3.   In the first full paragraph on page 115 Judge Posner says, "The main purpose of forbidding oral modifications is to prevent the promisor from fabricating a modification that will let him escape his obligations under the contract. . . ." He concludes that a modification is effective as a waiver only if there is reliance by the person offering to prove the modification. Judge Posner realizes that under that rule, there is "a danger of bootstrapping—of incurring a cost in order to make the case for a modification." But, he says, that course is risky and is less likely to happen than merely testifying to a conversation.

Judge Easterbrook rejects reliance as a requirement for waiver, and, in the first partial paragraph on page 121, says, "It might be sensible to treat claims of oral waiver with suspicion and insist on waiver by course of performance—for example accepting belated deliveries without protest."

In the following problem, which of the two tests for waiver do you prefer?

Problem. CaneCo and Sweets entered into a written contract in which CaneCo agreed to sell Sweets 10,000 pounds of sugar at 20 cents per pound, delivery on July 1st. The contract contained a "no-oral-modification" clause. CaneCo's owner claims that on June 30th she called the owner of Sweets and told him that, while performance was possible, it would involve some difficulties. "I told him on the phone," she testified, "that I could get the sugar to him the next day, but that would involve working my crew overtime and far into the night. I asked him if he really needed the sugar on July 1st, saying that if he did I would have it there. He said, 'No, I really don't need it July 1st. I don't want your crew to work all night. If you get the sugar to me by the 3rd, it will be ok.' I thanked him." When CaneCo tendered delivery on July 2nd, Sweets rejected on the ground that the sugar had been delivered late and denied ever having participated in the alleged phone conversation. CaneCo sues.

    a.   How would Judge Posner decide this case?

    b.   How would Judge Easterbrook decide it?

    c.   Would it make a difference if the price of sugar had dropped to 12 cents per pound on July 1st? What if the price drop occurred on June 25th? What if, conversely, the price of sugar had risen during this period?

4.   The possibility of waiver creates a dilemma for one party to a contract when the other is performing but not exactly as required by the contract. With respect to delay, for example, it often is more efficient for the buyer to hang in there with a slowly performing seller than it would be to cancel the contract and find another supplier. What should the buyer do to encourage the seller to complete performance without waiving the contract provision that requires performance by a specified date?

5.   **Section 2–209 and electronic communication.** If a contract states, "No modification of this contract shall be binding unless made in writing and signed by the parties," is a change in the terms of performance enforceable if it is made in the course of an exchange of e-mails? In addition to the relevant provisions of Article 2, see UETA §§ 5, 7.

6.   **CISG and oral modification of contract.** Article 29(2) of the Convention on Contracts for the International Sale of Goods reads: "A contract in writing which contains a provision requiring any modification or termination by agreement to be in writing may not be otherwise modified or terminated by agreement. However, a party may be precluded by his conduct from asserting such a provision to the extent that the other party has relied on that conduct." That language sounds as if it might require some conduct by the party against whom the modification is offered other than the oral agreement itself as a condition of proof. However, Professor Honnold has offered this gloss on the section:

> The role of the second sentence of Article 29(2) may be illustrated as follows:
>
>   *Example 29A. A written contract called for Seller to manufacture 10,000 units of a product according to specifications that were supplied by Buyer and set forth in the contract. The contract provided: "This contract may only be modified by a writing signed by the parties." Before Seller started production, the parties by telephone agreed on a change in the specifications. Seller produces 2,000 units in accordance with the new specifications; Buyer refused to accept these units on the ground that they did not conform to the specifications in the written contract.*

Because of the contract provisions, under Article 29(2) the oral agreement to the change in specifications, by itself, was ineffective to modify the contract. However, Buyer's oral agreement could be held to constitute "conduct" that would preclude him from invoking the contract clause "to the extent that the other party has relied on that conduct"; Seller's production of the 2,000 units in accordance with the oral agreement could constitute such reliance. However, Buyer is precluded only "to the extent" of the reliance; he should be able to insist on the original specifications for further production.

J. Honnold, Uniform Law for International Sales § 204, at 230–31 (4th ed.2009). Under this view, Article 29(2) really adopts a position like the one advanced by Judge Posner under 2–209(5).

7. Section 2–209 and the statute of frauds. Would the result in *Wisconsin Knife* have been different if the contract had not contained a no-oral-modification clause? Does 2–209(3) require that modifications like that claimed to have been made in *Wisconsin Knife* be in writing? If so, would "reliance" on an oral modification take it out of the statute of frauds? Under 2–201 itself, only specified forms of reliance make the contract enforceable in the absence of a writing. Only delivery and acceptance, payment, or the commencement of manufacture of specially manufactured goods have that effect. But cases like Decatur Cooperative Association v. Urban (Note 4, page 70 supra) hold that detrimental reliance makes the agreement enforceable even in the absence of a writing that satisfies 2–201.

It is possible to read 2–209(3) as requiring a writing for any modification of a contract for more than $500, but this reading creates an anomaly. Under 2–201 itself not all the terms of a contract have to be evidenced by a writing: the only essential term is a quantity term. Oral evidence can be offered showing all the other terms. Therefore, if the parties agree originally that delivery will be on July 5th, that term need not be evidenced by a writing. But if they later orally modify their agreement to require delivery on June 30, this reading of 2–209(3) would render the modification unenforceable. Therefore, perhaps 2–209(3) only states the obvious: that contracts for more than $500 must meet the requirements of 2–201. This would mean that any increase in the quantity term must be evidenced by a writing, since a contract is not enforceable beyond the quantity shown in the writing. And it would mean that if the price increases from less than $500 to $500 or more, there must be a writing that satisfies 2–201(1).

In spite of the incongruity with 2–201, the casual reader of 2–209(3) is likely to conclude that if the contract is subject to 2–201, any modification of it has to be in writing. Several courts have held just that, though they often immediately go on to suggest that even though the statute has not been satisfied, the modification may be effective as a "waiver." See, e.g. Cooley v. Big Horn Harvestore Systems, Inc., 767 P.2d 740 (Colo.App.1988).

In Article 2A the section on modification (2A–208) does not mention the statute of frauds.

8. Problem. Swift purchased an airplane to be used as an air taxi. The sales price was $45,000, to be paid $10,000 in cash and the balance at $1,000 per month for 35 months. After making six monthly payments, Swift told the seller, Cessna, that she needed to buy some additional equipment if she were to stay in business, but could not buy it unless the monthly payments were reduced to $600. Cessna orally agreed to the reduction in payments. The parties' written contract, however, provides that oral modifications are ineffective. Cessna accepted the reduced payments for six months and then notified Swift that future payments must be $1,000 per month and that the cumulative shortage in payment ($2,400, or $400 x 6) must be made up within 60 days. In the ensuing litigation, can Swift show an oral modification? If so, what are the contract terms now? What additional facts do you need, if any?

Can Cessna admit that the modification was made and nevertheless treat it as a "waiver" retractable under 2–209(5)? Or is the no-oral-modification provision treated like a private statute of frauds subject to the rule of 2–201 that an agreement is binding against a party who admits that the agreement was made?

On the facts of the problem, if Cessna were to deny that a modification was made, it would say either, "No, we didn't agree to a modification of the contract, but we did accept reduced payments for a time" or "We didn't agree to a permanently binding modification, what we did agree to was to accept reduced payments for a limited time." Observe that if Cessna makes the first assertion, and it is believed, it is a waiver situation to which 2–209(5) applies. See 1–303(f), which specifically refers to waivers by conduct and to 2–209 as relevant to them.

9. Modifications and the requirement of consideration. The common-law requirement of consideration often interfered with parties' attempts to modify an existing sales contract. Under the legal duty rule, also known as the pre-existing duty rule, a promise to do what one is already contractually obligated to do is not consideration for a return promise. Rationalized by a desire to prevent one party from coercing the other to do more (or accept less) than the contract requires, the rule is both over-inclusive and under-inclusive: it renders unenforceable good faith modifications when changed circumstances make the modification desirable to both parties, and it does not prevent true coercion when the coercing party includes some minor change that benefits the coerced party. Consequently, 2–209(1) provides that modifications can be binding even if there is no consideration for the modification. Instead, as Official Comment 1 states, the modification must satisfy the obligation of good faith, which is imposed in 1–304 and defined in 1–201(b)(20).

Problems.

a. Caneco contracted to sell Sweets 10,000 pounds of sugar, to be delivered in six months at a price equal to the market price at the time of delivery. When the contract was made, the market price was 60 cents per pound. During the period between the time of formation and the time of performance, the price of sugar rose to $5.00 per pound. Shortly before the date for performance the buyer's president approached the seller's president and told her that an insistence on strict performance of the contract would result in bankrupting him, but that he could pay $3.00 per pound and remain solvent. He proposed that they modify the price to $3.00.

Caneco's president was unhappy with the proposition, but since she had plenty of sugar on hand, which she had acquired at 50 cents a pound, she told Sweets that she would agree to the change. Sweets took delivery and paid $30,000 (i.e. $3.00 per pound). Four months later Caneco sued for $20,000, the excess of the original contract price over the amount Sweets actually paid. How should this case be decided?

b. Tronics obtained a contract to supply sensitive electronic equipment to Agrico for installation in farm tractors. Tronics then formed a contract with Caseco in which Caseco would design and fabricate 1,000 custom-made cases to house the electronic equipment. The price was $50 per case. Because of the rough conditions in which tractors operate, the cases required special insulation to protect the fragile electronics. When Caseco submitted a case for testing, Tronics determined it was not satisfactory. Caseco redesigned the case, using different materials. The redesign caused Caseco's cost of performance to rise from $25 per case to $40 per case. Caseco refused to produce and deliver the cases unless Tronics agreed to pay $65 per case. Tronics protested but ultimately agreed, and Caseco delivered the 1,000 cases. Tronics paid $50,000, and Caseco sued for $15,000. What result?

H. OPTIONS WITHOUT CONSIDERATION (FIRM OFFERS)

Friedman v. Sommer

New York Court of Appeals, 1984.
63 N.Y.2d 788, 481 N.Y.S.2d 326, 471 N.E.2d 139.

■ MEMORANDUM. . . .

Appellant and her late husband sponsored an offering plan to convert the 360-unit residential apartment building known as "The Sovereign" to cooperative ownership. By the terms of the sixteenth amendment to the plan dated April 14, 1981, the sponsor increased the purchase prices for all unsold apartments. That amendment also contained the following provision: "However, each tenant is granted the nonexclusive right to purchase his or her apartment at the price set forth in the Twelfth Amendment to the Offering Plan for a period of thirty (30) days from the presentation of this Sixteenth Amendment." Thereafter, but prior to May 12, 1981, the sponsor in oral communications to respondent tenant withdrew the offer to her with respect to her apartment 45G. Nevertheless, on May 12, 1981 the tenant undertook by a letter addressed to the sponsor to accept the offer contained in the sixteenth amendment and sought to purchase her apartment at the lower price. The determinative issue on this appeal is whether the sponsor's offer of April 14 was irrevocable. The tenant contends that it was and that she has an enforceable contract for the purchase of her apartment, and her position has been upheld by the lower courts. We, however, agree with the sponsor that the offer was revocable and that it was withdrawn prior to the tenant's purported acceptance.

It is conceded that there was no consideration for the offer and that it would therefore have been revocable at the common law. The tenant contends however that the offer was made irrevocable by statute.

A contract for the sale of a cooperative apartment, in reality a sale of securities in a cooperative corporation, is governed by the Uniform Commercial Code (Weiss v. Karch, 62 N.Y.2d 849, 850, 477 N.Y.S.2d 615, 466 N.E.2d 155). The applicable section of the Code is § 2–205 which provides in pertinent part: "An offer . . . in a signed writing which by its terms gives assurance that it will be held open is not revocable, for lack of consideration, during the time stated." The offer here gave no such assurance. Quite the contrary, it expressly provided that it was "non-exclusive." Thus, the sponsor explicitly reserved the right to sell the tenant's apartment to others at any time during the 30-day period— precisely the opposite of an assurance that the tenant would have the right at any time during that period to purchase the apartment for herself.

Inasmuch as the sponsor's offer was revocable, its withdrawal prior to acceptance by the tenant precluded the formation of a contract of purchase and requires dismissal of the tenant's complaint seeking specific performance or, in the alternative, damages for the breach of such contract.

QUESTIONS AND NOTES

1. By what reasoning does the court in *Friedman* conclude that Article 2 of the Code applies to the sale of a cooperative apartment? Does it apply?

Assuming that Article 2 does apply, is the court suggesting that if the offer had not contained the word "nonexclusive" it would have been a firm offer under 2–205? Do you think that if the offer had not stated that it was nonexclusive it should be treated as irrevocable during the 30 day period? Is there an alternative way of explaining the reference to 30 days in the offer?

2. **Technical requirements of firm offers.** It is a mistake to assume that all written offers, or even those that the parties have intended to be irrevocable, are firm without consideration. Note the technical requirements of 2–205.

How strictly should these requirements be construed? For example, is not the purpose behind the requirement that a firm offer be stated in a signed writing to insure that a merchant has deliberately intended such effectiveness? If so, is it possible to argue persuasively that a signed writing should not be needed if other kinds of conclusive evidence can be adduced to prove this deliberate intention? If a merchant, for example, admits that he made an oral promise not to revoke his offer, would the offer be firm under the rules of 2–205?

Is 2–205 limited to transactions involving the sale of goods? Suppose a merchant in writing offers to sell some shares of stock that are listed on the securities exchange and promises to keep the offer open for thirty days. Is this offer firm under 2–205? Would it make a difference if the shares were not listed on any exchange? If the offer were part of a takeover bid or proxy fight in which the offeror was seeking to acquire control of a company?

What is the purpose of the "merchant" limitation in 2–205? Suppose a practicing lawyer makes a written promise to keep open for 30 days an offer to sell part of her law library. Suppose it can be shown that this lawyer knows more about these particular books, and more about the law of firm offers and the doctrine of consideration, than anyone in the publishing business. Is her offer firm under 2–205?

Would it matter if the lawyer practices in the area of trusts and estates and has forgotten everything she ever learned about the law of firm offers and the doctrine of consideration?

Suppose a merchant makes a written offer to sell goods and promises in writing to keep it open for six months. Is the offer firm under 2–205? If so, for how long? Suppose an offer that is firm under 2–205 for a three-month period contains an automatic renewal clause that provides, in effect, that it will be extended for an additional three months unless the offeror gives written notice prior to the ending of the first three-month period that no extension will be granted. If the offeror does not give the written notice-of-no-extension within the time limit, is the offer revocable at the four-month point?

3. Many of the questions posed above have not been answered to date by judicial decisions. Some of them can be avoided by good drafting. There are other firm-offer difficulties, too, that can be handled by good drafting. Suppose, for example, a merchant in New York on April 1st mails a letter to a merchant in Los Angeles in which the offeror promises to keep the offer open for 30 days. Suppose the offeree in Los Angeles receives the letter on April 3rd and mails a purported acceptance on May 3rd at 11:00 P.M., P.S.T. (which is, of course 2:00 A.M., E.S.T., May 4th). Is there a contract?

If the offeree in Los Angeles mails the purported acceptance on May 5th, is it absolutely clear that there is no contract?

How would you draft a firm offer to avoid these problems?

4. **Problem.** SharpUSA makes an offer to sell OfficePro 100 DX-C381 Digital Photocopiers for $1,800 each. In a writing that complies with 2–205, SharpUSA assures OfficePro the offer is good for 30 days. This writing is dated May 1. On May 15 OfficePro informs SharpUSA that sales are slow and it will not be buying the copiers. Soon thereafter, sales pick up, and on May 25 OfficePro sends its purchase order purporting to accept SharpUSA's offer to sell the 100 copiers. Is SharpUSA obligated to deliver? At common law, rejection of an option contract does not terminate the offeree's power of acceptance. Is this true also under 2–205?

5. **Section 2–205 and promissory estoppel.** What if an offer does not comply with 2–205: may it nevertheless be irrevocable? In E.A. Coronis Associates v. M. Gordon Construction Co., 90 N.J.Super. 69, 216 A.2d 246

(App.Div.1966), the court rejected an argument by the offeree that the offeror had made a firm offer under 2–205. It then continued as follows:

> Defendant also argues that even if plaintiff's writing of April 22 is not a firm offer within the meaning of section 2–205, justice requires that we apply the doctrine of promissory estoppel to preclude its revocation. Restatement, Contracts, § 90 provides:

> "A promise which the promisor should reasonably expect to induce action or forbearance of a definite and substantial character on the part of the promisee and which does induce such action or forbearance is binding if injustice can be avoided only by enforcement of the promise."

Defendant argues that it relied on plaintiff's bid in making its own bid and that injustice would result if plaintiff could now revoke. Thus, defendant contends that plaintiff's bid is made irrevocable by application of the doctrine of promissory estoppel.

> . . .

> To successfully establish a cause of action based on promissory estoppel Gordon must prove that (1) it received a clear and definite offer from Coronis; (2) Coronis could expect reliance of a substantial nature; (3) actual reasonable reliance on Gordon's part, and (4) detriment. Restatement, Contracts, § 90.

> The Law Division did not think promissory estoppel would apply in the situation *sub judice*. Therefore we reverse. We also remand since it is necessary to determine if the elements of a promissory estoppel case are present. They are essentially factual and inappropriate to a summary judgment. Gordon must show the existence of an offer. The April 22 letter is subsequent in time to Gordon's bid to the Port Authority. It cannot furnish the basis for this suit since it would have been impossible for Gordon to have relied on it when making its bid. However, it is alleged that the letter merely confirmed prior oral agreements. The true facts must await a full hearing.

> Similarly, Gordon must show that Coronis could reasonably expect Gordon to rely on the bid. This will depend on Coronis' actual knowledge or the custom and usage in the trade. Gordon must also show actual reliance.[2] And we note that if Coronis' bid was so low as to put Gordon on notice that it was erroneous it cannot claim reliance. Finally, of course, detriment must be shown.

Should promissory estoppel apply with respect to offers that fail to meet the standards of 2–205?

6. CISG and firm offers. Under Article 16 of the Convention on Contracts for the International Sale of Goods, an offer is irrevocable "if it

---

[2] We do not consider whether the existence of section 2–205 of the Uniform Commercial Code precludes reliance on an offer not conforming to its provisions.

indicates, whether by stating a fixed time for acceptance or otherwise, that it is irrevocable."

CHAPTER 4

TERMS OF THE SALES CONTRACT

The preceding chapter considered whether express terms proposed by one of the parties become part of the contract. The focus there was on the process of contract formation and the means by which an express term was adopted. This chapter resumes consideration of the terms of the contract, but the focus is somewhat different. Here the concerns are (1) the enforceability of a term that appears in the written contract or that was expressly agreed to but does not appear in the written contract, and (2) the omission of a term that later turns out to be important.

If one had asked a Nineteenth Century lawyer what the parties' obligations under a written contract were, he probably would have said: "Show me the contract and I'll show you the obligations." This response would correctly reflect the jurisprudence of the times: that the "courts should not make a contract for the parties." Arising out of that jurisprudence were the ideas that courts should avoid supplying missing terms and that the total contractual obligation should be set forth within the four corners of the written document and read as a conveyancer reads deeds—meaning that anything not included is deemed excluded. As stated by a contracts treatise of the time: "for whenever the contract is reduced into writing, nothing that is not found impressed upon it can be considered as forming part of the contract." C. Addison, Law of Contracts 159 (1847).

This jurisprudential position may have resulted in great certainty, but at the expense of penalizing the parties who had agreed on a matter, either explicitly or implicitly, but failed to write the term into the contract. It also resulted in the courts voiding a number of contracts on grounds of uncertainty, lack of mutuality of obligation, or illusory promise. To avoid these drastic results, the courts gradually began to shift away from this position, culminating in the enactment of the UCC. The philosophy of Article 2 concerning missing terms is almost diametrically opposed to the views of the Nineteenth Century. Its drafters felt that a better result is achieved by supplying missing terms than by voiding the contract or by distorting its true meaning by enforcing it without the missing terms. This change has improved the law by giving greater effect to the intent of the parties, but it has been made at the cost of certainty and therefore has been subjected to criticism.

In any event, a consideration of the terms of a contract governed by Article 2 involves studying not only the ways in which explicit contractual provisions are interpreted, but also the methodology for determining missing terms and how these terms relate to express terms and to one another.

As a starting point in determining the terms of the contract, note that 1–201(b)(12) defines the word "contract" to mean "the total legal obligation which results from the parties' *agreement* as affected by this Act and any other applicable rules of law." (Emphasis added). What is meant by "agreement"? Are any and all kinds of agreements permissible? Suppose the parties have not, in fact, agreed on a matter that later proves to be important. Does the UCC impose a term on the parties in that case, enforce the contract where possible without the term, or chuck the whole thing out as being too indefinite to permit enforcement? Finally, how do the parties protect their written contract against the contention that there are missing terms in it which should be supplied in one way or another?

A. TERMS OF THE AGREEMENT

1. THE CONCEPT OF AGREEMENT

The term "agreement" is defined by 1–201(b)(3) to mean "the bargain of the parties in fact as found in their language or inferred from other circumstances, including course of performance, course of dealing, or usage of trade as provided in Section 1–303." Compare 1–201(b)(12), defining "contract."

The definitions of "agreement" and "contract" make it clear that not all agreements are effective and that the agreement itself consists of the express and implied terms constituting the actual bargain of the parties. But questions remain:

- Although a written term is an "express term," does "express term" mean "written term"?

- The definition makes it clear that implied terms may be developed by inference from course of performance, course of dealing, and usage of trade, but are implied terms limited to these sources?

In considering these questions, we start with express terms and then turn to course of performance, course of dealing, and usage of trade.

2. EXPRESS TERMS AND THE LIMITATIONS ON THEM

When an agreement is in writing, one naturally starts with the writing in ascertaining the terms of the contract. As will be seen below, the Code gives express terms preeminence over other terms, and written terms certainly are express terms. Moreover, as we shall see, written express terms displace any contradictory oral express terms that are made before or at the same time as the execution of the written contract. Thus it may be said that terms found in a written contract become the basic foundation on which the deal rests and that other express and implied terms, if enforceable, become the superstructure on this foundation.

Article 2 adopts the general principle of freedom of contract, which means, among other things, that written terms in a sales contract are generally to be taken at face value and understood according to the normal techniques of legal interpretation. But there are limits on freedom of contract. We will consider two of them here. In considering these limits, please start by reading 1–302(a) and (b), 2–302, and the Official Comments to those sections.

a. UNCONSCIONABILITY

The doctrine of unconscionability originated in equity, and for centuries courts of equity have possessed and exercised the power to refuse to enforce agreements that are so extreme in nature as to appear unconscionable in light of business practices and mores. This refusal is illustrated by Campbell Soup Co. v. Wentz, cited in Official Comment 1 to 2–302, in which the court refused to order specific performance of a contract for delivery of a farmer's crop because of the one-sided nature of the contract's provisions on the farmer's obligations and the buyer's remedies. It is illustrated also by mortgage cases, in which an equity of redemption was found to exist in spite of express words to the contrary in the contract, and by cases in which the courts refused to enforce penalties and forfeitures provided by the contract.

The doctrine of unconscionability was available, however, only in equity; it was not available to courts of law. Hence, at law the courts policed against outrageous contracts by using such concepts as fraud and duress. In addition, the fluidity of the rules of offer, acceptance, consideration, and conditions, along with the power of the courts to interpret contract language, often enabled them to avoid the enforcement of outrageous contracts by manipulating the rules or the construction of the contract to get a "right" result. These techniques, however, had the bad effect of leaving twisted law on the books to perplex and mislead lawyers and judges considering subsequent cases in which the same fireside equities were not present.

The manipulation of the law and the adverse construction of contract language as covert devices to prevent unconscionable results had other bad effects as well. Three of these unfortunate consequences were emphasized by Professor Karl Llewellyn (the principal drafter of Article 2) as the primary justification for developing 2–302 and allowing courts of law to explicitly consider claims of unconscionability. First, by avoiding a direct holding on unconscionability, the courts implied that unconscionable contracts are not really bad, thereby encouraging drafters to reword these offensive contracts and try again. Second, by evading the real issues, the courts failed to set minimum standards of decency for the commercial community. And, third, by disguising the methods of policing against these contracts, the courts generated confusion respecting proper methods of contract interpretation. See K. Llewellyn, The Common Law Tradition 362–63 (1960).

Official Comment 1 to 2–302 reveals that the section is designed to correct these deficiencies, particularly the matter of adverse construction of contractual and statutory language.

Official Comment 1 also attempts to give some meaning to the term "unconscionability" by listing some pre-Code cases designed to illustrate its meaning. Notice that these cases have to do with warranty disclaimers and efforts to limit the remedies of the parties. These are two of the principal matters to which the courts have applied 2–302.

———

A & M Produce Co. v. FMC Corp.

California Court of Appeal, 1982.
135 Cal.App.3d 473, 186 Cal.Rptr. 114.

■ WIENER, ASSOCIATE JUSTICE.

. . .

A & M, a farming company in the Imperial Valley, is solely owned by C. Alex Abatti who has been farming all of his life. In late 1973, after talking with two of his employees, Mario Vanoni and Bill Billingsley, he decided to grow tomatoes. Although they had grown produce before, they had never grown tomatoes or any other crop requiring a weight-sizer and were not familiar with weight-sizing equipment. At the suggestion of Billingsley, they first spoke with a salesman from Decco Equipment Company regarding the purchase of the necessary equipment. The salesman explained A & M would need a hydrocooler in addition to a weight-sizer and submitted a bid of $60,000 to $68,000 for the equipment. Abatti thought the Decco bid was high, and Billingsley suggested Abatti contact FMC for a competitive bid.

In January 1974, A & M called FMC whose representative, John Walker, met with them at A & M's office. Walker admitted he was not an expert on the capacity or specifics of weight-sizing equipment. Later he brought Edgar Isch of FMC into the negotiations to assist in making the determination on the proper type of equipment. Isch did not say a hydrocooler was required. According to Abatti, Isch recommended FMC equipment because it operated so fast that a hydrocooler was unnecessary thereby saving A & M about $25,000.

The parties discussed the capacity of the sizing equipment recommended by Isch. Walker and Isch proposed a preliminary bid of $15,299.55 for the weight-sizer. They obtained Abatti's signature to a "field order" for the equipment to "secure Abatti's consent" to order the equipment. The field order did not state the final price nor list all the necessary material and equipment. The order was on a standard form, printed on both sides, the terms of which were identical to the written contract which Abatti later received. Along with the order, Abatti delivered his $5,000 check as a deposit. Walker and Isch left a copy of the capacity chart for FMC weight-sizers which had been referred to in the negotiations.

The field order was sent to FMC where the proposed lay-out of the packing shed was analyzed by the engineering department, and a final list of essential materials was compiled. Abatti then received a copy of the form contract in the mail. It contained a list of all the equipment and materials being purchased, either typed in blanks on the front of the contract, or handwritten on an attached order sheet. The total bill was for $32,041.80. . . .

For our purposes the provisions of the agreement which are important are: paragraph 3, "Seller's Remedies" outlining the buyer's obligation to pay seller's reasonable attorney's fees in connection with any defaults by the seller; paragraph 4, "Warranty" containing a disclaimer of warranties, in bold print; and paragraph 5, "Disclaimer of Consequential Damages" stating in somewhat smaller print that "Seller in no event shall be liable for consequential damages arising out of or in connection with this agreement * * *."

Abatti signed the agreement and returned it to FMC with his check for an additional $5,680.60 as a down payment. He never paid the $21,361.20 due "on delivery of equipment." In April 1974 FMC delivered and installed the machinery. A 20-foot extension to A & M's packing house was required to house the equipment. A & M's problems with the FMC equipment began during the third week of May, when it started to pick the tomatoes. Tomatoes piled up in front of the singulator belt which separated the tomatoes for weight-sizing. Overflow tomatoes had to be sent through the machinery again, causing damage to the crop. The damage was aggravated because the tomatoes were not cooled by a hydrocooler, allowing a fungus to spread more quickly within the damaged fruit. Walker was called out and managed to control the overflow by starting and stopping the machine. This effort was counterproductive, however, because it significantly reduced the processing speed. Unlike the Decco machinery, the FMC equipment did not have a speed control.

Abatti unsuccessfully attempted to get additional equipment from FMC and/or Decco. There was insufficient time to set up a new packing shed to hand-pick the tomatoes. Moreover, a search for other packing operators to handle A & M's tomatoes was unavailing. On June 17, A & M closed its shed because the return on the fruit—some of which had been damaged—was inadequate to cover costs. Some tomatoes were sold to a canning plant; most were rejected because they were not cannery tomatoes.

Shortly thereafter, A & M offered to return the weight-sizer to FMC provided FMC would refund A & M's down payment and pay the freight charges. FMC rejected this offer and demanded full payment of the balance due.

A & M then filed this action for damages against FMC for breach of express warranties, breach of implied warranty for a particular use and misrepresentation. A & M dismissed the misrepresentation cause of action at trial. By stipulation the trial was bifurcated to permit the judge to decide FMC's cross-complaint for the balance due on the purchase price and the issue of attorney's fees after the jury returned its verdict on the complaint.

This appeal is the result of a third trial. In the earlier two cases special verdict forms were used. The first case resulted in a hung jury; a new trial was ordered in the second.

After hearing evidence presented to the jury, and additional evidence in the absence of the jury on the nature of the contract's formation and the bargaining position of the respective parties, the court ruled:

> "[I]t would be unconscionable to enforce [the waivers of warranties and waiver of consequential damage] provisions of the agreement, and further that they are not set out in a conspicuous fashion.

> "The Court's ruling is based on all of the circumstances in this case in connection with how the negotiations were conducted, the fact that initially a down payment of—a substantial down payment of $5,000 was made and later on the contract was signed."

Accordingly, the jury viewed only the front of the contract, not the reverse side with its lengthy provisions.

The jury returned a general verdict for $281,326 which the parties agreed to reduce by $12,090.70, the amount already paid to FMC for the machinery. The court found for FMC on its cross-complaint, but awarded plaintiff $45,000 in attorney's fees and prejudgment interest from September 18, 1976.*

. . . FMC asserts the trial court erred in applying [the doctrine of unconscionability] to the disclaimer of warranties. It contends unconscionability is irrelevant to warranty disclaimer provisions, having been eliminated by the specific statutory requirements of section 2316. (See J. White and R. Summers, [Uniform Commercial Code] 475–481 [2d ed. 1980]; Leff, Unconscionability and the Code—The Emperor's New Clause (1967) 115 U.Pa.L.Rev. 485, 516–528.) Alternatively, FMC suggests the California Legislature's failure to adopt the general Uniform Commercial Code section on unconscionability (§ 2–302) as part

---

*   Cal. Civ. Code § 1717 provides that if a contract provides for the recovery of attorney's fees in the event of successful litigation by one of the parties to the contract, then the other party is entitled to recover attorney's fees if he or she is the successful party.—Eds.

of California's Commercial Code precludes the trial court's reliance on the doctrine in this instance.

While FMC's argument is not without force, we conclude that an unconscionable disclaimer of warranty may be denied enforcement despite technical compliance with the requirements of section 2316. (See FMC Finance Corp. v. Murphree, [(5th Cir.1980) 632 F.2d 413, 420].) Unconscionability is a flexible doctrine designed to allow courts to directly consider numerous factors which may adulterate the contractual process. Uniform Commercial Code section 2–302 specifies that "any clause of the contract" may be unconscionable. The policing provisions of section 2316 are limited to problems involving the visibility of disclaimers and conflicts with express warranties. But oppression and unfair surprise, the principal targets of the unconscionability doctrine may result from other types of questionable commercial practices. Moreover, the subtle distinction between an "implied" warranty and an "express" warranty may do precious little to mitigate the exploitation of a party with inferior bargaining power. Yet as long as the warranty remains "implied," section 2316's policing provisions are ineffective.

. . .

We now turn to the principal question involved in this appeal: Whether the trial court erred in concluding that FMC's attempted disclaimer of warranties and exclusion of consequential damages was unconscionable and therefore unenforceable. Before we can answer that question however, we must first concern ourselves with the nature of the unconscionability doctrine.

The Uniform Commercial Code does not attempt to precisely define what is or is not "unconscionable." Nevertheless, "[u]nconscionability has generally been recognized to include an absence of meaningful choice on the part of one of the parties together with contract terms which are unreasonably favorable to the other party." (Williams v. Walker-Thomas Furniture Company (D.C.Cir.1965) 350 F.2d 445, 449, fn. omitted.) Phrased another way, unconscionability has both a "procedural" and a "substantive" element.

The procedural element focuses on two factors: "oppression" and "surprise." "Oppression" arises from an inequality of bargaining power which results in no real negotiation and "an absence of meaningful choice." (Williams v. Walker-Thomas Furniture Company, supra, 350 F.2d at p. 449.) "Surprise" involves the extent to which the supposedly agreed-upon terms of the bargain are hidden in a prolix printed form drafted by the party seeking to enforce the disputed terms. Characteristically, the form contract is drafted by the party with the superior bargaining position.

Of course the mere fact that a contract term is not read or understood by the non-drafting party or that the drafting party occupies a superior bargaining position will not authorize a court to refuse to enforce the contract. Although an argument can be made that contract terms not actively negotiated between the parties fall outside the "circle of assent"[11] which constitutes the actual agreement, commercial practicalities dictate that unbargained-for terms only be denied enforcement where they are also *substantively* unreasonable. No precise definition of substantive unconscionability can be proffered. Cases have talked in terms of "overly-harsh" or "one-sided" results. (See, e.g., Schroeder v. Fageol Motors, Inc. (1975) 86 Wash.2d 256, 544 P.2d 20, 23; Weaver v. American Oil Company (1972) 257 Ind. 458, 276 N.E.2d 144, 146.) One commentator has pointed out, however, that " * * * unconscionability turns not only on a 'one-sided' result, but also on an absence of 'justification' for it." (Eddy, [On the "Essential" Purposes of Limited Remedies: The Metaphysics of UCC Section 2–719(2), 65 Cal.L.Rev. 28, 45 (1977)]), which is only to say that substantive unconscionability must be evaluated as of the time the contract was made. (See U.Com.Code, § 2–302.) The most detailed and specific commentaries observe that a contract is largely an allocation of risks between the parties, and therefore that a contractual term is substantively suspect if it reallocates the risks of the bargain in an objectively unreasonable or unexpected manner. (Murray, Unconscionability: Unconscionability (1969) 31 U.Pitt.L.Rev. 1, 12–23; see also Eddy, supra, 65 Cal.L.Rev. at pp. 45–51.) But not all unreasonable risk reallocations are unconscionable; rather, enforceability of the clause is tied to the procedural aspects of unconscionability such that the greater the unfair surprise or inequality of bargaining power, the less unreasonable the risk reallocation which will be tolerated.

. . . [We] must now determine whether the trial court in this case was correct in concluding that the clauses in the FMC form contract disclaiming all warranties and excluding consequential damages were unconscionable. In doing so, we keep in mind that while unconscionability is ultimately a question of law, numerous factual inquiries bear upon that question. The business conditions under which the contract was formed directly affect the parties' relative bargaining power, reasonable expectations, and the commercial reasonableness of the risk allocation as provided in the written agreement. To the extent there are conflicts in the evidence or in the factual inferences which may be drawn therefrom, we must assume a set of facts consistent with the court's finding of unconscionability if such an assumption is supported by substantial evidence.

---

[11] In the words of Professor Murray:

"One of the fundamental concepts of contract law is the concept of *assent*. The basic idea that parties exercise their volition by committing themselves to future action and that the law provides their *circle of assent* with the status of a private law is fundamental to any discussion of contracts. The two basic questions raised are: (1) Did the parties agree to any future action or inaction? (2) If they did agree, what are the terms of their agreement (or, what is their circle of assent)"?

(Murray on Contracts (2d ed.1974) § 352, p. 743; first italics in original, second italics added.)

Turning first to the procedural aspects of unconscionability, we note at the outset that this contract arises in a commercial context between an enormous diversified corporation (FMC) and a relatively small but experienced farming company (A & M). Generally, " * * * courts have not been solicitous of businessmen in the name of unconscionability." (White and Summers, supra, § 4–9 at p. 170.) This is probably because courts view businessmen as possessed of a greater degree of commercial understanding and substantially more economic muscle than the ordinary consumer. Hence, a businessman usually has a more difficult time establishing procedural unconscionability in the sense of either "unfair surprise" or "unequal bargaining power."

Nevertheless, generalizations are always subject to exceptions and categorization is rarely an adequate substitute for analysis. With increasing frequency, courts have begun to recognize that experienced but legally unsophisticated businessmen may be unfairly surprised by unconscionable contract terms (see, e.g., Weaver v. American Oil Company, supra, 257 Ind. 458, 276 N.E.2d 144; Schroeder v. Fageol Motors, Inc., supra, 544 P.2d at p. 24), and that even large business entities may have *relatively* little bargaining power, depending on the identity of the other contracting party and the commercial circumstances surrounding the agreement. (See, e.g., Graham v. Scissor-Tail, Inc., [(1981)] 28 Cal.3d [807,] 818–819, 171 Cal.Rptr. 604, 623 P.2d 165; Allen v. Michigan Bell Telephone Company (1969) 18 Mich.App. 632, 171 N.W.2d 689, 693; Industralease Automated & Scientific Eq. Corp., Etc., [(1977) 58 A.D.2d 482], 396 N.Y.S.2d [427,] 432.) This recognition rests on the conviction that the social benefits associated with freedom of contract are severely skewed where it appears that had the party actually been aware of the term to which he "agreed" or had he any real choice in the matter, he would never have assented to inclusion of the term.

Both aspects of procedural unconscionability appear to be present on the facts of this case. Although the printing used on the warranty disclaimer was conspicuous, the terms of the consequential damage exclusion are not particularly apparent, being only slightly larger than most of the other contract text. Both provisions appear in the middle of the back page of a long preprinted form contract which was only casually shown to Abatti. It was never suggested to him, either verbally or in writing, that he read the back of the form. Abatti testified he never read the reverse side terms. There was thus sufficient evidence before the trial court to conclude that Abatti was in fact surprised by the warranty disclaimer and the consequential damage exclusion. How "unfair" his surprise was is subject to some dispute. He certainly had the opportunity to read the back of the contract or to seek the advice of a lawyer. Yet as a factual matter, given the complexity of the terms and FMC's failure to direct his attention to them, Abatti's omission may not be totally unreasonable. In this regard, the comments of the Indiana Supreme

Court in Weaver v. American Oil Company, supra, 276 N.E.2d at pp. 147–148 are apposite:

> "The burden should be on the party submitting [a standard contract] in printed form to show that the other party had knowledge of any unusual or unconscionable terms contained therein. The principle should be the same as that applicable to implied warranties, namely that a package of goods sold to a purchaser is fit for the purposes intended and contains no harmful materials other than that represented."

Here, FMC made no attempt to provide A & M with the requisite knowledge of the disclaimer or the exclusion. In fact, one suspects that the length, complexity and obtuseness of most form contracts may be due at least in part to the seller's preference that the buyer will be dissuaded from reading that to which he is supposedly agreeing. This process almost inevitably results in a one-sided "contract."

Even if we ignore any suggestion of unfair surprise, there is ample evidence of unequal bargaining power here and a lack of any real negotiation over the terms of the contract. Although it was conceded that A & M was a large-scale farming enterprise by Imperial Valley standards, employing five persons on a regular basis and up to fifty seasonal employees at harvest time, and that Abatti was farming some 8,000 acres in 1974, FMC Corporation is in an entirely different category. The 1974 gross sales of the Agriculture Machinery Division alone amounted to $40 million. More importantly, the terms on the FMC form contract were standard. FMC salesmen were not authorized to negotiate any of the terms appearing on the reverse side of the preprinted contract.[13] Although FMC contends that in some special instances, individual contracts are negotiated, A & M was never made aware of that option. The sum total of these circumstances leads to the conclusion that this contract was a "bargain" only in the most general sense of the word.

Although the procedural aspects of unconscionability are present in this case, we suspect the substantive unconscionability of the disclaimer and exclusion provisions contributed equally to the trial court's ultimate conclusion. As to the disclaimer of warranties, the facts of this case support the trial court's conclusion that such disclaimer was commercially unreasonable. The warranty allegedly breached by FMC went to the basic performance characteristics of the product. In attempting to disclaim this and all other warranties, FMC was in essence

---

[13]   The transcript of FMC salesman John Walker's testimony reads as follows:

"Q All right. Now do you negotiate the terms of those contracts, or are they preprinted and that's the way you use them?

"A They are sent by our legal department, with the exception of payment terms are negotiable, but not the 'Whereases' and Wherefores."

"Q So you don't separately negotiate the terms on the back and the other terms, other than payment terms?

"A I'm not empowered to do that, sir."

guarantying nothing about what the product would do. Since a product's performance forms the fundamental basis for a sales contract, it is patently unreasonable to assume that a buyer would purchase a standardized mass-produced product from an industry seller without any enforceable performance standards. From a social perspective, risk of loss is most appropriately borne by the party best able to prevent its occurrence. Rarely would the buyer be in a better position than the manufacturer-seller to evaluate the performance characteristics of a machine.

In this case, moreover, the evidence establishes that A & M had no previous experience with weight-sizing machines and was forced to rely on the expertise of FMC in recommending the necessary equipment. FMC was abundantly aware of this fact. The jury here necessarily found that FMC either expressly or impliedly guaranteed a performance level which the machine was unable to meet. Especially where an inexperienced buyer is concerned, the seller's performance representations are absolutely necessary to allow the buyer to make an intelligent choice among the competitive options available. A seller's attempt, through the use of a disclaimer, to prevent the buyer from reasonably relying on such representations calls into question the commercial reasonableness of the agreement and may well be substantively unconscionable. The trial court's conclusion to that effect is amply supported by the record before us.

As to the exclusion of consequential damages, several factors combine to suggest that the exclusion was unreasonable on the facts of this case. Consequential damages are a commercially recognized type of damage actually suffered by A & M due to FMC's breach.[14] A party " * * * should be able to rely on their existence in the absence of being informed to the contrary, * * *." (Schroeder v. Fageol Motors, Inc., supra, 544 P.2d at p. 24.) This factor is particularly important given the commercial realities under which the contract was executed. If the seller's warranty was breached, consequential damages were not merely "reasonably foreseeable"; they were explicitly obvious. All parties were aware that once the tomatoes began to ripen, they all had to be harvested and packed within a relatively short period of time.

Another factor supporting the trial court's determination involves the avoidability of the damages and relates directly to the allocation of risks which lies at the foundation of the contractual bargain. It has been suggested that "[r]isk shifting is socially expensive and should not be

---

[14] In the absence of an exclusion, the code provides that consequential damages are generally recoverable. (§§ 2714, subd. (3) and 2715, subd. (2).) The general rule regarding limitations on available remedies was stated by the court in Chemetron Corporation v. McLouth Steel Corporation (N.D.Ill.1974) 381 F.Supp. 245, 250:

"While parties may agree to limit the remedies for breach of their contract, the policy of the Uniform Commercial Code disfavors limitations and specifically provides for their deletion if they would act to deprive a contracting party of reasonable protection against breach." (Fn. omitted.)

undertaken in the absence of a good reason. An even better reason is required when to so shift is contrary to a contract freely negotiated." (S.M. Wilson & Co. v. Smith Intern., Inc. (9th Cir.1978) 587 F.2d 1363, 1375.) But as we noted previously, FMC was the only party reasonably able to prevent this loss by not selling A & M a machine inadequate to meet its expressed needs. "If there is a type of risk allocation that should be subjected to special scrutiny, it is probably the shifting to one party of a risk that *only* the other party can avoid." (Eddy, supra, 65 Cal.L.Rev. at p. 47, italics in original.)

In summary, our review of the totality of circumstances in this case, including the business environment within which the contract was executed, supports the trial court's determination that the disclaimer of warranties and the exclusion of consequential damages in FMC's form contract were unconscionable and therefore unenforceable. When non-negotiable terms on preprinted form agreements combine with disparate bargaining power, resulting in the allocation of commercial risks in a socially or economically unreasonable manner, the concept of unconscionability as codified in Uniform Commercial Code sections 2–302 and 2–719, subdivision (3), furnishes legal justification for refusing enforcement of the offensive result. . . .

The Judgment is affirmed.

QUESTIONS AND NOTES

1. In the third full paragraph on page 143 the court states that unconscionability has both a procedural and a substantive element. This characterization of unconscionability originated in Williams v. Walker-Thomas Furniture Co., 350 F.2d 445 (D.C.Cir.1965), and Leff, Unconscionability: The Emperor's New Clause, 115 U.Pa.L.Rev. 485 (1967). The characterization has proven very durable, and courts continue to rely on it.

A persistent question is whether both elements are essential to a finding of unconscionability. Some courts have held they are. Others have held they are, but there is a sliding scale: the more one element is present, the less the other is necessary. And still others have held that one element by itself may suffice. E.g., Maxwell v. Fidelity Financial Servs., 184 Ariz. 82, 907 P.2d 51, 58–59 (1995):

> Many courts, perhaps a majority, have held that there must be some quantum of *both* procedural and substantive unconscionability to establish a claim, and take a balancing approach in applying them. Other courts have held that it is sufficient if *either* is shown. . . .
>
> The cases that require a showing of both procedural and substantive unconscionability appear to be rather fact-specific, based more on the historical reluctance of courts to disturb contracts than on valid doctrinal underpinning. . . . Additional evidence that the dual requirement position is more coincidental than doctrinal is found within the very text of the statute on

unconscionability, which explicitly refers to "the contract *or any clause* of the contract." § [2–302] (emphasis added). Conspicuously absent from the statutory language is any reference to procedural aspects. That the U.C.C. contemplated substantive unconscionability alone to be sufficient is the most plausible reading of the language in § [2–302], given that the Code itself provides for *per se* unconscionability if there exists, without more, a substantive term in the contract limiting consequential damages for injury to the person in cases involving consumer goods. See § [2–719(3)]. It is wholly inconsistent to assert that unconscionability under § [2–302] requires some procedural irregularity when unconscionability under § [2–719] clearly does not.

Therefore, we conclude that under § [2–302], a claim of unconscionability can be established with a showing of substantive unconscionability alone, especially in cases involving either price-cost disparity or limitation of remedies.

2. Why does the court in *A & M Produce* conclude that the substantive element of unconscionability is present? Since 2–316 explicitly permits the seller to disclaim implied warranties, how can the court reach this conclusion? In view of the court's conclusion, is it possible for a seller to disclaim implied warranties: notwithstanding 2–316, when will a disclaimer *not* be unconscionable?

3. With respect to the procedural element of unconscionability, the court mentions oppression and surprise. In what way was there oppression in *A & M Produce*? In what way was there surprise?

Would the reasoning or the result in *A & M Produce* have been affected if plaintiff had seen the disclaimer and objected to it, but assented when defendant replied, "Look, this is the way we do business. Once we install the equipment, we're finished. Fine tuning and maintenance are up to you. Do you still want it"?

4. Unconscionability in commercial transactions. A few other courts have held contracts between two business entities to be unconscionable, but in most commercial cases the courts have rejected claims of unconscionability. E.g., Keystone Aeronautics Corp. v. R.J. Enstrom Corp., 499 F.2d 146 (3d Cir.1974) ("A social policy aimed at protecting the average consumer by prohibiting blanket immunization of a manufacturer or seller through the use of standardized disclaimers engenders little resistance. But when the setting is changed and the buyer and seller are both business entities, in a position where there may be effective and fair bargaining, the social policy loses its raison d'etre"); Potomac Elec. Power Co. v. Westinghouse Electric Corp., 385 F.Supp. 572 (D.D.C.1974) ("The negotiated agreement between these parties was not a contract between two small unknowledgeable shopkeepers but between two sophisticated corporations each with comparable bargaining power and fully aware of what they were doing. The negotiations leading to the consummation of the contract were deliberate, detailed and consumed more than two years. [The buyer's] representatives were experienced and the final agreement was reviewed by their corporate legal staff. While the evidence shows that other than Westinghouse, there was only one other domestic manufacturer with the capability of marketing the turbine-generator, there is nothing to indicate that [the buyer] was precluded from contracting with that manufacturer or even foreign manufacturers. Nor is there any evidence in the record showing that [the buyer] was a reluctant and unwilling purchaser, overreached and forced to yield to onerous terms imposed by Westinghouse"); KKO, Inc. v. Honeywell, Inc., 517 F.Supp. 892 (N.D.Ill.1981) ("Although plaintiffs have argued vigorously that Honeywell's conduct in this matter was deceitful, fraudulent and in violation of its obligations under the warranty clause, they have all but ignored the factual issue critical to unconscionability claims: the relative bargaining positions of the parties and the consequences of those relative strengths when the contract was entered into. . . . Plaintiffs have been in the business of manufacturing and selling commercial cooking equipment for over forty years and are among the largest distributors of fryers in the country.") Additional cases are collected in J. White & R. Summers, Uniform Commercial Code, 6th ed. (2010), § 5–9 nn. 2, 23–24.

5.   Unconscionability in consumer transactions. Buyers in consumer transactions have had somewhat more success in arguing unconscionability. In one early case, the court held that the price term was unconscionable but had difficulty justifying its conclusion. Jones v. Star Credit Corp., 59 Misc.2d 189, 298 N.Y.S.2d 264 (Spec.Term 1969) ("Concededly, deciding the issue is substantially easier than explaining it.") For the most part, however, the courts have applied the two-part test articulated in *A & M Produce*.

In recent years the most frequently raised issues of unconscionability have concerned contract provisions pertaining to dispute resolution, such as Hill v. Gateway 2000, Inc., on page 91 supra. Was the procedural element of unconscionability present in *Hill*? Was the substantive element present? In considering unconscionability in the context of arbitration clauses, courts have focused on the extent to which the agreement

- imposes costs on the consumer that are higher than the costs to litigate;
- specifies a situs of arbitration that, as a practical matter, forecloses participation by the consumer;
- removes common-law or statutory remedies, such as the right to punitive damages or attorney's fees, that would be available in litigation;
- shortens the period for asserting a claim; or
- obligates the consumer to arbitrate but leaves the merchant free to litigate.

In 2011 the Supreme Court held that the Federal Arbitration Act preempts application of the law of unconscionability to agreements to arbitrate insofar as that law interferes with the fundamental attributes of arbitration or stands as an obstacle to the accomplishment of the objectives of the Act. AT&T Mobility, L.L.C. v. Concepcion, 563 U.S. 333 (2011).

6.   UCCC. An alternative approach to unconscionability in consumer transactions appears in the Uniform Consumer Credit Code (UCCC, or U3C), which was drafted 45 years ago during the period in which Article 2 was being widely enacted. Sections 5.108 and 6.111 of the UCCC authorize courts to grant relief from an unconscionable contract. Section 6.111(3) elaborates:

> (3) In applying this section, consideration shall be given to each of the following factors, among others:
>
> (a) belief by the creditor at the time consumer credit sales, consumer leases, or consumer loans are made that there was no reasonable probability of payment in full of the obligation by the debtor;
>
> (b) in the case of consumer credit sales or consumer leases, knowledge by the seller or lessor at the time of the sale or lease of the inability of the buyer or lessee to receive substantial benefits from the property or services sold or leased;
>
> (c) in the case of consumer credit sales or consumer leases, gross disparity between the price of the property or services sold or leased and the value of the property or services measured by the price at which similar property or services are readily obtainable in credit transactions by like buyers or lessees;
>
> (d) the fact that the creditor contracted for or received separate charges for insurance with respect to consumer credit sales or consumer loans with the effect of making the sales or loans, considered as a whole, unconscionable; and
>
> (e) the fact that the respondent has knowingly taken advantage of the inability of the debtor reasonably to protect his interests by reason of physical or mental infirmities, ignorance, illiteracy or inability to understand the language of the agreement, or similar factors.

7. Unconscionability in lease transactions. In 2A–108(1) Article 2A tracks 2–302. That section also, however, contains provisions that go further. Subsection (2) provides that, in a consumer lease, the court can grant appropriate relief if a lease contract or any provision of it has been induced by unconscionable conduct. In addition, it provides that relief can be granted for unconscionable conduct in the collection of a claim arising under a lease contract. Subsection (4) permits an award of attorney's fees to a consumer who successfully asserts an unconscionability claim under 2A–108.

8. CISG and unconscionability. The Convention on Contracts for the International Sale of Goods does not contain a provision like 2–302. However, Article 4 of the Convention provides that the Convention "is not concerned with: (a) the validity of the contract or of any of its provisions or of any usage." Unconscionability may be viewed as an issue of "validity." If a contract, under conflict-of-law rules, is subject to the law of a state of the United States, the court could appropriately apply 2–302 and find the contract or a clause thereof unconscionable, i.e. invalid.

9. Mandatory Code rules that cannot be varied by agreement. Section 1–302(b) is clear in its provision that the parties are not competent to disclaim the "obligations of good faith, diligence, reasonableness, and care prescribed by" the UCC. They may, however, determine the standards by which the performance of these obligations is to be measured, so long as those standards are not manifestly unreasonable. For example, a provision in a sales contract required a commercial buyer to give notice of any defect in goods within 15 days after their receipt, on pain of losing all remedies for breach. A court held this standard to be manifestly unreasonable and therefore not permitted by this section, even though the seller and buyer were commercial giants. Neville Chemical Co. v. Union Carbide Corp., 422 F.2d 1205 (3d Cir.1970). Presumably, an agreement giving the buyer a longer period in which to discover defects but requiring it to report them promptly by certified mail would satisfy 1–302(b). Compare Prompt Electrical Supply Co., Inc. v. Allen-Bradley Co., 492 F.Supp. 344 (E.D.N.Y.1980) (notice of breach required by 2–607 cannot be waived, but the parties are competent to agree that the notice must be given in writing so that oral notice of breach was not sufficient).

Note that 1–302(a) grants the parties broad authorization to vary the effect of provisions of the UCC. But this authorization has limits. One limit is found in the introductory language of subsection (a), "except as otherwise provided in subsection (b)"; another is found in the rest of that introductory language, "or elsewhere in [the Uniform Commercial Code]." In other words, the provisions of the UCC can be varied by agreement unless the section or rule that the parties seek to vary provides otherwise. This means that some sections can be varied by agreement while others cannot. In this respect it is a difficult task to determine which provisions are mandatory and which are permissive, and the drafters have been criticized for not making this matter clear. Perhaps some clarity can be developed by looking at the history of the subsection.

The 1949 draft of the UCC, the first one seriously considered by the sponsors of the Code, contained a provision that was almost diametrically opposed to the thrust of present 1–302(a). Section 1–108 of the 1949 draft provided that "The rules enunciated in this Act are mandatory and may not be waived or modified by agreement unless the rule is qualified by the words 'unless otherwise agreed' or their equivalent."

This restrictive approach was justified on the ground of uniformity— that uniformity would be defeated if the parties were given the right to change the rules of the UCC, itself. On the other hand, it was recognized that many of the terms of Article 2 are really not rules of law but contractual terms to be imposed where the parties had failed to provide for the matter in their contract. These "gap-filling" rules could be varied or completely displaced by agreement. Explaining this, the official comment to the 1949 section stated that "This Act contains two types of rules: (1) Rules which are mandatory, that is, intended to govern the contract; (2) Rules which are intended merely to substitute for matters not expressed by the parties to the contract. The former may not be modified or waived by agreement. The latter may be waived or modified at will. The failure of the courts to distinguish between these two types of rules in interpreting prior Acts has led to complete lack of uniformity. Accordingly, great care has been used in specifying those rules which may be modified or waived by agreement. In all other cases, it is intended that the rules shall be mandatory."

This prohibitory approach ran into strong opposition, and it was substantially changed by the first official draft of the UCC in 1952. That draft (1–102(3)) provided that all provisions of the Code could be varied by agreement, except for matters falling within three categories, listed as subsections (a), (b) and (c) of 1–102(3) in the 1952 UCC: "(a) Definitions and formal requirements such as those determining what constitutes a negotiable instrument, a bona fide purchaser, a holder in due course, or due negotiation of documents of title are not subject to variation by agreement; (b) Except as otherwise provided by this Act the rights and duties of a third party may not be adversely varied by an agreement to which he is not a party or by which he is not otherwise bound; (and) (c) The general obligations prescribed by this Act such as good faith, due diligence, commercial reasonableness and reasonable care may not be disclaimed by agreement but the parties may by agreement determine the standards by which the performance of such obligations is to be measured if such standards are not manifestly unreasonable."

In implementing this change, the 1952 Code provided additionally that "Provisions of this Act which are qualified by the words 'unless otherwise agreed' or words of similar import may be waived or modified by agreement and the absence of such words contains no negative implication." 1–102(3)(d) (1952).

While the changes in 1952 were major steps away from a restrictive approach and toward the goal of freedom of contract, they did not go far enough to satisfy critics who were fearful of the language *"general obligations such as* good faith, due diligence . . ." (emphasis added). These people thought there was a danger that an unduly wide range of provisions might be interpreted as "general obligations," thus preventing them from being varied by agreement. This criticism was accepted by the sponsors in 1955 and subsection 1–102(3) was amended to make clear that the matters of good faith, diligence, and care were not mere illustrations of general obligations that cannot be disclaimed by agreement but rather constitute the only general obligations that cannot be so disclaimed.

Even this change did not satisfy the New York Law Revision Commission which recommended that 1–102(3)(a) and (b) of the 1952 Code be deleted as unnecessary. This suggestion was accepted, the deletion was made in 1956, but the drafters of the Code prepared a new comment to section 1–102 to carry forward the ideas that formerly had been expressed in the text of subsection (3)(a) and (b).

Does this legislative history and Official Comment 1 (which, except for stylistic changes, is identical to the original Official Comment) help one identify mandatory terms? If in doubt, would you say that a Code provision should be construed as mandatory or permissive with regard to its variability by agreement, in view of the legislative history of the section? The answer to this question is important, because there is a large gray area between those sections which are clearly subject to variation and those which are clearly not subject to variation. Code sections prefaced by the words "unless otherwise agreed" or the like are definitely subject to variation. There are quite a few provisions having this prefatory language, a carry-over in most cases from the 1949 draft. There are far fewer clearly mandatory provisions on the other extreme. For an example of one, look at 2–725 which is mandatory in some, but not all, respects.

Is 2–201 mandatory? Could the parties orally agree that the statute of frauds would not apply to their deal? Is 2–302 mandatory? Could the parties agree that the doctrine of unconscionability had no role to play in their contract? If you answered that these sections are mandatory, how did you reach that conclusion? Consider whether that same process of reasoning will apply to the variability of other sections of the Code.

b. CHOICE OF LAW

The doctrine of unconscionability imposes a limit on the permissible terms of an agreement. Several other provisions also place limits. Section 1–304 declares an obligation of good faith on the parties in the performance and enforcement of their contract. Section 1–302(b) prohibits the parties from disclaiming this obligation (though they may agree on the standards for determining good faith). Another limitation appears in 1–301(a), which empowers the parties to choose the state whose law will govern their contract. But this power is not unlimited: "when a transaction bears a reasonable relation to this state and also to another state . . . the parties may agree that the law either of this state or of such other state . . . shall govern their rights and duties." Thus the parties may not agree to be governed by the law of just any third state.

Wright-Moore Corporation v. Ricoh Corporation

United States Court of Appeals, Seventh Circuit, 1990.
908 F.2d 128.

■ FLAUM, CIRCUIT JUDGE.

[Plaintiff had a one year distributorship agreement with defendant under which it had a right to distribute certain Ricoh copiers nation wide. Plaintiff was an Indiana corporation headquartered in Fort Wayne Indiana. Defendant was incorporated in New York and had its principal place of business in New Jersey. Under the agreement, plaintiff, at its expense, had to train employees of retailers to whom it sold Ricoh copiers to service the copiers. At the end of the year, defendant notified plaintiff that it would not renew the arrangement because it had decided to undertake itself all national distribution of the copiers. Plaintiff claimed that it had been assured that the distributorship arrangement would be long term as long as plaintiff performed its obligations under the agreement and that it had performed those obligations during the year.

Plaintiff alleged violation of the Indiana franchise law, breach of contract, fraud, misrepresentation, and estoppel. The contract contained a provision that the courts of Manhattan had exclusive jurisdiction over any dispute arising out of the agreement and that the law of New York would govern any dispute. The trial court, among other things, held that application of New York law would be inconsistent with the public policy of Indiana as reflected in its franchise law. It applied Indiana law but held that under the Indiana franchise law the distributorship had been cancelled in good faith and that, therefore, defendant had no liability under the franchise law. It also held that all other claims were groundless and gave summary judgment for defendant. Plaintiff appealed.]

. . .

A.   Indiana Franchise Law Claims

Wright-Moore's appeal raises several significant issues under the Indiana franchise laws. Ind. Code §§ 23–2–2.5–1, et seq., 23–2–2.7–1, et seq. Wright-Moore argues that the district court erred as a matter of law in holding that non-renewal for the economic purposes of the franchisor constitutes good cause under Ind. Code § 23–2–2.7–1(7). In addition, Wright-Moore claims that summary judgment was improper because there were material issues of fact with respect to Ricoh's good faith during termination and with respect to the claim of discrimination. Ricoh supports the district court's holding but argues in the alternative that the contractually chosen New York law applies rather than Indiana law and, in addition, that Wright-Moore was not a franchise.

1.   Choice of Law

We begin with the choice of law question. Wright-Moore claims Indiana franchise law applies, despite the choice of New York law in the agreement, on the ground that the Indiana franchise statutes prohibit waiver of its protections and prohibit "limiting litigation brought for breach of the [franchise] agreement in any manner whatsoever." Ind. Code § 23–2–2.7–1(10). Ricoh argues that the express choice of law provision of the contract should govern. The district court held that Indiana has articulated a strong public policy against allowing parties to contract out of the protections of its franchise law and that this public policy overrides the choice of law provided for in the agreement.

Indiana has long adhered to the "most intimate contacts" test for choice of law. W.H. Barber v. Hughes, 223 Ind. 570, 63 N.E.2d 417 (1945). This approach has since been elaborated in the Restatement (Second) Conflict of Laws § 188 (the "Restatement"). Under this approach, "the court will consider all acts of the parties touching the transaction in relation to the several states involved and will apply as the law governing the transaction the law of that state with which the facts are in most intimate contact." W.H. Barber, 63 N.E.2d at 423. This approach also recognizes that parties may expressly choose the applicable law through a contract. "The law of the state chosen by the parties to govern their contractual rights and duties will be applied if the particular issue is one which the parties could have resolved by an explicit provision in their agreement directed to that issue." Restatement § 187(1). Typical issues that cannot be determined by explicit agreement include capacity, formalities, substantial validity, and illegality, but the set issues which cannot be contractually chosen is determined by local law. *Id.* at comment d. If the issue is one which could not have been explicitly resolved by the contract, the choice of law provisions of the contract will still apply unless the "chosen state has no substantial interest" in the litigation or "application of the law of the chosen state would be contrary to a fundamental policy of a state which has a materially greater interest than the chosen state in the determination of the particular issue and which, under the rule of § 188, would be the state of applicable law in the absence of an effective choice of law by the parties." *Id.* at § 187(2).

We agree with the district court that enforcement of the choice of law provision in the distributorship agreement would be contrary to Indiana's express public policy. Indiana has made it unlawful to enter into a franchise agreement "requiring the franchisee to prospectively assent to a release . . . [or] waiver . . . which purports to relieve any person from liability to be imposed by this chapter" or to enter into an agreement "limiting litigation brought for breach of the agreement in any manner whatsoever." Ind. Code § 23–2–2.7–1(10). We owe deference to the district judge's interpretation of the law of the state in which the judge sits, and the district judge here found that these provisions articulated a strong state policy against allowing contractual choice of law provisions to control the applicability of these provisions to Indiana franchises. The public policy, articulated in the nonwaiver provisions of the statute is clear: a franchisor, through its superior bargaining power, should not be permitted to force the franchisee to waive the legislatively provided protections, whether directly through waiver provisions or indirectly through choice of law. This public policy is sufficient to render the choice to opt out of Indiana's franchise law one that cannot be made by agreement.

Indiana law, following the Restatement, however, permits state public policy to override the contractual choice of law only if the state has a materially greater interest in the litigation than the contractually chosen state. Thus, for the Indiana public policy to control the choice of law, Indiana must have a materially greater interest in the litigation than does New York. We conclude that this is the case here. Wright-Moore is potentially a franchisee and is incorporated and located in the state of Indiana; its witnesses and documents are there; the contract negotiations occurred there; and the contract was, in part, performed there. New York's only connection to this litigation is that the defendant is incorporated in New York. The defendant's principal place of business is New Jersey. Indiana, therefore, has a materially greater interest in the litigation than New York. Since Indiana has a materially greater interest than New York and application of New York law would be contrary to a fundamental Indiana policy, Indiana franchise law governs this case.

. . .

3.   Nonrenewal of the Distributorship Agreement

Ind. Code §§ 23–2–2.7–1(7) and (8) declare unlawful any provision in a franchise agreement which permits the franchisee to be terminated or not renewed "without good cause or in bad faith." The district court found that Wright-Moore did not put forth sufficient evidence to show that its nonrenewal was in bad faith. The court found instead that Wright-Moore's nonrenewal was based on economic reasons internal to Ricoh, which the court held was good cause in compliance with Ind.Code § 23–2–2.7–1(7). The district court also found that Wright-Moore was not discriminated against in violation of Ind.Code § 23–2–2.7–2(5) because none of Ricoh's national distributors were renewed and consequently Wright-Moore cannot show treatment different from similarly situated franchises.

. . .

[As to the lack of good cause,] Wright-Moore also argues that the district court erred in holding that termination for the franchisor's own economic reasons constitutes good cause. The statute defines good cause to "include[ ] any material violation of the franchise agreement." Ind. Code § 23–2–2.7–1(7). There is no evidence that Wright-Moore breached the franchise agreement, so Ricoh's actions did not fall within the plain terms of the statute. Good cause, however is defined to *include* breach of the franchise agreement. The language of the statute does not indicate that it is limited to breach. The question is whether good cause also includes termination for the benefit of the franchisor's balance sheet.

Indiana courts have not yet considered this issue. We believe, however, that the language and structure of the Indiana law, along with the guidance provided by interpretation of franchise laws in other states, compel a conclusion that the internal economic reasons of the franchisor are not, by themselves, good cause for termination or nonrenewal of a franchise. Primarily, Ricoh's suggested conclusion that the franchisor's economic reasons would constitute good cause directly contravenes the very purpose of franchise statutes and would render the statutes ineffective. As noted above, franchise statutes are designed to prevent franchisors from extracting quasi-rents from franchisees. They are designed to ensure fair dealing between the parties. If the business reasons of the franchisor were sufficient, the protections of the statute would be meaningless since it is in the franchisor's short term business interest (and therefore good cause) to act opportunistically. (While this may not be effective in the long term as the franchisor may lose reputation or good will, a court is unlikely to make this determination.) Even absent opportunistic behavior, a franchisor could virtually always claim a plausible business reason for termination. Without a smoking gun, it would be difficult, if not impossible, for a franchisee to prove that a particular action is not in the business interests of the franchisor. Ricoh's suggested reading would, therefore, allow franchisors to extract rents from franchisees, the very behavior the statutes are designed to prevent.

This reasoning is supported by the decisions of several courts. In Kealey Pharmacy & Home Care Services, Inc. v. Walgreen Co., 761 F.2d 345 (7th Cir.1985), we held that Walgreen's termination of all its Wisconsin franchises and replacement with Walgreen-owned stores was not supported by good cause. Walgreen had valid business reasons to make this change. Nevertheless, we held that because Walgreen intended to appropriate the good will established by the franchisees, Walgreen's behavior was opportunistic and therefore, economic justifications alone were not sufficient. *See also* Remus v. Amoco Oil Co., 794 F.2d 1238, 1241 (7th Cir.1986) (good cause is limited to faults with the franchisee).

In addition, the structure of the Indiana statute indicates that good cause refers only to problems with the performance of the franchisee. Sections 23–2–2.7–1(7) and (8) prohibit termination or nonrenewal without good cause and list material violations of the franchise agreement as an example of good cause. The language of the statute is inclusive; the statute does not say material violations of the agreement are the sole legal cause for termination. The statute simply says that good cause *includes* material violations of the agreement. But as an example of the type of cause that the legislature had in mind, this indicates that the statute may be limited to other problems with the performance of the franchisee. Economic reasons internal to the franchisor do not fit this pattern; they generally have nothing to do with the performance of the franchisee.

. . .

[The court remanded the case to the district court for further consideration of the good faith termination issue.]

NOTES

You will observe that the court does not mention the UCC. The reason is that Article 2 does not apply to franchise contracts. See Note 6, page 34 supra. Nevertheless, the court's discussion of the choice-of-law issue is apropos of the rule of the UCC, found in 1–301.

3. THE HIERARCHY OF THE VARIOUS COMPONENTS OF AGREEMENT

Section 1–201(b)(3) defines "agreement" as "the bargain of the parties in fact as found in their language or inferred from other circumstances, including course of performance, course of dealing, or usage of trade. . . ." To identify the agreement, then, one must consider several sources: oral interactions, written communications and documents, course of performance, course of dealing, usage of trade, and other circumstances. Official Comment 3 adds, "Whether an agreement has legal consequences is determined by applicable provisions of the Uniform Commercial Code and, to the extent provided in Section 1–103, by the law of contracts." In other words, some parts of the agreement may not count, may not have legal consequences. Further, if a term supplied by one of these sources conflicts with a term supplied by one of the other sources, it becomes necessary to determine which term is part of the contract. The materials in this section examine how to make that determination.

In deciding what parts of the agreement count and do not count, particular attention is directed to 2–202 and 1–303. Please read these sections and the Official Comments to them. In the event of a conflict between terms supplied by the various components of an agreement, which term displaces which: what is the hierarchy of sources of terms under Article 2?

In your study of the law of contracts, you encountered the parol evidence rule, which limits the enforceability of agreements formed prior to or contemporaneously with the parties' adoption of a written agreement that they intend as the final expression of all or part of their deal. Article 2's version of this rule appears in 2–202. It addresses both partial integrations and complete integrations. If a writing is a complete integration, then the writing discharges all contemporaneous oral agreements and all prior oral *or written* agreements.

Problem. In a detailed, completely integrated agreement, Cartco contracted to deliver 50 golf carts to Sunrise Country Club on February 1 for a specified price. The writing is silent on the time of payment. Cartco tendered delivery on February 1 and demanded payment. Sunrise stated that it would pay by March 1. Cartco insisted that payment was due on delivery (see 2–310(a)) and refused to leave the carts at the Club. In the ensuing litigation, Sunrise wants to prove that it had purchased golf carts from Cartco four times during the preceding two years, that each time Cartco had delivered them without insisting on payment, and that each time Sunrise had paid within 30 days. Should the court entertain Sunrise's argument?

a.   THE PAROL EVIDENCE RULE

ARB, Inc. v. E-Systems, Inc.

United States Court of Appeals, District of Columbia Circuit, 1980.
663 F.2d 189.

[ARB, a corporation engaged in television and radio research, brought suit against E-Systems, a designer of electronic systems, for breach of a negotiated contract that was more than fifty pages in length. During the negotiations ARB had submitted a draft contract containing the following term: "If, as a result of default of performance by the Seller (E-Systems), this contract is terminated in whole or in part and if it is necessary to procure any of the specified products or services elsewhere, then Seller will be liable for any re-procurement charges which exceed the amount which would have been due the Seller if he had satisfactorily completed this order." This proposed term, providing for "cover" damages, was deleted at E-Systems's request.

The case was tried to a special master, who found that E-Systems had breached the contract, but denied ARB cover damages on the ground that it had bargained them away. The District Court adopted the master's report.]

■ TAMM, CIRCUIT JUDGE.

. . .

Misapplication of Parol Evidence Rule

ARB challenges the district court's conclusion that it "bargained away" its right to cover under section 2–712. It contends primarily that the evidence relied upon by the master in reaching this conclusion should have been excluded under Md.Com. Law Code Ann. § 2–202 (1975), the statutory parol evidence rule. As discussed below, ARB's contention on this point is well-founded, and this case will be remanded to the district court for the calculation of "cover" damages.

. . .

Two issues are raised by the application of [section 2–202] to the present facts: first, was the written contract "intended * * * as a complete and exclusive statement of the terms of the agreement," such that no evidence is admissible to explain or supplement it? Second, if not, and the contract was the "final expression of their agreement with respect to such terms as are included therein," should the specific evidence considered by the master have been barred as "contradict[ory]" or as not constituting a "consistent additional term"?

We believe that the written contract was "intended * * * as a complete and exclusive statement of the terms of the agreement." Two factors support this conclusion: first and most important is that the written contract contains an integration clause, and integration clauses are generally to be given effect under section 2–202. See Franz Chemical Corp. v. Philadelphia Quartz Co., 594 F.2d 146, 149 (5th Cir.1979); United States v. Haas & Haynie Corp., 577 F.2d 568, 572 (9th Cir.1978).[12] The integration clause in question here is not susceptible of any other reasonable interpretation; it states: "This Contract * * *

---

[12] See also the discussion by Professors White and Summers of the "special value" of the integration clause in the situation in which

the parties negotiate over a period of time, making and withdrawing numerous proposals. They finally reach an agreement and reduce it to writing. Here there is special need for a merger clause to protect against the risk that one party will, honestly or dishonestly, seek to resurrect some proposal that did not show up in the final writing.

J. White and R. Summers, Handbook of the Law of the Uniform Commercial Code 90 (2d ed.1980) constitutes the entire agreement between Buyer and Seller." (Contract at 35, § 6.19.) When combined with two other clauses in the contract, explicitly preserving "other or further remedies provided in law or in equity" (Contract at 29, § 6.8; Contract at 33, § 6.13), and a clause reserving to ARB the power "to avail itself cumulatively of all remedies provided in law or in equity," (Contract at 31, § 6.11), it makes the addition of a non-written term eliminating an "other * * * remed[y] provided in law" an error.

This decision to give effect to the integration clause is consistent with non-U.C.C. Maryland law, which holds that integration clauses, although not "absolutely conclusive," are "indicative of the intention of the parties to finalize their complete understanding in the written contract * * * that there was no other prior or contemporaneous agreement not included in the written contract." Pumphrey v. Kehoe, 261 Md. 496, 505, 276 A.2d 194, 199 (1971). Maryland law further requires, however, that the circumstances surrounding the making of the contract be considered to discover whether the integration clause in question does, in fact, express the genuine intention of the parties to make the written contract the complete and exclusive statement of their agreement. Shoreham Developers, Inc. v. Randolph Hills, Inc., 248 Md. 267, 271–72, 235 A.2d 735, 739 (1967); Rinaudo v. Bloom, 209 Md. 1, 9, 120 A.2d 184, 190 (1956). Thus, the issue is not whether the deletion of a given sentence antecedent to the making of the written contract was an agreement as to the matter deleted, but whether the integration clause, at the time it was agreed upon, represented the intentions of the parties.[13] Here, the bulk of the evidence suggests that the parties intended the written contract to be the complete and exclusive statement of the terms of their agreement. The length of the contract, its exhaustive detail, and the prolonged period of negotiation preceding its signing, collectively considered, support this conclusion. At the same time, E-Systems has offered no persuasive evidence supporting a determination that the parties intended, at the time of contracting, that non-written terms be part of the overall agreement.

Even if the written contract had not been "intended * * * as a complete and exclusive statement of the terms of the agreement," however, we believe that section 2–202 would bar evidence of the deletion

---

[13] Professor Corbin explained the effect of an integration clause in this way:

A provision that there are no previous understandings or agreements not contained in the writing is, on its face, a statement of fact; but it is more than such a statement. By limiting the contract to the provisions that are in writing, the parties are definitely expressing an intention to nullify antecedent understandings or agreements. They are making the document a complete integration. Therefore, even if there had in fact been an antecedent warranty or other provision, it is discharged by the written agreement.

3 A. Corbin, Corbin on Contracts § 578 (1960). Professor Corbin suggests that the declaration of completeness contained in an integration clause is "conclusive as long as [the clause] has itself not been set aside by a court on grounds of fraud or mistake, or on some ground that is sufficient for setting aside other contracts." Id. (footnote omitted).

of the reprocurement provision on the grounds that this evidence is not a "consistent additional term" within the meaning of section 2–202(b). We reach this conclusion by applying the appropriate test of consistency under Maryland law. This test is based not on the standard of simple non-contradiction of an express term of the contract applied by the master, but on a stricter standard requiring a substantially greater agreement between the contract and the proffered additional terms. The Court of Special Appeals explained it this way in Snyder v. Herbert Greenbaum & Assoc., Inc., 38 Md.App. 144, 380 A.2d 618 (1977):

> we hold that the additional terms offered by appellants are inconsistent with the contract itself. In doing so we reject the narrow view of inconsistency * * * that to be inconsistent the "additional terms" must negate or contradict express terms of the agreement.
>
> This interpretation of "inconsistent" is itself inconsistent with a reading of the whole of § 2–202. Direct contradiction of express terms is forbidden in the initial paragraph of § 2–202. The [narrow] interpretation renders that passage a nullity, a result which is to be avoided * * *.
>
> Rather we believe "inconsistency" as used in § 2–202(b) means the absence of reasonable harmony in terms of the language and respective obligations of the parties * * *.

380 A.2d at 623. We think that application of this test to the term here disputed indicates clearly that consideration of this "additional term"—the no-cover provision—would disrupt the delicate balance, the harmony, that the written contract establishes among the "respective obligations" of the parties.

Moreover, this conclusion is reinforced by application of the standard set out in Official Comment 3 to section 2–202 and expressly endorsed by the Maryland courts. See, e.g., Snyder v. Herbert Greenbaum & Assoc., Inc., 38 Md.App. 144, 380 A.2d 618, 623 (1977). It states in relevant part: "If the additional terms are such that, if agreed upon, they would certainly have been included in the document in the view of the court, then evidence of their alleged making must be kept from the trier of fact." We believe, for the reasons set out above in our discussion of the contract as a complete and exclusive statement of the agreement, that under all the circumstances of this case a term limiting the cover remedy, if agreed upon, would certainly have been included in the contract. In support, we note further that cover—referred to by White and Summers as "chief" among the general remedies of the buyer set out in section 2–711—occupies the central place in the U.C.C. remedy scheme.[16]

---

[16] Because . . . we decide the "cover" question on the basis of the parol evidence rule, we . . . do not consider [the master's] findings of fact as to the intentions of the parties on August 24, 1973, the day that the sentence upon which he based his decision was deleted from an earlier draft of the contract. We note, however, that were we to reach these fact findings, we would have reservations about the conclusion that the deletion "bargained away" cover, given the

QUESTIONS

1. The court in *ARB* determines that the writing is a complete integration and therefore concludes that any agreement concerning the availability of cover damages is not enforceable. The court goes on to conclude that even if the writing is only a partial integration, the agreement is not enforceable. Under 2–202(b) the latter conclusion is correct only if the agreement concerning cover is not a "consistent additional term."

Why does the court conclude that the agreement concerning the availability of cover damages is not consistent with the writing? What test(s) does the court apply to determine if the agreement is consistent with the writing?

The relevant language of 2–202 is

Terms . . . set forth in a writing . . . may not be contradicted by evidence of any prior agreement . . . but may be explained or supplemented . . . by evidence of consistent additional terms. . . .

Note that in the case of a partial integration, the statute excludes terms that "contradict" the writing but enforces terms that are "consistent" with the writing. Thus it seems to create two categories of terms, contradictory and consistent. This is true, however, only if "consistent" means "does not contradict the writing." If, as the court in *ARB* holds, "consistent" means something other than "does not contradict," viz., "is harmonious with," then the statute creates *three* categories: contradictory, harmonious, and non-contradictory but non-harmonious. Are terms in this third category enforceable? What basis for your answer is there in 2–202?

2. How helpful is Official Comment 3? Does it address the question whether the additional term is consistent or whether the writing is completely integrated?

3. Assume the court in *ARB* concludes that the writing is not a "complete and exclusive statement of the terms of the agreement." Even if the court is wrong in holding that the test for "consistent" is whether the prior agreement is "harmonious with" the writing, the court reached the correct result. Do you see why?

Noble v. Logan-Dees Chevrolet-Buick, Inc.

Mississippi Supreme Court, 1974.
293 So.2d 14.

■ SUGG, JUSTICE. . . .

Logan-Dees filed suit against Noble and alleged that it sold Noble a 1972 Buick Electra for the following consideration: trade-in of one 1970 wrecked Chevrolet El Camino, trade-in of one 1971 Dodge Charger and delivery to Logan-Dees of the proceeds of an insurance check covering the

---

differences in scope—broader as to the kind of expenses included, narrower as to application (the deleted sentence applied only to a contract default)—between the reprocurement provision of the contract and the "cover" remedy under the U.C.C.

wrecked 1970 Chevrolet El Camino in the amount of $1,532.66 and payment of $2,150.00 cash. Logan-Dees further alleged that it delivered Noble the 1972 Buick, accepted delivery of the two automobiles traded in, accepted payment of $2,150 with the promise of Noble to deliver the insurance check as soon as he received it. [When Noble failed to turn over the insurance check, Logan-Dees sued and recovered $1,532.66. The intermediate appellate court affirmed.]

At the trial Logan-Dees introduced its contract with Noble entitled "Retail Buyer's Order" prepared by it showing that Noble agreed to purchase a new automobile which was described only by stock number, model and color and to pay the following consideration:

Total cash price		$6,615.00
Cash down payment	46.40	
Used car allowance	4,418.60	
		4,465.00
Balance payable		$2,150.00

The contract was duly executed by both parties and contained the following provision:

> This order is not binding on dealer until accepted by dealer in writing. I have read the matter printed on the back hereof and agree to it as a part of this order the same as if it were printed above my signature. *The front and back of this order comprises the entire agreement pertaining to this purchase and no other agreement of any kind, verbal understanding or promise whatsoever, will be recognized.* Receipt of a copy of this order is hereby acknowledged. (Emphasis supplied.)

The contract was prepared and signed after oral negotiations between Noble and King, the salesman who handled the transaction for Logan-Dees. There is a conflict in the testimony as to when the contract was signed. King testified that it was signed at the time the 1972 Buick was delivered to Noble, but Noble testified that it was signed on a date previous to the delivery of the automobile. Regardless of the date the contract was signed, it is a writing expressing the contract between the parties.

Before delivery of the automobile, Noble paid Logan-Dees $46.40 and on the day of delivery gave the salesman a check for $2,150 and transferred title to the 1971 Charger and 1970 El Camino mentioned in the contract.

King testified that, when the Buick was delivered and the contract signed, Noble agreed to deliver the insurance check to Logan-Dees as part of the consideration. The insurance check is not mentioned in the contract and Noble objected on the ground that such testimony was an effort to alter the terms of a written agreement by parol evidence. The objection was overruled and judgment entered as aforesaid.

Noble contends that under the provisions of Miss.Code Ann. § 75–2–202 (1972) the court erred by permitting parol testimony contradicting the terms of the agreement of the parties as expressed in the contract. Logan-Dees contends that it was entitled to offer parol testimony under subsections (a) and (b) of the statute.

We hold that, under the facts as disclosed by the record, Logan-Dees was not entitled to offer parol testimony under subsection (a) because the evidence does not disclose a course of dealing and usage of trade as defined in Miss.Code Ann. § 75–1–205 [revised 1–303(b)–(c)] neither does it disclose a course of performance as defined by Miss.Code Ann. § 75–2–208 (1972) [revised 1–303(a)].

We hold that Logan-Dees was not entitled to introduce parol testimony under subsection (b) because the evidence offered was not of consistent additional terms, but the evidence offered would show a different consideration from that expressed in the writing. We also hold that parol evidence was not admissible under subsection (b) because the contract, by its own terms, was a complete and exclusive statement of the terms of the agreement of the parties.

If Logan-Dees expected to receive the proceeds of the insurance check as part of the consideration for the car sold to Noble, it would have been a very simple matter to include such a provision in the contract. Where parties, without any fraud or mistake, have deliberately put their contract in writing, the writing is not only the best, but the only, evidence of their agreement.

We hold that the court erred in receiving parol evidence to vary the terms of the written contract and that the parol evidence was not admissible either under Miss.Code Ann. § 75–2–202 (1972) or under the common-law parol evidence rule.

Reversed and rendered.

QUESTIONS

1.   The decision of the court benefits the consumer in this case. But the decision is potentially very disadvantageous to consumers generally. Do you see why?

2.   The Retail Buyer's Order stated simply, "Used car allowance," evidently referring to the trade-ins. What if the transaction had fallen apart when Noble came to pick up his new Electra, tendering just the Charger and the $2,150 cash: would Logan-Dees be allowed to prove that "Used car allowance" means the Charger and the El Camino? If so, what are the implications of this conclusion on the actual case?

Does 2–202 permit evidence of the private understanding or agreement of the parties as to the meaning of a term if the term is found to be ambiguous? On what statutory language do you rely to support the conclusion you reach? Is it possible to argue that, under the Code, evidence of the private agreement or understanding of the parties is admissible without a prior finding of ambiguity?

3.   Is the writing in *Noble* a complete integration or a partial integration? Compare the approach of the court in *ARB* to resolving this question.

4.   The court states that if the writing is viewed as a partial integration, the alleged agreement concerning the insurance proceeds is not a "consistent additional term." What test does the court use to arrive at this conclusion. Is the conclusion consistent with the approach in *ARB*?

5.   According to the court, the salesman testified that the Retail Buyer's Order was signed when Noble picked up his new car and dropped off the trade-ins. Noble, on the other hand, testified that they signed it when they struck the deal, some time before delivery of the new car. The court disregarded this difference, evidently believing it was irrelevant. Why was the court wrong?

6.   CISG and the parol evidence rule. The Convention on Contracts for the International Sale of Goods does not contain a parol evidence rule. Instead, it addresses the matter in terms of interpreting the understanding of the parties. It leaves each of the parties free to attempt to persuade the court that they agreed on matters that do not appear in the written contract.

With respect to interpreting the language of a contract, Article 8 adopts a qualified objective approach. Section (2) calls for statements and conduct of a party to be interpreted according to the understanding of a reasonable person in the position of the other party. In arriving at this understanding, section (3) requires the court to give due consideration to "all relevant circumstances of the case," including the negotiations, any course of dealing or usage of trade, and the subsequent conduct of the parties. It specifically states that the court may take negotiations into account in determining the meaning of a contract provision. All this, however, is subject to the provision in section (1) that statements and conduct are to be interpreted according to one party's subjective intention if the other party knew of that intent (or could not have been unaware of it). Please read Article 8.

In MCC-Marble Ceramic Center, Inc. v. Ceramica Nuova d'Agostino, S.P.A., 144 F.3d 1384 (11th Cir.1998), a U.S. buyer (MCC) contracted in Italy with an Italian supplier of ceramic tile. The buyer signed a contract written in Italian, which the buyer could not read. The contract specified that the buyer was aware of and agreed to terms on the reverse side. A dispute arose, and the seller asserted a claim under one of those terms. In response, the buyer relied on Article 8(1) and pointed to affidavits by representatives of both the buyer and the seller that the buyer did not intend for the terms on the reverse side to be part of the contract and that the seller knew that this was not the buyer's intent. The District Court rejected this argument, applied the parol evidence rule to exclude any agreement that the terms on the reverse side would not apply, and gave summary judgment for the seller. The buyer appealed, and the appellate court reversed:

> Contrary to the magistrate judge's report, which the district court
> endorsed and adopted, article 8(1) does not focus on interpreting

the parties' statements alone. Although we agree with the magistrate judge's conclusion that no "interpretation" of the contract's *terms* could support MCC's position, article 8(1) also requires a court to consider subjective intent while interpreting the *conduct* of the parties. The CISG's language, therefore, requires courts to consider evidence of a party's subjective intent when signing a contract if the other party to the contract was aware of that intent at the time. This is precisely the type of evidence that MCC has provided through the Silingardi, Copelli, and Monzon affidavits, which discuss not only Monzon's intent as MCC's representative but also discuss the intent of D'Agostino's representatives and their knowledge that Monzon did not intend to agree to the terms on the reverse of the form contract. This acknowledgment that D'Agostino's representatives were aware of Monzon's subjective intent puts this case squarely within article 8(1) of the CISG, and therefore requires the court to consider MCC's evidence as it interprets the parties' conduct.[11]

II. PAROL EVIDENCE AND THE CISG

Given our determination that the magistrate judge and the district court should have considered MCC's affidavits regarding the parties' subjective intentions, we must address a question of first impression in this circuit: whether the parol evidence rule, which bars evidence of an earlier oral contract that contradicts or varies the terms of a subsequent or contemporaneous written contract, plays any role in cases involving the CISG. We begin by observing that the parol evidence rule, contrary to its title, is substantive rule of law, not a rule of evidence. See II E. Allen Farnsworth, Farnsworth on Contracts, § 7.2 at 194 (1990). The rule does not purport to exclude a particular type of evidence as an "untrustworthy or undesirable" way of proving a fact, but prevents a litigant from attempting to show "the fact itself—the fact that the terms of the agreement are other than those in the writing." Id. As such, a federal district court cannot simply apply the parol evidence rule as a procedural matter—as it might if excluding a particular type of evidence under the Federal Rules of Evidence, which apply in federal court regardless of the source of the substantive rule of decision. Cf. id. § 7.2 at 196.[13]

---

[11] Without this crucial acknowledgment, we would interpret the contract and the parties' actions according to article 8(2), which directs courts to rely on objective evidence of the parties' intent. On the facts of this case it seems readily apparent that MCC's affidavits provide no evidence that Monzon's actions would have made his alleged subjective intent not to be bound by the terms of the contract known to "the understanding that a reasonable person . . . would have had in the same circumstances." CISG, art 8(2).

[13] An example demonstrates this point. The CISG provides that a contract for the sale of goods need not be in writing and that the parties may prove the contract "by any means, including witnesses." CISG, art. 11. Nevertheless, a party seeking to prove a contract in such a manner in federal court could not do so in a way that violated in the rule against hearsay. See Fed. R. Evid. 802 (barring hearsay evidence). A federal district court applies the Federal Rules of Evidence because these rules are considered procedural, regardless of the source of the law

The CISG itself contains no express statement on the role of parol evidence. It is clear, however, that the drafters of the CISG were comfortable with the concept of permitting parties to rely on oral contracts because they eschewed any statutes of fraud provision and expressly provided for the enforcement of oral contracts. Compare CISG, art. 11 (a contract of sale need not be concluded or evidenced in writing) with U.C.C. § 2–201 (precluding the enforcement of oral contracts for the sale of goods involving more than $500). Moreover, article 8(3) of the CISG expressly directs courts to give "due consideration . . . to all relevant circumstances of the case including the negotiations . . ." to determine the intent of the parties. Given article 8(1)'s directive to use the intent of the parties to interpret their statements and conduct, article 8(3) is a clear instruction to admit and consider parol evidence regarding the negotiations to the extent they reveal the parties' subjective intent.

. . .

Our reading of article 8(3) as a rejection of the parol evidence rule . . . is in accordance with the great weight of academic commentary on the issue. As one scholar has explained:

> The language of Article 8(3) that "due consideration is to be given to *all relevant* circumstances of the case" seems adequate to override any domestic rule that would bar a tribunal from considering the relevance of other agreements. . . . Article 8(3) relieves tribunals from domestic rules that might bar them from "considering" any evidence between the parties that is relevant. This added flexibility for interpretation is consistent with a growing body of opinion that the "parol evidence rule" has been an embarrassment for the administration of modern transactions.

Honnold, Uniform Law § 110 at 170–71.[17] . . . [A]lthough jurisdictions in the United States have found the parol evidence rule helpful to promote good faith and uniformity in contract, as well as an appropriate answer to the question of how much consideration to give parol evidence, a wide number of other States Party to the CISG have rejected the rule in their domestic jurisdictions. One of the primary factors motivating the negotiation and adoption of the CISG was to provide parties to international contracts for the sale of goods with some degree of certainty as to the principles of law that would govern potential disputes and remove the previous doubt regarding which party's legal system

that governs the substantive decision. Cf. Farnsworth on Contracts § 7.2 at 196 & n. 16 (citing cases).

[17] See also Louis F. Del Duca, et al., Sales Under the Uniform Commercial Code and the Convention on International Sale of Goods, 173–74 (1993); Henry D. Gabriel, A Primer on the United Nations Convention on the International Sale of Goods: From the Perspective of the Uniform Commercial Code, 7 Ind. Int'l & Comp. L. Rev. 279, 281 (1997) ("Subjective intent is given primary consideration . . . . [Article 8] allows open-ended reliance on parol evidence"). . . .

might otherwise apply. See Letter of Transmittal from Ronald Reagan, President of the United States, to the United States Senate, reprinted at 15 U.S.C. app. 70, 71 (1997). Courts applying the CISG cannot, therefore, upset the parties' reliance on the Convention by substituting familiar principles of domestic law when the Convention requires a different result. We may only achieve the directives of good faith and uniformity in contracts under the CISG by interpreting and applying the plain language of article 8(3) as written and obeying its directive to consider this type of parol evidence.

This is not to say that parties to an international contract for the sale of goods cannot depend on written contracts or that parol evidence regarding subjective contractual intent need always prevent a party relying on a written agreement from securing summary judgment. To the contrary, most cases will not present a situation (as exists in this case) in which both parties to the contract acknowledge a subjective intent not to be bound by the terms of a pre-printed writing. In most cases, therefore, article 8(2) of the CISG will apply, and objective evidence will provide the basis for the court's decision. Consequently, a party to a contract governed by the CISG will not be able to avoid the terms of a contract and force a jury trial simply by submitting an affidavit which states that he or she did not have the subjective intent to be bound by the contract's terms. . . . Moreover, to the extent parties wish to avoid parol evidence problems they can do so by including a merger clause in their agreement that extinguishes any and all prior agreements and understandings not expressed in the writing.[19]

Considering MCC's affidavits in this case, however, we conclude that the magistrate judge and the district court improperly granted summary judgment in favor of D'Agostino. Although the affidavits are, as D'Agostino observes, relatively conclusory and unsupported by facts that would objectively establish MCC's intent not to be bound by the conditions on the reverse of the form, article 8(1) requires a court to consider evidence of a party's subjective intent when the other party was aware of it, and the Silingardi and Copelli affidavits provide that evidence. This is not to say that the affidavits are conclusive proof of what the parties intended. A reasonable finder of fact, for example, could disregard testimony that purportedly sophisticated international merchants signed a contract without intending to be bound as simply too incredible to believe and hold MCC to the conditions

---

[19] See Ronald A. Brand & Harry M. Fletchner, Arbitration and Contract Formation in International Trade: First Interpretations of the U.N. Sales Convention, 12 J.L. & Com. 239, 252 (1993) (arguing that article 8(3) of the CISG will not permit the consideration of parol evidence when the parties have expressly excluded oral modifications of the contract pursuant to article 29); see also I Albert Kritzer, Guide to Practical Applications of the United Nations Convention on Contracts for the International Sale of Goods 125 (1989) (counseling the use of a merger clause to compensate for the absence of a parol evidence rule in the CISG).

printed on the reverse of the contract. Nevertheless, the affidavits raise an issue of material fact regarding the parties' intent to incorporate the provisions on the reverse of the form contract. If the finder of fact determines that the parties did not intend to rely on those provisions, then the more general provisions of the CISG will govern the outcome of the dispute.

———

b.   TRADE USAGE, COURSE OF DEALING, COURSE OF PERFORMANCE

Problem. In August 2018 Pulaski Packaging, a newcomer to the bottling industry, contracted to sell 500,000 plastic bottles to Sodas Supreme. The contract was embodied in a lengthy written document stating that it contained the complete agreement of the parties. The document specified a price and stated that the bottles were to be delivered during calendar year 2019 from time to time as requested by Sodas. By January 2020 Sodas had not requested delivery, and Pulaski now sues for profits lost as a result of Sodas' nonperformance. Sodas wants to introduce evidence that the custom in the bottle industry is for a seller of bottles to deliver samples, to demonstrate that it is capable of producing commercially acceptable bottles, and that Pulaski never delivered any samples. Pulaski claims that the written contract is a complete integration, that it is not ambiguous, and that the evidence should not be admitted or considered. What should the court do: does 2–202 preclude consideration of this evidence?

Nanakuli Paving & Rock Co. v. Shell Oil Co., Inc.

United States Court of Appeals, Ninth Circuit, 1981.
664 F.2d 772.

■ HOFFMAN, DISTRICT JUDGE.

Appellant Nanakuli Paving and Rock Company (Nanakuli) initially filed this breach of contract action against appellee Shell Oil Company (Shell) in Hawaiian State Court in February, 1976. Nanakuli, the second largest asphaltic paving contractor in Hawaii, had bought all its asphalt requirements from 1963 to 1974 from Shell under two long-term supply contracts [in which the price was specified as Shell's posted price on the date of each delivery]; its suit charged Shell with breach of the later 1969 contract. The jury returned a verdict of $220,800 for Nanakuli on its first claim, which is that Shell breached the 1969 contract in January, 1974, by failing to price protect Nanakuli on 7200 tons of asphalt at the time Shell raised the price for asphalt from $44 to $76. Nanakuli's theory is that price-protection, as a usage of the asphaltic paving trade in Hawaii, was incorporated into the 1969 agreement between the parties, as demonstrated by the routine use of price protection by suppliers to that trade, and reinforced by the way in which Shell actually performed the 1969 contract up until 1974. Price protection, appellant claims, required that Shell hold the price on the tonnage Nanakuli had already committed because Nanakuli had incorporated that price into bids put out to or contracts awarded by general contractors and government agencies. The District Judge set aside the verdict and granted Shell's motion for judgment n.o.v., which decision we vacate. We reinstate the jury verdict because we find that, viewing the evidence as a whole, there was substantial evidence to support a finding by reasonable jurors that Shell breached its contract by failing to provide protection for Nanakuli in 1974. . . .

Nanakuli [argues that] Shell's failure to offer price protection in 1974 was a breach of the 1969 contract. [It argues that] all material suppliers to the asphaltic paving trade in Hawaii followed the trade usage of price protection and thus it should be assumed, under the U.C.C., that the parties intended to incorporate price protection into their 1969 agreement. This is so, Nanakuli continues, even though the written contract provided for price to be "Shell's Posted Price at time of delivery," F.O.B. Honolulu. . . . Nanakuli points out that Shell had price protected it on the two occasions of price increases under the 1969 contract other than the 1974 increase. In 1970 and 1971 Shell extended the old price for four and three months, respectively, after an announced increase. This was done, in the words of Shell's agent in Hawaii, in order to permit Nanakuli to "chew up" tonnage already committed at Shell's old price.

. . .

[W]e hold that although the express price terms of Shell's posted price of delivery may seem, at first glance, inconsistent with a trade usage of price protection at time of increases in price, a closer reading shows that the jury could have reasonably construed price protection as consistent with the express term. We reach this holding for several reasons. First, we are persuaded by a careful reading of the U.C.C., one of whose underlying purposes is to promote flexibility in the expansion of commercial practices and which rather drastically overhauls this particular area of the law. The Code would have us look beyond the printed pages of the contract to usages and the entire commercial context of the agreement in order to reach the "true understanding" of the parties. Second, decisions of other courts in similar situations have managed to reconcile such trade usages with seemingly contradictory express terms where the prior course of dealings between the parties, trade usages, and the actual performance of the contract by the parties showed a clear intent by the parties to incorporate those usages into the agreement or to give to the express term the particular meaning provided by those usages, even at times varying the apparent meaning of the express terms. Third, the delineation by thoughtful commentators of the degree of consistency demanded between express terms and usage is that a usage should be allowed to modify the apparent agreement, as seen in the written terms, as long as it does not totally negate it. We believe the usage here falls within the limits set forth by commentators and generally followed in the better reasoned decisions. The manner in which price protection was actually practiced in Hawaii was that it only came into play at times of price increases and only for work committed prior to those increases on non-escalating contracts. Thus, it formed an exception to, rather than a total negation of, the express price term of "Shell's Posted Price at time of delivery." Our decision is reinforced by the overwhelming nature of the evidence that price protection was routinely practiced by all suppliers in the small Oahu market of the asphaltic paving trade and therefore was known to Shell; that it was a realistic necessity to operate in that market and thus vital to Nanakuli's ability to get large government contracts and to Shell's continued business growth on Oahu; and that it therefore constituted an intended part of the agreement, as that term is broadly defined by the Code, between Shell and Nanakuli.

. . .

V. Scope of Trade Usage

The validity of the jury verdict in this case depends on [several] legal questions. First, how broad was the trade to whose usages Shell was bound under its 1969 agreement with Nanakuli: did it extend to the Hawaiian asphaltic paving trade or was it limited merely to the purchase and sale of asphalt, which would only include evidence of practices by Shell and Chevron.[a] Second, were the two instances of price protection of Nanakuli by Shell in 1970 and 1971 waivers of the 1969 contract as a matter of law or was the jury entitled to find that they constituted a course of performance of the contract? Third, could the jury have construed an express contract term of Shell's posted price at delivery as reasonably consistent with a trade usage and Shell's course of performance of the 1969 contract of price protection, which consisted of charging the old price at times of price increases, either for a period of time or for specific tonnage committed at a fixed price in non-escalating contracts? . . .

We approach the first issue in this case mindful that an underlying purpose of the U.C.C. as enacted in Hawaii is to allow for liberal interpretation of commercial usages. . . .

The Code defines usage of trade as "any practice or method of dealing having such regularity of observance in a *place, vocation or trade* as to justify an expectation that it will be observed with respect to the transaction in question." Id. § 490:1–205(2) [revised 1–303(c)] (emphasis supplied). We understand the use of the word "or" to mean that parties can be bound by a usage common to the *place* they are in business, even if it is not the usage of their particular vocation or trade. . . . The drafters' Comments say that trade usage is to be used to reach the " * * * commercial meaning of the agreement * * * " by interpreting the

---

    a   Only Chevron and Shell sold asphalt on Oahu.—Eds.

language "as meaning what it may fairly be expected to mean to parties involved in the particular transaction *in a given locality or* in a given *vocation or trade.*" Id., Comment 4 [revised 1–303(c), Comment 3] (emphasis supplied). The inference ... is that a usage need not necessarily be one practiced by members of the party's own trade or vocation to be binding *if* it is so commonly practiced in a locality that a party should be aware of it.... A party is always held to conduct generally observed by members of his chosen trade because the other party is justified in so assuming unless he indicates otherwise. He is held to more general business practices to the extent of his actual knowledge of those practices or to the degree his ignorance of those practices is not excusable: they were so generally practiced he should have been aware of them.

. . .

[E]ven if Shell did not "regularly deal" with aggregate supplies,[b] it did deal constantly and almost exclusively on Oahu with one asphalt paver. It therefore should have been aware of the usage of Nanakuli and other asphaltic pavers to bid at fixed prices and therefore receive price protection from their materials suppliers due to the refusal by government agencies to accept escalation clauses. Therefore, we do not find the lower court abused its discretion or misread the Code as applied to the peculiar facts of this case in ruling that the applicable trade was the asphaltic paving trade in Hawaii. In so ruling, the judge undoubtedly took into account Shell's half-million dollar investment in Oahu strictly because of a long-term commitment by Nanakuli, its actions as partner in promoting Nanakuli's expansion on Oahu, and the fact that its sales on Oahu were almost exclusively to Nanakuli for use in asphaltic paving. The wisdom of the pre-trial ruling was demonstrated by evidence at trial that Shell's agent in Hawaii stayed in close contact with Nanakuli and was knowledgeable about both the asphaltic paving market in general and Nanakuli's bidding procedures and economics in particular.

Shell argued not only that the definition of trade was too broad, but also that the practice itself was not sufficiently regular to reach the level of a usage and that Nanakuli failed to show with enough precision how the usage was carried out in order for a jury to calculate damages. The extent of a usage is ultimately a jury question. The Code provides, "The existence and scope of such a usage are to be proved as facts." Haw.Rev.Stat. § 490:1–205(2) [revised 1–303(c)].[27] The practice must have "such regularity of observance * * * as to justify an expectation that it will be observed * * *." A "regularly observed" practice of protection, of which Shell "should have been aware," was enough to constitute a usage

---

[b] Asphalt and aggregate are the two components of asphalt paving. There was evidence that aggregate suppliers also provided price protection in the same way that Chevron and Shell did.—Eds.

[27] Written trade codes, however, are left to the court to interpret.

that Nanakuli had reason to believe was incorporated into the agreement.[28]

Nanakuli went beyond proof of a regular observance. It proved and offered to prove[29] that price protection was probably a universal practice by suppliers to the asphaltic paving trade in 1969.[30] . . .

Shell next argues that, even if such a usage existed, its outlines were not precise enough to determine whether Shell would have extended the old price for Nanakuli for several months or would have charged the old price on the volume of tonnage committed at that price. The jury awarded Nanakuli damages based on the specific tonnage committed before the price increase of 1974. Shell says the jury could not have ascertained with enough certainty how price protection was carried out to calculate such an award for Nanakuli. The argument is not persuasive. The Code provides, "The remedies provided by this chapter shall be liberally administered to the end that the aggrieved party may be put in as good a position as if the other party had fully performed * * *." Id. § 490:1–106(1) [revised 1–305(a)]. The Comments list as one of three purposes of this section "to reject any doctrine that damages must be calculable with mathematical accuracy. Compensatory damages are often at best approximate: they have to be proved with whatever definiteness and accuracy the facts permit, but no more." Id., Comment 1. Nanakuli got advance notices of each but the disputed increase by Shell, as well as an extension of several months at the old price in 1970, 1971, 1977, and 1978. Shell protests that in 1970 and 1971 Nanakuli's protected tonnage only amounted to 3,300 and 1,100 tons, respectively. Chevron's price protection of H.B.[c] in 1969 however, is also part of the trade usage; H.B.'s protection amounted to 12,000 tons. The increase in Nanakuli's tonnage by 1974 is explained by its growth since the 1970 and 1971 increases.

In addition, the scope of protection offered by a particular usage is left to the jury:

In cases of a well established line of usage varying from the general rules of this Act where the precise amount of the variation has not been worked out into a single standard, the party relying on the usage is entitled, in any event, to the minimum variation demonstrated. The whole is not to be disregarded because no particular line of detail has been

---

[28] White and Summers write that Code requirements for proving a usage are "far less stringent" than the old ones for custom. "A usage of trade need not be *well known,* let alone 'universal.' It only needs to be regular enough that the parties expect it to be observed." White & Summers, supra § 3–3 at 87 (emphasis supplied). "Note particularly in 1–205(1) & (2) [revised 1–303(c)] that it is not necessary for both parties to be consciously aware of the trade usage. It is enough if the trade usage is such as to 'justify an expectation' of its observance." Id. at 84.

[29] Nanakuli made an offer of proof, which the judge rejected as not sufficiently relevant to the asphaltic paving trade, that cement suppliers routinely price protected pavers for years.

[30] All evidence was that trade usage continued to be universally practiced after 1969, even by Shell.

[c] Nanakuli's major competitor.—Eds.

established. In case a dominant pattern [of usage] has been fairly evidenced, the party relying on the usage is entitled * * * to go to the trier of fact on the question of whether such dominant pattern has been incorporated into the agreement.

Id. § 490:1–205, Comment 9 [revised 1–303, Comment 8]. . . .

VI. . . . Course of Performance

Course of performance under the Code is the action of the parties in carrying out the contract at issue, whereas course of dealing consists of relations between the parties *prior* to signing that contract. Evidence of the latter was excluded by the District Judge; evidence of the former consisted of Shell's price protection of Nanakuli in 1970 and 1971. Shell protested that the jury could not have found that those two instances of price protection amounted to a course of performance of its 1969 contract, relying on two Code comments. First, one instance does not constitute a course of performance. "A single occasion of conduct does not fall within the language of this section * * *." Haw.Rev.Stat. § 490:2–208, Comment 4. Although the Comment rules out one instance, it does not further delineate how many acts are needed to form a course of performance. The prior occasions here were only two, but they constituted the only occasions before 1974 that would call for such conduct. In addition, the language used by a top asphalt official of Shell in connection with the first price protection of Nanakuli indicated that Shell felt that Nanakuli was entitled to some form of price protection. On that occasion in 1970 Blee, who had negotiated the contract with Nanakuli and was familiar with exactly what terms Shell was bound to by that agreement, wrote of the need to "bargain" with Nanakuli over the extent of price protection to be given, indicating that some price protection was a legal right of Nanakuli's under the 1969 agreement.

. . . The jury's interpretation of those acts as a course of performance was bolstered by evidence offered by Shell that it again price protected Nanakuli on the only two occasions of post-1974 price increases, in 1977 and 1978.[31]

VII. Express Terms As Reasonably Consistent With Usage and Course of Performance

Perhaps one of the most fundamental departures of the Code from prior contract law is found in the parol evidence rule and the definition of an agreement between two parties. Under the U.C.C., an agreement goes beyond the written words on a piece of paper. " 'Agreement' means the bargain of the parties in fact as found in their language or by

---

[31] Bohner testified on direct for Shell at the 1978 trial that the two later instances of price protection occurred "this" year and "last" year, by which he could have meant 1976 and 1977. Bohner's testimony was that on those later occasions Shell gave Nanakuli six and three or four months' notice of an increase to allow Nanakuli to buy tonnage it had committed at the old price. He defined Shell's actions as "in effect carryover pricing." The jury's finding was reasonable in light of the circumstances of universal price protection by asphalt and aggregate suppliers, as well as by Shell on all price increases except 1974.

implication from other circumstances including course of dealing or usage of trade or course of performance as provided in this chapter. . . ." Id. § 490:1–201(3) [revised 1–201(b)(3)]. Express terms, then, do not constitute the entire agreement, which must be sought also in evidence of usages, dealings, and performance of the contract itself. The purpose of evidence of usages, which are defined in the previous section, is to help to understand the entire agreement.

> [Usages are] a factor in reaching the commercial meaning of the agreement which the parties have made. The language used is to be interpreted as meaning what it may fairly be expected to mean to parties involved in the particular commercial transaction in a given locality or in a given vocation or trade * * *. Part of the agreement of the parties * * * is to be sought for in the usages of trade which furnish the background and give particular meaning to the language used, and are the framework of common understanding controlling any general rules of law which hold only when there is no such understanding.

Id. § 490:1–205, Comment 4 [revised 1–303, Comment 3]. . . .

A commercial agreement, then, is broader than the written paper and its meaning is to be determined not just by the language used by them in the written contract but "by their action, read and interpreted in the light of commercial practices and other surrounding circumstances. The measure and background for interpretation are set by the commercial context, which may explain and supplement even the language of a formal or final writing." Id., Comment 1 [revised 1–303, Comment 1]. Performance, usages, and prior dealings are important enough to be admitted always, even for a final and complete agreement; only if they cannot be reasonably reconciled with the express terms of the contract are they not binding on the parties. "The express terms of an agreement and an applicable course of dealing or usage of trade shall be construed wherever reasonable as consistent with each other; but when such construction is unreasonable express terms control both course of dealing and usage of trade and course of dealing controls usage of trade." Id. § 490:1–205(4) [revised 1–303(e)].

. . .

Our study of the Code provisions and Comments, then, form the first basis of our holding that a trade usage to price protect pavers at times of price increases for work committed on nonescalating contracts could reasonably be construed as consistent with an express term of seller's posted price at delivery. Since the agreement of the parties is broader than the express terms and includes usages, which may even add terms to the agreement, and since the commercial background provided by those usages is vital to an understanding of the agreement, we follow the Code's mandate to proceed on the assumption that the parties have included those usages unless they cannot reasonably be construed as consistent with the express terms.

. . .

Some guidelines can be offered as to how usage evidence can be allowed to modify a contract. First, the court must allow a check on usage evidence by demanding that it be sufficiently definite and widespread to prevent unilateral post-hoc revision of contract terms by one party. The Code's intent is to put usage evidence on an objective basis. . . .

Evidence of a trade usage does not need to be protected against perjury because, as one commentator has written, "an outside standard does exist to help judge the truth of the assertion that the parties intended the usage to control the particular dispute: the existence and scope of the usage can be determined from other members of the trade." [R. Kirst, Usage of Trade and Course of Dealing: Subversion of UCC Theory, 1977 University of Ill. L.F. 811, 839.] . . . [Another author] writes, "Astonishing as it will seem to most practicing attorneys, under the Code it will be possible in some cases to use custom to contradict the written agreement * * *. Therefore usage may be used to 'qualify' the agreement, which presumably means to 'cut down' express terms although not to negate them entirely." [J. Levie, Trade Usage and Custom Under the Common Law and The Uniform Commercial Code, 40 N.Y.U. L.R. 1101, 1112 (1965).] Here, the express price term was "Shell's Posted Price at time of delivery." A total negation of that term would be that the buyer was to set the price. It is a less than complete negation of the term that an unstated exception exists at times of price increases, at which times the old price is to be charged, for a certain period or for a specified tonnage, on work already committed at the lower price on nonescalating contracts. Such a usage forms a broad and important exception to the express term, but does not swallow it entirely. Therefore, we hold that, under these particular facts, a reasonable jury could have found that price protection was incorporated into the 1969 agreement between Nanakuli and Shell and that price protection was reasonably consistent with the express term of seller's posted price at delivery.

. . . [W]e reverse the judgment of the District Court and reinstate the jury verdict for Nanakuli in the amount of $220,800, plus interest according to law.

Reversed and remanded with directions to enter final judgment.

QUESTIONS AND NOTES

1. What does it take for a term to become part of a contract by reason of course of dealing? In *Belden v. AEC* (reproduced in part at page 75 supra, on 2–207), in which the term in question (a limitation on damages in the event of a breach) had appeared without objection in more than 100 transactions before the transaction at issue in that case. The court stated:

Our research shows that most cases involving the repeated exchange of forms does not in and of itself establish a course of dealing between the parties that incorporates the terms of those forms into the parties' contract under Section 2–207(3). See Step-Saver Data Sys., Inc. v. Wyse Tech., 939 F.2d 91, 103–04 (3rd Cir.1991); PCS Nitrogen Fertilizer, L.P. v. Christy Refractories, L.L.C., 225 F.3d 974, 982 (8th Cir.2000) ("Moreover, the fact that Christy repeatedly sent its customer acknowledgment form to PCS does not establish a course of dealing; the multiple forms merely demonstrated Christy's desire to include the arbitration clause as a term of the contract.").

We agree ... Belden's repeated sending of the order acknowledgement containing the same limitation on damages and same requirement of assent by AEC does not in and of itself establish a course of dealing between the parties showing that the parties agreed to Belden's terms and conditions of sale. At best, it shows that Belden wanted AEC to assent to its terms and conditions, which AEC never did.

885 N.E.2d 751, 759–60 (Ind.App.2008).

2.   Please look at 2–202. Under what circumstances does 2–202 provide that an oral agreement that is consistent with the writing is not part of the contract?

Under what circumstances does 2–202 provide that a trade usage is not part of the contract?

3.   Note the difference in phrasing of 2–202(a) and 1–303(d). Does the difference have any significance?

4.   Problem. Miller Paving Co. phoned Mobil Petroleum to inquire about purchasing its requirements of asphalt for the next three years. After extensive discussion, they agreed that Mobil would supply Miller with its requirements of asphalt, at Mobil's posted price at the time of delivery, for three years. In confirmation of this agreement, Miller sent its standard form. In the small print on the back of Miller's form is a term stating that in the event of non-delivery of asphalt, Miller is entitled to an order of specific performance.

a.   Assume there is a trade usage that when asphalt sellers raise their posted prices, they hold to the pre-raise price with respect to asphalt that the buyers already have committed to third parties. Is this trade usage part of the agreement between Miller and Mobil?

b.   During the phone call described above, Mobil told Miller, "You're talking about a very large quantity of asphalt. Therefore, I can't give you the usual price protection." Miller replied, "I understand." Under 2–202 is the trade usage part of the contract? Under 1–303?

5.   In what way does 1–303(e) qualify 1–303(d)? What is the price term in *Nanakuli*? The court holds that even though the writing is a complete integration, the price-protection trade usage is part of the contract, because it is not a "total negation" of the price term in the writing. Is this consistent with *ARB v. E-Systems*? See 2–202, Official Comment 2. Are both courts correct?

6. Revised Article 1 moved the content of 2–208 out of Article 2 and into 1–303, thereby consolidating course of performance, course of dealing, and trade usage in one section, applicable to the entire Code. When states enacted revised Article 1, they repealed 2–208 in its entirety. Many of the Official Comments to 2–208 have been moved to revised 1–303, but, notably not Comment 4, quoted in Part VI of the *Nanakuli* opinion (a single occasion of conduct is not a course of performance).

B. TERMS OUTSIDE THE AGREEMENT: "STATUTORY TERMS"

Article 2 provides, mainly (but not exclusively) in Part 3, a number of statutory terms to be used to fill gaps in the contract when missing terms cannot be supplied through resort to course of performance, course of dealing, or usage of trade. Parties may omit a term through inadvertence or ignorance, or they may omit it by design, planning to agree on it at a later time but then not being able to come to an agreement. By setting forth statutory terms, the Code supplies a commonly accepted term on the matter and perhaps prevents the contract from failing for lack of a reasonable basis for enforcement.

Statutory terms are of three types. Some are gap fillers, as described above, when the parties fail entirely to address a particular term, such as the place or time for performance. Others elaborate or set parameters on express terms. Examples include 2–305, which elaborates on the price term when the parties do not fix it at the outset, and 2–306, which places limits on the quantity term when the quantity is specified as the requirements of the buyer or the output of the seller. The third type appears in 1–304 and dictates how the parties are to go about performing their obligations and enforcing their rights under the contract. It provides, "Every contract or duty within the Uniform Commercial Code imposes an obligation of good faith in its performance and enforcement." The force of this section is pervasive: it affects every obligation of the parties, whether that obligation arises by virtue of express agreement, usage of trade, or gap filler.

In case of conflict, it is clear that the gap fillers are subordinated in rank to course of performance, course of dealing, and usage of trade, and this is sound because course of performance, course of dealing, and usage of trade are methods to find implied terms of the contract. These implied terms are part of the agreement itself ("bargain of the parties in fact"), whereas the gap fillers are not. In this connection, it is essential to heed the statement of 1–303, Official Comment 3, which speaks of usage of trade but is equally applicable to course of performance and course of dealing. Please read that Comment now.

Many statutory terms are signaled by the phrase, "unless otherwise agreed." This language makes it clear that the provision that follows is to be used only in those cases where the parties have not expressly or impliedly agreed on the matter at hand. It would have been good draftsmanship to have flagged all the statutory terms in the UCC in this manner, but unfortunately this was not done. No negative inference is to be drawn, however, from the fact that some terms are prefaced with the unless-otherwise-agreed language and others are not, because 1–302(c) provides, "The presence in certain provisions of the Uniform Commercial Code of the phrase 'unless otherwise agreed' or words of similar import, does not imply that the effect of other provisions may not be varied by agreement under this section." Indeed, the parties have the competence to displace most provisions of Article 2. Only mandatory provisions, like good faith, diligence, reasonableness, care, unconscionability, and others that are specifically made generally or partially binding irrespective of the expressed will of the parties, cannot be disclaimed by agreement. (E.g., the parties have no competence under 2–725 to lower the period of the statute of limitations below one year.) This indicates that all non-mandatory provisions are, basically, gap fillers to be used only when the parties have not come to a different express or implied agreement regarding a particular term.

For purposes of applying statutory terms, therefore, two propositions may be stated: (1) all "unless-otherwise-agreed" terms are optional and are deferred in ranking to express and implied terms; (2) most other provisions of Article 2 are optional and are similarly deferred unless the context of the section in which they appear or some strong social policy in favor of them makes it clear that they are to be imposed irrespective of the wishes of the parties. Mandatory provisions, such as the statute of frauds, unconscionability, and the statute of limitations, displace express and implied terms of an agreement.

Assuming there is no express or implied agreement, not all missing terms may be filled by statutory terms. The rationale underlying the use of statutory terms is that they represent ordinary understanding about common matters and therefore most likely would have been used by the parties had they considered the term when they made their agreement. In short, statutory terms presuppose that normally the parties have omitted, through haste, ignorance, or forgetfulness, a routine term that subsequently has become important and that the fairest method to fill that missing term is to impose upon the parties the kind of term that normally is used by most parties in common, unexceptional deals. Therefore, controversial or exceptional terms will not be imposed in this manner. For example, a party who claims the contract calls for an arbitration of disputes would have to establish that contention by proving an express or implied term. In the absence of that proof, the party could not resort to a statutory term because Article 2 contains no provision calling for disputes to be resolved by arbitration.

The failure to establish an alleged missing term may mean that the contract cannot be enforced because of indefiniteness, but this is not necessarily the result. The court may enforce the contract despite the missing term if the total situation shows that the parties nevertheless intended to be contractually bound and if there is a reasonably certain basis for giving an appropriate remedy (2–204(3)). Parties fully aware of the importance of a term may omit it with the intention of adding it at a later time. This kind of missing term is often called an open term. If the parties can come to an agreement with respect to the open term at the later time, they will then add it in accordance with their agreement, and no problems result. But if they cannot come to an agreement, the contract is left with a missing term that almost always is one of great importance. To save these contracts, the Code drafters took the position that statutory terms should be provided to fill open terms when the parties themselves were unable or unwilling to do so. Open terms, however, will be filled only when it is appropriate to conclude that the parties wanted to be contractually bound in spite of the fact that they were unable to come to an agreement on what the open term should specify.

The most common open terms involve price and details of performance.

1. PRICE

a. BACKGROUND

In most sales contracts a definite price is fixed, or course of dealing or usage of trade clearly indicates that a "reasonable" or "market" price is contemplated, as for example, where a homeowner phones a fuel company and asks to have her fuel tank filled with heating oil. In that case there is an implied term in the contract that the buyer will pay the going price charged by the seller. Cases in which the price is fixed in this way by an implied term have presented no difficulty for the courts.

Nevertheless, open-price contracts often have been troublesome. Since price is such an important term, the parties seldom will forget it completely. Why, then, do they leave the term open? One reason is suggested by the example above. Another common reason involves a conscious effort by both parties not to shift the risk of a possible fluctuating market. This risk is present whether the price is fixed or left open, but it may be shifted from one party to the other or retained, depending upon the agreement. Prior to entering into a fixed-price contract the seller has the risk that the price of his goods will decline before he can sell them, and the buyer has the risk that the price will increase before he can buy them. Once the contract is made with a fixed-price term these risks are shifted. Now the buyer has the risk that the value of the goods will decline, whereas the seller has the risk that their value will rise. In an open-price contract, the parties retain these risks.

What might motivate the parties to agree that the price is the going price at the time of delivery?

The courts have not always understood the economics of open-price terms and the justifications for them. At common law the use of open-price terms frequently resulted in the avoidance of an otherwise valid contract on grounds of indefiniteness, illusory promise, or lack of mutuality of obligation. E.g., Wilhelm Lubrication Co. v. Brattrud, 197 Minn. 626, 268 N.W. 634 (1936); Brooks v. Federal Surety Co., 24 F.2d 884 (D.C.Cir.1928).

Article 2 acknowledges the usefulness of open-price contracts. Please read 2–305 (and the Official Comments to that section). Which part of 2–305 governs the price term in the heating oil example in the introductory paragraph to this section?

b. VARIABLE-PRICE TERMS

Variable prices that depend on the happening or non-happening of stated contingencies are sometimes described by courts as "open-price" terms, but they are open only in the sense that the parties do not know at the time the contract is executed what the ultimate price will be. Good examples of variable price terms are agreements to sell at the market price or at the price charged by a particular seller on the day in question. If the external price standard becomes non-existent or otherwise fails to operate in the anticipated manner, a court is left with difficult decisions. First, it must determine whether the parties intended to be bound should their valuation scheme not operate. Secondly, if the court determines that the parties did intend to be bound (i.e. that the agreed-upon method of valuation is not a condition precedent to the existence of the obligation), what factors should it consider in setting the price? Of course, it would be better for the parties to agree in advance on these matters, but they do not always do so.

When the price is made to vary on the happening of a contingency that bears little or no relationship to the subject matter of the contract, a wager usually is involved, and it will not be enforced because of public policy. For example, suppose a barrel of flour usually sells for $50, that Black Beauty is running in the Kentucky Derby, and that the odds against Black Beauty winning the Derby are quoted at ten to one. Suppose, under these circumstances, the seller and buyer agree on the sale of a barrel of flour, the price to be $500 if Black Beauty wins the Derby but two cents if she loses. Is there any doubt that this "sale" is really a disguised wager?

Suppose, however, that before the Derby is run the owner of Black Beauty agrees to sell her to a buyer after the race, the price to be $5,000 if she loses, but $50,000 if she wins. Any "gambling" problem in that case?

In the second version of the hypothetical, what if Back Beauty is withdrawn from the race: is the agreement enforceable? If so, at what price?

c.   DRAFTING OPEN-PRICE TERMS

Section 2–305 enables the parties to a sales contract to preserve flexibility with respect to establishing the price of the transaction. It goes a long way toward eliminating the common-law objections to a contract with an indeterminate price. But problems may remain, if there is doubt concerning the factual questions posed by subsections (1) and (4): do the parties intend for there to be a contract even though they have not agreed on the price and even though they ultimately do not agree on the price? To avoid the problems, it is wise for the parties to address these questions of intent in the contract. They should make it clear whether they consider themselves contractually bound in the event that the price is not fixed in accordance with their agreement. For example, suppose they have agreed that the price is to be fixed by the prices set by a designated market and no such prices are set. Is the contract to fail in that event, or is the court to fix a reasonable price?

Furthermore, it usually is a good idea for the parties to state the factors that should be used in determining a "reasonable price" in the event that a court is called on to make this determination. Unhappiness with open-price contracts in the commercial community often is the result of courts' setting prices without taking into account certain factors that are important to merchants. These factors ought to be stated in the agreement.

Finally, there may be minimum and maximum amounts beyond which the parties do not contemplate the price should be set. For example, the seller and buyer may not be able to agree on a precise price but both may be thinking in terms of a fairly limited range, such as some point between $8,000 and $10,000. If so, it is only common sense for them to state this range *in advance* of difficulties by placing the inside and outside limits in the contract itself. A court knowing from the contract itself that the parties intend to be bound even though they have not been able to agree on the price, that certain factors are critical in determining the price, and that the parties have set maximum and minimum limits, may arrive at a price different from that which the seller or buyer regards as proper, but working under these constraints it will seldom sorely disappoint either party.

d.   MUTUALITY OF OBLIGATION

Note that 2–305(2) permits the parties to agree that the price may be fixed in good faith by one party alone. Does this rule represent an exception to the basic contract concepts of mutuality of obligation or illusory promise?

The concept of bilateral contract includes the idea of mutual commitment, and this means that if one party has not really made any commitment, then there is no contract. In that case, the apparent but unreal commitment is illusory and is not consideration for the return promise. This idea has proved troublesome in sales law because often one of the parties to a sales agreement may wish to provide for "a way out" if certain contingencies occur or do not occur. For example, a buyer may wish to condition his obligation to buy upon obtaining satisfactory financing and a seller may want to reserve the right to cancel if certain events happen. Many courts were hostile to agreements that they thought left one of the parties free to perform or withdraw from the transaction at his own unfettered discretion, and their adverse decisions on these matters threatened the right of the parties to agree that one of them alone could determine such things as satisfaction, details of performance, price, cancellation, and good cause.

Section 2–305 does not allow the parties to agree effectively that the price may be set through the unfettered discretion of either. Discretion to set the price is limited by good faith. The drafters of the Code believed that this limitation was sufficient to satisfy the requirements of the concept of mutuality of obligation, and that any party giving the other the power to set the price should assume the risk that it will be set at an unexpectedly high or low point (from his point of view) so long as the power is exercised in good faith. Is this not a great risk for the party to undertake? How can the flexibility of such an open price term be preserved without so great an assumption of risk?

A common example of an open-price term to be set by one of the parties alone is found in the American steel industry where the standard contract gives the seller the right to set the price at the amount that is charged to all customers on the day of delivery. Under these contracts, the particular buyer is protected by the fact that it will get the same price other buyers got on the day in question. Is this enough to satisfy the requirements of mutuality of obligation? Is the buyer also protected by the seller's obligation to act in good faith? Any problem under 2–305(2)?

Specific attacks on the common law requirement of mutuality of obligation can be found not only in 2–305 but also in 2–306 (dealing with output and requirements contracts) and 2–311 (dealing with options and cooperation respecting details of performance). How far can these sections be used by way of analogy to resolve other mutuality problems, as, for example, the problem of "satisfaction"? To illustrate, assume a seller and buyer enter into a contract in which a machine is sold and delivered on a "satisfaction-guaranteed" basis. Assume also that the buyer is not satisfied but the evidence establishes that the overwhelming number of people in the buyer's position would have been satisfied? If the buyer really is satisfied but wants to get out of the deal for other reasons and thus reports that he is dissatisfied, what result should the court reach? How can the fact finder determine whether the buyer really is dissatisfied with the machine?

———

Mathis v. Exxon Corporation

United States Court of Appeals, Fifth Circuit, 2002.
302 F.3d 448.

■ JERRY E. SMITH, CIRCUIT JUDGE.

This is a breach of contract suit brought by fifty-four gasoline station franchisees against Exxon Corporation ("Exxon") for violating the Texas analogue of the Uniform Commercial Code's open price provision. We affirm.

Exxon markets its commercial gas bound for retailers primarily through three arrangements: franchisee contracts, jobber contracts, and company operated retail stores ("CORS.") A franchisee rents Exxon-branded gas stations and enters into a sales contract for the purchase of Exxon-brand gas. The contract sets the monthly quantity of gas the franchisee must purchase and allows Exxon to set the price he must pay. The franchisee pays the dealer tank wagon price ("DTW") and takes delivery of the gas at his station.

A jobber contract requires the purchaser to pay the "rack price," which usually is lower than the price charged to franchisees.[a] There is no sale of gas to CORS by Exxon, because the stores are owned by Exxon and staffed by its employees. Instead, an intra-company accounting is recorded that is equivalent to the price charged franchisees in the same price zone.

All the plaintiff franchisees operate stations in the greater Houston, Texas, and Corpus Christi, Texas, areas. The genesis of the dispute is the allegation that Exxon has violated the law and its contracts with these franchisees for the purpose of converting their stores to CORS by driving the franchisees out of business.

Since 1994, franchisees have been barred from purchasing their gas from jobbers, so all their purchases have been governed by the terms of the Retail Motor Fuel Store Sales Agreement, under which the "DEALER agrees to buy and receive directly from EXXON all of the EXXON-branded gasoline bought by DEALER, and at least seventy-five percent (75%) of the volume shown in [a specified schedule] . . . DEALER will pay EXXON for delivered products at EXXON's price in effect at the time of the loading of the delivery vehicle." This "price in effect," also known as

———

[a] A jobber is an intermediate distributor, in this case acquiring gasoline from Exxon and reselling it to independent service stations. "Rack price" is the price charged to buyers who take delivery of the gasoline at the seller's distribution center and transport it from there at their own expense. The "dealer tank wagon price," or DTW, is the price charged when the seller delivers the gasoline to the buyer's location.—Eds.

the dealer tank wagon price ("DTW,") forms the heart of the present dispute. Exxon claims this arrangement is the industry standard and that almost all franchisor-franchisee sales of gasoline are governed by a similar price term. Plaintiffs respond that the DTW price charged under this clause is "consistently higher" than the rack price paid by jobbers plus transportation costs.

. . . The thrust of [plaintiffs'] testimony was that Exxon had set the DTW price at an uncompetitive level to drive them out of business (so as to replace their stores with CORS). Some of the plaintiffs testified that their franchises were unprofitable; they presented documents and witnesses to show that Exxon intended that result to drive them out of business.

The franchisees also submitted a market study showing that 62% of the franchisees in Corpus Christi were selling gas below the DTW price. The franchisees supported their theory of the case by calling Barry Pulliam as an expert witness on the economics of the gasoline market in Houston and Corpus Christi. [He] concluded that Exxon's DTW price was not commercially reasonable from an economic perspective because it was a price that, over time, put the purchaser at a competitive disadvantage. . . .

[His] conclusion rested on two main facts. First, he showed that 75% of the franchisee's competitors were able to purchase gasoline at a lower price. Second, he calculated a commercially reasonable DTW price by adding normal distribution charges to the average rack price of gasoline charged by Exxon and its competitors. He concluded that Exxon's DTW price exceeded the sum of these other prices by four or more cents per gallon.

Exxon countered with [its own expert], who testified that Exxon's DTW price was commercially reasonable because it reflected the company's investment in land, the store, transportation, and managers. [He] explained that Exxon recovers these costs through rent and the sale of gas.

The jury awarded $5,723,657. . . . [Exxon appeals on the ground that the] court should have granted Exxon's motion for [judgment as a matter of law (j.m.l.)]. . . .

II.

Exxon contends that because it charged its franchisees a DTW price comparable to that charged by its competitors, the breach of contract claim is precluded as a matter of law.

A j.m.l. is appropriate where "a party has been fully heard on an issue and there is no legally sufficient evidentiary basis for a reasonable jury to find for that party on that issue." Fed.R.Civ.P. 50(a). We review the denial of j.m.l. *de novo.* . . .

III.

Texas law, which tracks the Uniform Commercial Code, implies a good faith component in any contract with an open price term. [§ 2.305]. The parties agree that the franchise agreement term governing the purchase of gasoline is an open price term.

. . .

The key disagreement is over what constitutes a breach of the duty of good faith. Exxon contends it has satisfied that duty because it has charged the plaintiffs a DTW price within the range of its competitors' DTW prices, thereby satisfying the "commercial reasonableness" meaning of good faith. Plaintiffs respond that good faith encompasses both objective and subjective duties. Even if Exxon is right, and its prices are within the range of its competitors,' the argument runs, a subjective intent to drive the franchisees out of business would abridge the good faith duty of the open price term.

The pivotal provision is comment 3 to § 2.305. . . . In the absence of comment 3, there is no doubt Exxon would be subject to both the subjective "honesty in fact" good faith of § 1.201(19) and the objective "commercial reasonableness" good faith of § 2.103. The difficult question is whether comment 3 creates an exception to the normal principles of good faith governing the sale of goods.

The Code employs two standards of good faith. Section 1–201(19) [of original Article 1] states the generally applicable "subjective" ("white heart and empty head") standard which concentrates on the actual state of mind of the party rather than on the state of mind a reasonable man would have had under the same circumstances. Thus, the section defines good faith as "honesty in fact in the conduct or transaction concerned." In the case of merchants, however, or at least those merchants governed by Article 2 on Sales, an objective element is added to their good faith duties. Section 2–103(1)(b) provides that " '[g]ood faith' in the case of a merchant means honesty in fact and the observance of reasonable commercial standards of fair dealing in the trade." This definition imposes a duty on merchants to meet good faith requirements that are measured both subjectively and objectively.[b]

No court in this circuit, and no Texas state court, has squarely addressed this question. Fortunately, because the Texas open price provision replicates that of the UCC, we can seek guidance from other courts.

---

[b]   Original 1–201(19) defined "good faith" as "honesty in fact in the conduct or transaction concerned." Section 2–103(1)(b) added an objective standard, "and the observance of reasonable commercial standards of fair dealing." Revised Article 1, 1–201(b)(20), defines good faith as having both the subjective (honesty in fact) and objective (reasonable commercial standards of fair dealing) components.—Eds.

To decide whether comment 3 creates an exception, we turn first to the text of the comment and the related sections of the Texas version of the UCC. In full, comment 3 reads,

> Subsection (2), dealing with the situation where the price is to be fixed by one party rejects the uncommercial idea that an agreement that the seller may fix the price means that he may fix any price he may wish by the express qualification that the price so fixed must be fixed in good faith. Good faith includes observance of reasonable commercial standards of fair dealing in the trade if the party is a merchant. (Section 2–103). But in the normal case a "posted price" or a future seller's or buyer's "given price," "price in effect," "market price," or the like satisfies the good faith requirement.

The bare text offers little to resolve the question. First, the comment notes that good faith "includes" reasonable commercial standards. This implies that the good faith required of a merchant setting an open price term encompasses both objective and subjective elements. The comment also creates a good faith safe harbor for such merchants when they use various sorts of fixed prices. But this safe harbor is applicable only in the "normal case." This suggests the safe harbor is not absolute, but it does nothing to define what takes a case out of the safe harbor.

As we will explain, we conclude that the "normal case" of comment 3 is coextensive with a merchant's residual "honesty in fact" duty embodied in §§ 1.201(19) and 2.103. Thus, the comment embraces both the objective (commercial reasonableness) and subjective (honesty in fact) senses of good faith; objective good faith is satisfied by a "price in effect" as long as there is honesty in fact (a "normal case"). This conclusion finds support in three sources: the structure of the UCC, its legislative history, and the caselaw.

Reading comment 3 to embody two different meanings of "good faith" tracks the general structure of the UCC. Courts and commentators have recognized that the meaning of "good faith" is not uniform throughout the code. The cases and commentary treat the "good faith" found in article 1 as subjective and the good faith found only in article 2 as objective. Thus, there is nothing inconsistent in comment 3's using "good faith" in both the objective and the subjective senses.

The history of comment 3 bolsters this conclusion. Some drafters of the UCC worried that for the "great many industries where sales are not made at fixed prices," such as the steel industry, where "practically every contract" is made at "the seller's price in effect," if § 2–305 "is to apply . . . it means that in every case the seller is going to be in a lawsuit . . . or he could be, because there isn't any outside standard at all." Proceedings of Enlarged Editorial Bd. of Am. Law Inst. (Sunday Morning Session, Jan. 28, 1951) (statement of Bernard Broeker). The drafters considered wholly exempting such contracts from § 2–305, or stating that for a price in effect, the only test is whether the merchant engaged in price discrimination. One drafter explained that the steel industry wanted to make "clear that we do not have to establish that we are fixing reasonable prices, because that gets you into the rate of return of profit, whether you are using borrowed money, and all those questions." *Id.*

The committee responded to these worries with the current comment 3: "[I]n the normal case a 'posted price' or a future seller's or buyer's 'given price,' 'price in effect,' 'market price,' or the like satisfies the good faith requirement." The drafter's solution was to avoid objective good faith challenges to prices set by reference to some "price in effect," while preserving challenges to discriminatory pricing. *See* Hearing Before the Enlarged Editorial Board January 27–29, 1951, 6 Business Lawyer 164, 186 (1951) (explaining this intent). Nothing in the proceedings leading to the addition of comment 3 suggests that the overall *subjective* good faith duty of §§ 1–201 and 2–103 was to be supplanted; the evidence is quite to the contrary.

The drafters ultimately rejected two suggested addendums to § 2–305:

> An agreement to the effect that the price shall be or be adjusted to, or be based upon, or determined by reference to the seller's going price, price in effect, regular price, market price, established price, or the like, at the time of the agreement or at any earlier or later time, is not an agreement to which this subsection is applicable.
>
> . . .
>
> An agreement such as this is an agreement under which the seller or the buyer does not have any burden of showing anything other than that he has not singled out the particular other party for discrimination. Proceedings of Enlarged Editorial Bd. (statement of Bernard Broeker).

Both of these recommendations are more sweeping than is the language ultimately adopted. The first would have omitted any mention of the good faith duty for open price provisions; the second would have limited the duty of the price-setter to that of avoiding discrimination.

The existing comment, however, avoids challenges to prices set according to an open price term unless that challenge is outside the normal type of case. Although price discrimination was the type of aberrant case on the minds of the drafters, price discrimination is merely a subset of what constitutes such an aberrant case. Any lack of subjective, honesty-in-fact good faith is abnormal; price discrimination is only the most obvious way a price-setter acts in bad faith—by treating similarly-situated buyers differently.

The caselaw supports this interpretation of comment 3. Courts that have addressed the normalcy question have consistently held that a lack of subjective good faith takes a challenge outside the bounds of what is normal.[11]

Like the plaintiffs in *Nanakuli, Allapattah, and Wayman,* the franchisees here are alleging a breach of good faith grounded not in Exxon's failure to price in accord with an established schedule, but in its failure to set the price in good faith. Suits recognizing such a cause of action are rare, and with good reason: We would be ill-advised to consider a case to be outside the norm based only on an allegation of improper motive by the party setting the price.

Plaintiffs produced enough evidence to escape comment 3's "normal case" limitation. They showed, for example, that Exxon planned to replace a number of its franchises with CORS, that the DTW price was higher than the sum of the rack price and transportation, that Exxon prevented the franchisees from purchasing gas from jobbers after 1994, and that a number of franchisees were unprofitable or non-competitive.

For example, one Exxon document stated that the company's "Marketing Strategy for 1992–1997 is to reduce Dealer stores (est. 30%)." Another document set forth Exxon's plans to reduce dealer stations in Houston from 95 to 45, and to increase CORS from 83 to 150, between 1997 and 2003. James Carter, the Regional Director of the Exxon/Mobil Fuels Marketing Company, testified that Exxon made more of a profit from a CORS than from an independent lessee store. These plans and observations were validated by the fact that the number of dealer stations steadily declined.

An exhibit called the "Houston Screening Study" evaluated the strategy of "surplusing" (i.e., eliminating) 21 of 37 locations inside the Highway 610 loop. Of the 93 lessee-dealer stations, 69 would be done away with, but 73 of the 91 CORS would be kept.

Further indication of plans to shift from dealer-lessees to CORS is shown by Exxon's dissatisfaction with outlets featuring service bays. Exxon documents showed that service bays—generally associated with lessee-dealer locations—were becoming less profitable, while stations with convenience stores—generally associated with CORS—were the wave of the future. A document entitled "Retail Store Chain Outlook" revealed Exxon's plan to reduce stations with service bays from 2,506 to 190 from 1991 to 2005. That document included a plan to "[e]xpand CORS to improve profitability and to compete efficiently with private

---

[11] *See, e.g.,* Nanakuli Paving & Rock Co. v. Shell Oil Co., 664 F.2d 772, 806 (9th Cir.1981) (stating that "the dispute here was not over the amount of the increase—that is, the price that the seller fixed—but over the manner in which that increase was put into effect"); Allapattah v. Exxon Corp., 61 F.Supp.2d 1308, 1322 (S.D.Fla.1999) ("Because the parties' dispute is not over the actual amount of the purchase price Exxon charged for its wholesale gasoline to its dealers, but rather over the manner in which the wholesale price was calculated without considering the double charge for credit card processing, the instant action is not the 'normal' case."); *cf.* Wayman v. Amoco Oil Co., 923 F.Supp. 1322, 1349 (D.Kan.1996), *aff'd,* 145 F.3d 1347 (10th Cir.1998) ("[T]his court believes the present case is a normal case. If there was evidence that Amoco had, for example, engaged in discriminatory pricing or tried to run plaintiffs out of business, then the court's decision might be different.").

brands/distributors" and "[e]mphasize CORS operations in markets with high level of rack to retail competition."

Exxon's answer on appeal is that these documents "say nothing about *using pricing* to accomplish a 'plan' to eliminate dealers." Although that is so, there was sufficient evidence on this issue to go to the jury, which was free to, and apparently did, draw the inference connecting pricing to the elimination of dealer-lessees. The consequence of the jury's decision is that this case exceeds the "normal case" limit of § 2.305 comment 3. We still, however, must examine the content of the duty of subjective good faith. Although no Texas or Fifth Circuit case has squarely addressed the meaning of the good faith clause of § 2.305, Texas courts repeatedly have held that the "honesty in fact" definition of good faith found in § 1.201(19) is tied to the actual belief of the participant in the transaction. Thus, the same version of the facts accepted by the jury—that Exxon intended to drive the franchisees out of business—that takes this case out of the "normal" set of cases for purposes of comment 3 also satisfies the criteria for bad faith.

Exxon's bad faith, in this regard, is shown by the record. Facing the competition of self-service stations that were either selling food and other goods or had bare pumps with no overhead costs incurred in servicing vehicles, Exxon decided years ago that retail marketing through franchise dealers was becoming economically unsound. Although Exxon decided to move to CORS in Houston and jobbers in Corpus Christi, this decision was not communicated to its franchisees. Because of profit from their other sales, CORS could, and did, sell gas for less than the franchise dealers paid to Exxon for their gas. And the jobbers delivered Exxon gas to their dealers for less than Exxon franchisees were required to pay for their delivered gas, but Exxon prohibited its franchisees from buying at this lower price from the jobbers.

The loss of competitive position and profit to plaintiff franchisees was inevitable and foreseeable to Exxon. Although Exxon witnesses denied receiving complaints, its dealers testified that they had complained often and for years, without success, until the very eve of trial.

Accordingly, the jury's finding that Exxon breached its duty of good faith in setting the DTW price it charged the plaintiffs is not without foundation in the law or the evidence. As we have recounted, plaintiffs offered ample evidence tending to prove their version of price-setting. Accordingly, there is no error in the refusal to grant Exxon j.m.l. on the breach of contract claim.

. . .

QUESTIONS AND NOTES

1.   The jury evidently concluded that Exxon lacked the good faith required by 2–305(2). As a practical matter, does this mean that Exxon may not

charge more than its competitors charge their franchisees? more than it charges the jobbers who purchase its gasoline? If Exxon charges its franchisees the same price that it charges jobbers, but raises the franchise fee by an amount equal to 4 cents per gallon, would Exxon violate 2–305?

2. In *Nanakuli* (page 170), the buyer claimed that the seller breached their contract for the sale of asphalt by failing to provide price protection when the market price increased dramatically. The court held that usage of trade and course of performance supported the buyer's claim. The court also held that the buyer was entitled to price protection by virtue of the seller's obligation under 2–305(2) to set the price in good faith and by its obligation under 1–203 [revised 1–304] to act in good faith in the performance and enforcement of the contract:

VIII.   *Good Faith in Setting Price*

Nanakuli offers an alternative theory why Shell should have offered price protection at the time of the price increases of 1974. Even if price protection was not a term of the agreement, Shell could not have exercised good faith in carrying out its 1969 contract with Nanakuli when it raised its price by $32 effective January 1 in a letter written December 31st and only received on January 4, given the universal practice of advance notice of such an increase in the asphaltic paving trade. The Code provides, "A price to be fixed by the seller or by the buyer means a price for him to fix in good faith," Haw.Rev.Stat. § 490:2–305(2). For a merchant good faith means "the observance of reasonable commercial standards of fair dealing in the trade." Id. § 490:2–103(1)(b). The comment to Section 2–305 explains, "[I]n the normal case a 'posted price' . . . satisfies the good faith requirement." Id., Comment 3. However, the words "in the normal case" mean that, although a posted price will usually be satisfactory, it will not be so under all circumstances. In addition, the dispute here was not over the amount of the increase—that is, the price that the seller fixed—but over the manner in which that increase was put into effect. It is true that Shell, in order to observe the good faith standards of the trade in 1974, was not bound by the practices of aggregate companies, which did not labor under the same disabilities as did asphalt suppliers in 1974. However, Nanakuli presented evidence that Chevron, in raising its price to $76, gave at least six weeks' advance notice, in accord with the long-time usage of the asphaltic paving trade. Shell, on the other hand, gave absolutely no notice, from which the jury could have concluded that Shell's manner of carrying out the price increase of 1974 did not conform to commercially reasonable standards. In both the timing of the announcement and its refusal to protect work already bid at the old price, Shell could be found to have breached the obligation of good faith imposed by the Code on all merchants. "Every contract or duty within this chapter imposes an obligation of good faith in its performance or enforcement," id. § 490:1–203 [revised 1–304], which for merchants entails the observance of commercially reasonable standards of fair dealing in the trade. The Comment to 1–203 reads:

> This section sets forth a basic principle running throughout this Act. The principle involved is that in commercial transactions good faith is required in the performance and enforcement of all agreements or duties. Particular applications of this general principle appear in specific provisions of the Act. . . . It is further implemented by Section 1–205 [revised 1–303] on course of dealing and usage of trade.

Chevron's conduct in 1974 offered enough relevant evidence of commercially reasonable standards of fair dealing in the asphalt trade in Hawaii in 1974 for the jury to find that Shell's failure to give sufficient advance notice and price protect Nanakuli after the imposition of the new price did not conform to good faith dealings in Hawaii at that time.

3.   Subsection 2–305(2) is but a particularization of 1–304, which states that every contract imposes an obligation of good faith in its performance. Official Comment 1 to that section states, "While the duty [of good faith] is explicitly stated in some provisions of the Uniform Commercial Code, the applicability of the duty is broader than merely these situations and applies generally, as stated in this section, to the performance or enforcement of every contract or obligation within this Act." As we continue exploring Article 2, you should be alert to how 1–304 may affect the application of the sections being studied.

4.   The definition of good faith in 2–103(1)(b) applies only to merchants, so only merchants must observe reasonable commercial standards of fair dealing in the trade. The definition in 1–201(b)(20) applies to all persons, so even in the case of a non-merchant, good faith includes the observance of reasonable commercial standards. When states enacted revised Article 1, they were supposed to repeal 2–103(1)(b). In several states, however, the legislature enacted revised Article 1 without the new definition of good faith (so that it continues to be defined as just honesty in fact). In these states, there was no repeal of 1–203(1)(b). So in these states the objective component of the definition, reasonable commercial standards of fair dealing, applies only to merchants.

5.   In Shell Oil Co. v. HRN, Inc., 144 S.W.3d 429, 435–37 (Tex.2004), the Supreme Court of Texas rejected the holding of *Mathis*. As in *Mathis*, plaintiffs claimed that Shell set the price to its franchisees at a level that was designed to drive them out of business. The court held as a matter of law that plaintiffs failed to state a claim:

> The Dealers themselves concede that Shell is not obligated to price its gasoline with their interests in mind or to protect them from competition. They further explain that their theory in this case does not turn on the DTW price set by Shell but rather on the reason why Shell chose to charge that price. Likewise, the court of appeals concludes that this is not the normal case because the price, although commercially in line with that charged by other

refiners to their lessee dealers, may have been motivated by an improper underlying purpose to eliminate some dealerships.

It is not apparent, however, why the intent behind a commercially reasonable, non-discriminatory price should matter for purposes of a breach of contract claim under section 2.305(b). Dealers do not contend that they are entitled to any particular price and do not disagree that Shell's DTW price is within the range charged by other refiners to their dealers. Thus, if these Dealers were charged the same DTW price by another refiner who did not have a similar plan to thin their ranks, presumably the price would pass muster under the Dealers' view of section 2.305. Premising a breach of contract claim solely on assumed subjective motives injects uncertainty into the law of contracts and undermines one of the UCC's primary goals—to "promote certainty and predictability in commercial transactions."

. . .

The reasoning in *Mathis* and the court of appeals in this case negates the effect of Comment 3's "safe harbor" by concluding that circumstantial evidence of "any lack of subjective, honesty-in-fact good faith" is sufficient to create an "abnormal" case in which the posted-price presumption no longer applies. The effect is to allow a jury to determine in every section 2.305(b) case whether there was any "improper motive animating the price-setter," even if the prices ultimately charged were undisputedly within the range of those charged throughout the industry. This result appears to conflict with the drafters' desire to eliminate litigation over prices that are nondiscriminatory and set in accordance with industry standards. Although the subjective element of good faith may have a place elsewhere in the Code, we do not believe this subjective element was intended to stand alone as a basis for a claim of bad faith under section 2.305. Rather we conclude that allegations of dishonesty under this section must also have some basis in objective fact which at a minimum requires some connection to the commercial realities of the case.

. . .

The Dealers maintain, however, that even though Shell used a posted price it nevertheless violated its duty of good faith by setting its DTW price too high with the conscious intention of driving some of its franchisees out of business. And the court of appeals agreed that there was enough circumstantial evidence to raise a fact issue about Shell's subjective motives and therefore its good faith. According to the court, this evidence generally included: (1) the DTW price itself, which was on the high end of the wholesale pricing spectrum, (2) the "captive" nature of relationship between Shell and its franchisees, and (3) the general decline in the business fortunes of Shell franchisees.

. . .

We agree with Shell that [this] list of circumstantial factors [is] not evidence that Shell lacked good faith when fixing its DTW price. The DTW price, the captive nature of the franchisee relationship, and the business losses suffered by the Dealers are variations of the same theme: Shell's DTW price is too high for the Dealers to compete with other gasoline retailers. But good faith under section 2.305(b) does not mandate a competitive price for each individual Dealer, nor could it. The competitive circumstances of each Dealer in the same pricing zone may vary from station to station, and yet Shell must treat them all the same.

The court of appeals, however, suggests that because the Dealers paid more than most of the other gasoline retailers in Houston, the DTW price itself is some evidence of Shell's subjective bad faith ("73–80% of [the Dealers'] Houston competition paid rack price—or lower—for gas. . . ."). We cannot agree that a relatively high, yet commercially reasonable, price is evidence of bad faith. A good-faith price under section 2.305 is not synonymous with a fair market price or the lowest price available.

Each Dealer contractually agreed to buy gasoline at the DTW price applicable only to Shell-branded lessee-dealers. The court of appeals' wholesale cost analysis indiscriminately compares Shell's DTW price to prices available to other classes of trade, with different contractual buying arrangements. Included in the comparison are branded and unbranded jobbers who pick up their gasoline at terminals, open dealers who own their own premises, and company-owned stores operated by other refiners. Evidence that different prices are available to different classes of trade is not evidence of bad faith under section 2.305.

Which court is right?

In *Mathis* the federal court applied Texas law. According to Casserlie v. Shell Oil Co., 902 N.E.2d 1, 5 (Ohio 2009), after the decision of the Texas Supreme Court in *HRN*, *Mathis* is "no longer good law." This may be true in Texas and Ohio, but some other courts have found the reasoning in *Mathis* to be persuasive. E.g., Stephenson Oil Co. v. Citgo Petroleum Corp., 2010 WL 2998604 (N.D.Okla.2010). And see Marcoux v. Shell Oil Products Company LLC, 524 F.3d 33 (1st Cir.2008), another case in which franchisees alleged that their franchisor adopted pricing to force them out of business. After citing the language in Official Comment 3 that "in the normal case 'a posted price' . . . satisfies the good faith requirement," the court stated:

> . . . The defendants and amici urge us to read this comment as providing an absolute safe harbor for nondiscriminatory posted prices in open price term contracts. This we will not do.

> For one thing, the very comment on which the defendants and amici rely expressly invokes the general notion of "reasonable commercial standards of fair dealing." If the comment meant that only discriminatory pricing would be disallowed it certainly could have said that. For another, it is clear to us that a situation in

which one merchant is raising its prices in order to force a customer out of business is hardly the "normal case." The Eleventh Circuit allowed this question to go to a jury in a class action involving another oil company's pricing policies. *Allapattah Servs. v. Exxon Corp.*, 333 F.3d 1248, 1262 n. 16 (11th Cir.2003) (conceding that in a "normal case" nondiscriminatory pricing is protected, but holding that where the allegation was that an oil company was trying to drive service stations out of business, "whether this case constituted a normal case was a factual issue necessary to determine whether Exxon acted in good faith" and therefore rightly submitted to the jury). More recently, the Fifth Circuit upheld the denial of a motion for judgment as a matter of law on the basis that setting gasoline prices in bad faith to drive franchisees out of business violated the UCC. *Mathis v. Exxon Corp.* , 302 F.3d 448, 457–59 (5th Cir.2002) ("[T]he jury's finding that Exxon breached its duty of good faith in setting the DTW price it charged the plaintiffs is not without foundation in the law or the evidence."); *see also Bob's Shell, Inc. v. O'Connell Oil Assocs.*, 2005 WL 2365324, 2005 U.S. Dist. LEXIS 21318 (D.Mass. Aug. 31, 2005); *Wayman v. Amoco Oil Co.*, 923 F.Supp. 1322, 1349 (D.Kan.1996) (finding that the case before it was a "normal case" but noting that "[i]f there was evidence that Amoco had, for example, engaged in discriminatory pricing or tried to run plaintiffs out of business, then the court's decision might be different"). *But see Shell Oil v. HRN, Inc.*, 144 S.W.3d 429, 435–38 (Tex.2004) (holding absence of price discrimination created presumption of good faith notwithstanding allegations that that oil company set prices in bad faith as part of a plan to drive franchisees out of business).

Commerce is predicated on the idea that a transaction is good for both buyer and seller. The comment recognizes that allowing one party complete control over the price would be "uncommercial." We do not think the only reason for this is the risk of price discrimination. The drafters of the UCC and amici here are rightly concerned about a flood of litigation second-guessing every price set in an open price term contract. Mere allegations of bad faith will never be enough to survive summary judgment. But this case comes to us after a jury verdict finding bad faith and commercial unreasonableness.

Id. at 50–51.

6. In the penultimate paragraph on page 194, the court in *HRN* states, "Although the subjective element of good faith may have a place elsewhere in the Code, we do not believe this subjective element was intended to stand alone as a basis for claim of bad faith under section 2.305." Is this assertion consistent with Official Comment 6?

7. Section 2–304 states that the price may be made payable in money, goods, realty, or otherwise. What is the purpose of this section? Is it really a scope section? If Julio agrees to trade his HDTV set to Marissa in return for Marissa's exercise equipment, does Article 2 govern the transaction? If so, who is the seller and who is the buyer? (The answer to this question is important because many of the rules of Article 2 are directed to buyers or to sellers but not both). If Bob agrees to trade a small plot of land to Sally for $10,000 and a boat, is the transaction covered by Article 2? All of the transaction? Part of it?

8.   Open-price problems compounded by other uncertain terms. The open-price contract may be the result of a decision by the buyer and seller as to allocation of market risks, or it may come about as part and parcel of a bigger problem involving uncertainty as to the description of the subject matter, the quantity of goods to be taken, or both. The problem may be further exacerbated when the open price is to be set by some standard other than "reasonable price" or "market price."

Consider Royal Store Fixture Co. v. Bucci, 48 Pa.D. & C.2d 696 (Pa. Co.1969). Defendant purchased real estate with the intention of erecting a restaurant on it. Plaintiff was an executive of the Royal Store Fixture Co., which specialized in selling restaurant equipment, and he had expertise as a planner of restaurants and stores. Plaintiff and defendant entered into an agreement in which plaintiff agreed to work up the plans and specifications for the new restaurant and defendant promised to buy all his restaurant equipment from plaintiff "at prices competitive with other Manufacturers' equipment of equality and specifications." Plaintiff made the plans for defendant's restaurant and submitted a list of items of equipment that would be needed in it, but without specifications as to make and model. The first list totaled $29,004; the second list (different equipment) was $14,347; and third and fourth lists were in different amounts. Defendant rejected these bids and bought his equipment from another seller.

Plaintiff sued for breach of contract, arguing that his prices were competitive for the items he had listed. He conceded that there were many items of equipment that could be used by defendant, and that he (plaintiff) had no way of knowing whether his prices were competitive with prices that others would charge unless that equipment could be identified. He also indicated that he was willing to dicker the price. In explaining the overall price he testified that (referring to the second bid of $14,347) "this is normally only the beginning of a sale, because you then sit down with your customer, and then he starts to haggle, and before you know it, your fourteen thousand three forty five price might be down to thirteen thousand three hundred."

Was there a contract? The court held not. Was the court right? Is 2–204(3) relevant? How about 2–306? How do these sections relate, if at all, to 2–305? Stated differently, assume a quantity term is vague in some respects but meets the standards of 2–306, and a price term is vague in some respects, but meets the standards of 2–305. If these two terms are combined in the same contract, is the contract too indefinite to be enforced? Do you add up the sum total of vagueness in determining whether the standard of 2–204(3) is met?

9.   CISG. Article 55 of the Convention on Contracts for the International Sale of Goods states:

> Where a contract has been validly concluded but does not expressly or implicitly fix or make provision for determining the price, the parties are considered, in the absence of any indication to the contrary, to have impliedly made reference to the price generally charged at the time of the conclusion of the contract for such goods sold under comparable circumstances in the trade concerned.

Thus it substitutes "the price generally charged at the time of the conclusion of the contract" for the "reasonable price" of 2–305. Which formulation is preferable?

Consider Article 14, which states, in part, "A proposal is sufficiently definite if it indicates the goods and expressly or implicitly fixes or makes provision for determining the quantity and the price." Under Article 14, if a proposal does not expressly or implicitly fix, or make provision for determining, the price, can its acceptance result in a contract? If not, then what is the effect of Article 55?

2. QUANTITY

a. INTRODUCTION

Unlike price, which the parties might decide to leave for determination at some time after the contract is formed, one would expect the parties to specify the quantity of goods at the outset. And typically they do. But sometimes they do so with a degree of indefiniteness. A case in point is Riegel Fiber Corp. v. Anderson Gin Co., 512 F.2d 784 (5th Cir.1975). Riegel contracted to purchase cotton from the sellers, who were two gin companies and multiple farmers. The contracts called for delivery of "all the . . . cotton produced during the crop year 1973" on 4,222 acres. The problem was that 4,222 acres were only a fraction of the land that the sellers had under cultivation, and the contract did not specify the precise locations from which the cotton was to come. When the market price rose and the sellers threatened to breach, the buyer obtained a preliminary injunction requiring the sellers to deliver the cotton (and requiring the buyer to post a bond to protect the sellers in the event that the court ultimately determined that the agreement was not enforceable). Relying on 2–204(3), the court stated,

> . . . The official comment to this section adds that "commercial standards on the point of 'indefiniteness' are intended to be applied." Thus, we view our inquiry as limited to the question whether these contracts contained quantity terms acceptable to the majority of buyers and sellers knowledgeable in the cotton trade.
>
> Unfortunately, the parties directed their arguments more to technical contract doctrine than to the commercial reasonableness of the method used in these agreements to designate quantity. A review of the record, briefs, and argument of counsel convinces us, however, that the quantity terms as

stated in the contracts can meet the Code's test for definiteness. Significantly, the record is clear that [the sellers] themselves supplied the actual quantity provisions on the forms tendered by [the buyer]. . . . The evidence shows no objections made by any [seller] to the forms at the time the contracts were entered into; likewise, it reveals no attempt by [the sellers] to insert what they now argue would be more definite terms, even though they clearly had the opportunity to do so. Moreover, although we do not give controlling weight to this factor, it cannot be ignored that [the sellers] successfully identified and allocated contract and non-contract cotton when required to do so by the lower court's injunction.

The district court relied heavily on the impossibility of determining from the face of the master contracts the specific fields covered by the agreements. . . . Yet we find no evidence that any of the parties believe that such specificity is commercially necessary or even desirable. For its part, [the buyer] is apparently willing to rely to a large extent on the farmers' good faith and commercial reasonableness in choosing which of their acres are to be used to grow contract cotton. Likewise, the record contains no hint of why the individual farmers or the ginners might prefer as a normal practice to contract as to rigidly specified fields.[18] We think [the buyer's] evidence clearly makes out a prima facie case that the quantity terms in the master contracts . . . conform to acceptable practice in the cotton trade.

Id. 791–92.

b. REQUIREMENTS AND OUTPUT CONTRACTS

A requirements contract is one in which a buyer promises to purchase its requirements of a good from a seller. The buyer may be acquiring the goods for resale or for use in a manufacturing operation. Conversely, an output contract is one in which a seller promises to sell its entire production of a good to a buyer.

A requirements contract is advantageous to the buyer because it assures the buyer of having just the right amount of goods on hand. The buyer does not have to guess at what its needs will be, with the risk that

---

[18] [The sellers] have pitched almost their entire argument on "unique" technical faults allegedly present in the particular arrangements chosen by [the buyer] here. They offer little to buttress their argument except hypotheticals showing a supposed lack of mutuality in the agreements. When asked directly at oral argument whether it is commercially important to know the specific fields covered by cotton contracts, counsel for the farmers responded only that it was important to these contracts. Significantly, the testimony of [one of the sellers] revealed with regard to his individual cotton acreage that (1) he had no specific fields in mind when he signed the contract; (2) he never designated any fields as "contract" acres; (3) his intent when contracting was to sell half of his production; and (4) when his production turned out to be less than he anticipated, he nevertheless delivered under the contract half of the cotton he did produce without protest on Riegel's part. Appendix at 169–71. . . .

too high an estimate will result in an unusable supply of goods, and too low an estimate will result in the buyer's being unable to meet resale or manufacturing opportunities. The seller, on the other hand, suffers the disadvantage of not knowing the quantity to be sold and is likely to sell fewer goods to the buyer than would be the case under a contract that fixed the amount of quantity at a definite amount. What does the seller gain by a requirements contract, and what does the buyer lose?

Consider the converse situation with an output contract. It has obvious advantages for the seller, because it assures that the seller will have a market for all the goods it produces. It is disadvantageous to the buyer in that the buyer may end up buying more goods than needed. What are the disadvantages to the seller, and what are the advantages to the buyer under an output contract?

Some common-law courts struck down sales contracts as illusory if they contained terms measuring the quantity of the goods by the seller's output or the buyer's requirements. These decisions were based on the view that an output or requirements agreement leaves one of the parties completely free to fix the amount of goods to be sold, and thus completely free to avoid the contract altogether by fixing the amount at zero. Even adopting this assumption, however, other courts sustained these contracts on the ground that to set the quantity at zero would mean that the output seller would have to completely curtail manufacturing (thus having no output) and the requirements buyer would have to cease the activity for which it needed the goods, and that cessation of activities, of itself, amounts to consideration for the return promise. Moreover, the promise to purchase one's requirements (or sell one's output) means that the promisor is surrendering its right to do business with anyone else. This restraint on its future conduct is consideration. Section 2–306 validates output and requirement contracts.

1.   **Problem.** Albany and Billings agreed that Albany would sell to Billings at a fixed price an amount of cottonseed sufficient to meet all reasonable requirements of Billings, and that Billings would purchase cottonseed from Albany in an amount that from time to time it reasonably required. Is this a requirements contract?

The agreement also stated that Billings "shall have the exclusive right to dispose of all cottonseed acquired by Albany and that any such seed sold directly to farmers must be sold through Billings; or if not sold through Billings, Albany is to pay one half the profits realized from the sale." Does this "exclusive right" create an output contract?

2.   **Problem.** MyBaby, a manufacturer of dolls, needs nylon to produce its product. MyBaby agrees with Fabrico to purchase from Fabrico at a fixed price at least 50% of the nylon it needs for the next two calendar years. Is this agreement an enforceable requirements contract?

3.   **Problem.** MyBaby agrees with Fabrico to purchase its requirements of nylon for two calendar years, up to a total of 30,000 yards per year. In

December before the first year, Fabrico announces that it will not accept orders from MyBaby. MyBaby purchases its requirements for those two years from another supplier and sues Fabrico for the excess cost of 30,000 yards per year. Is the agreement enforceable?

4.   Problem. Bates and Sylvestri agreed that for five calendar years Sylvestri would supply Bates with its requirements of helium and Bates would buy its requirements of helium from Sylvestri. The price was to be $1 per cubic foot, except that if Bates purchased less than 1 million cubic feet per calendar year, the price was to be $1.05 per cubic foot and if Bates purchased more than 2 million cubic feet the price was to be $.90 per cubic foot. Further, if Bates purchased less than 800,000 cubic feet, the price would be $1.10; and if Bates purchased more than 1.2 million cubic feet, the price would be $.95. In years one, two, and three, Bates purchased 1.6, 1.9, and 2.1 million cubic feet, respectively. In the first eight months of year four, Bates ordered and Sylvestri delivered 2.3 million cubic feet. In October Bates placed an order for an additional .5 million cubic feet, but Sylvestri failed to deliver. During the remainder of that year, Bates purchased .5 million cubic feet from another source, and in year 5 purchased 3 million cubic feet from that source, all at a cost of $1.15 per cubic foot. Bates sued Sylvestri for the excess cost it incurred for those purchases. As we will see later, Article 2 permits recovery of a buyer's excess cost of buying replacement goods when a seller breaches. But in this case, for what quantity? See 2–306(1).

5.   The good-faith limitation of 2–306(1) prevents the parties from arbitrarily increasing or decreasing their output or requirements for ulterior reasons. Is good faith a sufficient safeguard?

Prudent business operators often feel that they are best safeguarded in output and requirements deals by including in the contract a stated estimate of what the output or requirements will be. Greater protection may be obtained by a statement giving a range within which the output or requirements must fall. This protection, however, comes at a cost, limiting the parties to their stated quantity. Moreover, if one of the parties is a new business enterprise, this safeguard may not be practicable.

6.   Subsection (1) states that in a requirements contract the quantity is the buyer's "actual . . . requirements as may occur in good faith." It goes on to add, "except that no quantity unreasonably disproportionate to any . . . normal or otherwise comparable prior output or requirements may be tendered or demanded." Official Comment 2, however, states that "good faith variations from prior requirements are permitted even when the variation may be such as to result in discontinuance." Can you reconcile this statement in the Comment with the language in the statute?

———

Empire Gas Corp. v. American Bakeries Co.

United States Court of Appeals, Seventh Circuit, 1988.
840 F.2d 1333.

■ POSNER, CIRCUIT JUDGE.

. . .

Empire Gas Corporation is a retail distributor of liquefied petroleum gas, better known as "propane." It also sells converters that enable gasoline-powered motor vehicles to operate on propane. The sharp rise in gasoline prices in 1979 and 1980 made American Bakeries Company, which operated a fleet of more than 3,000 motor vehicles to serve its processing plants and bakeries, interested in the possibility of converting its fleet to propane, which was now one-third to one-half less expensive than gasoline. . . . [The parties entered a contract] "for approximately three thousand (3,000) [conversion] units, more or less depending upon requirements of Buyer, consisting of Fuel Tank, Fuel Lock Off Switch, Converter & appropriate Carburetor & Small Parts Kit," at a price of $750 per unit. American Bakeries agreed "to purchase propane motor fuel solely from EMPIRE GAS CORPORATION at all locations where EMPIRE GAS has supplied carburetion and dispensing equipment as long as EMPIRE GAS CORPORATION remains in a reasonably competitive price posture with other major suppliers." The contract was to last for four years.

American Bakeries never ordered any equipment or propane from Empire Gas. Apparently within days after the signing of the contract American Bakeries decided not to convert its fleet to propane. No reason has been given for the decision.

Empire Gas brought suit against American Bakeries for breach of contract and won a jury verdict for $3,254,963, representing lost profits on 2,242 conversion units (the jury's estimate of American Bakeries' requirements) and on the propane fuel that the converted vehicles would have consumed during the contract period. . . .

The heart of this case is the instruction concerning American Bakeries' obligation under the contract. If there were no legal category of "requirements" contracts and no provision of the Uniform Commercial Code governing such contracts, a strong argument could be made that American Bakeries agreed to buy 3,000 conversion units or *slightly* more or *slightly* less, depending on its actual needs, and hence that it broke the contract by taking none. This is not only a semantically permissible reading of the contract but one supported by the discussions that the parties had before the contract was signed . . . , in which American Bakeries assured Empire Gas that it was planning to convert its entire fleet. American Bakeries insisted on adding the phrase "more or less depending upon requirements of Buyer" just in case its estimate of 3,000 was off, and this is quite different from supposing that the phrase was added so that American Bakeries would have no obligation to buy any units at all.

The parties agree, however, that despite the negotiating history and the inclusion in the contract of a specific estimate of quantity, the quoted phrase sorted the contract into the legal bin labeled "requirements contract" and thereby brought it under the governance of section 2–306(1) of the Uniform Commercial Code, which provides:

> A term which measures the quantity by the output of the seller or the requirements of the buyer means such actual output or requirements as may occur in good faith, except that no quantity unreasonably disproportionate to any stated estimate or in the absence of a stated estimate to any normal or otherwise comparable prior output or requirements may be tendered or demanded.

Over American Bakeries' objection the judge decided to read the statute to the jury verbatim and without amplification, remarking to the lawyers,

> Now, I have nothing to do with the fact that there may be some ambiguity in 2–306. If there is ambiguity, well, that is too bad. This is the law that the legislature has adopted. With due respect to all these great judges that [American Bakeries' counsel] has cited and these great academic lawyers he has called to my attention, well, good, they have a lot of time to mull over these problems.

> But I have the problem of telling this jury what the law is, and the law is right here, right here in this statute, and I have a good deal of faith in this jury's ability to apply this statute to the facts of this case.

> It is not true that the law is what a jury might make out of statutory language. The law is the statute as interpreted. The duty of interpretation is the judge's. Having interpreted the statute he must then convey the statute's meaning, as interpreted, in words the jury can understand. If section 2–306 means something different from what it seems to say, the instruction was erroneous.

The interpretive question involves the proviso dealing with "quantity unreasonably disproportionate to any stated estimate." This limitation is fairly easy to understand when the disproportion takes the form of the buyer's demanding more than the amount estimated. If there were no ceiling, and if the price happened to be advantageous to the buyer, he might increase his "requirements" so that he could resell the good at a profit. This would place him in competition with the seller—a result the parties would not have wanted when they signed the contract. So the "unreasonably disproportionate" proviso carries out the likely intent of the parties. The only problem is that the same result could easily be reached by interpretation of the words "good faith" in the preceding clause of section 2–306(1), thus making the proviso redundant. But redundancies designed to clarify or emphasize are common in legal drafting; and anyway the Uniform Commercial Code has its share of ambiguities, see *Wisconsin Knife Works v. National Metal Crafters,* 781 F.2d 1280, 1288 (7th Cir.1986).

The proviso does not distinguish between the buyer who demands more than the stated estimate and the buyer who demands less, and therefore if read literally it would forbid a buyer to take (much) less than the stated estimate. Since the judge did not attempt to interpret the statute, the jury may have read it literally, and if so the judge in effect directed a verdict for Empire Gas. The stated estimate was for 3,000 units; American Bakeries took none; if this was not unreasonably disproportionate to the stated estimate, what buyer shortfall could be?

So we must decide whether the proviso should be read literally when the buyer is demanding less rather than more than the stated estimate. There are no cases on the question in Illinois, and authority elsewhere is sparse, considering how often (one might think) the question must have arisen. But the clearly dominant approach is not to construe the proviso literally, but instead to treat the overdemanding and underdemanding cases differently [citing cases from five jurisdictions]. We think this is right. We also note that it was the common law approach: "the seller assumes the risk of all good faith variations in the buyer's requirements even to the extent of a determination to liquidate or discontinue the business." *HML Corp. v. General Foods Corp.,* 365 F.2d 77, 81 (3rd Cir.1966).

Granted, there is language in the Official Comments . . . which points to symmetrical treatment of the overdemanding and underdemanding cases: "the agreed estimate is to be regarded as a center around which the parties intend the variation to occur." UCC § 2–306, comment 3. But there is no elaboration; and the statement is in tension with the statement in comment 2 that "good faith variations from prior requirements are permitted even when the variation may be such as to result in discontinuance," for if that principle is sound in general, why should it cease to be sound just because the parties included an estimate of the buyer's requirements? A tiny verbal point against the symmetrical interpretation is the last word of the proviso—"demanded." The statement that "no quantity unreasonably disproportionate to any stated estimate . . . may be . . . demanded" is more naturally read as applying to the case where the buyer is demanding more than when he is reducing his demand below the usual or estimated level.

More important than this verbal skirmishing is the fact that the entire proviso is in a sense redundant given the words "good faith" in the main clause of the statute. The proviso thus seems to have been designed to explicate the term "good faith" rather than to establish an independent legal standard. And the aspect of good faith that required explication had only to do with disproportionately *large* demands. If the buyer saw an opportunity to increase his profits by reselling the seller's goods because the market price had risen above the contract price, the exploitation of that opportunity might not *clearly* spell bad faith; the proviso was added to close off the opportunity. There is no indication that the draftsmen were equally, if at all, concerned about the case where the buyer takes less than his estimated requirements, provided, of course, that he does not buy from anyone else. We conclude that the Illinois courts would allow a buyer to reduce his requirements to zero if he was acting in good faith, even though the contract contained an estimate of those requirements.

This conclusion would be greatly strengthened . . . if the only purpose of a requirements contract were to give the seller a reasonably assured market for his product *by forbidding the buyer to satisfy any of his needs by buying from another supplier.* . . .

. . . If the obligation were not just to refrain from buying a competitor's goods but to buy approximately the stated estimate (or, in the absence of any estimate, the buyer's "normal" requirements), the contract would be altogether more burdensome to the buyer. Instead of just committing himself not to buy from a competitor even if the competitor offered a better product or terms of sale, he would be committing himself to go through with whatever project generated the estimate of required quantity, no matter what happened over the life of the project save those exceptional events that would excuse performance under the related excuses of *force majeure,* impossibility, impracticability, or frustration. This would be a big commitment to infer from the inclusion in the contract of an estimated quantity, at least once the parties concede as they do here that their contract really is a requirements contract and not a contract for the estimate itself—not, in other words, a fixed-quantity contract.

Both extreme interpretations—that the buyer need only refrain from dealing with a competitor of the seller, and that the buyer cannot go significantly beneath the estimated quantity except in dire circumstances—must be rejected, as we shall see. Nevertheless the judge should not have read the "unreasonably disproportionate" proviso in section 2–306(1) to the jury. The proviso does not apply . . . where the buyer takes less rather than more of the stated estimate in a requirements contract.

This error in instructions requires reversal and a new trial on liability unless it is clear either that American Bakeries acted in good faith or that it acted in bad faith, since the statute requires the buyer to take his "good faith" requirements from the seller, irrespective of proportionality. The Uniform Commercial Code does not contain a definition of "good faith" that seems applicable to the buyer under a requirements contract. Compare section 2–104(1) with section 2–103(1)(b) [revised 1–201(b)(20)]. Nor has the term a settled meaning in law generally; it is a chameleon. See, e.g., *Bosco v. Serhant,* 836 F.2d 271, 278 (7th Cir.1987); *In re TCI Ltd.,* 769 F.2d 441, 445 (7th Cir.1985). Clearly, American Bakeries was acting in bad faith if during the contract period it bought propane conversion units from anyone other than Empire Gas, or made its own units, or reduced its purchases because it wanted to hurt Empire Gas (for example because they were competitors in some other market). Equally clearly, it was not acting in bad faith if it had a business reason for deciding not to convert that was independent of the terms of the contract or any other aspect of its relationship with Empire Gas, such as a drop in the demand for its bakery products that led it to reduce or abandon its fleet of delivery trucks. A harder question is whether it was acting in bad faith if it changed its mind about conversion for no (disclosed) reason. There is no evidence in the record on why it changed its mind beyond vague references to "budget problems" that, so far as appears, may have been nothing more than a euphemism for a decision by American Bakeries not to allocate funds for conversion to propane.

If no reason at all need be given for scaling back one's requirements even to zero, then a requirements contract is from the buyer's standpoint just an option to purchase up to (or slightly beyond, i.e., within the limits of reasonable proportionality) the stated estimate on the terms specified in the contract, except that the buyer cannot refuse to exercise the option because someone offers him better terms. . . . The statement of an estimate invites the seller to begin making preparations to satisfy the contract, and although no reliance expense was incurred by the seller in this case, a seller is entitled to expect that the buyer will buy something like the estimated requirements unless it has a valid business reason for buying less. More important than the estimate . . . is the fact that ordinarily a requirements contract is terminated after performance has begun, rather than before as in the present case. Whether or not the seller can prove reliance damages, the sudden termination of the contract midway through performance is bound to disrupt his operations somewhat. The Illinois courts interpret a requirements contract as a sharing of risk between seller and buyer. The seller assumes the risk of a change in the buyer's business that makes continuation of the contract unduly costly, but the buyer assumes the risk of a less urgent change in his circumstances, perhaps illustrated by the facts of this case where so far as one can tell the buyer's change of mind reflected no more than a reassessment of the balance of advantages and disadvantages under the contract. American Bakeries did not agree to buy conversion units and propane for trucks that it got rid of, but neither did Empire Gas agree to forgo sales merely because new management at American Bakeries decided that its capital would be better employed in some other investment than conversion to propane.

The general distinction that we are trying to make is well illustrated by *Southwest Natural Gas Co. v. Oklahoma Portland Cement Co.,* 102 F.2d 630 (10th Cir.1939), which to the drafters of the Uniform Commercial Code exemplified "reasonable variation of an extreme sort" (at least in the absence of an estimate, but that is irrelevant, for reasons we have explained). UCC § 2–306, comment 2. A cement company agreed to buy all of its requirements of gas from the seller for 15 years. Seven years later, the cement company replaced its boiler, which had worn out, with more modern equipment; as a result its need for gas fell by 80 percent. The court deemed this a bona fide change in the cement company's requirements. It would have been unreasonable to make the company replace its worn-out plant with an obsolete facility.

It is a nice question how exigent the buyer's change of circumstances must be to allow him to scale down his requirements from either the estimated level or, in the absence of estimate, the "normal" level. Obviously it need not be so great as to give him a defense under the doctrines of impossibility, impracticability, or frustration, or under a *force majeure* clause. Yet, although more than whim is required, . . . how much more is unclear. There is remarkably little authority on the question. This is a good sign; it suggests that, while we might think it unsatisfactory for the law to be unclear on so fundamental a question, the people affected by the law are able to live with the lack of certainty. The reason may be that parties linked in an ongoing relationship—the usual situation under a requirements contract—have a strong incentive to work out disagreements amicably rather than see the relationship destroyed by litigation.

The essential ingredient of good faith in the case of the buyer's reducing his estimated requirements is that he not merely have had second thoughts about the terms of the contract and want to get out of it. Whether the buyer has any greater obligation is unclear, but need not be decided here. Once it is decided (as we have) that a buyer cannot arbitrarily declare his requirements to be zero, this becomes an easy case, because American Bakeries has never given any reason for its change of heart. It might seem that once the district judge decided to instruct the jury in the language of the statute, American Bakeries was foreclosed from arguing that it had scaled down its requirements in good faith; a reduction to zero could never be proportionate if, as the instruction implied, the proviso on disproportion applies to reductions as well as increases in the buyer's takings. But the judge did not make this decision until the instructions conference. Until then American Bakeries had every opportunity and incentive to introduce evidence of why it decided not to convert its fleet to propane. It introduced none, and even at the argument in this court its counsel could give no reason for the change of heart beyond a hint that it was due to a change in management, which would not be enough by itself to justify a change in the buyer's requirements.

Even though Empire Gas had the burden of proving breach of contract and therefore (we may assume) of proving that American Bakeries acted in bad faith in reducing its requirements from 3,000 conversion units to zero, no reasonable jury could have failed to find bad faith, and therefore the error in instructing the jury on proportionality was harmless. Empire Gas put in evidence, uncontested and incontestable, showing that American Bakeries had not got rid of its fleet of trucks and did have the financial wherewithal to go through with the conversion process. After this evidence came in, American Bakeries could avoid a directed verdict only by introducing some evidence concerning its reasons for reducing its requirements. It not only introduced no evidence, but as is plain from counsel's remarks at argument it has no evidence that it would care to put before the jury—no reasons that it would care to share with either the district court or this court. It disagrees with the standard of good faith, believing that so long as it did not buy conversion units elsewhere or want to hurt Empire Gas it was free to reduce its requirements as much as it pleased. It does not suggest that it has a case under the standard we have adopted, which requires at a minimum that the reduction of requirements not have been motivated solely by a reassessment of the balance of advantages and disadvantages under the contract to the buyer.

. . .

The judgment is affirmed . . . .

■ KANNE, CIRCUIT JUDGE, dissenting:

I agree with the majority that the error in giving the instruction regarding the "unreasonably disproportionate" proviso in Illinois' Uniform Commercial Code § 2–306(1) requires a reversal and new trial, "unless it is clear either that American Bakeries acted in good faith or that it acted in bad faith. . . ." The fundamental problem is that there was no evidence of either good or bad faith as those terms are normally defined. For different reasons neither Empire Gas nor American Bakeries produced evidence of American Bakeries' honesty or dishonesty or fair or unfair dealing in regard to its reduction of its requirements to zero.

As in *Massey-Ferguson, Inc. v. Helland,* 105 Ill.App.3d 648, 61 Ill.Dec. 142, 146, 434 N.E.2d 295, 299 (1982), ". . . the material testimony in this case did not reveal any lies, deceit, overreaching or other examples of dishonesty in fact in the transaction . . . nor was any evidence adduced regarding reasonable commercial standards of fair dealing in the trade." In *Massey-Ferguson,* the Illinois Appellate Court found that a plaintiff's failure to introduce specific evidence as to bad faith constituted a failure to carry its burden of proof on the issue of bad faith.

The majority in the case before us assumes that Empire Gas bears the burden of proof on the issue of American Bakeries' bad faith. The majority then presumes that Empire meets this burden of showing bad faith by simply presenting evidence that "American Bakeries had not got rid of its fleet of trucks and did have the financial wherewithal to go through with the conversion." I do not agree that from this scant evidence "no reasonable jury could have failed to find bad faith," and thus the district court's failure to instruct the jury properly on this issue was not harmless error. In reality, at trial, Empire Gas was never required to shoulder—let alone carry—any actual burden of proof on bad faith. The majority thus transforms the seller's theoretical burden of proof on bad faith (unarticulated to the jury) into an actual presumption of the buyer's bad faith (articulated post-trial).

Empire Gas, if actually put to the test, may or may not be able to produce evidence of bad faith. Likewise, we do not know whether American Bakeries would be able to produce evidence to support a good faith reduction to zero. Absent the majority's presumption, at trial no one knew, at least based on the evidence, that it had become American Bakeries' burden to go forward with proof of its good faith.

Clearly American Bakeries' reduction of its requirements for conversion units from 3,000 to zero was "unreasonably disproportionate" on its face. However, the court (correctly I believe) holds today that what appears to be a buyers' unreasonably disproportionate reduction of requirements is not enough to determine liability under § 2–306— evidence of a buyer's good or bad faith is also necessary.

It is not this standard, but its practical application to the trial of this case, which causes me to part company with my brethren.

If, as the majority apparently holds—the seller has the burden of proof on the issue of the buyer's bad faith—I would reverse and remand for new trial because Empire Gas did not bear that burden and the trial record discloses no facts ordinarily found necessary by Illinois courts to prove bad faith.

If, on the other hand, the majority actually holds (again correctly I believe)—a buyer's assertion of an unreasonably disproportionate reduction in his requirements creates a bad faith presumption which may be rebutted by the buyer's proof of good faith—I would also reverse and remand for a new trial because this new rebuttable presumption of bad faith was not the Illinois rule under which the trial was conducted.

QUESTIONS AND NOTES

1. American Bakeries evidently said to Empire Gas, "We're interested in converting our gas vehicles to propane. If we decide to do that, what deal can you give us on supplying our requirements of converter kits and propane?" The parties then formed a contract for American Bakeries' requirements. In this context, should American Bakeries be able to declare that it does not have any requirements after all?

2. Was it appropriate for the court, in effect, to excise the "except" clause from 2–306(1)?

3. What do you suppose Judge Posner has in mind when, at the bottom of page 205, he states that the Code "does not contain a definition of 'good faith' that seems applicable to the buyer under a requirements contract?" Why does the court endorse the finding of good faith in Southwest Natural Gas (at pages 207–207) but conclude that American Bakeries was in bad faith?

4. The majority states that the "except no unreasonably disproportionate quantity" clause does not apply to the case of a reduction in quantity. How then can a large reduction create a presumption of bad faith?

5. Official Comment 2 states,

> Reasonable elasticity in the requirements is expressly envisaged by this section and good faith variations from prior requirements are permitted even when the variation may be such as to result in discontinuance. A shut-down by a requirements buyer for lack of orders might be permissible when a shut-down merely to curtain losses would not. The essential test is whether the party is acting in good faith.

A manufacturer may enter a requirements contract for a component or raw material it needs in order to manufacture one of its products. Over time an increase in the manufacturer's other costs of production, or a decline in the price for which it can sell its finished product, or the appearance on the market of a competing product based on different technology may make continued production unprofitable. Would it be reasonable for the manufacturer to discontinue production of this product?

Would the manufacturer be in good faith in ceasing to purchase the component or raw material needed for that line of business? The three sentences quoted above from Official Comment 2 seem internally consistent. In Simcala, Inc. v. American Coal Trade, Inc., 821 So.2d 197 (Ala.2001), the court held that a buyer that purchased only 41% of its estimated requirements breached a requirements contract. The court acknowledged that the buyer's reduction was in good faith, but it gave independent effect to the "unreasonably disproportionate" language:

> Simcala emphasizes official comment 2 in support of its argument that § 7–2–306(1) prohibits only unreasonably disproportionate increases. Comment 2 states:
>
>> "Reasonable elasticity in the requirements is expressly envisaged by this section and *good faith variations from prior requirements are permitted even when the variation may be such as to result in discontinuance.* A shut-down by a requirements buyer for lack of orders might be permissible when a shut-down merely to curtail losses would not. *The essential test is whether the party is acting in good faith.*"

(Emphasis in Simcala's brief.) While comment 3 begins with the words, "If an estimate . . . is included . . . ," comment 2 does not mention estimates. Comment 2 addresses the general limitation of "good faith," which applies when there is no agreed-upon estimate. The specificity of comment 3, however, dealing with estimates, displaces the generality of comment 2. Comment 3 therefore applies in the special case, like this one, where the parties have agreed on an estimate. Thus, the drafters' comments to § 7–2–306 support the conclusion that the statute applies both to unreasonably disproportionate increases and decreases from agreed-upon estimates.

. . .

As we have repeatedly stated, the function of the Court is "to say what the law is, not what it should be." To hold as Simcala requests we do—that the statute forbids only unreasonably disproportionate increases but not decreases—would require us to presume that the Legislature did not intend the ordinary meaning of the words that it chose to use in its enactment. We conclude that the interpretation supported by the plain meaning of the language of the statute and by the official comments is that § 7–2–306(1) prohibits unreasonably disproportionate decreases made in good faith. If adverse effects on market conditions warrant a different result, it is for the Legislature, not this Court, to amend the statute.

Id. at 201, 203.

6.   Problem. National Bakeries and BP Oil had a requirements contract for all the gasoline that National Bakeries needed for its fleet of trucks. The term of this contract was five years, and the price was BP's posted price at the time of delivery. After two years the market price of gasoline increased by 30%. Responding to this dramatic increase, National Bakeries converted its trucks to run on propane and purchased no more gasoline from BP (or anyone else). Did National Bakeries breach its contract with BP?

7.   Problem. Fuller Chemicals manufactures refrigerant, for which it needs chloroform. After difficult negotiations with Madison Gas, in which Fuller was unable to persuade Madison to reduce its price to less than $5 per pound, Fuller agreed to purchase its requirements of chloroform for five years at $5 per pound. After three years of performance, Fuller informed Madison that it had been losing money and would continue to do so unless Madison reduced the price to $3 per pound. Madison declined to lower the price of the chloroform. In response, Fuller closed its manufacturing facility and ceased manufacturing the refrigerant. Did Fuller breach?

What if Fuller desired to continue selling refrigerant, so although it no longer manufactured refrigerant, it contracted with another manufacturer for that manufacturer to produce the refrigerant for it. What result if Madison sues for breach of the requirements contract?

8.   Exclusive-dealing contracts. Exclusive dealing contracts are a variant of requirements contracts, in which the buyer is given the exclusive right to sell the product produced by the seller in a given territory and the seller promises to supply the buyer's requirements of that product. Unless the contract provides to the contrary, the buyer is free to sell other products in that territory and to acquire those products from different sellers. Thus, a buyer may have an exclusive right to sell Prada shoes in a particular town, but may be free to sell other shoes as well. Are such contracts too one-sided (in favor of the buyer) to be enforceable? Section 2–306(2) answers this question in the negative. What does the seller gain by such an arrangement? If the buyer is selling several different products that compete with the seller's product, is there a conflict of interest? If so, does 2–306(2) adequately resolve the conflict?

9.   "More or less" quantity terms. Sometimes a contract of sale is made in which the quantity term is qualified by words such as "more or less" or "about" (e.g. "about 1,000 bales of cotton.") Obviously, the purpose of the qualifying word or words is to protect the seller against variations in the number, measure, or weight of the described goods. Usually, when these qualifying words are used the variations will be slight, but suppose they are great: is there a contract in that case? If so, for what amount? Does it make a difference that the described goods can be identified by reference to independent circumstances? (E.g., "The entire lot of goods located in XYZ warehouse, more or less 10 tons." Suppose only two tons of goods comprise the entire lot in XYZ warehouse.) Compare: ("I will sell you all the goods I have, believed to be ten tons more or less," and it turns out that the seller only has two tons) with ("I will sell you ten tons, more or less," and the seller tenders two tons).

3.   PAYMENT

The payment term should not be confused with the price term. The price term deals with "how much" must be paid. The payment term deals with "where, when, and how" that payment is to be made. Unlike the price term, which is usually stated in a sales contract, the payment term often is omitted. In that event, differences of opinion may result as to when the buyer is obliged to pay, where the payment is to be made, and in what manner (e.g. cash, check, certified check, etc.). These gaps, of course, can be filled in some cases by resort to course of performance, course of dealing, or usage of trade. In other cases statutory terms found in 2–310, 2–507, and 2–511 provide answers.

Sections 2–507(1) and 2–511(1) embrace the common-law doctrine of constructive conditions. The obligation of the seller to deliver the goods and the obligation of the buyer to pay for them are concurrently conditional. That is, the seller's obligation to deliver is conditional on the buyer's tender of payment, and the buyer's obligation to pay is conditional on the seller's tender of delivery. Section 2–310(a) reinforces this by requiring payment at the time and place at which the buyer receives the goods, regardless of whether delivery occurs at the buyer's location, the seller's location, or elsewhere. Each of these rules, of course, may be varied by agreement of the parties.

Please reconsider Southwest Engineering v. Martin Tractor, page 52 supra. The seller argued that because the parties had never agreed on the time for payment, there was no contract. The court held that the parties did have a contract because they intended that a contract exist even though they had not settled on a payment term. The court observed that if the parties do not agree on the payment term, 2–310 supplies one.

Since the deal collapsed before delivery of the goods, it was not necessary to determine when payment was due. But what if the seller had tendered delivery of the goods and refused to leave them unless the buyer paid the entire price: would it be appropriate to conclude that payment was due on delivery? Section 2–310(a) states that "unless otherwise agreed" payment is due at the time and place where the buyer is to receive the goods. In the context of *Southwest Engineering*, exactly what does the quoted phrase mean?

4. DELIVERY

Delivery is an essential element in a sales contract, because if the transaction is really a sale the seller must at some time and some place and in some manner deliver the goods to the buyer. In well-written sales contracts these aspects of time, place, and manner are described. Unfortunately, not all contracts are well drafted, and some or all of these matters may be omitted.

Unlike open price and quantity terms, courts applying the common law did not take a dim view of open delivery terms. That is to say, they did not regard the delivery term as so material that its inclusion was deemed necessary to make the agreement enforceable. Rather, the courts used the same techniques for determining this missing term that Article 2 now adopts for many terms. The courts looked first to course of performance, course of dealing, and usage of trade to ascertain any implied understanding relating to delivery. If that produced no satisfactory answer, they used a set of rules, said to be based on common practices, to fill the gap. This approach, of course, is identical to the one employed by Article 2. With few exceptions, the statutory delivery terms of Article 2, found in 2–307, 2–308, and 2–309, carry forward the rules developed at common law.

Some of these rules, however, may seem strange to one not fully conversant with commercial practices. How would you handle this hypothetical: Powers in St. Louis agreed to sell to Dominion in Chicago a 20,000-lb. turbine needed for Dominion's manufacturing operations. Nothing was said about place of delivery. At the proper time Powers called Dominion and said, "The machine is ready. Come down and get it." Dominion refused, "You must bring it to my plant." Powers refused to deliver the machine to Dominion's plant. Which party, if either, has breached the contract?

Suppose the hypothetical involved a sofa that a consumer bought from a retail furniture store. Any change in result? If so, where do you find that change in the UCC?

———

Luedtke Engineering Co., Inc. v.
Indiana Limestone Co., Inc.

United States Court of Appeals, Seventh Circuit, 1984.
740 F.2d 598.

■ BAUER, CIRCUIT JUDGE. Plaintiff Luedtke Engineering Company brought this diversity action against defendant Indiana Limestone Company, alleging that Indiana Limestone breached its contract to sell breakwater stone to Luedtke. The district court held in favor of Indiana Limestone, and Luedtke appeals. We affirm.

I

In December 1977, the Army Corps of Engineers (the Corps) solicited bids for repair of the breakwater in the Milwaukee harbor. The Corps approved two sources from which bidders could purchase stone: Indiana Limestone and another quarry located in Indiana. The Corps earlier had given Indiana Limestone information about the repair project, including details of the Corps' time schedule. That schedule anticipated that work on the project would begin in March 1978 and be completed by November 1979.

The Corps also sent Indiana Limestone a list of the general contractors who planned to bid on the project; the list included Luedtke. Indiana Limestone and Luedtke had engaged in at least five other projects together. After receiving the list, Indiana Limestone sent Luedtke a letter containing a price quotation. Indiana Limestone's letter, dated February 20, 1978, contained the following proposals:

(1) Indiana Limestone would supply Luedtke with 70,000 tons of stone at $10.15 per net ton;

(2) The price would apply to shipments made during 1978 and 1979;

(3) Luedtke would be obligated to negotiate the freight rate for stone shipped in 1979 with the railroad company.

Luedtke relied on Indiana Limestone's quote to formulate its bid for the project. On April 12, 1978, the Corps awarded the contract to Luedtke.

After it received the Corps contract, Luedtke located a different quarry that offered to sell breakwater stone for $5.25 per ton. Because this quarry had not been approved by the Corps, Luedtke made several attempts to obtain permission from the Corps to buy stone from this quarry. When Indiana Limestone learned that Luedtke wanted to buy from another source, an Indiana Limestone official phoned Luedtke and offered to lower his company's price to $5.50 per ton. On the same day, the Corps denied Luedtke's request to purchase stone from the unapproved quarry.

On July 1, 1978, Luedtke issued a purchase order to Indiana Limestone for 70,000 tons of stone at $5.50 per ton. The order stated that Indiana Limestone should "ship at 1500 tons/day starting 24 July 1978."

At this rate, shipping would be completed by November 1978. For a variety of reasons, Indiana Limestone did not ship the stone at the specified rate; Luedtke instead received the last shipment in August 1979. Luedtke nevertheless finished the job in September 1979, seven weeks before the Corps' scheduled completion date of November 15.

Luedtke brought suit alleging that Indiana Limestone breached its contract by failing to ship the breakwater stone at the rate of 1,500 tons per day. Luedtke claimed that it incurred damages of $797,700 as a result of untimely and delayed deliveries. Indiana Limestone countered that it was unaware of Luedtke's intention to finish the project by November 1978, that it believed the shipping rate of 1,500 tons per day was merely an optimal goal, and that its delays in delivery were caused by factors beyond its control, including insufficient rail service, labor strikes, and bad weather.

The district court held in favor of Indiana Limestone. The court ruled that Indiana Limestone's February 20 quote letter was an offer to sell breakwater stone to Luedtke, and that Luedtke's purchase order was an acceptance of that offer. The court found that Luedtke's specific delivery requirement was a "material alteration" of the offer under Indiana law, and thus the parties had not agreed to a shipping rate. As a result, the court turned to the parties' course of dealing and trade usage in the industry to evaluate Indiana Limestone's performance. The court determined that Indiana Limestone delivered the stone in a reasonable time and thus did not breach the contract. Alternatively, the court held that even if Luedtke's shipping term was part of the contract, course of dealing and trade usage could help interpret the contract, and Indiana Limestone still would not be liable.

II

This case is governed by the Indiana Commercial Code, Ind. Code § 26–1–1–101 (1979), which is identical to the Uniform Commercial Code in all sections relevant to this dispute. Under § 2–207, an additional term in an acceptance to a contract between merchants becomes part of the contract unless the offer expressly limits acceptance to the offer's specific terms, the offeror objects to the additional term, or the additional term materially alters the contract. Luedtke argues that the district court erred in concluding that the delivery term in Luedtke's purchase order was a material alteration.

. . . Comment 4 to § 2–207 defines "material alteration" as a term that would "result in surprise or hardship if incorporated without express awareness by the other party." Determining this requires the trial court to make a factual evaluation of the parties' positions in each case. . . .

The evidence in the record supports the district court's conclusion that enforcing a delivery rate of 1,500 tons per day would have resulted in surprise and hardship for Indiana Limestone. The court based its finding on two factors. First, the court concluded that the delivery rate was based on Luedtke's intention to complete the Milwaukee breakwater project by November 1978, but that Indiana Limestone did not know of Luedtke's intention. The evidence amply supports this finding. In the summer of 1977, the Corps told Indiana Limestone that the completion date of the project was November 1979. Indiana Limestone made two references to 1979 prices in its offer to Luedtke and there is no evidence that Luedtke communicated to Indiana Limestone its desire to complete the project by November 1978. Indeed, in June 1978 Luedtke submitted a construction project chart to the Corps showing a July 1979 completion date.

. . . [T]he district court found that expecting Indiana Limestone to deliver stone at a consistent rate would have been contrary to the parties' other dealings. Evidence of prior dealings was admissible here to help supplement the terms of the contract under § 1–205 [revised 1–303]. Again, the record supports the court's conclusion. Intervening factors such as railroad problems, bad weather, and labor disputes apparently prevented Luedtke from receiving prompt, consistent shipment of stone from this quarry in the past. Steven Zachmann, Luedtke's chief engineer, testified at trial that 1,500 tons per day was an "arbitrary in-between quantity" that he derived from the different rates proposed by the parties during negotiation. Both Zachmann and Luedtke's President, Karl Luedtke, admitted that they did not expect Indiana Limestone to meet the delivery rate. In addition, Indiana Limestone's sales representative, Robert New, and Indiana Limestone's quarry supervisor, Athol Bennett, both testified that they considered 1,500 tons per day to be the maximum rate up to which Indiana Limestone would ship stone to Luedtke.

Luedtke nevertheless argues that Indiana Limestone's conduct after receiving the purchase order shows that Indiana Limestone understood the delivery rate to be part of the contract. Luedtke notes that New wrote on the purchase order that twenty-five railroad cars would be needed to ship 1,500 tons per day, that New ordered twenty-five cars per day from the Milwaukee Railroad, and that he sent this information to the quarry. Luedtke also notes that during the contractual period Indiana Limestone never claimed that it had no responsibility to ship 1,500 tons per day as a justification for its sporadic deliveries. These arguments, however, challenge Indiana Limestone's motives and the credibility of its witnesses. The district court has broad discretion in making these factual determinations and we decline to re-try them on appellate review. As discussed, the district court's determinations are not clearly erroneous. (Incidentally, the factors Luedtke cites are entirely consistent with Indiana Limestone's contention that it considered the shipping rate to be a goal, not a requirement.)

Luedtke next argues that if we accept the district court's conclusion that the contract did not contain a shipping rate, then § 2–307 applied and Indiana Limestone was required to ship all the stone in a single delivery. Section 2–307 provides in part that "[u]nless otherwise agreed all goods called for by a contract for sale must be tendered in a single delivery." Yet § 2–307 contains an exception to the single delivery requirement "where the circumstances give either party the right to make or demand delivery in lots," and Comment 4 to § 2–307 states that the phrase "unless otherwise agreed" includes surrounding circumstances, usage of trade, course of dealing, and course of performance. The circumstances here indicate that both parties expected delivery in lots. Luedtke does not contend that Indiana Limestone could have delivered all 70,000 tons of stone in one shipment, and such delivery obviously was not contemplated or desired by either party.

The absence of a specific delivery term in the contract required Indiana Limestone to deliver the stone within a reasonable time. Ind.Code § 26–1–2–309 (1979). The district court found that Indiana Limestone's delivery rate was reasonable, both because Indiana Limestone delivered the stone in time for Luedtke to finish the project before the Corps' deadline, and because Indiana Limestone's delivery delays were caused by factors beyond its control and expected by both parties in light of their previous dealings and industry practice. These conclusions are not clearly erroneous, and thus we affirm the court's ruling that Indiana Limestone's delivery was reasonable under the circumstances.

III

In summary, Luedtke's delivery term was a material alteration of Indiana Limestone's offer, and thus the contract did not include an express delivery term. Because Indiana Limestone delivered the breakwater stone within a reasonable time under the circumstances, Indiana Limestone did not breach its contractual obligations. . . . The district court's order is affirmed.

QUESTIONS

1. **Problem.** Printers, Inc., located in San Francisco, contracted to manufacture and sell to Big Box, located in Minneapolis, 10,000 printer cartridges at $50 per cartridge. Normal production time for this quantity was 30 days, but neither the negotiations nor the contract mentioned a time of delivery. The day after forming this contract, Printers realized it made a very bad deal, but that its loss from performing would be far less than its liability for breaching. So Printers worked its regular crew overtime and hired additional employees to get Big Box's order ready as soon as possible. When complete, Printers loaded the goods on its trucks, sent them on their way, and tendered delivery seven days after the contract was formed. Big Box phoned Printers to say that it was not expecting the cartridges for at least another two weeks and that it had not yet talked to its bank about financing the transaction. Big Box offered a post-dated check, which Printers refused, and Printers instructed the truck drivers to bring the cartridges back to San Francisco. Who, if anyone, has breached the contract, and why?

2.   Problem. Printers, Inc. agreed to sell printer cartridges to Office Supplies, a reseller, for $50 per cartridge. The first shipment was to be of 1,000 cartridges, to be delivered in 10 days and paid for on delivery. Office Supplies was to submit orders from time to time thereafter, but the agreement said nothing about the duration of the agreement, the time of shipment, or the time of payment. Office Supplies hired additional sales personnel to handle the new product. For how long does Office Supplies have the right to purchase cartridges from Printers?

A month after formation of the agreement, Printers' board of directors decided to change its method of distribution and open its own retail stores. Printers notified Office Supplies that it would not deliver any more cartridges. Is this a breach?

3.   Problem. Printers, Inc. agreed to sell printer cartridges to Desks & More, for as long as Desks & More wants to buy them, at $50 per cartridge, except that the price is to increase to the extent of any increase in Printers' direct costs. For how long does Desks & More have the right to purchase cartridges from Printers?

What is the relevance of the price-adjustment clause?

Three years later Printers informed Desks & More that it would deliver no more cartridges. Was this a breach?

4.   FOB Terms. Section 2–308(a) provides that, unless otherwise agreed, delivery is to occur at the seller's place of business (or residence), which means that the buyer must travel there to pick up the goods. Very often, however, the parties agree otherwise. This they may do if the seller has one or more vehicles for the purpose of delivering goods to its customers. They also may do this by calling on the services of a common carrier. If they do, they then must decide whether the seller's obligation to deliver is discharged when the seller delivers the goods to the carrier or when the carrier delivers the goods to the buyer. If the former, the contract is called a shipment contract; if the latter, a destination contract. If the parties do not decide, Official Comment 5 to 2–503 states that the contract is a shipment contract, i.e. the seller's delivery obligation is discharged upon proper delivery to the carrier. In a commercial transaction, the parties typically will use the term "FOB" to signal their intention, either "FOB Seller's location" or "FOB Buyer's location." Please read Section 2–319(1).

5. RISK OF LOSS

Who should have the risk of loss when goods are lost, damaged, or destroyed? The common law and Uniform Sales Act said the owner should have this risk, just as the owner stands to benefit if the goods appreciate in value. Losses and gains in the value of the goods were thought to be normal aspects of ownership. Since the seller was the owner of goods that ultimately would be owned by the buyer, risk of loss passed from one to the other at the precise moment that title was transferred from the seller to the buyer, unless the contract otherwise provided. Because the parties seldom made express agreements as to either risk of loss or the time that title passes from the seller to the buyer, the pre-Code law had to develop rules to determine passage of title when the goods had been damaged or destroyed. It made the "intention of the parties" preeminent in determining when title passed, but since that intention was seldom expressed, a number of presumptive rules were developed to determine it. Thus, if the goods were specific and nothing remained to be done to put them into a deliverable state, title passed when the bargain was struck. On the other hand, if the goods were unascertained (i.e. not yet identified as the goods constituting the subject matter of the contract), or if something remained to be done to them to make them deliverable, passage of title was postponed until the goods were "appropriated" to the contract and made deliverable.

These presumptions had a ring of certainty about them, but results in particular cases were far from certain, and a great deal of unnecessary litigation resulted. Consider Radloff v. Bragmus, 214 Minn. 130, 7 N.W.2d 491 (1943), in which a farmer contracted to sell a poultry dealer a flock of approximately 700 turkeys. The turkeys were to be graded by the parties and characterized by them as #1 or #2 and sold for a fixed price, which was 3 cents per pound more for the #1 birds than for the #2 birds. The contract was made on November 9th and the birds were to be delivered on November 13th. On November 11th a blizzard destroyed half of the turkeys and damaged the others. Who had the risk of loss? The court held that the risk passed to the buyer on November 9th, since the turkeys were sufficiently specific and nothing remained to be done to them to put them into deliverable condition. The weighing and grading process was described as merely ministerial, and not something "remaining to be done" so as to prevent the passage of title. The court was aided, of course, by the fact that the turkeys were frozen and thus still available for counting, grading, and weighing. What would have been the result if the turkeys had been destroyed by fire? How could the court have worked out the price? In that case, the court might well have found that the risk of loss remained with the seller since something important (i.e., determination of the price) remained to be done to make the birds deliverable.

Radloff v. Bragmus, and many common law and USA cases like it, also raised other policy problems that the passage-of-title concept did not take into account. For example, the farmer was in a better position to prevent the loss of the turkeys than the poultry dealer, and the farmer was more likely to have insurance on the birds. These facts favor placing the risk of loss on the seller.

In one of its most significant changes, Article 2 scrapped the passage-of-title, or property, approach to risk of loss and replaced it with what its drafters called a contractual approach. Official Comment 1 to 2–509. By using an FOB term, the parties contractually allocate the risk of loss. If they do not use an FOB term, 2–509 and 2–510 state rules on where the risk will fall. What factors do these rules emphasize? Under

2–509(1) why should the risk of loss depend on whether the contract is a shipment contract or a destination contract?

Under 2–509 the risk of loss depends in the first instance on whether the seller is required or authorized to ship the goods by carrier. If the seller is so required or authorized, then the risk of loss depends on where the seller is to deliver the goods. This is logical because the place of delivery normally is the point at which the seller's responsibilities for the goods end and the buyer's begin. Often the place of delivery is expressed by use of a mercantile term, such as "f.o.b.," "c.i.f.," "ex ship," etc. The most important mercantile terms are elaborately defined in 2–319 through 2–325. When the parties use one of these terms they are making an express contract, and in this respect 2–319 through 2–325 serve a different function from most of the other statutory terms found in Part 3 of Article 2. The definitions of mercantile terms found in 2–319 through 2–325 make it possible for the parties to express with a short symbol an entire range of rights and obligations that otherwise might take a full page to state. For example, 2–319(1) uses some 180 words to define the "f.o.b." term. Use of the symbol "f.o.b." creates an express term to do the things stated in all those words. The economy is obvious, and it accounts for the widespread use of the mercantile terms. Note that these terms are express terms of the parties' agreement, unlike the implied-in-law terms supplied by the gap fillers in Part 3 of Article 2, which insert terms when there is no express or implied-in-fact term covering the matter.

The term "f.o.b." (or "FOB") typically is used in connection with stating the price, because it indicates which party is to pay the cost of transporting the goods from the seller to the buyer. Under 2–319(1) if the contract is "FOB buyer's plant," who is to pay the freight charge? If the contract is "FOB seller's plant," who is to pay it? On what language do you rely for your conclusion?

———

A.M. Knitwear Corp. v. All America Export-Import Corp.

New York Court of Appeals, 1976.
41 N.Y.2d 14, 390 N.Y.S.2d 832, 359 N.E.2d 342.

■ COOKE, JUDGE. . . .

In June of 1973, the buyer All America Export-Import Corp., placed an order with the seller, A.M. Knitwear Corp., for several thousand pounds of yarn. The buyer used its own purchase order form, dated June 4, 1973, and typed thereon a description of the goods, a statement that partial shipments would be accepted, a description of how to mark the cartons, the quantity in pounds, and the dollar amount of the order. In addition, at the place on the buyer's form where the words "Ship Via" are printed, the buyer typed the instructions: "Pick Up from your Plant to

Moore-McCormack Pier for shipment to Santos, Brazil." Further, in the price column on the form, the buyer typed: "FOB PLANT PER LB. $1.35". . . . However, left blank by the buyer was the place on the form where the letters F.O.B. are printed and space is provided for the entry of F.O.B. terms.

In support of its contention that it had fully performed when the goods were loaded in the container, the seller quotes from an examination before trial of the buyer's vice-president, who stated:

"Q. What about the second order?

"A. After the first order was completed, Mr. Lubliner said he has more on hand.

"I said 'What do you mean by hand? Do you have again at the pier'?

"He says 'No. I have the same type of merchandise in my warehouse.' He says 'I could make you a similar offer, the same amount of cartons, 352 cartons. I do not know the weight. The weight may vary, at the same price.'

"I said, 'Okay,' We bought it. I accepted it.

"He asked me, what should I do.

"I said, 'As you know, most of the goods being shipped to South America is being containerized. I have to order a container or a trailer, whatever is the simplest expression. And then in turn you will have to put it into the container.'

"Mr. Lubliner said, 'This is no problem. Just send down the container. I will try to help you.' "

In preparation for shipping the goods to South America, the buyer phoned International Shipper's Co. of New York, a customs house broker and freight forwarder, and a third-party defendant in this action, to arrange for a local truckman to pick up and deliver the goods to the pier. International Shippers engaged a local truckman, Ability Carriers, Inc., another third-party defendant in this action, which as part of its services picked up an empty container from the Moore-McCormack Lines.

On Friday, June 22, 1973, the local truckman [delivered] the empty container . . . to the seller for loading.

On Monday, June 25, 1973, the seller had the goods loaded in the container and, on the same day, notified the buyer that the loading had been completed. The buyer then advised its freight forwarder to have the local truckman pick up the loaded container and deliver it to the Moore-McCormack pier. At around 8:00 p.m. that evening, prior to the arrival of the local truckman engaged by the buyer's freight forwarder, an individual driving a tractor arrived at the . . . premises where the container was located and hooked up the trailer containing the loaded container to his tractor. The tractor driven by this individual had no descriptive markings thereon or anything to identify its owner. Before leaving the premises, the driver signed a bill of lading, but the signature was indecipherable. It appears that this individual was a thief and had stolen the goods.

Sometime after June 25, the buyer delivered to the seller a check dated July 2, 1973 in the sum of $24,119.10 in payment for the goods loaded in the container. Payment on the check was thereafter stopped by the buyer, apparently when it was learned that the goods had not been received, and the seller brought an action against the buyer to recover payment for the goods.

At Special Term, both the seller and the buyer moved for summary judgment. That court found that the seller's undertaking was to load the goods in a deliverable condition into the carrier's container and that, by doing so and notifying the buyer, delivery was made in conformity with the agreement of the parties. Special Term thus determined that the risk of loss of the goods had passed to the buyer and granted the seller's motion for summary judgment.

The Appellate Division reversed Special Term and granted the buyer's motion for summary judgment, on the basis that there was neither physical delivery to the carrier nor delivery within the meaning of the Uniform Commercial Code. Both courts relied on subdivision (2) of section 2–401 and section 2–509, but the Appellate Division also relied on the holding in Avisun Corp. v. Mercer Motor Frgt., 37 A.D.2d 517, 321 N.Y.S.2d 658. We affirm the order of the Appellate Division which granted the buyer's motion for summary judgment.

Although the seller contends that the F.O.B. term on the buyer's form did not have its ordinary meaning, the Uniform Commercial Code provides that, unless otherwise agreed, the term F.O.B. at a named place "even though used only in connection with the stated price, is a delivery term" (Uniform Commercial Code, § 2–319, subd. [1]). Where the term F.O.B. the place of shipment is used, as in this case with the term F.O.B. plant, the code provides that the seller must ship the goods in the manner provided in section 2–504 of the Uniform Commercial Code and "bear the expense and risk of putting them into the possession of the carrier" (Uniform Commercial Code, § 2–319, subd. [1], par. [a]).

With respect to shipment by the seller, the code provides that where the seller is "required or authorized" to send the goods, but not required to deliver them to a particular destination, then "unless otherwise agreed" the seller must "put the goods into the possession of * * * a carrier" (Uniform Commercial Code, § 2–504, subd. [a]). Further, with respect to the risk of loss, the code provides that where the contract requires or authorizes the seller to ship the goods by carrier "if it does not require him to deliver them at a particular destination, the risk of loss passes to the buyer *when the goods are duly delivered to the carrier*" (Uniform Commercial Code, § 2–509, subd. [1], par. [a]; emphasis added). The risk of loss provision is, however, "subject to contrary agreement of the parties" (Uniform Commercial Code, § 2–509, subd. [4]). Although the seller contends that section 2–509 is not applicable because the agreement between the parties does not "require" the seller to "ship the goods by carrier," it should be noted that the section applies where the seller is "required or authorized" to ship the goods by carrier and is thus applicable here.

The effect of the provisions of the Uniform Commercial Code may be varied by agreement, with exceptions not applicable here (Uniform Commercial Code, § 1–102, subd. [3]) [revised 1–302(a)]. Furthermore, the provisions relevant to this action provide that the requirements set forth therein apply "unless otherwise agreed" or "subject to contrary agreement of the parties," though the absence of these words in the specific provisions was not intended to imply that the effect of such provisions may not be varied by agreement (Uniform Commercial Code, § 1–102, subd. [4] [revised 1–302(c)]). In this respect, the Official Comment to one provision states that "[c]ontrary agreement can also be found in the circumstances of the case, a trade usage or practice, or a course of dealing or performance" (Official Comment 5, § 2–509; see, also, Uniform Commercial Code, § 1–205 [revised 1–303] ("Course of Dealing and Usage of Trade."))

Despite the provisions of the code which place the risk of loss on the seller in the F.O.B. place of shipment contract until the goods are delivered to the carrier, here the seller contends that the parties "otherwise agreed" so that pursuant to its agreement, the risk of loss passed from the seller to the buyer at the time and place at which the seller completed physical delivery of the subject goods into the container supplied by the buyer for that purpose. In support of this contention, the seller alleges that the language of the purchase order "Pick Up from your Plant" is a specific delivery instruction and that the language "FOB PLANT PER LB. $1.35," which appears in the price column, is a price term and not a delivery term. Further support for the seller's contention is taken from the fact that the space provided in the buyer's own purchase order form for an F.O.B. delivery instruction was left blank by the buyer. Thus, the seller contends its agreement with the buyer imposed no obligation on it to make delivery of the loaded container to the carrier.

As often happens in commercial transactions, the parties to this action did not prepare an extensive written agreement, but merely made an arrangement that, under normal circumstances, would have been entirely satisfactory. The intervention of a wrongdoer who stole the goods that were the subject of the agreement forces the court to determine who should bear the loss resulting from the theft. In this respect, although the seller argues that only to the extent that the agreement is silent should the code apply, it should be noted that the underlying purpose and policy of the code is "to simplify, clarify and modernize the law governing commercial transactions" (Uniform Commercial Code, § 1–102, subd. [2], par. [a] [revised 1–103(a)(1)]). To this end, the code provides a framework for analyzing a variety of commercial transactions.

The seller's contention, that the parties intended the F.O.B. term as a price term and not a delivery term, conflicts with the code provision that states that the F.O.B. term is a delivery term "even though used *only* in connection with the stated price" (Uniform Commercial Code § 2–319, subd. [1]; emphasis added). That the F.O.B. term was not inserted in the space provided for such an expression in the buyer's own purchase order form does not require a determination that the F.O.B. term was intended as a price term, since the drafters of the code recognized that the term F.O.B. will often be used in connection with the stated price. Thus, the place where the term F.O.B. was typed on the buyer's form is not sufficient to suggest that the parties intended a price term, particularly when one considers that the relevant code provision was specifically intended to negate the decisions which treated this term as "merely a price term" (Official Comment 1, § 2–319.)

Since the term "FOB PLANT" was a delivery term, the risk of loss was on the seller until the goods were put into the possession of the carrier—unless the parties "otherwise agreed" or there was a "contrary agreement" with respect to the risk of loss. In this respect, the holding in Avisun v. Mercer Motor Frgt., cited by the Appellate Division, is illustrative. There, the question was whether the defendant carrier was liable as bailee for goods that were loaded in its trailer but were stolen before it arrived to pick them up. The Appellate Division there determined that until the acceptance of the goods by the defendant carrier, there was no bailment and that making available a vehicle for "possible temporary storage" was not an "acceptance." The seller contends that the *Avisun* case has no relevance to this case because it involves the issue as to when a bailment arises as a matter of law. The seller's interpretation is, however, too limited. The *Avisun* case is relevant here because, in the same sense that loading the trailer was not an "acceptance" of a bailment by the carrier, the loading of the container by the seller is not "delivery" to the carrier for purposes of the code, unless the parties so agree.

With respect to the agreement of the parties, the seller contends that the statements in the affidavits of the parties and a portion of an examination before trial of the buyer's vice-president manifest that the parties intended that the seller's performance would be complete when the goods were loaded into the container and the buyer was notified thereof. That this was the agreement of the parties is, according to the seller, further suggested by the fact the buyer issued a check, the payment of which was subsequently stopped, in payment for the goods.

The issuance of the check by the buyer gives little support to the seller's view. The making of payment is as consistent with the buyer's expectation that delivery had been made to the proper carrier as it is with the seller's contention that payment was made because the buyer considered the seller's performance to be completed upon loading the container.

With respect to the seller's contention as to the meaning of the statements of the buyer's vice-president, the seller has a formidable task in trying to prove that the parties did not intend the ordinary meaning of the term "FOB PLANT," i.e., delivery to the carrier. Although the only written expression in the transaction was the buyer's purchase order form on which the buyer typed the F.O.B. term, if the seller did not agree to this term, the seller should have expressed its disagreement after it received the purchase order form. For example, the seller should have indicated that the term "FOB PLANT" was merely a price term and not a delivery term or that the risk of loss was on the buyer after loading. The code anticipates that a written confirmation by a party may state terms additional to, or even different from, those offered and agreed upon, which terms, depending on certain factors, may become part of the contract (see Uniform Commercial Code, § 2–207). Yet here the seller did not seek to modify the F.O.B. term typed on the buyer's purchase order, but apparently relied on its own understanding of the agreement.

The provisions of the code with respect to risk of loss are subject to the "contrary agreement" of the parties (Uniform Commercial Code, § 2–509, subd. [4]). In this respect, the Official Comment states that " '[c]ontrary' is in no way used as a word of limitation and the buyer and seller are left free to readjust their rights and risks * * * in any manner agreeable to them" (Official Comment 5, § 2–509). It is, however, a recognized principle that "if the parties have made a memorial of their bargain * * * the law does not recognize * * * their intent, unless it is expressed in, or may fairly be implied from, their writing" (4 Williston, Contracts [3d ed.], § 600A, p. 286). It has also been established that when words have a well-understood meaning the courts are not permitted to search for the intent of the parties. The term "FOB PLANT" is well understood to require delivery to the carrier and does not imply any other meaning. If a contrary meaning was intended, an express statement varying the ordinary meaning is required. The statements made by an officer of the buyer and the other circumstances of this case are not enough to show that the term did not mean what it does in ordinary commercial transactions. One of the principal purposes of the code is to simplify, clarify and modernize the law governing commercial transactions (Uniform Commercial Code, § 1–102, subd. [2], par. [a] [revised 1–103(a)(1)]). To allow a commonly used term such as F.O.B. to be varied in meaning, without an express statement of the parties of an intent to do so, would not serve that purpose.

Accordingly, the order of the Appellate Division which granted the buyer's motion for summary judgment should be affirmed with costs.

QUESTIONS AND NOTES

1. The seller contended that "FOB Plant per lb. $1.35," as used in the contract, was a price term, not a delivery term. In view of the language in 2–319(1) that specifies the meaning of FOB "even though used only in connection with the stated price," how can the seller make this argument?

Note that 2–319(1)(a) requires the seller to ship the goods in the manner required by 2–504. Please read subsection (a) of 2–504. Is that section relevant to the court's reasoning in *A.M. Knitwear*?

2. Section 2–319 assigns a meaning to "f.o.b." but permits the parties to agree otherwise, i.e. to assign a different meaning to the term. Why does the court reject the seller's argument that the parties changed it in this case?

3. Problem. Zhang agreed to purchase furniture form Mellos Furniture Mfg. Co. Mellos' order form stated the price as "$8,416 + del'y" and called for transport to Zhang's residence "truck prepaid." On the way to Zhang's residence, the truck crashed, destroying the furniture. Zhang failed to pay, and Mellos sued. Who bore the risk of loss? Since the parties did not use an FOB term, 2–319 does not apply. Under 2–509(1) who should win? Is this a shipment or a destination contract?

In thinking about this problem, please consider Windows, Inc. v. Jordan Panel Systems Corp., 177 F.3d 114 (2d Cir.1999), in which a contract for window units between a seller in South Dakota and a buyer in New York provided, "All windows to be shipped properly crated/packaged/boxed suitable for cross-country motor-freight transit and delivered to New York City." The windows were damaged in transit.

> We conclude that this was a shipment contract. To overcome the presumption favoring shipment contracts, the parties must have explicitly agreed to impose on [the seller] the obligation to effect delivery at a particular destination. The language of this contract did not do so. Nor did [the buyer] use any commonly recognized industry term indicating that a seller is obligated to deliver the goods to the buyer's specified destination."

Id. at 117. The court held that under 2–509(1)(a) the buyer had the risk of loss.

Would the answer change if the contract contemplated that Mellos would use its own truck to deliver the furniture?

Notwithstanding the strong presumption favoring shipment contracts, an agreement displacing that presumption need not be express. For example, in Brunswick Box Co. v. Coutinho, Caro & Co., 617 F.2d 355 (4th Cir.1980), the seller was able to establish by the parties' course of dealing that "F.A.S." meant in the dock area, rather than "alongside the vessel" as provided in 2–319(2)(a).

4. The merchant-non-merchant distinction in 2–509(3). Under 2–509(3) if a consumer purchases goods from a merchant, risk of loss does not pass to the buyer until the buyer receives the goods. On the other hand, if a consumer purchases from another consumer, risk of loss passes upon tender of delivery. Often tender occurs an instant before the buyer receives the goods. But sometimes the buyer may not receive the goods until sometime after the seller tenders delivery. For example, the buyer may leave the goods with the seller for a time, as when a car dealer calls a buyer to set up a time for the buyer to pick up her newly arrived car, or when a buyer of furniture at a garage sale promises to return the next day with a truck. Is the distinction between merchants and non-merchants made by 2–509(3) justified? Are non-merchant sellers less likely to insure than merchant sellers? Are buyers from non-merchants more likely to insure goods tendered but not "received" by the buyer?

5.   It is common for the seller to send goods to the buyer by common carrier, and one of the parties must bear the risk of loss or damage to the goods in transit. (Of course, the party who bears the risk may have a claim against the carrier, but that is a different question.) Under 2–503, 2–504, and 2–509, the risk ordinarily passes from the seller to the buyer when the goods are placed in the hands of the carrier. That position is exemplified by the court in the *Windows* case. However, in order to shift the risk to the buyer, the seller must "put the goods in the hands of such a carrier and make such a contract for their transportation as may be reasonable having regard to the nature of the goods and other circumstances of the case" (2–504, and see Official Comment 3). In Cook Specialty Co. v. Schrlock, 772 F.Supp. 1532 (E.D.Pa.1991), the buyer argued that the seller had not made a reasonable contract with the carrier because the seller did not make sure that the carrier had insurance covering the full value of the shipment. (The carrier had shown the seller an insurance policy with a face-value coverage of $100,000 but in the particular circumstances, the policy covered only $5,000 of a $28,000 loss.) The court held that the seller had no responsibility to ascertain that the carrier's insurance would cover the full loss and that the seller had made a reasonable contract with the carrier.

6.   Section 2–509(4) recognizes, perhaps redundantly, that the parties are competent to allocate the risk of loss by their agreement. Thus, the parties could agree to split any loss on a 50–50 basis or some other fractional division or cast the entire burden on one party or the other. In the last major paragraph of its opinion, the court in *AM Knitwear* rejects the seller's argument that the parties did so in that case. Was this proper?

7.   If the court concluded that the parties had changed the meaning of "FOB Seller's Plant," what section would govern risk of loss, 2–319, 2–504, or 2–509?

8.   C.I.F. and C & F terms and risk of loss. C.I.F. and C. & F. terms are frequently employed in marine shipments. In almost all cases the place named by the term is the destination point. Thus, if the seller is in London and the buyer in New York, the contract employing c.i.f. or c. & f. terms would almost always provide "c.i.f. New York." What do these terms mean? The answer is found in section 2–320. Subsection (1) states that c.i.f. "means that the price includes in a lump sum the cost of the goods and the insurance and freight to the named destination. The term C. & F. or C.F. means that the price so includes cost and freight to the named destination." Thus a contract between a London seller and New York buyer which provided "$50,000 c.i.f. New York" would mean that for a price of $50,000, the London seller agrees to sell the goods to the buyer, pay the freight (and other costs) to New York, and purchase insurance on the goods in favor of the buyer. The c. & f. term is identical, except that the London seller has no obligation to purchase insurance.

Who has the risk of loss under these terms? At common law and under the USA, the buyer was said to have the risk of loss during the transit period (i.e. after the goods had been loaded on board in London) even though the contract required delivery in New York and for the seller to pay the freight. The conclusion was derived from the insurance term. Since, it was argued, the seller is obliged to purchase insurance in favor of the buyer, the parties must have agreed that the buyer had the risk of loss. Otherwise, it was questioned, why would he want insurance?

Apply this reasoning to the c. & f. contract, and a different result is reached. Here the seller is paying the freight; a destination point is named in the contract; and there is no duty on his part to provide insurance for the buyer. To some courts, at least, the "c. & f. New York" contract looked suspiciously like the "f.o.b. New York" contract and they, accordingly, put the risk of loss for the transit period on the seller. For an interesting case on this point, see Pittsburgh Provision & Packing Co. v. Cudahy Packing Co., 260 Pa. 135, 103 A. 548 (1918).

How does Article 2 assign risk of loss under c.i.f. and c. & f. contracts?

It makes no commercial sense to treat the c. & f. contract the same as if it were an f.o.b. contract, because the various mercantile symbols are intended by merchants to be short-hand expressions of different kinds of contracts. Two important factors in sales contracts are expense of transportation (is it included in the price or does the buyer have to pay it in addition to the price?) and risk of loss. Risk of loss becomes unimportant if there is insurance against it. If a seller, for example, has insurance against loss in any shipment made by him, he is well advised to make c.i.f. contracts. On the other hand, if the buyer has insurance against loss in transit, the c. & f. or f.o.b. origin contracts may be appealing to him. Note how the parties can allocate the risk of loss and cost of shipment by using f.o.b. and c.i.f. or c. & f. terms. Suppose the seller is in London and the buyer in New York. Which mercantile terms would you use to accomplish the following:

(1)   Buyer is willing to take the transit risk and to pay the freight charges;

(2)   Seller is willing to take the transit risk and pay the freight charges;

(3)   Buyer is willing to take the risk (because he already has insurance), but he wants the seller's price to include the transit charges;

(4)   Buyer is willing to take the risk if the seller will take out insurance for him, but he wants the seller to assume (as part of the price) the transit charges;

(5)   Buyer is willing to pay the transit charges but wants seller to assume the risk of loss.

A little reflection will indicate that the price will vary depending on which of the five contracts stated above is selected by the parties. In this connection the use of *pro forma* invoices is common, particularly in international trading. After coming to an agreement as to the basic price of goods at the factory in London, the London seller may be requested by the New York buyer to supply *pro forma* invoices showing what the price will be under some mercantile symbols. For example, the buyer may ask the seller to give him a *pro forma* invoice on "f.o.b. London" and "c. & f. New York." These invoices are usually considered to be offers, and the buyer is free to accept the one that best suits its needs.

9.   Sharpening the risk and expense points. London and New York are large cities. What happens when a term reads "f.o.b. London" or "c.i.f. New York" and the loss occurs in those cities themselves. Suppose, for example, the contract reads "f.o.b. London" and the goods are destroyed as they are being moved from the seller's plant in London to a ship anchored in the harbor? Suppose the goods are delivered to the shipowner at his dock, but they are destroyed as he tries to load them on board. Suppose they are put on board but are destroyed before the ship hoists its anchor or leaves the harbor. Similar hypotheticals easily can be developed for any mercantile term. Answers are of great importance, because many losses occur as goods are being loaded or unloaded from carriers, transported to and from carriers, and the like. How does Article 2 handle these problems?

The parties can better assure themselves as to where the risk will be placed by sharpening the points used in conjunction with mercantile terms. Thus, for example, instead of using a term "f.o.b. London," the parties might prefer to use a term such as "f.o.b. seller's plant London" or "f.o.b. dock London." Note also the additional mercantile terms that are available (because defined) for easy use where the parties want to pinpoint the risk of loss.

In terms of the London seller and the New York buyer, notice the continuum of risk points from the seller's plant in London to the buyer's plant in New York, and how the parties may make these points the ones at which the risk of loss will pass, through the use of mercantile terms:

(1)   There is a risk that the goods will be damaged or destroyed in loading them on a truck at the seller's plant. If the buyer is to take the risk after this point the contract might specify "f.o.b. truck seller's plant London";

(2)   There is a risk that the truck will be involved in an accident between the seller's plant and the loading dock. If the buyer is to take the risk after this point, the contract might specify "f.o.b. dock London";

(3)   There is a risk that the goods will be destroyed moving them from the dock onto a lighter to be used to transport them to the ship in the river. If the buyer is to take the risk after this point, the contract might specify "f.o.b. lighter London";

(4)   There is a risk that the lighter will be involved in an accident before it gets to the ship. If the buyer is to take the risk after this

point, the contract might provide "f.a.s. Jolly Jack London" (see 2–319(2) for the meaning of "f.a.s.");

(5)   There is a risk that the goods will be destroyed loading them onto the ship from the lighter. If the buyer is to have the risk after this point, the contract might read "f.o.b. Jolly Jack London."

By the same token, the various risk points thereafter (i.e. transit; unloading onto lighter in New York; unloading from lighter to dock; loading from dock onto truck; unloading from truck and loading onto boxcar; train transit; unloading from boxcar; loading onto truck in buyer's city; truck transit; unloading from truck at buyer's plant, etc.) can be identified in the contract as the risk-passing point. Obviously the price will vary depending on the risk assumed by the parties.

10. Incoterms. In 1936 the International Chamber of Commerce adopted a set of mercantile terms to establish a common worldwide understanding of those terms and the obligations of the seller and buyer thereunder. The most recent version of the Incoterms was promulgated in 2010 and contains 11 terms, including some that appear in Article 2, but also a number of additional ones. As to terms used in Article 2, the Incoterms 2010 defines them differently than Article 2 does. The Incoterms 2010 are intended for international, rather than domestic, trade, and the definitions reflect this difference.

To the extent Incoterms have become a usage of trade (or a course of dealing or course of performance), the definitions in Incoterms displace the definitions in Article 2 by virtue of the "unless-otherwise-agreed" exception of 2–319 to 2–324.

11. Risk of loss on bailed goods. Probably the most frequent occurrences of casualty are theft or accidents during transit. But occasionally a fire or theft will occur at the seller's place of business, as in *AM Knitwear*. When this happens the seller may try to place the loss on the buyer. Unless the parties have agreed otherwise, section 2–509(1) pretty clearly forecloses this: if the seller is to ship the goods by carrier, whether it is a shipment contract or a destination contract, the risk of loss is on the seller at least until the seller places the goods in the possession of the carrier. If the seller is not to ship by carrier, 2–509(3) places the risk of loss on the seller at least until the seller tenders the goods (and if the seller is a merchant, until the buyer receives the goods). So if the casualty occurs while the goods are still in the possession of the seller, the risk of loss remains on the seller.

On the other hand, 2–509(2) addresses the situation in which the goods are in the possession of a third party and are to remain there until the buyer claims them. Examples include goods in a warehouse, grain in a silo, and perishable goods that are in a refrigerated storage facility. In each of these examples, the goods are in the possession of a bailee.

The UCC defines "bailee" (7–102(a)(1)), but does not define "bailment." The dictionary defines "bailment" as "a delivery of personal property by one person (the *bailor*) to another (the *bailee*) who holds the property for a certain purpose, [usually] under an express or implied-in-fact contract." Black's Law Dictionary (11th ed.2019). In commercial transactions, the most common and useful kinds of bailments involve the shipment or storage of goods. The shipper or storer is the bailor; the carrier or the warehouse is the bailee. Usually when goods are shipped or stored, the bailee issues a document of title covering them. In the case of shipment, this document is called a "bill of lading"; in the case of storage, it is called a "warehouse receipt." These documents have three aspects. They are receipts for the goods; they are contracts describing the bailee's duty of care and the bailor's obligations to pay for that care; and they are "documents," meaning pieces of paper that control the goods. The documentary aspect is derived from the fact that the warehouse or carrier promises to deliver the goods only to the person who is in possession of the warehouse receipt or bill of lading under circumstances in which the promise runs to that person either directly, or through indorsement over to that person.

Not all bills of lading and warehouse receipts are documents. Usually they may be said to have documentary aspects only when they are negotiable, because the paper does not necessarily control the goods if it is non-negotiable. This distinction is considered in greater detail in Chapter 12 in conjunction with documentary sales.

One who has stored goods with a warehouse may want to sell them to a buyer who wants to leave them in the warehouse. This can be accomplished very easily if a negotiable warehouse receipt has been issued. In that case, the bailor "negotiates," i.e. transfers, the warehouse receipt to the buyer by indorsing and delivering it to the buyer. Thereafter, the buyer is entitled to take possession of the goods by surrendering the receipt to the bailee-warehouse. Under 2–509(2)(a) the risk of loss passes from the seller to the buyer when the seller delivers the warehouse receipt. If the warehouse receipt or bill of lading is non-negotiable, the transfer of the paper does not necessarily mean that the buyer will be able to get the goods, and thus this transfer, in and of itself, does not pass the risk of loss. The acknowledgment of the bailee that it will hold the goods for the buyer, rather than for the original bailor-seller, is the kind of assurance needed by the buyer of a non-negotiable warehouse receipt or bill of lading. Under 2–509(2)(b) this acknowledgment is the risk-passing event. But the rule is qualified. The buyer must obtain the acknowledgment or dishonor of the bailee within a reasonable time. If the buyer delays and waits more than a reasonable time before attempting to get the acknowledgment, the risk of loss passes as of the moment that the reasonable time period expires. This qualification is stated in 2–509(2)(c), which incorporates by reference 2–503(4)(b).

To repeat, when the document issued by the bailee is non-negotiable, 2–509(2)(b) provides that the risk of loss passes when the bailee acknowledges to the buyer that it is holding the goods for the buyer. If the goods suffer casualty while still in the possession of the seller, this rule incentivizes the seller to argue that it is a bailee and that it has given notice to the buyer (i.e., acknowledged) that it is holding the goods for the buyer. So, the argument concludes, risk of loss falls on the buyer. The courts uniformly reject this argument. E.g., Silver v. Wycombe, Meyer & Co., Inc., 124 Misc.2d 717, 477 N.YS.2d 288 (City Ct. N.Y. City 1984), holding that the rule of subsection (2) is limited to goods in the possession of a third party.

12. Organization of the sections on risk of loss. In the absence of contrary agreement, 2–509 states rules that apply depending on which of four categories is applicable to the transaction in question: Category one covers transactions in which the contract requires or authorizes the seller to ship the goods by carrier. Rules for this category are found in 2–509(1). Category two applies to transactions in which goods are held by a bailee to be delivered without being moved. Rules for this category are found in 2–509(2). Category three is residual. All transactions not in categories one and two fall into category three. Rules for this category are found in 2–509(3). Category four is transactions in which one of the parties has breached the contract before the loss or destruction of the goods, and the rules for these transactions are in 2–510.

Jakowski v. Carole Chevrolet, Inc.

New Jersey Superior Court, Law Division, 1981.
180 N.J.Super. 122, 433 A.2d 841.

■ NEWMAN, J.S.C.

Plaintiff seeks summary judgment on count I of the complaint alleging breach of a new car sales contract by defendant Carole Chevrolet, Inc.

The essential facts are not in dispute. On March 8, 1980 plaintiff Jakowski (hereinafter "buyer") entered into a contract of sale with defendant Carole Chevrolet, Inc. (hereinafter "seller,") calling for the purchase of one new 1980 Chevrolet Camaro. The parties also agreed that the car would be undercoated and that its finish would have a polymer coating. While there is some disagreement as to exactly when the buyer ordered the coatings, it is undisputed that prior to delivery the seller agreed to deliver the car with the coatings applied. Likewise, it is undisputed that the car in question was delivered to the buyer without the required coatings on May 19, 1980.

The next day, May 20, 1980, the seller contacted the buyer and informed him that the car delivered to him lacked the coatings in question and seller instructed buyer to return the car so that the coatings could be applied. On May 22, 1980 the buyer returned the auto to the seller for application of the coatings. Sometime during the evening of May 22 or the morning of May 23 the car was stolen from the seller's premises and it was never recovered. Seller has refused to either provide a replacement auto to buyer or to refund the purchase price. Buyer remains accountable on the loan, provided through GMAC, for the purchase of the car.

The narrow question thus presented is upon whom, as between buyer and seller, this loss should fall. In U.C.C. terminology, on May 22, 1980, which party bore the risk of the car's loss.

Seller argues that the risk of loss passed to the buyer upon his receipt of the auto. This is consistent with U.C.C. § 2–509(3) pursuant to which the risk of loss passes to the buyer upon his receipt of the goods. Section 2–509(4), however, expressly provides that the general rules of § 2–509 are subject to the more specific provisions of § 2–510 which deals with the effect of breach upon risk of loss.

Buyer relies upon § 2–510(1) which provides:

Where a tender or delivery of goods so fails to conform to the contract as to give a right of rejection the risk of their loss remains on the seller until cure or acceptance.

Application of this section to the instant facts requires that three questions be answered. First, did the car "so fail to conform" as to give this buyer a right to reject it? If so, did the buyer "accept" the car despite the nonconformity? Finally, did the seller cure the defect prior to the theft of the auto?

The first question must be answered in the affirmative. The contract[1] provided that the car would be delivered with undercoating and a polymer finish, and it is undisputed that it was delivered without these coatings. The goods were thus clearly nonconforming and, despite seller's assertion to the contrary, the degree of their nonconformity is irrelevant in assessing the buyer's concomitant right to reject them. N.J.S.A. 12A:2–106 is clear in its intent to preserve the rule of strict compliance, that is, the "perfect tender" rule:

Goods * * * are "conforming" or conform to the contract when they are in accordance with the obligations under the contract. [N.J.S.A. 12A:2–106(2), emphasis supplied. See also, Comment 2 to § 2–106].

The language of § 2–510(1), "so fails to conform," is misleading in this respect: no particular quantum of nonconformity is required where a single delivery is contemplated. The allusion is to § 2–612 which substitutes a rule of substantial compliance where, *and only where*, an installment deal is contemplated. White & Summers, Uniform Commercial Code (2nd ed.1980), § 5.5 at 187–188.

Secondly, did buyer "accept" the auto by taking possession of it? This question was presented in Zabriskie Chevrolet, Inc. v. Smith, 99 N.J.Super. 441, 240 A.2d 195 (Law Div.1968). In *Zabriskie* it was held that the mere taking of possession by the purchaser is not equivalent to acceptance. Before he can be held to have accepted, a buyer must be afforded a "reasonable opportunity to inspect" the goods. N.J.S.A. 12A:2–606.

Seller's actions in this matter preclude analysis in conventional "acceptance" terms. Buyer had no opportunity, indeed no reason, to reject, given seller's own communication to buyer shortly after delivery,

---

[1] Seller makes much of the fact that the original sales order failed to specify the coatings in question. It is undisputed, however, that seller, subsequent to execution of the order, agreed to supply the coatings prior to delivery. As such, the coatings were clearly part of the "contract," as that term is defined by the Code. N.J.S.A. 12A:1–201(11) [revised 1–201(b)(12)].

to the effect that the goods did not conform and that the seller was exercising its right to cure said nonconformity. See N.J.S.A. 12A:2–508 (seller's right to cure). This communication, in effect an acknowledgment of nonconformity, obviated the need for a formal rejection on buyer's part, if, indeed, § 2–510(1) imposes such an obligation. Put another way, it precluded the buyer from rejecting the car. Consistent with this analysis, I find as a matter of law that there was no acceptance by buyer of this nonconforming auto.

As to the final question of whether the seller effected a cure, there is no evidence—in fact defendant does not even contend—that cure was ever effected.

Given the undisputed facts, the operation of § 2–510(1) is inescapable. The goods failed to conform, the buyer never accepted them and the defect was never cured. Accordingly, the risk of loss remained on the seller and judgment is granted for plaintiff.

A further note on the law is in order. It is possible to conjure up a host of hypotheticals leading to seemingly perverse results under § 2–510. The section has been the subject of some scholarly criticism. See e.g., White & Summers, supra, § 5.5 at 187. Williston, "The Law of Sales in the Proposed Uniform Commercial Code," 63 Harv.L.Rev. 561, 583 (1950).

The fact is, however, that those courts considering it have had little difficulty in applying it as written [citing cases from four states].

The rule is simple enough: under N.J.S.A. 12A:2–510(1), where goods fail to conform to the contract of sale the risk of loss remains on the seller until the buyer accepts the goods or until the seller cures the defect. Such was the result in the aforecited cases, even though in all of them the goods were still in the *buyer's* possession at the time of their destruction.

For present purposes it is adequate to hold simply that where a seller obtains possession of the goods in an effort to cure defects in them so as to comply with his end of the bargain, he is under a contractual duty to redeliver them to the buyer. In failing to do so, he has breached the contract.

Pursuant to N.J.S.A. 12A:2–711 buyer is entitled to a refund of so much of the purchase price as has been paid to seller. Included in the cost of the automobile are the finance charges incurred by the buyer, who secured financing from GMAC pursuant to a retail installment sales contract entered into with the seller. There is no dispute about including these charges in the purchase cost, and the buyer, as of March 30, 1981, indicated the total amount due on any judgment to be $9,398.75. However, since this case was first heard some additional time has passed and a current pay-off figure should be obtained for inclusion in this judgment.

QUESTIONS AND NOTES

1.   Problem. Bonita contracted to purchase a new car from Carson Chevrolet, to be ordered from the manufacturer. When it arrived, Carson prepared it for delivery in accordance with the manufacturer's protocol and phoned Bonita to come pick it up. Before Bonita could get there, the car was severely damaged by hail. Who bore the risk of this casualty?

2.   In *Jakowski* the seller phoned the buyer on May 20 to bring the car back so that the seller could apply the coatings, and the car was stolen on May 22 after the buyer had returned it. What if the car had been stolen from the buyer's garage on May 21st: who would have had the risk of loss?

3.   Problem. Blake contracted to purchase a new car from Carson Chevrolet, to be ordered from the factory. In due course, Carson phoned Blake to say that the car had arrived. Blake went to pick it up and saw that the car had a racing stripe, which Blake did not order and did not want. Carson said, "I won't charge you for it; or, if you like, I can order in another car. It'll only be 6–8 weeks." Blake did not want to wait that long and said, "Oh, I'll take it that way." Carson then persuaded Blake to add undercoating, for another $250, and told Blake to return the next day after 5:00 to pick it up. Late that night the car was stolen. Who had the risk of loss?

4.   Problem. Taylor's Timepieces and Premiere Packaging entered into a contract under which Taylor's was to accept delivery of plastic pellets at the rate of 1,000 pounds per day for 120 days, beginning July 1. Before July 1st, Premiere produced the full quantity of 120,000 pounds, placed the pellets in its warehouse, and identified it to the particular contract. Taylor's told Premiere that it would not be able to accept delivery starting on July 1, but that it would be able to begin taking deliveries on July 10th. On July 7th, Premiere's warehouse burned and the entire stock of pellets was destroyed. To what extent, if any, is Taylor's liable to Premiere for the price of the goods? See 2–709.

What if Taylor's took delivery of the pellets on July 1–7, but the remainder of the pellets were destroyed by fire during the early morning hours on July 8? Taylor's must pay for the pellets it received (see 2–607(1)), but must it pay the rest of the price, i.e. who has the risk of loss?

5.   The court's statement at the bottom of page 233, that the "language of § 2–510(1), 'so fails to conform,' is misleading," is itself misleading, as we will see when we consider the buyer's right to reject nonconforming goods.

6.   CISG and risk of loss. Article 69 of the Convention on Contracts for the International Sale of Goods reads as follows:

(1)   . . . [In cases in which the contract of sale does not involve carriage of the goods or sale of goods in transit], the risk passes to the buyer when he takes over the goods, or, if he does not do so in due time, from the time when the goods are placed at his disposal and he commits a breach by failing to take delivery.

(2)   However, if the buyer is bound to take over the goods at a place other than a place of business of the seller, the risk passes

when delivery is due and the buyer is aware of the fact that the goods are placed at his disposal at that place.

(3) If the contract relates to goods not then identified, the goods are not considered to be placed at the disposal of the buyer until they are clearly identified to the contract.

What result under the Convention in Problem 4 above?

See Articles 67 and 68 of the Convention as to passage of risk in carriage contracts. Article 67 contains rules like those of 2–509 on carriage contracts. The Convention does not state a rule as to goods being held by bailees.

Article 70 of the Convention deals with the effect of seller's breach on risk of loss. It provides: "If the seller had committed a fundamental breach of contract, Articles 67, 68 and 69 do not impair the remedies available to the buyer on account of the breach." So the buyer may have the risk of loss but retains its remedies for the seller's fundamental breach. (See Article 25 for definition of "fundamental breach.")

7. Problem. REI, located in the United States, contracted to purchase 4,000 bicycles from Dengfu, located in China. Dengfu's delivery obligation was to put the bicycles on board a ship at Canton, and it did so. When the goods arrived in San Francisco, REI discovered that 1,000 of the bicycles were unusable because of warped wheels. Also, another 500 of the bicycles were soaked by seawater on the voyage and are essentially worthless. The warped wheels were in that condition when loaded on the vessel. Can REI reject the entire shipment of bicycles? See CISG Articles 49, 51 and 82.

May REI accept the bicycles and shift the risk of loss as to the seawater-damaged bicycles to Dengfu? Assume that there are no relevant sections other than those already cited here and in Note 6? Compare UCC 2–510.

8. Risk of loss vs. ultimate loss. The concept of "risk of loss" does not refer to ultimate loss. Rather, it is used to determine which party takes the initial loss. Often the initial loss can be shifted to the other party to the sales contract or to a carrier, warehouseman, or insurance company. For example, if the buyer has the risk and a loss occurs because of the seller's negligence, the seller is liable for its negligence and will suffer the ultimate loss. The initial loss is put on the buyer, but, on straight tort principles, the buyer can recover from the seller. Consideration of the liability of the carrier appears in Chapter 12.

6. SPECIAL ARRANGEMENTS

a. SALE OR RETURN; SALE ON APPROVAL

Buyers of goods for their own use will frequently want a trial period before deciding whether to purchase. Sections 2–326 and 2–327(1) define and describe the incidents of such "sales on approval." Notice particularly that title and risk of loss do not shift to the buyer until acceptance of the goods (which is not the same thing as acceptance of the seller's offer to sell). If the buyer does not accept the goods, their return is at the expense and risk of the seller. Also, goods on approval are not subject to the claims of buyer's creditors until the buyer accepts them. Therefore, for example, if a judgment creditor of the buyer has the sheriff seize goods that the buyer has "on approval" but has not yet accepted, the seller would be able to reclaim the goods from the sheriff.

A buyer who purchases goods for resale may want the right to return the goods to the seller for credit if the buyer is unable to sell them. Sections 2–326 and 2–327(2) also define and describe the incidents of such "sale or return" transactions. In a sale or return, title to the goods passes to the buyer under the ordinary rules of 2–401 (which we will study later), and the goods are subject to claims of the buyer's creditors while the goods are in the hands of the buyer. Therefore, the seller runs the risk of losing the goods to the buyer's creditors who get an interest in them while the goods are in the possession of the buyer. Also, in a sale or return transaction, return is at the buyer's risk and expense.

Note 2–326(4), which seeks to discourage buyers from falsely claiming that they have the right to return unsold goods.

b.   AUCTIONS

Please reread Hoffman v. Horton, page 40 supra.

Drew v. John Deere Co. of Syracuse, Inc.

New York Supreme Court, Appellate Division, 1963.
19 A.D.2d 308, 241 N.Y.S.2d 267.

■ HALPERN, JUSTICE. . . . [The defendant repossessed a tractor because the owner defaulted in his obligation to pay for it. State law requires a repossessing creditor to resell the tractor] at public auction (Personal Property Law, § 79). The defendant advertised the auction sale, stating that the property would be sold to the highest bidder at the sale. The plaintiff bid $1500 at the sale but the auctioneer did not accept the bid; instead he announced that the defendant itself had bid $1600 and accordingly the property was struck down to the defendant.

The plaintiff claims that the defendant was disqualified to bid because it had not announced in advance that it intended to bid pursuant to section 102, subdivision 4, of the Personal Property Law. Hence, the plaintiff argues, his bid was the highest lawful bid and therefore a contract of sale came into existence between the plaintiff and the defendant for the sale of the tractor at the price bid.

The plaintiff's whole case rests upon the theory that the auction was one "without reserve." At such an auction, the owner of the property has no right to withdraw the property after bidding has commenced. It is also necessarily implicit in an auction "without reserve," that the owner of the property may not himself bid in the property, as this would be equivalent to withdrawing it from sale (Restatement of Contracts, § 27). Various legal theories have been advanced for the holding that the announcement that [an] auction would be "without reserve" imposes a binding legal obligation upon the owner, but the best view seems to be that the owner, by making such an announcement, enters into a collateral contract with all persons bidding at the auction that he will not withdraw the property from sale, regardless of how low the highest bid might be (Gower, "Auction Sales of Goods Without Reserve," 68 Law Quarterly Review 457; Warlow v. Harrison (1859) 1 E. and E. 295, 309). Therefore, the highest bona fide bidder at an auction "without reserve" may insist that the property be sold to him or that the owner answer to him in damages.

On the other hand, in an auction sale not expressly announced to be "without reserve," the owner may withdraw the property at any time before it is actually "knocked down" to a bidder by the auctioneer. There is no contract until the offer made by the bidder is accepted by the auctioneer's "knocking down" the property to him (Personal Property Law, § 102, subd. 2). "An auction 'with reserve' is the normal procedure" (Comment 2 to section 2–328, Uniform Commercial Code).

In our case, there was no express statement that the auction would be "without reserve." The statement that the sale would be made to the highest bidder is not the equivalent of an announcement that the auction would be "without reserve" (cf. Personal Property Law, § 102(2); Uniform Commercial Code, § 2–328, subd. 3). "An announcement that a person will sell his property at public auction to the highest bidder is a mere declaration of intention to hold an auction at which bids will be received" (7 C.J.S. Auctions and Auctioneers § 1a, p. 1240).

Corbin writes that the auctioneer at an auction sale in asking for bids, does not make an operative offer. "This is true even though the seller or his representative has issued advertisements or made other statements that the article will be sold to the highest bidder, or is offered for sale to the highest bidder. Such statements are merely preliminary negotiation, not intended and not reasonably understood to be intended to affect legal relations. When such is the case, the seller or his representative is as free to reject the bids, highest to lowest, as are the bidders to withdraw them. The seller may at any time withdraw the article from sale, if he has not already accepted a bid. He need give no reasons; indeed, he rejects all bids by merely failing to accept them—by doing nothing at all. It is not necessary for him to say that 'the privilege is reserved to reject any and all bids.' Such a statement is merely evidence that the goods are not being offered 'without reserve'" (1 Corbin on Contracts, § 108, pp. 338–40).

Since, upon the present record, the auction sale appears to have been "with reserve," no contract of sale came into existence, even if we assume that the plaintiff was the highest lawful bidder. Concededly, the plaintiff's bid was never accepted. Therefore, the plaintiff's papers upon his motion for summary judgment fail to make out a cause of action for breach of contract.

. . .

The plaintiff's motion for summary judgment was therefore properly denied. The defendant asks us to go further and to grant a summary judgment in favor of the defendant. We do not believe that this should be done. The plaintiff relied upon the announcement that the sale would be to the highest bidder as showing that the auction sale was to be "without reserve." As we have seen, the announcement was insufficient of itself for that purpose but the plaintiff should be given an opportunity to produce any other evidence he may have on that subject. For that reason, summary judgment for the defendant should be denied.

QUESTIONS AND NOTES

1. For an Article 2 case reaching the same result as Hoffman v. Horton (reopening the bidding to receive a bid made as the hammer is falling), see Callimanopulos v. Christie's, Inc., 621 F.Supp.2d 127 (S.D.N.Y.2009).

2.   Shill bidding or puffing. Secret bidding at auctions by the seller or one acting on his behalf is known as "shill bidding" or "puffing," a practice that is considered fraudulent because it creates a misleading impression that there is greater competition for the goods than actually exists. The practice also may violate the obligations of one conducting an auction without reserve, for it permits the shill to overbid the highest bona fide bidder and deprive that bidder of the goods. Further, it enables the seller to convert an auction "without reserve" into one "with reserve," by purporting to sell the goods to the shill and by that subterfuge in effect withdraw them from the sale. How does the UCC police against this practice?

3.   Problem. Sylvia, a retailer of second-hand clothing, often disposes of slow-moving items by selling them at auction. She offered a fur coat for sale at an auction announced to be "without reserve." Beth attended the auction and bid $100 for it. Schiller, an employee of Sylvia who was instructed "to keep the bidding going unless otherwise signaled by the auctioneer," bid $110. The auctioneer, knowing Schiller's true role, accepted the bid. Beth then bid $120. Seeing the great interest manifested in the goods by Beth and Schiller, Clark became interested in the coat and bid $130. Schiller then bid $140, and Beth topped that with a bid of $150. At that point Schiller received the signal from the auctioneer and made no further bid. The goods were knocked down to Beth at $150. Does Beth have to pay? If so, or if Beth elects to take the goods, how much must she pay for them?

Would it make any difference if the auction were announced to be "with reserve"?

In Nevada National Leasing Co. v. Hereford, 36 Cal.3d 146, 203 Cal.Rptr. 118, 680 P.2d 1077 (1984), the owner's agent bid without the knowledge of others at the auction. Hereford bought three items of equipment at bid prices of $10,000, $6,100 and $8,600 respectively. His last bids before the agent started bidding were $6,000, $3,500 and $500 respectively. Hereford was given a judgment for the excess of the prices he paid over his last bid before the agent started bidding. Hereford was also awarded $10,000 in punitive damages for the fraud of owner. The court did not state whether other persons submitted bids between the agent's first bid and Hereford's accepted bid. However, the awarding of punitive damages suggests that the court would not have accepted an argument that recovery under 2–328 should be limited to the excess of Hereford's high bid over the next highest bid of a third party "good faith" bidder.

CHAPTER 5

WARRANTIES

A. INTRODUCTION

Caveat emptor—literally "buyer beware"—means that the buyer takes all risk concerning the quality of the goods being purchased, even including the risk that the goods are not as described. At one time the doctrine of caveat emptor was the law. For more than a century, however, the doctrine has not applied to the law of sales. For a judicial description of the evolution and abandonment of the doctrine at common law, see the 1934 case, Smith v. Zimbalist, 2 Cal.App.2d 324, 38 P.2d 170 (1934).

Today, of course, the matter is governed by Article 2, under which a merchant seller who deals in goods of the kind has an obligation that, unless the parties otherwise agree, the goods be of a certain quality. This obligation, a "warranty of merchantability," arises independently of any overt representations by the seller concerning the goods. Since it does not depend upon any affirmative statements or acts by the seller, it is referred to as an "implied warranty." Article 2 also provides for another implied warranty, the "warranty of fitness for particular purpose," which arises if the seller has reason to know that the buyer is relying on the seller to select for the buyer goods that are suitable for the buyer's purposes. Also, another warranty, an "express warranty" arises if the seller makes promises or representations as to the goods in such a manner as to become a part of "the basis of the bargain."

The core idea underlying these provisions is that the buyer is entitled to have the quality that the buyer reasonably expects under the contract. While it has sometimes been suggested that the Code warranty scheme is too complicated and could better have provided merely that a buyer is entitled to the quality that the buyer reasonably expects (the approach later taken by the CISG), the Code division of warranties of quality into three categories does rest on relatively easily distinguishable core factual differences. The following examples show the differences:

(a) Express warranty (2–313). Seller says to Buyer: "This pick-up truck is a 2018 model." It actually is a 2017 model. Seller has breached an express warranty.

(b) Implied warranty of merchantability (2–314). The truck in the above example is a 2018 model as represented but it has three cracked pistons, a differential ring gear with 10% of its teeth missing, and an inoperative automatic transmission pump (these are fairly serious problems). If Seller is a dealer in motor vehicles, Seller undoubtedly has breached the warranty of merchantability, even if Seller said nothing at all about the quality of the vehicle. We can view the merchant seller as impliedly representing that any goods it sells are of usual or normal quality. A person who is not a dealer in goods of the kind, on the other hand, does not impliedly warrant the merchantable quality of the goods. (Note, however, that a seller—whether merchant or non-merchant—may be liable in tort for failing to disclose defects of which the seller is aware.)

(c) Implied warranty of fitness for particular purpose (2–315). Buyer tells Seller that she needs a truck capable of towing her sailboat from her home to the various lakes in the region. Seller directs her to the truck in question. If the strain of towing the sailboat causes the truck's transmission to seize, there probably is a breach of the warranty of fitness for particular purpose.

The foregoing warranties relate primarily to the quality of the goods being sold. In addition to these warranties, Article 2 also provides a warranty of title (2–312), to protect a buyer's expectation that third parties will not disturb the buyer's possession of the goods.

Warranty is one of the areas of the law where tort and contract overlap. The same facts may require analysis under both bodies of law. The focus of this book, of course, is contract. But you should be aware of the need to consider tort doctrine as well. For example, a representation of fact (such as, "This is a 2018 model") gives rise to an express warranty. If that representation is false, it is actionable as a breach of warranty, and it may also be actionable as deceit, negligent misrepresentation, or innocent misrepresentation (if the other elements of those torts are present). Similarly, if goods are defective and cause personal injuries, the seller may be subject to strict liability in tort as well as liability in contract for breach of the implied warranty of merchantability.

B. EXPRESS WARRANTIES

Before reading the next case, please read 2–313(1)(a) and identify the facts that must exist in order for there to be an express warranty.

———

Doug Connor, Inc. v. Proto-Grind, Inc.

Florida District Court of Appeal, 2000.
761 So.2d 426.

■ PETERSON, J. . . .

Connor is in the land clearing business. In 1997, Doug Connor ("Doug"), the president of Connor, Inc., became interested in acquiring a large commercial grinding machine called a Proto-Grind 1200 manufactured by Proto-Grind, Inc. ("Proto-Grind"). Proto-Grind's brochure describes the machine as the toughest grinder on the market and capable of grinding "trouble free" a wide variety of debris. The brochure specifically lists timber, stumps, and railroad ties as items capable of being reduced to mulch and contains pictures of a large log being processed by the grinder. The brochure does not describe any type of timber or stumps as being incapable of being reduced to mulch.

Doug attended a demonstration of the machine in Atlanta, Georgia, during which a large log was reduced to mulch. During the demonstration, Doug told George Protos, the president of Proto-Grind, that he would need "a machine that would handle my land clearing operation . . . in Melbourne, Florida. . . . I told him that I needed it to grind, be able to grind palmettos, palm trees, oak trees, pine trees, pepper trees, whatever type of land clearing that's out there, that's what I needed the machine to do." Doug testified that he explained to Protos that he mainly conducted large land clearing in his business, approximately 15 acres to up to 100 acres, and that Protos assured him that "the machine would do what I needed it to do, large jobs, small jobs, whatever I needed."

In April 1997, Connor contracted to purchase a Proto-Grind 1200 for $226,000. Upon delivery, Connor employed it in a land clearing job which consisted of pepper and oak trees, but not palm trees or palmettos. The contract for the purchase of the grinder provided for a two-week trial period in which Connor could use the machine and, only if satisfied with its performance during the trial run, would he be irrevocably committed to purchasing the grinder. However, Doug could not resist the incentive offered by Protos only three days after the delivery that eliminated Connor's first installment payment of $5,500 in exchange for the elimination of the trial period.

Unfortunately, the grinder proved not to be as tough as advertised or represented. Connor experienced repeated mechanical difficulty but the most serious problem was the inability of the machine to discharge the mulch from cabbage palm trees and palmettos.

Connor's mechanic talked to representatives of Proto-Grind about the problem and was advised that some new grates, "demo grates," would perform better with not only the cabbage palms but other land clearing debris. The mechanic ordered the demo grates. The new grates "worked a little better as far as the land clearing debris, with the exception of cabbage palms." The mechanic testified that when grinding cabbage palms the mulch would simply not pass through the grates. During this period, from April to June, Connor wrote several letters to Protos complaining about the deficiencies.

In July 1997, Connor filed its complaint and alleged in Count III, that Proto-Grind breached an express oral warranty that the machine purchased would grind organic materials effectively, including palmettos, and that the machine "would be free from defects for a period of six months upon delivery and that should service be necessary, that defendant would promptly come to Florida to fix the machine at plaintiff's location."

The matter proceeded to a jury trial, but the trial court granted Proto-Grind's motion for directed verdict at the conclusion of Connor's case-in-chief. . . .

Connor alleged in Count III, that "at the time of sale . . . as an inducement to cause plaintiff to purchase the Proto-Grind 1200, defendant . . . through its agents, expressly, orally warranted to plaintiff that the Proto-Grind 1200 would grind, in an efficient and effective manner, organic waste materials from Florida land clearing operations, including the grinding and disposition of palmettos." At trial, Doug testified that the agents of Proto-Grind "all assured me all day long that the machine would do what I needed it to do here in Florida." Doug, during his meeting with Protos, informed Protos that he typically cleared large tracts of land—anywhere from 15 to 100 acres. Doug also told him that he needed to grind palmettos, palm trees, oak trees, pine trees and pepper trees. Doug's mechanic testified that during his inspection of a Proto-Grind machine in Tampa, company officials "had assured us that the machine would grind cabbages, because they had already done it."

Proto-Grind argues that the oral affirmations made by the Proto-Grind agents merely constituted puffing, sales talk, or otherwise non-actionable opinion and that in order to satisfy the threshold of an affirmation of fact, the statement must be detailed and specific. *See* Miles v. Kavanaugh, 350 So.2d 1090 (Fla. 3d DCA 1977). In *Miles,* the court found that a seller of an airplane, by reference to his logbook, had warranted the accuracy of the information contained in the book. Proto-Grind states that the principle of that case is that the threshold of making a factual affirmation is that the statement be specific and detailed. Contrarily, *Miles* seems to support the opposite conclusion by providing a broad definition of an express warranty. The court wrote:

> [A]n express warranty need not be by words, but can be by conduct as well, such as, the showing of a blueprint or other description of the goods sold to the buyer. Moreover, fraud is not an essential ingredient. . . . It is sufficient that the warranty was made which formed part of the basis of the bargain. *Id.* at 1093.

We believe that the statements made by Proto-Grind could amount to more than puffing or sales talk. Proto-Grind specifically understood the buyer's needs and represented to Connor that the Proto-Grind 1200 would meet those needs. The trier of fact should have had the opportunity to consider whether Proto-Grind made the express warranty that the Proto-Grind 1200 could, without modification of its basic components, reduce palmettos and palm trees to mulch on a regular basis. Connor's evidence that an unmodified Proto-Grind 1200 would only mulch palm trees 50% of the time without jamming, presented a jury question as to whether Proto-Grind's pre-purchase representations regarding mulching palm trees and palmetto brush were met.

Proto-Grind further argues that an express warranty generally arises only where the seller asserts a fact of which the buyer is ignorant prior to the beginning of the transaction, and on which the buyer reasonably relies as part of the basis of the bargain. It is not clear from the record, however, that when Connor purchased the Proto-Grind 1200 he was aware that it was ill-equipped to mulch palm trees and palmetto brush.

On a similar note, Proto-Grind argues that because Doug knew that a competitor was, at times, quite dissatisfied with his Proto-Grind 1200, Connor was on equal footing with Proto-Grind with respect to knowledge of the machine's capability. Doug testified that the Proto-Grind was the first grinder that Connor ever purchased. Even if Doug was more savvy than he acknowledged, the manufacturer of an expensive product should be well aware of the product's attributes and deficiencies before it offers it to the public. We conclude that the relative knowledge of the parties is a matter for the jury to consider, not a complete bar to recovery by Connor.

We conclude that the trial court erred in dismissing Connor's count alleging a breach of an express warranty. . . . [T]he finder of fact could reasonably conclude that the alleged oral promises made were more than mere puffing, that the product failed to meet the promise that it would sufficiently grind palm trees and palmettos, that Connor relied on these affirmations, and that because the deficiency of the product was not cured, Proto-Grind breached this express warranty.

The directed verdict in favor of Proto-Grind on Count III is vacated and the matter is remanded to the trial court for further proceedings.

QUESTIONS

1. Defendant argued that it had not made the affirmation of fact required by 2–313(1)(a) for there to be an express warranty. In view of subsection (2) and Official Comment 8, why does the court reject that argument?

2. In the second paragraph on this page, the court suggests that the relative knowledge of the parties is relevant. To what is it relevant?

Royal Business Machines, Inc. v. Lorraine Corp.

United States Court of Appeals, Seventh Circuit, 1980.
633 F.2d 34.

■ BAKER, DISTRICT JUDGE.

[Plaintiff purchased 128 photocopiers from defendant. Dissatisfied with the performance of the copiers, plaintiff sued and won. Defendant appealed.]

We first address the question whether substantial evidence on the record supports the district court's findings that Royal made and breached express warranties to Booher [the plaintiff]. The trial judge found that Royal Business Machines made and breached the following express warranties:

(1) that the [copiers] and their component parts were of high quality;

(2) that experience and testing had shown that frequency of repairs was very low on such machines and would remain so;

(3) that replacement parts were readily available;

(4) that the cost of maintenance for each RBC machine and cost of supplies was and would remain low, no more than 1/2 cent per copy;

(5) that the RBC machines had been extensively tested and were ready to be marketed;

(6) that experience and reasonable projections had shown that the purchase of the RBC machines by Mr. Booher and Lorraine Corporation and the leasing of the same to customers would return substantial profits to Booher and Lorraine;

(7) that the machines were safe and could not cause fires; and

(8) that service calls were and would be required . . . on the average of every 7,000 to 9,000 copies, including preventive maintenance calls.

. . .

The decisive test for whether a given representation is a warranty or merely an expression of the seller's opinion is whether the seller asserts a fact of which the buyer is ignorant or merely states an opinion or judgment on a matter of which the seller has no special knowledge and on which the buyer may be expected also to have an opinion and to exercise his judgment. General statements to the effect that goods are "the best," Thompson Farms, Inc. v. Corno Feed Products, 173 Ind.App. 682, 366 N.E.2d 3 (1977), or are "of good quality," Olin-Mathieson Chemical Corp. v. Moushon, 93 Ill.App.2d 280, 235 N.E.2d 263 (1968), or will "last a lifetime" and be "in perfect condition," Performance Motors, Inc. v. Allen, 280 N.C. 385, 186 S.E.2d 161 (1972), are generally regarded as expressions of the seller's opinion or "the puffing of his wares" and do not create an express warranty.

No express warranty was created by Royal's affirmation that [the copiers] and their component parts were of high quality. This was a statement of the seller's opinion, the kind of "puffing" to be expected in any sales transaction, rather than a positive averment of fact describing a product's capabilities to which an express warranty could attach.

Similarly, the representations by Royal that experience and testing had shown that the frequency of repair was "very low" and would remain so lack the specificity of an affirmation of fact upon which a warranty could be predicated. These representations were statements of the seller's opinion.

The statement that replacement parts were readily available is an assertion of fact, but it is not a fact that relates to the goods sold as required by Ind.Code § 26–1–2–313(1)(a) and is not an express warranty to which the goods were to conform. Neither is the statement about the future costs of supplies being 1/2 cent per copy an assertion of fact that relates to the goods sold, so the statement cannot constitute the basis of an express warranty.

It was also erroneous to find that an express warranty was created by Royal's assurances to Booher that purchase of the RBC machines would bring him substantial profits. Such a representation does not describe the goods within the meaning of U.C.C. § 2–313(1)(b), nor is the representation an affirmation of fact relating to the goods under U.C.C. § 2–313(1)(a). It is merely sales talk and the expression of the seller's opinion. See Regal Motor Products v. Bender, 102 Ohio App. 447, 139 N.E.2d 463, 465 (1956) (representation that goods were "readily saleable" and that the demand for them would create a market was not a warranty).

On the other hand, the assertion that the machines could not cause fires is an assertion of fact relating to the goods, and substantial evidence in the record supports the trial judge's findings that the assertion was made by Royal to Booher. The same may be said for the assertion that the machines were tested and ready to be marketed. See Bemidji Sales Barn v. Chatfield, 312 Minn. 11, 250 N.W.2d 185 (1977) (seller's representation that cattle "had been vaccinated for shipping fever and were ready for the farm" constituted an express warranty). See generally R. Anderson, Uniform Commercial Code § 2–313:36 (2d ed. 1970) (author asserts that seller who sells with seal of approval of a third person, e. g., a testing laboratory, makes an express warranty that the product has been tested and approved and is liable if the product was in fact not approved). The record supports the district court's finding that Royal represented that the machines had been tested.

As for findings 8 and the maintenance portion of Number 4, Royal's argument that those statements relate to predictions for the future and cannot qualify as warranties is unpersuasive. An expression of future capacity or performance can constitute an express warranty. In Teter v. Shultz, 110 Ind.App. 541, 39 N.E.2d 802, 804 (1942), the Indiana courts held that a seller's statement that dairy cows would give six gallons of milk per day was an affirmation of fact by the seller relating to the goods. It was not a statement of value nor was it merely a statement of the seller's opinion. The Indiana courts have also found that an express warranty was created by a seller's representation that a windmill was capable of furnishing power to grind 20 to 30 bushels of grain per hour in a moderate wind and with a very light wind would pump an abundance of water. Smith v. Borden, 160 Ind. 223, 66 N.E. 681 (1903). . . .

Whether a seller affirmed a fact or made a promise amounting to a warranty is a question of fact reserved for the trier of fact. Substantial evidence in the record supports the finding that Royal made the assertion to Booher that maintenance cost for the machine would run 1/2 cent per copy and that this assertion was not an estimate but an assertion of a fact of performance capability.

Finding Number 8, that service calls on the RBC II would be required every 7,000 to 9,000 copies, relates to performance capability and could constitute the basis of an express warranty. There is substantial evidence in the record to support the finding that this assertion was also made.

While substantial evidence supports the trial court's findings as to the making of those four affirmations of fact or promises, the district court failed to make the further finding that they became part of the basis of the bargain. Ind. Code § 26–1–2–313(1) (1976). While Royal may have made such affirmations to Booher, the question of his knowledge or reliance is another matter.[7]

This case is complicated by the fact that it involved a series of sales transactions between the same parties over approximately an 18-month period and concerned two different machines. The situations of the parties, their knowledge and reliance, may be expected to change in light of their experience during that time. An affirmation of fact which the buyer from his experience knows to be untrue cannot form a part of the basis of the bargain. City Machine & Mfg. Co. v. A. & A. Machinery Corp., 4 UCCRS 461 (E.D.N.Y.1967). See generally R. Anderson, Uniform Commercial Code, § 2–313:18 (2d ed.1970). Therefore, as to each purchase, Booher's expanding knowledge of the capacities of the copying machines would have to be considered in deciding whether Royal's representations were part of the basis of the bargain. The same representations that could have constituted an express warranty early in the series of transactions might not have qualified as an express warranty in a later transaction if the buyer had acquired independent knowledge as to the fact asserted.

The trial court did not indicate that it considered whether the warranties could exist and apply to each transaction in the series. Such an analysis is crucial to a just determination. Its absence renders the district court's findings insufficient on the issue of the breach of express warranties.

---

[7] The requirement that a statement be part of the basis of the bargain in order to constitute an express warranty "is essentially a reliance requirement and is inextricably intertwined with the initial determination as to whether given language may constitute an express warranty since affirmations, promises and descriptions tend to become a part of the basis of the bargain. It was the intention of the drafters of the U.C.C. not to require a strong showing of reliance. In fact, they envisioned that all statements of the seller become part of the basis of the bargain unless clear affirmative proof is shown to the contrary. See Official Comments 3 and 8 to U.C.C. § 2–313." Sessa v. Riegle, 427 F. Supp. 760, 766 (E.D.Pa.1977), aff'd without op. 568 F.2d 770 (3d Cir.1978).

Since a retrial on the questions of the breach of express warranties and the extent of damages is necessary, we offer the following observations. The court must consider whether the machines were defective upon delivery. Breach occurs only if the goods are defective upon delivery and not if the goods later become defective through abuse or neglect.

In considering the promise relating to the cost of maintenance, the district court should determine at what stage Booher's own knowledge and experience prevented him from blindly relying on the representations of Royal. A similar analysis is needed in examining the representation concerning fire hazard. . . . The court also should determine when that representation was made. If not made until February 1975, the representation could not have been the basis for sales made prior to that date. . . .

QUESTIONS AND NOTES

1.   Why does the court conclude that the statements concerning availability of replacement parts and the future cost of supplies do not relate to the goods? How is the statement concerning the cost of maintenance different?

2.   At the end of the excerpt, the court asserts that the representation concerning fire hazard could not give rise to an express warranty in those sales made before the seller made the representation. Intuitively this seems correct. But is it actually correct?

3.   The distinction between an affirmation of fact and a statement of the seller's opinion has been critical in a very large number of decisions. Long ago Judge Learned Hand wrote of the distinction as follows:

> An opinion is a fact, and it may be a very relevant fact; the expression of an opinion is the assertion of a belief, and any rule which condones the expression of a consciously false opinion condones a consciously false statement of fact. When the parties are so situated that the buyer may reasonably rely upon the expression of the seller's opinion, it is no excuse to give a false one. Bigler v. Flickinger, 55 Pa. 279. And so it makes much difference whether the parties stand "on an equality." For example, we should treat very differently the expressed opinion of a chemist to a layman about the properties of a composition from the same opinion between chemist and chemist, when the buyer had full opportunity to examine. The reason of the rule lies, we think, in this: There are some kinds of talk which no sensible man takes seriously, and if he does he suffers from his credulity. If we were all scrupulously honest, it would not be so; but, as it is, neither party usually believes what the seller says about his own opinions, and each knows it. Such statements, like the claims of campaign managers before election, are rather designed to allay the suspicion which would attend their absence than to be understood as having any relation to objective truth. It is quite true that they induce a

compliant temper in the buyer, but it is by a much more subtle process than through the acceptance of his claims for his wares.

Vulcan Metals Co. v. Simmons Manufacturing Co., 248 F. 853, 858 (2d Cir.1918).

To distinguish warranty from puffery, the court in Avola v. Louisiana-Pacific Corp., 991 F.Supp.2d 381, 392–94 (E.D.N.Y.2013), stated that courts look to factors of vagueness, subjectivity, and ability to influence the buyer's expectations:

> The "vagueness" factor applies when the disputed statements fail to describe a specific characteristic of the product on which the claims are based. . . . General descriptions about the product—*e.g.*, high-speed internet service as the "fastest, easiest way to get online"; a truck as the "most dependable, long-lasting"; or an insurance policy as providing that its policyholders are "in Good Hands"—can constitute puffery. . . .

> The "subjectivity" factor applies when the disputed statements may not be measured on an objective basis, such as by reference to clinical studies or comparison with the product's competitors. . . . Examples of puffery [include] statements that a stereo system reflects the "most life-like reproduction of orchestral and vocal sounds" or that a chain of hotels maintains "standards proud enough to bear [the founder's] name."

> The "inability to influence" factor applies when, among other things, the disputed statements are made by all of the product's competitors, or these statements cannot mean everything that they suggest. . . . For instance, a statement that a sports beverage will "Upgrade your game" is plainly an exaggeration, because no buyer truly believes that consuming this beverage "result[s] in improved athletic abilities." Similarly, a statement that "you can grow thick, beautiful grass ANYWHERE" with a specific type of grass seed is "so exaggerated as to preclude reliance by consumers."

Thus the court in *Royal Business Machines* stated, "General statements to the effect that goods are 'the best,' or are 'of good quality,' or will 'last a lifetime' and 'be in perfect condition' are generally regarded as expressions of the seller's opinion and do not create an express warranty." Do not overlook the word "generally" in this sentence.

Consider Morehouse v. Behlmann Pontiac-GMC Truck Service, Inc., 31 S.W.3d 55, 57–60 (Mo.App.2000), in which plaintiff purchased a used minivan. She returned the vehicle five times for repair of numerous problems. When the engine overheated and seized while plaintiff was driving on the highway, she sued.

> Morehouse and her mother, Dorothy Williams, went to the Behlmann dealership to look at used cars. Ed Bogosian . . . , a Behlmann salesperson with forty-two years of experience selling vehicles, offered to help Morehouse. Morehouse told him that she was looking for a reliable and lasting van priced around ten or

twelve thousand dollars. Bogosian told her that he had years of experience selling vehicles and that he knew what was good.

After looking at several vehicles, Morehouse focused on a Chevrolet Astro minivan because it had less than 100,000 miles and the color appealed to her. Bogosian told her that the minivan was in excellent condition, had been well maintained, and that it would be reliable.

Following this conversation, Morehouse and her mother test drove the minivan. Morehouse noticed a "jerking of the engine" and the brake pedal pressing almost to the floor. Her mother thought that the engine felt sluggish. After the test drive, Morehouse advised Bogosian of these complaints. Bogosian replied that the vehicle was in good condition but agreed to go with Morehouse on a second test drive. Bogosian said that he could not feel or hear anything wrong with the engine and that the roughness was standard. He also said that since a minivan drives more like a truck than a car and she was not used to driving a truck, she should not be concerned about the roughness of the engine. . . .

A seller may puff his wares or express his opinion as to the quality and value of his goods even to the point of exaggeration without incurring a warranty obligation. *Guess v. Lorenz*, 612 S.W.2d 831, 833 (Mo.App.1981). Conversely, if the representation is a statement of fact, a petition alleging such a representation may sufficiently state a claim for breach of express warranty or fraudulent misrepresentation. *Carpenter v. Chrysler*, 853 S.W.2d 346, 358 (Mo.App.1993). A given representation can be an expression of opinion or a statement of fact depending upon the circumstances surrounding the representation.

In *Carpenter v. Chrysler Corp.*, a salesman told a customer that a car was "a good car, reliable, brand new. This might be what you're looking for. This is the kind of car to have." In fact, the dealer had repaired a leak in the power steering system and the car had been subject to a recall. We held that the salesman's statements to the customer were statements of fact.

Similarly, here Bogosian represented to Morehouse that the minivan was "in excellent condition," "in good condition," "in tip-top shape" and would be "reliable." Also as in *Chrysler,* the salesperson here referred specifically to the minivan in attesting to its soundness and reliability. As we held in *Chrysler,* these statements conveyed sufficient definite information about the quality of the vehicle for that representation to be considered material. They are not merely statements of opinion. . . .

Conversely, in *Guess v. Lorenz,* we held that an automobile seller's statements that the car was "in good shape" and that a noise in the rear end of the vehicle "was just something the car does" were expressions of opinion. An integral part of that holding, however, was that the buyer and the seller were on equal footing in terms of knowledge of car mechanics and the seller gave no impression of knowledge about cars. *Id.* In the present case, Morehouse told Bogosian several times that she was an inexperienced car buyer and that she had no idea what to look for in a car. Bogosian responded that he had years of experience selling cars and knew what was good. Given Bogosian's advantage in experience and his representation thereof, his statements to Morehouse about the condition of the car conveyed sufficient information to be representations of fact, and not merely statements of opinion. We hold that Bogosian's statements to Morehouse were actionable representations of fact.

4. An automobile manufacturer states, "For 3 years or 36,000 miles, whichever comes first, we will repair or replace any part that is defective in material or workmanship under normal use." Does this create an express warranty? If so, precisely what is it? Please consider 2–313, Official Comment 4 (first sentence).

Problem. Hudson Motor Co. distributes an owner's manual with each car it manufactures. The owner's manual contains the language quoted above. Hudson learns that a seal in the engine in certain of its models is prone to fail after four-to-five years of operation. This is far short of the expected life of the engine (or a properly designed seal). Hudson continues selling the cars in this condition, accompanied by the language quoted above. Wilkens purchases one of these models and drives it 42,000 miles, at which time the engine is destroyed because of the faulty seal. May Wilkens recover for breach of express warranty? Is 2–725(2) relevant to this issue?

Several courts have concluded that an automobile warranty limited as above to a specified duration or mileage means that for a breach to occur, the defect must become manifest within the specified period. E.g., Daugherty v. American Honda Motor Co., 144 Cal.App.4th 824, 51 Cal.Rptr.3d 118 (2006). On the other hand, the sale of a product with knowledge that a major part is likely to fail long before the expiration of the useful life of the product may violate a consumer fraud statute that prohibits the knowing concealment or omission of a material fact with intent that others rely upon the nonexistence of that material fact. E.g., Maniscalco v. Brother International Corp., 627 F.Supp.2d 494 (D.N.J.2009). Contra, *Daugherty.*

5. Under the Uniform Sales Act, the predecessor to Article 2, the buyer's reliance on the seller's statement was an essential element of express warranty. The drafters of Article 2 specifically departed from expressing the requirement in terms of reliance. Instead, they created the phrase, "basis of the bargain." What does it take for an affirmation of fact to become part of the basis of the bargain? The court in *Royal Business Machines* addresses this briefly in footnote 7. Please reread that footnote and the Official Comments cited there.

6. In Rogath v. Siebenmann, 129 F.3d 261 (2d Cir.1997), plaintiff purchased a painting from defendant for $570,000. After the exchange, the authenticity of the painting was questioned, and plaintiff sued. The trial court granted plaintiff's motion for summary judgment, holding that defendant breached express warranties. Defendant appealed, acknowledging that he made the affirmations but claiming that at the time of the purchase plaintiff knew that the affirmations were false. The court wrote:

> The Bill of Sale provides:
>
>> In order to induce David Rogath to make the purchase, Seller . . . makes the following warranties, representations and covenants to and with the Buyer.
>>
>> 1.   That the Seller is the sole and absolute owner of the painting and has full right and authority to sell and transfer same; having acquired title as described in a copy of the Statement of Provenance signed by Seller annexed hereto and incorporated herein; [and] that the Seller has no knowledge of any challenge to Seller's title and authenticity of the Painting. . . .
>
> Because the Bill of Sale was a contract for the sale of goods, Rogath's breach of warranty claims are governed by Article Two of the Uniform Commercial Code ("UCC"). Section 2–313 of the UCC provides that "any description of the goods which is made part of the basis of the bargain creates an express warranty that the goods shall conform to the description."
>
> Whether the "basis of the bargain" requirement implies that the buyer must rely on the seller's statements to recover and what the nature of that reliance requirement is are unsettled questions. See Note, "Express Warranties under the Uniform Commercial Code: Is There a Reliance Requirement"? 66 N.Y.U. L. Rev. 468, 469 (1991); see also Annotation, "Purchaser's Disbelief in, or Nonreliance upon, Express Warranties Made by Seller in Contract for Sale of Business as Precluding Action for Breach of Express Warranties," 7 A.L.R. 5th 841 (1992). Not surprisingly, this same confusion haunted the New York courts for a time.
>
> Some courts reasoned that the buyer must have relied upon the accuracy of the seller's affirmations or promises in order to recover.
>
> Other courts paid lip service to a "reliance" requirement, but found that the requirement was met if the buyer relied on the seller's promise as part of "the basis of the bargain" in entering into the contract; the buyer need not show that he relied on the truthfulness of the warranties.
>
> Finally, some courts reasoned that there is a "reliance" requirement only when there is a dispute as to whether a warranty was in fact given by the seller. These courts concluded that no reliance of any kind is required "where the existence of an express warranty in a contract is conceded by both parties." CPC Int'l Inc. v. McKesson Corp., 134 Misc.2d 834, 513 N.Y.S.2d 319, 322 (Sup.Ct.1987). In these cases, the buyer need establish only a breach of the warranty.

In 1990 New York's Court of Appeals dispelled much of the confusion when it squarely adopted the "basis of the bargain" description of the reliance required to recover for breach of an express warranty. In CBS Inc. v. Ziff-Davis Publishing Co., 75 N.Y.2d 496, 553 N.E.2d 997, 554 N.Y.S.2d 449 (N.Y.1990), the court concluded that "this view of 'reliance'—i.e., as requiring no more than reliance on the express warranty as being a part of the bargain between the parties—reflects the prevailing perception of an action for breach of express warranty as one that is no longer grounded in tort, but essentially in contract." 553 N.E.2d at 1001. The court reasoned that "the critical question is not whether the buyer believed in the truth of the warranted information . . . but whether [he] believed [he] was purchasing the [seller's] promise [as to its truth]." Id. 1000–01 (quotations omitted and some insertions altered).

CBS was not decided on the basis of the UCC, probably because the sale of the magazine business at issue did not constitute the sale of goods. Nevertheless, the court relied heavily on UCC authorities, expressly noting that "analogy to the Uniform Commercial Code is 'instructive.' " Id. at 1002 n.4.

In 1992, in a case also involving the sale of a business, we followed the New York Court of Appeals and delineated fine factual distinctions in the law of warranties: a court must evaluate both the extent and the source of the buyer's knowledge about the truth of what the seller is warranting. "Where a buyer closes on a contract in the full knowledge and acceptance of facts *disclosed by the seller* which would constitute a breach of warranty under the terms of the contract, the buyer should be foreclosed from later asserting the breach. In that situation, unless the buyer expressly preserves his rights under the warranties . . . , we think the buyer has waived the breach." Galli v. Metz, 973 F.2d 145, 151 (2d Cir.1992) (emphasis added). The buyer may preserve his rights by expressly stating that disputes regarding the accuracy of the seller's warranties are unresolved, and that by signing the agreement the buyer does not waive any rights to enforce the terms of the agreement. See Galli, 973 F.2d at 150.

On the other hand, if the seller is not the source of the buyer's knowledge, e.g., if it is merely "common knowledge" that the facts warranted are false, or the buyer has been informed of the falsity of the facts by some third party, the buyer may prevail in his claim for breach of warranty. In these cases, it is not unrealistic to assume that the buyer purchased the seller's warranty "as insurance against any future claims," and that is why he insisted on the inclusion of the warranties in the bill of sale. Galli, 973 F.2d at 151.

In short, where the seller discloses up front the inaccuracy of certain of his warranties, it cannot be said that the buyer—absent the express preservation of his rights—believed he was purchasing the seller's promise as to the truth of the warranties. Accordingly, what the buyer knew and, most importantly, whether he got that knowledge from the seller are the critical questions.

The court held that the granting of plaintiff's motion for summary judgment was improper because the affidavits of the parties in connection with that motion raised genuine questions of fact concerning what defendant told plaintiff about challenges to the authenticity of the painting.

7.   Problem. After taking it for a test drive, Kit and Carl Christal purchased a ten-year-old car with 196,000 miles from a used-car dealer for $800. The dealer told them that the car was "mechanically sound," was "in good condition," and had "no problems." On their way home after the purchase, the car did not seem to operate properly. They took it to a mechanic, who said that it needed $1,500 in repairs to be made safe to drive. The Christals sued, claiming breach of express warranty. What result?

8.   Problem. To sell a used crane, Equipco ran the following advertisement:

> "CRANE-Railroad 30 ton. McMyler Cummins diesel engine; 55 ft. hvy. duty boom; complete with generator for magnet work. Good condition."

a.   The owner of Pauli Construction looked at the crane and was told by one of Equipco's employees that it was "in very good condition." Pauli purchased the crane and, when delivered, it was inoperable. Did Equipco make an express warranty as to condition?

b.   Assume that the advertisement and oral statement as to good condition created an express warranty. Assume also that at the time of sale, Pauli and Equipco signed a document that reads as follows:

Contract of Sale

Seller agrees to sell and Buyer agrees to buy the following equipment:

> 1 Used Locomotive Crane, Manufactured by McMyler, 30-ton capacity, 55-ft. boom, complete with Cummins Diesel Engine and Generator.

Price F.O.T. Chicago—$4,000

Buyer understands that the contract between the parties hereto consists solely and completely of the terms found in this instrument.

_____
s/Buyer

_____
s/Seller

Does this document affect Pauli's ability to enforce the earlier statements as express warranties?

c.   Assume that the document also states,

> "Buyer hereby waives all warranties, express or implied, including the implied warranty of merchantability, or any warranty given by

operation of law, statutory or otherwise, regarding the subject matter of this contract."

Now what result? See 2–316(1).

d. Assuming the same contract of sale, what result if the boom turned out to be only 45 feet long? (Assume that Pauli was reasonable in not noticing that fact)?

If Pauli had noticed that the boom did not look like it was 55 feet long but had said nothing to Equipco about that fact before entering the contract, what result?

e. Suppose that the crane was as described above in problem (b), but a conspicuous clause in the body of the contract states:

"All equipment is subject to inspection and the descriptions are approximate and intended to serve as a guide."

If the crane will lift only seven tons, is there a breach of express warranty?

9. Preemption. Statutes other than the UCC may preempt warranty liability under 2–313. An example is the Food, Drug, and Cosmetics Act. With respect to medical devices, the Act states that "no State . . . may establish . . . any requirement (1) which is different from, or in addition to, any requirement applicable under this chapter to the device . . . ."[a] Pursuant to this provision, if the FDA has approved a manufacturer's representation about a product, the state may not impose liability for that representation. But, notwithstanding the prohibition against requirements "in addition to" the FDA's, a state may impose liability for representations that go beyond what the FDA has approved.[b] In Wildman v. Medtronic, Inc., 874 F.3d 862 (5th Cir.2017), plaintiff was injured when a neurostimulater malfunctioned less than two years after it was implanted in his back. He sued for breach of an express warranty that the neurostimulator had a useful life of at least nine years. In its approval process, the FDA approved the manufacturer's statement that the device's battery life was nine years. Medtronic argued that plaintiff's claim was preempted. But since the FDA had evaluated the longevity of the battery but not any other components, the court rejected the argument. It concluded that the warranty went "above and beyond any guarantee the FDA expressly or implicitly approved." Even though the device's primary component may have been the battery, Medtronic's warranty referred not just to the battery, but also to the "many components" of the device.

10. Leases. Except for stylistic improvements, 2A–210 is identical to Article 2's provision on express warranties. Consequently, the foregoing materials on sales transactions are equally applicable to lease transactions.

11. CISG. The Convention on Contracts for the International Sale of Goods uses different terminology than Article 2. Section (1) of Article 35 declares, "The seller must deliver goods which are of the quantity, quality and description required by the contract and which are contained or packaged in

---

a   21 U.S.C. § 360k(a)(2018).

b   Gomez v. St. Jude Medical Daig Division Inc., 442 F.3d 919 (5th Cir.2006).

the manner required by the contract." To what extent does this cover the same ground as 2–313(1)?

Section (2) proceeds to articulate several gap-filling quality terms, using some of the terminology found in Article 2, mostly in the sections on *implied* warranties. At this time, note subsection (2)(c), which resembles 2–313(1)(c). We will return to this section in connection with implied warranties.

C. THE IMPLIED WARRANTY OF MERCHANTABILITY

1. HISTORICAL BACKGROUND

By 1830 the courts of England had recognized an implied warranty of merchantability in contracts for the sale of goods. The courts of the United States had not. For example, in 1833 a merchant sold a large quantity of flour. When the flour proved to be of unsatisfactory quality, the buyer sued, and lost. On appeal, three members of New York's highest court wrote opinions; here is an excerpt from one of them, in which the judge described the evolution of the law of implied warranty in England:

> I have been accustomed to suppose that the rules as to the liability of vendors, on sales of personal property, were clearly defined and firmly settled, at least in this State; but I am getting to learn that the spirit of the age, which is disposed to consider nothing settled that it imagines susceptible of improvement—a spirit which regards nothing as too ancient to be attacked— nothing as too new to be attempted, is extending its influences to the oldest and deepest rooted principles of the common law. This event might not be so much regretted, if it were proposed to be brought about only through the open and responsible agency of legislation; but when pursued through the devious and occult process of judicial exceptions and qualifications, it becomes a subject of some solicitude and apprehension. Ld. Eldon wisely remarked, that instead of struggling by little circumstances to take cases out of a general rule, it is more wholesome to struggle not to let little circumstances prevent the application of the general rule. But this principle, in modern times, has been so poorly maintained, that the profession of the law, it seems to me, is fast becoming a matter of memory rather than of reason and judgment; and the study of it is already so much more the study of the exceptions and evasions of general principles, than of general principles themselves, that I am sometimes induced to think that as a science, the law would be better understood, and as a rule of right, more justly administered, if the reports of judicial decisions for the last half century were struck out of existence. We see continually that the qualification or relaxation of a general principle, established by one reported case, is made the place of departure for

ascertaining a new position in another, and this in a third, and so on, until the original rule, the natural standard of the law, is obscured and utterly lost sight of, by means of intervening artificial measures of supposed particular justice. The consequence to be feared is that judicial reports, instead of being what, no doubt it is intended they should be, beacons and landmarks to guide the public into quiet havens of security and repose, may become false lights to decoy into the whirls and shoals of litigation. . . .

In the earliest history of the common law, the distinction between its rules and those of the civil law in respect to the liability of vendors, was marked and acknowledged. More than 200 years ago, Ld. Coke, in speaking of it, says: "The civil law binds every man to warrant the thing he selleth, albeit there be no express warranty; but the common law bindeth him not, unless there be a warranty in deed or in law." . . .

Originally, the only implied warranty or warranty in law, as distinguished from a warranty in fact on the sale of personal property, was that of ownership by the vendor. Afterwards the sale of goods by sample was held to imply a warranty that the bulk of the goods corresponded in quality with the specimen exhibited; then, in case of goods not present at the sale, and consequently not susceptible of inspection by the buyer, a warranty was implied that they were of the general denomination or nature represented; then, though the goods were present and susceptible of inspection by the buyer, yet if not actually inspected, a warranty was implied that they were of the description and quality represented in the invoice or sale bill, this, however, is rather on the ground that the writing amounts to an express warranty in fact. Then, where goods are sold by the manufacturer of them, a warranty has been implied that they are of a merchantable quality; then, where goods are sold for a particular purpose, a warranty that they are fit for that purpose. Finally, in Jones v. Bright, 5 Bing., 533, Ch.J. Best is disposed to consider the law as resolving itself into this: "that if a man sells generally, he undertakes [warrants] that the article is fit for some purpose, viz.: that it is merchantable; and if he sells for a particular purpose, he undertakes [warrants] that it is fit for that particular purpose." Thus the English courts, in a circle of about 200 years, by the process of finding a new principle in each departure from the old one, by extending each case a little beyond the rule of the case immediately preceding it, instead of measuring it by the original standard principle, have gradually but completely subverted the common law maxim of *caveat emptor,* and effectually, though perhaps undesignedly, substituted for it the repudiated principle of the civil law, which, as Ld. Coke quaintly but correctly states it "binds every man to warrant the thing he selleth, albeit there be no express warranty." Some cases [in this state] would seem to indicate that our courts are upon the same pilgrimage; but [they are not].

Wright v. Hart, 18 Wend. 449 (N.Y.Ct. Errors 1837) (Tracy, Sen.).

————

Senator Tracy spoke too soon: courts in New York and elsewhere continued to find new principles in departures from the old, and in sales of goods by merchants implication of warranties of merchantability became the rule rather than the exception.

The Uniform Sales Act, drafted by Professor Samuel Williston and approved by NCCUSL in 1906, provided: "Where goods are bought by description from a seller who deals in goods of that description (whether he be the grower or manufacturer or not), there is an implied warranty that the goods shall be of a merchantable quality." [§ 15(2)]. Williston had lifted that language from section 14 of the British Sale of Goods Act, adopted in England in 1894.

Under the Uniform Sales Act, an implied warranty of merchantability would arise in a fact situation like that in Wright v. Hart, but note that section 15 created the implied warranty only "where goods are bought by description. "Hence, the warranty might not arise in a case in which a buyer purchased specific barrels of flour that were on hand at the time of the purchase: there it might be concluded that the sale was not "by description." See generally, Williston on Sales, Revised Edition, §§ 227–32 (1948).

2. THE STANDARDS

The Uniform Commercial Code dropped the sale-by-description limitation on the warranty of merchantability: now the warranty arises under 2–314 against any merchant who deals in goods of the kind in any sales transaction unless there is an effective disclaimer. In addition, the Code provides in 2–315 for an implied warranty of fitness for particular purpose. Please review these sections now.

1.   Problem. To promote sales of its high-end Viking stoves, Superior Appliances advertised that it would give anyone who purchased a Viking stove a free Dyson hand-held vacuum cleaner. Martinez purchased one of the stoves, installed it in his kitchen, and plugged the Dyson into an outlet in his walk-in pantry. The Dyson short circuited and caused a small fire, quickly extinguished. Has Superior breached an implied warranty?

2.   Problem. Needing to replace some of the windows in her house, Skubic purchased six double-paned thermal windows from World Windows. After installation Skubic discovered that the seal was defective, water had gotten between the panes, and the glass was foggy. World Windows replaced the six windows with new ones. The replacement windows had a sound seal, but the insulating gas between the panes was defective, causing the glass to appear cloudy. Can Skubic recover for breach of the implied warranty of merchantability?

3.   Problem. A new-car dealership renovated its mechanical and body repair shops. To make room for a new spray-paint machine, it sold its old sprayer to Denton's, an independent body-repair shop, for $6,000. Denton's installed the sprayer in its shop, but when operated at full speed the machine sprayed unevenly. To perform in an acceptable manner, it had to be used at 50% of its capacity. Denton's sued for breach of the implied warranty of merchantability. What result?

––––––

Ambassador Steel Co. v. Ewald Steel Co.

Michigan Court of Appeals, 1971.
33 Mich.App. 495, 190 N.W.2d 275.

■ FITZGERALD, JUDGE. . . .

Plaintiff and defendant are both merchants in the business of the sale of steel. On or about October 4 and 5, 1966, plaintiff sold a certain amount of steel to defendant. The purchase price of the steel was $9,856.44, of which defendant paid $4,107.60, leaving an unpaid balance of $5,748.84. Plaintiff brought an action in the common pleas court to recover the balance due, waiving all amounts over $5,000 so as to bring the matter within the jurisdiction of that court.

Defendant admitted the purchase price of the steel, but claimed a set-off, alleging that plaintiff breached its implied warranty of merchantability in that plaintiff failed to supply defendant with "commercial quality" steel, that is, steel with a carbon content of 1010 to 1020. The defect came to light when the company to whom the defendant in turn sold the steel informed defendant that the steel cracked after being welded on to railroad cars. As a result of this, defendant's customer charged back its losses to defendant. Defendant thus claimed the set-off against plaintiff.

The trial court allowed defendant to set off the entire amount of the charge-back, with the exception of a claim for overhead, and entered a judgment for plaintiff in the amount of $1,055.78. Plaintiff appealed to the circuit court, contending the judgment was inadequate. The circuit court affirmed, plaintiff applied for leave to appeal to this court and we granted it.

Plaintiff on appeal raises four issues which will be dealt with *seriatim.*

The first issue can be stated in the following form:

As between dealers in steel, is there an implied warranty that the steel is merchantable for the purpose for which it is used, where plaintiff was not advised by defendant of the use to which the steel was to be put?

Plaintiff contends on appeal that because defendant did not inform plaintiff of the purposes for which the steel was to be used, defendant cannot claim that it was not fit for the purpose for which it was used. Defendant, however, appears to be relying on a different implied warranty, that of merchantability, and not that of particular fitness.

Section 2–314 of the Uniform Commercial Code provides. . . .

This section is further explained in [Comment 2], which states:

"2. The question when the warranty is imposed turns basically on the meaning of the terms of the agreement as recognized in the trade. Goods delivered under an agreement made by a merchant in a given line of trade must be of a quality comparable to that generally acceptable in that line of trade under the description or other designation of the goods used in the agreement."

Thus, unless there is an exclusion or modification, when, as here, a merchant sells such goods, an implied warranty arises that the goods would pass without objection in the trade under the contract description; also, that they are fit for the ordinary purposes for which the goods are used.

The implied warranty of merchantability is decidedly different from the implied warranty for a particular purpose that arises under M.C.L.A. § 440.2315. The particular purpose warranty is defined by the official UCC comment as:

"2. A 'particular purpose' differs from the ordinary purpose for which the goods are used in that it envisages a specific use by the buyer which is peculiar to the nature of his business whereas the ordinary purposes for which goods are used are those envisaged in the concept of merchantability and go to uses which are customarily made of the goods in question. For example, shoes are generally used for the purpose of walking upon ordinary ground, but a seller may know that a particular pair was selected to be used for climbing mountains."

It appears, then, that the warranty of merchantability warrants that the goods sold are of average quality within the industry, whereas a warranty of fitness for a particular purpose warrants that the goods sold are fit for the purposes for which they are intended. The latter is also further qualified by the requirement that the seller must know, at the time of sale, the particular purpose for which the goods are required and also that the buyer is relying on the seller to select or furnish suitable goods.

In the instant case, it is undisputed that the plaintiff was not made aware of the purpose for which the steel was to be used. Therefore, the implied warranty of fitness for a particular purpose did not arise under M.C.L.A. § 440.2315.

The question then becomes whether or not the steel sold by plaintiff to defendant was subject to the implied warranty of merchantability under M.C.L.A. § 440.2314. Although defendant sold the goods to a third party, M.C.L.A. § 440.2314 Comment 1 states that the warranty of merchantability applies to goods sold for resale as well as those for sale. And, as we previously stated, Comment 2 of the same section states that the question of when the warranty is imposed turns basically on the meaning of the terms as recognized in the trade.

M.C.L.A. § 440.1205(2) [revised 1–303(c)] defines a usage of trade as "any practice or method of dealing having such regularity of observance in a place, vocation or trade as to justify an expectation that it will be observed with respect to the transaction in question."

M.C.L.A. § 440.1205(3) [revised 1–303(d)] provides, "A course of dealing between parties and any usage of trade in the vocation in which they are engaged or of which they are or should be aware give particular meaning to and supplement or qualify terms of an agreement."

Testimony in the transcript indicates that defendant made no specific request concerning the particular quality of steel they ordered. However, there was also ample testimony below to the effect that when an order is placed without specification as to the particular quality desired, custom and usage of the steel business is that a "commercial quality" steel, that is, steel with a carbon content between 1010 and 1020, is to be used. Further testimony was to the effect that if one desired steel other than "commercial quality" it must be specified in the order, according to local custom and usage. The testimony indicated that the steel sold by plaintiff to defendant was not within the commercial range, thus the steel cracked after being welded. Therefore, plaintiff breached the implied warranty of merchantability in selling to defendant steel of a different quality than ordinarily sold in the custom and usage of the steel business, and not fit for the ordinary purposes for which such goods are used. M.C.L.A. § 440.2314.

Plaintiff raises the point that they were not notified of the purpose to which the steel was to be put. Apparently plaintiff implies that the use made of the steel was a particular purpose and thus not an ordinary purpose. We have already held that plaintiff is not liable for any implied warranty for fitness for a particular purpose. Furthermore, we need not decide whether this was a particular purpose, because the quality of steel that should have been delivered under the general warranty of merchantability, but was not, was sufficient to satisfy the use in the instant case.

. . .

Plaintiff next raises the issue that defendant did not sustain the burden of proving that plaintiff had breached the contract. We agree; defendant did not sustain the burden of proving plaintiff had breached the contract. However, defendant did not need to do so. What defendant needed to do, and what the record shows he did do, was prove that plaintiff had breached its implied warranty of merchantability. Defendant proved below that plaintiff impliedly warranted the steel sold as being of "commercial quality," that the plaintiff did not, in fact, sell to defendant steel that was of "commercial quality," and that if the steel had been of "commercial quality" it would not have cracked after being welded on to the railroad cars. This is sufficient to sustain an action for breach of warranty. See U.C.C., Sec. 2–314, Official Comment 13.

. . .

Therefore, the lower court should be, and hereby is, affirmed. Costs to appellees.

QUESTIONS AND NOTES

1.   Section 2–314 articulates six examples of merchantability standards. Which of them did the steel fail to meet?

2.   In the last paragraph of its opinion, the court says that buyer did not prove that seller breached the contract, but did prove that seller had breached the implied warranty of merchantability. Is it appropriate to say that breach of warranty is not breach of contract? See 1–201(b)(12). What difference would it make whether the court views a breach of warranty as a breach of contract?

3.   Non-uniform amendments regarding livestock. At least 24 states in the Midwest, South, and West have limited the existence or scope of implied warranties in the sale of livestock, either by amending 2–316 or by enacting a separate statute for that purpose. The statutes vary as to the animals included in the amendment, but cattle and hogs are always included. Most include horses, and some include sheep and poultry, and at least one includes rabbits. Most say there is no warranty as to freedom from disease, but a few exclude all implied warranties. Many condition the exclusion on compliance with any applicable state and federal regulations.

————

Bethlehem Steel Corp. v. Chicago Eastern Corp.

United States Court of Appeals, Seventh Circuit, 1988.
863 F.2d 508.

■ FLAUM, CIRCUIT JUDGE.

[Plaintiff sued for the price of two orders of steel sold to defendant. Defendant counterclaimed that the warranty of merchantability had been breached. The trial court gave judgment on a verdict for plaintiff, and defendant appealed.]

. . .

The second issue on appeal is whether the district court properly granted Bethlehem's motion for a directed verdict on Chicago Eastern's claim that Bethlehem breached the implied warranty of merchantability applicable to the steel acquired in the first purchase. . . .

Under Illinois law, if the seller of goods is a merchant of goods of the kind being sold, a warranty that the goods are "merchantable" is implied into a contract for their sale as a matter of law, unless otherwise expressly excluded or modified. Ill.Rev.Stat. ch. 26, para. 2–314(1) and 2–316. Chicago Eastern and Bethlehem agree that the first purchase included an implied warranty that the steel sold by Bethlehem would be "merchantable." The minimum criteria for determining merchantability are set forth in paragraph 2–314(2)(a)–(f). Chicago Eastern claims that the factors particularly relevant to the present dispute are those enumerated "(b)" and "(c)" in the statute. Paragraph 2–314(2)(b) requires that goods, if fungible, be of "fair average quality within the [contract] description," while 2–314(2)(c) states that goods must be "fit for the ordinary purposes for which such goods are used." Chicago Eastern contends that it introduced evidence at trial from which a reasonable juror could conclude that the steel acquired from Bethlehem in the first purchase failed to satisfy these two requirements and that the district court therefore erred in granting Bethlehem's motion for a directed verdict.

Prior to trial, Bethlehem and Chicago Eastern stipulated to a number of facts. The parties agreed that Chicago Eastern submitted an order for steel sheets to be manufactured by Bethlehem and that confirmation of the first purchase was memorialized on two Chicago Eastern purchase orders. The first purchase order, dated February 4, 1976, states that Chicago Eastern ordered sheet steel of a type designated by the American Society of Testing Materials (ASTM) as "446 Grade C." The second confirmation, a supplement to the first confirmation, did not use the ASTM designation; rather it specified a certain chemical composition and maximum yield strength: ".14–.20 carbon yield to 40,000 PSI after roll forming."

Chicago Eastern acknowledges that it received steel that complied with the requirements necessary to qualify as ASTM 446 Grade C and the requirements specified in the second purchase order. Chicago Eastern also acknowledged at oral argument that the steel would pass without objection in the trade under the contract description. It argues, however, that the steel was not merchantable because the steel was subjected to a renitrogenization process—a process not traditionally used with steel of this designation. Under this process, the nitrogen content of the steel was substantially increased. This increased the yield strength of the steel, but also made the steel more brittle and more susceptible to fracturing upon sudden impact. In other words, Chicago Eastern admits that the steel it received from Bethlehem did indeed possess the properties necessary to comply with the ASTM designation it ordered, but argues that the steel also possessed additional properties as a result of the renitrogenization process that made the steel unmerchantable. In the procedural posture of this case, the specific inquiry is whether Chicago Eastern introduced evidence from which a reasonable juror could conclude that steel which admittedly was ASTM 446 Grade C steel, was also less than "fair average quality within the [contract] description" and not "fit for the ordinary purposes for which such goods are used."

Chicago Eastern points to the testimony of its expert, Professor David W. Levinson, as evidence introduced at trial from which a reasonable juror could conclude that the steel acquired from Bethlehem in the first purchase was not merchantable. Levinson testified that although there was no specific prohibition against using the renitrogenization process in the production of ASTM 446 Grade C steel, the amount of nitrogen was 25 to 50 times higher than the level found in typical steel of this designation and that this amount of nitrogen "is added to very few steels." He further testified that this amount of nitrogen increased the yield strength of the steel, but also raised the "transition temperature" of the steel. Levinson explained that the transition temperature is the temperature below which fractures in a steel are substantially brittle and above which they are substantially ductile. This distinction is important because steel above the transition temperature stretches before it fractures. More pressure is therefore required to cause a ductile fracture than a brittle fracture.

Levinson testified that after examining samples of the fractured steel from the grain bins that it was his opinion that the fractures were brittle and not ductile. He also noted that tests conducted by third parties indicated that the transition temperature of the fractured steel was substantially higher because of the renitrogenization process than it otherwise would have been. Chicago Eastern's direct examination of Levinson culminated with his agreement that the renitrogenized steel was unsuitable "for use as a wall sheet in a grain tank which could be erected anywhere in the United States." Chicago Eastern contends that this was evidence which indicated that the steel acquired from Bethlehem was not of fair-average quality under the contract description and that the steel was not fit for the ordinary purposes for which such steel is used. In Chicago Eastern's view, Levinson's testimony provided sufficient evidence that the Bethlehem steel was not merchantable and therefore the warranty of merchantability issue should have been presented to the jury.

Even viewing the evidence presented at trial in the light most favorable to Chicago Eastern, we hold that no reasonable juror could conclude that the steel acquired from Bethlehem was not merchantable. All the evidence introduced by Chicago Eastern, including Levinson's testimony, was directed towards showing that the steel acquired in the first purchase was unfit for use as wall sheets in grain storage bins.

Merchantability, however, does not look only at the particular use to which the buyer puts the goods. Rather, Uniform Commercial Code Comment 7 states that paragraph 2–314(2)(a) and (b) are to be read together and refer "to the standards of that line of the trade which fits the transaction and the seller's business." Ill.Rev.Stat. ch. 26, para. 2–314 comment 7. It is therefore appropriate to analyze the transaction from the selling merchant's perspective. Bethlehem is in the business of selling unfinished steel products, including ASTM 446 Grade C steel. Chicago Eastern was required to show the ordinary purposes for which this type of steel is used and that the renitrogenization made the steel acquired from Bethlehem unfit for these purposes. This Chicago Eastern did not do.

Chicago Eastern has not pointed to any evidence presented at trial on the ordinary uses of this type of steel or how the renitrogenization affected these uses, nor has Chicago Eastern directed us to any place in the record where it introduced evidence showing that use as wall sheets in grain bins was in fact an ordinary use of this type of steel. In addition, Chicago Eastern did not introduce evidence that the increased nitrogen made the steel below fair-average quality. Levinson's testimony indicated that the nitrogen increased the transition temperature and made the steel more brittle, but that it also increased the yield strength of the steel. The steel was therefore not defective in the typical warranty of merchantability sense because the nitrogen that allegedly made the product defective by making the steel too brittle also had the seemingly desirable effect of making the steel stronger. It seems possible that different uses of steel require a different balancing of the apparent tradeoff between strength and brittleness. We do not hold that steel subjected to this process is merchantable under the ASTM 446 Grade C description, rather we hold only that Chicago Eastern failed to offer evidence that it was not. Chicago Eastern was required to introduce evidence that the brittleness of the steel, regardless of the improved strength, made this steel unfit for the ordinary uses of ASTM 446 Grade C steel; no such evidence was introduced.[9]

QUESTIONS AND NOTES

1.   In the penultimate paragraph of its opinion, the court quotes Official Comment 7 and asserts that it therefore is appropriate to analyze the transaction from the seller's perspective. Official Comment 7 addresses subsections (2)(a) and (b). Is this the proper perspective from which to analyze a transaction involving subsection (2)(c)? the other provisions of subsection (2)?

---

[9]   Indeed, Chicago Eastern conceded at oral argument that the steel it acquired would pass without objection under the contract description of ASTM 446 Grade C steel. Although this designation does not speak to brittleness or provide for a particular level of nitrogen, if the steel was in fact too brittle to be used for ordinary purposes it is difficult to understand how it would pass without objection in the trade.

2. What level of quality is required by the standard "merchantability"? Subsection (2) lists several translations. Notably, the word "defective" does not appear among them. Is a showing that the goods contain some defect tantamount to a showing that they are not fit for their ordinary purposes or will not pass without objection in the trade? Consider Fargo Machine & Tool Co. v. Kearney & Trecker Corp., 428 F.Supp. 364 (E.D.Mich.1977), in which Fargo purchased a complex milling machine from Kearney & Trecker for approximately $150,000. During the first two years of the machine's operation, a large number of service calls were made by seller in response to complaints by buyer. The court stated:

> Fargo's complaint alleges that the H-100 is "defective in material and workmanship" and "has required numerous and repetitive repairs, including some thirty-seven separate repair jobs." Certainly, however, every mechanical failure in a new and complex machine does not constitute a breach of warranty. N.C.R. v. Adell, 57 Mich.App. 413, 225 N.W.2d 785 (1975). At the outset then, it is necessary to distinguish and segregate those defects which merely required that work be performed and those legally significant defects which either remained uncured after reasonable opportunity to correct them or which are otherwise related to plaintiff's damage claims. Fargo does not contend that it was entitled to a perfect machine, nor that the installation and break-in period should have been completely service free. Exactly what Fargo was entitled to is governed by the Uniform Commercial Code unless permissibly modified by agreement between the parties.

> . . . Fargo's complaints must be read in terms of their significance in the machining trade and relative to what would normally pass in the trade without objection under the contract description. Notably, with regard to repairs, Fargo's expert, Fassey, testified not only that Fargo's $850.00 total expenditures through 1976 were remarkably low, but in addition, that a high degree of debugging is required on such machines and that normally the first five years of a machine of this nature often generate $5,000 to $10,000 in maintenance costs. As noted earlier, case law recognizes that such mechanical failures in new and complex machines are expected, and to the extent that deficiencies and corrective service performed were routine for so sophisticated a machine, no breach occurs. Indeed, McCaffrey conceded from the stand that, although numerous problems developed at one time or another, most were of a minor nature, almost all were fixed by Kearney & Trecker promptly, and Fargo is left with relatively few defects which have any operational impact. Both the service reports and the lists of defects prepared by McCaffrey for payment conferences with Kearney & Trecker support this conclusion. Nearly all of the service reports, bearing McCaffrey's signature as chief engineer of Fargo, indicate the precise problems for which the service call was made and whether or not the job was completed. An uncompleted job was indicated only seven times after installation had been finished and

four of these jobs were satisfactorily completed on follow-up calls. . . .

The court concluded, however, that there were three remaining serious problems with the machine which the seller had been unable to correct and which did constitute breaches of warranty.

To similar effect is Taterka v. Ford Motor Co., 86 Wis.2d 140, 271 N.W.2d 653 (1978), in which the taillight assembly gaskets in plaintiff's new 1972 Mustang had been installed in a manner that allowed water to enter. The problem was common to all Mustangs of that year. The presence of water in the taillight assembly caused rust. Plaintiff sued for breach of the implied warranty of merchantability:

> Where automobiles are concerned the term "unmerchantable" has only been applied where a single defect poses a substantial safety hazard or numerous defects classify the car as a "lemon." *See e.g.,* Zabriskie Chevrolet, Inc. v. Smith, 99 N.J.Super. 441, 240 A.2d 195 (1968); Henningsen v. Bloomfield Motors, Inc., 32 N.J. 358, 161 A.2d 69 (1960). The ordinary purpose for which a car is intended is to provide transportation. Where a car can provide safe, reliable transportation it is generally considered merchantable.
>
> . . .
>
> The automobile here involved had been driven for 33 months and in excess of 75,000 miles without a serious misadventure. In fact, it had been driven 90,000 miles at the time of the hearing on the motion for summary judgment in 1976. The only inference that can reasonably be drawn from the undisputed facts is that the rust problem described in this case did not render the car unfit for the purpose of driving and therefore unmerchantable. Since conflicting inferences did not arise from the undisputed facts, summary judgment was appropriate.

Would the result in *Taterka* be different if the problem had been with the paint, so that the rust appeared on the hood (the panel covering the engine compartment) of the car?

3. *Bethlehem Steel* illustrates the importance—and the difficulty—of establishing not only the quality standard envisioned by a particular subsection of 2–314(2), but also the failure of the goods to meet that standard. Use of expert witnesses is one way, but it is not the only way. A buyer may be able to establish by circumstantial evidence that goods are not fit for their ordinary purposes. Consider these excerpts from Nelson v. Wilkins Dodge, Inc., 256 N.W.2d 472 (Minn.1977):

> The elemental facts are not in dispute. On August 16, 1972, plaintiffs, William and Cheryl Nelson, bought a new 1972 Toyota Hilux 4-cylinder half-ton pickup truck from Wilkins Dodge, Inc. (Wilkins), a Toyota dealer in St. Paul. Before making this purchase, Mr. Nelson, concerned about the size of a 4-cylinder engine, told a salesman at Wilkins that he needed a vehicle that could withstand constant freeway speeds. Plaintiff needed a sturdy vehicle because as an ironworker he was required to travel long distances to and

from various jobs. The salesman replied that the pickup was fine for freeway driving and that it could be driven at 65 miles per hour all the time.

After purchasing the pickup, plaintiffs experienced numerous difficulties with it in its use as the family car. The difficulties included the following:

(1)   Within a month of purchase and within its first 2,000 miles of use, bubbles appeared in the paint covering the seam on the back part of the pickup.

(2)   Within the same period of time, the taillights failed to function. Mr. Nelson noticed that the taillight covers had been installed upside down, enabling rain to enter the assembly and short out the lights. He inverted the covers himself and experienced no problem with the lights thereafter.

(3)   In the middle of October 1972, with approximately 7,500 miles on the pickup, as Mr. Nelson was driving through Wisconsin during a rainstorm the windshield-wiper blade and arm flew off into the night, forcing him to negotiate the last 100 miles of his journey at a slow speed keeping watch from the side window. The next day he discovered that the bolts from the windshield-wiper motor were loose and tightened them; he later had a new wiper blade and arm installed.

(4)   In February 1973, with approximately 12,000 miles on the pickup, Mr. Nelson noticed oil leakage from the front and rear of the pickup. . . .

(5)   In March of 1973 . . . the horn bracket broke causing the horn to fall out, and the shift lever became loose preventing engagement of the transmission.

> . . .

Defendant asserts that the evidence supported inconsistent inferences as to the causes of the condition of the pickup. If the state of the evidence was such that the jury would have had to speculate among possible causes of the pickup's condition, then plaintiffs would have failed to sustain their burden of production, and the court's ruling would be correct. In Heil v. Standard Chemical Mfg. Co., 301 Minn. 315, 324, 223 N.W.2d 37, 42 (1974), we quoted approvingly the following language . . . :

> Where the record shows that there are several possible causes of an injury, for one or more of which the defendant was not responsible, and it is just as reasonable and probable that the injury was the result of the latter, the plaintiff may not recover, since he has failed to prove that the defendant's breach caused the injury.

Plaintiffs assert that there can be no question that proximate cause has been demonstrated with respect to the paint bubbles, the inverted taillight covers, and the loosened windshield-wiper blade and arm and shift lever. Defendant suggests that the paint bubbles and the loosened windshield wiper, horn bracket, and shift lever just as probably resulted from the continuous and hard use to which plaintiffs put the pickup as from any defect inhering in the vehicle when plaintiffs purchased it. Although liability for breach of warranty attaches only when a defect existing in the goods causes a breakdown in quality, generally no specific defect need be alleged, and a defective condition can be proved by circumstantial evidence. No direct evidence was introduced as to the causes of the conditions in question. It is reasonable to suppose, however, that vehicles that are fit for ordinary purposes probably do not display these defects this early, even if they are driven a great deal within a short period of time. Thus, the causes of the faulty paint, windshield wiper, horn bracket, and shift lever were questions that should have been decided by the jury. A fortiori, the cause of the inverted taillight covers was a jury question.

Plaintiffs have also cited antifreeze and oil leaks as being further defects of the pickup. Defendant correctly asserts that there was no probative evidence of an antifreeze leak and thus there could be no breach in that respect. The question of the oil loss is less clear. Although defendant contends that the jury might reasonably have inferred that the oil leakage was caused by an earlier improper oil change, this contention is unavailing because the record does not indicate that anyone other than defendant performed an earlier oil change. Therefore, the cause of the oil loss was also a question for the jury.

4.   What level of quality must a new car meet in order to be merchantable? The cases in Note 2 suggest that the car need not be free of all defects or nonconformities. How much nonconformity does it take to amount to a breach of the warranty? In Isip v. Mercedes-Benz USA, LLC, 155 Cal.App.4th 19, 65 Cal.Rptr.3d 695 (2007), plaintiff purchased a new 2004 Mercedes-Benz for $46,000. Shortly after the purchase, she began experiencing problems, which included the following:

> The air-conditioning emitted an offensive smell every time it was turned on, giving [plaintiff] a headache and making her sister sneeze. The car made a loud tugging noise when she engaged the gear, and it made a clanking noise when [she] released the brake in reverse. When the car automatically shifted gears to pick up speed, the car pulled back, hesitated, and then took off like a slingshot. It also hesitated and pulled back before slowing down. The engine made a loud knocking sound and there were fluid leaks. White smoke came out of the exhaust system.

Id. at 696. Does this amount to a breach of the implied warranty of merchantability? Claiming that it does not, defendant asked the trial court to instruct the jury:

> In the case of automobiles, the implied warranty of merchantability can be breached only if the vehicle manifests a defect that is so basic

that it renders the vehicle unfit for its ordinary purpose of providing transportation.

Id. at 697. Is that the correct standard? The court thought not:

> ... [Defendant's] attempt to define a vehicle as unfit only if it does not provide transportation is an unjustified dilution of the implied warranty of merchantability. We reject the notion that merely because a vehicle provides transportation from point A to point B, it necessarily does not violate the implied warranty of merchantability. A vehicle that smells, lurches, clanks, and emits smoke over an extended period of time is not fit for its intended purpose.

Id. at 700. Accord, Hodges v. Johnson, 199 P.3d 1251 (Kan.2009), in which plaintiffs purchased a ten-year-old Mercedes with 135,000 miles for $15,900. Within months of the purchase, plaintiffs discovered that the air conditioning did not work and would cost more than $3,400 to repair. On appeal from the trial court's decision for the plaintiffs, the intermediate appellate court held as a matter of law that in connection with the sale of a used car, the implied warranty extends only to "the operation of major components that are necessary for the vehicle to operate, such as the engine and transmission," and stated that "it is the responsibility of the buyer to ensure that the components incidental to operation are in working condition."

The Supreme Court reversed. It held that whether the warranty is breached requires a case-by-case determination, so it was error for the lower court to decide the issue as a matter of law. Further, it rejected that court's articulation of the standard required by the warranty:

> Although there can be little doubt that the primary purpose of a vehicle is transportation, the Court of Appeals' opinion ignores the reality that a buyer may purchase a particular vehicle for a number of other purposes—among which may be safety, fuel economy, utility, or comfort in traveling to and from various destinations. . . . The determination as to whether the implied warranty has been breached turns on a number factors, including "[t]he buyer's knowledge that the goods are used, the extent of their prior use, and whether the goods are significantly discounted." . . . The broad range of used goods that may be covered by the implied warranty of merchantability underscores the wisdom of this court's previous recognition that a "late model, low mileage car, sold at a premium price, is expected to be in far better condition and to last longer than an old, high mileage, 'rough' car . . . sold for little above its scrap value."

Id. at 1260–61.

5. If the problem with the car implicates safety, a minor defect may breach the warranty. In Brand v. Hyundai Motor America, on a buyer's first day with a new car, the sunroof spontaneously and repeatedly opened and closed, beyond the control of the buyer. Rejecting the argument that a car is fit for its ordinary purposes so long as it has the capability of "getting from point 'A' to point 'B,'" the court held that

> a reasonable jury could conclude that a vehicle sunroof that opens and closes *on its own* creates a substantial safety hazard. [The buyer] described how on the freeway the papers in his car suddenly swirled about in the passenger compartment without notice, creating a dangerous distraction. . . . A jury therefore reasonably could infer a multitude of similar unsafe scenarios: a driver suddenly distracted, buffeted, or even incapacitated by unexpected incoming rain, sleet, snow, dust, or blinding sun, or endangered by objects shooting through or out of the cabin.

173 Cal.Rptr.3d 454, 461 (Cal.App.2014). The court reversed the trial court's nonsuit of the plaintiff, even though the problem, once properly diagnosed, was easily fixed.

Problem. Carey purchased a new boat. Immediately after purchase, cracks begin emerging in the finish of the boat. Carey had them repaired, but new cracks emerged, requiring repairs on three occasions over the next year, and still more cracks continued to emerge. Has there been a breach of the implied warranty?

In Carey v. Chaparral Boats, Inc., 514 F.Supp.2d 1152, 1156 (D.Minn.2007), the basis for this problem, the court held not, granting the seller's motion for summary judgment:

> Under Minnesota law, an implied warranty of merchantability requires that goods be "fit for the ordinary purposes for which such goods are used." . . . In this case, the overwhelming evidence demonstrates that the cracks in the boat's finish are a cosmetic problem and in no way impact the boat's ordinary use. [A fiberglass specialist] testified that the cracks are a "cosmetic issue," as did [another witness] who stated that the cracks could be characterized as a cosmetic problem that does not impact the structural integrity of the boat. Further, there is no evidence in the record that the cracks have prevented [plaintiff] from using his boat. Accordingly, there is no genuine issue as to whether [defendant] breached its implied warranty of merchantability.

What is the flaw in this analysis?

6.   Problem. Ellis ordered a plate of chicken enchiladas at a Mexican restaurant. As she was chewing on a forkful of enchilada, she bit down on a chicken bone and chipped a tooth. Is the restaurant liable for breach of the implied warranty of merchantability?

Would it matter if she had ordered vegetarian enchiladas?

7.   Problem. Kemp was preparing a dish pursuant to a recipe in a cookbook. The recipe called for an ingredient known as elephant's ear plant root. It is common for consumers to snack on or taste ingredients while they cook. Kemp casually ate a small piece of the uncooked ingredient. She became violently ill because, in its raw form, the elephant's ear plant root is highly toxic. Is the cookbook merchantable?

In connection with this problem, you may be interested to know that in 1978,

> Random House recalled some 3,000 copies of "Woman's Day Crockery Cuisine" by Sylvia Vaughn Thompson and mounted a media campaign to warn purchasers of approximately 10,000 additional copies of the book. That action came after it was discovered that the recipe for Silky Caramel Slices, if followed exactly as printed in the book, could cause an explosion.

N.Y. Times, p. 19, Dec. 14, 1983. Is this relevant to determining the answer to the problem?

8. Fried food at fast-food restaurants has a notoriously high level of trans fat, which is recognized by the medical community to be very bad for one's health. Does Chollie's Chickens, a fast-food restaurant, breach an implied warranty of merchantability with respect to its chicken or french fries?

9. Problem. Gupta purchased from Hughes Cars, a used-car dealer, two 2014 Ford Mustang GT Coupes, one at a price of $20,000 and the other at a price of $14,000. Hughes made no express warranties other than that the automobiles were 2014 Mustangs, as indeed they were. A few weeks after purchase, Gupta discovered that both cars required a $1,200 replacement of the engine's head gasket. Assume that this amounts to a breach of the implied warranty of merchantability as to the $20,000 car. Does this necessarily mean that there is a similar breach of warranty as to the $14,000 car? What arguments can you make on behalf of Hughes? Gupta?

10. Problem. Denbow purchased a used 2013 Honda Accord from Hughes Cars, a used-car dealer, for $18,000. Unknown to Hughes, the car had been in a serious accident and had been declared a total loss by the company that had insured it. The car wound up in the hands of a rebuilder, who made enough cosmetic and mechanical repairs to be able to sell it. Structurally, however, the car is not safe to drive. Hughes knew nothing of this prior history of the car. When Denbow experienced excessive tire wear, she investigated and discovered that the car had been declared a total loss by its insurer and sold as salvage. Did Hughes breach the implied warranty of merchantability?

11. The car in Problem 10 manifested a condition—tire wear—that is not normal. It has not yet manifested another defect, viz., collapse of the frame in the event of a collision. Under what circumstances should a flaw in the goods which has not yet—and may never—become apparent constitute a breach of the implied warranty of merchantability? Consider Everett v. TK-Taito, L.L.C., 178 S.W.3d 844 (Tex.App.2005), in which plaintiffs sued because their 10-year-old vehicles were equipped with seat belt buckles that the buckle manufacturer admitted had a propensity to engage only partially and therefore to release during a collision. This propensity had not yet manifested itself in plaintiffs' vehicles.

> We begin our analysis by drawing a distinction between manifested product defects and unmanifested product defects—like the one alleged by the Everetts—because most of the cases relied

upon by the Everetts involve manifested defects, not unmanifested defects; therefore, those cases are not controlling.

The Texas Supreme Court has not yet addressed which claims, if any, a plaintiff possesses standing to assert based on an unmanifested product defect that causes only economic damages. Our sister courts, as well as out-of-state courts, have reached different conclusions concerning which, if any, theories of recovery are available to a plaintiff seeking economic benefit-of-the-bargain or cost-of-replacement damages based on an unmanifested product defect.

... Because this is a statutory cause of action, we apply statutory standing principles. The statutory elements of the Everetts' breach of implied warranty of merchantability are (1) that their vehicles' seat belt buckles are defective as unfit for their purpose because of a lack of what was required for adequacy, (2) that the alleged defect existed when the buckles left the manufacturer's and the seller's possession, and (3) that the alleged defect proximately caused the injuries for which the Everetts seek damages. See id. §§ 2.314 & cmt. 13, 2.607(c)(1), 2.714–.715. ...

In determining whether the allegations show that the defect caused injury, we recognize that the defect in an implied warranty of merchantability case may not be the same as the defect in a strict products liability case. In the context of an implied warranty of merchantability case, the word "defect" means a condition of the goods that renders them unfit for the ordinary purposes for which they are used because of a lack of something necessary for adequacy. In the area of strict products liability, however, the word "defect" means a condition of the product that renders it unreasonably dangerous. A defective design may render a product unreasonably dangerous for strict liability purposes, but may not render a product unfit for the ordinary purposes for which it is used if the product works properly when used for its ordinary purpose. [E.g.,] Sears, Roebuck & Co. v. Kunze, 996 S.W.2d 416, 422 (Tex. App. 1999) (involving products liability suit based on unreasonably dangerous radial saw—defective for lack of a lower blade guard— but obviously fit for sawing, the ordinary purpose for which it was used).

The Everetts pleaded a breach of the implied warranty of merchantability cause of action, but they pleaded a products liability defect—a defective design of the buckle giving it a "*propensity* to partially latch and *potentially* provide insufficient restraint during a crash." [Emphasis added.] A product that performs its ordinary function adequately is not defective in the implied warranty of merchantability context simply because it does not function as well as the buyer would like, or even as well as it could. That is, for a defect to cause redressable damages in a breach of the implied warranty of merchantability action, it must cause the product not to function adequately in the performance of its ordinary function for the plaintiff. Compare Microsoft Corp., 914 S.W.2d 602, 610 (holding software that could not successfully perform data compression—regardless of whether plaintiff attempted to use this feature—did not or would not perform adequately in its ordinary function so that a "defect" existed causing injury and loss of benefit-of-the-bargain damages). . . .

Here, the Everetts' vehicles are many years old; Pete's Nissan truck is a 1994 model and Marcella's Isuzu Rodeo is a 1991 model. Although the vehicles are over a decade old, the Everetts do not allege that the TK-52 buckles in their vehicles have ever only partially latched when they latched them or have ever provided them with insufficient restraint. They instead seek economic damages based on the "buckles' *propensity* to partially latch and *potentially* provide insufficient restraint during a crash." [Emphasis added.] To cause redressable injuries in the breach of the implied warranty of merchantability context, a "defect" must either have manifested during the product's normal use or such manifestation must be inevitable when the defective feature of the product is used—such as the software data compression feature in Manning. Although the Everetts' vehicles are over a decade old, the defect that they allege has caused them economic injuries has not manifested itself, nor do the Everetts claim that it will inevitably manifest itself.

Instead, the Everetts have pleaded for contract-based damages from the alleged breach of the implied warranty of merchantability while alleging a tort-based products liability defect. This mixing of liability and damage theories does not establish an injury. Consequently, we hold that the Everetts have not pleaded facts demonstrating the type of injury that is redressable within the context of their breach of the implied warranty of merchantability claim.

. . . The statute implicitly defines a buyer's injury as the product's defect, that is, the condition of the product or good that renders it unfit for the ordinary purposes for which it is used because of a lack of something necessary for adequacy. See § 2.314 & cmt. 13. An actual malfunction of the product or good is not required to establish an injury; what is required is an allegation that the alleged defect will inevitably manifest itself in the ordinary use of the product and that the defect renders the product unfit for the ordinary purposes for which the product is used. Such an allegation would make the plaintiff's injury personal and nonspeculative, establishing the plaintiff's statutory standing to assert a claim for breach of the implied warranty of merchantability. Here, as discussed above, the Everetts have pleaded only an unmanifested defect. They have not pleaded or established that the alleged defective design of the TK-52 buckles will inevitably cause the buckle to malfunction; they have pleaded that the buckles have a propensity to partially latch and to potentially provide insufficient restraint during a crash. Because the buckles' alleged propensity to partially latch and their potential to ineffectively restrain have not occurred—despite over a decade of ordinary use of the TK-52 buckles—we cannot agree that the Everetts have pleaded the existence of a defect that renders their seat belt buckles unfit for the ordinary purposes for which they were intended. The TK-52 buckles in the Everetts' vehicles, by performing as they were supposed to for over ten years have lived up to that "minimum level of quality" implied by section 2.314(b), (c). For the reasons stated, we . . . hold that the Everetts do not possess statutory standing to assert a claim for breach of the implied warranty of merchantability.

Accord, Gutierrez v. Carmax Auto Superstores California, 248 Cal.Rptr.3d 61 (Cal.App.2018). Plaintiff purchased a used car that was subject to a safety recall to replace a brake light switch. Plaintiff's complaint alleged that the existence of the safety recall constituted breach of the implied warranty of merchantability. The trial court sustained defendant's demurrer, and the appellate court affirmed. The switch in plaintiff's car had not failed and plaintiff did not state facts showing that the switch in her car was defective or made the car unsafe.

> The existence of the safety recall does not adequately allege a substantial safety hazard. . . . There is no allegation that the switch was actually defective or failed to function . . . . Furthermore, we located no allegation explaining how [plaintiff's] use of the vehicle was restricted or otherwise affected by the existence of the recall. For example, [she] did not allege she became aware of the safety recall on a particular date and thereafter was reluctant to drive the [car] due to safety concerns related to the stop lamp switch."

Id. at 75–76.

12. Implied warranties supplied by trade usage. Subsection (3) of 2–314 provides that implied warranties also may arise by virtue of usage of trade or course of dealing. Thus in Gindy Mfg. Corp. v. Cardinale Trucking Corp. (page 322 infra), in a contract for the sale of new trucks, the court pointed to 2–314(3) to find an implied warranty that the seller will repair all defects, no matter how trivial.

13. Hybrid and services transactions. As we saw in Chapter 2, transactions in which a person supplies both goods and services pose a problem for determining what law to apply. An example is contracts for the fabrication of machines or buildings or parts of them. It frequently is difficult to categorize these transactions. A number of courts have held that, on the facts of the particular case, the transaction is not a sale of goods but instead is a sale of services and that no implied warranties arise in sales of services. E.g., Milau Associates, Inc. v. North Ave. Development Corp., 42 N.Y.2d 482, 398 N.Y.S.2d 882, 368 N.E.2d 1247 (1977). As we saw in Chapter 2, some courts have held that implied warranty liability does arise as to the goods components of hybrid transactions. E.g., Franklin v. Northwest Drilling Co., Inc., 215 Kan. 304, 524 P.2d 1194 (1974); Worrell v. Barnes, 87 Nev. 204, 484

P.2d 573 (1971). Some courts have gone further and held that there is warranty liability even as to the services component of fabrication or construction contracts. E.g., Insurance Co. of North America v. Radiant Electric Co., 55 Mich.App. 410, 222 N.W.2d 323 (1974); O'Laughlin v. Minnesota Natural Gas Co., 253 N.W.2d 826 (Minn.1977). Compare *Northwest Drilling* (implied warranty that services will be performed in a workmanlike manner with the skill that ordinarily is expected in the profession) with Air Heaters, Inc. v. Johnson Electric, Inc., 258 N.W.2d 649 (N.D.1977) (warranty as to the total resulting structure whether the failure is based on a defect in the component materials or in the services involved in assembling the components).

In "pure" services transactions, to which Article 2 does not apply, there is no implied-warranty liability for non-negligent mistakes or failures. E.g., Lemley v. J & B Tire Co., 426 F.Supp. 1378 (W.D.Pa.1977) (failure of brakes after defendant repaired them); Strong v. Retail Credit Co., 38 Colo.App. 125, 552 P.2d 1025 (1976) (inaccurate credit report); Lewis v. Big Powderhorn Mountain Ski Corp., 69 Mich.App. 437, 245 N.W.2d 81 (1976) (tow-rope on ski lift snapped).

3. THE IMPLIED WARRANTY OF MERCHANTABILITY AND STRICT LIABILITY IN TORT

As *Ambassador Steel* establishes, if goods fail to meet applicable industry standards, the goods are not merchantable. But what if the goods do meet industry standards: can they still be unmerchantable? In most states the answer is "yes." If the goods cause personal injury or property damage, they may be found to be not merchantable even though they meet industry standards. Often the courts analyze the issue under the rubric of products liability or strict liability in tort. Traditionally sellers were liable in tort for defective products only if they were negligent. But the law evolved, as it did with respect to implied warranty (pages 257–258] supra), culminating in 1960 with promulgation of the Restatement (Second) of Torts § 402A, which imposed liability on sellers for personal injuries caused by defects in the products they sell regardless of the absence of negligence. The test for whether a product was defective was whether the product failed to meet the reasonable expectations of the consumer. And the courts applied this test without regard to the kind of defect, whether it be a defect in manufacturing or a defect in design. Over the years, however, some courts became dissatisfied with this test as applied to design defects, because it places liability on manufacturers for injuries that they could not have foreseen and could not have avoided or prevented. In 1998 the American Law Institute promulgated the Restatement (Third) of Torts—Products Liability. It provides:

§ 1. Liability of Commercial Seller or Distributor for Harm Caused by Defective Products.

One engaged in the business of selling or otherwise distributing products who sells or distributes a defective product is subject to liability for harm to persons or property caused by the defect.

§ 2. Categories of Product Defect.

A product is defective when, at the time of sale or distribution, it contains a manufacturing defect, is defective in design, or is defective because of inadequate instructions or warnings. A product:

(a) contains a manufacturing defect when the product departs from its intended design even though all possible care was exercised in the preparation and marketing of the product;

(b) is defective in design when the foreseeable risks of harm posed by the product could have been reduced or avoided by the adoption of a reasonable alternative design by the seller or other distributor, or a predecessor in the commercial chain of distribution, and the omission of the alternative design renders the product not reasonably safe;

(c) is defective because of inadequate instructions or warnings when the foreseeable risks of harm posed by the product could have been reduced or avoided by the provision of reasonable instructions or warnings by the seller or other distributor, or a predecessor in the commercial chain of distribution, and the omission of the instructions or warnings renders the product not reasonably safe.

These provisions, unlike their predecessor in the Restatement (Second), distinguish between manufacturing defects and design defects. Under the Restatement (Second), one looks to the reasonable expectations of the buyer to determine whether the product is defective. Under the Restatement (Third), however, the existence of a design defect requires the availability of a reasonable alternative design that would have made the product reasonably safe.

At the beginning of this chapter, we pointed out that the basic purpose of warranty law is to give the buyer the quality of goods that the buyer reasonably expects under the contract. The next case points out the difference between the "consumer-expectations" test of sales law and the "reasonable-alternative-design" test of the Restatement (Third) to determine whether a product design is defective.

Denny v. Ford Motor Company

New York Court of Appeals, 1995.
87 N.Y.2d 248, 639 N.Y.S.2d 250, 662 N.E.2d 730.

■ TITONE, JUDGE.

Are the elements of New York's causes of action for strict products liability and breach of implied warranty always coextensive? If not, can the latter be broader than the former? These are the core issues presented by the questions that the United States Court of Appeals for the Second Circuit has certified to us in this diversity action involving an allegedly defective vehicle. On the facts set forth by the Second Circuit, we hold that the causes of action are not identical and that, under the circumstances presented here, it is possible to be liable for breach of implied warranty even though a claim of strict products liability has not been satisfactorily established.

I.

. . . [T]his action arises out of a June 9, 1986 accident in which plaintiff Nancy Denny was severely injured when the Ford Bronco II that she was driving rolled over. The rollover accident occurred when Denny slammed on her brakes in an effort to avoid a deer that had walked directly into her motor vehicle's path. Denny and her spouse sued Ford Motor Co., the vehicle's manufacturer, asserting claims for negligence, strict products liability and breach of implied warranty of merchantability (*see* UCC 2–314[2][c]; 2–318). The case went to trial in the District Court for the Northern District of New York in October of 1992.

The trial evidence centered on the particular characteristics of utility vehicles, which are generally made for off-road use on unpaved and often rugged terrain. Such use sometimes necessitates climbing over obstacles such as fallen logs and rocks. While utility vehicles are traditionally considerably larger than passenger cars, some manufacturers have created a category of down-sized "small" utility vehicles, which are designed to be lighter, to achieve better fuel economy and, presumably, to appeal to a wider consumer market. The Bronco II in which Denny was injured falls into this category.

Plaintiffs introduced evidence at trial to show that small utility vehicles in general, and the Bronco II in particular, present a significantly higher risk of rollover accidents than do ordinary passenger automobiles. Plaintiffs' evidence also showed that the Bronco II had a low stability index attributable to its high center of gravity and relatively narrow track width. The vehicle's shorter wheel base and suspension system were additional factors contributing to its instability. Ford had made minor design changes in an effort to achieve a higher stability index, but, according to plaintiffs' proof, none of the changes produced a significant improvement in the vehicle's stability.

Ford argued at trial that the design features of which plaintiffs complained were necessary to the vehicle's off-road capabilities. According to Ford, the vehicle had been intended to be used as an off-road vehicle and had not been designed to be sold as a conventional passenger automobile. Ford's own engineer stated that he would not recommend the Bronco II to someone whose primary interest was to use it as a passenger car, since the features of a four-wheel-drive utility vehicle were not helpful for that purpose and the vehicle's design made it inherently less stable.

Despite the engineer's testimony, plaintiffs introduced a Ford marketing manual which predicted that many buyers would be attracted to the Bronco II because utility vehicles were "suitable to contemporary life styles" and were "considered fashionable" in some suburban areas. According to this manual, the sales presentation of the Bronco II should take into account the vehicle's "suitability for commuting and for suburban and city driving." Additionally, the vehicle's ability to switch between two-wheel and four-wheel drive would "be particularly appealing to women who may be concerned about driving in snow and ice with their children." Plaintiffs both testified that the perceived safety benefits of its four-wheel-drive capacity were what attracted them to the Bronco II. They were not at all interested in its off-road use.

At the close of the evidence, the District Court Judge submitted both the strict products liability claim and the breach of implied warranty claim, despite Ford's objection that the two causes of action were identical. With respect to the strict products liability claim the court told the jury that "[a] manufacturer who places a product on the market in a defective condition is liable for injury which results from use of the product when the product is used for its intended or reasonably foreseeable purpose." Further, the court stated:

"A product is defective if it is not reasonably safe. * * * It is not necessary for the plaintiffs to prove that the defendant knew or should have known of the product's potential for causing injury to establish that the product was not reasonably safe. Rather, the plaintiffs must prove by a preponderance of the evidence that a reasonable person * * * who knew of the product's potential for causing injury and the existence of available alternative designs * * * would have concluded that such a product should not have been marketed in that condition. Such a conclusion should be reached after balancing the risks involved in using the product against the product's usefulness and its costs against the risks, usefulness and costs of the alternative design as compared to the product defendant did market."

With respect to the breach of implied warranty claim, the court told the jury:

"The law implies a warranty by a manufacturer which places its product on the market that the product is reasonably fit for the ordinary purpose for which it was intended. If it is, in fact, defective and not reasonably fit to be used for its intended purpose, the warranty is breached.

"The plaintiffs claim that the Bronco II was not fit for its ordinary purpose because of its alleged propensity to rollover and lack of warnings to the consumer of this propensity."

Neither party objected to the content of these charges.

In response to interrogatories, the jury found that the Bronco II was not "defective" and that defendant was therefore not liable under plaintiffs' strict products liability cause of action. However, the jury also found that defendant had breached its implied warranty of merchantability and that the breach was the proximate cause of Nancy Denny's injuries. Following apportionment of damages, plaintiff was awarded judgment in the amount of $1.2 million.

Ford subsequently moved for a new trial . . . arguing that the jury's finding on the breach of implied warranty cause of action was irreconcilable with its finding on the strict products liability claim. The trial court rejected this argument, holding that it had been waived and that, in any event, the verdict was not inconsistent.

On defendant's appeal, a majority at the Second Circuit held that defendant's trial conduct had not resulted in a waiver of the inconsistency issue. Reasoning that the outcome of the appeal depended upon the proper application of New York law, the court certified the following questions for consideration by this Court (1) whether the strict products liability claim and the breach of implied warranty claim are identical; (2) whether, if the claims are different, the strict products liability claim is broader than the implied warranty claim and encompasses the latter; and (3) whether, if the claims are different and a strict liability claim may fail while an implied warranty claim succeeds, the jury's finding of no product defect is reconcilable with its finding of a breach of warranty.

II.

In this proceeding, Ford's sole argument is that plaintiffs' strict products liability and breach of implied warranty causes of action were identical and that, accordingly, a defendant's verdict on the former cannot be reconciled with a plaintiff's verdict on the latter. This argument is, in turn, premised on both the intertwined history of the two doctrines and the close similarity in their elements and legal functions. Although Ford recognizes that New York has previously permitted personal injury plaintiffs to simultaneously assert different products liability theories in support of their claims, it contends that the breach of implied warranty cause of action, which sounds in contract, has been subsumed by the more recently adopted, and more highly evolved, strict products liability theory, which sounds in tort. Ford's argument has much to commend it. However, in the final analysis, the argument is flawed because it overlooks the continued existence of a separate *statutory* predicate for the breach of warranty theory and the subtle but important distinction between the two theories that arises from their different historical and doctrinal root.

When products liability litigation was in its infancy, the courts relied upon contractual warranty theories as the only existing means of facilitating economic recovery for personal injuries arising from the use of defective goods. . . . [T]he courts posited the existence of an implied warranty arising as an incident of the product's sale and premised a cause of action for consequential personal injuries based on breaches of that warranty.

Eventually, the contractually based implied warranty theory came to be perceived as inadequate in an economic universe that was dominated by mass-produced products and an impersonal marketplace. Its primary weakness was, of course, its rigid requirement of a relationship of privity between the seller and the injured consumer—a requirement that often could not be satisfied (*see,* Martin v. Dierck Equip. Co., 43 N.Y.2d 583, 589–590, 403 N.Y.S.2d 185, 374 N.E.2d 97). Some courts (including ours) recognized certain narrow exceptions to the privity requirement in an effort to avoid the doctrine's harsher effects. (Prosser and Keeton, Torts § 96, at 682 [5th ed.1984]). However, the warranty approach remained unsatisfactory, and the courts shifted their focus to the development of a new, more flexible tort cause of action: the doctrine of strict products liability.

The establishment of this tort remedy has, as this Court has recognized, significantly diminished the need to rely on the contractually based breach of implied warranty remedy as a means of compensating individuals injured because of defective products. Further, although the available defenses and applicable limitations principles may differ, there is a high degree of overlap between the substantive aspects of the two causes of action. . . .

Nonetheless, it would not be correct to infer that the tort cause of action has completely subsumed the older breach of implied warranty cause of action or that the two doctrines are now identical in every respect. The continued vitality of the warranty approach is evidenced by its retention and expansion in New York's version of the Uniform Commercial Code (UCC 2–314[2] [c]; 2–318). The existence of this statutory authority belies any argument that the breach of implied warranty remedy is a dead letter.[2]

Although the products liability theory sounding in tort and the breach of implied warranty theory authorized by the UCC coexist and are

---

[2] Indeed, the statutory provision for personal injury recovery as an element of "consequential damages" (UCC 2–715[2][b]) makes it illogical to conclude, as the *amicus* Product Liability Advisory Council suggests, that the breach of implied warranty theory should be confined to recovery for economic loss.

often invoked in tandem, the core element of "defect" is subtly different in the two causes of action. Under New York law, a design defect may be actionable under a strict products liability theory if the product is not reasonably safe. Since this Court's decision in Voss v. Black & Decker Mfg. Co., 59 N.Y.2d 102, 108, 463 N.Y.S.2d 398, 450 N.E.2d 204, the New York standard for determining the existence of a design defect has required an assessment of whether "if the design defect were known at the time of manufacture, a reasonable person would conclude that the utility of the product did not outweigh the risk inherent in marketing a product designed in that manner." This standard demands an inquiry into such factors as (1) the product's utility to the public as a whole, (2) its utility to the individual user, (3) the likelihood that the product will cause injury, (4) the availability of a safer design, (5) the possibility of designing and manufacturing the product so that it is safer but remains functional and reasonably priced, (6) the degree of awareness of the product's potential danger that can reasonably be attributed to the injured user, and (7) the manufacturer's ability to spread the cost of any safety-related design changes. The above-described analysis is rooted in a recognition that there are both risks and benefits associated with many products and that there are instances in which a product's inherent dangers cannot be eliminated without simultaneously compromising or completely nullifying its benefits (see, Prosser and Keeton, op. cit., § 99, at 699). In such circumstances, a weighing of the product's benefits against its risks is an appropriate and necessary component of the liability assessment under the policy-based principles associated with tort law.

The adoption of this risk/utility balance as a component of the "defectiveness" element has brought the inquiry in design defect cases closer to that used in traditional negligence cases, where the reasonableness of an actor's conduct is considered in light of a number of situational and policy-driven factors.[3] While efforts have been made to steer away from the fault-oriented negligence principles by characterizing the design defect cause of action in terms of a product-based rather than a conduct-based analysis, the reality is that the risk/utility balancing test is a "negligence-inspired" approach, since it invites the parties to adduce proof about the manufacturer's choices and ultimately requires the fact finder to make "a judgment about [the manufacturer's] judgment" (Birnbaum, Unmasking the Test for Design Defect: From Negligence [to Warranty] to Strict Liability to Negligence, 33 Vand.L.Rev. 593, 610, 648). In other words, an assessment of the manufacturer's conduct is virtually inevitable, and, as one commentator

---

[3] In design defect cases, the alleged product flaw arises from an intentional decision by the manufacturer to configure the product in a particular way. In contrast, in strict products liability cases involving manufacturing defects, the harm arises from the product's failure to perform in the intended manner due to some flaw in the fabrication process. In the latter class of cases, the flaw alone is a sufficient basis to hold the manufacturer liable without regard to fault.

observed, "[i]n general, * * * the strict liability concept of 'defective design' [is] functionally synonymous with the earlier negligence concept of unreasonable designing" (Schwartz, *New Products, Old Products, Evolving Law, Retroactive Law*).

It is this negligence-like risk/benefit component of the defect element that differentiates strict products liability claims from UCC-based breach of implied warranty claims in cases involving design defects. While the strict products concept of a product that is "not reasonably safe" requires a weighing of the product's dangers against its over-all advantages, the UCC's concept of a "defective" product requires an inquiry only into whether the product in question was "fit for the ordinary purposes for which such goods are used" (UCC 2–314[2][c]). The latter inquiry focuses on the expectations for the performance of the product when used in the customary, usual and reasonably foreseeable manners. The cause of action is one involving true "strict" liability, since recovery may be had upon a showing that the product was not minimally safe for its expected purpose—without regard to the feasibility of alternative designs or the manufacturer's "reasonableness" in marketing it in that unsafe condition.

This distinction between the "defect" analysis in breach of implied warranty actions and the "defect" analysis in strict products liability actions is explained by the differing etiology and doctrinal underpinnings of the two distinct theories. The [warranty action] originates in contract law, which directs its attention to the purchaser's disappointed expectations; the [products liability action] originates in tort law, which traditionally has concerned itself with social policy and risk allocation by means other than those dictated by the marketplace.

The dissent takes issue with the foregoing conclusion, arguing, in essence, that any residual distinction that exists between the two causes of action should be eliminated and that the analysis for "defect" in implied warranty claims should be deemed to encompass the risk/utility analysis that has previously been incorporated in tort causes of action. This argument is predicated on the dissent's view that the common history of the two causes of action and the perceived advantages of risk/utility analysis counsel in favor of the use of a unitary standard. The dissent has even gone so far as to suggest that the breach of implied warranty cause of action should be treated like a tort claim despite the fact that it is based on the provisions of the Uniform Commercial Code.

What the dissent overlooks is that, as long as that legislative source of authority exists, we are not free to merge the warranty cause of action with its tort-based sibling regardless of whether, as a matter of policy, the contract-based warranty claim may fairly be regarded as a historical relic that no longer has any independent substantive value. Rather, we must construe and apply this separate remedy in a manner that remains consistent with its *current* roots in contract law (*see,* Codling v. Paglia, [32 N.Y. 2d 330, 345 N.Y.S.2d 461, 298 N.E. 2d 622] [recognizing a tort cause of action to avoid stretching the breach of implied warranty theory to the point where it no longer reflects its origin as part of the bargain between the consumer and seller]).

. . .

Contrary to the dissent's suggestion, the current version of UCC 2–318 . . . [does not] manifest an intention by our State's Legislature to engraft a tort cause of action onto a UCC article that concerns itself principally with the contract-based obligations (*see,* dissenting opn., at [casebook pages 237–38]). Indeed, the Law Revision Commission Staff Notes, which the dissent cites, clearly state that the proposed amendments to UCC 2–318 "would * * * allow recovery by the [strict products liability] plaintiffs *on a different cause of action*" (Bill Jacket, L.1975, ch. 774, Mem of N.Y.Law Rev.Commn, Staff Notes relating to A–3070 [emphasis supplied]). Similarly, the Sponsoring Memorandum on which the dissent relies states that the bill's purpose was to "extend more intelligently the warranty provided to a purchaser of goods under the UCC" (Mem of Assemblyman Silverman, reprinted in 1975 NY Legis Ann, at 110). In fact, it is evident from the legislative materials accompanying the bill's passage that its purpose was to expand the class of plaintiffs who can avail themselves of the Code's warranty remedies and not to transform those remedies into a new tort cause of action (*see,* 1A U.L.A. 558 [Master ed.], UCC 2–318, Official Comment).

. . . [W]hile the commentators on which the dissent relies criticize the consumer-expectation-based tests for product defect and argue instead for the use of a risk/utility approach, their arguments are addressed to tort causes of action alone. One of the cited commentators, for example, argues that the consumer expectation test is a "blunt instrument" "when it comes to recognizing and maximizing the * * * goals, objectives, interests and values *important to modern tort law*" (Kennedy, The Role of the Consumer Expectation Test under Louisiana's Products Liability Tort Doctrine, 69 Tul.L.Rev. 117, 152 [emphasis supplied]). The same commentator also acknowledges that different standards might be appropriate for different theories of recovery where other objectives and values are pertinent (*id.*). Another commentator cited by the dissent contends that the risk/utility analysis should be used in place of a consumer-expectation test, but the argument is, once again, premised on the assumption that the latter "is *not a tort way* of looking at the problem of product defect" (Birnbaum, *op. cit.,* at 646 [emphasis supplied]). This commentator also affirmatively criticizes courts that have failed "to separate conceptually the notions of strict liability, negligence, warranty, and absolute liability" (*id.* at 601).

. . .

In any event, while the critics and commentators may debate the relative merits of the consumer-expectation and risk/utility tests, there is no existing authority for the proposition that the risk/utility analysis is appropriate when the plaintiff's claim rests on a claimed breach of implied warranty under UCC 2–314(2)(c) and 2–318. Further, the absence of authority for the dissent's position is not surprising since the negligence-like risk/utility approach is foreign to the realm of contract law.

As a practical matter, the distinction between the defect concepts in tort law and in implied warranty theory may have little or no effect in most cases. In this case, however, the nature of the proof and the way in which the fact issues were litigated demonstrates how the two causes of action can diverge. In the trial court, Ford took the position that the design features of which plaintiffs complain, i.e., the Bronco II's high center of gravity, narrow track width, short wheel base and specially tailored suspension system, were important to preserving the vehicle's ability to drive over the highly irregular terrain that typifies off-road travel. Ford's proof in this regard was relevant to the strict products liability risk/utility equation, which required the fact finder to determine whether the Bronco II's value as an off-road vehicle outweighed the risk of the rollover accidents that could occur when the vehicle was used for other driving tasks.

On the other hand, plaintiffs' proof focused, in part, on the sale of the Bronco II for suburban driving and everyday road travel. Plaintiffs also adduced proof that the Bronco II's design characteristics made it unusually susceptible to rollover accidents when used on paved roads. All of this evidence was useful in showing that routine highway and street driving was the "ordinary purpose" for which the Bronco II was sold and that it was not "fit"—or safe—for that purpose.

Thus, under the evidence in this case, a rational fact finder could have simultaneously concluded that the Bronco II's utility as an off-road vehicle outweighed the risk of injury resulting from rollover accidents *and* that the vehicle was not safe for the "ordinary purpose" of daily driving for which it was marketed and sold. Under the law of this State such a set of factual judgments would lead to the concomitant legal conclusion that plaintiffs' strict products liability cause of action was not viable but that defendant should nevertheless be held liable for breach of its implied promise that the Bronco II was "merchantable" or "fit" for its "ordinary purpose." Importantly, what makes this case distinctive is that the "ordinary purpose" for which the product was marketed and sold to the plaintiff was *not* the same as the utility against which the risk was to be weighed. It is these unusual circumstances that give practical significance to the ordinarily theoretical difference between the defect concepts in tort and statutory breach of implied warranty causes of action.

From the foregoing it is apparent that the causes of action for strict products liability and breach of implied warranty of merchantability are not identical in New York and that the latter is not necessarily subsumed by the former. It follows that, under the circumstances presented, a verdict such as the one occurring here—in which the manufacturer was found liable under an implied warranty cause of action and not liable under a strict products cause of action—is theoretically reconcilable under New York law.

Accordingly, certified question No. 1 should be answered in the negative, certified question No. 2 in the negative and certified question No. 3 in the affirmative.

■ SIMONS, JUDGE (dissenting).

I agree with the majority that causes of action in strict products liability and breach of implied warranty are not identical. In my view, however, the strict products liability claim is substantively broader than and encompasses the implied warranty claim and, thus, the jury's verdict of no defect in the products liability cause of action is not reconcilable with its finding of breach of implied warranty. Accordingly, I would answer the first two questions certified to the Court no and yes and find it unnecessary to answer the third question.

I

Liability without fault may be imposed against a manufacturer or supplier of a defective product and in favor of one injured by the product. The product may be defective because it is improperly made, because its design is defective or because the manufacturer's warnings against foreseeable risks in using it are inadequate. The members of the Court agree that strict products liability and implied warranty are similar in the sense that both causes of action require that, before plaintiff may recover, the product be defective, i.e., there must be something wrong with it. We disagree, however, over how defectiveness is determined. The question does not appear to have been previously addressed by the Court in the context of personal injury litigation.

The majority concludes that the implied warranty and strict products liability causes of action are different because the existence of an actionable defect is determined by two different analyses. Viewing implied warranty from a contract perspective, it would define defectiveness by whether the product lived up to the consumer's expectations whereas defectiveness, for strict products liability purposes, is determined by application of the risk/utility standard. In my judgment, the consumer expectation standard, appropriate to commercial sales transactions, has no place in personal injury litigation alleging a design defect and may result in imposing absolute liability on marketers of consumers' products. Whether a product has been defectively designed should be determined in a personal injury action by a risk/utility analysis.

. . . Breach of implied warranty and strict liability in tort developed from separate legal doctrines but are not materially different when applied to personal injury claims involving design defects. While breach of implied warranty retains its contractual law characteristics when applied to commercial transactions, it has been consistently recognized that it is a tort when applied to personal injury litigation and that tort principles should apply. To introduce a new test of defectiveness into tort litigation—one based on contract principles—can only destabilize the well-settled law in this area. Both causes of action are torts and defectiveness for both should be determined by the same standard.

. . .

Nevertheless, the idea that contractual principles inhere in breach of implied warranty claims for personal injuries has persisted, producing conceptual difficulties and anomalies when the courts tried to apply the cause of action in a tort setting (*see,* Prosser and Keeton, Torts § 97, at 692 [5th ed.1984]). In Codling v. Paglia, 32 N.Y.2d 330, 345 N.Y.S.2d 461, 298 N.E.2d 622, we were confronted with a claim in implied warranty seeking to impose liability against a manufacturer in favor of a nonuser bystander injured by a defective automobile. We had long since abandoned the privity requirement in many personal injury claims based on implied warranty and incrementally extended the duty of manufacturers and suppliers not only to purchasers and users, but to users' family members, to remote purchasers, to an airline passenger suing the manufacturer of a defective component part of an airplane, and to rescuers suing the manufacturer of a defective oxygen mask. In *Codling* we recognized the difficulties in adopting implied warranty principles in personal injury claims and, abandoning privity entirely, recognized a new cause of action under the broad principle of strict products liability, as other courts before us had done, to hold the manufacturer liable to the bystander.

This new cause of action was not separate from implied warranty but an amalgam which had been constructed by the courts to establish a cause of action for liability without fault by merging warranty concepts (to avoid fault analysis) with negligence concepts (to avoid privity). . . . It makes little sense, therefore, to perpetuate a legal distinction between them based upon the method for determining defectiveness, particularly when the flaws in the consumer expectation standard for measuring defectiveness are recognized.

II

The majority has not attempted to define the consumer expectation standard, nor did the District Court use the phrase in its charge. Under one formulation, however, the standard provides that a product is defective, i.e., it is unreasonably dangerous, if it is "dangerous to an extent beyond that which would be contemplated by the ordinary consumer who purchases it, with the ordinary knowledge common to the community as to its characteristics" (*see,* Restatement [Second] of Torts § 402A, comment *i; see also,* Kennedy, The Role of the Consumer Expectation Test under Louisiana's Products Liability Tort Doctrine, 69 Tul.L.Rev. 117, 120 [1994]). The consumer expectation standard originated from the sales notion that a seller could agree, expressly or impliedly, to indemnify a buyer if the purchased product did not satisfy the buyer's purposes. The obligation to "indemnify" applied only to the parties to the sale, those in privity, and did not "run with the goods" (*see,* 5 Harper, James and Gray, *op. cit.,* § 28.16, at 454). As evolving social policy sought to hold manufacturers and sellers liable for personal injuries caused by defective products, however, the requirement of privity was narrowed and then eliminated, and the courts extended liability as far as social policy required (*id.*). With these developments, it made little sense to think in terms of the buyer's bargain or expectations. In many, if not most, cases the buyer was not litigating.

By contrast, the standard usually employed to determine design defectiveness in strict products liability claims requires a balancing of the risks attendant on using the product with the utility of the product when used as intended. As we stated in Robinson v. Reed-Prentice Div. of Package Mach. Co., 49 N.Y.2d 471, 479, 426 N.Y.S.2d 717, 403 N.E.2d 440: "Where a product presents an unreasonable risk of harm, notwithstanding that it was meticulously made according to detailed plans and specifications, it is said to be defectively designed. This rule, however, is tempered by the realization that some products, for example knives, must by their very nature be dangerous in order to be functional. Thus, a defectively designed product is one which, at the time it leaves the seller's hands, is in a condition not reasonably contemplated by the ultimate consumer and is unreasonably dangerous for its intended use; that is one whose utility does not outweigh the danger inherent in its introduction into the stream of commerce."

. . .

If the [consumer expectations] test is applied to determine the actual buyer's expectations, as in contract law, it can result in imposing absolute liability upon manufacturers and sellers making them insurers of the product's safety merely because the product did not live up to the consumer's subjective expectations. If the test is used objectively, it is beyond the experience of most lay jurors to determine what an "ordinary consumer" expects or "how safe" a sophisticated modern product could or should be made to satisfy those expectations unless the jury is allowed to consider the cost or impracticality of alternative designs or, indeed whether any alternative design for the product was available.

The test can also produce bad results. For example, if the risk is one that is easily understood and appreciated by the average consumer, the manufacturer might not be liable even if the defect could be eliminated by available and inexpensive design changes. Conversely, if the defect was not apparent, liability might attach even if the product was in fact state of the art.

. . .

III

The majority maintains, however, that the consumer expectation standard must be applied because breach of implied warranty is a statutory cause of action and the Court is not free to ignore the statute's provisions or draw a distinction between its application to commercial claims and personal injury claims.

Implied warranties have been a part of our statutory law since at least 1911, long before any serious attempt was made to base tort liability on them (*see,* former Personal Property Law § 96; now UCC 2–314). Section 96, and its successor provisions in the Uniform Commercial Code, were enacted to address problems arising in commercial transactions. For many years they had no significant impact upon personal injury litigation because of the rules of privity. However, in 1975, shortly after *Codling v. Paglia, supra,* was decided, *section 2–318* of the Uniform Commercial Code was amended to harmonize it with existing case law by eliminating the requirement of privity in personal injury claims. The amendment had no relevance to commercial claims; it was proposed by the Legislature, and widely supported, because it acknowledged and encouraged the judicial development of a separate category of warranty providing a tort remedy for personal injuries (*see,* 1975 N.Y.Legis.Ann., at 110; *see also,* Bill Jacket, L.1975, ch. 774, Mem of State Consumer Protection Board, July 14, 1975; Mem of NY Law Rev Commn, Staff Notes Relating to A–3070; Mem of New York State Trial Lawyers Assn, May 12, 1975). The Legislature's recognition of a distinction between the statutory cause of action for personal injury claims and commercial claims based on implied warranty is further manifested by the Legislature's decision to adopt alternative B of the three formulations proposed by the National Conference of the Commissioners on Uniform State Laws, the alternative which removed the requirement of privity in personal injury claims based upon implied warranty, rather than alternative C which extends the rule (abolishing privity) to warranty claims other than those dealing with injuries to the person (*see* UCC 2–318, Official Comment 3).

Moreover, no words in the statute either before or after the amendment, provide that the defectiveness of the product in tort claims, or commercial claims for that matter, is to be measured by the consumer's expectations. That standard has been developed by the courts. It may accurately assess the terms and conditions of the bargain between the parties to a sale but it can hardly extend beyond them to address defectiveness in the sense that something is "wrong" with the product. The thing "wrong" with the product in the consumer expectation test is that it has not lived up to the consumer's expectations and this is so even if the design of the product is perfection itself. The standard may retain some vitality when applied to commercial transactions but its individualized concept of injury is entirely foreign to tort doctrine underlying this area of law which is based upon the broad concept of enterprise responsibility to protect the public at large from harm.

... Nothing has prevented us in the past from construing and applying the provisions of the Uniform Commercial Code to supplement and advance the policy concerns underlying strict products liability generally, and we should not construe the statute now to establish a standard for determining defectiveness which is inconsistent with the present law in this area (*see generally,* UCC 1–103 [revised 1–103(b)]).

Accordingly, I dissent.

QUESTIONS AND NOTES

1.   The Restatement differentiates between manufacturing defects and design defects. Comment *a* elaborates:

> In contrast to manufacturing defects, design defects and defects based on inadequate instructions or warnings are predicated on a different concept of responsibility. In the first place, such defects cannot be determined by reference to the manufacturer's own design or marketing standards because those standards are the very ones that plaintiffs attack as unreasonable. Some sort of independent assessment of advantages and disadvantages, to which some attach the label "risk-utility balancing," is necessary. Products are not generically defective merely because they are dangerous. Many product-related accident costs can be eliminated only by excessively sacrificing product features that make products useful and desirable. Thus, the various trade-offs need to be considered in determining whether accident costs are more fairly and efficiently borne by accident victims, on the one hand, or, on the other hand, by consumers generally through the mechanism of higher product prices attributable to liability costs imposed by courts on product sellers.

2.   Comment *n* addresses the relationship between warranty and tort liability:

> The rules in this Section and in other provisions of this Chapter define the bases of tort liability for harm caused by product defects existing at time of sale or other distribution. The rules are stated functionally rather than in terms of traditional doctrinal categories. Claims based on product defect at time of sale or other distribution must meet the requisites set forth in Subsection (a), (b), or (c), or the other provisions in this Chapter. As long as these requisites are met, doctrinal tort categories such as negligence or strict liability may be utilized in bringing the claim.

> Similarly, a product defect claim satisfying the requisites of Subsection (a), (b), or (c), or other provisions in this Chapter, may be brought under the implied warranty of merchantability provisions of the Uniform Commercial Code. It is recognized that some courts have adopted a consumer expectations definition for design and failure-to-warn defects in implied warranty cases involving harm to persons or property. This Restatement contemplates that a well-coordinated body of law governing liability for harm to persons or property arising out of the sale of defective products requires a consistent definition of defect, and

that the definition properly should come from tort law, whether the claim carries a tort label or one of implied warranty of merchantability.

The comment goes on to say that since the factual predicate for a breach of the warranty of merchantability and strict-tort liability are the same in both manufacturing defect and design-defect cases, claims on both theories should not be submitted to a jury simultaneously. However, according to the comments, the plaintiff can choose whether to assert a claim in strict tort or in contract for breach of the warranty of merchantability. One or the other causes of action may be more favorable for other reasons, such as the statute of limitations.

Express warranties and the warranty of fitness for particular purpose depend on specific representations by the seller and, therefore, a claim for breach of those warranties is not duplicative of strict-tort liability and can be asserted along with a claim for strict-tort liability.

The Restatement takes the position that the strict-liability tort rules adopted by the Restatement apply to personal injury and to injury to property other than the thing being sold (Restatement of Torts (Third) § 21). Defects that injure only the property being sold are left to the law of contract, including warranty law. Therefore, if the defect injures the product being sold and also injures persons or other property, the plaintiff's claim would be in warranty as to the product itself and could be in tort as to the injury to person or property. (The leading case holding that warranty law, not the strict-liability doctrine of tort law, applies to defects that injure the property itself is East River Steamship Corp. v. Transamerica Delaval, Inc., 476 U.S. 858, 106 S.Ct. 2295, 90 L.Ed.2d 865 (1986)). Under the Restatement (Third), then, if an SUV rolls over when the plaintiff attempts to avoid a deer on the road, the plaintiff may assert breach of the implied warranty of merchantability for the destruction of the vehicle, but may recover damages for the defective design that caused her personal injuries and the destruction of the new TV she had just purchased only if she establishes that the design is defective under the standard of Restatement (Third) section 2(b). Should different standards apply to the different kinds of injuries resulting from the same alleged design defect?

3.   **Problem.** In early November Kathi saw a TV advertisement for the Jumbo Roaster, a large roasting pan shown being used to cook a 25-pound turkey. Kathi purchased the Jumbo Roaster and used it to roast a large turkey on Thanksgiving. When the turkey was done, she donned insulated mittens to remove it from the oven. The handles on the pan were only large enough, however, for her to use two fingers of each hand to grip them. As she removed the pan from the oven, she lost control of it, and the pan tipped toward her, spilling hot drippings on her feet and ankles. She sued, alleging both products liability and breach of implied warranty of merchantability. The trial court held that the two claims were duplicative, and it submitted only the products liability claim to the jury. Based on evidence that the pan functions well to cook lasagna, stuffed potatoes, casseroles, cutlets, cookies, cake, and other low-weight dishes, the jury returned a verdict for the seller. The trial court entered judgment on the verdict, and Kathi now appeals,

alleging that the trial court erred in refusing to submit the warranty claim to the jury. What should the appellate court do?

D. THE IMPLIED WARRANTY OF FITNESS FOR PARTICULAR PURPOSE

Tyson v. Ciba-Geigy Corp.
North Carolina Court of Appeals, 1986.
82 N.C.App. 626, 347 S.E.2d 473.

[Plaintiff, intending to plant no-till soybeans, contacted defendant Farm Chemical intending to order the herbicides Lasso and Lorox. After plaintiff had described the characteristics of his land and indicated that he wanted to plant no-till soybeans, a Farm Chemical salesman told him that Dual 8E, mixed with Paraquat would be as good as and less expensive than Lasso or Lorox. Plaintiff thereupon purchased Dual 8E. The mixture recommended by Farm Chemical did not kill crabgrass and, as a result, plaintiff had a very low yield of soybeans. Plaintiff sued Farm Chemical and Ciba-Geigy Corp., the manufacturer of Dual 8E. The trial court directed a verdict in favor of both defendants.]

■ HEDRICK, CHIEF JUDGE.

. . .

Plaintiff argues that he presented sufficient evidence for the jury to find that Farm Chemical breached express warranties relating to the effectiveness of Dual 8E, to kill crabgrass in the no-till cultivation of soybeans. Plaintiff contends that the statements of the sales representative of Farm Chemical that the Dual 8E, when mixed with Paraquat and a surfactant, would "do a good job" created an express warranty.

. . . A salesman's expression of his opinion in "the puffing of his wares" does not create an express warranty. Performance Motors, Inc. v. Allen, 280 N.C. 385, 186 S.E.2d 161 (1972). Thus, statements such as "supposed to last a lifetime" and "in perfect condition" do not create an express warranty. Id. Similarly, the statement made by the salesman in the present case that the Dual 8E would "do a good job" is a mere expression of opinion and did not create an express warranty.

Finally, plaintiff contends that the trial court erred in granting defendant Farm Chemical's motion for directed verdict on the issue of breach of implied warranty. We agree with this contention. . . .

The evidence in the present case, when considered in the light most favorable to plaintiff, tends to show that plaintiff contacted defendant Farm Chemical to order the herbicides Lasso and Lorox, for the no-till cultivation of soybeans. He spoke with Mr. Gregory, an employee of Farm Chemical, on the telephone and told him that he was planning the no-till cultivation of soybeans on 145 acres of his land and described the type of soil on the land. Mr. Gregory gave Dual 8E a good recommendation and told plaintiff that it would "do a good job," would be less expensive to use than the chemicals he had used the previous year and would also be less risky to use on plaintiff's type of land. He further told plaintiff that Dual 8E could be mixed with Paraquat and a surfactant to replace Lasso and Lorox. He also told plaintiff the amount of Dual 8E per acre that he should use. Plaintiff testified that based upon Mr. Gregory's recommendation and his past business dealings with Farm Chemical, he decided to use Dual 8E and ordered thirty-five gallons from Farm Chemical. Vance Tyson testified that he mixed the chemicals in accordance with Mr. Gregory's instructions, but that the Dual 8E was ineffective in killing crabgrass. Plaintiff also introduced evidence tending to show that Dual 8E must be mixed with Sencor, Lexone or Lorox and either Ortho Paraquat CL or Roundup. This evidence is sufficient to support a finding that the seller, Farm Chemical, had reason to know of the particular purpose, the no-till cultivation of soybeans, for which the product was required and that plaintiff was relying on its recommendation when he ordered the Dual 8E. There is no evidence in the record indicating that defendant Farm Chemical disclaimed any warranties relating to the Dual 8E. Thus, the evidence in the record is sufficient for a jury to find that Farm Chemical made an implied warranty relating to the fitness of the Dual 8E for plaintiff's purpose and that this warranty was breached. We hold, therefore, that the trial court erred in directing a verdict for defendant Farm Chemical on the issue of breach of an implied warranty of fitness for particular purpose.

. . .

QUESTIONS AND NOTES

1.   Why does the court in *Tyson* hold that the statement by the salesman did not create an express warranty? Do you agree? Characterization of the warranty as "express" would make a difference if the seller had effectively disclaimed the implied warranty of fitness for particular purpose. See 2–316(1).

2.   What are the elements of the implied warranty of fitness for a particular purpose? Was each present in *Tyson*?

3.   **Problem.** Reynolds told Carr's Autos that she needed a vehicle capable of towing her boat, which with its trailer weighed 6,500 pounds. Carr's recommended a particular model of GMC pick-up trucks, and Reynolds purchased it. Is there an implied warranty of fitness for the buyer's particular purpose? Is there an implied warranty of merchantability?

As Reynolds was driving (with her boat and trailer) to her vacation destination 500 miles from her home, the transmission seized. Is there a breach of the implied warranty of fitness? Is there a breach of the implied warranty of merchantability? If you need additional facts, what are they?

When Reynolds sued Carr's for breach of implied warranty, Reynolds testified on cross examination that she visited the web sites of GMC, Ford, and Toyota to learn about the various models offered by these manufacturers. She also testified that she discussed the choice of pick-ups with other boat owners. Does this testimony preclude recovery for breach of implied warranty of fitness for particular purpose?

In A.S. Leavitt v. Monaco Coach Corp., 241 Mich.App. 288, 294, 616 N.W.2d 175, 180 (2000), the court upheld recovery by the purchaser of a motorhome:

> Defendant points out that the evidence indicates that plaintiff never negotiated for specific speed capabilities and that the coach in question could, in fact, negotiate the steepest mountain grades while fully loaded, albeit at slow speeds. However, the evidence that plaintiff communicated his wish to traverse mountain roads while keeping up with commercial buses was sufficiently specific to support a finding that plaintiff articulated to defendant his particular need for engine power. Likewise, plaintiff's testimony about having communicated his problems with brakes in the past while seeking defendant's advice in the matter, along with having described the mountainous areas in which he wished to drive the coach, was sufficient to support a finding that defendant articulated to defendant his particular braking needs.
>
> Concerning plaintiff's reliance on defendant in selecting the coach for his special needs, defendant points to evidence that suggests that plaintiff relied primarily on his own judgment, not defendant's, in the matter. However, plaintiff's insistence that he relied mainly on defendant for the choice of engine, and for deciding against upgrading the brakes, is sufficient to support a finding that plaintiff relied on defendant's expertise in selecting a coach that suited his needs.

Back to the GMC pick-up problem: assume that further investigation reveals that the manufacturer ran out of one of the components used in fabricating the transmission. To keep its production line operating, it obtained substitutes from an alternate supplier, and these components were substandard and failed in most of the 1,000 transmissions in which they were used. Did Seller breach an implied warranty of merchantability? an implied warranty of fitness for the buyer's particular purpose? What does Official Comment 2 to 2–315 suggest?

4. Would the buyer in *Bethlehem Steel* (page 263 supra) have had better luck arguing breach of the implied warranty of fitness for particular purpose? What factual inquiries would you make if you were trying to determine the buyer's chances of successfully asserting that claim in *Bethlehem Steel*? Should there be any obligation on the part of the seller to notify the buyer that this steel was more brittle at lower temperatures than most steel of the designated grade?

5. In Wilson v. Massey-Ferguson, Inc., 21 Ill.App.3d 867, 315 N.E.2d 580 (1974), plaintiff purchased a farm tractor. Claiming that the tractor could not handle heavy duty plowing and that the engine failed earlier than it should have, he sued for breach of the warranty of merchantability and the warranty of fitness for particular purpose. The court responded:

> [T]here was no evidence to support a warranty for a particular purpose. The Illinois Code Comment to section 2–315 indicates that:
>
> > "Thus, where the goods are to be put to ordinary use, the concept of merchantability and not particular purpose is involved." (S.H.A., ch. 26, Sec. 2–315, p. 239.)
>
> The Uniform Commercial Code Comment similarly indicates that:
>
> > "2. A 'particular purpose' differs from the ordinary purpose for which the goods are used in that it envisages a specific use by the buyer which is peculiar to the nature of his business whereas the ordinary purposes for which goods are used are those envisaged in the concept of merchantability and go to uses which are customarily made of the goods in question. For example, shoes are generally used for the purpose of walking upon ordinary ground, but a seller may know that a particular pair was selected to be used for climbing mountains." (Id. at p. 240.)
>
> In this case, the tractor was sold and used for ordinary farm work, which includes, without question, heavy duty plowing. Thus, section 2–315 is not relevant in this case, and the implied warranty of merchantability (Sec. 2–314), is the only relevant concept here.

Compare Tennessee Carolina Transportation, Inc. v. Strick Corp., 283 N.C. 423, 196 S.E.2d 711 (1973), in which plaintiff purchased truck trailers from defendant. When the trailers collapsed while carrying normal loads on normal roads, plaintiff sued for breach of warranty of fitness for particular purpose. Applying the law of Pennsylvania, the court stated:

> At trial, plaintiff stipulated that it was not relying on the implied warranty of merchantability, Pa.Stat.Ann. tit. 12A, Sec. 2–314 (1970). Therefore, the suit was only for breach of the implied warranty of fitness for a particular purpose, Pa.Stat.Ann. tit. 12A, Sec. 2–315 (1970). Defendant now contends that such a suit is tenable only where the goods were purchased for a *particular* purpose. It further contends that this term does not embrace purchases of goods for the *general* purpose for which goods of that kind are used. Thus, defendant urges that plaintiff has failed to make out a case for the jury since it bought the trailers not for a particular purpose but rather for the general or ordinary purpose of hauling cargo. For this reason defendant assigns as error the overruling of its motions for directed verdict.
>
> We find no merit in this assignment. Although the primary purpose of Pa.Stat.Ann. tit. 12A, Sec. 2–315 (1970) is indeed to protect a buyer who purchases goods with the intention of using them in a "particular" manner, meaning a manner in which they would not normally be expected to be used, we do not think that section is limited exclusively to purchases of such a nature. That

warranty also protects a buyer when his particular purpose *is* the general or ordinary purpose.

Although no cases have been found either expressly adopting or rejecting this construction of "particular purpose," Professor Nordstrom so construes that term. See Nordstrom Sales Sec. 78 (1970): "[I]f the buyer's use of the goods is the ordinary use of those goods, * * * the buyer's particular purpose coincides with the ordinary use of the goods, and *either section 2–314 or section 2–315* will give the buyer the protection he needs." (Emphasis added) Such was also the rule at common law. See 46 Am.Jur. Sales § 346 (1943).

Despite the lack of authority expressly adopting this interpretation of "particular purpose," several cases have done so impliedly, without discussion of the issue. *See* Annot. 17 A.L.R.3d 1010, 1071 (1968). Among these is Adams v. Scheib, 408 Pa. 452, 184 A.2d 700 (1962). There, the Pennsylvania Supreme Court held that where plaintiff bought pork sausage for the purpose of consumption—obviously the ordinary purpose—an implied warranty arose, citing *both* Pa.Stat.Ann. tit. 12A, Sec. 2–314 *and* Sec. 2–315. See also L & N Sales Co. v. Stuski, 188 Pa.Super. 117, 146 A.2d 154 (1958), where whiskey pourers were bought for the ordinary purpose of pouring drinks, and the Pennsylvania Superior Court, assuming that a warranty of fitness for a particular purpose arose under Pa.Stat.Ann. tit. 12A, Sec. 2–315, held that such warranty was not excluded by an express warranty of merchantability or by a disclaimer contained in the purchase money security agreement executed after the sale.

Therefore, we think it beyond dispute that in Pennsylvania the warranty of fitness does protect a buyer whose particular purpose *is* the general or ordinary one.

Which court is right, *Wilson* or *Tennessee Carolina Transportation*? What is the relevance of 2–315, Official Comment 2: is it addressing the issue in these cases, or some other issue?

What difference does it make whether a warranty of fitness for particular purpose can arise where the buyer's purpose is the ordinary and normal purpose for which the goods are used?

6.   If recovery for breach of the implied warranty of fitness for the buyer's particular purpose is not permitted when that purpose coincides with the ordinary purpose of the goods, the court may be called upon to draw very fine distinctions between the ordinary purpose and the buyer's particular purpose. In Golden v. Den-Mat Corp., 276 P.3d 773 (Kan.App. 2012), plaintiff Golden sought dental veneers that would give her teeth what she described as a "super white" appearance. (Veneers are synthetic panels cemented to the front of the teeth.) She discussed this with Dr. Gill, a dentist, who obtained and installed porcelain veneers on her teeth. The veneers became discolored and failed to adhere. She sued for breach of both implied

warranties. The trial court gave summary judgment for defendant, but the appellate court reversed:

> Courts sometimes point out that warranties of merchantability apply to the fundamental functions or core attributes of the goods rather than matters of aesthetics or appearance. Those cases would be factually inapposite here given the ordinary use of dental veneers. The veneers are, by their very purpose, cosmetic. If certain veneers fail of that purpose in a manner atypical of that product generally, they likely would not meet standards of merchantability under the UCC.
>
> Dr. Gill also argues the veneers were not covered by . . . any implied warranty of fitness for a particular purpose. . . . While Golden had identified the Cerinate veneers as the product she believed would best fit her needs, she had not already contracted to purchase them when she met with Dr. Gill. According to Golden, they discussed her desire for very white teeth. Dr. Gill recalled suggesting Golden might prefer a more natural shade for the veneers, since the whitest ones might look artificial. Golden, nonetheless, asked Dr. Gill to order the brightest veneers Den-Mat made.
>
> The evidence would support a jury determination that Golden had a particular purpose in mind beyond simply some cosmetic improvement in the appearance of her teeth. She wanted strikingly white teeth, even if some people, apparently including Dr. Gill, might find them unnatural and unflattering. On its face, that looks to be a particular purpose in contrast to a generic characteristic of veneers. Dr. Gill certainly knew of that purpose and knew of Golden's plan to buy Cerinate veneers. In turn, Golden's request of Dr. Gill for some assurance that the veneers would satisfy that purpose and Dr. Gill's purported response that porcelain dental appliances do not discolor or stain could be construed as creating an implied warranty of fitness for a particular purpose. Golden made clear a specific need she wanted the veneers to satisfy and sought affirmation from Dr. Gill the Cerinate veneers would work. The communication may not have been pointed, detailed, or extended. . . . The jury should be permitted to make the call on whether there was an implied warranty of fitness for a particular purpose under K.S.A. 84–2–315 and whether the veneers breached that warranty.
>
> Breaches of implied warranties of merchantability and of fitness for a particular purpose are not mutually exclusive. That is, depending on the facts, a seller may be liable for breaching both in a single transaction, although a buyer may not recover duplicative damages. For example, a pair of shoes sold to a person requesting footwear for mountain climbing may have a claim for a breach of warranty for a particular purpose if they fall apart halfway up [a mountain in Alaska]. If the sole on one of them starts flapping while the person walks through the . . . airport to get on [the] flight to

Alaska, the shoes likely breach an implied warranty of merchantability for footwear generally and necessarily breach the more specific and more demanding warranty for the particular purpose of mountain climbing. Here, the claims for breach are more closely connected. The asserted warranty of merchantability related to durability, including resistance to chipping, retention in place, and constancy of color and appearance. The warranty of fitness for a particular purpose appears to depend on constancy of color and appearance alone. That overlap, however, does not impose a legal bar to either claim. The jury, properly instructed, ought to determine the existence and scope of the warranties and any concomitant breach.

7. Could the buyer in *Denny* (page 279) have asserted breach of the implied warranty of fitness for particular purpose?

8. Problem. Chollie's Chicken places language on its web site that its potato products do not contain dairy products, wheat, or gluten. That language may create an express warranty, and if Chollie's fries are not free of those substances, there may be a breach of express warranty. Is there also a breach of the implied warranty of fitness for particular purpose?

9. CISG. The introduction to this chapter pointed out that the division of warranty into express warranties and implied warranties of merchantability and fitness for a particular purpose is somewhat artificial and that perhaps the Code should merely have said that the buyer is entitled to the quality he reasonably expected. The Convention on Contracts for the International Sale of Goods deals with seller's obligation as to quality of goods in Article 35. That provision does not use the term warranty, and it does not distinguish between express and implied obligations. Please read Article 35.

Is the formulation in the Convention better than the one in Article 2? Why or why not?

Article 35, section 2(a) tracks 2–314, but section 2(b) does not exactly track 2–315. Exactly how does it differ?

E. IMPLIED WARRANTIES IN LEASES

Article 2A recognizes two kinds of leases. In one, the lessor typically maintains an inventory of the goods, retains the title to the goods, and gets them back at a time when they still have meaningful value. These might be characterized as true leases, and they are analogous to sales. Before the promulgation of Article 2A in 1989, when called upon to decide whether there were warranties in this kind of lease transaction, the courts held that Article 2 warranties apply to leases. In 2A–210 to –213, Article 2A confirms this result. Section 2A–212, for example, provides for an implied warranty of merchantability identical to the warranty for sales under 2–314. Like sales, this form of lease is a mechanism for putting goods into the possession of the user of the goods.

The other kind of lease is as much a mechanism for financing a transaction as it is a mechanism for putting goods into the possession of the user. In this kind of lease, the lessor has no inventory of goods, may know nothing about the goods it leases, and provides no repair or other services with respect to those goods. Rather, the lessor is a financial institution and is purely a source of financing for the user of the goods. By way of illustrating the differences among various kinds of leases and purchases, a person who wants to acquire goods but does not have ready cash has several options:

(1) purchase from a seller on credit and promise to pay the price in monthly installments:

(2) borrow the needed funds from a lender, use the loan proceeds to purchase the goods, and promise to repay the lender in monthly installments:

(3) lease the goods from a person who has an inventory of the goods and promise to make monthly payments:

(4) enter an arrangement with a financial institution in which the financial institution purchases the goods specified by the lessee, leases them to the lessee, and is repaid by the lessee in the form of monthly lease payments:

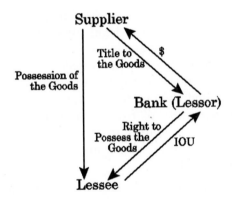

The lessee may have tax, accounting, or other business reasons for preferring to structure the transaction this last way, in what is known as a finance lease. The following case arose before enactment of Article 2A and concerns the applicability of the implied warranty of merchantability to a finance lease.

All-States Leasing Co. v. Bass

Idaho Supreme Court, 1975.
96 Idaho 873, 538 P.2d 1177.

[Defendant Bass, doing business as Bass Phillips "66" Service Station in Boise, Idaho, contacted Auto Laundry Manufacturing Company about the purchase of a coin-operated car wash machine. Two salesmen for the company contacted Bass and, when Bass said he wanted the machine, suggested that a lease arrangement be worked out. The salesmen filled out two forms for a leasing arrangement: a lease application form and the lease agreement itself. Both forms showed the name of plaintiff conspicuously on the front. Plaintiff approved the transaction, purchased the machine from Auto Laundry, and leased it to defendant.

The car wash system was delivered and Bass signed a completion certificate acknowledging that the system was properly installed and was in proper condition. Defendant made two payments but then refused to make any further payments: among the reasons given for this refusal was that there were breaches of warranty as to the machine. Plaintiff brought suit for rent due under the lease. Bass asserted as a defense that plaintiff had breached warranties of fitness and merchantability.

The trial court found that plaintiff had breached implied warranties "in the nature of fitness." It rescinded the agreement, but allowed plaintiff to retain payments already made as compensation for the use of the machine by defendant. Plaintiff appeals.]

■ MCQUADE, C.J.

. . .

Appellant contends that it is unsettled in Idaho whether the lease of personal property has the same legal effect with respect to implied warranties as does a sale of goods. Appellant concedes that there is authority in other jurisdictions to that effect, but maintains that even if this be the rule of law in this state, the trial court committed reversible error when it concluded that under the facts of this case there existed either an implied warranty of fitness for a particular purpose or an implied warranty of merchantability. In the alternative, appellant argues that any warranties which may have been applicable were effectively disclaimed by it.

Before answering appellant's contentions, we must first determine whether the trial court was correct in applying warranty doctrine to a lease transaction.

[In an omitted part of the opinion, the court held that implied warranty principles should apply to leases of goods.]

. . .

By analogy in a lease transaction, in order for such an implied warranty [of fitness for particular purpose] to arise it must be shown that: (1) the lessor was made aware of the lessee's need, (2) that the lessor recommended a product, and (3) that the lessee leased the product as recommended.

In the instant case, the record indicates that while appellant lessor may have been aware of respondent lessee's need, it made no suggestion or recommendation as to a choice of car wash system to meet this need. Furthermore there is no evidence that respondent made his selection on any basis other than his own inspection of the manufacturer's literature describing the equipment and his impressions of the equipment based upon the statements made by the manufacturer's salesmen which the trial court correctly found did not bind appellant lessor. This being the case, we conclude that no implied warranty of fitness for a particular purpose existed.

Turning our inquiry next to the question of whether appellant impliedly warranted that the car wash system would be of merchantable quality, we conclude that no such implied warranty existed in the instant case. . . .

In a lease transaction, in order for such an implied warranty of merchantability to exist it must be shown that the lessor is a "merchant" with respect to the goods which he leases.

. . .

The official comment following [section 2–104] notes:

> "On the other hand, in Section 2–314 on the warranty of merchantability, such warranty is implied only 'if the seller is a merchant with respect to goods of that kind.' Obviously this qualification restricts the implied warranty to a much smaller group than everyone who is engaged in business and requires a professional status as to particular kinds of goods."

It is true that prior to the execution of the lease in issue, appellant handled between forty to fifty transactions over a period of six to eight months, concerning the same Budg-O-Matic Car Wash System that is the subject of this dispute. However, this in our mind does not make All-States Leasing a "merchant" for purposes of the Code. The record discloses that appellant does not build, manufacture or sell any equipment or machines of any kind, but rather is in the business of purchasing or financing the purchase of equipment specifically selected and specified by an approved lessee. Mr. Lorenz, the Chairman of the Board of Directors and Vice President of appellant company testified:

> Q.   "Now, what business—what is the business nature of All-States Leasing Company?
>
> A.   "We are a capital equipment lessor. We provide equipment to people who make application to use for a lease, if we grant it, we buy the equipment that they specify from the people that they want us to buy it from and we lease it to them.
>
> Q.   "Does All-States Leasing Company manufacture any kind of equipment?
>
> A.   "No.
>
> Q.   "Does All-States Leasing Company broker or distribute any kind of equipment?
>
> A.   "No.
>
> Q.   "Do you distribute any kind of merchandise at all?

A. "None.

Q. "Do you manufacture any kind of merchandise?

A. "None.

Q. "In other words, your business or All-States Leasing Company is strictly a company that leases or buys equipment that people specify and, then, lease that to them?

A. "That's correct."

. . .

[A]s one law journalist has noted:

"Section 2–314 presents several obstacles to the imposition of liability on the finance lessor. First, the implied warranty of merchantability applies only to 'merchants.' The Code defines a merchant as one who deals in goods of the kind, or holds himself out as having knowledge peculiar to the goods, involved in the transaction. Since the finance lessor neither deals in goods of the kind being leased nor holds himself out as knowledgeable in the field, the finance lessor does not fit the Code definition of a merchant. Hence, it would appear at the outset that the UCC's implied warranty of merchantability cannot be applied by analogy to the finance lessor."[11]

In light of our conclusion that appellant was a finance lessor and not a merchant for purposes of IC § 28–2–314, it is unnecessary to pass upon the validity of the disclaimer clause, as it has no bearing on the merits of this appeal.

We do not have to decide whether respondent would have a cause of action against the manufacturer, as the manufacturer was not joined as a party to this action.

Judgment reversed. . . .

■ SHEPARD, J., dissenting. SCOGGIN, D.J. (retired) concurs in dissent.

I disagree with that portion of the majority opinion that holds that the lessor is not a "merchant." I cannot agree that the appellant who purchased and thereafter leased large numbers of car wash systems was not "a person who deals in goods of the kind." Although the appellant here did not build or manufacture such equipment, neither do most retailers. The sole distinction in this case is that appellant, being a lessor rather than a vendor, retained title to the equipment. The majority's purported change in rule permitting a lessor, in some circumstances, to be held to an implied warranty of merchantability is in reality no change at all. If a person must "sell" and divest himself of title to become a "merchant" and thus subject himself to implied warranty liability, a lessor can never be subjected to such liability on implied warranty.

---

[11] Comment, Finance Lessor's Liability for Personal Injuries, Univ. of Ill. Law Forum, Vol. 1, 154, 158 (1974).

Questions and Notes

1. *All-States Leasing* was decided 3 to 2. If All-States Leasing had sold 40 of the machines over six to eight months, is there any doubt that it would have been a merchant for purposes of the warranty of merchantability? More specifically, suppose that Auto Laundry's method of doing business was to have its personnel handle all customer contacts and then transfer title to All-States Sales Co., which in turn would sell to the buyers of the machines. (Perhaps business might be handled this way to avoid having to comply with requirements for doing business in the state.) Could All-States argue that it was not a merchant in that case?

2. Idaho adopted Article 2A in 1993, two decades after the transaction in *All-States Leasing*. If the case arose today, how would it be decided? The applicable section is 2A–212. Ignoring for the moment the five introductory words of that section, would there be an implied warranty of merchantability?

3. The introductory words to 2A–212 mean that with respect to the implied warranty of merchantability, Article 2A puts a finance lessor in the same category as a lender: there is no implied warranty. In both kinds of transactions, the plaintiff who is acquiring the goods must look to the person that sold the goods, that is, sold to either the plaintiff or the lessor. "Finance lease" is defined in 2A–103(g). Please read that definition now.

For a lease to be a finance lease, three elements must be present. It appears that the lease in *All-States Leasing* would not have qualified as a "finance lease" under the definition in Article 2A because, although the first two elements were present, the third element was not: Bass did not receive a copy of the contract between Auto Laundry and All-States Leasing, the transaction was not conditional upon his approval of that contract, and he had not received a statement of the rights against Auto Laundry. If the case arose today, how strong an argument does All-States Leasing have that it still has no implied warranty of merchantability liability because it is not a merchant?

Even if a lessor is not a finance lessor under Article 2A, it can still avoid warranty liability by an effective disclaimer. See 2A–214.

4. Problem. When Atlas Construction Co.'s fifteen-year-old crane became unreliable, Atlas decided to replace it by leasing a new one. After identifying the crane it wanted to acquire, Atlas approached Worldbank Leasing, Inc., about financing the transaction. Worldbank was amenable, telling Atlas that its experience with leasing Craneco equipment had been excellent and that Craneco's equipment is the best on the market. Worldbank Leasing and Atlas Construction entered a ten-year lease contract for the crane, and Worldbank acquired the equipment from Craneco, pursuant to a contract containing several express warranties. Atlas took possession of the crane and made payments for six years, at which time the crane collapsed and could not be repaired. Does Atlas have a claim against Worldbank Leasing for breach of warranty? against Craneco?

The right of a remote buyer to recover for breach of warranty from a person with whom it has no contract is considered in Chapter 6, pages 334–

372 infra. For the right of a *lessee* to recover from the person with whom it has no contract, see 2A–209, which gives the lessee in a finance lease a direct cause of action against the "supplier" of the goods. For the definition of "supplier," see 2A–103(x).

5.   Insulation of the financer. Finance leases frequently include so-called "hell or high water" clauses under which the lessee promises to pay the lessor even though the leased goods are defective. These clauses recognize that the finance lessor is really a supplier of money rather than a supplier of goods and provide that the lessor is entitled to be repaid, whether or not the leased goods are defective. Similar devices are available to sellers and lenders. For example, a sales contract may contain a waiver-of-defenses clause, by which the buyer agrees not to assert against an assignee of the contract those claims or defenses (e.g., breach of warranty) that it has against the seller. In the loan context, the holder-in-due-course doctrine achieves the same result. (A holder in due course takes a negotiable instrument—a promissory note—free of the claims and defenses that the promisor may have against the seller who received the instrument or its proceeds.)

For the Article 2A rule as to a lessee's right to assert defenses against a finance lessor, see 2A–407. What are the lessee's rights under that section as against a finance lessor prior to the lessee's acceptance of the goods? Observe that 2A–407 is a statutory "hell or high water" provision that is effective even though the contract itself does not contain a "hell or high water" provision. Should the section have merely validated contractual clauses?

In consumer transactions a number of courts have held that it may be unfair or contrary to public policy for the buyer to have to pay the assignee of a contract or promissory note for goods that were never delivered or that were grossly defective, when the assignee or note holder is little more than an extension of the seller. E.g., Unico v. Owen, 50 N.J. 101, 232 A.2d 405 (1967). After determining that it is inefficient to externalize the costs of the seller's breach from the consumer's obligation to pay, the Federal Trade Commission adopted the Trade Regulation Rule Concerning Preservation of Consumers' Claims and Defenses (often called the Holder Rule). This Rule requires sellers to include the following language in their contracts:

> Any holder of this consumer credit contract is subject to all claims and defenses which the debtor could assert against the seller of goods or services obtained pursuant hereto or with the proceeds hereof. . . .

With respect to loans directly from a lender to a consumer, if the lender is closely related to the seller, the Rule permits sellers to accept loan proceeds only if the loan contract contains that language. The Holder Rule does not apply to leases, but in Mercedes-Benz Credit Corp. v. Lotito, 306 N.J.Super. 25, 703 A.2d 288 (App.Div.1997), the court extended the reasoning underlying Unico v. Owen and the Holder Rule to consumer lease transactions.

F. WARRANTY OF TITLE

1. THE OBLIGATION TO PROVIDE GOOD TITLE

As in land transactions, personal property may be sold on a quit-claim basis, giving the buyer all the risks of ownership. Sales of goods on this basis, however, are rare, and thus, in the absence of an express agreement to the contrary, 2–312 requires the seller to give more.

Subsection (1)(a) provides that the seller warrants "good" title. Good title is not defined by the Code, but Official Comment 1 states that a good title is one that is not exposed to a lawsuit. Good title means not just that the buyer can defeat the third party in a lawsuit. It also means that the buyer's title is not unreasonably exposed to the claim of the third person. The warranty is breached if the party is exposed to a non-frivolous claim of infringement even if the claim ultimately is determined to not be valid. Pacific Sunwear of California, Inc. v. Olaes Enterprises, Inc., 167 Cal.App.4th 466, 84 Cal.Rptr.3d 182 (2008). A breach of the warranty of title entitles the buyer to cancel the sale or to recover from the seller the costs of defending the title.

The operation of this subsection is illustrated by Jefferson v. Jones, 286 Md. 544, 549–54, 408 A.2d 1036, 1039–42 (1979), in which plaintiff purchased a motorcycle from defendant. The vehicle identification number (VIN) on the title certificate did not match the VIN stamped on the motorcycle, and the police seized it. Plaintiff obtained return of the vehicle and then sued defendant, claiming breach of the warranty of title. The court agreed:

> . . . [T]he U.C.C.'s warranty of title requirement is to protect a vendee from legal claims which may arise concerning his ownership of the purchased goods. The type or nature, however, of a third party's claim of title or right to possession giving rise to a breach of the warranty is not further delineated by the statute. Consequently, we will now proceed to determine the nature of the claims which the legislature intended should have the protection of the warranty of title provided for in section 2–312.
>
> The intermediate appellate and trial court's answer to this query was that a breach of section 2–312(1) (a) occurs only when a purchaser establishes the existence of a "superior or paramount" title in a third party. These rulings are in accord with the showing that was required at common law before a breach of the implied warranty of title could be found. However, it is our view that the legislature intended, in accord with the design of the drafters, that the Code's warranty of title would provide a buyer with greater protection than its common law counterpart. Our determination in this regard here is amply supported by the statement in the comments that "[disturbance]

of quiet possession, . . . [which at common law required interference by a holder of a superior or paramount title before a breach was declared] is one way, *among many*, in which the breach of the warranty of title may be established." § 2–312, comment 1 (emphasis added). Again, finding nothing to the contrary, we therefore conclude that the General Assembly intended that section 2–312's protection, unless waived by the purchaser, applies to third party claims of title no matter whether eventually determined to be inferior or superior to the buyer's ownership. . . .

Our holding here, that proof of a superior title is not necessary, does not mean, however, that all claims, no matter how unfounded, which may be made against the buyer's title should result in a breach of the warranty. "Good title" is "usually taken to mean that the title which the seller gives to the buyer is 'free from reasonable doubt, that is, not only a valid title in fact, but [also] one that can again be sold to a reasonable purchaser or mortgaged to a person of reasonable prudence.'" [citation omitted] As such, "there is some point at which [a] third party's claim against the goods becomes so attenuated that we should not regard it as an interference against which the seller has warranted." [citation omitted] All that a purchaser should expect from a seller of property is that he be protected from colorable claims against his title and not from all claims. Spurious title claims can be made by anyone at any time. . . . Thus, before a third party's claim against the title of another will result in a breach of the warranty of title, the claim must be colorable, nonspurious and of such a nature as to produce a reasonable doubt as to the title's validity. . . .

. . . When analyzing the legal questions presented, a court, in our opinion, may profitably draw upon the principles which this Court has developed over the years for deciding whether title to real property is marketable. Decisions of this Court, stretching back for over 100 years, have discussed the reasonable doubt concept in this regard as it pertains to real property. The criteria which have developed essentially require a determination of whether the claim is of such a substantial nature that it may reasonably subject the buyer to serious litigation. While such a standard may be considered vague, it is one which courts have successfully applied for many years. Furthermore, the public policy considerations underlying this standard concerning marketability of title to realty are similar to those which section 2–312 was designed to foster in the sales of personalty—to balance the needs of the purchaser concerning title with the litigious nature of our society and the seller's needs for a limit to his liability.

When we examine the facts of the case now before us, in light of the legal standard just mentioned, we conclude that, as a matter of law, there exists a warranty of title that has been breached here. . . . Whenever the title to personal property is evidenced by a document which is an aid to proving ownership, as is true in the case of motor vehicles, any substantial defect in that document necessarily creates a reasonable doubt as to that ownership. A certificate of title, which, with limited exceptions, all owners of motor vehicles must have in this State, is prima facie evidence of ownership. To be valid, such a certificate must include, among other things, the vehicle's identification number; and while the owner of the vehicle may prove his title by means other than the certificate, any seller of a motor vehicle who executes . . . an assignment of the vehicle's certificate of title that contains identifying information that is different from that on the vehicle itself, knows or should know that problems concerning the buyer's ownership would arise. Without a valid title certificate, the owner of a vehicle cannot register, drive or sell it, and if problems do arise, as in this case, the seller is responsible for any damages caused. In other words, a breach of the warranty of title occurs whenever a seller of a motor vehicle fails to provide his purchaser with adequate proof of ownership because of the reasonable doubts which faulty documentation raise as to the validity of the buyer's title.

Another illustration of the operation 2–312 is Saber v. Dan Angelone Chevrolet, Inc., 811 A.2d 644 (R.I.2002). A buyer experienced mechanical difficulties shortly after purchasing a five-year-old red Corvette with an automatic transmission. Upon researching the prior ownership of the car, he discovered a document that described it as a black Corvette with a manual transmission. Further investigation revealed that the VIN— which appears on the chassis, engine, and other components—was not the same in all the places where it appeared. Suspecting that the car or some of its parts were stolen goods, the police impounded the car. In fact, the parts were not stolen. Instead, the car had been declared a total loss following a fire and then been rebuilt using parts from various other cars. It was not clear whether the seller of the car knew of this prior history. Nevertheless, the court held that the seller had breached the warranty of title:

> [We] acknowledge that "there is some point at which [a] third party's claim against the goods becomes so attenuated that we should not regard it as an interference against which the seller has warranted." White & Summers, [Uniform Commercial Code,] § 9–12 at 537 [(4th ed.1995)]. Here, the car and its parts were not stolen and defendant did indeed have and deliver a legally valid title to plaintiff. We are satisfied, however, that under the facts in this case, the claim made against plaintiff's

car—the state police's impoundment—was not too far attenuated. Lieutenant Costa's inspection of the Corvette revealed that it had contradicting VINs and a missing . . . sticker. Based on those facts Lt. Costa reasonably, albeit mistakenly, believed that the car was composed of stolen parts, and therefore impounded it. By doing so, the state police called plaintiff's ownership into question, thereby "casting * * * a substantial shadow over his title.

The Corvette in this case reminds us of a passage attributed to Abraham Lincoln when he asked, "[h]ow many legs does a dog have if you count his tail as a leg? Four. You can call a tail a leg if you want to, but that doesn't make it a leg." Just as a dog's tail is not a leg, this car is not a typical 1985 Corvette. Although defendant argues that the car is a 1985 Corvette, the car has several "unique" qualities that distinguish it from most other 1985 Corvettes. Without knowing the colorful past associated with this car, plaintiff could not get the benefit of his bargain when he made his purchase. The Corvette was rebuilt after having previously been declared a total loss because of fire damage. Various parts were replaced from an assortment of other vehicles. Vehicle identification numbers embossed on certain parts did not correspond to one another. We conclude that those distinctive characteristics associated with the car and its title would lower its value in the eyes of a reasonably prudent purchaser. By imposing liability for breach of warranty of title in this scenario, the trial justice allayed buyers' fears of encountering a similar situation. Thus, we uphold the trial justice's ruling that defendant breached the warranty of title.

Id. at 651–52. The court affirmed the trial court's judgment on the jury's verdict in the amount of the purchase price.

Subsection 2–312(1)(b) requires that the goods be free from any security interest, lien, or encumbrance of which the buyer has no actual knowledge. If there is a security interest, then, the seller breaches the warranty of title, but only if the buyer does not know of the security interest. The knowledge limitation reflects the fact that a person buying goods with actual knowledge of a possible outstanding interest in them will pay less for them, in return for which it is fair for that person to assume the title risks. But the buyer is not charged with knowledge of a security interest merely because it is on the public record by virtue of a financing statement filed pursuant to Article 9 (which deals with security interests). Whether the buyer takes free of the perfected security interest, however, is determined by other law. This aspect of the transaction is addressed in Chapter 11.

2. DISCLAIMER OF THE WARRANTY

Subsection (2) of 2–312 sets out requirements for disclaiming the warranty of title. A disclaimer of title can be only by specific language. The word "only" in subsection (2) means that the warranty of title cannot be disclaimed by using broad disclaimer language, which we will see is authorized by 2–316(2)–(3) to disclaim the implied warranties of merchantability and fitness for particular purpose. Rather, the seller must use specific language calling the buyer's attention to the fact that the warranty of title is being disclaimed. This requirement is for the protection of the buyer because general disclaiming language usually suggests only that the buyer assumes quality risks and not that the buyer assumes title risks as well.

Subsection (2) also provides that no warranty of title exists when the circumstances of the sale give the buyer reason to know that the seller does not claim to have title or purports to be selling only whatever ownership the seller may have. Sales by sheriffs, executors, and pawnbrokers, for example, are of such nature that a buyer is not entitled, by virtue of sale alone, to the personal obligation of the seller respecting good title to the merchandise. Article 9, however, provides that creditors foreclosing under Article 9 make title warranties that by operation of law accompany a voluntary disposition of collateral of the kind being sold (9–610(d)). Therefore, the warranties of 2–312 apply to foreclosure sales. Subsections 9–610(e) and (f) provide that the creditor may disclaim the warranty of title in the manner specified in 2–312 or by giving the buyer a statement that "there is no warranty relating to title, possession, quiet enjoyment, or the like in this disposition."

3. WARRANTY AGAINST INFRINGEMENT

Subsection 3 provides that a merchant dealing in goods of the kind that are being sold warrants that the goods will be free from infringement claims by third persons which may arise out of violations of patents, trademarks, and similar rights. If the goods infringe a third party's patent, the seller breaches the warranty. But the warranty protects not just against infringement, but also against claims of infringement. All claims? No, in the words of the statute, only "rightful" claims. What is a rightful claim?

The court in EZ Tag Corp., v. Casio America, Inc., 861 F.Supp.2d 181 (S.D.N.Y.2012), had to answer this question. EZ Tag purchased a device supplied by Casio, which EZ Tag then resold to others. A third party, Raylon LLC, sued EZ Tag in Texas, alleging that EZ Tag's sales violated a Raylon patent. The court rejected this allegation, holding that the Casio device did not infringe Raylon's patent and neither did EZ Tag's sales of it. EZ Tag then sued Casio in New York for Casio's alleged breach of its warranty against infringement under 2–312(3), seeking to recover the $150,000 EZ Tag had spent defending against Raylon's infringement claim. The dispositive issue was whether Raylon's claim of patent infringement was "rightful." The court held not:

> . . . [T]he claim asserted in the Raylon Action cannot be considered "rightful" under any of the definitions of the term put forth by courts around the country.
>
> In 84 Lumber Co. v. MRK Technologies, Ltd., 145 F.Supp.2d 675 (W.D.Pa.2001), the court determined that the question of whether or not a claim was "rightful" would involve a comparison of the patent with the goods at issue to determine "that there was an adequate basis for [claimant]'s assertion that defendants' products infringed his patents." The court stated that "[i]f claims of patent infringement are seen as marks on a continuum, whatever a 'rightful claim' is would fall somewhere between purely frivolous claims, at one end, and claims where liability has been proven, at the other."
>
> The court in Sun Coast Merchandise Corp. v. Myron Corp., 393 N.J.Super. 55, 922 A.2d 782, 796–97 (2007) agreed with the court in *84 Lumber* that the patent and claim of infringement must be examined to determine whether or not a claim was "rightful." . . . The "buyer must establish that the infringement claim is of a substantial nature that is reasonably likely to subject the buyer to litigation, and has a significant and adverse effect on the buyer's ability to make use of the goods in question." . . . The Raylon Action, which the Texas court described as "stretch[ing] the bounds of reasonableness," does not rise to that level.
>
> All of the claims of the 589 patent that was the subject of the Raylon Action require a "display being pivotally mounted" on the device housing. To sustain Raylon's patent infringement claim, the court would have had to define "pivotally mounted" broadly enough to encompass moving one's arm or wrist so that the entire device is moved and the viewer's perspective is altered. As the court in Texas found, this interpretation is "contrary to the specification and the plain meaning of the claim," which required that the display be pivotally mounted relative to the housing, rather than to the viewer. Raylon's claims, therefore, while not so frivolous as to be sanctionable, surely were not so substantial as to impose a significant and adverse effect on EZ Tag's ability to make use of the goods. As Raylon's claim of infringement against EZ Tag was not "rightful" within the meaning of NY-UCC 2–312(3), Casio had no duty to indemnify EZ Tag for the expenses incurred in the Raylon Action.

Note that if the buyer furnishes the specifications for the goods that the seller is to deliver, the buyer does not get the protection against infringement. On the contrary, the buyer must hold the seller harmless against any such claims that arise out of compliance with the specification. In other words, in this case it is the buyer who gives the warranty that no harm will come to the seller through compliance with the specifications.

4. LEASES

Though modeled on 2–312, the warranty in 2A–211 reflects the fact that in lease transactions the title does not pass to the lessee. Therefore, 2A–211 imposes a warranty of quiet possession: that no person holds a claim or interest arising from an act or omission of the lessor which will interfere with the lessee's enjoyment of the leasehold interest. Further, except in a finance lease, the warranty also protects against claims of infringement. As with the warranty of title in sales transactions, this warranty may be excluded or modified. Unlike its analog in Article 2, however, the provision authorizing disclaimer of the warranty of quiet possession appears in the section authorizing disclaimers of other implied warranties (2A–214(4)).

5. CISG

The Convention on Contracts for the International Sale of Goods requires the seller to hand over any documents relating to the goods, as required by the contract and the Convention (Articles 30, 34). Most often this refers to documents pertaining to possession of the goods, such as bills of lading, but it also encompasses certificates of title for goods that have them. Article 41 requires the seller, unless the parties have agreed otherwise, to deliver the goods free from any right or claim of a third party. Though not denominated a warranty, this imposes on the seller obligations similar to those imposed by Article 2.

CHAPTER 6

DISCLAIMERS AND OTHER LIMITATIONS ON WARRANTIES

A. DISCLAIMERS

Consistent with the underlying freedom-of-contract philosophy of Article 2, the provisions that create implied warranties (2–314 and 2–315) are simply default provisions. The parties are free to agree otherwise, viz., that there will be no implied warranties in their particular transaction. Section 2–316 provides the mechanism for implementing this agreement. Please read that section, noting the different language dealing with express warranties, the implied warranty of merchantability, and the implied warranty of fitness for a particular purpose.

Sierra Diesel Injection Service, Inc. v. Burroughs Corporation

United States Court of Appeals, Ninth Circuit, 1989.
874 F.2d 653.

■ STEPHENS, SENIOR DISTRICT JUDGE.

Sierra Diesel Injection Service, Inc. (Sierra Diesel) is a family owned and operated business that services the fuel injection portions of diesel engines and sells related diesel engine parts. In September 1977, 19-year-old Caroline Cathey, the daughter-in-law of the Sierra Diesel's owner and operator James Cathey, worked as the company bookkeeper. She went to the Reno, Nevada branch office of the Burroughs Corporation (Burroughs) to purchase a posting machine to speed up Sierra Diesel's invoicing and accounting. The salespeople at Burroughs told Caroline Cathey that Sierra Diesel should buy a B-80 computer (B-80) instead of a posting machine. Caroline and James Cathey attended a demonstration of the B-80 at the Burroughs office. . . .

In October 1977, Mr. Cathey decided to purchase the B-80. Sierra Diesel and Burroughs signed various contracts for the sale of hardware and software and for maintenance service. Mr. Cathey's highest level of formal education was a high school degree. At the time he bought the B-80 he was not knowledgeable about computers. He had a general knowledge of warranties and their limitations from the warranty service work Sierra Diesel did for diesel component parts manufacturers, but he did not understand the meaning of "merchantability." He read the contracts from Burroughs to see that they contained the correct price information and product description and he glanced at the back of the contract to see, as he put it, that "I'm not actually signing away the deed to my home or something of this nature."

The B-80 computer did not perform the invoicing and accounting functions for which it had been purchased. It experienced basic equipment breakdowns and was unable to "multiprogram." Sierra Diesel personnel complained to the Burroughs service personnel. Burroughs responded to these complaints and its staff attempted to solve the problems and also attempted to repair the system during their regularly scheduled visits under the Maintenance Agreement. Eventually, the Burroughs staff recommended to Sierra Diesel that it purchase a different Burroughs computer (B-91) to remedy the problems. Sierra Diesel purchased the B-91 and took delivery in February 1981. The B-91 computer was no better able to perform the invoicing and accounting functions than the B-80. After additional unsuccessful attempts by Burroughs employees to correct the problems, Sierra Diesel employed an independent computer consultant who concluded that the Burroughs computers would never perform the functions for which they had been purchased. Sierra Diesel bought another computer from a different company. In 1984, Sierra Diesel initiated the present litigation.

Sierra Diesel sued Burroughs. . . . Burroughs moved for summary judgment on the grounds that . . . the warranties had been excluded. . . . After the trial, the court held that the exclusion of warranties clauses were not conspicuous. . . .

     . . .

Warranty exclusions are permitted under the UCC § 2–316 to allow parties to bargain to allocate the risk of loss. However, exclusions of warranties are generally disfavored, and standardized take it or leave it form contracts such as the one in this case are construed against the drafter. They are subject to the general obligation of good faith and of not imposing unconscionable terms upon a party. Restatement (Second) of Contracts § 211. Nevada has adopted the UCC waiver of warranty language in NRS § 104.2316. According to official comment one the purpose of the warranty waiver section is to "protect a buyer from unexpected and unbargained language of disclaimer by denying effect to such language when inconsistent with language of express warranty and permitting the exclusion of implied warranties only by conspicuous language or other circumstances which protect the buyer from surprise."

Conspicuousness is defined by NRS § 104.1201(10) [revised 1–201(b)(10)]: "A term or clause is conspicuous when it is so written that a reasonable person against whom it is to operate ought to have noticed it. . . . Language in the body of a form is 'conspicuous' if it is in larger or other contrasting type or color." Official Comment 10 notes that "the test is whether attention can reasonably be expected to be called to it."

"Whether a term or clause is 'conspicuous' or not is for decision by the court." NRS § 104.1201(10) [revised 1–201(b)(10)]. Review of the trial court's finding is de novo.

Both the hardware and software agreements contained the following warranty disclaimer, "EXCEPT AS SPECIFICALLY PROVIDED HEREIN, THERE ARE NO OTHER WARRANTIES, EXPRESS OR IMPLIED, INCLUDING, BUT NOT LIMITED TO, ANY IMPLIED WARRANTIES OF MERCHANTABILITY OR FITNESS FOR A PARTICULAR PURPOSE." In the hardware agreement the disclaimer appeared in the middle of the page at the left hand column in all capital bold type. It is one of the three paragraphs on the reverse side in all capital bold type. There are 15 separately numbered sections. The warranty exclusions clause is in section 4. There is no heading to identify it as a warranty section.

On the front of the software agreement a sentence standing alone in large capital bold letters directs the signor to read the warranty terms on the back, "THE TERMS AND CONDITIONS, INCLUDING THE WARRANTY AND LIMITATION OF LIABILITY, ON THE REVERSE SIDE ARE PART OF THE AGREEMENT." The back of the contract contains 14 separately numbered and titled sections, some of which are further divided into paragraphs. The ninth section, entitled **WARRANTY**, contains the exclusion clause in the fourth paragraph of the section. The clause is in all capital letters, but it is not bold type. The only words in bold on the back of the form are the title headings and the words **TERMS AND CONDITIONS** at the top of the page.

Whether a disclaimer is conspicuous is not simply a matter of measuring the type size or looking at the placement of the disclaimer within the contract. A reviewing court must ascertain that a reasonable person in the buyer's position would not have been surprised to find the warranty disclaimer in the contract. One factor to consider is the sophistication of the parties. See e.g., Collins Radio v. Bell, 623 P.2d [1039,] 1051 [(Okla.Civ.App.1980)] ("we note that the disclaimer [in capital letters] is of *minimal* compliance, and we do not venture to state what factors might alter this determination in future cases outside of the sophistication of the buyer") (emphasis in the original). Also relevant as to whether a reasonable person would have noticed a warranty disclaimer are the circumstances of the negotiation and signing.

The trial court found that Mr. Cathey was not familiar with computers or with contracts. Mr. Cathey read the front of the contracts, but did not notice the warranty disclaimer clauses on the back. Given Mr. Cathey's lack of sophistication in the field of contracts and the written and oral representations made by Burroughs, it is not surprising that it would require more than a collection of standardized form contracts on various subjects involved in a transaction to notify a reasonable person in Mr. Cathey's position that the B-80 came without any warranty of merchantability.

Burroughs faults the trial court for holding that all warranty disclaimers must be in capital letters and in bold type, but the trial court did not rule in so mechanistic a fashion. The trial court's rulings consider type size and boldness as factors in an overall analysis and also the fact that the disclaimers were on the back of the page. Cf. Sellman Auto, Inc. v. McCowan, 89 Nev. 353, 513 P.2d 1228, 1230 (1973) (Under Uniform Sales Act, a waiver of an express warranty printed on the back of a contract is not effective unless the buyer is actually aware of it.) The trial court also considered the relative sophistication of the parties.

Burroughs points to two Nevada cases interpreting NRS § 104.2316. In Bill Stremmel Motors, Inc. v. IDS Leasing Corp., 89 Nev. 414, 514 P.2d 654 (1973), the Nevada Supreme Court affirmed a trial court judgment holding that a warranty exclusion clause in all capital letters was conspicuous. In *Stremmel* the trial court found that both parties were sophisticated, that there was no evidence that the buyer had not read the contract, and that the disclaimer was conspicuous. There is a marked difference in the dispute between Burroughs and Sierra Diesel. The district court found that Mr. Cathey was not a sophisticated buyer, he had not read the contract, and the trial court found that the disclaimers were not conspicuous. In the second case, Sierra Creek Ranch v. J. I. Case, 97 Nev. 457, 634 P.2d 458 (1981), the Nevada Supreme Court again affirmed a trial court finding that an exclusion clause was conspicuous. Both *Stremmel* and *Sierra Creek* show that a disclaimer in capital letters that mentions merchantability can be effective to exclude warranties. They do not hold that capital letters as a matter of law will be effective in all cases.

In the circumstances of this case, the district court's finding that the warranty disclaimer clauses were not conspicuous is not erroneous.

. . .

■ CANBY, CIRCUIT JUDGE, concurring in part and dissenting in part: . . .

My disagreement with the majority concerns the question whether the disclaimers of implied warranties were conspicuous. On that issue, our standard of review is de novo. My own view of the contracts leads me to conclude that the clauses are conspicuous within the meaning of Nev.Rev.Stat. § 104.1201(10) [revised 1–201(b)(10)].

The software agreement is the clearest. In a separate paragraph, in large, capital bold type immediately above the signature line on the face page, there appears the following sentence: "THE TERMS AND CONDITIONS, INCLUDING THE WARRANTY AND LIMITATION OF LIABILITY, ON THE REVERSE SIDE ARE PART OF THIS AGREEMENT." That language is possibly the most conspicuous single item in the entire agreement. On the reverse side, under the section headed "WARRANTY" appears the disclaimer of implied warranties, in a separate paragraph, all in capital letters. These provisions, in my view, would call a reasonable buyer's attention to the disclaimer.

The disclaimer in the hardware agreement presents a closer question. There is no reference to warranties or limitation of liability on the front of the contract, but the last line, in capitals, before the signature states that the customer has agreed to all terms and conditions including those on the reverse side. The reverse side contains 15 numbered sections, in print of small size and low contrast that discourages reading. Nevertheless, in the middle of the left column, in much larger print and all capitals, there appears the separate paragraph stating: "EXCEPT AS SPECIFICALLY PROVIDED IN THIS AGREEMENT, THERE ARE NO OTHER WARRANTIES EXPRESS OR IMPLIED INCLUDING BUT NOT LIMITED TO ANY IMPLIED WARRANTIES OF MERCHANTABILITY OF FITNESS FOR A PARTICULAR PURPOSE." By location and prominence, this clause is probably the most conspicuous one on the page. I conclude that it would notify the reasonable buyer. . . . The fact that the disclaimer was on the back side of the contract ought not to render it ineffective, so long as the language on the front side prominently referred to the terms and conditions on the back. . . .

QUESTIONS AND NOTES

1. To be effective under 2–316(2), a disclaimer of the implied warranty of merchantability must mention "merchantability." What do you suppose is the rationale for this requirement?

2. To be effective under 2–316(2), a disclaimer of the implied warranty of merchantability must be conspicuous, which is defined in 1–201(b)(10). In *Sierra Diesel* the disclaimer was in capital letters. Given the definition in 1–201, by what reasoning can the court conclude that the disclaimer was not conspicuous? In the penultimate paragraph on page 317 the court asserts that "whether a disclaimer is conspicuous is not simply a matter of measuring the type size or looking at the placement of the disclaimer in the contract." Is this statement defensible?

3. In Hamilton v. O'Connor Chevrolet, Inc., 399 F.Supp.2d 860 (N.D.Ill. 2005), a car dealer included language of disclaimer in its retail installment sales contract. When the purchasers sued for breach of warranty, the dealer argued that the disclaimer was effective. The court agreed:

In the case *sub judice,* the disclaimer mentioned "merchantability" in writing that is conspicuous. The disclaimer specifically states, in bold: **"Warranties Seller Disclaims. You understand that the Seller is not offering any warranties and that there are no implied warranties of merchantability, or fitness for a particular purpose, or any other warranties, express or implied by the Seller. . . ."** The bold-faced writing is not hidden or obscured; in fact, it is free-standing and set forth in its own paragraph out from the remainder of the text. In addition, below the disclaimer, the Retail Contract provides a definition of implied warranty of merchantability. ("An implied warranty of merchantability generally means that the vehicle is fit for the ordinary purpose for which such vehicles are generally used.")

The fact that the disclaimer is on the back side of the Retail Contract does not, in this case at least, alter the result of the analysis about whether a reasonable person would be expected to notice it. *Accord, e.g.,* Larry J. Soldinger, Assocs., Ltd. v. Aston Martin Lagonda of N. Am., Inc., 1998 WL 151817 at *4 (N.D.Ill., 1998) ("The fact that the disclaimer is on the back side of the bill of sale does not make it invalid."). Like the bill of sale in *Soldinger,* the front side of the Retail Contract directs the reader in bold-face type to the back side of the contract "for other important agreements." In addition, in at least three other places, the front side of the Retail Contract directs the reader to the back side of the agreement. The front side of the Retail Contract also states in bold-face type: "Notice to the buyer. 1. Do not sign this agreement before you read it or if it contains any blank spaces. 2. You are entitled to an exact copy of the agreement you sign. . . ." In short, with respect to the language directing the reader to the back side of the Retail Contract, a "reasonable person would have read the back side of the [agreement] and noticed the disclaimer."[8]

4. *Sierra Diesel* and *Hamilton v. O'Connor* present two very different attitudes toward contract formation. Which of the two more closely represents your view?

In thinking about this question, please consider the following excerpts. The first is from an opinion deciding an issue under a bankruptcy statute that requires a "clear and conspicuous" statement of specified information. Commenting on the definition of "conspicuous" in Article 1, the court stated:

> True, the UCC specifies that "[a] printed *heading* in capitals" is normally conspicuous. (emphasis added) This has given rise to the canard that all language in capitals is automatically conspicuous, and the fallacy that language not in capitals isn't conspicuous. . . . The use of capitals as a talisman of conspicuousness has survived intact despite decades of improved literacy and technology. Even some web page "click-through" agreements have clauses written in capitals, though there are better ways of making text stand out in a web browser window.
>
> Lawyers who think their caps lock keys are instant "make conspicuous" buttons are deluded. In determining whether a term is conspicuous, we look at more than formatting. A term that appears in capitals can still be inconspicuous if it is hidden on the back of a contract in small type. *See, e.g.,* Sierra Diesel, 890 F.2d at 114. Terms that are in capitals but also appear in hard-to-read type may flunk the conspicuousness test. *See, e.g., id.*; Lupa v. Jock's,

---

[8] Moreover, although not necessary to the result of the analysis, the Court notes that the contract at issue in this appears to be an oversized document—8.5 inches by perhaps as much as 22 inches—such that a reader would naturally be curious about the document and be inclined to flip it over, even if it did not expressly and repeatedly direct the reader to do so, as this one did.

131 Misc.2d 536, 500 N.Y.S.2d 962, 965 (N.Y. City Ct.1986). A sentence in capitals, buried deep within a long paragraph in capitals will probably not be deemed conspicuous. Formatting does matter, but conspicuousness ultimately turns on the likelihood that a reasonable person would actually see a term in an agreement. Thus, it is entirely possible for text to be conspicuous without being in capitals.

In re Bassett, 285 F.3d 882, 886 (9th Cir.2002).

The second excerpt is from a case concerning the sale and installation of a used engine in a consumer's automobile. The contract included the statement, "the undersigned purchaser understands and agrees that dealer . . . disclaims all warranties, including warranties of merchantability. . . ." Speaking to the conspicuousness of this statement, the court stated:

The provision is set off to one side of the page with the heading "Exclusion of Warranties" in all capital letters. The heading's capital letters are greater in size than the provision's extremely small lettering, but they are smaller than other capitalized words on the page. Indeed, the heading is smaller than the word "Signed," which follows the provision and calls for [the consumer's] signature, noting her agreement that warranties are excluded. As discussed below, [she] did not sign her acknowledgment of this provision, and therefore did not agree that the warranties could be excluded.

[Moreover], even if it was conspicuous, the exclusion is without force. The exclusion provision explicitly calls for an affirmative act; it requires that the customer agree to the exclusion of warranties. The exclusion provision states that "[t]he *undersigned* purchaser understands and agrees that dealer makes no warranties of any kind, express or implied, and disclaims all warranties, including warranties of merchantability." (Emphasis added.) Directly under the provision are lines for date and signature. Both lines are blank. A signature does appear on another portion of the document that specifically authorizes repairs. However, while Salazar may have signed the document to authorize repairs, she did not sign agreeing to exclude warranties from the transaction.

. . . Thus, when reviewing exclusion provisions, we must look both to the provision's form and its language. In this case, we cannot ignore the specific language in the provision that requires a buyer's agreement in order to exclude warranties.

Salazar v. D.W.B.H., Inc., 144 N.M. 828, 192 P.3d 1205, 1210 (2008).

5.   Problem. Carr's Audi sold Lee a used car, along with a two-year service contract. The retail installment sales contract conspicuously stated:

Disclaimer. We expressly disclaim all warranties, express or implied, including any implied warranties of merchantability and fitness for a particular purpose, unless we enter into a service contract with you at the time of, or within 90 days of, the date of this transaction.

Two weeks after Lee took possession, the car's transmission failed, and Carr's refused to repair. When Lee referred to the service contract, Carr's pointed out that the service contract was between Lee and Extended Care Company (ECC), an independent entity with no ownership connection to Carr's, and that Carr's signed the service contract as agent of ECC and sent ECC the price that Lee paid for the service contract. Carr's asserted that Lee's claim under the service contract must be made against ECC, not Carr's, and that Lee has no claim against Carr's because it disclaimed all warranties. Does Carr's have a good argument: can Lee recover from Carr's Audi for breach of the implied warranty of merchantability?

6. Problem. Bradley negotiated the purchase of a new automobile from Carr's Audi. Upon completion of the negotiations, Carr's presented a standard-form retail sales contract. This document was two-sided, on the back side of which was a disclaimer, in red letters and larger than the other type on the back side. On the front side was the statement, "This sale is subject to the terms and conditions on the reverse side." Carr's put this document in front of Bradley, front-side up, pointed to the signature line, and said, "Sign here." Bradley signed where indicated. Is the disclaimer effective?

7. Problem. Purcell purchased a truck-tractor from Hi-Way Sales. The tractor required repairs shortly after the purchase, and Purcell sued for breach of implied warranty. Hi-Way Sales claimed that the warranty was disclaimed by language in the contract of sale executed by the parties. The disclaimer language was in the same size and kind of type as the rest of the contract. Purcell, however, admitted that she had read the disclaimer clause before signing the document. Can she successfully argue that the disclaimer is not effective because it is not conspicuous?

––––––––

Gindy Manufacturing Corp. v. Cardinale Trucking Corp.

New Jersey Superior Court, Law Division, 1970.
111 N.J.Super. 383, 268 A.2d 345.

■ BOTTER, J.S.C. This is an action by the seller (Gindy) of twenty-five 1967 semi-trailers for a deficiency of $13,052.37 after repossession and resale following defendant's default in payment under a conditional sales contract. The defense and counterclaim are based on the assertion that the trailers were delivered with faulty radius rods which caused premature tire wear and consequent monetary loss.

The matter is before the court on plaintiff's motion for summary judgment. Plaintiff contends that the installment sales contract expressly excluded all warranties. Accordingly, plaintiff seeks a judgment for the amount of the deficiency, with interest and costs, and a dismissal of the counterclaim.

On or about June 1, 1967, the parties entered into a written installment sales contract in the total sum of $141,756, inclusive of finance charges. The contract, provided by plaintiff, was a one-page form contract with considerable close print. The only additions were by typewriter to show the name and address of the buyer, the various charges and installment payments involved, and the due date of the first installment. Also, in prominent position, a description of the trailers was typed in under various headings in the printed form as shown below, with the typewritten portions indicated by my use of italics:

New Or Used	Year	Make or Manufacturer's Trade Name	Description	Model	Serial No.
New	*1967*	*Gindy*	*semi-trailer*	*C240AV9*	*38480 thru 38504*

The printed form also contained the following paragraph:

H. WARRANTIES. Buyer is buying the vehicle "as is" and no representations or statements have been made by Seller except as herein stated, so that no warranty, express or implied, arises apart from this writing. Buyer warrants that any property which is offered in trade for the vehicle is free from any lien, claim, encumbrance or security interest.

Plaintiff contends that the above clause, particularly the provision that the vehicles are sold "as is," excludes all warranties. Plaintiff further contends that the recital in the contract that the "writing contains the full, final and exclusive statement of the agreement of the parties" precludes any modification by oral agreement or otherwise of the specific provision excluding warranties. There was also a separately signed provision that: "No modification of this contract may be made except in writing signed by Seller." Since defendant failed to meet installment payments due for May, June, July and August of 1968, defendant was in default under the agreement, and plaintiff had the right to repossess and resell the trailers and sue for the deficiency. The only question, therefore, is whether defendant can assert as an offset or by way of counterclaim damages caused by the alleged defects in the vehicles furnished.

Defendant asserts that it has been doing business with Gindy for 20 years and had purchased hundreds of trailers, none of which were purchased "as is." Defendant asserts that in past dealings with Gindy and in accordance with the custom of the trade all defects in the manufacture of the trailers were the responsibility of Gindy. Defendant further asserts that in the past Gindy did correct at its own cost manufacturing defects whenever they appeared; that in the present transaction, when the defect caused by faulty radius rods appeared, Gindy agreed to replace them and ordered defendant to take the trailers to the Husky Trailer Company with whom Gindy contracted to have the repairs made at Gindy's expense; that Gindy sent new parts to be installed in the trailers in question in replacement of the defective parts; that every trailer which defendant purchased from Gindy was purchased brand new; that Gindy knew defendant's operation and, in fact, when Gindy started in business the founders of defendant corporation helped Gindy in designing the trailers; that defendant was not aware of the existence of the "as is" provision in the contract; that on June 12, 1967 another installment sales contract in an amount in excess of $200,000 entered into with Gindy by a corporation related to defendant did not have an "as is" clause; that the inclusion of the "as is" clause is contrary to the custom in the trade which provides implied warranties that all *new* equipment will perform as represented and will do the job for which it was purchased; that *used* equipment may be purchased "as is," and the absence of warranties in such case is reflected in the price of the equipment; and that at no time in the dealings between the parties during the period when defects arose on the trailers did Gindy ever take the position that the equipment had been purchased "as is." These assertions in the affidavit of defendant's president are uncontroverted in the record before me.

. . .

Defendant asserts without contradiction that it has always been the custom in the trade and in defendant's relationship with Gindy that all manufacturing defects were the responsibility of Gindy and that, when such defects appeared, Gindy in the past did make the necessary corrections or repairs at its own expense. In this transaction, too, Gindy undertook to correct the defects in the trailers. The express terms of an agreement should be construed where reasonable as consistent with the custom of the trade or a course of dealing evidenced by previous conduct of the parties. N.J.S.A. 12A:1–205 [revised 1–303(e)]. Moreover, a course of performance is relevant to the interpretation of an agreement. N.J.S.A. 12A:2–208 [revised 1–303(d)]. The express terms of an agreement and a course of performance, course of dealing and usage of trade "shall be construed whenever reasonable as consistent with each other * * *." N.J.S.A. 12A:2–208(2) [revised 1–303(e)].

Defendant asserts that the trailers were delivered with faulty radius rods. In the answer and counterclaim defendant asserts that the defects caused premature tire wear and loss of use of the equipment, presumably while repairs were being made. From the facts at hand it is not clear whether the defects were so serious as to make the vehicles unmerchantable. . . . Repairs undertaken by plaintiff, the usage of trade and prior dealings of the parties offer strong evidence of plaintiff's obligation to make such repairs, whether in satisfaction of an implied warranty of merchantability or in satisfaction of a stricter implied warranty claimed by defendant under N.J.S.A. 12A:2–314(3), . . . namely, an implied warranty to repair all defects in manufacture regardless of their seriousness. Code Comment 12 has been interpreted to indicate that "other implied warranties" arising under section 2–314(3) by course of dealing or usage of trade are not limited to "what might ordinarily be regarded as warranties but also include collateral obligations related to a seller's performance." 1 Anderson Uniform Commercial Code, Sec. 2–314:10, p. 209 (1961). Accordingly, unless properly disclaimed pursuant to section 2–316, there arose in this transaction an implied warranty on the part of Gindy to accept responsibility for defects in manufacture, at least to the extent of repair or replacement.

Plaintiff contends that an appropriate disclaimer of all warranties was expressly provided by Paragraph H of the agreement quoted above. Plaintiff also relies upon the separately signed agreement that a modification of the contract cannot be made except in writing. N.J.S.A. 12A:2–209(2).

. . .

To disclaim an implied warranty of merchantability, section 2–316(2) of the Code requires the use of the word "merchantability," and requires, in a written contract, that such exclusion must be in "conspicuous" language. "Conspicuous" is defined by N.J.S.A. 12A:1–201(10) [revised 1–201(b)(10)] to include such writing "that a reasonable person against whom it is to operate ought to have noticed it." The definition provides that "a printed heading in capitals * * * is conspicuous," and that "conspicuous" writing includes larger print or other contrasting type or color. This section also provides that conspicuousness is to be determined by the court.

The definition also provides that "in a telegram any stated term is conspicuous." The definition of "conspicuous" is not exhaustive nor does it mean that in all circumstances ordinary print cannot be conspicuous. See Code Comment 10, Sec. 1–201 [revised 1–201(b)(10), Official Comment 10] which says that "the test is whether attention can reasonably be expected to be called to it."

In the case at hand an implied warranty of merchantability has not been excluded in a manner that conforms to N.J.S.A. 12A:2–316(2). The word "merchantability" is not used and the exclusion is not conspicuous. Paragraph H does not contain larger or different type in the exclusionary provision; the only large type is the printed heading which reads, "WARRANTIES." The use of that heading did not make the *exclusion* conspicuous; if anything, it would suggest to a buyer who does not read the fine print that warranties are included, not excluded. In fact, there is an express warranty in the clause, but not by the seller. It is a warranty by the buyer as to clear title of a vehicle given in trade.

Plaintiff contends, however, that the "as is" provision is sufficient to disclaim all implied warranties. On the other hand, defendant contends that the "as is" clause is inoperative because it is not appropriate to the transaction, involving the sale of new vehicles, and because the clause is not in conspicuous language.

Subsection (3) does not use the term "conspicuous." Subsection (2), which requires the use of conspicuous language in written agreements to exclude or modify implied warranties of merchantability or fitness, is expressly made subject to subsection (3). The introductory language of subsection (3) also suggests the supremacy of its provisions over subsection (2). Thus, reading the two subsections literally would eliminate the requirement of "conspicuous" language as a condition for the exclusion of all implied warranties where expressions like "as is" are used. On the other hand, the intent may have been simply to provide in subsection (3) a qualification of subsection (2) so as to permit the use of commonly understood terms in substitution for the term "merchantability" or terms respecting fitness, without eliminating the requirement of conspicuous language where the agreement is in writing. . . . [T]he basic purpose of the Code [is] to protect the buyer from surprise. Code Comment 1, Sec. 2–316. See also Code Comment 11, Sec. 2–314, which says in part:

> The warranty of merchantability, wherever it is normal, is so commonly taken for granted that its exclusion from the contract is a matter threatening surprise and therefore requiring special precaution.

The original draft of section 2–316 contained a single paragraph (2) which provided for the exclusion of warranties with three exceptions comparable to sub-paragraphs (a), (b) and (c) now contained in subsection (3). U.C.C.Supp. No. 1 (1952), Sec. 2–316. The amendment of section 2–316 to its present form broke subsection (2) into two parts. One part remained section (2) and the exceptions became section (3). To section (2) was added the requirement of conspicuous language where a disclaimer is in writing. In addition, section (2) was amended to require that a disclaimer of an implied warranty of fitness must always be in writing, and the requirement of specific language to avoid a warranty of fitness was changed.

The drafters of the Code made the following comment upon the redrafting of subsection (2):

> *Reason*: Former subsection (2) was rewritten and divided into subsections (2) and (3) in Supp. No. 1 to relieve the seller from the requirement of disclaiming the warranty of fitness in specific language and yet afford the buyer an adequate warning of such disclaimer. Subsequently, subsection (1) was rewritten and subsections (3)(a) and (3)(b) changed for clarification and to meet criticism by the New York Commission. U.C.C., 1956 Recommendations, at 40.

No comment was made regarding the applicability of the conspicuous language requirement to subsection (3), and no case has been found in New Jersey or elsewhere which deals with the problem. Nor is it dealt with in the Code Comments or in the New Jersey Study Comment. . . .

The metamorphosis of section 2–316 and the reason given in the legislative history mentioned above suggest that the use of expressions like "as is" was intended merely to give effect to common terms in addition to those specified in subsection (2) as a means for disclaiming certain warranties. There is no evidence of a legislative purpose to require conspicuous language in one case and not when expressions like "as is" are used.

It appears desirable to read into section 2–316(3) the requirement of conspicuousness when the attempted disclaimer is in writing. This would avoid surprise to a buyer and fulfill a fundamental purpose of the Code. However, one of the difficulties is that subsection (2) deals expressly with disclaiming the implied warranties of merchantability and fitness. It does not deal with disclaimer of other implied warranties arising from a course of dealing or usage of trade under N.J.S.A. 12A:2–314(3). While subsection (2) deals with two types of implied warranties and expressly imposes the requirement of conspicuous language in writings as to them, subsection (3)(a) specifically refers to "all implied warranties" and does not contain the requirement of conspicuous language. ... If the requirement of "conspicuous" language had been intended, being a term defined by the Code itself in section 1–201(10), the draftsmen should have expressly included that term in subsection (3). Perhaps it is a matter of poor draftsmanship or oversight. But it always presents a problem for the court when the omission of a provision that could so easily have been included seems to conflict with an underlying purpose of the legislation.

It does not make sense to require conspicuous language when a warranty is disclaimed by use of the words "merchantability" or "fitness" and not when a term like "as is" is used to accomplish the same result. It serves no intelligible design to protect buyers by conspicuous language when the term "merchantability" is used, but to allow an effective disclaimer when the term "as is" is buried in fine print. Nor does it make sense to require conspicuous language to disclaim the implied warranties of merchantability and fitness and not impose a similar requirement to disclaim other implied warranties that arise by course of dealing or usage of trade. The expectations of the buyer need as much protection in one case as in another. My preference, therefore, is to find that there is a requirement of conspicuousness when terms like "as is" are used to exclude an implied warranty of merchantability or fitness. It seems reasonable to say that to avoid these implied warranties the requirements of subsection (2) must be met, except that expressions like "as is" will be given effect in addition to the expressions specified in subsection (2). This interpretation, nevertheless, would still leave intact the exclusion of implied warranties arising from a course of dealing or usage of trade by expressions like "as is," whether conspicuous or not. It would appear desirable, to eliminate all doubt in this area, for the legislature to amend N.J.S.A. 12A:2–316 so as to include an express requirement of conspicuous language when a writing is used to exclude or modify any and all implied warranties. In any case, an interpretation requiring conspicuousness to avoid the warranties of merchantability and fitness still leaves open the effect of the disclaimer clause here on the implied warranties arising under section 2–314(3). My holding below on this issue is dispositive of this motion.

The agreement in question is at least ambiguous as to the applicability of the "as is" clause in this transaction. Subsection (3)(a) of section 2–316 gives force to an "as is" clause "unless the circumstances indicate otherwise." Moreover, by the terms of that section the "as is" clause must call the buyer's attention to the exclusion of all warranties and make that result "plain." Ambiguity arises by virtue of the fact that at the beginning of the contract, before the description of the vehicles sold, there is a clause providing, "Buyer accepts delivery in good condition." (Defendant claims that this provision provides an express warranty of quality.) Moreover, the form contract provided by the seller by its terms was applicable to the sale of either a new vehicle or a used vehicle. Defendant's uncontradicted affidavit recites that an "as is" clause by custom of the trade may be expected in the sale of used vehicles but not in the sale of new vehicles. Accordingly, whether or not the provision for "delivery in good condition" was intended to create an express warranty of quality, that clause, together with the inappropriateness of the "as is" clause in the sale of new trailers, would not "make it plain" to a buyer that the "as is" clause was intended to disclaim all implied warranties in this transaction. A buyer could reasonably expect that the clause in question was to apply only when the form contract was employed in the sale of used vehicles. This interpretation would make the provisions of the contract consistent with prevailing usage of trade and the previous course of dealing between the parties. Also, Gindy's undertaking to supply replacement parts and to have the vehicles repaired at its own cost, without disclaiming responsibility, without reliance on the "as is" clause, shows an interpretation by Gindy of this contract consistent with defendant's position.

The "as is" clause employed in the contract, even augmented by language stating "that no warranty express or implied arises apart from this writing," appears inappropriate to this transaction, given the usage of the trade and the dealings of the parties. All of that language was not sufficient to call attention and make plain to defendant that there was no implied warranty intended by the seller with respect to the sale of new vehicles as distinguished from used vehicles. Significantly, almost without exception, "as is" and similar expressions construed by the courts are found in cases dealing with the sale of used vehicles, articles or equipment. . . .

The effectiveness of an "as is" clause as a disclaimer is conditioned by the preamble of Section 2–316(3), namely, "unless the circumstances indicate otherwise." In the case at hand the circumstances do indicate otherwise. One buying a new vehicle under a contract requiring acceptance of delivery "in good condition" could readily say that in these circumstances "as is" means new and in good mechanical condition. This is exactly the interpretation which the parties gave to this instrument.

Accordingly, the "as is" clause in this contract is not effective to disclaim an implied warranty of merchantability, nor an implied warranty arising by usage of trade or course of dealing. . . . [T]he buyer should be assured of reasonable performance and not be deprived thereof by unexpected terms in a form contract.

For the foregoing reasons plaintiff's motion for summary judgment is denied. An appropriate order shall be submitted.

QUESTIONS AND NOTES

1. What warranty did plaintiff allegedly breach?

2. Based in part on the legislative history, the court concludes that the conspicuousness requirement in subsection (2) also exists in subsection (3). Please reread the court's recitation of this legislative history. Can you construct another interpretation of it, one that does not necessarily lead to the conclusion that the conspicuousness requirement exists in subsection (3)?

3. The court states (last paragraph on page 327) that it does not make sense to require conspicuousness in subsection (2) and not require it in subsection (3). The court's assertion of that proposition does not necessarily make the proposition true. See if you can construct an argument for the opposite proposition, viz., that there is a reason to require conspicuousness under subsection (2) but not require it under subsection (3). Is your argument persuasive?

4. Problem. Dillard's Dodge sold a used car to Hong, using a bill of sale that provided, on its face, "This vehicle is sold as is." As it turned out, the car was not fit to drive and would not pass without objection in the trade. Is the disclaimer effective?

5. Should "as is" be sufficient to disclaim implied warranties in transactions with consumers? According to several surveys commissioned by the Federal Trade Commission in the 1970s, approximately 25–50% of consumers do not understand the legal effect of that phrase. Many believe the phrase applies to apparent or disclosed defects (e.g., dings and dents) but not to latent defects. FTC, Staff Report, Sale of Used Motor Vehicles 263–65 (1978).

6. In Murray v. D & J Motor Company, Inc., 958 P.2d 823 (Okla.App.1998), plaintiff told defendant's salesman that she needed a reliable van so that she could transport her ailing, disabled daughter. When plaintiff noticed a rattling noise during a test drive, the salesman told her that the engine had been replaced, that it had been inspected by a mechanic, and that there was nothing wrong with it. Plaintiff purchased the van, pursuant to documents that stated the vehicle was sold "as is." Within a day of the purchase, the engine broke down. The court stated:

> [A]mong the circumstances that could render a purported "as is" or "with all faults" disclaimer unreasonable and ineffective are fraudulent representations or misrepresentations concerning the condition, value, quality, characteristics or fitness of the goods sold that are relied upon by the Buyer to the Buyer's detriment. Therefore if the disclaimer . . . [is] tainted with, or by, such misrepresentations or false representations, that then is a "circumstance" that will preclude an effective disclaimer. To hold otherwise would allow a seller to profit from his fraud and to be effectively granted a license to mislead or conceal facts.

Id. at 830 (reversing the action of the trial court in upholding defendant's demurrer to the evidence). Accord Sorchaga v. Ride Auto, LLC, 909 N.W.2d 550 (Minn.2018) (fraud is a circumstance that indicates otherwise).

7.   Problem. The purchasing officer for Office Supplies called at Standard Furniture's warehouse for the purpose of purchasing a large number of tables and chairs. One entire floor of the warehouse was covered with tables and chairs, and the purchasing officer selected several of them at random and inspected them. The parties agreed on the terms, and Office Supplies purchased the entire floor of merchandise. After delivery of the merchandise, Office Supplies discovered that many of the tables and chairs were defective. Is there a breach of warranty? Are additional facts necessary to resolve this problem? If so, what facts?

8.   Inconsistency between a disclaimer and an express warranty. A contract may contain an express warranty along with a disclaimer along the lines of, "This warranty is in lieu of all other warranties, whether express or implied, including the implied warranty of merchantability and the implied warranty of fitness for particular purpose." Subsection (1) of 2–316 directs the court to construe words that create warranties as consistent with words negating warranty whenever it is reasonable to do so. If that is not possible, the disclaimer is "inoperative." Please read 2–316(1). The directive in 2–316(1) was in issue in AEP Industries Inc. v. Thiele Technologies Inc., 2016 WL 4591902 (E.D.Wis.2016). Thiele sent AEP a written proposal to sell a line of manufacturing equipment, stating that the equipment was to be capable of producing 720 units per minute. Included in the "terms and conditions" was the following language in bold typeface:

> Seller warrants that the products sold are free from defects in materials and workmanship . . . for a period of one year . . . . The Warranties set forth herein are in lieu of all other warranties, whether expressed, implied or statutory, including but not limited to implied warranties of merchantability and fitness for a particular purpose.

AEP responded with a purchase order, and Thiele delivered and installed the equipment. Over the next six months, Thiele's engineers and other personnel were unable to make the equipment produce 720 units per minute. AEP sued, inter alia, for breach of express and implied warranties, seeking return of the purchase price and damages. Denying Thiele's motion to dismiss, the court wrote:

> . . . [The disclaimer] is sufficient to disclaim any implied warranties. It follows that AEP's breach of implied warranty claim should be dismissed.
>
> The same conclusion does not follow, however, as to AEP's claim for breach of express warranty. . . . Thiele's proposal, which upon acceptance by AEP became the contract between the parties, specified the maximum speeds the [equipment] would be able to operate . . . . The amended complaint alleges that "[t]hese processing times were critical to Plaintiff's production requirements and Plaintiff materially relied on those representations in connection with its decision to purchase the [equipment]." Thus, it would appear that the maximum speeds of the [equipment] specified in Thiele's proposal constituted an express warranty. Yet, the warranty provision of Thiele's terms and conditions purports to limit express warranty to defects in material and workmanship . . . .
>
> The amended complaint alleges that the [equipment] Thiele delivered has never been able to reach the speeds promised. Though the complaint does not allege why the [equipment] has not performed at the promised speeds, it seems unlikely it is due to a defect in material or workmanship, since Thiele engineers, installers and repairmen have been unable to get it to operate at those speeds. Instead, based on the allegations of the complaint and the description of the work Thiele personnel performed in their efforts to get the [equipment] to perform as promised, it appears more likely the problem is a design defect. Regardless of the cause, however, it is doubtful that Thiele's limitation of its express warranties would bar AEP from obtaining any form of relief for Thiele's breach of this warranty.
>
> . . . As explained in the official comment to [2–316], its purpose is "to protect a buyer from unexpected and unbargained language of disclaimer by denying effect to such language when inconsistent with language of express warranty and permitting the exclusion of implied warranties only by conspicuous language or other circumstances which protect the buyer from surprise." Comment 1.
>
> Applying that section to the facts alleged here yields two possible outcomes. First, the Court could reconcile Thiele's express warranty of the speeds of the [equipment] with its effort to limit its warranties by noting that the limitation language is ambiguous. The limitation states that "[t]he Warranties set forth herein are in lieu of all other warranties . . . ." It is unclear, however, whether the phrase "Warranties set forth herein" refers only to the warranties set forth in the Warranty provision of the Terms and Conditions of Sale or to those set forth anywhere in the entire proposal. If it refers to the entire proposal, then Thiele's express

warranty of the speed of the [equipment] survives. It would be one of the "Warranties set forth herein" and would not be excluded.

Alternatively, if the Court concluded it could not reconcile the words creating the express warranty with the words limiting it, the limitation would be inoperative. This follows because it would be unreasonable to permit a seller to create an express warranty in its offer and then add a term or condition at the end that effectively excludes the very warranty it created.

9. Even if a disclaimer meets the requirements of 2–316, it may nevertheless not be effective, in which event the buyer may recover for breach of implied warranty.

a.   Personal injuries. If the buyer seeks to recover for personal injuries, the action may be in tort or in contract (warranty). In either case, the buyer is likely to recover. E.g., Henningsen v. Bloomfield Motors, Inc., 32 N.J. 358, 161 A.2d 69 (1960).

The Restatement (Third) of Torts, section 18 states that disclaimers or limitations of remedies do not bar or limit liability claims for injury to persons. However, the comments to that section state that it takes no position on whether disclaimers are effective as to injury to property. That is left to developing case law. The comments also state that nothing prevents sellers in the distributive chain from contracting among themselves as to who bears the risk of product liability claims. One of the basic assumptions about the development of the strict tort rules is that they prevent effective contract disclaimers, at least as to personal injury. It is highly likely, therefore, that even if a claim for personal injury is brought in warranty, the court will hold that any warranty disclaimer is ineffective to bar the claim.

b.   Economic loss. As to recovery of economic loss, failure to comply with 2–316 is not the only basis for concluding that a disclaimer of implied warranties is unenforceable. Another basis is unconscionability. In a landmark article, Professor Arthur Leff argued that a court cannot properly conclude that a disclaimer meeting the requirements of 2–316 is unconscionable. Leff, Unconscionability and the Code: The Emperor's New Clause, 115 U.Pa.L.Rev. 485, 516–528 (1967). As we have seen, the courts disagree. *A & M Produce v. FMC*, page 140 supra. See also Martin v. Joseph Harris Co., 767 F.2d 296 (6th Cir.1985):

> A threshold problem in this context is whether under Michigan law warranty disclaimers which comply with U.C.C. § 2–316 are limited by U.C.C. § 2–302. In holding Harris Seed's disclaimer clause unconscionable under the facts of this case, the district court implicitly held that U.C.C. § 2–302 is a limitation on U.C.C. § 2–316. Harris Seed argues that by enacting § 2–316 the Michigan Legislature "unequivocally [authorized the] exclusion or modification of the implied warranty of merchantability by disclaimer." We have been presented with no Michigan cases resolving this issue; however, a number of arguments support the district court's conclusion that § 2–316 is not insulated from review under § 2–302. First, § 2–302 provides that "any clause" of a

contract may be found unconscionable. Similarly, "section 2–316 does not state expressly that all disclaimers meeting its requirements are immune from general policing provisions like section 2–302. . . ." J. White & R. Summers, Handbook of the Law Under the Uniform Commercial Code, § 12–11, at 476 (2d Ed. 1980). Had the drafters of the Uniform Commercial Code or the Michigan Legislature chosen to limit the application of § 2–302, language expressly so stating could easily have been included. Furthermore, as pointed out by Professors White and Summers:

> Comment 1 [to § 2–302] lists and describes ten cases which are presumably intended to illustrate the underlying basis of the section: In seven of those cases disclaimers of warranty were denied full effect. It is difficult to reconcile the intent on the part of the draftsman to immunize disclaimers from the effect of 2–302 with the fact that they used cases in which courts struck down disclaimers to illustrate the concept of unconscionability.

Id. (footnotes omitted). Therefore, because this issue is unsettled under Michigan law and according the district court's conclusion "considerable weight," we hold that the district court correctly relied upon § 2–302 as a limitation on § 2–316.

10. Other legislation impairing the effectiveness of 2–316. The federal government and many states also have adopted special rules governing warranties in consumer transactions. Section D, page 380 infra, addresses these statutes. In some states, non-uniform legislation modifies 2–316 for all contracts, commercial as well as consumer. For example, Mississippi has deleted 2–316 entirely. Implied warranties of merchantability and fitness for a particular purpose arise under 2–314 and 2–315, but the phrase "unless excluded or modified" has been deleted from both sections. In 1987 Mississippi added a provision (2–315.1) that specifically states that written or oral disclaimers of the warranties of merchantability or fitness or attempts to limit liability for breach of the warranties are unenforceable. There is an exception for the sale of motor vehicles that are six or more years old or that have been driven more than 75,000 miles. In those transactions the seller may disclaim warranties or limit remedies by using a form prescribed by the state attorney general.

South Carolina permits disclaimers of implied warranties, but its non-uniform 2–316(2) provides that language to exclude implied warranties must be specific. Expressions such as "as is" and "with all faults" are not effective to disclaim warranties.

11. Electronic transactions. The requirement of conspicuousness for effectiveness of a disclaimer of implied warranties applies to transactions that are formed on the Internet or by e-mail. How can a seller ensure that its disclaimer will satisfy the definition of "conspicuous"?

In the context of commercial transactions, some contracts are formed electronically without any human intervention whatsoever: a purchaser programs its computer so that, upon the occurrence of some event, the purchaser's computer will place an order by communicating with the seller's computer, which the seller will have programmed to book the order and direct shipment of the goods. How can a seller satisfy the conspicuousness requirement when the parties contemplate that no human will see any term before formation of the contract is complete?

Do you think that a "click here to proceed" provision is sufficient to call an Internet buyer's attention to a disclaimer? Do you think that a clause, "sign here only if you have read the terms on the back," in a face-to-face transaction is sufficient to make a disclaimer conspicuous if it is not otherwise conspicuous? Are the two situations analogous?

12. Problem. In need of a new home, Jamerson went to Miller Mobile Home Sales. Of the mobile homes that she viewed there, one was much more appealing than the rest. She told Miller that she wanted to buy a mobile home just like that one. "Ah," the salesman said, "that's the Dreamland, we can order you one just like it." Jamerson and Miller signed a retail installment sales contract, for the sale of a Dreamland for $46,000, to be set up by Miller on a lot to be designated by Jamerson. On the front side was a prominent provision, "Seller disclaims all warranties, express or implied, including the implied warranty of merchantability." The Dreamland arrived and was installed, but it lacked several features of the home viewed by Jamerson at Miller's lot: the heating and air conditioning system were less efficient than the one in the home on the lot; the bedroom was somewhat smaller; and shortly after set-up a wall separated from the ceiling, allowing cold air and rain to leak into the home. When Jamerson complained, Miller told her to take it up with the manufacturer of the mobile home. Jamerson comes to you for assistance. Does she have a claim against Miller Mobile Home Sales for breach of warranty?

Would it affect your analysis if, immediately above the signature line, the following appeared: "Please read this contract carefully. Do not sign it if it contains any blanks. This contract is the entire agreement of parties and there are no other representations, warranties, or agreements."

13. Leases. Section 2A–214 is the analog of 2–316 for leasing contracts. Subsection (2) requires that any disclaimer of the warranty of merchantability be conspicuous and in writing, and subsection (3)(a) imposes those same requirements on "as is" or "other similar language" disclaimers.

14. CISG. Unlike the UCC, the Convention on the International Sale of Goods does not contain a separate section governing disclaimers. But Article 35, which requires what UCC Article 2 calls implied warranties, contains the qualifying language, "except where the parties have agreed otherwise." See section (2). Hence, the parties may agree that the goods need not be fit their ordinary purposes. Please read Article 35, sections (1)–(2). As a seller, what language would you use to avoid liability for the failure of the goods to be of the quality expected by the buyer?

B. PRIVITY AND WARRANTY

A buyer contracts to purchase a car from a seller. If the car is not merchantable, the seller has breached a warranty, and the buyer may recover for the loss sustained as a result of the breach. If the buyer has permitted her daughter to use the car, may the daughter recover from the seller for loss she sustained as a result of the seller's breach of warranty? Alternatively, if a manufacturer sells a car to a retailer, who resells it to a consumer, may the consumer recover from the manufacturer? In neither of these situations does the person responsible for the injury have a contract with the injured person. They are not in privity of contract. This section considers the liability of a seller to persons who purchase or are affected by the goods but who are not in privity of contract with the seller. In discussing the rights of parties who did not contract with the defendant being sued, courts distinguish vertical privity from horizontal privity.

Vertical privity refers to a chain of sellers: e.g., Manufacturer-Distributor-Wholesaler-Retailer-Consumer, and raises the issue whether a buyer (typically from a retailer) can assert a warranty claim against a remote seller (typically a manufacturer).

Horizontal privity deals with the question whether a non-buyer can assert a claim against the immediate seller of goods to a buyer. Examples of such a non-buyer include people who have relationships such as the following with the buyer: donee of the goods, user of the goods, person in the buyer's family or household, guest of the buyer, or bystander.

As we will see, the rights of the non-privity plaintiff may depend on

(1) whether the plaintiff asserts breach of express warranty or breach of implied warranty;

(2) whether the plaintiff seeks damages for personal injuries, other direct damages, or consequential damages; and

(3) whether the relationship between the plaintiff and the defendant concerns vertical privity or horizontal privity.

———

1. EXPRESS WARRANTY

Randy Knitwear, Inc. v. American Cyanamid Co.
New York Court of Appeals, 1962.
11 N.Y.2d 5, 226 N.Y.S.2d 363, 181 N.E.2d 399.

■ FULD, JUDGE. "The assault upon the citadel of privity," Chief Judge Cardozo wrote in 1931, "is proceeding in these days apace." (Ultramares Corp. v. Touche, 255 N.Y. 170, 180, 174 N.E. 441, 445, 74 A.L.R. 1139.) In these days, too, for the present appeal, here by leave of the Appellate Division on a certified question, calls upon us to decide whether, under the facts disclosed, privity of contract is essential to maintenance of an action against a manufacturer for breach of express warranty.

American Cyanamid Company is the manufacturer of chemical resins, marketed under the registered trade-mark "Cyana," which are used by textile manufacturers and finishers to process fabrics in order to prevent them from shrinking. Apex Knitted Fabrics and Fairtex Mills are manufacturers of fabrics who were licensed or otherwise authorized by Cyanamid to treat their goods with "Cyana" and to sell such goods under the "Cyana" label and, with the guaranty that they were "Cyana" finished. Randy Knitwear, a manufacturer of children's knitted sportswear and play clothes, purchased large quantities of these "Cyana" treated fabrics from Apex and Fairtex. After most of such fabrics had been made up into garments and sold by Randy to customers, it was claimed that ordinary washing caused them to shrink and to lose their shape. This action for breach of express warranty followed. . . . [Defendant alleged that plaintiff lacked privity of contract with it and moved for summary judgment. The trial court denied the motion, and the intermediate appellate court affirmed, certifying to the Court of Appeals the question whether privity of contract is necessary in order for a buyer of goods to assert a breach of express warranty against the manufacturer of the goods.]

Insofar as relevant, the complaint alleges that Cyanamid "represented" and "warranted" that the "Cyana" finished fabrics sold by Fairtex and Apex to the plaintiff would not shrink or lose their shape when washed and that the plaintiff purchased the fabrics and agreed to pay the additional charge for the cost involved in rendering them shrink-proof "in reliance upon" Cyanamid's representations. However, the complaint continues, the fabrics were not as represented since, when manufactured into garments and subjected to ordinary washing, they shrank and failed to hold their shape. The damages suffered are alleged to be over $208,000.

According to the complaint and the affidavits submitted in opposition to Cyanamid's motion, the representations relied upon by the plaintiff took the form of written statements expressed not only in numerous advertisements appearing in trade journals and in direct mail pieces to clothing manufacturers, but also in labels or garment tags furnished by Cyanamid. These labels bore the legend,

"A
CYANA
FINISH
This Fabric Treated for
SHRINKAGE CONTROL
Will Not Shrink or
Stretch Out of Fit
CYANAMID,"

and were issued to fabric manufacturers using the "Cyana Finish" only after Cyanamid had tested samples of the fabrics and approved them. Cyanamid delivered a large number of these labels to Fairtex and Apex and they, with Cyanamid's knowledge and approval, passed them on to garment manufacturers, including the plaintiff, so that they might attach them to the clothing which they manufactured from the fabrics purchased.

... Cyanamid moved for summary judgment dismissing the complaint against it on the ground that there was no privity of contract to support the plaintiff's action. The court at Special Term denied the motion and the Appellate Division unanimously affirmed the resulting order.

Thirty-nine years ago, in Chysky v. Drake Bros. Co., 235 N.Y. 468, 139 N.E. 576, 27 A.L.R. 1533, this court decided that an action for breach of implied warranty could not succeed, absent privity between plaintiff and defendant and, some time later, in Turner v. Edison Storage Battery Co., 248 N.Y. 73, 161 N.E. 423, we reached a similar conclusion with respect to express warranties, writing, "There can be no warranty where there is no privity of contract" (p. 74, 161 N.E. p. 424).[2] This traditional privity limitation on a seller's liability for damage resulting from breach of warranty has not, however, been adhered to with perfect logical consistency and, just a year ago, in Greenberg v. Lorenz, 9 N.Y.2d 195, 213 N.Y.S.2d 39, 173 N.E.2d 773, we noted the definite shift away from the technical privity requirement and recognized that it should be dispensed with in a proper case in the interest of justice and reason. More specifically, we held in Greenberg that, in cases involving foodstuffs and other household goods, the implied warranties of fitness and merchantability run from the retailer to the members of the purchaser's household, regardless of privity of contract. We are now confronted with the further but related question whether the traditional privity limitation shall also be dispensed with in an action for breach of express warranty by a remote purchaser against a manufacturer who induced the purchase by representing the quality of the goods in public advertising and on labels which accompanied the goods.

It was in this precise type of case, where express representations were made by a manufacturer to induce reliance by remote purchasers, that "the citadel of privity" was successfully breached in the State of

---

[2] These decisions proceed, manifestly, from a characterization of the breach of warranty action as one essentially *contractual* in nature. The soundness of this characterization becomes highly questionable, however, when the problem is seen against the backdrop of legal history. The action for breach of warranty "was, in its origin, a pure action of tort." (Ames, Lectures on Legal History [1913], p. 136, reprinted, with revisions, from 2 Harv.L.Rev. 1, 8). Indeed, the earliest reported case upon a warranty arose in 1383 (Fitz. Abr. Monst. de Faits, pl. 160), a century before special assumpsit found its place among the forms of action. And it was not until 1778 that the first decision was reported in which an action on a warranty was brought in assumpsit. (Stuart v. Wilkins, 1 Dougl. 18.) Accordingly, for some 400 years the action rested not on an enforceable promise but on a wrong or tort. In the historical development of the law of warranty, however, as so often happens in law and life in general, accident was evidently confused with essence: from the fact that the cases which arose involved contractual relationships and represented enforceable promises, the courts seem to have concluded that the contract was of the essence of the action. The occasion for the warranty was constituted a necessary condition of it.

Washington in 1932. (See Baxter v. Ford Motor Co., 168 Wash. 456, 12 P.2d 409, 15 P.2d 1118.) It was the holding in the Baxter case that the manufacturer was liable for breach of express warranty to one who purchased an automobile from a retailer since such purchaser had a right to rely on representations made by the manufacturer in its sales literature, even though there was no privity of contract between them. And in the 30 years which have passed since that decision, not only have the courts throughout the country shown a marked, and almost uniform, tendency to discard the privity limitation and hold the manufacturer strictly accountable for the truthfulness of representations made to the public and relied upon by the plaintiff in making his purchase, but the vast majority of the authoritative commentators have applauded the trend and approved the result.

The rationale underlying the decisions rejecting the privity requirement is easily understood in the light of present-day commercial practices. It may once have been true that the warranty which really induced the sale was normally an actual term of the contract of sale. Today, however, the significant warranty, the one which effectively induces the purchase, is frequently that given by the manufacturer through mass advertising and labeling to ultimate business users or to consumers with whom he has no direct contractual relationship.

The world of merchandising is, in brief, no longer a world of direct contract; it is, rather, a world of advertising and, when representations expressed and disseminated in the mass communications media and on labels (attached to the goods themselves) prove false and the user or consumer is damaged by reason of his reliance on those representations, it is difficult to justify the manufacturer's denial of liability on the sole ground of the absence of technical privity. Manufacturers make extensive use of newspapers, periodicals and other media to call attention, in glowing terms, to the qualities and virtues of their products, and this advertising is directed at the ultimate consumer or at some manufacturer or supplier who is not in privity with them. Equally sanguine representations on packages and labels frequently accompany the article throughout its journey to the ultimate consumer and, as intended, are relied upon by remote purchasers. Under these circumstances, it is highly unrealistic to limit a purchaser's protection to warranties made directly to him by his immediate seller. The protection he really needs is against the manufacturer whose published representations caused him to make the purchase.

The policy of protecting the public from injury, physical or pecuniary, resulting from misrepresentations outweighs allegiance to an old and out-moded technical rule of law which, if observed, might be productive of great injustice. The manufacturer places his product upon the market and, by advertising and labeling it, represents its quality to the public in such a way as to induce reliance upon his representations. He unquestionably intends and expects that the product will be purchased and used in reliance upon his express assurance of its quality and, in fact, it is so purchased and used. Having invited and solicited the use, the manufacturer should not be permitted to avoid responsibility, when the expected use leads to injury and loss, by claiming that he made no contract directly with the user.

It is true that in many cases the manufacturer will ultimately be held accountable for the falsity of his representations, but only after an unduly wasteful process of litigation. Thus, if the consumer or ultimate business user sues and recovers, for breach of warranty, from his immediate seller and if the latter in turn, sues and recovers against his supplier in recoupment of his damages and costs, eventually, after several separate actions by those in the chain of distribution, the manufacturer may finally be obliged "to shoulder the responsibility which should have been his in the first instance." (Hamon v. Digliani, 148 Conn. 710, 717, 174 A.2d 294, 297; see Kasler & Cohen v. Slavouski [1928], 1 K.B. 78, where there was a series of 5 recoveries, the manufacturer ultimately paying the consumer's damages, plus a much larger sum covering the costs of the entire litigation.) As is manifest, and as Dean Prosser observes this circuity of action is "an expensive, time-consuming and wasteful process, and it may be interrupted by insolvency, lack of jurisdiction, disclaimers, or the statute of limitations." (Prosser, The Assault upon the Citadel [Strict Liability to the Consumer], 69 Yale L.J. 1099, 1124.)

Indeed, and it points up the injustice of the rule, insistence upon the privity requirement may well leave the aggrieved party, whether he be ultimate business user or consumer, without a remedy in a number of situations. For instance, he would be remediless either where his immediate seller's representations as to quality were less extravagant or enthusiastic than those of the manufacturer[5] or where—as is asserted by Fairtex in this very case—there has been an effective disclaimer of any and all warranties by the plaintiff's immediate seller. Turning to the case before us, even if the representations respecting "Cyana" treated fabric were false, the plaintiff would be foreclosed of all remedy against Fairtex, if it were to succeed on its defense of disclaimer, and against Cyanamid because of a lack of privity.

. . .

We perceive no warrant for holding—as the appellant urges—that strict liability should not here be imposed because the defect involved, fabric shrinkage, is not likely to cause personal harm or injury. Although

---

[5] Typical of this would be a case where the consumer, relying on representations contained on labels or in advertisements for which the manufacturer is responsible, purchases a brand-name article from the shelves of the retailer. In such a case, the retailer ordinarily makes no express warranty and the purchaser may not even invoke an implied warranty of fitness. Consequently, if privity were prerequisite to an action by the consumer against the manufacturer, whose representations induced his purchase, he would (absent proof of negligence) be denied all redress except, perhaps, for breach of the implied warranty of merchantability (Personal Property Law, § 96, subd. 2).

there is language in some of the opinions which appears to support Cyanamid's contention, most of the courts which have dispensed with the requirement of privity in this sort of case have not limited their decisions in this manner. (See, e.g., Burr v. Sherwin Williams Co., 42 Cal.2d 682, 696–697, 268 P.2d 1041 [insecticide; damage to crops]; State Farm Mut. Auto Ins. Co. v. Anderson-Weber, Inc., 110 N.W.2d 449 [Iowa], [automobile; property damage]; [additional citations omitted].) And this makes sense. Since the basis of liability turns not upon the character of the product but upon the representation, there is no justification for a distinction on the basis of the type of injury suffered or the type of article or goods involved.

. . .

Nor may it be urged that section 93 of the Personal Property Law renders privity of contract necessary. The Legislature has there defined a warranty as an "affirmation" (or "promise") made by a seller, but the section nowhere states that liability for breach of express warranty extends only to the warranting seller's immediate buyer and cannot extend to a later buyer who made the purchase from an intermediate seller but in foreseeable and natural reliance on the original seller's affirmations. Indeed, we made the matter clear in Greenberg v. Lorenz when, after observing that the rule requiring a direct contractual relationship between the plaintiff and the defendant is of "judicial making," we went on to say, "our statutes say nothing at all about privity" (9 N.Y.2d 195, 200, 213 N.Y.S.2d 39, 42, 173 N.E.2d 773, 775).

In concluding that the old court-made rule should be modified to dispense with the requirement of privity, we are doing nothing more or less than carrying out an historic and necessary function of the court to bring the law into harmony "with modern-day needs and with concepts of justice and fair dealing." (Bing v. Thunig, 2 N.Y.2d 656, 667, 163 N.Y.S.2d 3, 11, 143 N.E.2d 3, 9.)

The order appealed from should be affirmed, with costs, and the question certified [whether privity of contract is necessary in an action for breach of express warranty] answered in the negative.

QUESTIONS AND NOTES

1. *Randy Knitwear* arose shortly before New York adopted the UCC, so the applicable law was the Uniform Sales Act. As originally enacted, 2–318 consisted of what is now labeled 2–318 (Alternative A). It answers the first question posed at the beginning of this section, viz., is the seller of goods liable for breach of warranty to a person who the buyer permits to use the goods. What answer does it provide?

2. In 1966 the sponsoring organizations revised 2–318 to add two additional versions of that section. Please read those alternatives and the Official Comments. By far the most states have adopted Alternative A, but several states have adopted one of the others.

3. If a seller breaches an express warranty, the ultimate user may suffer direct economic loss, in the form of paying the price of conforming goods but receiving only nonconforming goods. See 2–714(2). In addition, the user may sustain consequential loss. See 2–714(3) and 2–715(2). In *Randy Knitwear* plaintiff suffered both kinds of loss. And in denying defendant's motion for summary judgment, the court apparently believed that plaintiff can recover for both. Compare Beyond the Garden Gate, Inc. v. Northstar Freeze-Dry Manufacturing, Inc., 526 N.W.2d 305 (Iowa 1995), in which a manufacturer of a machine for freeze-drying flowers made affirmations of fact concerning the machine to the plaintiff, who then purchased one of the machines from another person. When the machine failed to operate as represented, plaintiff asserted breach of express warranty against the manufacturer. The jury awarded no damages for direct loss, but awarded $40,000 for lost profits and other consequential loss. In holding that a nonprivity plaintiff may at most recover for direct loss, the court quoted extensively from the White and Summers treatise:

> "Courts allow a nonprivity buyer to recover for direct economic loss damages if the remote seller has breached an express warranty." [James J. White & Robert S. Summers, *Uniform Commercial Code* § 11–5, at 538 (3d ed. 1988)]. "On the other hand, courts are split on whether to allow a nonprivity buyer to recover consequential economic loss damages." *Id.* at 539. White and Summers make a good argument for siding with those courts that have refused to allow remote or nonprivity buyers from recovering consequential economic loss damages:

> "We agree with those courts that have refused to allow recovery of consequential economic loss by remote buyers. Even if relevant policies justify allowing nonprivity consumers to recover for direct economic loss, there can be no justification in the usual case for allowing nonprivity consumer buyers to recover for consequential economic losses they sustain. Remote buyers may use a seller's goods for unknown purposes from which enormous losses might ensue. Since the remote seller cannot predict the purposes for which the goods will be used he faces unknown liability and may not be able to insure himself. Insurers are hesitant to insure against risks they cannot measure. Moreover, here more than in personal injury and property damage cases, it is appropriate to recognize the traditional rights of parties to make their own contract. If a remote seller wishes to sell at a lower price and exclude liability for consequential economic loss to sub-purchasers, why should we deny him that right? Why should we design a system that forces him to bear the unforeseeable consequential economic losses of remote purchasers? Indeed, by forcing the buyer to bear such losses we may save costly law suits and even some economic losses against which buyers, knowing they have the responsibility, may protect themselves. In short, we believe that a buyer should pick his seller with care and recover any economic loss from that seller and not from parties remote from

the transaction. Put another way, we believe the user is often the 'least cost avoider.' By placing the loss on him or by forcing him to bargain with his immediate seller about the loss, we may minimize the total loss to society. If the manufacturer is not the least cost risk avoider, but must nevertheless bear the loss, we may cause him to spend more of society's resources than are optimal to avoid the loss and may unnecessarily increase the cost of the commodity sold." *Id.* at 539–40. We agree and now hold that nonprivity buyers who rely on express warranties are limited to direct economic loss damages.

Are you persuaded by the argument lifted from *White & Summers*? Granted that a manufacturer that places a tag on its goods or circulates a brochure about its product cannot foresee all uses to which remote buyers may put the product, was that the case in *Garden Gate*? Please read 2–715(2), defining "consequential damages." How, if at all, is this definition relevant to the court's reasoning?

4. *Garden Gate* concerns an individualized affirmation made to a specific individual. In this context it is questionable whether lack of privity should defeat a claim of express warranty. In most sales, however, affirmations to persons not in privity occur in an anonymous, mass distribution context. Thus, a manufacturer that includes a "warranty in the box" intends to create an express warranty in favor of, not its immediate purchaser, but rather the ultimate purchaser at retail, i.e., the person who will use the goods. Conceptually there is a difficulty applying the warranty provisions of Article 2, because, e.g., 2–313(1)(a) speaks of an affirmation "made by the seller to *the* buyer." But here the warranty is made by the manufacturer to its buyer, who is not the ultimate buyer-user. Official Comment 2 to 2–313 literally contemplates only sales in a privity context, as does 2–318. Not surprisingly, although not literally covered by 2–313 or 2–318, this conceptual difficulty has not troubled the courts, perhaps because remote sellers rarely have the temerity to say that an express warranty that it intended a retailer to deliver to the ultimate purchasers of its products should be treated as something other than what it purports to be, an express warranty to the ultimate purchaser. When one remote seller did dare to argue lack of privity, the court stated that the "argument is nothing if not audacious," concluding, "It is simply unconscionable to say that this Warranty, which accompanies each new car, is unenforceable against the warrantor. It defies logic to say that [the] warranty flows to the first retail purchaser, but that there is no such person." Morano v. BMW of North America, LLC, 928 F.Supp.2d 826, 835, 837 (D.N.J.2013).

Notwithstanding the lack of privity of contract, courts routinely permit retail purchasers to enforce express warranties that are packaged with goods as they travel from manufacturer to distributor to retailer to consumer. Indeed, there are surprisingly few cases even considering the propriety of imposing liability for breach of express warranty in the absence of privity. For other cases holding remote sellers liable for breaching their express warranties, see U.S. Tire-Tech, Inc. v. Boeran, 110 S.W.3d 194 (Tex.App. 2003); Prairie Production, Inc. v. Agchem Div.-Pennwalt Corp., 514 N.E.2d

1299 (Ind.App.1987); and Ferguson v. Sturm, Ruger & Co., 524 F.Supp. 1042 (D.Conn.1981). Contra Copiers Typewriters Calculators, Inc. v. Toshiba Corp., 576 F.Supp. 312 (D.Md.1983) (under Maryland law a remote seller is not liable for breach of express warranty). Georgia courts reject express-warranty liability to remote parties unless, through such facts as the manufacturer's authorization to the retailer to deliver written warranties to the buyer, it appears that the remote seller intends the remote buyer to be the beneficiary of its warranties. In the absence of this intent, there is no warranty liability. To the extent that the defective product damaged other property, however, a strict tort action would lie. Lamb v. Georgia-Pacific Corp., 194 Ga.App. 848, 392 S.E.2d 307 (1990).

To be distinguished from cases in which a manufacturer creates an express warranty that it contemplates will be communicated to the ultimate retail purchaser are cases in which the first retail purchaser sells the now-used goods to another person. When the purchaser of the used goods sues the manufacturer, lack of privity is not a defense. Collins Company, Ltd. v. Carboline Co., 125 Ill.2d 498, 127 Ill.Dec. 5, 532 N.E.2d 834 (1988) (express warranty); MAN Engines & Components, Inc. v. Shows, 434 S.W.3d 132 (Tex.2014) (implied warranty of merchantability).

For a suggestion that it might be more rational to treat cases in which a buyer relies on representations by a remote seller, in advertising or otherwise, as involving the tort of misrepresentation. See Hill, Damages for Innocent Misrepresentation, 73 Colum.L.Rev. 679 (1973).

5.   In Minnesota Mining & Manufacturing Co. v. Nishika Ltd., 565 N.W.2d 16 (Minn.1997), 3M, a manufacturer of photo-finishing emulsion, expressly warranted to two photo-processing companies that the emulsion would work well in their process for producing 3-dimensional images. In fact, it did not work well at all, and the purchasers went out of business. The manufacturer also communicated the express warranty to two camera companies whose business depended on the ability of the photo-processors to process the photographs taken by the cameras they produced. These camera companies also failed, and they sued 3M for the consequential damages (i.e. lost profits) they sustained. The dispute was governed by the law of Minnesota, which has adopted a variant of Alternative C of 2–318:

> A seller's warranty whether express or implied extends to any person who may reasonably be expected to use, consume or be affected by the goods and who is injured by breach of the warranty. A seller may not exclude or limit the operation of this section.

Denying recovery, the court stated:

> We agree with 3M that the statute is not so clear and free from ambiguity that we may disregard legislative intent, the aims of section 336.2–318 at the time of enactment, or the consequences of a particular construction. The unadorned term "injured" is not defined in the U.C.C., nor is it used elsewhere in the text of Article 2. As applied to [plaintiffs], the reach of section 336.2–318 is unclear. We must therefore interpret the statute consistent with

legislative intent and in a sensible manner that avoids unreasonable, unjust, or absurd results.

Under section 336.2–318, this court has sanctioned the recovery of lost profits (one form of economic loss) by a third-party beneficiary whose damages arose from a remote seller's breach of warranty. We have also indicated that plaintiffs who never used, purchased, or otherwise acquired defective goods may qualify as third-party beneficiaries when they suffer property damage.

But this court has never gone so far as to hold that section 336.2–318 reaches a plaintiff who is seeking lost profits unaccompanied by physical injury or property damage and who never used, purchased, or otherwise acquired the goods in question. To do so, we believe, would expand warranty liability well beyond the limits contemplated by the legislature.

When placed in historical context, it seems clear that the primary motivation for the current version of section 336.2–318 was concern for injured consumers. A prevalent legal conflict at the time of enactment was how best to protect consumers from dangerous products. One route was to expand the doctrine of "warranty" to reach subpurchasers and others injured in person by defective products. During the 1960s, however, the preferred course was to recognize that the concept of "warranty" had been outgrown and to legitimize recovery in tort. See William L. Prosser, The Fall of the Citadel (Strict Liability to the Consumer), 50 Minn. L. Rev. 791, passim (1966) (recounting the legal battle to break down the barrier of "privity," which culminated in widespread adoption of strict products liability in tort). Despite the promulgation of Restatement of Torts (Second) § 402A in 1965 . . . , the drafters of the model U.C.C. presented states with Alternative C of the third-party beneficiaries provision, which was intended to follow the trend of strict products liability and extend warranty protection "beyond injuries to the person." U.C.C. § 2–318 cmt. 3. But the expansion of warranty protection to certain classes of noncontracting parties in the U.C.C. cannot be completely detached from the concerns that motivated our legislature in 1969.

Our understanding of the background and aims of section 336.2–318 leads us to conclude that the scope of a seller's liability for breach of warranty should recede as the relationship between a "beneficiary" of the warranty and the seller's goods becomes more remote. . . . [T]hose who purchase, use, or otherwise acquire warranted goods have standing to sue for purely economic losses. Those who lack any such connection to the warranted goods must demonstrate physical injury or property damage before economic losses are recoverable. This line comports with legislative intent, provides a clear rule of law, and identifies a sensible limit to liability without disrupting settled precedent.

Any other result implies almost unlimited liability for sellers of warranted goods. If section 336.2–318 were interpreted as the [plaintiffs] advocate, it seems that the [plaintiffs'] individual employees, or perhaps even their families, would have standing to sue 3M for causing the loss of their jobs or even a decline in their wages. The [plaintiffs'] reading also appears to allow recovery on the facts of Nebraska Innkeepers, Inc. v. Pittsburgh-Des Moines Corp., 345 N.W.2d 124 (Iowa 1984), in which plaintiffs connected with motel, restaurant, bar, and retail businesses invoked Iowa's third-party beneficiaries provision in an attempt to sue solely for economic losses arising from a bridge closing; the closing was allegedly caused by the defendant-seller's defective steel. That attempt to expand the scope of the U.C.C. was rejected. The [plaintiffs] appear to advocate warranty recovery as a catch-all alternative for [persons] with no viable legal basis for suit. The risk, however, is that the fortuitous existence of a warranty—between some seller and some buyer, somewhere—would allow remote yet foreseeable parties to recover for their hampered expectations, while others in similar circumstances—but who could not identify a warranty—would not. Cf. Cunningham v. Kartridg Pak Co., 332 N.W.2d 881, 885 (Iowa 1983) ("Plaintiff is not an injured consumer; he was a shareholder of a corporation whose expectations did not materialize. To allow a shareholder to use products liability law as the vehicle to a direct cause of action otherwise denied by general corporate law would be an injustice to both areas of the law.").

Confronted with liability of this magnitude, sellers would be encouraged to attempt to disclaim warranties or exclude consequential damages remedies—affecting both the immediate buyer and third-party beneficiaries alike.

We therefore reject the [plaintiffs'] reading of the statute—an interpretation that would likely lead to a variety of unreasonable, unjust, and absurd results that we cannot imagine were intended by the legislature. In light of the statute's language and purpose, and consistent with the legislature's apparent intent, the best reading of section 336.2–318 is that noncontracting parties who never used, purchased, or otherwise acquired the seller's warranted goods may not seek lost profits, unaccompanied by physical injury or property damage, for breach of warranty under the statute. [Plaintiffs] are simply not within the class of warranty "beneficiaries" protected by section 336.2–318.

In the first full paragraph on page 344 and in the last paragraph of the excerpt, the court refers to non-privity buyers who suffer physical injury or property damage as a result of a remote seller's breach of express warranty. For an example of such a case, see City of Wyoming v. Proctor & Gamble Co., 210 F.Supp.3d 1137 (D.Minn.2016), in which several municipalities sued several manufacturers of what were labeled and advertised as flushable wipes. The wipes did not break down like toilet paper; rather, they clogged up the sewer systems and damaged the treatment facilities. Even though the cities had not purchased the wipes from the defendants, or anyone else for that matter, they were third party beneficiaries of the contracts between the defendants and the persons to whom the wipes were sold.

---

2. IMPLIED WARRANTIES

The foregoing materials primarily concern liability to nonprivity plaintiffs for breach of express warranty. Section 2–318 refers to a "seller's warranty whether express or implied." How does the section apply to implied warranty? Please consider the following: Simmons Seating sells a large number of chairs to Dollar Discount, which sells one of them to Benton, a consumer. Benton's adult son suffers personal injury when the chair collapses as a result of a manufacturing defect. How does 2–318 (Alternative A) apply to the son's claim for compensation against Simmons Seating?

Tex Enterprises, Inc. v. Brockway Standard, Inc.
Washington Supreme Court, 2003.
149 Wash.2d 204, 66 P.3d 625.

■ EN BANC. OWENS, J. A commercial purchaser seeks to recover economic damages from a manufacturer for breach of implied warranties under Article 2 of the Uniform Commercial Code, Title 62A RCW (UCC). The plaintiff asserts that implied warranties arose out of the manufacturer's verbal assurances as to the quality of his product, made directly to the plaintiff. However, the plaintiff ultimately purchased the product from an intermediate distributor, not the manufacturer. Furthermore, an agreement between the manufacturer and the distributor contained a disclaimer of all warranties. Thus, absent privity between the plaintiff and the manufacturer, and without reliance on the contract between the manufacturer and the distributor as a third party beneficiary, we hold that such assurances do not give rise to implied warranties.

FACTS

Brockway Standard, Inc. (Brockway) is a Georgia corporation that manufactures three-and five-gallon unlined steel containers, treated only with a rust inhibitor. J.F. Shelton Company (Shelton) is a Washington distributor of Brockway products. Tex Enterprises, Inc. (Tex) is a Washington corporation that purchases three-and five-gallon containers in which it ships and stores Spantex, a liquid coating used to seal decks and other exterior surfaces. Brockway sells its containers to Shelton, who in turn sells them to Washington purchasers like Tex. [When Shelton placed an order with Brockway,] Brockway would ship the goods and mail an invoice. On the back of the invoice, terms and conditions were printed which warranted only that the goods would be free from defects in workmanship and materials. The terms explicitly disclaimed all other warranties, express or implied, and limited damages to refund of the purchase price and cost of return shipping. An additional clause required that Georgia law govern the agreement. Although Shelton had received multiple invoices over the course of its relationship with Brockway, these terms were never negotiated, and Shelton was unaware of their existence until the inception of this lawsuit.

Similarly, Tex's practice was to place verbal orders with Shelton for Brockway products. No party has referred to any written agreement between Tex and Shelton. Furthermore, because Tex never ordered directly from Brockway, Tex was unaware of the disclaimer, remedy limitation clause, and choice of law clause printed on Brockway's invoices. No similar disclaimers or limitations were printed anywhere on Brockway products or their packaging, and Shelton never notified Tex that the disclaimers existed.

Prior to September 1997, Tex used Brockway one-gallon tin cans to store and ship Spantex, but used another company's three-and five-gallon steel containers. In September 1997, [a Shelton representative and a Brockway representative visited Tex's president], with the objective of persuading him to switch to Brockway three-and five-gallon containers for storing and shipping Spantex. [They] toured the Tex facility and examined the containers that Tex was using. [The Brockway rep] told [Tex's president] that Brockway containers were "just as good" for storing Spantex as the containers Tex was using. . . . Relying on these representations, [Tex] agreed to switch to Brockway containers. Ultimately, Tex purchased 4,800 Brockway containers in which it stored and shipped more than 22,000 gallons of Spantex to its customers.

In the spring of 1998, Tex began to receive complaints from retail and consumer customers. The Spantex that was stored in the three-and five-gallon Brockway containers had begun to thicken and solidify, rendering it useless. Tex claims that the problem was caused by a reaction between the Spantex and the rust inhibitor with which the containers were treated. Tex expected that its costs for replacing the ruined Spantex would exceed $440,000.

Tex sued both Brockway and Shelton, claiming that it was entitled to recovery under a variety of theories including breach of express warranty, breach of implied warranty of merchantability, breach of implied warranty of fitness for a particular purpose, and breach of contract (against Shelton only). Tex sought to recover its costs for replacing the ruined product, incidental and consequential damages, disposal costs, and attorney fees. Shelton settled with Tex and is no longer a party to this lawsuit.

Brockway responded that the language on its invoices limited the claims and remedies available to Tex. . . . [T]he trial court . . . dismissed all claims based upon the disclaimers printed on the Brockway invoices and lack of privity.

The Court of Appeals agreed that any third party beneficiary claims would depend upon Shelton's agreement with Brockway, which was limited by the language on Brockway's invoices. Still, the court reversed and remanded, holding instead that "direct representations to the purchaser can create express *and implied* warranties that run to the purchaser independent of any contract between the manufacturer and distributor." (emphasis added).

. . .

ISSUE

Can an implied warranty arise from a manufacturer's direct representation to a remote commercial purchaser, absent a contract between the parties or reliance as a third party beneficiary on the contract between the manufacturer and its immediate buyer?

ANALYSIS

When reviewing an order of summary judgment, this court engages in the same inquiry as the trial court. Thus, we must affirm the trial court's summary judgment on this issue if we determine that there is no genuine issue of material fact and Brockway is entitled to judgment as a matter of law. The facts and reasonable inferences from the facts must be considered in the light most favorable to Tex as the nonmoving party.

Article 2 of the UCC, as adopted in Washington, governs. . . . [L]ack of privity has historically been a defense to claims of breach of warranty. There are two types of plaintiffs for whom lack of privity has been a concern. A " 'horizontal' non-privity plaintiff" is not a buyer of the product in question, but is one who consumes or is affected by the goods. The " 'vertical' non-privity plaintiff" is a buyer who is in the distributive chain, but who did not buy the product directly from the defendant. Tex is a vertical nonprivity plaintiff.

By adopting alternative A of section 2–318 . . . , the Washington Legislature chose to eliminate the privity requirement for horizontal nonprivity plaintiffs under certain circumstances. . . . UCC comment 3 to section 2–318, as adopted in Washington, notes that this provision is silent with regard to vertical privity, but the section "is not intended to enlarge or restrict the developing case law on whether the seller's warranties, given to his buyer who resells, extend to other persons in the distributive chain." RCWA 62A.2–318 U.C.C. cmt. 3, at 207 (purpose); see also RCWA 62A.2–318 Wash. cmt. at 206 (noting comment 3 is emphatic that the section was intended to be neutral with regard to vertical privity). Thus, questions regarding the extension of warranties to vertical nonprivity plaintiffs are left to the courts.

In Baughn v. Honda Motor Co., 107 Wn.2d 127, 727 P.2d 655 (1986), this court upheld a trial court's summary judgment order in favor of a manufacturer, dismissing the remote purchasers' claims for breach of implied warranty. The *Baughn* court adopted the traditional rule that a plaintiff may not bring an implied warranty action under the UCC without contractual privity. It is important to note that the *Baughn* court would have allowed a plaintiff's express warranty claim to proceed because "[t]he privity requirement is relaxed . . . when a manufacturer makes express representations, in advertising or otherwise, to a plaintiff." Id. at 151–52

A few years later in [Touchet Valley Grain Growers, Inc. v. Opp & Seibold General Construction, Inc., 119 Wn.2d 334, 831 P.2d 724 (1992)], this court created an exception to the privity requirement for implied warranties. The *Touchet Valley* court allowed a vertical nonprivity plaintiff to recover where the plaintiff was the intended third party beneficiary of the implied warranty that the manufacturer gave to its intermediate dealer. Notably, the *Touchet Valley* court did not overturn *Baughn*. Instead, it distinguished *Baughn* based in part on the fact that "the analysis was not based on a third party beneficiary argument." Thus, we conclude that *Touchet Valley* carved a third party beneficiary exception out of the general rule that a vertical nonprivity plaintiff cannot recover from a remote manufacturer for breach of implied warranty.

The Court of Appeals in this case held that a manufacturer's direct verbal representations to a remote purchaser can create express and implied warranties that run to the remote purchaser, independent of any contract between the manufacturer and the intermediate distributor. However, allowing implied warranties to arise without reliance on an underlying contract is inconsistent with both the plain language of RCW 62A.2–314 and –315 and this court's prior approach to implied warranties.

First, the plain language of both RCW 62A.2–314 and –315 requires that implied warranties arise only out of contractual relationships. RCW 62A.2–314 states that the warranty that goods shall be merchantable is "implied in a contract for their sale." Similarly, RCW 62A.2–315 explains that the implied warranty of fitness for a particular purpose arises based on the seller's understanding "at the time of contracting." This language can be contrasted with RCW 62A.2–313 (express warranties), the language of which does not refer to an underlying "contract." Thus, the plain meaning of this statutory language forecloses application of implied warranties where there is no underlying contract to which the purchaser is a party or an intended third party beneficiary.

In addition, Tex has failed to cite to any case in which this court has allowed a vertical nonprivity plaintiff to recover economic damages for breach of implied warranty without reliance on some underlying contract. Such a restriction is justified because, to be enforceable, contractual relationships under the UCC must be formed according to the Code's safeguards, making contractual relationships comparatively formalized. See, e.g., RCW 62A.2–201 (statute of frauds). In contrast, express representations, made in advertisements or otherwise, require no formalities. Thus, we recognize that allowing implied warranties to arise out of express representations could leave a manufacturer unable to adequately predict when implied warranties will attach.

This court has also distinguished between express and implied warranties, restricting recovery for breach of implied warranty where it would have allowed recovery for breach of express warranty. See Baughn, 107 Wn.2d at 151–52. Because implied warranties arise by operation of law without specific adoption by the seller, we recognize that such warranties must be more closely guarded than express warranties, whose adoption requires some voluntary action.

The combination of the plain language of the statutory scheme and this court's prior treatment of implied warranties overcomes the reasoning of the Court of Appeals in this case. . . .

The Court of Appeals also adopted the reasoning of the Florida Court of Appeals in Cedars of Lebanon Hospital Corp. v. European X-Ray Distributors of America, Inc., 444 So. 2d 1068 (Fla.Ct.App.1984), a case involving a fact pattern similar to this one. The Cedars court reasoned that it would be "fundamentally unfair . . . to allow the manufacturer to hide behind the doctrine of privity when the product, which it induced the purchaser to buy, turns out to be worthless." Cedars, 444 So.2d at 1072. The Cedars court also hoped to avoid prolonged indemnity litigation, gradually advancing up the chain of privity. However, both of these concerns are easily alleviated where the plaintiff is allowed to pursue a claim under breach of express warranty, something that Washington law clearly allows in this case. Therefore, we find the Cedars reasoning unconvincing.

It is important to note that Tex and future vertical nonprivity plaintiffs are not left without recourse. We emphasize that this court has already clearly established that the privity requirement is relaxed where a manufacturer makes express representations to a plaintiff. In fact, the issue of whether an express warranty was made in this case still remains to be decided by the trial court. . . . Finally, where a commercial plaintiff can show that it is the intended third party beneficiary of a contract between the manufacturer and its direct purchaser, recovery may be available under a third party beneficiary analysis.

For all of the reasons discussed above, we hold that implied warranties do not arise out of express representations made by a manufacturer to a remote commercial purchaser absent privity or reliance on some underlying contract.

CONCLUSION

We reverse the Court of Appeals with regard to the implied warranty claim and hold that in cases where a commercial purchaser seeks to recover economic damages from a remote manufacturer, implied warranties do not arise absent privity or an underlying contract to which the remote commercial purchaser is a third party beneficiary.

Morrow v. New Moon Homes, Inc.

Alaska Supreme Court, 1976.
548 P.2d 279.

■ RABINOWITZ, CHIEF JUSTICE. . . .

In October of 1969, Joseph R. and Nikki Morrow bought a mobile home from Golden Heart Mobile Homes, a Fairbanks retailer of mobile homes. A plaque on the side of the mobile home disclosed that the home had been manufactured in Oregon by New Moon Homes, Inc. The Morrows made a down payment of $1,800, taking out a loan for the balance of the purchase price from the First National Bank of Fairbanks. The loan amount of $10,546.49, plus interest of 9 percent per year, was to be repaid by the Morrows in 72 monthly installments of $190.13 each.

At the time of the purchase, the Morrows inspected the mobile home and noticed that the carpeting had not been laid and that several windows were broken. Roy Miller, Golden Heart's salesman, assured them that these problems would be corrected and later made good his assurances. Miller also told the Morrows that the mobile home was a "good trailer," " * * * as warm as * * * any other trailer." After the sale, Miller moved the Morrows' mobile home to Lakeview Terrace, set it up on the space the Morrows had rented, and made sure that the utilities were connected. Then the troubles started.

On the first night that the mobile home's furnace was in use, the motor went out and had to be replaced. The electric furnace installed by the manufacturer had been removed by someone who had replaced the original with an oil furnace. The furnace vent did not fit, and consequently the "stove pipe" vibrated when the furnace was running. Subsequent events showed the furnace malfunction was not the primary problem with the mobile home.

About four days after the mobile home had been set up, the Morrows noticed that the doors did not close all the way and that the windows were cracked. The bathtub leaked water into the middle of the bedroom. In March of 1970 when the snow on the roof began to melt, the roof leaked. Water came in through gaps between the ceiling and the wall panels, as well as along the bottom of the wallboard. A short circuit developed in the electrical system; the lights flickered at various times. When it rained, water came out of the light fixture in the hallway. Other problems with the mobile home included the following: the interior walls did not fit together at the corners; the paneling came off the walls; the windows and doors were out of square; the door frames on the bedroom doors fell off and the closet doors would not slide properly; the curtains had glue on them; and the finish came off the kitchen cabinet doors.

Despite all these problems, the Morrows continued to live in the mobile home and make the loan payments. Golden Heart Mobile Homes was notified many times of the difficulties the Morrows were having with their mobile home. Roy Miller, the Golden Heart salesman with whom the Morrows had dealt, did put some caulking around the bathtub, but otherwise he was of little assistance. Finally, sometime before April 1, 1970, Nikki Morrow informed Miller that if Golden Heart did not fix the mobile home the Morrows wanted to return it. Miller said the Morrows would "[h]ave to take it up with the bank." Subsequently Golden Heart went out of business.

The First National Bank of Fairbanks was more sensitive to the Morrows' plight. Upon being informed by the Morrows that they intended to make no further payments on the mobile home, bank personnel went out and inspected the home several times. In addition on May 27, 1970, the bank wrote to New Moon Homes, Inc. in Silverton, Oregon. Its letter informed New Moon of the problems the Morrows were having with their New Moon mobile home and asked whether New Moon expected to send a representative to Fairbanks since Golden Heart, the dealer, was no longer in business. Apparently, New Moon did not respond to the bank's letter.

A short time later the Morrows' counsel wrote a letter to New Moon Homes notifying New Moon that the Morrows intended to hold the company liable for damages for breach of implied warranties. About a month later the Morrows separated, with Nikki Morrow continuing to live in the mobile home. She continued to make payments to First National because she "couldn't afford Alaskan rents." Nikki Morrow eventually moved out of the mobile home but made no effort to sell or rent it because she considered it "not fit to live in." In October of 1971 the Morrows filed this action against both New Moon Homes and Golden Heart Mobile Homes, alleging that defendants had breached implied warranties of merchantability and fitness for particular purpose in manufacturing and selling an improperly constructed mobile home. . . .

. . . The superior court granted the Morrows a default judgment against Golden Heart, but dismissed their claim against New Moon "for both failure of jurisdiction and failure of privity of contract." The Morrows then appealed from that portion of the superior court's judgment which dismissed their claim against New Moon.

The heart of this appeal concerns the remedies which are available to a remote purchaser against the manufacturer of defective goods for direct economic loss. The superior court held that the Morrows had no legal claim against New Moon because they were not in privity of contract with New Moon. The first argument advanced here by the Morrows amounts to an end run around the requirement of privity. The Morrows contend that their complaint asserted a theory of strict liability in tort. They further argue that they should have prevailed irrespective of any lack of privity of contract between New Moon and themselves, because lack of privity of contract is not a defense to a strict tort liability claim. . . . [T]he Morrows argue that strict liability should . . . apply in the situation where a consumer sues a manufacturer solely for economic loss attributable to the manufacturer's defective product. This precise contention presents a question of first impression in Alaska.

The issue whether strict liability in tort should extend to economic loss has prompted no small amount of discussion in legal journals. . . .

. . . Under the Uniform Commercial Code the manufacturer is given the right to avail himself of certain affirmative defenses which can minimize his liability for a purely economic loss. Specifically, the manufacturer has the opportunity, pursuant to AS 45.05.100 [2–316], to disclaim liability and under AS 45.05.230 [2–719] to limit the consumer's remedies, although the Code further provides that such disclaimers and limitations cannot be so oppressive as to be unconscionable and thus violate AS 45.05.072 [2–302]. In addition, the manufacturer is entitled to reasonably prompt notice from the consumer of the claimed breach of warranties, pursuant to AS 45.05.174(c)(1) [2–607(3)(a)].

In our view, recognition of a doctrine of strict liability in tort for economic loss would seriously jeopardize the continued viability of these rights. The economically injured consumer would have a theory of redress not envisioned by our legislature when it enacted the U.C.C., since this strict liability remedy would be completely unrestrained by disclaimer, liability limitation and notice provisions. Further, manufacturers could no longer look to the Uniform Commercial Code provisions to provide a predictable definition of potential liability for direct economic loss. In short, adoption of the doctrine of strict liability for economic loss would be contrary to the legislature's intent when it authorized the aforementioned remedy limitations and risk allocation provisions of Article II of the Code. To extend strict tort liability to reach the Morrows' case would in effect be an assumption of legislative prerogative on our part and would vitiate clearly articulated statutory rights. This we decline to do. Thus, we hold that the theory of strict liability in tort . . . does not extend to the consumer who suffers only economic loss because of defective goods.

The principal theory of liability advocated by the Morrows at trial was that New Moon had breached statutory warranties which arose by operation of law with the manufacture and distribution of this mobile home. Specifically, the Morrows rely upon AS 45.05.096 [2–314] and AS 45.05.098 [2–315] of the Uniform Commercial Code as enacted in Alaska. The former section provides for an implied warranty of "merchantability" in the sale of goods governed by the Code; the latter establishes an implied warranty that the goods are fit for the particular purpose for which they were purchased. The superior court was of the view that these Code warranties operated only for the benefit of those purchasing directly from a manufacturer or seller. Since the Morrows were not in privity of contract with New Moon, the superior court concluded that a warranty theory based on AS 45.05.096 and AS 45.05.098 could not serve as a basis for liability.

. . . The critical question in this case is whether the Morrows, as remote purchasers, can invoke the warranties attributable to the manufacturer which arose when New Moon passed title of the mobile home to the next party in the chain of distribution. In other words, do the implied warranties of merchantability and fitness run from a manufacturer only to those with whom the manufacturer is in privity of contract?

Although sometimes criticized, the distinction between horizontal and vertical privity is significant in this case. The issue of horizontal privity raises the question whether persons other than the buyer of defective goods can recover from the buyer's immediate seller on a warranty theory. The question of vertical privity is whether parties in the distributive chain prior to the immediate seller can be held liable to the ultimate purchaser for loss caused by the defective product. The Code addresses the matter of horizontal privity in AS 45.05.104 [2–318], extending the claim for relief in warranty to any " * * * person who is in the family or household of his buyer or who is a guest in his home if it is reasonable to expect that the person may use, consume, or be affected by the goods * * *." With regard to vertical privity, the Code is totally silent and strictly neutral, as Official Comment 3 to AS 45.05.104 makes eminently clear. The Code leaves to the courts the question of the extent to which vertical privity of contract will or will not be required.[25]

This court has never previously confronted the question whether a requirement of privity of contract will preclude a purchaser from recovering against the original manufacturer on a theory of implied warranties. . . . [I]n Clary v. Fifth Avenue Chrysler Center, Inc., 454 P.2d 244 (Alaska 1969), [we expressly held] that a manufacturer is strictly liable in tort for personal injuries attributable to his defective goods. In approving a theory based on strict liability in tort, we stressed the efficacy, simplicity, and comprehensiveness of that theory. Appellees in Clary had urged this court to limit the consumer's source of redress to possible application of the statutory provisions governing sales warranties, particularly AS 45.05.096 [2–314]. This we declined to do. As we have noted, under the statutory scheme an injured consumer is required to give notice of the defect to the warrantor within a relatively short period of time, and potential liability may be circumscribed by express disclaimers from the manufacturer. The Clary court was concerned that such provisions might operate as a trap for the unwary, and it expressed a preference for a tort theory more solicitous of the needs of the consumer in the modern, prepackaged, mass merchandised market

[25] By this statement we do not mean to intimate that the matter of horizontal privity is exclusively controlled by AS 45.05.104. The fact that a given plaintiff is not expressly authorized to sue for breach of warranty under that provision will not preclude this court from possibly holding at some future date, as a matter of case law, that plaintiff is not barred by a requirement of horizontal privity.

place. However, this preference was never intended to imply that reliance on the statutory warranty provisions was not available as an alternative vehicle for relief. There is nothing incompatible in affording parallel consumer remedies sounding in tort and in contract, and several jurisdictions which have adopted strict liability in tort also make available an implied warranty theory without regard to privity of contract.

The dispute here is whether the requirement of vertical privity of contract should be abolished in Alaska. This battle has already been waged in many jurisdictions, and the results are well known: the citadel of privity has largely toppled. The course of this modern development is familiar history and we need not recount it at length here. Contrived "exceptions" which paid deference to the hoary doctrine of privity while obviating its unjust results have given way in more recent years to an open frontal assault. The initial attack came in Spence v. Three Rivers Builders & Masonry Supply, Inc., 353 Mich. 120, 90 N.W.2d 873 (1958), but the leading case probably remains Henningsen v. Bloomfield Motors, Inc., 32 N.J. 358, 161 A.2d 69 (1960), in which the New Jersey Supreme Court held liable for personal injuries and property damages both the manufacturer of an automobile and the dealer who sold the vehicle. The rationale for the widespread abolition of the requirement of privity stems from the structure and operation of the free market economy in contemporary society; it was succinctly summed up not long ago by the Supreme Court of Pennsylvania:[31]

> Courts and scholars alike have recognized that the typical consumer does not deal at arms length with the party whose product he buys. Rather, he buys from a retail merchant who is usually little more than an economic conduit. It is not the merchant who has defectively manufactured the product. Nor is it usually the merchant who advertises the product on such a large scale as to attract consumers. We have in our society literally scores of large, financially responsible manufacturers who place their wares in the stream of commerce not only with the realization but with the avowed purpose, that these goods will find their way into the hands of the consumer. Only the consumer will use these products; and only the consumer will be injured by them should they prove defective.

The policy considerations which dictate the abolition of privity are largely those which also warranted imposing strict tort liability on the manufacturer: the consumer's inability to protect himself adequately from defectively manufactured goods, the implied assurance of the maker when he puts his goods on the market that they are safe, and the superior risk bearing ability of the manufacturer. In addition, limiting a consumer under the Code to an implied warranty action against his immediate

---

[31]   Kassab v. Central Soya, 432 Pa. 217, 246 A.2d 848, 853 (1968) (footnote omitted).

seller in those instances when the product defect is attributable to the manufacturer would effectively promote circularity of litigation and waste of judicial resources. Therefore, we decide that a manufacturer may be held liable for a breach of the implied warranties of AS 45.05.096 [2–314] and AS 45.05.098 [2–315] without regard to privity of contract between the manufacturer and the consumer.

The more difficult question before this court is whether we should extend this abolition of privity to embrace not only warranty actions for personal injuries and property damage but also those for economic loss. Contemporary courts have been more reticent to discard the privity requirement and to permit recovery in warranty by a remote consumer for purely economic losses. In considering this issue we note that economic loss may be categorized into direct economic loss and consequential economic loss, a distinction maintained in the Code's structure of damage remedies. One commentator has summarized the distinction:

> Direct economic loss may be said to encompass damage based on insufficient product value; thus, direct economic loss may be 'out of pocket'—the difference in value between what is given and received—or 'loss of bargain'—the difference between the value of what is received and its value as represented. Direct economic loss also may be measured by costs of replacement and repair. Consequential economic loss includes all indirect loss, such as loss of profits resulting from inability to make use of the defective product.*

The claim of the Morrows in this case is one for direct economic loss.

A number of courts recently confronting this issue have declined to overturn the privity requirement in warranty actions for economic loss. One principal factor seems to be that these courts simply do not find the social and economic reasons which justify extending enterprise liability to the victims of personal injury or property damage equally compelling in the case of a disappointed buyer suffering "only" economic loss.[37] There is an apparent fear that economic losses may be of a far greater magnitude in value than personal injuries, and being somehow less

---

* Note, Economic Loss in Products Liability Jurisprudence, 66 Colum. L. Rev. 917, 918 (1966).—Eds.

[37] See, e.g., State ex rel. Western Seed Prod. Corp. v. Campbell, 250 Or. 262, 442 P.2d 215 (1968) and Price v. Gatlin, 241 Or. 315, 405 P.2d 502 (1965). In the latter case Justice Holman tried to elucidate the distinction in a concurring opinion at 504:

> In establishing liability in personal injury cases courts have been motivated to overlook any necessity for privity because the hazard to life and health is usually a personal disaster of major proportions to the individual both physically and financially and something of minor importance to the manufacturer or wholesaler against which they can protect themselves by a distribution of risk through the price of the article sold. There has not been the same social necessity to motivate the recovery for strict economic losses where the damaged person's health, and therefore his basic earning capacity, has remained unimpaired.

foreseeable these losses would be less insurable, undermining the risk spreading theory of enterprise liability.

Several of the courts which have recently considered this aspect of the privity issue have found those arguments unpersuasive. We are in agreement and hold that there is no satisfactory justification for a remedial scheme which extends the warranty action to a consumer suffering personal injury or property damage but denies similar relief to the consumer "fortunate" enough to suffer only direct economic loss. Justice Peters' separate opinion in Seely v. White Motor Co., 63 Cal.2d 9, 45 Cal.Rptr. 17, 24, 403 P.2d 145, 152 (1965), persuasively establishes that the cleavage between economic loss and other types of harm is a false one, that each species of harm can constitute the "overwhelming misfortune" in one's life which warrants judicial redress. The Supreme Court of New Jersey is also in complete agreement with this view:

> From the standpoint of principle, we perceive no sound reason why the implication of reasonable fitness should be attached to the transaction and be actionable against the manufacturer where the defectively made product has caused personal injury and not actionable when inadequate manufacture has put a worthless article in the hands of an innocent purchaser who has paid the required price for it. In such situations considerations of justice require a court to interest itself in originating causes and to apply the principle of implied warranty on that basis, rather than to test its application by whether personal injury or simply loss of bargain resulted in the breach of the warranty. True, the rule of implied warranty had its gestative stirrings because of the greater appeal of the personal injury claim. But, once in existence, the field of operation of the remedy should not be fenced in by such a factor.[40]

The fear that if the implied warranty action is extended to direct economic loss, manufacturers will be subjected to liability for damages of unknown and unlimited scope would seem unfounded. The manufacturer may possibly delimit the scope of his potential liability by use of a disclaimer in compliance with AS 45.05.100 [2–316] or by resort to the limitations authorized in AS 45.05.230 [2–719]. These statutory rights not only preclude extending the theory of strict liability in tort, supra, but also make highly appropriate this extension of the theory of implied warranties. Further, by expanding warranty rights to redress this form of harm, we preserve " * * * the well developed notion that the law of contract should control actions for purely economic losses and that the law of tort should control actions for personal injuries."[41] We therefore hold that a manufacturer can be held liable for direct economic loss attributable to a breach of his implied warranties, without regard to

---

[40] Santor v. A. & M. Karagheusian, Inc., 44 N.J. 52, 60, 207 A.2d 305, 309 (1965).

[41] Comment, The Vexing Problem of Purely Economic Loss in Products Liability: An Injury in Search of a Remedy, 4 Seton Hall L.Rev. 145, 175 (1972).

privity of contract between the manufacturer and the ultimate purchaser.[42] It was therefore error for the trial court to dismiss the Morrows' action against New Moon for want of privity.

Our decision today preserves the statutory rights of the manufacturer to define his potential liability to the ultimate consumer, by means of express disclaimers and limitations, while protecting the legitimate expectation of the consumer that goods distributed on a wide scale by the use of conduit retailers are fit for their intended use. The manufacturer's rights are not, of course, unfettered. Disclaimers and limitations must comport with the relevant statutory prerequisites and cannot be so oppressive as to be unconscionable within the meaning of AS 45.05.072 [2–302]. On the other hand, under the Code the consumer has a number of responsibilities if he is to enjoy the right of action we recognize today, not the least of which is that he must give notice of the breach of warranty to the manufacturer pursuant to AS 45.05.174(c)(1) [2–607(3)(a)]. The warranty action brought under the Code must be brought within the statute of limitations period prescribed in AS 45.05.242 [2–725]. If the action is for breach of the implied warranty of fitness for particular purpose, created by AS 45.05.098 [2–315], the consumer must establish that the warrantor had reason to know the particular purpose for which the goods were required and that the consumer relied on the seller's skill or judgment to select or furnish suitable goods. In the case of litigation against a remote manufacturer, it would appear that often it will be quite difficult to establish this element of actual or constructive knowledge essential to this particular warranty.

. . .

Reversed and remanded for a new trial in accordance with this opinion.

QUESTIONS AND NOTES

1.   *Tex Enterprises* and *New Moon* reach different conclusions with respect to a seller's liability for economic loss for breach of implied warranty to a person not in privity of contract with the seller. What reason does each court give for its conclusion? Which opinion to you find more persuasive? Are the cases distinguishable?

2.   In *New Moon* the court holds that a buyer not in vertical privity with a remote seller may recover for direct loss caused by the remote seller's breach of implied warranty. Would the court permit recovery for consequential loss caused by a remote seller's breach of implied warranty, for example, if

---

[42]   We recognize that the arguments against the abolition of privity are more compelling when the injury alleged is damages of a consequential nature many times the value of the manufacturer's product. See, e.g., Note, Economic Loss in Products Liability Jurisprudence, 66 Colum.L.Rev. 917, 965–66 (1966). We do not speak today to the issue of consequential economic loss, other than to note that AS 45.05.222 [2–715] governs the recovery of such damages and requires, among other things, that said damages must have been foreseeable by the manufacturer.

plaintiffs had moved into an apartment while the mobile home was being repaired?

3. At least 12 states (Hawaii, Iowa, Maine, Massachusetts, Minnesota, New Hampshire, North Dakota, Rhode Island, South Dakota, South Carolina, Utah, and Virginia) have adopted Alternative C of 2–318 or similar statutory language that specifically extends sellers' warranty liability to remote buyers. Alternative C seems literally to cover both vertical and horizontal privity and there is no limitation to personal injury or property damage. The Supreme Judicial Court of Massachusetts has held, however, that the statute was intended to apply only to actions that are in essence products liability actions. Bay State-Spray & Provincetown S.S., Inc. v. Caterpillar Tractor Co., 404 Mass. 103, 533 N.E.2d 1350 (1989). On the other hand, courts in Minnesota and South Dakota have held that Alternative C permits remote buyers to recover for purely economic loss. Nelson v. International Harvester Corp., 394 N.W.2d 578 (Minn.App.1986); Cundy v. International Trencher Service, Inc., 358 N.W.2d 233 (S.D.1984).

4.   Hybrid transactions. If a transaction is predominantly for services, may the ultimate user of an item supplied during the course of those services successfully assert warranty claims against a remote seller of the item? Assume Walt owns a very old house in which the electrical wiring does not comply with the current building code. Walt engages Bender Electric to rewire his house, replacing the existing wiring with code-compliant wiring, converting his outlets to grounded outlets, and adding a new light fixture in his basement so that it is not so dark. Bender acquires the materials, including the light fixture, from Wisdom Electrical Supplies Co. If the new fixture is defective, may Walt recover from Bender Electric for breach of express or implied warranty? from Wisdom Electrical Supplies? from Regency, the manufacturer of the fixture?

5.   Statutory modifications of the Article 2 privity rules. A number of states have adopted statutes that protect intermediate sellers in the distributive chain from actions for personal injury, death, or property damage that result from defective products or from failure to properly warn of the dangers of products. These statutes usually protect only sellers who had no reasonable opportunity to examine the product, as would be the case with goods that are intended to be delivered to buyers in the original package. And they protect sellers only if the manufacturer is subject to the jurisdiction of courts of the state and is not insolvent. E.g., N.C.Gen.Stat. ch. 99B. The statutes typically also permit buyers to sue manufacturers directly for personal injury, death, or property damage caused by a breach of warranty.

6. Notwithstanding the argument by several authors that Article 2's warranty provisions preempt the field and should prevent courts from adopting common-law theories of strict tort liability for personal injuries, courts have embraced strict tort liability, which largely provides a remedy parallel to warranty liability. In Delaware, however, the Supreme Court concluded that adoption of the Code precludes the application of strict tort liability to sales transactions, even for personal injuries. Cline v. Prowler

Industries of Maryland, Inc., 418 A.2d 968 (Del.1980). Other courts have not followed Delaware's lead.

The Restatement (Third) of Torts extends the strict-liability rules only to personal injury and damage to property other than the defective product. Therefore, the Restatement does not authorize recovery in tort of purely economic loss. The courts agree.

7.   Leases. For ordinary leases, Article 2A pretty much tracks Article 2. But for finance leases, 2A–209 explicitly gives the lessee a direct cause of action against the supplier of the goods. The "supplier" is the person from whom the lessor buys the goods (2A–103(x)). In *All-States Leasing v. Bass*, page 301 supra, the court held that the lessee had no claim against the lessor for breach of the implied warranty of merchantability. Under Article 2A, would the lessee have a claim against Auto Laundry Mfg. Co., the supplier?

————

3.   DISCLAIMERS

Patty Precision Products Co. v. Brown & Sharpe Manufacturing Co.

United States Court of Appeals, Tenth Circuit, 1988.
846 F.2d 1247.

■ BARRETT, SENIOR CIRCUIT JUDGE. . . .

During April, 1974, Patty Precision was awarded a contract by the United States for the manufacture of bomb racks. Subsequently, Patty Precision contacted appellee (Brown & Sharpe) relative to the purchase of a vertical hydrotape machining center capable of producing the side plates for the bomb racks. Following its meeting with Brown & Sharpe, Patty Precision purchased from Marsuco, Inc., a Brown & Sharpe hydrotape vertical machining center equipped with a General Electric "G.E. 550 Mark Century Numerical Control."

. . .

It is uncontested that during Patty Precision's initial meeting with Brown & Sharpe that a Brown & Sharpe employee specifically recommended General Electric controls, that the employee stated that Brown & Sharpe had bought over 700 controls from General Electric, and that they had a lot of confidence in the General Electric controls. It is also uncontested that after Patty Precision had ordered the machines, but prior to their delivery, that Brown & Sharpe notified General Electric of the scheduled shipment of each machine including the serial number of each General Electric control being shipped to Patty Precision, that after the machines were shipped to Patty Precision's plant General Electric employees participated in the installation and start up of each machine, and that because of the volume of controls that General Electric supplied to Brown & Sharpe, General Electric "had a service engineer basically full time at Brown & Sharpe whose job was to assist in the start up of machines and provide any feedback" from customers.

From the outset, the three machines failed to perform in accordance with Patty Precision's expectations:

"In fact, because the machines needed almost constant repairs, defendants voluntarily extended the warranty period on the machines until June, 1977. Despite the alleged poor performance of the machines, plaintiff continued to use them to meet the deadlines of a government contract. After the warranties expired in June, 1977, plaintiff attempted to resolve its grievances by meeting with defendants in November, 1977. Those attempts were unsuccessful and plaintiff filed this diversity suit in May, 1978, more than three years after the purchase of the first machine."

Patty Precision v. Brown & Sharpe Mfg. Co., et al., 742 F.2d 1260, 1262 (10th Cir.1984) (*Patty Precision I*).

[Patty Precision sued Brown & Sharpe and General Electric for, among other things, breach of the implied warranty of merchantability. The trial court gave judgment on the verdicts for Patty Precision against Brown & Sharpe and against Patty Precision on its claim against General Electric. Patty Precision filed a motion for a new trial, alleging that the court had improperly excluded evidence and erroneously instructed the jury. The trial court denied this motion, and Patty Precision appealed.]

During the trial, General Electric was allowed, over Patty Precision's relevancy objection, to present evidence regarding the warranty between Brown & Sharpe and General Electric covering the General Electric numerical controls utilized in Machines No. 1, No. 2 and No. 3. A General Electric employee testified that General Electric's warranty on the controls extended only to Brown & Sharpe and that General Electric's "warranty policy has always excluded all consequential damages and has limited it to parts and repairs or replacement only." The employee also testified that, to his knowledge, there was never "any written document expressing a warranty given by the General Electric Company to the end user in this case, Patty Precision Products Company."

. . .

Patty Precision contends that the district court erred in permitting evidence of and instructing on any disclaimer from General Electric to Brown & Sharpe. We agree. Patty Precision argues that General Electric's disclaimer, as set forth in its Statement of Warranty (Appendix A herein), was disclosed only to Brown & Sharpe and could not, as a matter of law, be considered effective against Patty Precision. . . .

In response, General Electric argues that its disclaimer to Brown & Sharpe was effective as to Patty Precision as a subsequent purchaser and a valid defense as a matter of law. . . .

The parties agree that the dispositive issue is whether General Electric's disclaimer applies to Patty Precision. The disclaimer, according to General Electric's evidence, extended only to Brown & Sharpe. Patty Precision was not informed of the disclaimer prior to its purchases of the three machines, and the disclaimer was never expressed to Patty Precision in writing. The issue thus is whether the disclaimer of warranties can nonetheless be binding on Patty Precision and admissible herein. Based on our review of applicable Oklahoma law, we hold that General Electric's disclaimer to Brown & Sharpe was not binding on Patty Precision, that the disclaimer was irrelevant, and that the district court erred in admitting it in evidence and instructing on it.

. . .

The implied warranty of merchantability has been referred to as the most important warranty in the UCC. See White & Summers, [Handbook of the Law under the Uniform Commercial Code, 2d Edition], § 9–6, p. 343 (1984). One of the prime goals of the Code was to do away with the requirement of privity of contract consistent with "402A of the Restatement which abolishes the privity requirement only in cases of property damage and personal injury." Id. at 407. In our view, the broad-sweeping language used by the Supreme Court of Oklahoma in Old Albany Estates v. Highland Carpet Mills, [604 P.2d 849 (Okla.1979)], reiterated and enlarged upon in Elden v. Simmons, [631 P.2d 739 (Okla.1981)], rejected the majority view that a "vertical" non-privity plaintiff, i.e., one who buys within the distributive chain but who does not buy directly from the defendant, cannot maintain an action for breach of implied warranty. In both *Old Albany* and *Elden v. Simmons*, the claimed economic losses were alleged to have resulted from a builder-vendor's breach of implied warranty of habitability and construction in a workmanlike manner.

. . .

Thus, an ultimate consumer in the distribution chain in Oklahoma can bring a direct breach of warranty action against a manufacturer, notwithstanding his lack of privity. Since there is an implied warranty of merchantability under Sec. 2–314 and fitness for particular use under Sec. 2–315 unless excluded in accordance with Sec. 2–316, we hold that General Electric's disclaimer to Brown & Sharpe, undisclosed to Patty Precision, was irrelevant and that the district court erred in admitting it into evidence and instructing on it. General Electric's evidence showed that the disclaimer extended only to Brown & Sharpe and that it was never expressed in writing to Patty Precision. Patty Precision also presented evidence that the disclaimer was not related or disclosed to it prior to its purchase of the machines.

Furthermore, General Electric was fully aware of the use to be made of the numerical controls it sold to Brown & Sharpe, which were, in turn, sold to Patty Precision as part of the machines. General Electric employees participated in the installation and start up of the machines at Patty Precision's plant. There is nothing in the record indicating that the numerical controls sold by General Electric were specially designed. Thus, the fact that they were components of a machining center used by Patty Precision does not distinguish them from any other "goods" insofar as implied warranty of merchantability is concerned. The record demonstrates that General Electric knew of the intended use of the machines by Patty Precision and the system for which the component was to be an integral part. Under these circumstances, the implied warranty of merchantability under Sec. 2–314 applied and it was not "excluded or modified" by a conspicuous writing under Sec. 2–316. We hold that district court erred in admitting evidence of and instructing on General Electric's Statement of Warranty.

. . .

Reversed and remanded for a new trial.

QUESTIONS AND NOTES

1. How do you think the Alaska court that decided *Morrow v. New Moon* would have decided *Patty Precision*?

2. After the decision in *Patty Precision*, Oklahoma amended its version of 2–318 (Alternative A) by adding two paragraphs partially excerpted below:

(2) This section does not displace principles of law and equity that extend a warranty to or for the benefit of a buyer to other persons.

(3) . . . [A]n exclusion, modification, or limitation of the warranty, including any with respect to rights and remedies, effective against the buyer is also effective against any beneficiary designated under this section.

Presumably, paragraph 3 was intended to overrule the result in *Patty Precision*. What do you think about the policy issue? Should sellers be obligated to see that their purchasers pass along to their customers any limitations on warranties imposed by the first seller?

3. If a record packaged with goods is not read or called to the attention of the remote purchaser until after the purchase, are disclaimers of the implied warranty of merchantability or of fitness for particular purpose which appear in the record nevertheless binding on the remote purchaser? Would the disclaimer be effective if the immediate seller directs the remote purchaser to read the record before purchase even though the purchaser does not comply with the request? Would the disclaimer be effective if the remote purchaser asserts rights under the statements in the record which create express obligations?

4. The courts are split on the question whether warranty disclaimers that are effective against the immediate buyer are also effective against remote buyers. E.g., Wenner Petroleum Corp. v. Mitsui & Co. (U.S.A.), Inc., 748 P.2d 356 (Colo.App.1987) (yes); Hoffman v. Daimler Trucks North America, LLC, 940 F.Supp.2d 347 (W.D.Va.2013) (Virginia law) (yes); Spagnol Enterprises v. Digital Equipment Corp., 390 Pa.Super. 372, 568 A.2d 948 (1989) (no);

Patty Precision (no). Would a requirement that any warranty disputes be subject to arbitration bind a remote buyer who is entitled to the benefit of the warranty but does not know of the arbitration clause? See Recold, S.A. de C.V. v. Monfort of Colorado, Inc., 893 F.2d 195 (8th Cir.1990) (no, applying Colorado law).

The doctrine of unconscionability operates as a limit on the enforceability of a disclaimer of implied warranties. *A & M Produce*, page 140 supra. If a disclaimer is unconscionable and therefore ineffective against an immediate purchaser, presumably it also is ineffective against a remote purchaser. But how about the converse: if a disclaimer is effective against the immediate purchaser, can it be unconscionable with respect to a remote purchaser?

5. In *Morrow v. New Moon* suppose Golden Heart (the immediate seller) had discovered substantial defects in the trailer when it was delivered and New Moon (the manufacturer) settled Golden Heart's warranty claim by deducting $6,000 from the price. How would that affect the right of the plaintiffs to recover from New Moon?

Or, suppose that New Moon had sold the mobile home to Golden Heart as "factory defective" at a discount of 50% off the ordinary price. How should that affect the manufacturer's liability to the Morrows?

4. IS PRIVITY ENOUGH?

The foregoing materials address the question whether the supplier of goods is liable in the absence of privity with the ultimate user of the goods. Another question concerns the liability of an entity that facilitates the sale and purchase of goods but is not directly in the chain of distribution of those goods. This inquiry encompasses the liability of electronic platforms that facilitate transactions between remote sellers and buyers but which do not ever have title to the goods that are the subject of those transactions. The prime example is Amazon. In an opinion not addressing warranty liability, a federal court provided this description:

> [Amazon's] website is an online marketplace where Amazon retails its own products as well as those of more than one million third-party vendors. These third-party vendors decide which products to sell, the means of shipping, and product pricing. For its part, Amazon lists the products on the Amazon Marketplace, collects order information from consumers, and processes payments. In exchange for these services, Amazon collects fees from each third-party vendor.
>
> In order to use Amazon's services, a third-party vendor must assent to Amazon's Services Business Solutions Agreement. This Agreement governs every step of the sales process.
>
> Once a third-party vendor has assented to the Agreement, the vendor chooses which product or products it would like to

sell using Amazon's website. This choice is, with some notable exceptions, left to the discretion of the vendor. Among the exceptions are products that Amazon determines are illegal, sexually explicit, defamatory, or obscene.

When the third-party vendor has chosen a product that it wants to offer on Amazon's website, the vendor provides Amazon with a description of the product, including its brand, model, dimensions, and weight. Pursuant to the Agreement, the vendor must also provide Amazon with digital images of the product, as well as other information such as shipping and handling options, product availability, in-stock status, and any other information reasonably requested by Amazon.

Based on this information, Amazon formats the product's listing on its website. This function, too, is provided for in the Agreement, by which Amazon retains the right in its sole discretion to determine the content, appearance, design, functionality, and all other aspects of the Services, including by redesigning, modifying, removing, or restricting access to any of them. In fact, the Agreement grants Amazon a royalty-free, non-exclusive, worldwide, perpetual, irrevocable right and license to commercially or non-commercially exploit in any manner, the information provided by third-party vendors.

The third-party vendor can then choose which, if any, of Amazon's other services it will use in conjunction with listing its product on Amazon's website. For example, Amazon offers "Amazon Clicks," an advertising service in which Amazon highlights and promotes the vendor's product to customers. Amazon also offers a "Fulfillment by Amazon" service, in which it takes physical possession of third-party vendors' products and ships those products to consumers. Otherwise, the vendor itself is responsible for shipping products directly to consumers.

The listed price for the product is chosen by the third-party vendor, subject to one exception: Vendors may not charge more on Amazon than they charge in other sales channels. Nor, according to the Agreement, may third-party vendors offer inferior customer service or provide lower quality information about products than in other sales channels. To the extent that third-party vendors need to communicate with customers regarding their orders on Amazon, they must do so through the Amazon platform.

With these preliminaries completed, Amazon lists the product online and sales begin. As customers make purchases on Amazon's website, Amazon collects payment and delivers order information to the third-party vendor. At checkout, the customer can choose any shipping method offered by the third-party vendor, and any promises made by the vendor with respect to shipping date must be met. Amazon ensures compliance with this obligation by requiring the vendor to send Amazon shipping information for each order. In addition, vendors have a powerful interest in providing quality products and ensuring timely delivery, as Amazon allows shoppers to publicly rate the vendors and their products.

In exchange for its role in the transaction, Amazon collects two types of fees: one is a commission, typically between seven and fifteen percent of the overall sales price; the other is either a per-item or monthly fee, depending on the third-party vendor's preference. At least once every two weeks, Amazon remits all sales proceeds, minus fees, to the vendor. Pursuant to the Agreement, Amazon is classified as the third-party vendor's "agent for purposes of processing payments, refunds, and adjustments . . . receiving and holding Sales Proceeds on your behalf, remitting Sales Proceeds to Your Bank Account, charging your Credit Card, and paying Amazon and its Affiliates amounts you owe . . . ."

Throughout each step of the sales process, Amazon may at any time cease providing any or all of the Services at its sole discretion and without notice, including suspending, prohibiting, or removing any listing. Amazon also retains other important privileges. For example, Amazon can require vendors to stop or cancel orders of any product. If Amazon determines that a vendor's actions or performance may result in risks to Amazon or third parties, it may in its sole discretion withhold any payments to the vendor. Furthermore, Amazon requires that its vendors release it and agree to indemnify, defend, and hold it harmless against any claim, loss, damage, settlement, cost, expense, or other liability.

Oberdorf v. Amazon.com Inc., 930 F.3d 136, 140–42 (3rd Cir.2019) (opinion vacated and rehearing en banc granted).

Many of the vendors who use the Amazon platform are located outside the United States and have no facilities or representatives here. There may not be any way for the buyer to communicate with them or, if need be, serve them with process initiating litigation. If a consumer purchases an item on the Amazon website and item is defective, may the consumer assert a breach-of-warranty claim against Amazon?

———

Erie Insurance Co. v. Amazon.com, Inc.

Unites States Court of Appeals, Fourth Circuit, 2019.
925 F.3d 135.

■ NIEMEYER, CIRCUIT JUDGE.

. . .

I

On April 9, 2014, Trung Cao, a resident of Montgomery County, Maryland, purchased online an LED headlamp—"for cycling, camping, [and] hiking"—and gave it as a gift to his friends, Minh and Anh Nguyen, who lived in Burtonsville, also in Montgomery County. Two weeks later, the headlamp malfunctioned, supposedly from a defective battery or batteries, igniting the Nguyens' house and causing $313,166.57 in damages. Erie Insurance Company, the Nguyens' insurer, paid the loss.

Cao purchased the headlamp on Amazon's website, and the document evidencing the transaction stated that the headlamp was "sold by: Dream Light"—and "Fulfilled by: Amazon." There can be no dispute that this information was displayed to Cao on the website when he purchased the headlamp. The headlamp was paid for by credit card and delivered to Cao on April 11, 2014, by UPS Ground.

The arrangement between Dream Light and Amazon was governed by Amazon's comprehensive "Amazon Services Business Solutions Agreement" and included "fulfillment" services offered by Amazon. Under the fulfillment program, Amazon provided logistics services for a fee. The seller could ship its inventory to an Amazon warehouse for storage and, once an order was received online for a product, Amazon would retrieve the product from inventory, box it, and ship it to the purchaser. In this case, Dream Light shipped its headlamps to Amazon's warehouse in Virginia, and, when Cao's order for one came in, Amazon packaged and shipped it to Cao using the third-party shipper, UPS Ground. As part of its fulfillment services, Amazon also collected payment and, after withdrawing its service fee, remitted the balance to Dream Light. Dream Light set the price for the headlamp and created the content of the product's description used on the Amazon site. While Dream Light was also allowed under the program to "offer any warranty," apparently no explicit warranty information was provided in this case.

After paying the fire loss, Erie Insurance Company, as subrogee, commenced this action against Amazon, asserting [claims for negligence, breach of warranty, and strict liability in tort] based on its allegation that Amazon was the "seller" of the headlamp and therefore had the liability attributable to sellers of defective goods under Maryland law.

On Amazon's motion, the district court granted summary judgment to Amazon, concluding that Amazon was not the "seller" and therefore was not liable to Erie. . . .

III

On the merits, Erie contends that Amazon, like a brick-and-mortar store such as Home Depot, is a seller of products and therefore is liable under Maryland law for the defective products that it sells. While it acknowledges that the document evidencing the transaction in this case indicated that Dream Light was the seller, it argues that Amazon, through its fulfillment services program, took so much control over the transaction that it effectively became the seller and therefore became responsible under theories of negligence, breach of warranty, and strict liability in tort. As Erie states, Amazon controls "significant aspects of th[e] transaction," "put[ting] [it] in the position of a seller. It doesn't make [Amazon] any different than if you go to a Home Depot and . . . bought the same product from a Home Depot." The reality, it argues, was that Dream Light's role in the sale was "passive," while "Amazon was the actor, the controlling party." In support of this position, Erie notes:

> The purchaser ordered from Amazon, using Amazon's website. The purchaser paid Amazon directly. Amazon packaged the product, in Amazon's warehouse, delivered it to the carrier, assumed the risk of credit card fraud, received payment, collected Amazon's fee, and presumably forwarded any remaining balance to Dream Light. The purchaser never had direct contact—or, really, privity of any sort—with Dream Light. The contract was between him and Amazon, not between him and Dream Light.

Erie thus reasons, "The purchaser, of course, reasonably assumed that title passed directly from Amazon to him, inasmuch as all of his dealings were with Amazon."

As both parties observe, products liability under Maryland law, whether asserted under theories of negligence, breach of warranty, or strict liability in tort, is imposed on sellers and manufacturers (a manufacturer also being a seller). As Maryland courts have explained, "Irrespective of whether the theory of recovery is breach of warranty, negligence or strict liability, a plaintiff must show three product litigation basics—defect, *attribution of defect to seller*, and a causal relationship between the defect and the injury." Laing v. Volkswagen of Am., Inc., 180 Md.App. 136, 949 A.2d 26, 39 (Md. Ct. Spec. App. 2008) (emphasis added) (cleaned up). . . . The defect must be shown to exist at the time the product left the seller (whether manufacturer, distributor, or retailer) or at the time the sale was made. But in each case Maryland law imposes liability *on the seller. See, e.g.,* Md. Code, Com. Law § 2–314 (providing that a warranty that goods are merchantable is implied "in a contract for their *sale*" and providing that the "seller" includes "the manufacturer, distributor, dealer, wholesaler or other middleman or the retailer" (emphasis added)); *id.* § 2–315 (providing that the implied warranty of fitness for particular purpose is enforced against the "seller" of the goods). . . .

We also find no indication that the term "seller," as used in Maryland's products liability law, should be understood in any manner other than its ordinary meaning. And the ordinary meaning of "seller" is "one that offers [property] for sale," with "sale" defined as "the transfer of ownership of and the title to property from one person to another for a price." Merriam-Webster's Collegiate Dictionary 1129, 1097 (11th ed. 2007). Indeed, the Maryland Uniform Commercial Code adopts this definition precisely. *See* Md. Code, Com. Law § 2–103(1)(d) (defining a seller as "a person who sells or contracts to sell goods"); *id.* § 2–106 (defining a "sale" as "the passing of title from the seller to the buyer for a price").

We thus conclude that insofar as liability in Maryland for defective products falls on "sellers" and manufacturers (who are also sellers), it is imposed on owners of personal property who transfer title to purchasers of that property for a price. In this sense, a manufacturer, distributor, dealer, and retailer who own—*i.e.*, have title to—the products during the chain of distribution are sellers, whereas shippers, warehousemen, brokers, marketers, auctioneers, and other bailees or consignees, who do not take title to property during the course of a distribution but rather render services to facilitate that distribution or sale, are not sellers. *See, e.g.*, Musser v. Vilsmeier Auction Co., 522 Pa. 367, 562 A.2d 279, 283 (1989) (holding that auctioneers are not "sellers"). Consistent with this distinction, various courts have held that Amazon was not a seller under similar circumstances. . . .

In this case, no one has presented evidence to dispute that when Dream Light shipped its headlamp to Amazon's warehouse in Virginia, it was the owner of—*i.e.*, it had title to—the headlamp. And when it transferred possession of the headlamp to Amazon, without Amazon's payment of the headlamp's price or an agreement transferring title to it, Amazon did not, by that simple transfer, receive title. Moreover, after Amazon received the headlamp at its warehouse, there was no action or agreement that amounted to the consummation of a sale of the headlamp by Dream Light to Amazon. Indeed, even as Amazon possessed the headlamp in its warehouse, Dream Light set the price for the sale of the product to purchasers, designed the product description for the website, paid Amazon for its fulfillment services, and ultimately received the purchase price paid by the purchaser. In these circumstances, as Amazon explicitly posted on its site, Dream Light was the seller.

Moreover, the agreement between Dream Light and Amazon governing their relationship confirms this, as it repeatedly specifies and contemplates that Dream Light, not Amazon, retained title to the goods it stored in Amazon's warehouses as part of the fulfillment program. *See* . . . Md. Code, Com. Law § 2–401(1) ("[T]itle to goods passes from the seller to the buyer in any manner and on any conditions explicitly agreed on by the parties"). For example, under the agreement, if Dream Light were to request that Amazon dispose of the headlamps that it stored in

Amazon's warehouse, then, upon receipt of Dream Light's request, "title to each disposed unit [would] transfer to [Amazon]." Of course, this indicates that title otherwise remained with Dream Light.

. . .

While Amazon does in fact sell products that it owns on its website and thus would be considered a seller of *those* products, in this case it facilitated the sale for Dream Light under its fulfillment program. We thus conclude that Dream Light was the seller, as Cao was so informed on the site, and there is no evidence to indicate that title passed other than from Dream Light to Cao. Although Amazon's services were extensive in facilitating the sale, they are no more meaningful to the analysis than are the services provided by UPS Ground, which delivered the headlamp to Cao. Neither Amazon nor UPS Ground was a seller incurring liability for the defective product.

. . .

At bottom, we conclude that Amazon was not, in this particular transaction, a seller—one who transfers ownership of property for a price—and therefore does not have the liability under Maryland law that sellers of goods have. To be sure, when Amazon sells its own goods on its website, it has the responsibility of a "seller," just as any other retailer, such as Home Depot, would have. But when it provides a website for use by other sellers of products and facilitates those sales under its fulfillment program, it is not a seller, and it does not have the liability of a seller. . . .

■ DIANA GRIBBON MOTZ, CIRCUIT JUDGE, concurring:

I concur fully in the court's opinion rejecting Erie's claims that Amazon is a "seller" under Maryland law. I write separately to emphasize why this may not always be so.

Although at the moment, Maryland law supports the result we reach, much of the State's product liability law was adopted at a time when the American economy operated much differently than it does now. In a traditional supply chain, manufacturers transfer new goods to consumers through multiple links, with each link in the chain—from manufacturer to distributor to retailer—taking title to, and possession of, the product. Because seller liability extends to manufacturers, distributors, and retailers alike, the consumer at the end of this supply chain almost always has some legal recourse in the event of an injury, for some entity in this linear supply chain is clearly a "seller" and available for service of process within the United States.

But Amazon disrupts the traditional supply chain. By design, Amazon's business model cuts out the middlemen between manufacturers and consumers, reducing the friction that might keep foreign (or otherwise judgment-proof) manufacturers from putting dangerous products on the market. Today, Amazon makes up at least 46 percent of the online retail marketplace, selling more than its next twelve online competitors combined. Lina M. Khan, Note, *Amazon's Antitrust Paradox*, 126 Yale L.J. 710, 712–13 (2017). Yet Amazon's business model shields it from traditional products liability whenever state law strictly requires the exchange of title for seller liability to attach, in many cases forcing consumers to bear the cost of injuries caused by defective products (particularly where the formal "seller" of a product fails even to provide a domestic address for service of process).

Indeed, Amazon played an outsized role in the transaction at issue in this case. Trung Cao, the purchaser of the allegedly defective headlamp, ordered the product from Amazon's website and paid Amazon directly. Amazon took physical possession of the product, warehoused it, packaged it, and delivered it to the carrier. Amazon even assumed the risk of credit card fraud, received payment, and remitted a portion of that payment to the manufacturer. Nearly the only thing Amazon did not do was hold title.

I agree that, under Maryland law as it stands today, that final fact—which is surely no accident—resolves this case in Amazon's favor. But that may not always be so. Indeed, Maryland's highest court has repeatedly emphasized that considerations of public policy may justify a change in the common law when, "in light of changed conditions or increased knowledge, the former rule has become unsound in the circumstances of modern life." Miles Labs., Inc. Cutter Labs. Div. v. Doe, 315 Md. 704, 556 A.2d 1107, 1117 (1989); *see also* May v. Air & Liquid Sys. Corp., 446 Md. 1, 129 A.3d 984, 989–1000 (2015) (expanding duty to warn in asbestos case based on policy considerations). And the Supreme Court, interpreting federal antitrust law, recently held that consumers purchasing third-party digital applications on a marketplace operated by a major technology corporation nonetheless qualified as "direct purchasers" from that corporation. Apple Inc. v. Pepper, No. 17–204, ___ U.S. ___, 139 S.Ct. 1514, 203 L.Ed.2d 802, 2019 WL 2078087, at *3 (U.S. May 13, 2019).

A federal court sitting in diversity, however, must proceed with caution. Our charge is to take state law as we find it "or, if necessary, predict how the state's highest court would rule on an unsettled issue." Askew v. HRFC, LLC, 810 F.3d 263, 266 (4th Cir. 2016) (internal quotation marks omitted). Given the policy-intensive nature of this inquiry, the lack of on-point Maryland precedent, and Amazon's novel business model, I cannot confidently predict that Maryland courts would treat Amazon as a seller under state law. Nor do I believe it appropriate, in the absence of a request from either party, to certify this question to the Court of Appeals of Maryland on this court's own initiative.

Even so, nothing in today's holding prevents Maryland's own courts or legislators from taking up and resolving these difficult, fast-changing, and cutting-edge issues differently. To be sure, Amazon's strategy of removing nearly every products liability case to federal court has complicated this endeavor and arguably stunted the development of state law. But legislative reforms, non-removable lawsuits, and (in appropriate cases) certification remain available to consumers and state leaders who seek to confront these uniquely modern challenges.

QUESTIONS

1.   Article 2 defines "sale" as the passing of title from the seller to the buyer for a price (2–106)(1)). Since Amazon never held title to the goods, it is clear that there was no sale from Amazon to Cao. Therefore, both plaintiff and the court resort to analogies. Plaintiff analogizes Amazon to Home Depot, and the court analogizes Amazon to UPS. Which analogy is (more) apt?

2.   The concurring judge invites the Maryland Court of Appeals to consider whether an entity in the position of Amazon should be liable in this kind of case. In view of the statutory definitions in Article 2, by what reasoning could the Court hold Amazon liable?

3.   Should Amazon be liable on the facts of Erie Insurance v. Amazon?

C. CAUSATION, CONTRIBUTORY NEGLIGENCE, AND ASSUMPTION OF RISK

1. CAUSATION

For a buyer to recover for breach of warranty, the buyer must prove:

- that there is a warranty with respect to the goods,
- that the seller breached the warranty,
- that the buyer suffered a loss or injury,
- that the breach of warranty is the factual and legal cause of the injury, and
- the amount of the loss.

See 2–314, Official Comment 13. Thus it is not enough for the buyer to establish a warranty and a loss. The buyer also must establish a breach of the warranty, and the mere fact of injury does not establish that the seller breached the warranty. For example, in Heil v. Standard Chemical Manufacturing Co., 301 Minn. 315, 223 N.W.2d 37 (1974), a seller of a cattle-feed supplement made an express warranty that proper use of the product would produce a weight gain of two pounds per day for the cattle in the buyer's herd. When the cattle gained less than half that amount, the buyer sued for breach of express warranty. The trial court gave judgment for the buyer, and defendant appealed. Reversing, the Supreme Court of Minnesota stated:

> It is necessary that the breach has proximately caused the damages complained of by the plaintiff. The burden is upon the buyer to establish the breach. Minn. St. 336.2–607(4). Further:
>
> "In an action based on breach of warranty, it is of course necessary to show not only the existence of the warranty but the

fact that the warranty was broken and that the breach of the warranty was the proximate cause of the loss sustained." U.C.C. Comment 13 on U.C.C. § 2–314 (referring specifically to actions based upon implied warranties).

The defendant-appellant essentially contends that inasmuch as plaintiff failed to introduce evidence that exemplified this causal connection, the jury verdict could have only been based upon pure speculation. . . .

Several courts have indicated the importance of the element of causation. The result of this lack of proof is that an otherwise valid action for a breach of warranty will fail. In an action based upon the failure of a weed killer to perform as warranted, the Idaho Supreme Court stated:

" * * * Even if such a failure occurred, the plaintiffs still had to establish that the resulting weeds proximately caused the loss of their potato crop. * * *

"In an action based on breach of warranty, it is necessary to show that the breach of warranty was the proximate cause of the loss sustained. Where the record shows that there are several possible causes of an injury, for one or more of which the defendant was not responsible, and it is just as reasonable and probable that the injury was the result of the latter, the plaintiff may not recover, since he has failed to prove that the defendant's breach caused the injury." . . . Chisholm v. J.R. Simplot Co., 94 Idaho 628, 631, 495 P.2d 1113, 1116 (1972).

Further, the following result was reached by the Illinois Court of Appeals when it was requested to find that the explosives the defendant quarry operator had purchased from the plaintiff were the cause of the inadequate results obtained by the use of the product:

"On this evidence, we are left to speculate. It could be that the poor results were caused by the powder failing to measure up to an implied warranty of fitness for the purpose intended. It could also be that the poor results were caused by failing to remove the broken rock from the toe and the loading to within five feet of the top. There is even a possibility that the shot holes were improperly drilled or that a difference in the rock formation was the cause.

"We have no evidence in this record that anything was wrong with the explosive except by reasoning backward, i.e., the result was poor; therefore, something must have been wrong with the explosive. In view of the other possibilities this is not enough." Olin Mathieson Chemical

Corp. v. Moushon, 93 Ill.App.2d 280, 282, 235 N.E.2d 263, 264 (1968).

It appears that defendant has made a substantial argument for this court's determination. . . . It is a rather specious argument by plaintiff that the factors of weather, management, animal health, supervision of employees, and feeding procedures were not proven to have caused the failure, for that statement results in acceptance of the theory that since no other factor could have prevented realization of the expectations, the minimal results had to have been the product of the failure of the feed supplement. As shown above, proof of causation cannot be established through negative implication.

. . .

In the case before us, the factual disputes obviously open the door for many inferences to be drawn by a jury. However, the conclusion seems compelling that there was little evidence offered which would tend to allow the jury to conclude that defendant's feed supplement, and not one of the other factors which could adversely affect production of healthy animals, was the causation element. It cannot be doubted that causation should at least have been mentioned by the lower court in its instructions to the jury. Instead the jury instructions were the following: That it was the plaintiff's duty to follow the feeding instructions given by the defendant and to use reasonable skill and diligence in feeding and caring for the cattle; that the defendant would not be liable for any losses which were not the direct result of any failure of the defendant's product, but rather were the result of some failure on the part of the plaintiff to use this care and diligence; that the plaintiff could not recover unless he established by a fair preponderance of the evidence that there existed an express warranty that the feed supplement, if used as directed, would produce a 2-pound-per-day weight gain in the cattle; and finally, that the plaintiff could not recover unless there was a breach of this warranty. It appears that the statement to the jury that defendant's liability depends upon the damage being the direct result of its, and not plaintiff's, failure, is not sufficient without the more definite requirement of an affirmative finding under the special verdict that the breach of warranty proximately caused plaintiff's damages.

Without an affirmative finding by the jury on causation, the conclusion that the entire verdict is based upon speculation is well supported. For this reason, we therefore grant a new trial.

In another case, plaintiff purchased heart worm medication for her dog. The FDA subsequently asked the manufacturer to recall the drug because of adverse side effects suffered by many dogs to which it was administered. Plaintiff's dog suffered no side effects and did not develop heart worm. Nevertheless, plaintiff brought a class action alleging breach of the implied warranty of merchantability. The court acknowledged that the withdrawal of the drug from the market may establish that it was not fit for its ordinary purpose, but the breach of warranty did not cause any loss to plaintiff. Therefore, she was not a suitable representative for a class of plaintiffs whose dogs suffered as a result of the drug's lack of fitness. Rule v. Fort Dodge Animal Health, Inc., 607 F.3d 250 (1st Cir.2010).

On the other hand, the burden is not insuperable, even if the buyer cannot establish the cause of the product's failure to do what it is supposed to do. In Nevada Contract Services, Inc. v. Squirrel Companies, 119 Nev. 157, 68 P.3d 896 (2003), the buyer, NCS, purchased an electronically controlled system for dispensing liquor in its bar. The system was designed to control the quantity and price of servings, provide inventory management, prevent theft, and manage the revenue generated by liquor sales. Shortly after installation, the system failed to do these things, and NCS sued.

Prior to filing its complaint in the district court, NCS made numerous requests that the problems it was experiencing with the liquor-dispensing system be corrected. In response, service technicians from Vega, Squirrel, and BMS evaluated the liquor-dispensing system. Upon inspection, the technicians found a lack of dedicated power; water damage to the EasyBar system caused by a leaking water filter near the EasyBar system's control box; and employee misuse, namely the liquor-dispensing guns were submerged in water for cleaning and one of the pumps had a nail in it. The parties disputed whether these findings could have caused the liquor-dispensing system to malfunction. . . .

Following the inability [of NCS's expert witness] to opine as to the cause of the liquor-dispensing system's malfunction, respondents filed a motion for summary judgment, arguing that NCS could not sustain its causation burden. The district court expressed concern over the fact that NCS's own experts could not opine as to the probable cause of the liquor-dispensing system's malfunction. NCS responded that the experts were attempting to pinpoint the exact cause of the malfunction, not the probable cause, and argued that it did not have to prove the precise cause of the malfunction.

The district court disagreed [and] . . . granted summary judgment in favor of respondents. This appeal followed. . . .

In this appeal, we consider the degree of specificity required to meet the causation burden in a breach of warranty action. In Nelson v. Wilkins Dodge, Inc., [256 N.W.2d 472, 476 (Minn.1977),] the Minnesota Supreme Court observed that in a breach of warranty case, "generally no specific defect need be alleged, and a defective condition can be proved by circumstantial evidence." Likewise, in Hershenson v. Lake Champlain Motors, Inc., [139 Vt. 219, 424 A.2d 1075, 1078 (1981),] the Vermont Supreme Court observed:

"Circumstantial evidence may be resorted to . . . if there can be drawn therefrom a rational inference that [a defect in the defendant's product] was the source of the trouble. There must be created in the minds of the jurors something more, of course, than a possibility, suspicion or surmise, but the requirements of the law are satisfied if the existence of this fact is made the more probable hypothesis, when considered with reference to the possibility of other hypotheses."

We agree with those courts that hold that the specific cause of the malfunction need not be shown. Indeed, we reached a similar conclusion in Stackiewicz v. Nissan Motor Corp., [100 Nev. 443, 450–51, 686 P.2d 925, 929 (1984) (concluding that "evidence of a steering malfunction which resulted in the [plaintiff's] losing control of [her] vehicle might properly be accepted by the trier of fact as sufficient circumstantial proof of a defect . . . without direct proof of the mechanical cause of the malfunction")]. Although *Stackiewicz* is a products liability case, we are adopting a similar causation burden in breach of warranty actions. In *Stackiewicz*, we stated that requiring a plaintiff to prove the specific cause of a product defect or to negate alternative causes in order to establish that a product is defective is far too restrictive. Applying this reasoning, we conclude that it is too burdensome to require a plaintiff to prove precisely why a product does not work in a breach of warranty action, specifically in instances such as the one presented here, where a product integrating electronic and mechanical components is involved. [Cf. Capitol Dodge Sales v. Northern Concrete Pipe, 131 Mich.App. 149, 346 N.W.2d 535, 539 n.11 (1983) (holding that a new car's inoperability establishes its failure to conform to the contract of sale without showing the specific technical cause of the overheating); Eggl v. Letvin Equipment Co., 2001 ND 144, 632 N.W.2d 435, 439 (2001) (holding that evidence that a farm tractor was not fit for the ordinary purposes for which such goods are used was sufficient when it was shown that the tractor could not be used to pull an implement).]

Based on the testimony of the various technicians, we conclude that there was sufficient evidence to support a reasonable inference that respondents breached the warranty and caused NCS's damages. We acknowledge that NCS's experts could not opine as to the precise cause of the liquor-dispensing system's malfunction and that there is evidence of alleged misuse of the liquor-dispensing system that may have contributed to the malfunction; however, such evidence affects the weight of NCS's case. Thus, we conclude that a genuine issue of material fact exists, thereby precluding summary judgment.

We hold that a plaintiff need not show the specific technical cause of a product's malfunction in order to sustain its causation burden in a breach of warranty cause of action. Because NCS produced evidence creating an inference that the newly acquired liquor-dispensing system's problems were not related to misuse and may have resulted from respondents' breach of warranty, we conclude that NCS is entitled to litigate its case before a jury.

———

2. Contributory Negligence and Assumption of Risk

Sellers often defend warranty actions by asserting that even if the goods failed to conform to the warranty, conduct of the buyer caused or contributed to the injury. This is especially true when the breach results in personal injuries. The issues that arise include the applicability of comparative fault statutes, which provide that an injured person is not to be denied recovery merely because of contributory negligence but that the damages should be diminished in proportion to the comparative negligence of the parties. These statutes, which have been adopted in a majority of the states, were enacted to replace common law contributory-negligence rules under which a plaintiff whose own negligence was to any degree a cause of the injury was barred from recovery. The move to comparative fault was, therefore, a liberalizing rule that allowed previously barred plaintiffs to recover.

When applied to warranty actions, however, the effect is very different. Before adoption of the comparative-negligence statutes, most courts had taken the position of the Restatement (Second) of Torts § 402A, comment *n* that in implied-warranty and strict-tort actions, only assumption of the risk—not ordinary negligence—is a defense to a strict-tort (or warranty) action. Therefore, as to strict-tort or warranty actions, use of comparative-fault principles *reduces* plaintiffs' recoveries below what they would have been under prior law.

Hence, courts have differed on their willingness to extend the effect of the statutes to claims not based in negligence. (Recall that negligence is not an element of a breach of warranty.) For example, while acknowledging that an action for breach of implied warranty of merchantability to recover for personal injuries sounds in tort, the Supreme Judicial Court of Massachusetts has stated:

> Simply stated, the policy of negligence liability presumes that people will, or at least should, take reasonable measures to protect themselves and others from harm. This presumption

justifies the imposition of a duty on people to conduct themselves in this way. A person harmed by one whose conduct "falls below the standard established by law for the protection of others against unreasonable risk," Restatement (Second) of Torts § 282 (1965), may recover against the actor. However, if the injured person's unreasonable conduct also has been a cause of his injury, his conduct will be accounted for in apportioning liability or damages.

Strict liability is justified on a much different basis. "On whatever theory, the justification for the strict liability has been said to be that the seller, by marketing his product for use and consumption, has undertaken and assumed a special responsibility toward any member of the consuming public who may be injured by it; that the public has the right to and does expect, in the case of products which it needs and for which it is forced to rely upon the seller, that reputable sellers will stand behind their goods; that public policy demands that the burden of accidental injuries caused by products intended for consumption be placed upon those who market them, and be treated as a cost of production against which liability insurance can be obtained; and that the consumer of such products is entitled to the maximum of protection at the hands of someone, and the proper persons to afford it are those who market the products." Restatement (Second) of Torts § 402A, comment *c* (1965). Recognizing that the seller is in the best position to ensure product safety, the law of strict liability imposes on the seller a duty to prevent the release of "any product in a defective condition unreasonably dangerous to the user or consumer," into the stream of commerce. Restatement (Second) of Torts § 402A(1) (1965). This duty is unknown in the law of negligence and it is not fulfilled even if the seller takes all reasonable measures to make his product safe. The liability issue focuses on whether the product was defective and unreasonably dangerous and not on the conduct of the user or the seller. Given this focus, the only duty imposed on the user is to act reasonably with respect to a product which he knows to be defective and dangerous. When a user unreasonably proceeds to use a product which he knows to be defective and dangerous, he violates that duty and relinquishes the protection of the law. It is only then that it is appropriate to account for his conduct in determining liability. Since he has voluntarily relinquished the law's protection, it is further appropriate that he be barred from recovery. The absolute bar to the user for breach of his duty balances the strict liability placed on the seller. Other than this instance, the parties are not presumed to be equally responsible for injuries caused by defective products, and the principles of contributory or comparative negligence have no part in the strict liability scheme. Given this focus, the user's negligence does not prevent recovery except when he unreasonably uses a product that he knows to be defective and dangerous. In such circumstances, the user's conduct alone is the proximate cause of his injuries, as a matter of law, and recovery is appropriately denied. In short, the user is denied recovery, not because of his contributory negligence or his assumption of the risk but rather because his conduct is the proximate cause of his injuries.

Correia v. Firestone Tire & Rubber Co., 388 Mass. 342, 446 N.E.2d 1033, 1039–40 (1983).

That same year the court next door in Rhode Island disagreed. After citing the applicable statute, which stated that it applied to "*all* actions hereafter brought for personal injuries" (emphasis added), the court noted:

> We think it important to note an unfair and inequitable result that would occur were we to decide differently. If the comparative-negligence statute only applied to negligence actions, a defendant manufacturer found liable in strict liability or implied warranty could not have the damages apportioned because of plaintiff's culpable conduct. Ironically, defendant manufacturers found liable in negligence would have the damages apportioned, despite the fact that their conduct was clearly more culpable than the conduct of those defendants found liable in strict liability or implied warranty. We believe that the just outcome of a case should not be determined by adroit pleading or semantical distinctions. A defendant's culpability is the basis for an award of damages, whether that culpability is denominated negligence, strict liability, or breach of warranty. Similarly, a plaintiff's culpable conduct is the basis for an apportionment of those damages. In the present case there is a finding of fact by the jury in regard to plaintiff's culpability which cannot be dismissed by adverting to semantics.

Fiske v. MacGregor, Div. of Brunswick, 464 A.2d 719, 728 (R.I.1983).

Correia and *Fiske* reveal disagreement as to whether comparative fault ought to be applied in strict tort or warranty actions. What do you think? Does comparative fault undercut the policy behind strict tort and warranty liability? Is it possible to compare plaintiff's negligent conduct with defendant's non-negligence-based strict tort or warranty liability?

If comparative fault is to apply in strict tort or warranty actions, to what conduct of the plaintiff should it apply? In another part of the opinion, *Fiske* suggests that assumption of the risk should still be a complete defense. Do you agree? At the other extreme, should comparative fault mean assumption of the risk, so that other negligent conduct of the plaintiff is no defense at all?

How is comparative fault to be measured in a strict tort or warranty action? Should the comparison be of relative degrees of blameworthiness? Or should the comparison be of relative degrees of causation? or of both? or of neither? Observe that relative degrees of causation might be said to be also dealt with as a part of proximate cause. For a good discussion of the questions just asked, see the opinion of Justice Linde in Sandford v. Chevrolet Division of General Motors, 292 Or. 590, 642 P.2d 624 (1982). See also 2–314, Official Comment 13 (especially the last sentence). And consider the Texas statute:

> The trier of fact shall determine the percentage of responsibility . . . with respect to each person's causing or contributing to cause in any way the harm for which recovery of damages is sought, whether by negligent act or omission, by any defective or unreasonably dangerous product, by other conduct or activity that violates an applicable legal standard, or by any combination of these. . . .

Vernon's Tex. Code Ann., Civ. Prac. & Rem. § 33.003. In JCW Electronics, Inc. v. Garza, 257 S.W.3d 701 (Tex.2008), the court held that this statute applies to actions to recover for personal injuries, whether based on negligence, strict liability in tort, or breach of the implied warranty of merchantability.

D. FEDERAL AND STATE STATUTES APPLYING SPECIAL RULES TO CONSUMER TRANSACTIONS

1. THE MAGNUSON-MOSS CONSUMER WARRANTY ACT

a. INTRODUCTION

Dissatisfaction with the operation of certain UCC rules in consumer transactions led Congress in 1975 to enact the Magnuson-Moss Consumer Warranty Act. Primary among the points of dissatisfaction was the deception implicit in the ubiquitous practice of giving something with one hand (viz., an express warranty) while simultaneously taking away much more with the other (viz., disclaimer of implied warranties and exclusion of liability for damages for breach of the express warranty). To address the deception and perceived unfairness in this practice, the Act has three principal components: (1) disclosure; (2) a ban on disclaimers; and (3) enhanced remedies.

To understand the Act, careful attention to the definitions is essential. Please read the definition of "written warranty" (§ 101(6), 15 U.S.C.A. § 2301(6)). How does it differ from the definition of "express warranty" in Article 2? If a manufacturer of computers describes them as "Panorama capable," meaning that they are capable of running the designated software, has the manufacturer given a "written warranty"?

Please read the definitions of "supplier," "consumer," and "consumer product."

The Act does not require a supplier to give a written warranty. That remains entirely within the discretion of the supplier. If, however, the supplier does give a written warranty, the requirements of the Magnuson-Moss Act apply.

(1) Section 103 (15 U.S.C.A. § 2303) requires suppliers of consumer goods who give written warranties to label those warranties either "full" or "limited." To be a full warranty, the warranty must meet the standards specified in section 104 (15 U.S.C.A. § 2304). If a written warranty does not meet those standards, it may not properly be labeled "full warranty." If the supplier nevertheless labels it "full warranty," then it is deemed to incorporate all the standards specified for full warranties (§ 104(e), 15 U.S.C.A. § 2304(e)). In addition, the Act requires "full and conspicuous" disclosure of the terms of the warranty (§ 102(a), 15 U.S.C.A. § 2302(a)). The Federal Trade Commission is authorized to promulgate implementing regulations, and it has done so. FTC, Disclosure of Written Consumer Product Warranty Terms and Conditions, 16 C.F.R. §§ 701.1–701.4.

(2) Section 108 (15 U.S.C.A. § 2308) sweeps away disclaimers of implied warranties. If a supplier gives a written warranty, the supplier may not disclaim implied warranties. This is true even if the written warranty is a "limited warranty." The supplier may, however, be able to limit the duration of the implied warranties.

(3) Finally, if the warrantor breaches a written warranty or an Article 2 implied warranty, the consumer has a federal cause of action and, if successful, may recover attorney's fees (§ 110(d), 15 U.S.C.A. § 2310(d)). Article 2 contains no provision making attorney's fees available to a successful litigant, so the Magnuson-Moss Act provides a huge benefit to those who can assert its provisions.

Although the Act is entitled, "Consumer Warranty Act," its reach extends beyond consumer transactions. This is a function of the definitions of "consumer product" and "consumer." A "consumer product" is any goods that are normally used for personal, family, or household purposes. This means that an automobile or a television, for example, is within the definition even if the purchaser is a commercial entity. "Consumer" includes a buyer who purchases for use rather than resale. So when section 108 bans disclaimers on consumer products that are sold to consumers, it bans disclaimers on televisions sold to sports bars. And when section 110(d) gives a right of action to consumers, it confers a right of action on a corporation that purchases a car for its sales rep.

b. INVALIDATION OF DISCLAIMERS

The Act invalidates disclaimers of implied warranties, but only if the supplier makes a written warranty. "Supplier" includes the manufacturer of a consumer product, intermediate distributors, and the retailer. In any sale to a consumer, some of the suppliers may make written warranties and some may not. It is important to determine whether a particular supplier has made a written warranty. If it has, then the consumer may recover for any breach of an implied warranty by that supplier. Please read the definition of "implied warranty."

In Ventura v. Ford Motor Corp., 180 N.J.Super. 45, 433 A.2d 801 (App.Div.1981), plaintiffs purchased a new car that turned out to be defective. When repairs proved ineffective, plaintiffs sued the dealer (Marino Auto Sales) and the manufacturer, seeking to revoke their acceptance of the car and recover the price. The manufacturer warranted that the dealer would "repair or replace free any parts found . . . to be defective . . . within the earlier of 12 months or 12,000 miles." The contract between plaintiffs and the dealer contained a disclaimer of "all warranties" and a provision that "[t]he selling dealer . . . agrees to promptly perform and fulfill all terms and conditions of the [manufacturer's warranty]." The court granted the requested relief:

> We will first consider the application of this act to the dealer, Marino Auto. As quoted above, paragraph 7 of the purchase order contract provides that there are no warranties, express or implied, made by the selling dealer or manufacturer except, in the case of a new motor vehicle, "the warranty expressly given to the purchaser upon delivery of such motor vehicle. . . ." This section also provides: "The selling dealer also agrees to promptly perform and fulfill all terms and conditions of the owner service policy." . . . The provision in paragraph 7 in these circumstances is a "written warranty" within the meaning of § 101(6)(B) since it constitutes an undertaking in connection with the sale to take "remedial action with respect to such product in the event that such product fails to meet the specifications set forth in the undertaking. . . ." In our view the specifications of the undertaking include, at the least, the provisions of the limited warranty furnished by Ford. . . .

> . . . Accordingly, having furnished a written warranty to the consumer, the dealer as a supplier may not "disclaim or modify [except to limit in duration] any implied warranty to a consumer. . . ." The result of this analysis is to invalidate the attempted disclaimer by the dealer of the implied warranties of merchantability and fitness. Being bound by those implied warranties arising under state law, N.J.S.A. 12A:2–314 and 315, Marino Auto was liable to plaintiff for the breach thereof as found by the trial judge, and plaintiff could timely revoke his acceptance of the automobile and claim a refund of his purchase price. N.J.S.A. 12A:2–608 and N.J.S.A. 12A:2–711. . . .

> Plaintiff also could have recovered damages against Ford for Ford's breach of its written limited warranty. Marino Auto

was Ford's representative for the purpose of making repairs to plaintiff's vehicle under the warranty. . . .

One question posed by this case is whether recovery of the purchase price from the manufacturer was available to plaintiff for breach of the manufacturer's warranty. If the warranty were a full warranty plaintiff would have been entitled to a refund of the purchase price under the Magnuson-Moss Warranty Act. Since Ford's warranty was a limited warranty we must look to state law to determine plaintiff's right to damages or other legal and equitable relief. § 110(d)(1). Once privity is removed as an obstacle to relief we see no reason why a purchaser cannot also elect the equitable remedy of returning the goods to the manufacturer who is a warrantor and claiming a refund of the purchase price less an allowance for use of the product. . . .

c.   IMPACT ON THE REQUIREMENT OF PRIVITY

In the last paragraph of the *Ventura* excerpt, the court states that a consumer may sue a remote seller for the remote seller's breach of the implied warranty of merchantability. You will recall that as a matter of state law, the states are split on this question (pages 346–358 supra). Hence, *Ventura* suggests that section 110(d) eliminates any requirement of privity of contract for implied warranty. The Supreme Court of Illinois agreed:

> The Act broadly defines "consumer" in section 101(3) as "a buyer (other than for purposes of resale) of any consumer product, any person to whom such product is transferred during the duration of an implied or written warranty * * * and any other person who is entitled by the terms of such warranty * * * or under applicable State law to enforce against the warrantor * * * the obligations of the warranty." It has been suggested that this broad definition of "consumer" and the provisions of section 110(d)(1), which section authorizes a "consumer" to maintain a civil action for damages for failure of a "supplier" or "warrantor" to comply with any obligation of a written or implied warranty, effectively abolish vertical privity. We do not think we can focus on any one section of Magnuson-Moss but should read the sections referred to together to accomplish the purpose of Magnuson-Moss of furnishing broad protection to the consumer.

> . . . In cases where no Magnuson-Moss written warranty has been given, Magnuson-Moss has no effect upon State-law privity requirements because, by virtue of section 101(7), which defines implied warranty, implied warranty arises only if it does so under State law. However, if a Magnuson-Moss written warranty (either "full" or "limited") is given, by reason of the policy against disclaimers of implied warranty expressed in Magnuson-Moss and the provisions authorizing a consumer to

sue a warrantor, the nonprivity "consumer" should be permitted to maintain an action on an implied warranty against the "warrantor." . . . [A] warrantor, by extending a written warranty to the consumer, establishes privity between the warrantor and the consumer which, though limited in nature, is sufficient to support an implied warranty under sections 2–314 and 2–315 of the UCC. The implied warranty thus recognized, by virtue of the definition in section 101(7) of Magnuson-Moss, must be one arising under the law of this State.

Szajna v. General Motors Corp., 115 Ill.2d 294, 104 Ill.Dec. 898, 503 N.E.2d 760, 768–69 (1986).

Another court took a decidedly different approach:

Ford argues that State privity laws are preserved under the Act and must be considered by the Court before a plaintiff may assert an implied warranty claim under Magnuson-Moss. Ford bases its privity argument on the express provisions of the Act. It notes that although the Act provides for a Federal cause of action for breach of implied warranty, the Act defines implied warranty as "an implied warranty arising under State law (as modified by sections 108 and 104(a) of this act) in connection with the sale by a supplier of a consumer product." Section 101(7), 15 U.S.C. § 2301(7). . . .

In response plaintiffs have argued that State law privity doctrines do not apply under Magnuson-Moss because the Act creates a new Federal private cause of action for breach of implied warranty. Therefore, plaintiffs assert, the requirement that vertical privity exist between the purchaser and Ford is eliminated under the Act and cannot serve as a barrier for pursuing implied warranty claims. Specifically, plaintiffs cite to the Act's definition of "consumer," "supplier," and "warrantor" as a basis for arguing that state privity law has been superseded. When reading those definitions into section 110(d)(1), plaintiffs argue, the Court must conclude that any person to whom the vehicle is transferred during the life of the implied warranty is entitled to enforce that warranty by bringing suit.

Certainly, it is axiomatic that where the meaning of the statute is plain on its face, this Court need not take further inquiry into its purpose. Here, Congress has specifically provided that implied warranties "arise" under State law. Section 101(7), 15 U.S.C. 2301(7). If, in this action, there are to be any implied warranty claims at all under Magnuson-Moss, they must "originate" from or "come into being" from state law.[4]

---

[4] The Random House Dictionary of the English Language (Random House, N.Y. 1969) defines arise as "1. to come into being, action, or notice; originate; appear; spring up."

Therefore, if a State does not provide for a cause of action for breach of implied warranty where vertical privity is lacking, there cannot be a Federal cause of action for such a breach.

The statutory history in this matter is also clear. In a Senate report from the Committee on Commerce, the committee stated that:

> It is not the intent of the Committee to alter *in any way* the manner in which implied warranties are created under the Uniform Commercial Code. For instance, an implied warranty of fitness for a particular purpose which might be created by an installing supplier is not, in many instances, enforceable by the consumer against the manufacturing supplier. *The Committee does not intend to alter currently existing state law on these subjects.*

Senate Comm. on Commerce, S.Rep. No. 151, 93d Cong., 1st Sess. 21 (1973) (emphasis added). . . .

Plaintiffs, however, argue that the definitions "consumer," "supplier," and "warrantor" in section 101 abolish any state law privity requirements. They assert that by transposing these definitions into the subsection that provides for civil actions by consumers for breach of warranty, the Court is compelled to conclude that State privity requirements are abolished. When transposing these definitions of section 101, section 110(d)(1) provides:

> . . . a consumer [including "a buyer (other than for purposes of resale) of any consumer product, any person to whom such product is transferred"] who is damaged by the failure of a supplier ["any person engaged in the business of making a consumer product directly or indirectly available to consumers"] [or] warrantor ["any supplier or other person who . . . is or may be obligated under an implied warranty"] ["arising under State law"] . . . to comply with . . . an implied warranty ["arising under State law"] . . . may bring suit. . . .

In adding these definitions to section 110(d)(1), it is still evident to this Court that an action under Magnuson-Moss may be brought by a "consumer who is damaged by the failure of a supplier to comply with any obligation under [the act] . . . includ[ing] implied warranties arising under State law." H.R.Rep. No. 93–1107, 93d Cong., 2d Sess., reprinted in 1974 U.S.Code Cong. & Ad.News 7702, 7723. The definitions do not alter the requirement that an implied warranty, if it is to arise at all, must arise under State law and "[i]f state law requires vertical privity to enforce an implied warranty and there is none, then, like the yeastless souffle, the warranty does not 'arise.' " Feinstein v. Firestone Tire & Rubber Co., 535 F.Supp. at 605 n. 13.

Walsh v. Ford Motor Co., 588 F.Supp. 1513, 1524–26 (D.D.C.1984).

Which view is correct? Does the Magnuson-Moss Act override state law in those states that require vertical privity for implied-warranty liability?

In *Szajna* the Illinois Supreme Court believed that it is a question of state law whether the state's requirement of privity survives enactment of Magnuson-Moss. The federal courts disagree. For example, in Larry J. Soldinger Associates, Ltd. v. Aston Martin Lagonda of North America, Inc., 1999 WL 756174 (N.D.Ill.1999), the United States District Court for the Northern District of Illinois stated:

> . . . In Illinois, a plaintiff may pursue a UCC breach of implied warranty claim for economic damages only if he is in privity of contract with the seller. Rothe v. Maloney Cadillac, Inc., 119 Ill.2d 288, 292, 518 N.E.2d 1028, 1029–30 (1988) (noting that "with respect to purely economic loss, the UCC article II implied warranties give a buyer of goods a potential cause of action only against his immediate seller"). . . .

> Count II . . . alleges breach of implied warranty of merchantability [and] relies on the Magnuson-Moss Act. *See* 15 U.S.C. § 2310(d). . . . Defendant's argument, in a nutshell, is as follows. Section 2310(d) of the Act allows for suits based on breach of implied warranties; section 2301(7) defines implied warranties as "an implied warranty arising under State law (as modified by section 2308 and 2304(a) of this title)." 15 U.S.C. § 2301(7). Under Illinois law, as discussed above, contractual privity is a prerequisite for UCC breach of implied warranty claims. Plaintiff had no privity of contract with Aston Martin. Because Magnuson-Moss defines breach of implied warranty claims by reference to Illinois law, Defendant contends, Plaintiff's claims must fail. Defendant urges the court to follow several federal decisions that support this conclusion, including Walsh v. Ford Motor Co., 807 F.2d 1000, 1014 (D.C.Cir.1986), Abraham v. Volkswagen of Am., 795 F.2d 238, 247–48 (2d Cir.1986), Walsh v. Ford Motor Co., 106 F.R.D. 378, 395–96 (D.D.C.1985), *rev'd on other grounds,* 807 F.2d 1000 (D.C.Cir.1986), and Skelton v. General Motors Corp., No. 79 C 1243, 1985 WL 1860, at *2–3 (N.D.Ill. June 21, 1985).

> Plaintiff, on the other hand, contends that Defendant here ignores controlling law: in both *Rothe* and *Szajna,* the Illinois Supreme Court has ruled that contractual privity is not required to maintain a breach of implied warranty claim under the Act. These cases held that, although "the UCC article II implied warranties give a buyer of goods a potential cause of

action only against his immediate seller," Magnuson-Moss "broadens the reach of the UCC . . . affording consumers substantially greater protection," so implied warranty claims under the federal statute do not require contractual privity. Rothe, 119 Ill.2d at 293–95, 518 N.E.2d at 1030–31 (citing Szajna). In light of the "crystal clear pronouncements of the Illinois Supreme Court on what Illinois law requires," Plaintiff argues that an absence of privity of contract does not preclude his Magnuson-Moss breach of implied warranty claims. . . .

. . . After carefully considering the arguments of both sides, the court finds the *Abraham* line of authority more persuasive.

Szajna, on which Plaintiff relies, was the Illinois Supreme Court's seminal case. . . . Because the plaintiff was not in privity of contract with GM, and claimed only economic losses, the court decided that he could not proceed with his claim under the UCC.

Moving on to the Magnuson-Moss claim, the court perused the text of the statute, beginning with Section 2301(7), which defines implied warranties as those "arising under state law (as modified by section 2308 and 2304(a) of this title)." . . .

. . . The court's rationale was that by extending a written warranty, the manufacturer establishes a privity-like relationship with the consumer sufficient to support an implied warranty. This result, the court believed, was consistent with the broad policy goals of the statute: "Magnuson-Moss broadens the reach of the UCC article II implied warranties, affording consumers substantially greater protection against defective goods." Rothe, 119 Ill.2d at 295, 518 N.E.2d at 1031 (characterizing the reasoning of *Szajna*).

Several federal courts—*Abraham,* the court of appeals in *Walsh, Skelton*—have taken a view contrary to that of the Illinois Supreme Court. The Second Circuit's analysis in *Abraham* is the most comprehensive. . . . The court of appeals observed that the " 'arising under' phrase [in Section 2301(7) of the Act] strongly suggests that the obligations of the warranty are solely the creation of state law, an inference further strengthened by the explicit reference [in Section 2301(7)] to 'modifications' of such state law elsewhere in the Act, none of which deal with privity." [Abraham, 795 F.2d] at 247. Still, the court acknowledged that a liberal reading of the statutory text arguably "provide[s] for an action by a consumer without privity against a supplier on an implied warranty arising under the law of a state that does not allow transferees without privity to sue." *Id.* The court therefore considered the extent to which Magnuson-Moss added a new layer of federal law to existing state warranty doctrines.

Parsing the statute's legislative history, *Abraham* found "that with regard to written warranties . . . privity is not required," and that Congress clearly intended to limit the ability of sellers to disclaim implied warranties. Id. at 248. The *Abraham* court determined that Congress nevertheless intended that state law would govern the applicability of implied warranties, except where Sections 2308 and 2304(a) explicitly modified state law. . . .

The court concurs with the conclusion of *Abraham* for several reasons. First, although this court technically is not bound by a Second Circuit decision, *Abraham* holds greater sway than *Szajna,* since the Seventh Circuit asks that district courts give "substantial weight" to the "direct authority of a sister circuit." Richards v. Local 134, Int'l Bhd. of Electrical Workers, 790 F.2d 633, 636 (7th Cir.1986). Additionally, *Szajna's* decision to review and interpret not only Section 2308 but also Sections 2301(3) and 2310, while neglecting to consider 2304(a), is inconsistent with plain language of the touchstone Section 2301(7), which defines "implied warranty" by reference to state law and Sections 2308 and 2304(a) only.

. . .

Moreover, the decisions of these federal courts are consistent with the plain language of Section 2301(7), which refers to state law and Sections 2308 and 2304(a) to define the parameters of implied warranties. Sections 2308 and 2304(a) deal primarily with limitations on disclaimers, however; they do not discuss privity at all. What remains to guide the interpretation of the Act on the question of privity, then, is state law, which in Illinois is as follows: under the Illinois UCC, contractual privity is a prerequisite for recovery under a theory of breach of implied warranty. In sum, because Plaintiff was not in contractual privity with Aston Martin, summary judgment is appropriate. . . .

The Seventh Circuit endorsed this conclusion. Voelker v. Porsche Cars North America, Inc., 353 F.3d 516 (7th Cir. 2003). But is the conclusion correct? Section 101(7) defines "implied warranty" as "an implied warranty arising under state law." Under 2–314 when a manufacturer sells to a distributor, "a warranty that the goods shall be merchantable is implied." Does not this mean that a warranty "arises," that is, comes into being? UCC 2–314(2)(c) articulates the seller's obligation to provide its purchaser with goods that are fit for their ordinary purposes. Magnuson-Moss 110(d) permits a consumer to recover for a warrantor's failure "to comply with any obligation . . . under . . . [an] implied warranty." Perhaps the interpretation of the court in *Voelker* is wrong.

d. LEASES

The definition of "consumer" begins, "The term 'consumer' means a buyer. . . ." Similarly, the Act defines "written warranty" as an affirmation "made in connection with the sale of a consumer product. . . ." If a consumer acquires goods by means of a lease, does the consumer have the benefit of Magnuson-Moss? That issue was before the court in *Voelker*, and it stated:

> The Magnuson-Moss Act defines three categories of "consumer[s]"[1]: a category one consumer is "a buyer (other than for the purposes of resale) of any consumer product"; a category two consumer is "any person to whom such product is transferred during the duration of an implied or written warranty (or service contract) applicable to the product"; and, a category three consumer is "any other person who is entitled by the terms of such warranty (or service contract) or under applicable State law to enforce against the warrantor (or service contractor) the obligations of the warranty (or service contract)." 15 U.S.C. § 2301(3). Voelker claims to be a consumer under all three categories.

> The first category of consumer would require Voelker to be a "buyer," which presupposes a sale. The "sale" that Voelker identifies in his brief is the lease, which he argues is functionally equivalent to a sale. No binding authority governs the question of whether a lease can constitute a sale under the Magnuson-Moss Act. Persuasive authorities, for their part, are divided. See Szubski v. Mercedes-Benz, U.S.A., LLC, 796 N.E.2d 81 (Ohio Com. Pleas 2003) (collecting cases on both sides of the issue).

> As the Court of Appeals of New York has pointed out, the Act does not define "sale." DiCintio v. DaimlerChrysler Corp., 97 N.Y.2d 463, 768 N.E.2d 1121, 1124, 742 N.Y.S.2d 182 (N.Y. 2002). Under the Uniform Commercial Code, however, it is well established that a sale occurs only where there is a passing of title to a buyer. In common speech, similarly, a sale is typically understood to require the transfer of title. See Webster's Ninth New Collegiate Dictionary 1037 (1987) (defining "sale," in relevant part, as "the transfer of ownership of and title to property from one person to another for a price.") Against this backdrop, we conclude that no reasonable person reading the Magnuson-Moss Act would conclude that there is a sale to Voelker under the Act where title does not pass to him. Here, it is undisputed that title never passed to Voelker under the lease agreement, and so the lease cannot constitute a sale for purposes of making Voelker a category one consumer.

---

[1] For ease of reference, we refer to the three types of consumers as category one, two or three consumers, although the statute itself does not use this terminology.

When Voelker signed his lease, however, title had already passed from the car's manufacturer, Porsche, to the lessor, Copans. . . . Voelker argues that the sale needed to qualify him as a category one consumer occurred when the manufacturer sold the vehicle to Copans, who in turn became Voelker's lessor. We disagree because, for a sale to qualify a plaintiff as a category one consumer, it must be made to a buyer "*other than for purposes of resale.*" 15 U.S.C. § 2301(3) (emphasis added). In other words, it is a final sale to a user, not a sale to an intended reseller. But whenever a lessor takes title to a car, at least one of its purposes is, presumably, the actual resale of the vehicle. DiCintio, 768 N.E.2d at 1127. In this particular case, Voelker's lease, a copy of which is attached to the complaint, establishes that Copans took title of the vehicle with intent ultimately to resell it: Paragraph 17 gives Voelker first option to buy the car at the end of the lease term or even before the end of the lease term. . . .

In short, for Voelker to qualify as a category one consumer under the Magnuson-Moss Act, there must have been a sale of the automobile "other than for the purposes of resale," and that sale must have included the transfer of title. Here, the only sale alleged in relation to the car was between the manufacturer, Porsche, and the lessor, Copans, and that sale occurred for the purposes of resale. Accordingly, accepting all facts alleged in the complaint as true, the transfer of the possession of the car to Voelker was not a sale and thus he is not entitled to proceed under the Magnuson-Moss Act as a category one consumer.

The next question is whether Voelker has stated a claim as a category two consumer. In other words, has Voelker alleged facts that would show that he is "any person to whom such product is *transferred during the duration* of an implied or written warranty (or service contract) applicable to the product"? 15 U.S.C. § 2301(3) (emphasis added). The "written warranty . . . applicable to the product" that Voelker identifies is the New Car Limited Warranty, which Voelker has attached to his complaint. That warranty, however, did not begin until after possession of the car was transferred to Voelker, and not "during [the warranty's] duration." By its own terms, the warranty did not take effect until one of four antecedents occurred: "the date the car [was] first delivered to the first retail purchaser, or the date it was first used as a demonstrator, lease, or company car, whichever came first." The only triggering event that Voelker identifies is the date that the car was first used—by himself—as a lease car. Because the warranty did not begin until the date the car was "first used as a . . . lease" car, the warranty did not begin until after he took possession. Thus,

Voelker has failed to allege that the car was "transferred [to him] during the duration" of the New Car Limited Warranty, and, accepting all of the allegations in his complaint as true, he does not qualify as a category two consumer.

Finally, we consider whether Voelker has stated a claim as a category three consumer. That is, we ask whether he is "any other person who is entitled by the terms of such warranty (or service contract) or under applicable State law to enforce against the warrantor (or service contractor) the obligations of the warranty (or service contract)." 15 U.S.C. § 2301(3) (emphasis added). Copans, as the defendants assert, assigned to Voelker "all its rights under the Porsche Limited Warranty." Under the state law of Illinois, as an assignee of that warranty, a lessee like Voelker was entitled to enforce the rights arising from the warranty. Dekelaita v. Nissan Motor Corp., 343 Ill.App.3d 801, 799 N.E.2d 367 (Ill.App.2003). Therefore, Voelker qualifies as a category three consumer.

2. STATE STATUTES MODIFYING ARTICLE 2 FOR CONSUMER TRANSACTIONS

The Magnuson-Moss Act significantly limits a seller's right to disclaim warranties in consumer goods transactions *if* the seller gives a written warranty as defined in the Act: if the seller does not give a written warranty, the Magnuson-Moss limitations on disclaimers do not apply. However, many states have enacted legislation that limits or forbids warranty disclaimers whether or not the seller has given a written warranty. Most states that limit or forbid disclaimers have amended or eliminated UCC 2–316 and 2–719,[1] but others have adopted totally separate consumer protection acts.[2] In addition, one state has a consumer protection statute that is incorporated directly into the Article 2.[3]

Five eastern states (Connecticut, Maine, Maryland, Massachusetts, and Vermont), as well as the District of Columbia, have amended 2–316 to provide that 2–316 does not apply to sales of consumer goods or services.[4] The statutes provide that any language, oral or written, that

---

[1] Alabama, Ala.Code 1975 §§ 7–2–316(5), 7–2–719(4); Connecticut, Conn.Gen.Stat.Ann. § 42a–2–316(5); District of Columbia, D.C.Code § 28:2–316.01; Maine, Me.Rev.Stat.Ann. tit. 11, § 2–316(5); Maryland, Md.Code Com.Law § 2–316.1; Massachusetts, Mass. Ann.Laws ch. 106, § 2–316A; Mississippi, Miss.Code, §§ 75–2–314(1), (3), 75–2–315, 75–2–719(4); New Hampshire, N.H.Rev.Stat.Ann. § 382–A:2–316(4); South Carolina, S.C.Code tit. 36, § 2–316(5) (2002); Washington, Wash.Rev.Code § 62A.2–316(4), 62A.2–719(3).

[2] California, Cal.Civ.Code Ann. §§ 1790–1795.7; Kansas, Kan.Stat.Ann. §§ 50–639, 50–644; Minnesota, Minn.Stat.Ann. §§ 325G.17–325G.20; West Virginia, W.Va.Code §§ 46A–1–107, 46A–8–102.

[3] Rhode Island, R.I.Gen.Laws § 6A–2–329.

[4] Consumer goods and services are those which are used or bought primarily for personal, family, or household purposes (see UCC 9–109). The Connecticut and Vermont statutes provide that disclaimers of implied warranties are unenforceable only as to new or unused consumer

attempts to exclude or modify implied warranties as to consumer goods cannot be enforced. These sections also affect 2–719 (which generally permits modification or limitation of remedy) by providing that an exclusion or modification of consumer's remedies for breach of an implied warranty cannot be enforced.

Other states modify Article 2's disclaimer provisions, but most do not provide consumers with the kind of protection found in the statutes of the states discussed in the preceding paragraph. Several, notably California, Kansas, Minnesota, Rhode Island, and West Virginia, have adopted consumer-protection statutes that affect sellers' warranties. For example, under the California Song-Beverly Consumer Warranty Act, a manufacturer, distributor, or retailer who makes express warranties may not limit, modify, or disclaim the implied warranties of merchantability and fitness that arise in every sale of consumer goods. These implied warranties may not be disclaimed except on an "as is" or "with all faults" basis and then only if the seller strictly complies with the statute's provisions. To disclaim, the manufacturer must attach to the goods a conspicuous writing that clearly informs the buyer prior to the sale in simple and concise language that (1) the goods are being sold on an "as is" or "with all faults" basis, (2) the entire risk as to the quality and performance of the goods is with the buyer, and (3) the buyer will assume the entire cost of all necessary servicing or repair.

The bottom line is that there is great variation among the states concerning disclaimers of warranty in consumer transactions. One needs to look well beyond the UCC to understand the law of the jurisdiction concerning warranties. Breach of warranty gives rise to a cause of action under the UCC, and it also may give rise to a cause of action under other law. For example, the Texas Deceptive Trade Practices Act, which enumerates various kinds of conduct that amount to deceptive practices, provides that a consumer may recover under that Act for breach of express or implied warranty. Tex. Bus. & Com. Code § 17.50(a)(2). Moreover, every state has a statute, some modeled after the Federal Trade Commission Act, which broadly prohibits deception in consumer transactions. These statutes may apply in warranty-related situations. For example, a manufacturer of a temperature controller told a buyer that the product had been used only at a trade show. It actually had been sold and returned as defective. When the manufacturer resold it without any repair or reconditioning, a court in Massachusetts held that the seller violated the state's little-FTC act, Mass.Gen.L. ch. 93A, § 2. Polycarbon Industries, Inc. v. Advantage Engineering, Inc., 260

---

goods. As to used goods, the provisions of 2–316(2), (3), and (4) still operate to permit disclaimers of the implied warranties. In addition, the California and Rhode Island consumer protection statutes discussed below apparently apply only to sales of new consumer goods. The implied warranties of merchantability and fitness for a particular purpose do not arise in sales of used consumer goods under those statutes. The Maryland statute provides that disclaimers of implied warranties are effective as to certain used automobiles if the disclaimers meet specified requirements.

F.Supp.2d 296 (D.Mass.2003). Note that both the Texas and Massachusetts statutes apply these consumer-protection statutes in such a way as to encompass certain commercial buyers.

Finally, between 1983 and 1986 virtually every state enacted a warranty law pertaining solely to new motor vehicles. These statutes respond to a shortcoming in Article 2's remedial scheme. Known as "lemon laws," they offer additional protection to buyers of new cars when the dealer and manufacturer fail to make good on their promises to repair defects. We will return to these laws in Chapter 7 in connection with the buyer's remedies for breach of warranty.

CHAPTER 7

BUYER'S REMEDIES FOR BREACH BY THE SELLER

A. INTRODUCTION

Section 2–301 states the basic obligations of the parties as, respectively, "to transfer and deliver" and "to accept and pay," both "in accordance with the contract." Sections 2–507 and 2–511 elaborate: the seller must tender delivery of the goods, and until the seller does so, the buyer does not have to accept the goods or pay for them (2–507(1)). The buyer must tender payment, and until the buyer does so, the seller does not have to tender or complete delivery of the goods (2–511(1)). Putting these together, we see that Article 2 embraces the common-law rule that ordinarily the parties must perform simultaneously. This chapter considers the rights of the parties when the seller allegedly fails to perform in accordance with the contract and the UCC.

A seller may breach by repudiating the contract, by failing to deliver the goods, or by making a tender of delivery that does not conform to the contract. The nonconforming tender may consist of either a defect in the quality or quantity of the goods or a defect in the details of delivery (e.g., delivery that is at the wrong place or time). Article 2 gives the buyer several remedies for each of these kinds of breach, but not all of the remedies are available all the time:

- If a seller makes a nonconforming tender the buyer may be entitled to refuse to take the goods or refuse to keep the goods (these options are called "rejection" and "revocation of acceptance" of the goods). Sometimes, however, the buyer is obligated to accept the goods even though they do not conform to the contract.

- If the buyer rightfully rejects the goods or rightfully revokes acceptance of them, or if the seller repudiates the contract, the buyer may cancel the contract and recover damages (2–711(1)).

- If the buyer accepts nonconforming goods and keeps them, the buyer may not cancel the contract but may be able to recover damages.

This chapter considers each of these alternatives, starting with the right to reject or revoke acceptance when the goods or the tender do not conform to the contract.

B. Rejection, Cure, and Revocation of Acceptance

1. Single-Delivery Contracts

At common law, unless the parties have agreed otherwise, performance by each party is a condition of the other party's obligation to perform. This leads to the common-sense conclusion that if one party refuses to perform, the other need not perform either. But what if the party does not refuse to perform, but just does not perform exactly as required? In the eighteenth and nineteenth centuries, the courts developed the substantial-performance doctrine, under which substantial performance—albeit not complete or perfect—by one of the parties satisfies the condition and triggers the obligation of the other. The second party may refuse to perform only if the performance of the first falls short of substantial performance. This rule applies today in many kinds of contracts, e.g., contracts for construction. At one time it applied to contracts for the sale of goods, too. But that changed in 1877, with the English case of Bowes v. Shand, L.R. 2 App.Cas. 455 (H.L.1877). *Bowes* concerned a contract for the sale of 600 tons of rice, to be "shipped" in March or April of 1874. The seller tendered to the buyer 600 tons of merchantable rice, but almost all of the rice had been put on board the carrier ship in February, and only a small part of the rice was put on board in March. The House of Lords interpreted the term "shipped" to mean "put on board," and under this interpretation it held that the seller had breached by tendering rice that had been shipped in February and not in March or April as required by the contract. It held that this breach by the seller justified the buyer's rejection of all of the rice upon its arrival.

Seven years after *Bowes,* the United States Supreme Court followed its reasoning in two companion cases, Norrington v. Wright, 115 U.S. 188, 6 S.Ct. 12, 29 L.Ed. 366 (1885), and Filley v. Pope, 115 U.S. 213, 6 S.Ct. 19, 29 L.Ed. 372 (1885). *Norrington* concerned a contract for the sale of 5,000 tons of iron rails, to be shipped at the rate of about 1,000 tons per month, beginning in February of 1880, the whole of the contract goods to be shipped before August 1, 1880. The Supreme Court interpreted the contract to mean that the seller was obligated to ship as close to 1,000 tons as possible in the months of February–June and any deficiencies were to be made up by shipments in July. The seller shipped 400 tons in February and 885 tons in March. The Court held that the seller's actions constituted breach justifying rescission by the buyer, even though shipment at the rate of 1,000 tons thereafter would have achieved shipment of the whole of the 5,000 tons before August 1. In *Filley,* the seller agreed to ship Scotch iron from Glasgow as soon as possible. He was unable to obtain a vessel out of Glasgow, so he shipped the iron from Leith. The market price of iron declined, and the buyer rejected the goods when they arrived. The Supreme Court held the rejection rightful, stating that a court could not inquire into the reasons the parties had for stipulating shipment from Glasgow, or whether the place of shipment was of any moment to the parties. The fact that the tender was not in strict compliance with the terms of the contract was enough to justify rejection.

The rule of *Bowes, Norrington,* and *Filley* is known as the perfect-tender rule. The Uniform Sales Act adopted the perfect-tender rule, but courts in states that adopted the Act sometimes failed to follow its provisions. For example, in National Importing & Trading Co. v. E.A. Bear & Co., 324 Ill. 346, 155 N.E. 343 (1927), the buyer, relied on Bowes v. Shand to claim that the seller breached by loading eggs on March 31st when the contract called for the first shipment in April. It appeared that the market price for the eggs had declined sharply. Even though Illinois had adopted the Uniform Sales Act more than a decade earlier, the court did not refer to the Act and applied the substantial-performance rule.

For the position of the UCC on this question, see 2–601, which continues the perfect-tender rule in single-delivery contracts, and 2–612, which adopts a version of the substantial-performance rule in installment contracts (2–612), except as to defects in documents, where it adheres to the perfect-tender rule. The comments to 2–601 and 2–612 do not state any reason for the difference in treatment of single-delivery and installment-delivery contracts. Can you think of any justification for the different treatment?

D.P. Technology Corp. v. Sherwood Tool, Inc.

United States District Court, District of Connecticut, 1990.
751 F.Supp. 1038.

■ NEVAS, DISTRICT JUDGE. . . . On January 24, 1989, the defendant entered into a written contract to purchase a computer system, including hardware, software, installation and training, from the plaintiff. The complaint alleges that the computer system was "specifically" designed for the defendant and is not readily marketable. The contract, executed on January 24, 1989, incorporates the delivery term set forth in the seller's amended letter of January 17, 1989, stating that the computer system would be delivered within ten to twelve weeks. The delivery period specified in the contract ended on April 18, 1989. The software was delivered on April 12, 1989, and the hardware was delivered on May 4, 1989. On May 9, 1989, the defendant returned the merchandise to the plaintiff, and has since refused payment for both the software and the hardware. Thus, the plaintiff alleges that the defendant breached the contract by refusing to accept delivery of the goods covered by the contract while the defendant argues that it was rather the plaintiff who breached the contract by failing to make a timely delivery. [Defendant moved to dismiss plaintiff's complaint for failure to state a claim.]

. . .

Because the contract between the parties was a contract for the sale of goods, the law governing this transaction is to be found in Article 2 of the Uniform Commercial Code ("UCC"); Conn Gen.Stat. §§ 42a–2–101 et seq. In its motion to dismiss, the defendant argues that the plaintiff fails to state a claim upon which relief can be granted because the plaintiff breached the contract which provided for a delivery period of ten to twelve weeks from the date of the order, January 24, 1989. Since the delivery period ended on April 18, 1989, the May 4 hardware delivery was 16 days late. The defendant contends that because the plaintiff delivered the hardware after the contractual deadline, the late delivery entitled the defendant to reject delivery, since a seller is required to tender goods in conformance with the terms set forth in a contract. U.C.C. § 2–301; Conn.Gen.Stat. § 42a–2–301.

. . . [P]laintiff argues that the defendant relies on the perfect tender rule, allowing buyers to reject for any nonconformity with the contract. Plaintiff points out that the defendant has not cited one case in which a buyer rejected goods solely because of a late delivery, and that the doctrine of "perfect tender" has been roundly criticized. While it is true that the perfect tender rule has been criticized by scholars principally because it allowed a dishonest buyer to avoid an unfavorable contract on the basis of an insubstantial defect in the seller's tender, . . . the basic tender provision of the Uniform Commercial Code continued the perfect tender policy developed by the common law and embodied in the Uniform Sales Act. Section 2–601 states that with certain exceptions,[5] the buyer has the right to reject "if the goods or the tender of delivery fail *in any respect* to conform to the contract." (emphasis supplied). Conn.Gen.Stat. § 42a–2–601. The courts that have considered the issue have agreed that the perfect tender rule has survived the enactment of the Code. . . . Similarly, courts interpreting § 2–601 have strictly interpreted it to mean any nonconformity, thus excluding the doctrine of substantial performance.[6] Printing Center of Texas, Inc. v. Supermind Pub. Co., Inc., 669 S.W.2d 779, 783 (Tex.App.1984) (the term "conform" within § 2–601 authorizing the buyer to reject the whole if the goods or tender of delivery fail in any respect to conform to the contract does not mean substantial

---

[5]   See, e.g., §§ 2–508 (seller's limited right to cure defects in tender), 2–608 (buyer's limited right to revoke acceptance) and 2–612 (buyer's limited right to reject nonconforming tender under installment contract). See also Calamari and Perillo, Contracts, (2d ed.1972) at 413 n. 81 ("It has been suggested that these exceptions in fact represent a new rule, supplanting the traditional perfect tender rule in that despite § 2–601, the intent of the Code is to apply the doctrine of substantial performance to sales contracts.").

[6]   This interpretation allowing a buyer to cancel a contract for any nonconformity dates back to the common law interpretation of the perfect tender rule in the law of sales which differed from the law of contracts, which allows rescission only for material breaches. Ramirez v. Autosport, 88 N.J. 277, 284, 440 A.2d 1345, 1349 (1982). Thus, Judge Learned Hand stated in Mitsubishi Goshi Kaisha v. J. Aron & Co., Inc., 16 F.2d 185, 186 (2d Cir.1926), that "[t]here is no room in commercial contracts for the doctrine of substantial performance." While Judge Hand wrote in a pre-UCC context, modern courts have reiterated the view that perfect tender does not require substantial performance but complete performance.

performance but complete performance); Jakowski v. Carole Chevrolet, Inc., 180 N.J.Super. 122, 125, 433 A.2d 841, 843 (1981) (degree of nonconformity of goods is irrelevant in assessing buyer's concomitant right to reject them) [citations of two additional cases omitted]. These courts have thus found that the tender must be perfect in the context of the perfect tender rule in the sense that the proffered goods must conform to the contract in every respect. Connecticut, however, appears in this regard to be the exception. Indeed, in the one Connecticut case interpreting § 2–601, Franklin Quilting Co., Inc. v. Orfaly, 1 Conn.App. 249, 251, 470 A.2d 1228, 1229 (1984), in a footnote, the appellate court stated that "the 'perfect tender rule' requires a *substantial nonconformity* to the contract before a buyer may rightfully reject the goods." Id. at 1229 n.3, citing White & Summers, Uniform Commercial Code, (2d ed.), § 8–3 (emphasis supplied). Thus, the Connecticut Appellate Court has adopted "the White and Summers construction of § 2–601 as in substance a rule that does not allow rejection for insubstantial breach such as a short delay causing no damage." Id., (3rd ed.). § 8–3. See also National Fleet Supply, Inc. v. Fairchild, 450 N.E.2d 1015, 1019 n. 4 (Ind.App.1983) (despite UCC's apparent insistence on perfect tender, it is generally understood that rejection is not available in circumstances where the goods or delivery fail in some small respect to conform to the terms of the sales contract (citing White and Summers)); McKenzie v. Alla-Ohio Coals, Inc., 29 U.C.C.Rep.Serv. (Callaghan) 852, 856–57 (D.D.C.1979) (there is substantial authority that where a buyer has suffered no damage, he should not be allowed to reject goods because of an insubstantial nonconformity).

... [A] federal court sitting in diversity must apply the law of the highest court of the state whose law applies. Since this court has determined that Connecticut law governs, the next task is to estimate whether the Connecticut Supreme Court would affirm the doctrine of substantial nonconformity, as stated in *Orfaly*, an opinion of the Connecticut Appellate Court. When the highest state court has not spoken on an issue, the federal court must look to the inferior courts of the state and to decisions of sister courts as well as federal courts. As noted, the weight of authority is that the doctrine of substantial performance does not apply to the sale of goods. However, as noted by White and Summers, in none of the cases approving of perfect rather than substantial tender was the nonconformity insubstantial, such as a short delay of time where no damage is caused to the buyer. White and Summers, Uniform Commercial Code (3rd ed.), § 8–3 n.8. In the instant case, there is no claim that the goods failed to conform to the contract. Nor is there a claim that the buyer was injured by the 16-day delay. There is, however, a claim that the goods were specially made, which might affect the seller's ability to resell. Thus Connecticut's interpretation of § 2–601 so as to mitigate the harshness of the perfect tender rule reflects the consensus of scholars that the rule is harsh and needs to be mitigated. Indeed, Summers and White state that the rule has been so "eroded" by the exceptions in the Code that "relatively little is left of it; the law would be little changed if § 2–601 gave the right to reject only upon 'substantial' nonconformity," especially since the Code requires a buyer or seller to act in good faith. R. Summers and J. White, Uniform Commercial Code (3rd ed.1988), § 8–3, at 357. See also Alden Press Inc. v. Block & Co., Inc., 123 Ill.Dec. 26, 173 Ill.App.3d 251, 527 N.E.2d 489, 493 (1988) (notwithstanding the perfect tender rule, the reasonableness of buyer's rejection of goods and whether such rejection of goods is in good faith are ultimately matters for the trier of fact); Printing Center of Texas v. Supermind Pub. Co., Inc., 669 S.W.2d 779, 784 (Tex.App.1984) (if the evidence establishes any nonconformity, the buyer is entitled to reject the goods as long as it is in good faith); Neumiller Farms, Inc. v. Cornett, 368 So.2d 272, 275 (Ala.1979) (claim of dissatisfaction with delivery of goods so as to warrant their rejection must be made in good faith, rather than in an effort to escape a bad bargain). A rejection of goods that have been specially manufactured for an insubstantial delay where no damage is caused is arguably not in good faith.

Although the Connecticut Supreme Court has not yet addressed the issue of substantial nonconformity, it has stated, in a precode case, Bradford Novelty Co. v. Technomatic, 142 Conn. 166, 170, 112 A.2d 214, 216 (1955), that although "[t]he time fixed by the parties for performance is, at law, deemed of the essence of the contract," where, as here, goods have been specially manufactured, "the time specified for delivery is less likely to be considered of the essence . . . [since] in such a situation there is a probability of delay, and the loss to the manufacturer is likely to be great if the buyer refuses to accept and pay because of noncompliance with strict performance." Id. But see Marlowe v. Argentine Naval Com'n, 808 F.2d 120, 124 (D.C.Cir.1986) (buyer within its rights to cancel a contract for 6-day delay in delivery since "time is of the essence in contracts for the sale of goods") citing Norrington v. Wright, 115 U.S. 188, 203 n.6 (1885) ("In the contracts of merchants, time is of the essence.")

After reviewing the case law in Connecticut, this court finds that in cases where the nonconformity involves a delay in the delivery of specially manufactured goods, the law in Connecticut requires substantial nonconformity for a buyer's rejection under § 2–601, and precludes a dismissal for failure to state a claim on the grounds that the perfect tender rule, codified at § 2–601, demands complete performance. Rather, Connecticut law requires a determination at trial as to whether a 16-day delay under these facts constituted a substantial nonconformity. [Defendant's motion to dismiss is denied.]

QUESTIONS AND NOTES

1.   The perfect-tender rule can be defended on the grounds that (1) in the usual case the seller can resell the goods to someone else and therefore is not substantially harmed by the rejection, and (2) the rule avoids difficult fact

determinations as to whether any particular breach is material. However, in cases like *D.P. Technology*, when the goods are specially manufactured for the buyer, it seems unfair to the seller to permit the buyer to reject for inconsequential delay. The court in *D.P. Technology* applied a Connecticut rule requiring "substantial nonconformity" for the right to reject goods under the perfect-tender rule to override the apparent rigidity of 2–601. What would the court have done if the computer or the software contained some minor defect, which the seller could not fix?

2. **Problem.** Candyland contracted to buy 100,000 pounds of sugar from Caine at a price of 20 cents per pound, delivery May 15. Caine tendered the sugar on May 14th, at which time the price of sugar was 12 cents per pound. Candyland refused to accept the sugar, even though it had storage space and would have incurred no additional expense by accepting it. Was the rejection rightful?

3. **Good-faith limitation on the buyer's right to reject.** Section 1–304 provides, "Every contract or duty within [the Uniform Commercial Code] imposes an obligation of good faith in its performance or enforcement." Does this limit the buyer's right to reject goods under 2–601? Is rejection within the ambit of "performance or enforcement"? Consider the following excerpt from Honnold, Buyer's Right of Rejection, 97 U.Pa.L.Rev. 457, 475–476 (1949):

> The precise scope intended for [1–304] is not apparent. But its language is sufficiently vague to invite the argument that a rejection in a falling market was engendered by an ulterior motive to avoid the price decline and therefore was not made in "good faith."
>
> This new legal tool may be used to good effect to bar untoward rejection. But it gives little aid in determining whether in any specific case rejection is an appropriate remedy. In its customary setting in problems of *bona fide* purchase, a concept such as "good faith" is necessary, and reasonably workable. In dealing with the propriety of rejection, however, a legal test framed in terms of the buyer's state of mind is much more elusive. Presumably a rejection of goods which were seriously defective would not be held improper on evidence that the buyer was aware of a market decline and was delighted to have an avenue of escape from the purchase. In this field, less subjective tests are needed.

What is the flaw in this passage? What is the content of the obligation to act in good faith?

4. Exactly what does it mean to say that a buyer may reject goods if the goods or the tender "fail in any respect to conform to the contract"? How does the Code define "conform"? If a contract calls for the sale of 10,000 bushels of wheat, does the buyer have a right to reject if the seller delivers 10,001 bushels? 9,999 bushels?

While the case from which the following excerpt is taken did not concern an attempted rejection, the idea expressed may be relevant.

Fargo's complaint alleges that the H-100 is "defective in material and workmanship" and "has required numerous and repetitive repairs, including some thirty-seven separate repair jobs." Certainly, however, every mechanical failure in a new and complex machine does not constitute a breach of warranty. N.C.R. v. Adell, 57 Mich.App. 413, 225 N.W.2d 785 (1975). At the outset then, it is necessary to distinguish and segregate those defects which merely required that [repairs] be performed and those legally significant defects which either remained uncured after reasonable opportunity to correct them or which are otherwise related to plaintiff's damage claims. Fargo does not contend that it was entitled to a perfect machine, nor that the installation and break-in period should have been completely service free.

Fargo Machine & Tool Co. v. Kearney & Trecker Corp., 428 F.Supp. 364, 370 (E.D.Mich.1977).

5. **Cure.** Section 1–304 is not the only section that imposes some limits on a buyer's right to reject nonconforming goods or a nonconforming tender. Section 2–508 permits a seller, after a buyer has rejected goods, to cure the nonconformity for which the buyer rejected. In Problem 2, then, even if Candyland's rejection were proper, Caine could re-tender the goods on May 15. Hence 2–508 lessens the harshness of the perfect-tender rule. It does not eliminate the harshness, however, because (1) re-tender will cause at least some additional expense, and (2) it may not be possible for the seller to acquire the necessary information and take the necessary steps to make an appropriate re-tender, as, for example, when tender is being made by a third party.

6. **Problem.** Koll's ordered 5,000 electric knives from Silex. When the knives arrive, Koll's discovers that there are only 4,500 in the shipment. The 4,500 all seem to conform to the contract. May Koll's reject the shipment? What if Koll's wants to reject 2,500 and keep 2,000: may it do so? Please consult 2–307, 2–601, 2–612, 2–105(6), 2–106(2). Is 1–304 relevant, too?

If the shipment is the first of two 5,000-unit shipments under a single contract for 10,000 knives, may Koll's reject all or part of the shipment? What additional facts are relevant?

7. **Problem.** One morning as you are having your first mug of coffee, a long-time client, the owner of a chain of independent grocery stores, phones you. She tells you that she has a contract with a brewery for 1,000 cases of premium microbrew. The price is $25 per case FOB Seller's loading dock, and the delivery date is today. A truck driver has just arrived at her dock, but he has only 600 cases. He said the other 400 were stolen while he was in a truck stop having lunch. And, she reports, the seller permitted the trucking company to issue a bill of lading for the beer that limits the trucking company's liability to $20 per case. She asks, "What should I do?" How do you respond?

8. **Problem.** Stark, the plumbing subcontractor on a construction job requiring Kohler brand plumbing fixtures, contracted with Supplies, Inc. for delivery on March 1st of 100 Kohler faucets. The faucets arrive in shipping

cartons marked Kohler, but the individual boxes containing the faucets are marked American Standard. The faucets themselves contain no identifying marks. May the buyer rightfully reject them? Does it make a difference whether or not the faucets actually are Kohler? that Supplies, Inc. notifies Stark at the time of delivery that they are Kohler?

What if Stark operates a retail plumbing supply store and purchases the fixtures for resale?

9.   CISG. The Convention on Contracts for the International Sale of Goods rejects the perfect tender rule. See Articles 25, 49(1)(a), 46(2), 47, 51. But see Article 52 as to early delivery. The CISG does not use the term rejection, but the apparent assumption is that the buyer can properly reject the goods only if it is "avoiding" the contract, and a contract can be avoided only for "fundamental breach," which is defined in Article 25.

In international sales, sellers could be substantially inconvenienced if a buyer in the country of destination could reject for minor defects, leaving the seller to arrange for their disposition. This may be true of sellers in some domestic transactions, too. Would you be in favor of abandoning the perfect-tender rule in domestic sales?

2.   INSTALLMENT CONTRACTS

As noted above, although Article 2 nominally adopts the perfect-tender rule for single-delivery contracts, it adopts essentially the substantial-performance rule for installment contracts. Section 2–612(2) provides that the buyer may reject an installment only if:

- the installment has a nonconformity,
- the nonconformity substantially impairs the value of the installment, and
- the nonconformity cannot be cured.

If the nonconformity substantially impairs the value of the whole contract—as opposed to just the value of the installment—the buyer may cancel the contract and recover damages for total breach. 2–612(3), 2–711(1).

In Graulich Caterer, Inc. v. Hans Holterbosch, Inc., 101 N.J.Super. 61, 243 A.2d 253 (App.Div.1968), Holterbosch contracted with Graulich for a large quantity of frozen meals to be heated in microwave ovens and sold at the Lowenbrau Pavilion at the 1964 New York World's Fair. The first delivery was made on April 23, 1964. Holterbosch's personnel were "stunned" by the product initially delivered and complained immediately that the units did not match previously furnished samples. The first delivery was rejected as "bland, unpresentable, tasteless," and generally unsaleable. The second delivery was no better than the first. Holterbosch cancelled the contract and installed conventional ovens to prepare food. Graulich sued for lost profits, claiming unjustifiable termination of the contract. The trial court held for Holterbosch. The appellate court affirmed:

Since warranties of sample and description are characterized as "express warranties," the "whole of the goods shall conform to the sample or model." N.J.S. 12A:2–313(1)(c). The "goods" to "conform" to the sample or model must be "in accordance with the obligations under the contract," N.J.S. 12A:2–106(2); here, to comply with the standards established by the March 17 taste-test of the samples. . . . Additionally, the implied warranty of fitness for purpose attaches to contracts of this type, where, as here, they are not specifically excluded. A breach of these warranties triggers a buyer's rights following seller's breach as catalogued in N.J.S. 12A:2–711. These remedies include, but are not limited to, cancellation, N.J.S. 12A:2–711(1), 2–106(4), "if the breach goes to the whole of the contract." N.J.S. 12A:2–612(3).

. . .

Here, Holterbosch had the right to reject any installment that was nonconforming, provided that the nonconformity substantially impaired the value of that installment and could not be cured. N.J.S. 12A:2–612(2). "Cure," novel to New Jersey's jurisprudence, permits the seller to cure a defective tender through repair, replacement or price allowance if he reasonably notifies the buyer of his curative intention and, in effecting the cure, makes a timely conforming delivery. N.J.S. 12A:2–508(1).

. . . We find that Holterbosch was justified in rejecting Graulich's tender of the April 23 initial installment since the nonconformity of the tendered goods with the accepted sample was incurable, and thus substantially impaired the value of that installment.

Replacing considerations of anticipatory repudiation and the material injury with the test of substantial impairment, N.J.S. 12A:2–612 adopts a more restrictive seller-oriented approach favoring "the continuance of the contract in the absence of an overt cancellation." See Comment [6]. To allow an aggrieved party to cancel an installment contract, N.J.S. 12A:2–612(3) requires (1) the breach be of the whole contract which occurs when the nonconformity of "one or more installments substantially impairs the value of the whole contract"; and (2) that seasonable notification of cancellation has been given if the buyer has accepted a nonconforming installment.

What amounts to substantial impairment presents a question of fact. . . . Comment [4] states that "substantial impairment of the value of an installment can turn not only on the quality of the goods but also on such factors as time, quantity, assortment and the like. It must be judged in terms of the normal or specifically known purposes of the contract."

At the Lowenbrau Pavilion on April 23, 1964 plaintiff Graulich, timely noticed of the nonconforming initial tender, gave assurance that future tenders would be cured to match the original samples. Unequivocally committed to the microwave kitchen method, defendant lent plaintiff three members from its staff in aid of this adjustment. Since plaintiff was given the opportunity to cure, there is no need to touch upon the substantiality of the initial nonconforming installment.

The second installment tender was as unsatisfactory as the first. The meat was dry, the gravy "gooey" and the complaints abundant. After the nonconforming second delivery it became apparent that eleventh-hour efforts attempting to rework and adjust the platters failed. Translating this into legal parlance, there was a nonconforming tender of the initial installment on a contract for the sale of goods; upon tender the buyer Holterbosch notified the seller Graulich of the nonconformity and unacceptable nature of the platters tendered; the failure of the cure assured by plaintiff, seller, was evidenced by a subsequently defective nonconforming delivery. The second unacceptable delivery and the failure of plaintiff's additional curative efforts left defendant in a position for one week without food. Time was critical. Plaintiff knew that platters of maximum quality were required on a daily installment basis. Because of defendant's immediate need for quality food and plaintiff's failure to cure, we find that the nonconformity of the second delivery, projected upon the circumstances of this case, "substantially impair[ed] the value of the whole contract [and resulted in] a breach of the whole." N.J.S. 12A:2–612(3). If the breach goes to the whole contract the buyer may cancel the whole contract. N.J.S. 12A:2–711(1). Accordingly, we find that Holterbosch was justified in canceling the installment agreement signed on April 1, 1964.

QUESTIONS

1. The contract called for daily delivery. When the first delivery was nonconforming, the buyer rejected it. This was permissible only if the nonconformity substantially impaired the value of the installment—which it did—*and* the nonconformity could not be cured. Was the nonconformity non-curable?

2. The buyer rejected the first installment. The next day it properly rejected the next installment, and it also cancelled the contract. Granted that the quality of the food was wholly unacceptable, why does unsatisfactory performance on two of 180 installments justify cancellation of the entire contract? Is the court faithful to the rationale for the rule in 2–612(2)?

Midwest Mobile Diagnostic Imaging, L.L.C. v. Dynamics Corporation of America

United States District Court, Western District of Michigan, 1997.
965 F.Supp. 1003.

■ ENSLEN, CHIEF JUDGE. [After extensive negotiations, in August 1995 plaintiff (MMDI) contracted to purchase four trailers from Ellis & Watts (E & W), doing business as Dynamics Corp. The seller was to outfit each of the trailers to accommodate an MRI unit to be supplied by Phillips, which was to certify that the completed trailers were satisfactory. MMDI paid $63,000 of the price at the signing of the contract. The delivery dates initially were left open, but the parties subsequently fixed December 1 as the date for delivering the first fully-equipped trailer. MMDI thereupon scheduled patients for visits starting on December 4.

[In mid-November E & W completed assembly, including installation of the MRI units supplied by Phillips, and sent a bill to MMDI, which paid another $321,500. Upon inspection on November 28, Phillips concluded that the trailer did not meet the contract specifications because the walls were not sufficiently stable. E & W accepted this conclusion and attempted to cure the nonconformities. Its cure, tendered on December 13, however, consisted of a system of large steel beams that were aesthetically unpleasing and impeded the servicing of the machine. After an exchange of correspondence, MMDI cancelled the contract on December 18 and sued for damages caused by E & W's breach.]

ANALYSIS

A. Breach of contract

The primary issue for resolution by the Court is whether MMDI rightfully rejected E & W's tender of the first trailer and then subsequently canceled the contract, or if its actions in mid-December constituted anticipatory repudiation of the contract. . . .

1. Installment Contract

Before turning to the specific questions of rejection and cancellation, the Court must first resolve a threshold issue. Under the UCC, the parties' rights to reject, cure, and cancel under an installment contract differ substantially from those defined under a single delivery contract. Consequently, resolution of whether the contract is an installment contract is of primary concern. Section 2–612(1) defines an "installment contract" as "one which requires or authorizes the delivery of goods in separate lots to be separately accepted. . . ." The commentary following this section emphasizes that the "definition of an installment contract is phrased more broadly in this Article [than in its previous incarnation as the Uniform Sales Act] so as to cover installment deliveries tacitly authorized by the circumstances or by the option of either party." § 2–612, cmt. 1.

Plaintiff argues that the contract between itself and E & W does not constitute an installment contract because it authorizes delivery in commercial units, and not lots, as required by subsection (1). However, upon review of the Code section defining those terms, it becomes clear that those terms are not mutually exclusive. Section 2–105 defines a "lot" as a "parcel or single article which is the subject matter of a separate sale or delivery, whether or not it is sufficient to perform the contract." The same section defines a commercial unit as "such a unit of goods as by commercial usage is a single whole for purposes of sale and division of which materially impairs its character or value on the market or in use. A commercial unit may be a single article (as a machine) or a set of articles (as a suite of furniture or an assortment of sizes) or a quantity (as a bale, gross, or carload) or any other unit treated in use or in the relevant market as a single whole." Thus, a lot, which is the measure of goods that the contract states will be delivered together in one installment, can be a single commercial unit. Consequently, § 2–612 applies wherever a contract for multiple items authorizes the delivery of the items in separate groups at different times, whether or not the installment constitutes a commercial unit.

. . . [N]either party disputes that they agreed to have the trailers delivered at four separate times. Therefore, the Court finds that the contract in dispute is an installment contract.

2.   Right of Rejection

Section 2–612, therefore, is the starting point for the Court's analysis of MMDI's actions on December 13, 1995. Under § 2–612, the buyer's right to reject is far more limited than the corresponding right to reject under a single delivery contract defined under § 2–601. Under § 2–601, a buyer has the right to reject, "if the goods or tender of delivery fail in any respect to conform to the contract. . . ." Known as the "perfect tender" rule, this standard requires a very high level of conformity. Under this rule, the buyer may reject a seller's tender for any trivial defect, whether it be in the quality of the goods, the timing of performance, or the manner of delivery. To avoid injustice, the Code limits the buyer's correlative right to cancel the contract upon such rejection by providing a right to cure under § 2–508. § 2–508, cmt. 2. Under § 2–508, the seller has a right to cure if s/he seasonably notifies the buyer of the intent to do so, *and* either 1) the time for performance has not yet passed, or 2) the seller had reason to believe that the goods were in conformity with the contract. Thus, § 2–508's right to cure serves to temper the buyer's expansive right to reject under a single delivery contract.

Section 2–612 creates an exception to the perfect tender rule. Under subsection (2), a buyer may not reject nonconforming tender unless the defect substantially impairs the value of the installment. In addition, "if the nonconformity is curable and the seller gives adequate assurances of cure," the buyer must accept the installment. § 2–612, cmt. 5. But even if rejection is proper under subsection 2, cancellation of the contract is not appropriate unless the defect substantially impairs the value of the whole contract. § 2–612(3), cmt. 6. Because this section significantly restricts the buyer's right to cancel under an installment contract, there is no corresponding necessity for reference to § 2–508; the seller's right to cure is implicitly defined by § 2–612.[6]

a.   Delivery Date

Before proceeding with the analysis of MMDI's December 13 rejection, the Court initially notes that E & W's tender on December 13 constituted a cure attempt for the wall-flexing defect which delayed the delivery of the first trailer beyond the agreed upon delivery date. Although under § 2–612 the delivery date does not cut off the seller's right to cure, it does have an effect on the rights of the parties. *See* Graulich Caterer, Inc. v. Hans Holterbosch, Inc., [101 N.J.Super. 61, 243 A.2d 253, 261 (1968)].

In the instant case, the original, written contract included no definite delivery date. Instead, the contract left the delivery term to be agreed upon at a later date. At the time of execution, the parties both expected delivery of the first trailer to take place in October. During the months after the execution of the contract, however, the parties modified the deadline for the first installment of the contract on several occasions. As noted above, upon review of the testimony and documentary evidence, the Court finds that, whatever delivery date the parties had agreed upon prior to November 1995, by early November they had renegotiated their agreement to establish a December 1, 1995 delivery date. *See* § 2–209 (sales contract may be modified by oral or written agreement without consideration, so long as agreement does not state otherwise).

Defendant argues, however, that, even if the parties had at one point agreed upon a December 1, 1995 deadline, when the first trailer failed the Philips road test on November 28, 1995, the parties renegotiated the delivery term to allow E & W a reasonable time to cure the defect. While E & W is correct that, as of December 1, it had a reasonable time in which to cure the wall-flexing problem, the Court disagrees that MMDI's willingness to wait for a cure constitutes an agreement to extend the delivery deadline. Because the parties believed that the defect was curable and E & W, without solicitation, unequivocally promised to cure it, under § 2–612, MMDI had no choice but to accept an offer of cure. To reject the installment on November 28 would have constituted a violation of § 2–612. The Court, therefore, finds that any negotiations the parties engaged in regarding delivery after discovery of the wall-flexing problem,

---

[6] Courts of other jurisdictions have reached differing conclusions with regard to the interaction between §§ 2–612 and 2–508. *See, e.g.* Arkla Energy Resources v. Roye Realty & Dev., Inc., 9 F.3d 855 (10th Cir.1993). This Court does not find the arguments of these other courts persuasive, however, and notes that their decisions are not binding on this Court. Nevertheless, the Court also notes that, since the time for delivery of the first installment had already passed on December 1, 1995 . . . and defendant could not have reasonably believed and, in fact, did not believe that the trailer was in conformity with the contract on that date, defendant had no right to cure under § 2–508.

did not constitute a modification of the delivery date for the first installment, but rather involved negotiation regarding cure. Since no specific date for delivery of a cure was agreed upon during those negotiations, under section 2–309(1), E & W had a reasonable time to effectuate a cure. Although there is some question as to whether further delay would have been reasonable, the Court finds that, as of December 13, 1995, a reasonable time had not yet passed. Therefore, defendant's tender of a cure was timely.

b.   *Substantial Impairment of the Installment*

The Court's conclusion that E & W's December 13 tender was an attempt to cure the November 28 breach raises another question: which standard of conformity applies to cure under an installment contract, perfect tender or substantial impairment? Looking to the rationale behind § 2–612, the Court notes that the very purpose of allowing the seller time to cure under this section is to permit it additional time to meet the obligations of the contract. The assumption is that, because the parties have an ongoing relationship, the seller should be given an opportunity to make up the deficiency. This section was not designed to allow the seller to have a never-ending series of chances to bring the item into conformity with the contract. Nor was it enacted to force the buyer to accept a nonconforming product as satisfaction of the contract. Consequently, it is logical that a tender of cure should be required to meet the higher "perfect tender" standard. On its face, however, § 2–612, which generally defines a buyer's right to reject goods under an installment contract, requires . . . substantial impairment in this context as well. Thus, there is some question as to which is the appropriate standard. The answer is not crucial however, since the trailer in this case fails under *both* standards. Because a decision on this point will not affect the ultimate outcome in this case, the Court declines to address the issue. Instead, the Court proceeds with the substantial impairment analysis provided by § 2–612.

To establish substantial impairment of the value of an installment, the buyer " 'must present objective evidence that with respect to its own needs, the value of the goods was substantially impaired.' " Arkla Energy Resources v. Roye Realty & Dev., Inc., 9 F.3d 855, 862 (10th Cir.1993) (quoting Bodine Sewer, Inc. v. Eastern Illinois Precast, Inc., 143 Ill.App.3d 920, 97 Ill.Dec. 898, 906, 493 N.E.2d 705, 713 (1986)). *See also* § 2–612, cmt. 4. The existence of such nonconformity depends on the facts and circumstances of each case, and "can turn not only on the quality of the goods but also on such factors as time . . . , and the like." § 2–612, cmt. 4. *See eg.,* Colonial Dodge, Inc. v. Miller, 420 Mich. 452, 457–58, 362 N.W.2d 704 (1984) (holding missing spare tire in new car had special devaluing effect for the buyer and thus could constitute substantial impairment). Finally, whether nonconformity rises to the level of substantial impairment may be judged by reference to the concept of material breach under traditional contract law. *See* Durfee v. Rod Baxter Imports, Inc., 262 N.W.2d 349 (Minn.1977).

In the instant case, plaintiff alleges several aspects in which defendant's December 13 tender failed to conform to contract obligations. Plaintiff contends that the trailer tendered on December 13 with the bracing structure did not conform to the parties' agreement because: 1) it was not and could not be certified by Philips without conditions for use with the 1.5T scanner and 2) its interior design did not conform with the parties' agreements. Because of these defects, MMDI argues that the value of trailer was reduced substantially. Defendant, on the other hand, contends that the contract required only that the trailer meet the technical specifications provided by Philips, and that, therefore, the December 13 trailer was in complete compliance with its terms.

The written contract signed by the parties in this case is relatively skeletal and thus, requires interpretation. The Court's fundamental purpose in interpreting the terms of the contract is to give effect to the intent of the parties as it existed at the time the agreement was made. . . .

As instructed by the commentary to § 2–612, the Court begins the substantial impairment analysis by looking to the "normal and specifically known purposes of the contract." § 2–612, cmt. 4. Reviewing the evidence presented, the Court finds that the primary purpose of the contract was to provide the plaintiff with four trailers for use with the Philips 1.5T scanner. With that in mind, the parties agreed that the trailers would be constructed in accordance with the specifications provided by Philips and that the trailer would be not be ready for delivery until Philips certification had been received. Philips did not, however, ever certify the trailer for unconditional use with the bracing structure. Because the bracing structure prevented normal service of the scanner magnet, it was only approved as a temporary fix.

. . . The bracing structure's shape and orientation prevented removal of the outer panels from the scanner magnet and made some repairs to the magnet more difficult and more dangerous. Furthermore, in order to perform certain repairs, the steel brace would have to be unbolted and removed. Once removed, the scanner magnet would have to be recalibrated and retested. Consequently, Philips' decision to refuse certification was entirely justified. Having found no evidence of bad faith or dishonesty on the part of Philips, the Court finds that defendant's failure to meet this condition constituted a breach of the parties' agreement. . . . The Court, therefore, finds that this failure to conform to the parties' agreement, in and of itself, constituted a material breach.

In addition to violating the requirement that the trailer receive certification from Philips, plaintiff correctly asserts that defendant breached yet another term of the contract. The Court notes that the bracing structure also violated the parties' implied agreement regarding the design of the interior of the trailer. . . .

. . . [W]hen the contract was executed, the parties both understood that the trailer's interior was meant to be aesthetically pleasing. It is the very nature of a mobile MRI trailer to function as an extension of the hospital it services. Since E & W was in the business of constructing trailers for mobile medical uses, it no doubt understood that the appearance of the trailer's interior could impact the comfort of MMDI's patients. Indeed, it is apparent that E & W realized such aesthetics were important to the value of the trailer, since, in its initial negotiations with MMDI, E & W included a cut-away drawing of the interior of a mobile unit which read: "Spacious, efficient layout with clean, *aesthetically pleasing* interior." The Court, therefore, finds that the agreement between the parties required that the interior of the trailer be aesthetically pleasing.

Such a condition of satisfaction by one of the parties to the contract will only be excused if approval is withheld unreasonably. *See* American Oil Company v. Carey, 246 F.Supp. 773 (E.D.Mich.1965); Restatement (Second) of Contracts, § 228. In the instant case, upon review of photographs of the bracing structure and testimony of those experienced in this industry, and in light of the fact that the interior of the trailer should match that of a hospital and not a construction site, the Court finds that plaintiff's refusal to approve the aesthetics of the design was commercially reasonable. Given that an integral aspect of the trailer's function is to serve as a clinic for patients undergoing medical procedures, and given MMDI's clients' expectations after having viewed the trailer at [a preview before the unit was formally delivered in late November], such a defect in the trailer's interior also reduced the value of the trailer substantially.

Upon review of the evidence, the Court finds that the bracing structure substantially impaired the value of the first trailer. Although the trailer met the express technical Philips' specifications for wall-flexing, it was never certified by the manufacturer. The failure of this condition does not relieve defendant of liability because it was defendant's failure to properly construct the trailer that prevented certification. In light of the specific facts and circumstances of this case, the Court finds that this deficiency substantially impaired the value of the installment. When coupled with the trailer's failure to conform with the aesthetic requirements of the contract and the delay caused by the cure attempt, the Court holds that the cure attempt clearly constitutes a substantial breach within the meaning of § 2–612(2).

Substantial impairment, however, does not in itself justify rejection of the installment. As noted above, the buyer must still accept tender if the defect can be cured and the seller gives adequate assurances. . . . Defendant has failed in this regard. The Court notes that neither E & W's statements during the December 13 conference call nor the letter sent the following day constituted adequate assurances. On the contrary, during the December 13 conference call, Andrew Pike, the President of E

& W denied the existence of a defect, disclaimed any continuing obligation to cure under the contract, and stated that he did not believe a better design could be made which would remedy the wall-flexing problem. Furthermore, on December 14, Mr. Pike again ignored the servicing problems that the bracing structure had caused, ignored the fact that the bracing structure had not been approved for permanent use by Philips, and reiterated his doubt that the design could be constructed in a more aesthetically pleasing manner. Under these circumstances, the Court finds that MMDI's rejection of E & W's cure on December 13 constituted a rightful rejection under § 2–612(2).

3. Cancellation

a. *Substantial Impairment of Contract as a Whole*

The fact that rejection of one installment is proper does not necessarily justify cancellation of the entire contract. Under § 2–612(3) the right to cancel does not arise unless the nonconforming goods substantially impair the value of the *entire* contract. Indeed, as noted above, the very purpose of the substantial impairment requirement of § 2–612(3) is to preclude parties from canceling an installment contract for trivial defects.

Whether a breach constitutes "substantial impairment" of the entire contract is a question of fact. To make such a determination, the Court should consider "the cumulative effect of [the breaching party's] performance under the contract, based on the totality of the circumstances. . . ." Neufer v. Video Greetings, Inc., 931 F.2d 56, 1991 WL 65439 (6th Cir.1991) (unpublished). Ultimately, "[w]hether the nonconformity in any given installment justifies cancellation as to the future depends, not on whether such nonconformity indicates an intent or likelihood that future deliveries will also be defective, but whether the nonconformity substantially impairs the value of the whole contract." § 2–612, cmt. 6. Thus, the question is one of present breach which focuses on the importance of the nonconforming installment relative to the contract as a whole. If the nonconformity only impairs the aggrieved party's security with regard to future installments, s/he "has the right to demand adequate assurances but [ ] not an immediate right to cancel the entire contract." § 2–612, cmt. 6. The right to cancel will be triggered only if "material inconvenience or injustice will result if the aggrieved party is forced to wait and receive an ultimate tender minus the part or aspect repudiated." § 2–610, cmt. 3 (noting the test for anticipatory repudiation under § 2–610 is the same as the test for cancellation under § 2–612(3)).

In the instant case, there is substantial evidence that one of the primary purposes of this contract was to provide MMDI with a fourth mobile MRI trailer so that it could meet the growing demand for its services. Thus, impairment of one of the four installments would have a substantial negative impact on MMDI. Moreover, an early delivery time was of primary importance to MMDI, as E & W was well aware. By failing to cure the November 28 breach on the first installment, E & W substantially delayed completion of the remainder of the contract which delayed MMDI's ability to begin use of the 1.5T MRI trailer it had promised to its customers [on November 3 at the preview event]. Having found that substantial injustice would be done to plaintiff if it were required to accept the remaining three trailers after substantial delay as satisfaction of the contract, the Court finds that plaintiff rightfully canceled the contract on December 18, 1995. . . .

QUESTIONS AND NOTES

1. The court states that the date for delivery of the first trailer was December 1. Could MMDI have rejected the trailer on December 1? Was MMDI required to accept the trailer at that time? Could MMDI have argued that E & W had totally breached the contract on December 1, thereby allowing it to cancel the contract, as permitted by 2–711(1) when a breach goes to the whole contract?

2. Problem. Stratton contracted with Disaster Recovery to deliver six generators (one per month), each to be capable of producing 1,000 Kw/hour, plus or minus 2%. In due course, Stratton tendered delivery of a generator that produced 900 Kw/hour. Disaster Recovery refused to accept it. Was this proper?

Assume that when Disaster Recovery complained, Stratton agreed to correct the problem. A week after picking up the generator, Stratton returned it to Disaster Recovery. The generator produced 975 Kw/hour, and Stratton said, "That's the best we can do." May Disaster Recovery reject the generator?

3. In Holiday Mfg. Co. v. B.A.S.F. Systems, Inc., 380 F.Supp. 1096 (D.Neb.1974), the parties entered into a contract for the manufacture and sale of 6 million tape player cassettes. The cassettes were to be delivered at the rate of 500,000 per month. A year later, however, only 1.5 million cassettes had been delivered. In addition, the seller had a number of difficulties in producing those cassettes: there were depressions in the cassette surface, cracks, oversize cassettes, and tape leader misalignment. Each time a problem appeared, the buyer called it to the attention of the seller, and the seller was able to change the manufacturing process to correct it. Then, nearly a year after first deliveries under the contract were due, the seller delivered cassettes with a new defect, improper guide-hole spacing. At that point the buyer cancelled the contract claiming that, under § 2–612(3), the seller's delays and the numerous defects had substantially impaired the value of the whole contract.

The court held that the buyer improperly terminated. It stated that the buyer had not treated the delays as being serious but rather seemed willing to allow whatever time was needed to correct the various defects. As to the defects, the court said that all were corrected except the last and that under the circumstances there was no substantial impairment. This seems to suggest that as long as a seller is willing and able to remedy defects in its performance, the buyer must continue accepting that performance.

Compare the result in Rester v. Morrow, 491 So.2d 204 (Miss.1986), involving an attempt by the purchaser of an automobile to revoke acceptance of the goods in a single-delivery contract, pursuant to 2–608. That section employs a similar test for revocation of acceptance that 2–612(3) uses for the buyer's right to cancel an installment contract, viz., substantial impairment to the buyer of the value of the whole contract. Over the course of an entire year, the dealer had repaired a number of defects, but finally as to three defects that were themselves fairly trivial, the dealer did not make the repairs as promised. The court held that whether the value of the car to the buyer was substantially impaired was a jury question. The court said: "[On the day of revocation] Rester pointed out a soiled carpet, an unrepaired fuse panel, and an unreplaced piece of chrome. Unquestionably these are minor defects. . . . But our law does not allow a seller to postpone revocation in perpetuity by fixing everything that goes wrong with the automobile. There comes a time when enough is enough—when an automobile purchaser, after having to take his car to the shop for repairs an inordinate number of times and experiencing all of the attendant inconvenience, is entitled to say, 'That's all,' and revoke, notwithstanding the seller's repeated good faith efforts to fix the car."

Which of these decisions is more faithful to Article 2?

4.   Leases. Article 2A follows the approach of Article 2 to installment contracts. See 2A–510.

3.   PROCEDURE FOR EFFECTIVE REJECTION AND DUTIES AFTER REJECTION

If the goods and the tender conform to the contract, the buyer must accept them. If either the goods or the tender of them does not conform to the contract, in a single-delivery contract the buyer may reject them. Sections 2–513 and 2–602 govern rejection; the former provides that the buyer has a right to inspect the goods before accepting them, and the latter provides that rejection must occur within a reasonable time after tender and is ineffective unless the buyer gives timely notice to the seller. Section 2–606 governs acceptance of the goods and provides the ways in which acceptance may occur. Please read these sections, and note that under 2–606 acceptance does not depend on the buyer's intent to accept.

As a general rule, a person who brings a lawsuit must establish by a preponderance of the evidence every fact essential to the claim being asserted. This is true of actions under the UCC, so if the seller is suing because the buyer rejected the goods, one of the elements of the seller's claim is that the goods conform to the contract. Hence, the burden of proving that fact is on the seller. If, however, the buyer has accepted the goods and refuses to pay for them because they allegedly fail to conform to the contract, 2–607(4) places the burden of proving the fact of nonconformity on the *buyer*. This is true even if the issue arises in a lawsuit by the seller to recover the price of the goods. Sometimes it is not easy to determine whether the goods conform. In those instances, and some others as well, it is essential to know whether the buyer has accepted or rejected the goods.

———

Miron v. Yonkers Raceway, Inc.

United States Court of Appeals, Second Circuit, 1968.
400 F.2d 112.

■ J. JOSEPH SMITH, CIRCUIT JUDGE: Yonkers Raceway, Inc. and Saul Finkelstein appeal from a judgment of the District Court for the Southern District of New York, Richard H. Levet, Judge, entered after a trial without a jury, rendering them liable to plaintiffs for the purchase price of a horse and dismissing their counterclaims on the merits. . . .

I.

In September 1965, plaintiffs entered the horse "Red Carpet" in an auction called the "Old Glory Horse Sale," sponsored by Raceway. The contract by which Red Carpet was consigned to Raceway for sale provided that Raceway would act as plaintiffs' exclusive agent for the sale of the horse and would receive a commission of 10% on the accepted bid, and incorporated by reference the "Terms and Conditions of Sale." The Terms and Conditions of Sale provided, *inter alia:* that the horses were offered for sale according to the laws of New York, that title and "all risk and responsibility for the horse" pass to the buyer at the fall of the auctioneer's hammer, that "No delivery will be made until final settlement," and that "unless otherwise expressly announced at time of sale, there is no guarantee of any kind as to the soundness or condition or other quality of any horse sold in this Sale except that horses which are unsound in eyes or wind, or are 'cribbers,' must be announced at time of sale * * * Any horse whose condition is as aforesaid and is not so announced at time of sale, or where sex is incorrectly represented at time of sale, will be subject to return to Consignor * * * [provided that the buyer gives notice in writing] within seven days of sale. Any other representation, warranty or guarantee of the Consignor which is announced or otherwise given shall not extend beyond 24 hours after the fall of the Auctioneer's hammer or until final payment has been made, whichever is sooner."

Plaintiffs delivered Red Carpet to Raceway on October 17, 1965; the auction of the horse took place early in the afternoon of October 19. At $17,000 there was a lull in the bidding, whereupon Murray Brown, plaintiffs' employee, took the microphone and said:

> This horse has won 2 of his last 3 starts. On September 24, he raced on a muddy track, big stake race in Montreal * * * beating Mr. Sea Song. Now, you know what Mr. Sea Song has done this year * * * he's a top free-for-all horse and this horse beat him racing a good trip, and this is just recently. He's as sound—as,

as gutty a horse as you want to find anywhere. He'll race a good
mile for you every time. He's got loads of heart and you're way
off on the price of this horse.[2]

The bidding then resumed, and defendant Finkelstein submitted the
highest bid, which was $32,000.

By about 3:00 p.m. that day, Raceway delivered possession of Red
Carpet to Finkelstein without obtaining any part of the purchase price,
and Finkelstein immediately had the horse transported to his barn at
Roosevelt Raceway, Westbury, Long Island. The next morning, Cruise,
the trainer for Finkelstein's horses, took Red Carpet out of his stall and
hitched him to a jog cart. He observed some swelling of the horse's left
hind leg at that time, and when the horse was caused to walk and trot, it
limped and favored its left hind leg. Cruise returned Red Carpet to the
stall, and summoned Dr. Bernard F. Brennan, a veterinarian, who found
that Red Carpet's left hind leg was swollen, warm and sensitive.

Finkelstein notified Raceway, at about 11:30 a.m. that day, October
20, that Red Carpet was lame and not sound, and that afternoon an
official of Raceway notified Brown, at plaintiffs' stables, of Finkelstein's
complaint. Finkelstein subsequently demanded, as we have said, that
plaintiffs take back the horse because it was not sound, as warranted,
but they have continued to refuse to accept its return. Neither Raceway
nor Finkelstein has paid plaintiffs any part of the purchase price for Red
Carpet.

The basic factual issue tried below was whether Red Carpet was
sound, as warranted, at the time when the auctioneer's hammer fell and
all risks passed to Finkelstein as the buyer. The defendants' evidence on
this issue consisted of X-rays of the horse's left hind leg.

Dr. Brennan testified that he took X-rays of Red Carpet's leg on the
afternoon of October 20, and prints were introduced as the defendants'
Exhibits B, C, D1 and E1. The X-rays revealed a broken splint bone,
which, it was agreed by witnesses for all of the parties, is enough to
render a racehorse unsound. Both of the defendants' expert witnesses . . .
testified that Exhibits B and D1 revealed calcification around the site of
the fracture indicating that the fracture was two or three weeks old. The
plaintiffs' experts testified, however, that Exhibit D1, unlike Exhibit B,
did not show calcification, and concluded that the X-rays must have been
taken on different days. The defendants countered by offering testimony
that a difference in intensity between the exhibits explained the fact that
callus growth was less visible on D1 than on B, but the court found that
Exhibit D1 showed no calcification and that it therefore was not taken on
the same day as Exhibit B. The court also found that Exhibits D1 and E1
were undated, that Exhibits B and C were admittedly incorrectly dated,
and that no business records sufficient to prove the date on which the X-

---

[2] This statement was recorded on tape. Plaintiffs have conceded that it constituted a
warranty that the horse was sound.

rays were taken had been produced, and concluded that the exhibits lacked sufficient probative force to establish the date on which the fracture occurred. We see no reason why this conclusion should not stand.

The expert witnesses were in substantial agreement that the symptoms of a broken splint bone are swelling, heat which is perceptible to the touch, and sensitivity and lameness, and that these symptoms become apparent immediately or very soon after the occurrence of the fracture. Thus if Red Carpet's splint bone was broken at the time of sale, an examination of the horse after the sale would have disclosed that fact. Finkelstein testified that he was not an experienced horse buyer, and ordinarily has a trainer or veterinarian examine the legs of horses he buys, but he went to the auction on October 19, 1965 intending to buy two brood mares, and for that reason did not have his trainer or a veterinarian with him. Although he observed the horse when it was led into the ring at the auction, he did not examine it or look at its legs at the time of the sale. The court found that neither Finkelstein nor his agents inspected or examined the horse prior to the time when Cruise observed a swelling of its left hind leg on the day after the sale.

The plaintiffs offered, on the basic issue of the time of the fracture, testimony of persons who had observed and examined Red Carpet on the day of the sale. Roger White, a competitor of the Mirons, testified that he inspected the horse with the intention of buying it if the price was right, and that he couldn't see anything wrong with it. Dr. Rene Rosaire Gauthier, who accompanied White to the auction and examined Red Carpet for him, testified that when he examined Red Carpet's legs he observed no heat or swelling, and that he saw the horse trotting and walking without limping or manifesting any lameness. The court found, on the basis of this and other testimony, that "On October 19, 1965, prior to sale, the horse's left hind leg was neither swollen, hot, nor lame."[5]

The District Court's finding on the basic factual issue was expressed in terms of failure to carry the burden of proof. Concluding that under New York law Finkelstein had accepted Red Carpet and therefore had the burden of proving a breach of warranty, the court found: "Defendant Finkelstein has failed to prove by a fair preponderance of the credible evidence that the horse was not 'sound' at the time of its sale to him on October 19, 1965."

We will first consider the questions relevant to whether there was a breach of warranty, and then turn to the issues raised by the counterclaims.

---

[5]   The horse's groom, who cared for it from September 24, 1965 to October 19, exercising it and rubbing its legs daily, did not see any swelling on the left hind leg, and did not see the horse limping. An X-ray of the horse's left hind leg taken on September 30, 1965 showed that on that date Red Carpet did not have a broken splint bone. Red Carpet raced on September 24, 1965, finishing first; on October 2, 1965, finishing first; and on October 16, 1965, finishing sixth.

II.

We affirm the judgment below on the breach of warranty issue, because we agree with the District Court that under New York law Finkelstein had the burden of proving a breach of warranty and we find ample support in the record for the finding that Finkelstein did not carry that burden successfully. The plaintiffs have argued forcefully that we need not consider who had the burden of proof on the issue, but we must disagree.

. . .

The District Court based its determination that Finkelstein had the burden on New York Uniform Commercial Code ("U.C.C.") § 2–607(4), which provides: "The burden is on the buyer to establish any breach with respect to the goods accepted." The question thus is whether Finkelstein accepted the horse, and we turn for guidance to U.C.C. § 2–606(1), which states:

Acceptance of goods occurs when the buyer

(a)   after a reasonable opportunity to inspect the goods signifies to the seller that the goods are conforming or that he will take or retain them in spite of their nonconformity; or

(b)   fails to make an effective rejection (subsection (1) of Section 2–602), but such acceptance does not occur until the buyer has had a reasonable opportunity to inspect them; or

(c)   does any act inconsistent with the seller's ownership; but if such act is wrongful as against the seller it is an acceptance only if ratified by him.

It has not been argued that Finkelstein accepted the horse under subsection (a). We doubt he could be said to have done any act inconsistent with the plaintiffs' ownership of the horse, within the meaning of subsection (c), but we need not decide the applicability of that subsection, for we think the trial judge was right in finding that Finkelstein failed to make an effective rejection of the horse under U.C.C. § 2–602(1), thereby accepting it under subsection (b). U.C.C. § 2–602(1) provides: "Rejection of goods must be within a reasonable time after their delivery or tender. It is ineffective unless the buyer seasonably notifies the seller."

Finkelstein accepted the horse, then, if having had a reasonable opportunity to inspect it, he did not reject it within a reasonable time.[14]

---

[14] A "reasonable opportunity to inspect," U.C.C. § 2–606(1)(b), may of course encompass more than merely a reasonable time to inspect; here, there is no question that Finkelstein had the facilities for inspection available, and the only question on appeal was whether he waited too long.

A reasonable period for rejection overlaps a reasonable opportunity to inspect under U.C.C. § 2–606(1)(b). Thus if inspection discloses a defect, there remains the obligation to reject within a reasonable time. But in many cases where the buyer passes up a reasonable opportunity to inspect, he thus fails to reject within a reasonable time, and we think that this is one of those cases, for reasons stated in the text.

What is reasonable depends upon an evaluation of all of the circumstances, and we would therefore be reluctant to overturn the findings and conclusions of the trial judge on these issues. He has a feel for the circumstances of the case which we could not possibly have.[15] Moreover, the finding that Finkelstein did not reject the horse within a reasonable time seems to us to be clearly correct.

As the trial judge rightly pointed out, "The fact that the subject matter of the sale in this case was a live animal * * * bears on what is a reasonable time to inspect and reject." Finkelstein's own testimony showed that it is customary, when buying a racehorse, to have a veterinarian or trainer examine the horse's legs, and we agree that the existence of this custom is very important in determining whether there was a reasonable opportunity to inspect the horse. See Official Comment to U.C.C. § 1–204 [revised 1–205], para. 2. We gather from the record that the reason it is customary to examine a racehorse's legs at the time of sale is that a splint bone is rather easily fractured (there was testimony that a fracture could result from the horse kicking itself), and although the judge made no specific findings as to this, we assume that is generally what he had in mind when he pointed out that "a live animal is more prone to rapid change in condition and to injury than is an inanimate object." As we have said, Finkelstein did not have the horse examined either at the place of sale or at his barn later the day of the sale. He thus passed up a reasonable opportunity to inspect Red Carpet.

Finkelstein having had a reasonable opportunity to inspect Red Carpet on the day of the sale, we have no problem with the finding that the attempted rejection on the next day did not come within a reasonable time. In addition to our reluctance to question the trial judge's finding as to what is a reasonable time, we take into account that what is a reasonable time for rejection depends on the purpose of rejection. See U.C.C. § 1–204(2) [revised 1–205(1)]. Where goods are effectively rejected for breach of warranty, the burden of proving that they conform presumably remains on the seller,[17] whereas upon acceptance the buyer has the burden to establish any breach. U.C.C. § 2–607(4). In this case, the subject of the sale is a racehorse warranted to be sound, and the record clearly shows that an injury such as occurred here, rendering a horse unsound, may be a matter of chance, proof of the exact time of injury being very difficult to make. In these circumstances, the burden of

---

[15] Cf. the cases in which it has been said that what is a reasonable time for inspection is a question of fact for the jury; e.g., C.W. Anderson Hosiery Co. v. Dixie Knitting Mills, Inc., 204 F.2d 503, 505 (4 Cir.1953); see Annot., 52 A.L.R.2d 900 (1957).

[17] The official comment to U.C.C. § 2–602, para. 3, states that the section applies only to rightful rejection by the buyer. Yet acceptance may depend upon whether there has been a rejection under that section, and the allocation of the burden of proving whether there was a defect, and thus whether or not there was "rightful rejection," depends upon whether there has been acceptance. See U.C.C. §§ 2–606(1)(b) and 2–607(4). The only sensible construction of these sections would seem to be that non-acceptance, consisting of attempted rejection within a reasonable time after delivery or tender, amounts to rightful rejection if the seller fails to prove that the goods conform, but is a breach if the seller proves conformity.

proof on the issue of soundness at the time of sale cannot fairly rest on the seller where the buyer has taken possession of the horse, transported it to his barn, and kept it overnight before discovering the injury and informing the seller of it. We conclude that rejection did not take place within a reasonable time after delivery, and Finkelstein thus accepted the horse. In short, since one of the consequences of acceptance is that the buyer bears the burden of proving any breach, the fairness of allocating the burden one way or the other is relevant in determining whether acceptance has occurred—here, whether rejection took place within a reasonable time.

The defendants have argued strenuously that inspection and rejection on the day after the sale is certainly soon enough, and the argument would gain substantial strength if another sort of defect were involved and we took into account that the customary type of inspection at the time of sale might not disclose aspects of a horse's soundness other than the condition of its legs, and that these aspects, unlike the condition of the legs, would be very unlikely to change overnight. There is nothing in the record as to how much the customary inspection at the time of sale would show; Finkelstein testified only that he has a trainer or veterinarian examine the legs of horses he buys. In any case, if there are defects which are not discoverable by the inspection which the District Court found Finkelstein had a reasonable opportunity to make, the problem is taken care of by U.C.C. § 2–608(1), which provides in relevant part:

> The buyer may revoke his acceptance of a lot or commercial unit whose nonconformity substantially impairs its value to him if he has accepted it.

* * *

> (b) without discovery of such nonconformity if his acceptance was reasonably induced either by the difficulty of discovery before acceptance or by the seller's assurances.

The answer to the argument is that inspection is not necessarily final; where there are defects discoverable by a customary inspection at the time of sale, a buyer in Finkelstein's position will not be excused from making that inspection and rejecting the goods within a reasonable time, if a defect is disclosed, on the ground that there are possible critical defects which only a more thorough inspection would disclose. There are no conceptual problems involved in this approach, for there is nothing ultimate about any of the conceptions we are using. Since a finding of acceptance depends upon a finding that there was a reasonable opportunity to inspect, the question whether acceptance may be revoked as reasonably induced by the difficulty of discovery before acceptance, within the meaning of U.C.C. § 2–608(1), must be answered by reference to the scope of the inspection which there was a reasonable opportunity to make. Thus if Finkelstein had carried out the customary inspection and accepted the horse, and the defect allegedly rendering Red Carpet unsound at the time of sale were a defect not discoverable by inspection on the day of sale, rather than a broken splint bone, we may presume the District Court would not have placed the burden of proof on Finkelstein, and would have said that he had "revoked his acceptance."

The defendants argue that the provision in the Terms and Conditions of Sale that any warranty of the consignor "shall not extend beyond 24 hours after the fall of the Auctioneer's hammer or until final payment has been made, whichever is sooner," fixes by agreement, a reasonable time for rejection, U.C.C. § 1–204(1) [revised 1–302(b)], and that since Finkelstein rejected within 24 hours of the fall of the hammer, he did not accept Red Carpet under U.C.C. § 2–606(1)(b). There was considerable confusion over the meaning of this provision at the trial; Finkelstein submitted a memorandum in which it was argued that under the provision any defect violating the warranty appearing within 24 hours is presumed to be a defect existing at the time of sale, so that the seller must show that "some external, intervening cause occurred after the horse passed from its possession." The trial judge interpreted this as an argument that the provision converted any warranty into a 24-hour insurance policy, and, not surprisingly, rejected that notion. He concluded that "At most, the clause means that if any futuristic warranty is stated, it could extend no longer than the period mentioned."

We think this provision must be construed simply as setting a time within which defects must be reported in order for the warranty to be valid. The setting of such a deadline does not necessarily mean that any unreasonable delay in inspection or rejection is acceptable so long as it does not extend past the deadline. Had Red Carpet been obviously lame, hobbling badly at the time he was delivered to Finkelstein, and had Finkelstein nonetheless taken the horse away to his barn without comment, it would be unreasonable to say that Finkelstein nonetheless had twenty-four hours to report the defect, because of this provision. On our view of the case, whether rejection was within a reasonable time must be answered with reference to what inspection for defects is customary, and it appears that Finkelstein had no more excuse for taking the horse away without giving its legs the customary inspection than he would have had for taking it away without comment if it had been hobbling. We will not construe a provision which by its terms sets a maximum time for reporting defects to set a minimum time as well, for some defects may be more readily discoverable than others.

We conclude, then, that Finkelstein accepted the horse by failing to reject it within a reasonable time, and thus had the burden of proving any breach of warranty. As we have already said, we find ample support for the finding that he failed to prove a breach by a fair preponderance of the credible evidence. The only evidence submitted by the defendants to establish the time of the fracture was the X-rays discussed above, and we have explained why the trial judge found that these lacked sufficient probative force to establish the date of the fracture.[18]

. . .

Affirmed.

QUESTIONS AND NOTES

1. Assume that a consumer finds a car for sale on an Internet website that brings buyers and sellers together. After agreeing to a transaction, the buyer learns that the seller lives only a short distance away, and they agree that instead of handling payment and delivery of the car through the website's mechanism, the buyer will pick it up at the seller's home and pay for it with a cashier's check. When the buyer arrives at the seller's house, he asks to take the car for a little drive. The seller refuses to hand over the keys until the buyer hands over the check, and the buyer refuses to pay until he has a chance to drive the car. The seller sues, and the buyer counterclaims. Who wins?

2. Section 2–602(1), as explained by 1–205, requires that (a) rejection be within a reasonable time after delivery, and (b) notice of rejection occur within a reasonable time. Which of these is in issue in *Miron*?

The concepts of reasonable time for rejection and for notification of rejection are elastic. The resolution of the issue is normally one for the jury. It has been held that three hours after delivery was an unreasonably long time to defer rejection (Max Bauer Meat Packer, Inc. v. United States, 198 Ct.Cl. 97, 458 F.2d 88 (1972) (perishable goods)), and that 12 months was not unreasonably long. (Trailmobile Div. of Pullman, Inc. v. Jones, 118 Ga.App. 472, 164 S.E.2d 346 (1968) (motor vehicle)). What is a reasonable time in which to reject is closely related to what is a reasonable time in which to exercise the right to inspect before acceptance (see § 2–513(1)). This will vary with the nature of the goods, the kind of inspection that is required, and the ability of the buyer to make the necessary inspection. The reasonable time for inspection shrinks when the goods are perishable (Appeal of Mazur Bros. & Jaffe Fish Co., Inc., 3 UCC Rep.Serv. 419 (Veterans Administration Contract Appeals Board, VACAB-512, June 25, 1965)) or when the inspection consists of a simple measurement of the size of the goods delivered (Michael M. Berlin & Co., Inc. v. T. Whiting Mfg., Inc., 5 UCC Rep.Serv. 357 (N.Y.Tr.Ct.1968)). Also, when goods are seasonal, the time for inspection may be limited so that if the buyer rejects the goods, the seller still may dispose of the goods before they become obsolete (Société Nouvelle Vaskene v. Lehman Saunders, Ltd., 14 UCC Rep.Serv. 692 (N.Y.Sup.Ct.1974) (dresses)).

Rejection of the goods does not occur merely because the goods do not conform to the contract and the buyer notifies the seller of that fact. The buyer may, after all, desire to keep the goods despite the nonconformity. For example, in Ferraro v. Perry's Brick Co., 2011 WL 182088 (N.Y. City

---

[18] If Finkelstein, having accepted the horse, had met his burden of proof, he would have been entitled to damages for nonconformity; see U.C.C. § 2–714.

Civ.Ct.2011), the buyer contracted to purchase a solid oak door for $12,000, but the seller delivered a door with an oak veneer. The buyer first discovered that the door was not solid oak when it was installed shortly after it was delivered. He promptly complained that it was not what he had ordered. The court held that this did not amount to rejection:

> The court must ... assess whether plaintiff unequivocally communicated his intent to reject the door. ... A buyer's mere complaint about the goods does not constitute a clear and unequivocal act of rejection. ...

> Although Ferraro timely notified Perry's Brick that the door was defective and was not of solid wood, he never effectively rejected the door. His mere complaints that he never bargained for a veneer door do not constitute a rejection. His testimony was equivocal as to whether he ever told Perry he did not want the door. Furthermore, he was more focused on having the [manufacturer's] employees fix the various alleged defects in the door, such as the lock and spaces between the frame and door, than he was in returning the door due to its being veneer. Given the primary emphasis plaintiff placed upon the door not being made of solid wood, it begs all reason for him to have requested that Perry's repair the various defects in the door, since the composition of the door was unalterable and non-repairable.

When a buyer complains upon receiving delivery that the goods do not conform, the seller may promise to make the goods conform to contract specifications. In computing a reasonable time for rejection in this setting, courts discount the time during which the seller attempts to remedy the defect in the goods. See Trailmobile Div. of Pullman, Inc. v. Jones, 118 Ga.App. 472, 164 S.E.2d 346 (1968); Fablok Mills, Inc. v. Cocker Machine & Foundry Co., 125 N.J.Super. 251, 310 A.2d 491 (1973); Continental Concrete Pipe Corp. v. Century Road Builders, Inc., 195 Ill.App.3d 1, 142 Ill.Dec. 291, 552 N.E.2d 1032 (1990).

The contract may specify the period within which rejection must take place and that provision will be effective unless it is "manifestly unreasonable" (1–302(b)). If the time limitation is so short that the contract time for rejection would expire before the buyer has a reasonable chance to discover the defect, the time set is manifestly unreasonable. Neville Chemical Co. v. Union Carbide Corp., 422 F.2d 1205 (3d Cir.1970); Koch Supplies, Inc. v. Farm Fresh Meats, Inc., 630 F.2d 282 (5th Cir.1980).

3. Problem. Carpet World purchased a roll of carpet. It was delivered on June 1, and placed in Carpet World's warehouse. Nine months later, when Carpet World first had a customer who wished to buy that particular pattern, it was unrolled and was found to be defective. May Carpet World reject?

Would it matter if the contract had provided that notification of rejection must occur within 30 days after delivery?

4. It is not enough for the buyer to record its decision to reject. The rejection is ineffective unless the buyer communicates it to the seller. The reasons are obvious: upon rejection, the seller may have a right to cure the nonconformity but cannot do so unless informed of the problem. Even if the seller has no right to cure, the policy of the Code is to promote negotiation with respect to troublesome transactions. See, e.g., 2–607(3), which requires the buyer to give the seller notice of a breach even if the buyer already has accepted the goods and intends to keep them.

In *Miron* if the x-rays had proven that Red Carpet was lame at the time of the sale, would defendant's rejection have been effective?

In the typical case notification of rejection is virtually contemporaneous with rejection. If the rejection is within a reasonable time, then the notification will be held to have been seasonably made.

In DeJesus v. Cat Auto Tech Corp., 161 Misc.2d 723, 615 N.Y.S.2d 236 (N.Y. City Civ.Ct.1994), defendant took delivery of 10,000 printed certificates and paid for them by check. He then examined the certificates, concluded that they were defective, and stopped payment on the check. He did not notify the seller of this action nor of his rejection of the certificates. The seller did not learn of the problem until her bank returned the buyer's check to her. The court held that the stop order on the check was not an effective rejection because it did not give the seller a reasonable time and opportunity to cure. As authorized by 2–709(1)(a), the court gave the seller judgment for the balance of the contract price.

5.   Courts have sometimes confused rejection or revocation of acceptance with "rescission." (E.g., Sarnecki v. Al Johns Pontiac, 3 UCC Rep.Serv. 1121 (Pa.Com.Pl.1966); Menard & Holmberg Rambler, Inc. v. Shea, 44 Mass.App.Dec. 204 (1970)). However, rejection is merely a refusal to take the tendered goods: it need not be accompanied by a decision not to sue on the contract for breach. Rescission of the contract, on the other hand, is a choice among several available remedies for breach. A person who rescinds is seeking to escape from the contract and return to its pre-contract status, as opposed to enforcing the contract by seeking expectancy damages for the loss caused by the other person's breach.

Courts also have sometimes failed to distinguish between rejection and revocation of acceptance. Revocation of acceptance (authorized by 2–608) is an "undoing" of acceptance and is available in only limited circumstances. Rejection is a refusal to accept the goods and is much more readily available. While the carelessness of courts in this regard is understandable, since rejection and revocation of acceptance both force the goods back on the seller, you should not be similarly careless. The two concepts are different, they apply in different situations, and the standards for exercising the two remedies are different.

Rejection and revocation of acceptance are remedies, but the buyer's selection of either of them does not necessarily preclude the buyer from seeking other remedies as well. As stated with respect to remedies of the seller, "This Article rejects any doctrine of election of remedy as a fundamental policy and thus the remedies are essentially cumulative in nature and include all the available remedies for breach. Whether the pursuit of one remedy bars another depends entirely on the facts of the individual case." 2–703, Official Comment 1. Thus, after rejecting (or revoking acceptance of) goods, the buyer might seek to rescind the contract or might instead seek to enforce the contract by obtaining damages as provided in 2–712 or 2–713. Incidentally, asking for return of any of the purchase price paid would not necessarily be a request for rescission, since on breach-of-contract principles, a seller is not entitled to retain the price of goods not accepted. See 2–711 and Official Comment 1 to 2–608. (By the way, in the sentence starting at the very bottom of page 420, the court's assertion with respect to the burden of proof if defendant had revoked acceptance, is wrong. Do you see why?) Revocation of acceptance is covered in more detail later in this chapter.

6.   Acceptance by conduct inconsistent with the seller's ownership. The foregoing materials concern acceptance of goods under 2–606(1)(b), as a result of the buyer's failure to make an effective rejection. Acceptance of the goods also may occur even if the buyer purports to reject but then engages in conduct inconsistent with the seller's ownership (2–606(1)(c)).

Problem. Wellford purchased a dining room suite from Fein Furnishings, a furniture retailer. When the furniture arrived, it was the wrong color. Wellford immediately notified Fein that she did not want the furniture and that Fein should come pick it up. Several days later, before Fein had picked up the furniture, one of the pieces, a buffet, was substantially damaged by workers installing a new floor in Wellford's apartment. Wellford accepted a check for the full purchase price of the buffet from the insurance company for the flooring company and allowed the insurance company to take it. When Fein's truck arrived to pick up the furniture, the driver saw that the buffet was missing. He phoned Fein to report this, and Fein directed him to leave all the furniture where it was and to return to the store. Relying on 2–607(1) and 2–709(1)(a), Fein sued for the price of all the furniture. What result? (In addition to the sections already discussed, please consult 2–603 and 2–604.)

Suppose that, in the above problem, Fein is located in Los Angeles, Wellford lives in Bakersfield (110 miles away), and that after rejection Fein requested Wellford to make arrangements to return the suite of furniture to Los Angeles. Is Wellford obligated to do so?

7.   Use of the goods after rejection. In Bowen v. Young, 507 S.W.2d 600 (Tex.Civ.App.1974), Young purchased a mobile home from Bowen in El Paso, Texas. It was taken to Columbia, South Carolina, where Young had taken a job. When it was set up, Young discovered numerous defects and, 17 days after delivery, sent a notice of rejection. At the time of rejection, Young was paying rent on a space for the trailer, storage charges on his furniture, and rent on the place where he was living. When the seller failed to return his deposit, Young moved into the trailer to minimize his expenses. He spent $581.00 to make the heating system conform to the contract, lived in the trailer for a year, and then spent $1,880 to have it taken back to El Paso. The trial court held that Young had properly rejected. Reversing, the appellate court stated:

Section 2.602 requires that the rejection be within a reasonable time after delivery, with notice to the seller. Then in § 2.711 there is the following provision:

> "(c) On rightful rejection or justifiable revocation of acceptance a buyer has a security interest in goods in his possession or control for any payments made on their price and any expenses reasonably incurred in their inspection, receipt, transportation, care and custody and may hold such goods and resell them in like manner as an aggrieved seller."

In this case, Appellee received the mobile home in South Carolina on January 4, 1971. On January 21st, he rejected the unit and advised the seller. Where goods fail "in any respect" to conform to the contract the buyer may . . . reject the entire unit. Certainly the telegram dated January 21, 1971, was evidence to support the trial Court's finding that the Appellee rightfully rejected the mobile home. It did not conform in every respect to the one ordered, particularly with regard to the size of the air conditioner. The rejection within a few days after the unit had been connected up and all equipment tested, but before Appellee moved into it, was under the circumstances a rejection within a reasonable time and notice was given to the seller by telegram to comply with § 2.602.

Although § 2.711(c) gives a buyer a security interest in goods in his possession, and even a right to resell them, it does not give a right to continued use of the goods until the security interest is satisfied. The Appellee testified that after discovering the defects in the mobile home, he telephoned both the seller and manufacturer to obtain some satisfaction toward the repairs and change of the defects. When he sent his telegram on January 21st to the seller, he said therein "Unable to secure commitment from factory." A week earlier he had wired the seller and General Electric Credit Corporation, who was to originally finance the mobile home, that the unit was damaged and that he would not pay until it was completely repaired.

Failing to get satisfactory assurance from either the seller or manufacturer concerning the damaged and nonconforming mobile home, Appellee did not seek to foreclose his security interest for the down-payment, transportation and storage expense. Nor did he act in accordance with § 2.604, which provides: " * * * if the seller gives no instructions within a reasonable time after notification of rejection the buyer may store the rejected goods for the seller's account or reship them to him or resell them for the seller's account with reimbursement as provided in the preceding section. Such action is not acceptance or conversion." Instead, he decided sometime in February to move into the mobile home and spent nearly $600.00 to repair the heating unit and change from an electric to a gas heater. By doing so he accepted the goods under § 2.606, and under § 2.607 became obligated to pay at the contract

price for the goods accepted, retaining such rights, if any, as existed
for damages under § 2.714 and § 2.715.

Keeping in mind that the goods in question were a mobile home, exactly what
should Young have done? Why was his occupancy of it not an appropriate
response? We will return to this problem in connection with revocation of
acceptance.

8.   Problem. Coco's, a retail dress shop, contracted to purchase 15 "wet-
look" vinyl skirts from Sonjia. The skirts delivered were not "wet-look," and
Coco's immediately telephoned Sonjia and rejected them. Sonjia told Coco's
to try to sell the skirts. Instead of following that instruction, Coco's put the
skirts back in the packing boxes in which they were shipped and placed them
in a storage room. Sonjia sued for the price (2–607(1) and 2–709(1)(a)),
alleging that Coco's accepted the skirts. What result? Did Coco's act properly
after rejection?

9.   CISG and the burden of proving nonconformity. In disputes under
Article 2, allocation of the burden of proving whether goods conform to the
contract can be critical. The same is true of the Convention on Contracts for
the International Sale of Goods. For example, under Article 67(1), the risk of
loss passes to the buyer when the goods are delivered to the carrier. Under
Article 36(1) the seller is liable for any nonconformity that exists at the time
the risk passes to the buyer. In the case of perishable goods that, upon
arrival, the buyer discovers to be spoiled, it is critical to know whether the
goods already were spoiled when the seller delivered them to the carrier.
Who has the burden of proving that the goods did or did not conform to the
contract? This was an issue in Chicago Prime Packers, Inc. v. Northam Food
Trading Co., 408 F.3d 894 (7th Cir.2005), in which a U.S. seller sued a
Canadian buyer for the purchase price of pork ribs that arrived in a spoiled
condition. The court held that the burden of proof rested on the buyer:

> [The buyer] asserts that [the seller] should bear the burden of
> proving that the ribs were not spoiled at the time of transfer
> because the quality of the goods is an essential element of [the
> seller's] breach of contract claim. [The seller] counters that
> nonconformity is an affirmative defense for which [the buyer] has
> the burden of proof. Proper assignment of the burden of proof is a
> question of law that we review de novo.
>
> The CISG does not state expressly whether the seller or buyer
> bears the burden of proof as to the product's conformity with the
> contract. Because there is little case law under the CISG, we
> interpret its provisions by looking to its language and to "the
> general principles" upon which it is based. See CISG Art. 7(2); see
> also Delchi Carrier SpA v. Rotorex Corp., 71 F.3d 1024, 1027–28
> (2d Cir.1995). The CISG is the international analogue to Article 2
> of the Uniform Commercial Code. Many provisions of the UCC and
> the CISG are the same or similar, and "caselaw interpreting
> analogous provisions of Article 2 of the [UCC], may ... inform a
> court where the language of the relevant CISG provision tracks

that of the UCC." Delchi Carrier SpA, 71 F.3d at 1028. "However, UCC caselaw 'is not per se applicable.' " Id.

A comparison with the UCC reveals that the buyer bears the burden of proving nonconformity under the CISG. Under the UCC, the buyer may plead breach of the implied warranty of fitness for ordinary purpose as an affirmative defense to a contract action by the seller for the purchase price. In such an action it is the defendant-buyer's burden to prove the breach of the warranty.

Section 2–314 of the UCC provides that a warranty that goods are "fit for the ordinary purpose for which such goods are used" is implied unless the contract states otherwise. Mirroring the structure and content of this section, Article 35(2) of the CISG provides that unless the contract states otherwise, "goods do not conform with the contract unless they . . . are fit for the purposes for which goods of the same description would ordinarily be used." Accordingly, just as a buyer-defendant bears the burden of proving breach of the implied warranty of fitness for ordinary purpose under the UCC, under the CISG, the buyer-defendant bears the burden of proving nonconformity at the time of transfer. See Larry A. DiMatteo et al., The Interpretive Turn in International Sales Law: An Analysis of Fifteen Years of CISG Jurisprudence, 24 Nw.J.Int'l L. & Bus. 299, 400 (2004) (Under the CISG, "the buyer is allocated the burden of proving that the goods were defective prior to the expiration of the seller's obligation point"); see also R. Folsom, 1 International Business Transactions § 1.15, at 41 (2d ed.2002). The district court was correct to conclude that [the buyer] bears the burden of proving that the ribs were spoiled at the time of transfer.

Assuming that the court is correct in looking to Article 2 for guidance, what is the flaw in the court's reasoning?

4.   CURE

Under 2–612(2) a buyer in an installment contract may not reject an installment that contains nonconforming goods if the nonconformity can be cured. In a single-delivery contract, the matter is governed by 2–508. That section contemplates that although the buyer may reject goods that fail in any respect to conform to the contract (2–601), in some instances the seller has a right to cure. Under 2–508 the buyer's rejection of the goods is a prerequisite to the seller's right to cure. If the buyer accepts nonconforming goods and asserts a claim because of the nonconformity, 2–508 does not give the seller any right to cure (although the contract may provide otherwise). Please read 2–508. Note that subsection (1) governs the seller's right to cure when the buyer rejects the goods before the time for the seller's performance has expired. Subsection (2) applies when the time for the seller's performance has expired.

PROBLEMS

1. Loew's contracted to sell a Generac generator to Clarick for use in Clarick's construction business, delivery to Clarick's job site by May 1. After taking delivery April 28 and powering it up, Clarick discovered that the generator sputtered and did not run smoothly. It phoned Loew's to complain, and Loew's said it would send out a technician to investigate and repair the generator later that day. Clarick responded, "We don't want a repaired or rebuilt generator, we're entitled to a brand new generator that operates properly without repairs. Bring us a new generator to replace this defective one." Under 2–508 whose position is stronger?

2. Same facts as above, but when Clarick objected to Loew's offer to repair, Loew's responded, "OK, but we don't have any more Generacs in stock. We'll bring you a Honda with the same capacity and specifications." Clarick said, "Nothing doing. Come get your Generac. We'll find another supplier." Now whose position is stronger?

3. Fudgeland contracted to buy 100,000 pounds of sugar at a price of 20 cents per pound, delivery to be May 15. Caine tendered the sugar on May 14th. Fudgeland refused to accept the sugar because it was delivered early and Fudgeland did not have the space for it. (Compare Problem 2, page 401 supra.) What should Caine do?

4. Same contract as above, Caine tendered delivery of 96,000 pounds of sugar on May 15. Asserting that the contract calls for 100,000 pounds, Fudgeland refused to accept delivery.

    a. Is Fudgeland's refusal rightful?

    b. Does Caine have any rights under 2–508?

Zabriskie Chevrolet, Inc. v. Smith

New Jersey Superior Court, Law Division, 1968.
99 N.J.Super. 441, 240 A.2d 195.

■ DOAN, J.D.C. (temporarily assigned). This action arises out of the sale by plaintiff to defendant of a new 1966 Chevrolet automobile. Within a short distance after leaving the showroom the vehicle became almost completely inoperable by reason of mechanical failure. Defendant the same day notified plaintiff that he cancelled the sale and simultaneously stopped payment on the check he had tendered in payment of the balance of the purchase price. Plaintiff sues on the check and the purchase order for the balance of the purchase price plus incidental damages and defendant counterclaims for the return of his deposit and incidental damages.

The facts are not complex nor do they present any serious dispute.

On February 2, 1967 defendant signed a form purchase order for a new 1966 Chevrolet Biscayne Sedan which was represented to him to be a brand-new car that would operate perfectly. On that occasion he paid plaintiff $124 by way of deposit. On February 9, 1967 defendant tendered plaintiff his check for $2069.50 representing the balance of the purchase price ($2064) and $5.50 for license and transfer fees. Delivery was made to defendant's wife during the early evening hours of Friday, February 10, 1967, at which time she was handed the keys and the factory package of printed material, including the manual and the manufacturer-dealer's warranty, none of which she or her husband ever read before or after the sale was made, nor were the details thereof specifically explained to or agreed to by defendant. While en route to her home, about 2-1/2 miles away, and after having gone about 7/10 of a mile from the showroom, the car stalled at a traffic light, stalled again within another 15 feet and again thereafter each time the vehicle was required to stop. When about halfway home the car could not be driven in "drive" gear at all, and defendant's wife was obliged to then propel the vehicle in "low-low" gear at a rate of about five to ten miles per hour, its then maximum speed. In great distress, defendant's wife was fearful of completing the journey to her home and called her husband, who thereupon drove the car in "low-low" gear about seven blocks to his home. Defendant, considerably upset by this turn of events, thereupon immediately called his bank (which was open this Friday evening), stopped payment on the check and called plaintiff to notify them that they had sold him a "lemon," that he had stopped payment on the check and that the sale was cancelled. The next day plaintiff sent a wrecker to defendant's home, brought the vehicle to its repair shop and after inspection determined that the transmission was defective.

Plaintiff's expert testified that the car would not move, that there was no power in the transmission and in that condition the car could not move. Plaintiff replaced the transmission with another one removed from a vehicle then on plaintiff's showroom floor, notifying defendant thereafter of what had been done. Defendant refused to take delivery of the vehicle as repaired and reasserted his cancellation of the sale. Plaintiff has since kept the vehicle in storage at his place of business. Within a short period following these occurrences plaintiff and defendant began negotiations for a new 1967 Chevrolet, but these fell through when plaintiff insisted that a new deal could only be made by giving defendant credit for the previously ordered 1966 Chevrolet. This defendant refused to do because he considered the prior transaction as cancelled.

The issues in this case present problems for disposition under the Uniform Commercial Code (Code). The Code . . . provides that the act shall be liberally construed and applied to promote its underlying purposes and policies. N.J.S. 12A:1–102 [revised 1–103(a)][;] . . . that unless displaced by the particular provisions of the Code, the principles of law and equity or other validating or invalidating cause shall supplement its provisions, N.J.S. 12A:1–103 [revised 1–103(b)]; and . . . that the remedies provided by the Code shall be liberally administered to the end that the aggrieved party may be put in as good a position as if the other party had fully performed. N.J.S. 12A:1–106 [revised 1–305(a)].

. . .

Plaintiff urges that defendant accepted the vehicle and therefore under the Code (N.J.S. 12A:2–607(1)) is bound to complete payment for it. Defendant asserts that he never accepted the vehicle and therefore under the Code properly rejected it; further, that even if there had been acceptance he was justified under the Code in revoking the same. Defendant supports this claim by urging that what was delivered to him was not what he bargained for, i.e., a new car with factory new parts, which would operate perfectly as represented and, therefore, the Code remedies of rejection and revocation of acceptance were available to him. These remedies have their basis in breach of contract and failure of consideration although they are also viewed as arising out of breach of warranty. The essential ingredient which determines which of these two remedies is brought into play is a determination, *in limine,* whether there had been an "acceptance" of the goods by the buyer. Thus, the primary inquiry is whether the defendant had "accepted" the automobile prior to the return thereof to the plaintiff.

. . .

[Section 2–606 makes it] clear that a buyer does not accept goods until he has had a "reasonable opportunity to inspect." Defendant sought to purchase a new car. He assumed what every new car buyer has a right to assume and, indeed, has been led to assume by the high powered advertising techniques of the auto industry—that his new car, with the exception of very minor adjustments, would be mechanically new and factory-furnished, operate perfectly, and be free of substantial defects. The vehicle delivered to defendant did not measure up to these representations. Plaintiff contends that defendant had "reasonable opportunity to inspect" by the privilege to take the car for a typical "spin around the block" before signing the purchase order. If by this contention plaintiff equates a spin around the block with "reasonable opportunity to inspect," the contention is illusory and unrealistic. To the layman, the complicated mechanisms of today's automobiles are a complete mystery. To have the automobile inspected by someone with sufficient expertise to disassemble the vehicle in order to discover latent defects before the contract is signed, is assuredly impossible and highly impractical. Consequently, the first few miles of driving become even more significant to the excited new car buyer. This is the buyer's first reasonable opportunity to enjoy his new vehicle to see if it conforms to what it was represented to be and whether he is getting what he bargained for. How long the buyer may drive the new car under the guise of inspection of new goods is not an issue in the present case. It is clear that defendant discovered the nonconformity within 7/10 of a mile and minutes after leaving plaintiff's showroom. Certainly this was well within the ambit of "reasonable opportunity to inspect." That the vehicle was grievously defective when it left plaintiff's possession is a compelling conclusion, as is the conclusion that in a legal sense defendant never accepted the vehicle.

. . .

Nor did plaintiff have reasonable grounds to believe that a new automobile which could not even be driven a bare few miles to the buyer's residence would be acceptable. The dealer is in an entirely different position from the layman. The dealer with his staff of expert mechanics and modern equipment knows or should know of substantial defects in the new automobile which it sells. There was offered into evidence the dealer's inspection and adjustment schedule containing over 70 alleged items that plaintiff caused to be inspected, including the transmission. According to that schedule the automobile in question had been checked by the seller for the satisfaction of the buyer, and such inspection included a road test. The fact that the automobile underwent a tortured operation for about 2-1/2 miles from the showroom to defendant's residence demonstrates the inherent serious deficiencies in this vehicle which were present when the so-called inspection was made by plaintiff, and hence plaintiff was aware (or should have been) that the vehicle did not conform to the bargain the parties had made, and plaintiff had no reasonable right to expect that the vehicle in that condition would be accepted.

There having been no acceptance, the next issue presented is whether defendant properly rejected under the Code. That he cancelled the sale and rejected the vehicle almost concomitantly with the discovery of the failure of his bargain is clear from the evidence. [Section 2–601] delineates the buyer's rights following nonconforming delivery and reads as follows: . . .

Section 12A:2–602 indicates that one can reject after taking possession. Possession, therefore, does not mean acceptance and the corresponding loss of the right of rejection; nor does the fact that buyer has a security interest along with possession eliminate the right to reject. . . .

N.J.S. 12A:2–106 defines conforming goods as follows:

"(2) Goods or conduct including any part of a performance are 'conforming' or conform to the contract when they are in accordance with the obligations under the contract."

The Uniform Commercial Code Comment to that section states:

"2. Subsection (2): It is in general intended to continue the policy of requiring *exact performance* by the seller of his obligations as a condition to his right to require acceptance. However, the seller is in part safeguarded against surprise as a result of sudden technicality on the buyer's part by the provisions of Section 2–508 on seller's cure of improper tender or delivery. Moreover usage of trade frequently permits commercial leeways in performance and the language of the agreement itself must be read in the light of such custom or usage and also, prior course of dealing, and in a long term contract, the course of performance."

There was no evidence at the trial concerning any "custom or usage," although plaintiff in its brief argued that it is the usage of the automobile trade that a buyer accept a new automobile, although containing defects of manufacture, if such defects can be and are seasonably cured by the seller. Perhaps this represents prevailing views in the automobile industry which have, over the years, served to blanket injustices and inequities committed upon buyers who demurred in the light of the unequal positions of strength between the parties. The spirit of the [opinion in Henningsen v. Bloomfield Motors, Inc., 32 N.J. 358, 161 A.2d 69 (1960)] contemplated these conditions which cried out for correction. In the present case we are not dealing with a situation such as was present in Adams v. Tramontin Motor Sales, 42 N.J.Super. 313, 126 A.2d 358 (App.Div.1956). In that case, brought for breach of implied warranty of merchantability, the court held that minor defects, such as adjustment of the motor, tightening of loose elements, fixing of locks and dome light, and a correction of rumbling noise, were not remarkable defects, and therefore there was no breach. Here the breach was substantial. The new car was practically inoperable and endowed with a defective transmission. This was a "remarkable defect" and justified rejection by the buyer.

Lastly, plaintiff urges that under the Code, N.J.S. 12A:2–508, it had a right to cure the nonconforming delivery. . . .

The New Jersey Study Comment to 12A:2–508 reads:

"3. Subsection 2–508(2) has been applauded as a rule aimed at ending 'forced breaches.' See, Hawkland, Sales and Bulk Sales Under the Uniform Commercial Code, 120–122 (1958). * * *

"Section 2–508 prevents the buyer from forcing the seller to breach by making a surprise rejection of the goods because of some minor nonconformity at a time at which the seller cannot cure the deficiency within the time for performance."

The Uniform Commercial Code Comment to 12A:2–508 reads:

"2. Subsection (2) seeks to avoid injustice to the seller by reason of a surprise rejection by the buyer. However, the seller is not protected unless he had 'reasonable grounds to believe' that the tender would be acceptable."

It is clear that in the instant case there was no "forced breach" on the part of the buyer, for he almost immediately began to negotiate for another automobile. The inquiry is as to what is intended by "cure," as used in the Code. This statute makes no attempt to define or specify what a "cure" shall consist of. It would appear, then, that each case must be controlled by its own facts. The "cure" intended under the cited section of the Code does not, in the court's opinion, contemplate the tender of a new vehicle with a substituted transmission, not from the factory and of unknown lineage from another vehicle in plaintiff's possession. It was not the intention of the Legislature that the right to "cure" is a limitless one to be controlled only by the will of the seller. A "cure" which endeavors by substitution to tender a chattel not within the agreement or contemplation of the parties is invalid.

For a majority of people the purchase of a new car is a major investment, rationalized by the peace of mind that flows from its dependability and safety. Once their faith is shaken, the vehicle loses not only its real value in their eyes, but becomes an instrument whose integrity is substantially impaired and whose operation is fraught with apprehension. The attempted cure in the present case was ineffective.

Accordingly, and pursuant to N.J.S. 12A:2–711, judgment is rendered on the main case in favor of defendant. On the counterclaim judgment is rendered in favor of defendant and against plaintiff in the sum of $124, being the amount of the deposit, there being no further proof of damages.

Defendant shall, as part of this judgment, execute for plaintiff, on demand, such documents as are necessary to again vest title to the vehicle in plaintiff.

QUESTIONS

1.   Which subsection of 2–508 governs *Zabriskie*?

2.   The seller attempted to cure the nonconformity by replacing the defective transmission with one from another car. The court held that this was not sufficient. What could the seller have done to cure the nonconformity?

3.   **Shaken-faith doctrine.** The court created what has come to be known as the "shaken-faith doctrine." Some other courts have embraced it, too. But not all. For example, in Sinco, Inc. v. Metro-North Commuter Railroad Co., 133 F.Supp.2d 308 (S.D.N.Y.2001), Metro-North was undertaking a renovation of Grand Central Terminal in New York City. It invited proposals for a fall-restraint system to protect its workers when they were working high off the floor in the terminal. Ultimately, it contracted with Sinco for a system in which workers would wear a harness that would be connected to a cable system by metal clips. If a worker fell, the harness and cable system would prevent any serious injury or death. When Sinco came to the work site to show the system to the workers, one of the metal clips fell apart in a worker's hand. The worker's union asserted that its members would under no circumstances work with the Sinco system. The contract provided that on material breach, Sinco would have seven days to cure the breach. Sinco proposed a cure by reworking some clips and supplying others that did not have the flaw. Metro-North refused to accept this cure. When Sinco sued, Metro-North counterclaimed to recover the excess cost it paid another

supplier for a fall-restraint system. Each party filed a motion for summary judgment. The court's response:

> Metro-North alleges that Sinco's delivery of the defective Sayflinks was so material a breach that Metro-North was entitled to terminate the contract without even providing an opportunity for cure. This argument conflicts with both the language of the contract and the substantive law of New York. Article 7.01 of the contract provides that a "material breach" by Sinco may be considered an "Event of Default." "The remedy of termination—or, more accurately, the 'right' to terminate—is available only where one party has materially breached the contract. . . . Where a breach is material, the party is justified in refusing to go on, and thus the law provides that party with the right to terminate." ESPN, Inc. v. Office of the Comm'r of Baseball, 76 F.Supp.2d 383, 392 (S.D.N.Y.1999). It is well-settled under New York law that in order to justify termination, "a breach must be . . . so substantial and fundamental as to strongly tend to defeat the object of the parties in making the contract." Babylon Assocs. v. County of Suffolk, 101 A.D.2d 207, 475 N.Y.S.2d 869, 874 (App. Div.2d Dep't 1984). Termination is an "extraordinary remedy" to be permitted only when the breach goes to "the root of the agreement." Septembertide Publishing, B.V. v. Stein & Day, Inc., 884 F.2d 675, 678 (2d Cir.1989).

> An injured party's right of termination, however, is limited by the doctrine of cure. . . .

> . . . Metro-North argues that the delivery of defective Sayflinks was so severe a breach that it irremediably undermined Metro-North's confidence in the fall-protection system, rendering futile any attempt at cure. Following the discovery of the defect, Metro-North's unions reported that their members would not use the system, and the unions repeatedly expressed a complete lack of confidence in Sinco and its products. Metro-North contends that nothing Sinco did—no curative performance of any sort—could restore this lost confidence. In other words, the breach could not be cured.

> In support of this "shaken faith" or "loss of confidence" theory, Metro-North cites case law from states other than New York. I find these authorities not entirely applicable to the case before me.

> Zabriskie Chevrolet, Inc. v. Smith, 99 N.J.Super. 441, 240 A.2d 195 (N.J.Sup.Ct.1968) involved a car dealer's efforts to cure its delivery of new car with a faulty transmission by replacing the transmission with one removed from a showroom model. The court found that the substitution of a transmission "not from the factory and of unknown lineage" was "not within the agreement or contemplation of the parties." Id. at 458, 240 A.2d 195. In short, the cure did not conform to the terms of the contract. The court's discussion of "shaken faith" is not essential to its conclusion; it

appears from the text of the opinion that the attempted cure was objectively unreasonable.

Hemmert Agricultural Aviation, Inc. v. Mid-Continent Aircraft Corp., 663 F.Supp. 1546 (D.Kan.1987), decided under Kansas state law, better illustrates Metro-North's theory. The flaws in a "crop-duster" airplane purchased by the plaintiff created "fear and apprehension" in the pilot. The court held that, "[w]here the buyer's confidence in the dependability of the machine is shaken because of the defects and possibly because of seller's ineffective attempts to cure, revocation appears justified." Id. at 1552.

There appear to be no New York cases treating the "shaken faith" theory articulated in *Hemmert* under Kansas law. I am not prepared to hold that Sinco's breach rendered futile any potential cure. A materially breaching party generally is entitled, subject to the relevant terms and conditions of the contract and the Uniform Commercial Code, to cure its breach within a reasonable period of time. Cure, in this case, required not only the timely delivery of conforming replacement parts, but a convincing showing of the reliability of the equipment. Such a showing would have required a description of Sinco's manufacturing methods and a precise explanation of the reasons why the demonstration parts failed in relation to such methods. If Sinco had timely tendered such a cure, Metro-North would have been able to assess the reasons for the failure and the reliability of the cure. If, objectively, the cure was shown to be reliably safe, Metro-North would have been obligated to accept the cure, despite, perhaps, any lingering subjective misgivings of its employees. Ultimately, however, Sinco failed to cure and Metro-North justifiably terminated the contract.

. . .

It is undisputed that Sinco's attempted performance under the contract—its delivery of a fall-protection system that included the defective Sayflinks—did not satisfy its contractual obligations. Pursuant to the Code and the contract, Sinco had the opportunity following this breach to cure.

Sinco, as the party attempting to effect a cure, had the burden to show that its proffered cure did, in fact, conform to the terms of the contract. Those terms included stringent conditions regarding quality control and reliability. It is uncontested that the welded Sayflinks, manufactured and delivered within two days after the equipment failure, were not subjected to Sinco's internal quality controls. The contractual conditions regarding reliability also applied to the replacement Sayflinks that came from the regular assembly line that did not include the additional welding. Sinco had to show exactly what had caused the defect in the demonstration parts, that the underlying problem had been remedied, and that the defect would not recur. Furthermore, in order to conform to the contract, any replacement system had to be demonstrably reliable. In a situation such as this, involving the failure of vital safety equipment in front of the very individuals the equipment was designed to protect, the injured party did not have to accept at face value the word of the breaching party regarding the reliability of replacement equipment. Metro-North was entitled to objective evidence of such reliability.

Sinco did not satisfy that obligation by delivering to Metro-North a videotape of a welded and staked Sayflink surviving a single "pull test" of over 6200 pounds of stress. The replacement parts sent by Sinco included four Sayflinks that had been staked, and four that had been both welded and staked. The videotaped test was performed only on a Sayflink with the supplemental welding, not on a "standard" Sayflink that lacked the welding. Moreover, the test involved the application of stress in a different direction than the direction in which the failure occurred, and did not show reliability over time and frequent use. Finally, the videotape was produced by Sinco itself, not by a disinterested and objective third party. The videotaped stress test did not demonstrate the reliability of Sinco's attempted cure.

. . .

When Metro-North did not accept Sinco's first attempted cure, Sinco proposed several ideas for other possible cures during discussions with Metro-North. However, these mere offers of potentially curative performance did not adequately cure Sinco's breach.

Pursuant to Section 2–508(2) of the New York Uniform Commercial Code, Sinco had to notify Metro-North of its intention to cure and had to make a "conforming tender." "This clearly entails *more than a mere offer,* but less than actual physical delivery." Allied Semi-Conductors Int'l, Ltd. v. Pulsar Components Int'l, Inc., 907 F.Supp. 618, 624 (E.D.N.Y.1995) (emphasis added).

. . .

Sinco's bare offers of potentially curative performance were not enough. The contract called for reliable equipment to protect Metro-North's employees from grave injury or death, and Sinco's equipment had been shown to be unreliable. In order to effectuate a cure, Sinco was obliged to make a conforming tender—that is, to put a fall protection system and proof of its reliability at Metro-North's disposition, leaving it to Metro-North to accept the tender. In essence, Sinco had to take the initiative; it could not shift any part of its burden to Metro-North. It was not enough for Sinco merely to suggest possible solutions. Because Sinco failed to cure its breach, I deny its motion for summary judgment and grant Metro-North's motion for summary judgment on the issue of liability.

4. The court in *Sinco* suggests that when the first attempt at cure failed, Sinco had the right to try again. What language in 2–508 supports this position? How many attempts does the seller get?

5. Would appropriate cure in *Sinco* require the seller to convince the buyer's employees to use the seller's system?

6. The court in *Sinco* applies subsection (2) of 2–508, which applies when the seller has reasonable grounds to believe that the nonconforming tender would be acceptable. What basis is there for saying that Sinco had reasonable grounds to believe that the clips would be acceptable?

7. Subsection (2) gives a seller a right to cure if the seller had reasonable grounds to believe the tender would be acceptable "with or without a money allowance." The primary situation for application of the quoted phrase is a tender of a smaller quantity than the contract calls for, but not so much smaller that the seller should reasonably understand that it would fail to meet the buyer's needs. An example is the sugar contract in Problem 4, page 429, in which the seller may reasonably believe the smaller quantity would be acceptable if the seller reduced the price to reflect the shortfall.

8. Cure by repair vs. cure by substitution of new goods. In Wilson v. Scampoli, 228 A.2d 848 (D.C.App.1967), the buyer purchased a color TV in 1965 for $675. When delivered and set up, the picture had a red tinge. Two days later a service representative was unable to fix the problem and said he needed to take the chassis to the seller's shop. The buyer refused to permit this and demanded another brand new TV set. The seller refused to replace the TV unless it proved incapable of repair. The buyer demanded return of the purchase price and, when the seller refused, sued. The trial court granted the relief plaintiff requested, but the appellate court reversed. Citing 2–508, it stated:

> A retail dealer would certainly expect and have reasonable grounds to believe that merchandise like color television sets, new and delivered as crated at the factory, would be acceptable as delivered and that, if defective in some way, he would have the right to substitute a conforming tender. The question then resolves itself to whether the dealer may conform his tender by adjustment or minor repair or whether he must conform by substituting brand new merchandise. The problem seems to be one of first impression in other jurisdictions adopting the Uniform Commercial Code as well as in the District of Columbia.

> Although the Official Code Comments do not reach this precise issue, there are cases and comments under other provisions of the Code which indicate that under certain circumstances repairs and adjustments are contemplated as remedies under implied warranties. In L & N Sales Co. v. Little Brown Jug, Inc., 12 Pa.Dist. & Co.2d 469 (Phila.Cty.Ct.1957), where the language of a disclaimer was found insufficient to defeat warranties under §§ 2–314 and 2–315, the court noted that the buyer had notified the seller of defects in the merchandise, and as the seller was unable to remedy them and later refused to accept return of the articles, it

was held to be a breach of warranty. In Hall v. Everett Motors, Inc., 340 Mass. 430, 165 N.E.2d 107 (1960), decided shortly before the effective date of the Code in Massachusetts, the court reluctantly found that a disclaimer of warranties was sufficient to insulate the seller. Several references were made in the ruling to the seller's unsuccessful attempts at repairs, the court indicating the result would have been different under the Code.

While these cases provide no mandate to require the buyer to accept patchwork goods or substantially repaired articles in lieu of flawless merchandise, they do indicate that minor repairs or reasonable adjustments are frequently the means by which an imperfect tender may be cured. In discussing the analogous question of defective title, it has been stated that:

> The seller, then, should be able to cure [the defect] under subsection 2–508(2) in those cases in which he can do so without subjecting the buyer to any great inconvenience, risk or loss. Hawkland, Curing an Improper Tender of Title to Chattels: Past, Present and Commercial Code, 46 Minn.L.Rev. 697, 724 (1962).

Removal of a television chassis for a short period of time in order to determine the cause of color malfunction and ascertain the extent of adjustment or correction needed to effect full operational efficiency presents no great inconvenience to the buyer. In the instant case, appellant's expert witness testified that this was not infrequently necessary with new televisions. Should the set be defective in workmanship or parts, the loss would be upon the manufacturer who warranted it free from mechanical defect. Here the adamant refusal of [the buyer] to allow inspection essential to the determination of the cause of the excessive red tinge to the picture defeated any effort by the seller to provide timely repair or even replacement of the set if the difficulty could not be corrected. The cause of the defect might have been minor and easily adjusted or it may have been substantial and required replacement by another new set—but the seller was never given an adequate opportunity to make a determination.

... We therefore reverse the judgment of the trial court granting rescission and directing the return of the purchase price of the set.

9. Under 2–508(1) the seller's right to cure within the "time for performance" or "contract time" is absolute. After the "contract time," however, cure is available only if the seller had reasonable grounds to believe that the original, nonconforming tender would be acceptable. If the seller does not have reasonable grounds to believe that, it is critical to the seller's right to cure that the time for performance not have expired when the buyer rejects the goods.

When does the time for performance expire? Ordinarily, we would expect it to be the last date on which the seller could deliver the goods. But what if the seller also promises to provide some form of support for a specified period of time after delivery: does this mean that the "contract time" extends to the end of that period, so that if the goods do not conform, the seller may cure the nonconformity long after the deadline for delivery? One court has held just that. Peter Pan Seafoods, Inc. v. Olympic Foundry Co., 17 Wash.App. 761, 565 P.2d 819 (1977), but other courts have not adopted this position. See the Official Comments to 2–508.

The *Zabriskie* court discusses cure and seems to assume that any available cure would be under 2–508(2). This assumption rests on the conclusion that "time for performance" in 2–508(1) refers to the time when, under the contract, the goods must be delivered. Of course, it might be that February 10th, the day on which the automobile was delivered to Smith, was not the last day on which delivery could be made without a breach of the time provisions of the contract. If so, then if a delivery on, say, February 15th would have been within the contract time requirements, the seller might have had a right to cure under subsection (1) until at least the 15th. Assuming, however, that the contract time for delivery had expired in *Zabriskie* before the seller tendered the repaired automobile, did the seller have a right to cure?

10. The court in *Zabriskie*, in the first full paragraph on page 432, says that since the dealer claimed to have inspected the car prior to delivery, he knew "or should have known" that the car was defective. The next step in that line of reasoning, although the court does not overtly take it, is that since the dealer ought to have known he was selling a defective machine, he could not reasonably expect that it would be acceptable with or without money allowance, and thus had no right to cure. The reverse of that argument is that if the dealer neither knew nor had reason to know of the defect, he had a right to cure no matter how serious the defect is. Starting at the bottom of page 433, however, the court seems to take a somewhat different view of cure, suggesting that it is available after the time for performance has passed only if the rejection is an attempt to force a breach. Presumably, that idea is that cure is available only if the defect is so minor that ordinarily a buyer would go ahead and take the goods anyway "with or without money allowance." See Official Comment 2 to 2–508. In the view of most commentators, this "surprise rejection" situation is the only one contemplated by 2–508(2). R. Nordstrom, Law of Sales § 105, 317–322 (1970); R. Dusenberg & L. King, Sales and Bulk Transfers § 14.02 (1974); W. Hawkland, A Transactional Guide to the UCC § 1.37, at 198–200 (1964); Peters, Remedies For Breach of Contract Relating to the Sale of Goods Under the Uniform Commercial Code; A Roadmap For Article Two, 73 Yale L.J. 199, 209–216 (1963).

11. It will be a rare case in which a seller who was aware of substantial defects in tendered goods will be able to establish a reasonable belief that they would be acceptable so as to support a right to cure under 2–508(2). In Wilson v. Scampoli, however, the seller did not know of the defect in the television set, and the court held that he therefore was reasonable in believing that the set would be acceptable and thus had the right to cure whether or not the defect was substantial.

Under that view, the right to cure applies not only to trivial defects, but also to substantial ones if the seller is (reasonably?) unaware of the defects. See, in favor of the result in *Scampoli*, 1 J. White, R. Summers & R. Hillman, Uniform Commercial Code § 9:24 (6th ed.2012). For a commentary critical of the result, see R. Nordstrom, Sales 320–321 (1970). In Johannsen v. Minnesota Valley Ford Tractor Co., Inc., 304 N.W.2d 654 (Minn.1981), the court held that the right to cure is limited to cases in which the defects are minor and that after the time for performance has expired the seller has no right to cure defects that substantially impair the value of the goods.

12. Problem. Brandon contracted with Dreamland Homes for a new mobile home that Dreamland agreed to sell, deliver, and install on Brandon's lot on October 1. Dreamland warranted the home against defects and promised to repair or replace any defects in material or workmanship. Brandon paid $5,000 at the time of contracting and promised to pay the balance in monthly installments. During installation on October 1, Dreamland's employees noticed problems with the roof and frame, but they said nothing to Brandon. That very night it rained, and water leaked into the living quarters. Within a few days, the doors did not close properly, the gas furnace leaked, and other problems emerged. Brandon called Dreamland and demanded that it remove the home from his lot and refund his down payment. Dreamland refused to do so, but offered to fix everything that was wrong. Brandon refused this offer and announced he would not make any further payment. Dreamland sued to recover the balance of the price, and Brandon counterclaimed to recover the down payment. How should this dispute be resolved?

13. In Jakowski v. Carole Chevrolet, page 232 supra, the seller delivered a car without the undercoating required by the contract. The buyer brought the car back in for the seller to apply the undercoating, and while the car was on the dealer's lot, it was stolen. The court looked to 2–510 to determine the risk of loss because the car as delivered failed to conform to the contract. In view of 2–508, however, was the court right: should risk of loss have been governed by 2–509?

14. CISG and cure. Article 37 gives the seller the right to cure any nonconformity if (a) the cure is completed by the contractual date of delivery and (b) exercise of the right to cure does not cause the buyer "unreasonable inconvenience or unreasonable expense." If the seller effects cure, the seller remains liable for any loss caused before cure is complete. Unlike 2–508(2), CISG does not extend the time for performance, and its usefulness in long-distance transactions is diminished.

5. REVOCATION OF ACCEPTANCE

Once the buyer has accepted the goods, it is too late to reject them, even if they are grossly nonconforming. The buyer may, however, be able to revoke acceptance of them. Like rejection, revocation of acceptance has the effect of putting the goods back into the hands of the seller. To that extent, it may seem that it does not matter whether the buyer rejects or revokes acceptance. But it matters a lot: as noted earlier, the burden of proving whether the goods are nonconforming depends entirely on whether the buyer wants to reject them or revoke acceptance of them (2–607(4)). Furthermore, although rejection is permitted if the goods or the tender fail in any respect to conform to the contract, revocation of acceptance is permitted only under the circumstances specified in 2–608. Please read that section.

———

Jorgensen v. Pressnall

Oregon Supreme Court, 1976.
274 Or. 285, 545 P.2d 1382.

■ O'CONNELL, CHIEF JUSTICE. This is a suit for the rescission of a mobile home purchase contract and for the recovery of plaintiffs' down payment and damages. Defendants are Pressnall, the seller of the mobile home, and Commercial Credit Company, the company financing the transaction. Commercial Credit counterclaims for losses incurred in repossession of the mobile home and, in the event rescission is granted, seeks recovery of damages from Pressnall for breach of a warranty. The trial court found for plaintiffs against Pressnall and for Commercial Credit on its cross-complaint against Pressnall. Pressnall appeals.

Plaintiffs purchased a new mobile home from Pressnall, using their old mobile home as a down payment and financing the balance. Pressnall assigned the financing contract to Commercial Credit, warranting the enforceability of the assigned contract.

Pressnall represented the mobile home to plaintiffs as being of "good, sound construction," and of "medium quality." He also represented to plaintiffs that the mobile home was strong enough to stand up to frequent moves. Plaintiffs were assured that any defects present in the mobile home delivered to them from the factory would be repaired promptly.

The mobile home was delivered to plaintiffs' lot on November 1, 1972. Soon after they moved in plaintiffs discovered water and air leaks, gaps in the "tip out,"[1] as well as defective doors, cabinets, vents and walls. Plaintiffs promptly gave Pressnall a list of these defects and were assured by Pressnall that the problems would be corrected. Thereafter, a series of repair requests yielded no action except the appearance of workmen who were not prepared to make repairs. Finally, plaintiffs, having decided that it was futile to attempt to have the unit properly repaired through Pressnall's efforts, turned the matter over to their attorney and rejected Pressnall's further efforts to make repairs. Thereafter, negotiations were held with a representative of the mobile home manufacturer and as a result three repairmen worked approximately ten hours each repairing defects. However, plaintiffs were not satisfied with

———

[1] The "tip out" is a hinged section that is transported inside the mobile home and then tipped out to widen the living room when the mobile home is set up. This method of construction is necessitated by width limitations for transportation over highways.

the quality of repairs and when a release was tendered to them they refused to sign it. Although some of the defects were cured, the serious problems such as leakage continued and new problems were created.

Concluding that further requests to repair the unit would be futile, plaintiffs instructed their attorney on December 27th, 1972, to send letters to both defendants notifying them of plaintiffs' decision to rescind the purchase contract. Plaintiffs tendered back the new mobile home, subject to their security interest, and demanded return of the down payment as well as consequential damages. On advice of counsel plaintiffs continued to occupy the mobile home until November 15, 1973, approximately three weeks before the trial. The mobile home was repossessed by Commercial Credit in January of 1974 and resold at a loss.

Pressnall contends that plaintiffs did not prove facts sufficient to justify rescission, asserting (1) that there is no evidence of a material misrepresentation inducing plaintiffs' purchase; (2) that there is no evidence that the uncorrected defects were material or that they rendered the trailer unfit for use as a dwelling; (3) that rescission is not a proper remedy because plaintiffs refused to allow reasonable efforts to repair, and (4) that plaintiffs' continued possession and use of the mobile home constituted an assertion and exercise of the right of ownership inconsistent with their attempted revocation of acceptance.

The contract in question is governed by the Uniform Commercial Code. Specifically, the buyer's right to revoke acceptance is defined in ORS 72.6080. . . .

Plaintiffs' rescission letter constituted a revocation of acceptance within the meaning of the code. When cast in language of the Uniform Commercial Code, Pressnall's contentions are that there is no proof of nonconformities substantially impairing the value of the goods and that there has been no failure to seasonably cure the nonconformities.

Whether plaintiffs proved nonconformities sufficiently serious to justify revocation of acceptance is a two-step inquiry under the code. Since ORS 72.6080(1) provides that the buyer may revoke acceptance of goods "whose nonconformity substantially impairs its value *to him*," the value of conforming goods *to the plaintiff* must first be determined. This is a subjective question in the sense that it calls for a consideration of the needs and circumstances of the plaintiff who seeks to revoke; not the needs and circumstances of an average buyer.[3] The second inquiry is whether the nonconformity in fact substantially impairs the value of the goods to the buyer, having in mind his particular needs. This is an

---

[3]   See, Uniform Commercial Code § 2–608, comment 2: "The test is not what the seller had reason to know at the time of contracting; the question is whether the nonconformity is such as will in fact cause a substantial impairment of value to the buyer though the seller had no advance knowledge as to the buyer's particular circumstances." See also, Tiger Motor Co. v. McMurtry, 284 Ala. 283, 292, 224 So.2d 638 (1969): "We are aware that what may cause one person great inconvenience or financial loss, may not another."

objective question in the sense that it calls for evidence of something more than plaintiff's assertion that the nonconformity impaired the value to him; it requires evidence from which it can be inferred that plaintiff's needs were not met because of the nonconformity. In short, the nonconformity must *substantially* impair the value of the goods to the plaintiff buyer. The existence of substantial impairment depends upon the facts and circumstances in each case.

In the present case plaintiffs purchased the mobile home for the purpose of using it as their residence. Because of the defects described above and defendant's failure to cure them, the value of the mobile home to plaintiffs as a residence was substantially impaired. Defendant argues that since plaintiffs did not produce any evidence showing that the cost of repairs was substantial in relation to the purchase price, there was no proof of substantial impairment of value. This argument would have some force if the test for a substantial impairment of value were an objective one. However, since, as we have shown, the test is a subjective one, permitting revocation of acceptance if it is shown that the value *to the purchaser* is impaired, the relatively small amount of money needed to repair the defect is not necessarily relevant because the impairment of the value to the purchaser may be substantial even though the cost of curing the defect may be relatively small. Thus, in the present case, although the defects in the mobile home probably could have been repaired at a relatively small cost, plaintiffs were deprived of the benefits of a comfortable home for a substantial period of time as a result of defendant's failure to make timely repairs.

Defendant also seems to argue that impairment of value is not shown unless the goods are useless for the purchaser's purposes. This is not true; revocation of acceptance is permissible not only where there is complete impairment, but also where the impairment is substantial but not complete.

Pressnall contends that any failure to cure the nonconformities was excused because plaintiffs unreasonably refused to allow further attempts to repair the unit. The record indicates, however, that Pressnall had ample opportunity to cure the defects before the revocation of acceptance occurred, but that he did not act seasonably. A seller does not have an unlimited amount of time to cure the nonconformity.

Pressnall's final argument is that plaintiffs' use of the mobile home after the notice of rescission constituted a use of the goods inconsistent with the seller's ownership and that therefore a new acceptance of the goods occurred. The answer to this contention is that plaintiffs retained a security interest in the mobile home after the revocation of acceptance. This entitled them to continue in possession to preserve their collateral. Continued occupancy was the most feasible method of protecting the mobile home from water damage. The alternative was to find covered storage, which would have been expensive. Defendant suffered no loss as a result of plaintiffs' occupancy since the trial court awarded an offset to defendant for the rental value of the mobile home during plaintiffs' occupancy.

Plaintiffs having successfully revoked their acceptance of the mobile home, Pressnall thereby breached the warranty given on assignment of the financing contract to Commercial Credit. Damages were, therefore, properly awarded to Commercial Credit.

The decree of the trial court is affirmed.

QUESTIONS AND NOTES

1.   Is *Jorgensen* a subsection (1)(a) case or a subsection (1)(b) case?

2.   Subsection (2) permits revocation of acceptance only if the buyer acts within a reasonable time after discovering the grounds for it. Did the Jorgensens revoke within a reasonable time?

In Tiger Motor Co. v. McMurtry, 284 Ala. 283, 224 So.2d 638 (1969) (cited in footnote 3 of the *Jorgensen* opinion), the buyer was allowed to revoke his acceptance of a new automobile even though he had kept it for 344 days and driven it more than 14,000 miles. The buyer recovered all payments he had made, the court refusing to allow the seller any rental value as a set-off. The buyer testified that he had taken the automobile back to the dealer at least 30 times for repair and that it had been in the seller's shop for a total of 40 to 50 days.

On the other hand, in Green Chevrolet Co. v. Kemp, 241 Ark. 62, 406 S.W.2d 142 (1966), the court held that the buyer could not revoke his acceptance after keeping an automobile for six months and driving it 3,000 miles.

3.   Subsection (2) also requires that revocation occur "before any substantial change in condition of the goods which is not caused by their own defects." Was there no substantial change in the condition of the Jorgensens' mobile home as a result of their living in it for more than a year?

Problem. Papyrus, a manufacturer of paper office supplies, purchased on credit a large quantity of rolled paper from Intergon, a paper mill. Papyrus cut, packaged, and marketed the finished product as photocopy paper. When it turned out that the paper was defective, Papyrus' customers demanded refunds. Papyrus notified Intergon that the paper was defective, that Papyrus would not pay for it, and that Papyrus was revoking acceptance. It proceeded to sell the paper for scrap. Intergon has sued for the price, and Papyrus has counterclaimed for losses it incurred processing the rolled paper and dealing with customer complaints.

   a.   Under 2–608(1)(b) was revocation of acceptance permitted?

   b.   Does subsection (2) preclude revocation of acceptance? What is the effect of Official Comment 6?

   c.   What is the relevance of subsection (3)?

4.   **Continued use after revocation of acceptance.** In Bowen v. Young (Question 7, page 425 supra) the purchaser of a mobile home rejected it, but then moved into and occupied it for a year. The court held that after first

rejecting the home, the buyer's occupation of it amounted to acceptance under 2–606(1)(c). A similar issue arises with respect to revocation of acceptance. The court in *Jorgensen* concluded that the buyers' continued occupancy did not amount to acceptance. Why not?

Another court supplied a non-exhaustive list of factors to be considered in determining whether continued use undermines a buyer's revocation of acceptance:

- Upon notice of revocation, what instructions did the seller give the buyer concerning the goods?

- Did the buyer's business needs or personal circumstances compel the continued use?

- During the period of use by the buyer, did the seller assure the buyer that the defects would be cured or that provisions would be made to compensate the buyer for the inconvenience resulting from the defects?

- Did the seller act in good faith? and

- Was the seller unduly prejudiced by the buyer's continued use?

Cuesta v. Classic Wheels, Inc., 358 N.J.Super. 512, 521, 818 A.2d 448, 453 (App.Div.2003).

The existence of articulated criteria does not make the decisions easy, and they are not entirely consistent. For example, a consumer revoked acceptance of a car but continued using it because she did not have access to public transportation and could not afford to buy another one. The court held that it was not reasonable for her to have continued using the car indefinitely, driving it some 37,000 miles between the date of revocation and the date of the decision. Barrett v. Brian Bemis Auto World, 408 F.Supp.2d 539 (N.D.Ill.2005). In another case the owner of a golf course (Swan Lake) purchased 110 golf carts, many of which suffered premature battery failure. A year later the seller (Yamaha) replaced all the batteries, but some continued to fail, and 20 were replaced again. The court stated:

> The untimeliness of the revocation is, by itself, sufficient to grant summary judgment in favor of Yamaha. But even if Swan Lake's revocation had been timely, it would still not be a remedy available to Swan Lake because Swan Lake continued to use the carts after its attempted revocation. The general rule is that a buyer is not permitted to continue to use goods after an attempted revocation. This is because goods (such as golf carts) depreciate with each use. Think of how a car depreciates with each mile that is put on it. This rule underscores the central "purpose of revocation," namely "to cancel the sale and return the parties to *status quo ante.*" To hold otherwise would allow a plaintiff to have his cake and eat it too. A plaintiff could continue to use the supposedly nonconforming goods, cause them to depreciate in value, all the while continuing to press for the revocation of acceptance. That's precisely what Swan Lake has done here. The bottom line is that if Swan Lake did not want the carts, it should

have promptly revoked their acceptance and returned them to Yamaha. . . .

As with most rules, there are exceptions. A party may ask for the revocation of acceptance while continuing to use the goods when such use would amount to an absolute necessity. Indeed, this was the case in [Jones v. Abriani, 169 Ind.App. 556, 350 N.E.2d 635 (1976)], which involved the Plaintiffs' continued use of a mobile home that they had bought. Return of the mobile home was not feasible because it was where the Plaintiffs lived and returning the item would have subjected them to a substantial hardship— homelessness.

Swan Lake argues that its continued use of the carts after revocation was a "business necessity" that was "from a commercial standpoint . . . equivalent" to the necessity in *Abriani*. This is hardly persuasive. While Swan Lake needed golf carts to maintain the operations of its golf course, it had other options than to continue using the Yamaha carts it had revoked. First, the Yamaha golf carts are not, apparently, the only ones in Swan Lake's fleet. . . . Swan Lake also has 44 Club Car brand golf carts in its fleet. Second, Swan Lake could have purchased or leased additional golf carts. This may sound harsh—forcing Swan Lake to incur additional cost while sorting out its rights as to allegedly defective Yamaha carts—but the remedy of revocation demands, absent extraordinary circumstances, that the condition and integrity of the goods be maintained. . . .

Swan Lake was required to "search for and obtain any necessary replacements with dispatch" and was "not permitted to dawdle for well over a year" while continuing to use the carts. Swan Lake's continued use "was not justified and thus worked to invalidate any purported revocation. *"[A] buyer* who revokes acceptance . . . must begin the search for replacement goods with reasonable dispatch."

Swan Lake Holdings, LLC v. Yamaha Golf Cart Co., 2011 WL 781598 at *7 (N.D.Ind.2011).

On the other hand, *Jorgensen* permitted continued use, and so did the court in Fablok Mills, Inc. v. Cocker Machine & Foundry Co., 125 N.J.Super. 251, 310 A.2d 491 (1973). Plaintiff purchased 10 knitting machines that were delivered over a nine-month period. Before all were delivered, the plaintiff experienced problems with some of the machines and complained. The seller undertook to correct the defects and continued to make those efforts until two years after the last machines were delivered, at which point plaintiff notified defendant that it was revoking its acceptance of the machines. After this notification, the plaintiff stopped using some of the machines and put them in storage. It continued to use others (the court's opinion does not indicate the period of use). The trial court held that, as a matter of law, the revocation did not come within reasonable time and that use after the revocation was inconsistent with revocation. The appellate court reversed.

The attempts of the seller to repair may have induced the buyer reasonably to believe that the defects would be cured. What is a reasonable time within which to revoke is a matter for the jury. Further, whether use after revocation is inconsistent with revocation is also a matter for the jury. The court stated that the overriding requirement of reasonableness which permeates the Code counsels against any absolute rule against continued use after revocation of acceptance. Use may be the most appropriate means of mitigating damages. Here the seller was the only domestic maker of knitting machines: plaintiff's choice was to either close down its business or continue using some of the machines. The defendant did not show that it objected to the continued use, that the delay in stopping use prejudiced it, or that the buyer had any reasonable alternative. Accord, Toshiba Machine Co. v. SPM Flow Control, Inc., 180 S.W.3d 761, 772–75 (Tex.App.2005).

5. Revocation of acceptance and privity of contract. In Durfee v. Rod Baxter Imports, Inc., 262 N.W.2d 349 (Minn.1977), plaintiff purchased an imported automobile that proved to be seriously nonconforming. He sent the dealer and the manufacturer's U.S. distributor notice of revocation of acceptance and sued them both to recover the purchase price, as permitted by 2–711(1). The court permitted recovery:

> Defendant Saab-Scania suggests that it cannot be liable because, as the distributor of the Saab, it had no direct contractual relationship with plaintiff. If this is the case, plaintiff may well be left without relief, for Saab-Scania was unable to assure us at oral argument of the continued existence of Rod Baxter. Although the relevant sections of Article 2 of the Uniform Commercial Code seem to require a buyer-seller relationship, Saab-Scania does not escape liability on this ground in these circumstances.

> The existence and comprehensiveness of a warranty undoubtedly are significant factors in a consumer's decision to purchase a particular automobile. Saab-Scania evidently warrants its automobiles to increase retail sales and indirectly its own sales of Saab automobiles. When the . . . defects are substantial enough to justify revocation of acceptance, we think the buyer is entitled to look to the warrantor for relief. If plaintiff had sued Saab-Scania for breach of either express warranty or implied warranty, the absence of privity would not bar the suit despite the language of the pertinent Code sections. We see no reason why the result should differ merely because plaintiff has chosen to revoke his acceptance instead of suing for breach of warranty. The remedies of the Code are to be liberally administered. Minn.St. 336.1–106(1) [revised 1–305(a)]. We think liberal administration does not envision forcing a consumer to keep a car which is sufficiently defective so as to justify his returning it and then requiring him to sue the distributor for damages merely because the dealer is insolvent or no longer in business. The distributor of the automobile, who profits indirectly from retail sales, must take responsibility for the solvency of its dealers when its warranty is breached. A consumer cannot be expected to foresee the demise of local dealerships;

instead he is entitled to rely on the distributor who induced him to buy the automobile. The lack of privity between the parties does not relieve Saab-Scania of liability.

Compare Gasque v. Mooers Motor Car Co., Inc., 227 Va. 154, 313 S.E.2d 384 (1984):

> The remedy of revocation of acceptance . . . lies only against a seller of goods, not against a remote manufacturer. This is so because the remedy, where successful, cancels a contract of sale, restores both title to and possession of the goods to the seller, restores the purchase price to the buyer, and as fairly as possible, returns the contracting parties to the status quo ante. The remote manufacturer, having no part in the sale transaction, has no role to play in such a restoration of former positions.
>
> The buyers argue that this limitation on revocation revivifies the "archaic doctrine of privity." We disagree. A remote manufacturer is liable to a buyer for damages arising from negligence or from breach of warranty, and the defense of lack of privity has been abolished as to such cases. Code § 8.2–318. But the remedy of revocation of acceptance under Code § 8.2–608 is conceptually inapplicable to any persons other than the parties to the contract of sale sought to be rescinded.

Under the language of 2–608, which court is right?

———

Accettura v. Vacationland, Inc.

Illinois Court of Appeals, 2018.
112 N.E.3d 1054.

■ JUSTICE MCLAREN delivered the judgment of the court . . . .

¶ 2 I.   BACKGROUND

¶ 3 On April 19, 2014, plaintiffs bought [an] RV, a new 2014 Palomino trailer, from defendant for $26,000.25. On April 25, 2014, plaintiffs took possession of the RV. In June 2014, plaintiffs discovered water leaking into the RV from the emergency-exit window. Plaintiffs brought the RV to defendant for repair; defendant repaired the RV to plaintiffs' satisfaction, at no charge.

¶ 4 In July 2014, during a trip to Michigan, plaintiffs discovered a different leak in the RV. During a rainstorm, water leaked into the dinette area, damaging the walls and causing electrical failure. Plaintiffs brought the RV to defendant for repair on July 14, 2014. Defendant told plaintiffs that the RV needed to be sent to the manufacturer for repair. Defendant [stated] that it could not estimate how long the manufacturer would take to repair the RV. On August 2, 2014, [plaintiffs] verbally revoked acceptance of the RV. The manufacturer had the RV in repair from approximately August 4 through September 23, 2014. [It returned the RV to the dealer, who called plaintiffs to inform them that they could pick it up.] On September 28, 2014, plaintiffs' attorney sent defendant a letter revoking acceptance of the RV. . . .

¶ 6 On October 29, 2014, plaintiffs filed a . . . complaint against defendant, alleging the following. Since they purchased the RV, it had experienced numerous mechanical problems, including (a) water leakage through a defective emergency-exit window, (b) water leakage through a defective dinette window, (c) water leakage into a paneled wall, (d) an inoperative electrical system, (e) and "generally massive water leaks," which "have the potential of causing mold and serious health issues." Further, these "defects cannot be repaired. The [RV] was in repair for almost the entire summer of 2014, and still has not been repaired properly. * * * Prior to filing this suit, Plaintiff's [sic] revoked their acceptance of the RV and canceled their contract. * * * Defendant refused to return Plaintiffs' money."

¶ 7 Plaintiffs sought damages under the following theories: . . . revocation of acceptance and cancellation of contract, under sections 2–608(1)(b) and 2–711(1) of the UCC. They also sought to recover the purchase price, under section 2–711(1). . . .

¶ 9 On November 14, 2016, defendant filed a motion for summary judgment [arguing] that plaintiffs' failure to give defendant a reasonable opportunity to cure was fatal to their claims, as a matter of law. Plaintiffs responded that there was a genuine issue of material fact regarding whether the RV was repaired within a reasonable time. Defendant replied that plaintiffs failed to rebut material facts set forth in defendant's motion.

¶ 10 On February 10, 2017, the trial court granted defendant summary judgment . . . . The trial court stated that reasonableness is a question of fact but that, in this case, the record clearly showed that plaintiffs revoked acceptance sometime before August 2, 2014, which did not provide a reasonable time for defendant to cure. . . . Plaintiffs [appealed.]

¶ 15 II. ANALYSIS

. . .

¶ 19 B. Reasonable Opportunity to Cure

¶ 20 Plaintiffs argue that whether defendant had a reasonable opportunity to cure is a disputed issue of material fact. Defendant contends that the trial court correctly determined that plaintiffs did not provide defendant with a reasonable opportunity to cure, as a matter of law.

. . .

¶ 23 Typically, reasonableness is a question of fact. . . . When more than one inference could be drawn from undisputed facts, a triable issue exists and summary judgment may not be granted. However, where, as here, undisputed facts give rise to a single inference, summary judgment should be granted.

co_anchor_F42045610244_1¶ 24 Here, on defendant's motion for summary judgment, plaintiffs were obligated to establish facts that would satisfy their burden of showing that they provided defendant with a reasonable opportunity to cure. The undisputed facts establish that plaintiffs brought the RV to defendant in June 2014 because water leaked into the RV from the emergency-exit window. Defendant repaired this problem to plaintiffs' satisfaction. In early July 2014, a separate and distinct problem arose in the RV during a rainstorm; significant water leaked into the dinette area, causing electrical-system and other problems. Plaintiffs brought the RV to defendant for repair on July 14, 2014, and revoked acceptance, "sometime before August 2, 2014."

¶ 25 Although a plaintiff need not prove his case at the summary judgment stage, he must present a factual basis that would arguably entitle him to a judgment at trial. Mere speculation, conjecture, or guess is insufficient to survive summary judgment.

¶ 26 Here, plaintiffs have failed to point to any authority or facts to support their assertion that their revocation of acceptance, approximately two weeks after asking defendant to repair the RV, was reasonable. Rather, the undisputed facts give rise to only one inference: plaintiffs failed to provide defendant a reasonable opportunity to cure. There is no genuine issue of material fact on this question. . . .

¶ 35 E. Opportunity to Cure Under UCC Section 2–608(1)(b)

co_anchor_F92045610244_1¶ 36 Next, plaintiffs argue that the trial court erred by entering summary judgment in defendant's favor . . . because the trial court improperly determined that an opportunity to cure is a prerequisite for a claim under section 2–608(1)(b) of the UCC. . . .

¶ 38 Plaintiff contends that, although section 2–608(1)(a) requires an opportunity to cure, section 2–608(1)(b) does not. Plaintiff correctly notes that this is an issue of first impression.

¶ 39 When interpreting a statute, our primary objective is to ascertain and give effect to the legislature's intent. The best indication of the legislature's intent is the language used in the statute, which must be given its plain and ordinary meaning.

¶ 40 Section 2–608(1)(b) does not specify whether the seller has a right to cure prior to a proper revocation of acceptance. However, in *Belfour v. Schaumburg*, 306 Ill. App. 3d 234 at 241, 239 Ill.Dec. 383, 713 N.E.2d 1233 (1999), this court rejected the argument that the seller did not have a right to cure before the buyer revoked acceptance under section 2–608. We stated that, "[u]nder the UCC, the buyer must allow the seller time to cure before invoking revocation of acceptance." We explained, "courts will resort to revocation of acceptance only after attempts at adjustment have failed." *Id.* at 242, 239 Ill.Dec. 383, 713

N.E.2d 1233 (citing 2–608(1)(a), Uniform Commercial Code Comment [4]. We concluded that the buyer's revocation of acceptance was improper because the seller had offered a proper cure. In addition, our supreme court has stated that "[r]evocation of acceptance is a form of equitable relief."

co_anchor_F102045610244_1¶ 41 In this case, the record clearly establishes that on July 14, 2014, plaintiffs asked defendant to cure the defects discovered during their trip to Michigan and defendant offered plaintiffs a proper cure. Plaintiffs revoked acceptance about two weeks later, knowing that the RV was going to the manufacturer to be repaired under the warranty. Thus, the material facts are undisputed and all reasonable minds would agree that plaintiffs failed to allow defendant a reasonable time to cure before their purported revocation, as a matter of law. Accordingly, the trial court properly determined that plaintiffs' revocation was improper under section 2–608(1)(b). . . .

Accettura v. Vacationland, Inc.

Illinois Supreme Court, 2019.
__ N.E.3d __, 2019 IL 124285.

■ JUSTICE GARMAN.

[After reciting the facts and procedure as described in the lower court's opinion, the court continued:]

¶ 8 On appeal to this court, defendant does not dispute that the defect, without repair, substantially impaired the RV's value to plaintiffs. Plaintiffs' expert opined that the defective unit was worth a mere 10% of its purchase price. The record does not show that defendant rebutted this opinion. Rather, defendant relied on its argument that plaintiffs must have given it an opportunity to seasonably cure, which would have remedied any impairment of value.

¶ 9 Defendant likewise does not dispute that plaintiffs were unaware of the defect in the RV at the time they accepted it. Thus, subsection (1)(a) cannot apply, for that subsection, by its plain language, contemplates a buyer who accepted a good she knew to be nonconforming "on the reasonable assumption that its non-conformity would be cured." *Id.* § 2–608(1)(a). Thus, if plaintiffs can revoke their acceptance, they can do so because they accepted the RV "without discovery of such nonconformity" and their "acceptance was reasonably induced either by the difficulty of discovery before acceptance or the seller's assurances." *Id.* § 2–608(1)(b).

¶ 10 Plaintiffs brought the RV to defendant for repair on July 14. Before defendant sent the RV to the manufacturer, one of its employees gave plaintiffs what plaintiffs described as a "very vague and extended" timeline. Plaintiffs state that they then called the manufacturer, who referred them back to defendant. Upset with defendant's and the manufacturer's inability to give them a timeline for repair, plaintiffs thereafter called defendant to revoke their acceptance of the RV.

Defendant argues that plaintiffs were required to give it a reasonable time to cure before they could revoke acceptance.

¶ 11 Interpretation of subsection (1)(b) is an issue of first impression in Illinois. The standard of review for questions of statutory interpretation is *de novo*. The primary objective of our analysis is to ascertain and give effect to the legislative intent. The most reliable indicator of the legislature's intent is the statutory language itself, given its plain and ordinary meaning. We do not depart from the plain language of the statute by reading into it exceptions, limitations, or conditions that conflict with the expressed intent.

¶ 13 . . . The plain language of the statute evinces the General Assembly's intention to allow a buyer to revoke acceptance of a substantially impaired commercial unit under two separate and distinct circumstances. The first circumstance is when the buyer knows of the nonconformity, the buyer accepts the nonconforming unit with a reasonable assumption that the nonconformity will be cured, and the seller fails to seasonably cure it. 2–608(1)(a). The second is when the buyer accepts the nonconforming unit without knowledge of the nonconformity and either the nonconformity was difficult to discover or the seller assured her that the unit conformed to the specifications. *Id.* § 2–608(1)(b).

¶ 14 Both situations contemplate a nonconformity that substantially impairs the unit's value to the buyer. Where they diverge is in the buyer's expectation. The first contemplates a buyer who accepts a nonconforming unit and expects the seller to cure the nonconformity. When she does not get that cure seasonably, she can revoke her acceptance. The second contemplates a buyer who accepts what she believes to be a conforming unit. When she does not get that conforming unit, she can revoke her acceptance. Because we find this language plain and because subsection (1)(b) does not require that a buyer give the seller an opportunity to cure, we need not consider the requirements of other statutes that defendant argues are analogous.

. . .

¶ 17 Defendant argues that this case involves more than statutory interpretation of subsection (1)(b). Defendant claims that it offered and plaintiffs accepted repair as their remedy for the defect before plaintiffs revoked acceptance. Because they elected that remedy, defendant asserts, they were obligated to allow defendant a reasonable time to complete the repair.

¶ 18 Although a situation could arise in which a buyer acts unreasonably in revoking acceptance of a good after requesting that the seller cure a nonconformity, this is not such a situation. Nothing in the record indicates that plaintiffs agreed to an open-ended repair timeline. The fact that they considered allowing defendant to cure does not obligate them to accept an unreasonable cure. Further, it does not obviate their right to revoke under subsection 2–608(1)(b).

¶ 19 Defendant further argues that the cases plaintiffs cite do not comprise a majority of foreign jurisdictions. Rather, it contends, a split of authority exists. It argues that many jurisdictions, and "probably a majority of the commentators," find that the seller has a right to cure when a buyer attempts to revoke acceptance under subsection (1)(b).

¶ 20 Because we find the language plain, we need not look to our sister states' interpretations of this provision. Even if we review those decisions, however, our research indicates that, although a split of authority exists, a majority of other jurisdictions have interpreted their state's adoption of the statutory provision consistent with our decision today. See, *e.g.*, (citations of decisions from five states omitted).

¶ 21 Notably, although it appears that the courts in some of our sister states would rule to the contrary, we did not find a case in which a court expressly interpreted the statutory language and found that subsection (1)(b) required that the buyer give the seller an opportunity to cure. Rather, the decisions that run contra to ours seem to base their decision on policy grounds (see, *e.g.*, *Conte v. Dwan Lincoln-Mercury, Inc.*, 172 Conn. 112, 374 A.2d 144, 149 (1976) (" 'One policy of the Code is to encourage the parties to work out their differences and so to minimize losses resulting from defective performance.' " . . .)) or gloss over interpretation (see, *e.g.*, *Cuesta v. Classic Wheels, Inc.*, 358 N.J.Super. 512, 818 A.2d 448, 451 (N.J. Super. Ct. App. Div. 2003) (citing section 2–508 but not further elaborating) . . .).

¶ 22 Defendant next argues that when the language of the UCC is ambiguous, which it argues the statute here is, we may consider the committee comments. As we find the language unambiguous, we need not consider them. Even if we did, however, they do not support defendant's position. Defendant cites comment 4 of section 2–608, which states that revocation "will be generally resorted to only after attempts at adjustments have failed," and comment 5, which discusses "considerations of good faith, prevention of surprise, and reasonable adjustment." These comments both discuss the notice that a revoking buyer must give the seller. As the comment states, a court should consider that most buyers will usually seek a cure before revoking in determining whether the notice of revocation was timely. In determining whether the notice of revocation sufficiently notifies the seller of the nonconformity, the court should consider what information the seller has as a result of the buyer previously seeking a cure. Such consideration, however, is irrelevant to whether the buyer *must* seek a cure before revoking.

¶ 23 Finally, defendant argues that section 2–608(3), which states that "[a] buyer who so revokes has the same rights and duties with regard to the goods involved as if he had rejected them," invokes section 2–508. Some of our sister jurisdictions agree. See, *e.g.*, *Cuesta*, 818 A.2d at 451.

Section 2–508 allows a seller to cure a rejected nonconforming delivery if "the time for performance has not yet expired" or if "the seller had reasonable grounds to believe [the nonconforming tender] would be acceptable."

¶ 24 We disagree. Rather, we agree with the Michigan appellate court's analysis of this argument. See *Head v. Phillips Camper Sales & Rental, Inc.*, 593 N.W.2d 595, 600–01 (Mich.App. 1999) (interpreting UCC section 2–608, discussing the differences between rejection and revocation of acceptance, and finding that subsection (3) does not incorporate UCC section 2–508). Defendant's argument ignores the distinction between rejection and revocation of acceptance. A buyer may reject goods if they "fail in any respect to conform to the contract." § 2–601. Once the buyer accepts the goods, however, he may only revoke that acceptance if the "non-conformity substantially impairs its value to him." § 2–608(1). When a buyer rejects nonconforming goods, the seller may have a right to cure. *Id.* § 2–508. In the case of a revocation, however, as aptly stated by the *Head* court, "[t]he seller, in turn, loses the right to cure, but gains the benefit of the higher substantial impairment standard for revocation." 593 N.W.2d at 601. We further agree that the "rights and duties" referred to in section 2–608(3) are found in sections 2–602, 2–603, and 2–604, not section 2–508. See *Head*, 593 N.W.2d at 600. . . .

¶ 26 We hold that the plain language of subsection 2–608(1)(b) of the Illinois Commercial Code does not require that the buyer give the seller an opportunity to cure a substantial nonconformity before revoking acceptance. We reverse and remand for further proceedings consistent with this opinion.

QUESTIONS AND NOTES

1.   The Court of Appeals and the Supreme Court each cites Official Comment 4 to 2–608 to support its position. Which position does that Comment support?

2.   In Gappelburg v. Landrum, 654 S.W.2d 549 (Tex.App.1983), the court perceived a distinction between cure by repair and cure by replacement. It held that when a seller tried but failed to repair a very expensive large-screen projection TV, it had a right to cure by replacing the TV with a new one. The Texas Supreme Court reversed. "We are cited no good policy reason why different rules should attain as to cure by replacement instead of cure by repair. Indeed, we cannot envision any basis for a distinction. Thus, we state that once a buyer has properly revoked acceptance of a product, the seller has neither the right to cure by repair nor by replacement." 666 S.W.2d 88, 91 (Tex.1984).

3.   As stated in *Accettura*, the courts are split on the question whether the seller has a right to cure under 2–608(1)(b). Which position is preferable? And is there a basis for distinguishing between cure by repair and cure by replacement?

4.   Problem. On January 12 Benton contracted to purchase a 75-inch TCL TV from Schiller TV & Appliance. The contract specified that the TV was to be delivered to Benton's home by January 30 (in time for the Super Bowl) for $2,888. Schiller delivered the TV on January 22. Benton signed a receipt stating that she accepted the set. Two days later the screen became cloudy, making it difficult to see anything. In response to Benton's phone call, Schiller picked up the set and attempted to repair it, but informed Benton on January 26 that it was unable to do so. Benton told Schiller to keep the TV and return her purchase price. Schiller replied that it would deliver a new one the next day. Benton told Schiller not to bother, that she would not take delivery of it. When Schiller failed to return the purchase price, Benton sued. Who should win?

5.   CISG. Article 48 of the Convention on Contracts for the International Sale of Goods provides that even after the date of delivery the seller may "remedy at his own expense any failure to perform his obligations, if he can do so without unreasonable delay and without causing the buyer unreasonable inconvenience." But this right is "subject to article 49," which provides that the buyer may declare the contract avoided if the seller's failure to perform amounts to a "fundamental breach of contract." Article 25 defines "fundamental breach." Please read Articles 25, 48, and 49.

Problem. In a transaction governed by the CISG, Case contracts to sell a road grader to Bayer. The grader is delivered and placed in operation. In the second week of operation, the engine seizes up because of a failure of the oil pump. Cure would require replacement of the engine. Bayer notifies Case of the problem, and informs Case that it is avoiding the sale because of Case's fundamental breach. Case, in turn, asserts that Bayer cannot avoid the sale and states that it will replace the engine within two weeks. Bayer refuses to allow Case to do this. Has Bayer breached?

What additional facts are needed, if any? Is the CISG approach to cure preferable to that of Article 2?

C. REMEDIES WHEN THE BUYER DOES NOT HAVE THE GOODS

1. THE RIGHT TO GET THE GOODS

According to 2–711(2), "Where the seller fails to deliver or repudiates the buyer may . . .

     (a)   if the goods have been identified recover them as provided in this Article (Section 2–502); or

     (b)   in a proper case obtain specific performance or replevy the goods as provided in this Article (Section 2–716)."

Section 2–502 addresses some of the situations in which a buyer forms a contract with a seller who encounters financial difficulty before delivering the goods. The problem is especially acute for the buyer who has paid all or part of the price. Section 2–502 provides relief, and it establishes different rules for consumer buyers than for others. For consumer buyers, it permits the buyer to recover the goods from the seller regardless of the reason the seller fails to deliver, simply upon tendering the balance of the price. For commercial buyers, tendering the balance of the price is not the sole requirement. In addition, the seller must be insolvent, and the insolvency must have arisen within ten days after the buyer's first payment. If the seller becomes insolvent (defined in 1–201(b)(23)) outside the ten-day window, the buyer gains no rights under 2–502, even if the buyer had no reason to suspect the insolvency. The insolvency-within-ten-days limitation deprives the section of much of its utility, and even if 2–502 gives the buyer rights to the goods as against the seller, the seller's creditors also may have rights to them. These conflicts are resolved elsewhere in the Code and are the subject of Chapter 11.

Section 2–716(1) states that the buyer is entitled to specific performance "where the goods are unique or in other proper circumstances." Other than heirlooms, art objects, and certain collectibles, what goods are unique? In what other circumstances is specific performance appropriate? See Official Comment 2.

———

Sedmak v. Charlie's Chevrolet, Inc.

Missouri Court of Appeals, 1981.
622 S.W.2d 694.

■ SATZ, JUDGE. . . . In their petition, plaintiffs, Dr. and Mrs. Sedmak (Sedmaks), alleged they entered into a contract with defendant, Charlie's Chevrolet, Inc. (Charlie's), to purchase a Corvette automobile for approximately $15,000.00. The Corvette was one of a limited number manufactured to commemorate the selection of the Corvette as the Pace Car for the Indianapolis 500. Charlie's breached the contract, the Sedmaks alleged, when, after the automobile was delivered, an agent for Charlie's told the Sedmaks they could not purchase the automobile for $15,000.00 but would have to bid on it.

The trial court found the parties entered into an oral contract and also found the contract was excepted from the Statute of Frauds. The court then ordered Charlie's to make the automobile "available for delivery" to the Sedmaks.

Charlie's raises three points on appeal: (1) the existence of an oral contract is not supported by the credible evidence; (2) if an oral contract exists, it is unenforceable because of the Statute of Frauds; and (3) specific performance is an improper remedy because the Sedmaks did not show their legal remedies were inadequate.

. . . [T]he record reflects the Sedmaks to be automobile enthusiasts, who, at the time of trial, owned six Corvettes. In July, 1977, "Vette Vues," a Corvette fancier's magazine to which Dr. Sedmak subscribed, published an article announcing Chevrolet's tentative plans to manufacture a limited edition of the Corvette. The limited edition of approximately 6,000 automobiles was to commemorate the selection of the Corvette as the Indianapolis 500 Pace Car. The Sedmaks were interested in acquiring one of these Pace Cars to add to their Corvette collection. In November, 1977, the Sedmaks asked Tom Kells, sales manager at Charlie's Chevrolet, about the availability of the Pace Car. Mr. Kells said he did not have any information on the car but would find out about it. Kells also said if Charlie's were to receive a Pace Car, the Sedmaks could purchase it.

On January 9, 1978, Dr. Sedmak telephoned Kells to ask him if a Pace Car could be ordered. Kells indicated that he would require a deposit on the car, so Mrs. Sedmak went to Charlie's and gave Kells a check for $500. She was given a receipt for that amount bearing the names of Kells and Charlie's Chevrolet, Inc. At that time, Kells had a pre-order form listing both standard equipment and options available on the Pace Car. Prior to tendering the deposit, Mrs. Sedmak asked Kells if she and Dr. Sedmak were "definitely going to be the owners." Kells replied, "yes." After the deposit had been paid, Mrs. Sedmak stated if the car was going to be theirs, her husband wanted some changes made to the stock model. She asked Kells to order the car equipped with an L82 engine, four speed standard transmission and AM/FM radio with tape deck. Kells said that he would try to arrange with the manufacturer for these changes. Kells was able to make the changes, and, when the car arrived, it was equipped as the Sedmaks had requested.

Kells informed Mrs. Sedmak that the price of the Pace Car would be the manufacturer's retail price, approximately $15,000. The dollar figure could not be quoted more precisely because Kells was not sure what the ordered changes would cost, nor was he sure what the "appearance package"—decals, a special paint job—would cost. Kells also told Mrs. Sedmak that, after the changes had been made, a "contract"—a retail dealer's order form—would be mailed to them. However, no form or written contract was mailed to the Sedmaks by Charlie's.

On January 25, 1978, the Sedmaks visited Charlie's to take delivery on another Corvette. At that time, the Sedmaks asked Kells whether he knew anything further about the arrival date of the Pace Car. Kells replied he had no further information but he would let the Sedmaks know when the car arrived. Kells also requested that Charlie's be allowed to keep the car in their showroom for promotional purposes until after the Indianapolis 500 Race. The Sedmaks agreed to this arrangement.

On April 3, 1978, the Sedmaks were notified by Kells that the Pace Car had arrived. Kells told the Sedmaks they could not purchase the car for the manufacturer's retail price because demand for the car had inflated its value beyond the suggested price. Kells also told the Sedmaks they could bid on the car. The Sedmaks did not submit a bid. They filed this suit for specific performance.

Mr. Kells' testimony about his conversations with the Sedmaks regarding the Pace Car differed markedly from the Sedmaks' testimony. Kells stated that he had no definite price information on the Pace Car until a day or two prior to its arrival at Charlie's. He denied ever discussing the purchase price of the car with the Sedmaks. He admitted, however, that after talking with the Sedmaks on January 9, 1978, he telephoned the zone manager and requested changes be made to the Pace Car. He denied the changes were made pursuant to Dr. Sedmak's order. He claimed the changes were made because they were "more favorable to the automobile" and were changes Dr. Sedmak "preferred." In ordering the changes, Kells said he was merely taking Dr. Sedmak's advice because he was a "very knowledgeable man on the Corvette." There is no dispute, however, that when the Pace Car arrived, it was equipped with the options requested by Dr. Sedmak.

Mr. Kells also denied the receipt for $500 given him by Mrs. Sedmak on January 9, 1978, was a receipt for a deposit on the Pace Car. On direct examination, he said he "accepted a five hundred dollar ($500) deposit from the Sedmaks to assure them the first opportunity of purchasing the car." On cross-examination, he said: "We were accepting bids and with the five hundred dollar ($500) deposit it was to give them the first opportunity to bid on the car." Then after acknowledging that other bidders had not paid for the opportunity to bid, he explained the deposit gave the Sedmaks the "last opportunity" to make the final bid. Based on this evidence, the trial court found the parties entered into an oral contract for the purchase and sale of the Pace Car at the manufacturer's suggested retail price.

. . .

[The court's discussion of statute of frauds issues is omitted. It found that the $500 payment satisfied the statutory requirement.]

Finally, Charlie's contends the Sedmaks failed to show they were entitled to specific performance of the contract. We disagree. Although it has been stated that the determination whether to order specific performance lies within the discretion of the trial court, Landau v. St. Louis Public Service Co., 273 S.W.2d 255, 259 (Mo.1954), this discretion is, in fact, quite narrow. When the relevant equitable principles have been met and the contract is fair and plain, " 'specific performance goes as a matter of right.' " Miller v. Coffeen, 280 S.W.2d 100, 102 (Mo.1955). Here, the trial court ordered specific performance because it concluded the Sedmaks "have no adequate remedy at law for the reason that they cannot go upon the open market and purchase an automobile of this kind with the same mileage, condition, ownership and appearance as the automobile involved in this case, except, if at all, with considerable expense, trouble, loss, great delay and inconvenience." Contrary to defendant's complaint, this is a correct expression of the relevant law and it is supported by the evidence.

Under the Code, the court may decree specific performance as a buyer's remedy for breach of contract to sell goods "where the goods are unique or in other proper circumstances." § 400.2–716(1) RSMo 1978. The general term "in other proper circumstances" expresses the drafters' intent to "further a more liberal attitude than some courts have shown in connection with the specific performance of contracts of sale." § 400.2–716, UCC, Comment 1. This Comment was not directed to the courts of this state, for long before the Code, we, in Missouri, took a practical approach in determining whether specific performance would lie for the breach of contract for the sale of goods and did not limit this relief only to the sale of "unique" goods. Boeving v. Vandover, 218 S.W.2d 175 (Mo.App.1949). In *Boeving*, plaintiff contracted to buy a car from defendant. When the car arrived, defendant refused to sell. The car was not unique in the traditional sense but, at that time, all cars were difficult to obtain because of war-time shortages. The court held specific performance was the proper remedy for plaintiff because a new car "could not be obtained elsewhere except at considerable expense, trouble or loss, which cannot be estimated in advance and under such circumstances [plaintiff] did not have an adequate remedy at law." Id. at 177–178. Thus, *Boeving* presaged the broad and liberalized language of § 400.2–716(1) and exemplifies one of the "other proper circumstances" contemplated by this subsection for ordering specific performance. § 400.2–716, Missouri Code Comment 1. The present facts track those in *Boeving*.

The Pace Car, like the car in *Boeving*, was not unique in the traditional legal sense. It was not an heirloom or, arguably, not one of a kind. However, its "mileage, condition, ownership and appearance" did make it difficult, if not impossible, to obtain its replication without considerable expense, delay and inconvenience. Admittedly, 6,000 Pace Cars were produced by Chevrolet. However, as the record reflects, this is limited production. In addition, only one of these cars was available to each dealer, and only a limited number of these were equipped with the specific options ordered by plaintiffs. Charlie's had not received a car like the Pace Car in the previous two years. The sticker price for the car was $14,284.21. Yet Charlie's received offers from individuals in Hawaii and Florida to buy the Pace Car for $24,000 and $28,000 respectively. As sensibly inferred by the trial court, the location and size of these offers demonstrated this limited edition was in short supply and great demand. We agree, with the trial court. This case was a "proper circumstance" for ordering specific performance.

Judgment affirmed.

———

Hilmor Sales Co. v. Helen Neushaefer Div. of Supronics Corp.

New York Supreme Court, Queens County, 1969.
N.Y.L.J., April 21, 1969, Part I, p. 22, 6 U.C.C. Rep.Serv. 325.

■ CRISONA, J. Plaintiff moves by order to show cause for an order (1) enjoining the defendant from disposing of goods which the defendant has allegedly contracted to sell to plaintiff, and (2) directing that the defendant specifically perform its contract.

The subject matter of the contract in dispute here is a substantial quantity of lipsticks and containers of nail polish. The only claim made by plaintiff with respect to these chattels being unique is that they were purchased at close-out prices and cannot be replaced at the contract price.

Section 2–716(1) of the Uniform Commercial Code provides with respect to a buyer's right to specific performance that it may be decreed "where the goods are unique or in other proper circumstances." Plaintiff has failed to establish that there is anything unique about these chattels. It appears to the court that plaintiff can be adequately compensated for any breach of the contract herein by an award of money damages. In such a situation, "there should be no specific performance" (Glick v. Beer, 263 App.Div. 599, 600–601). Finally, plaintiff has failed to demonstrate that it will be irreparably damaged if the injunction which it seeks is not granted (cf. Camp v. Brengel, 286 App.Div. 1031).

For the foregoing reasons, the motion is denied. Settle order.

QUESTIONS AND NOTES

1.   Are the two preceding cases inconsistent with each other? What is the best ground you can think of for distinguishing them? If you think they are inconsistent, which reaches the better result?

2.   **A glimpse at the history of specific performance in contracts for the sale of goods.** Early case law limited specific performance of contracts for the sale of chattels to unique or one-of-a-kind goods (heirlooms, etc.), but there are a fair number of pre-Code cases giving specific performance of sales contracts in other situations. A sampling includes The Equitable Gas Light Co. of Baltimore City v. Baltimore Coal Tar & Manufacturing Co., 63 Md. 285, 3 A. 108 (1885) (specific performance granted on allegations that the goods were indispensable to plaintiff's business, were not available in Baltimore except from defendant, and if defendant did not perform plaintiff would have to procure the goods from distant cities); Eastern Rolling Mill Co. v. Michlovitz, 157 Md. 51, 145 A. 378 (1929) (specific performance granted in a 5-year output contract because the goods were not otherwise obtainable in the locale and the uncertainty concerning quantity makes damages so uncertain that an action for damages would be an inadequate remedy); Paullus v. Yarbrough, 219 Or. 611, 347 P.2d 620 (1959) (specific performance granted on a contract for the sale of standing timber because of the

increasing difficulty that small operators like plaintiff were having in finding timber tracts that they could purchase); and Strause v. Berger, 220 Pa. 367, 69 A. 818 (1908) (specific performance granted to the buyer of timber, because the quality of the timber and the difficulty of procuring timber of that quality in the locality in which his business was conducted gave it special value to the buyer).

As the court in *Sedmak* states, 2–716 represents a liberalization of the availability of specific performance. In Groeb Farms, Inc. v. Alfred L. Wolff, Inc., 68 UCC Rep.Serv.2d 539, 2009 WL 500816 (E.D.Mich.2009), defendant formed two contracts in which it promised to deliver large quantities of honey originating in Korea and in India. Instead of performing as agreed, defendant attempted to import honey that originated in China, but anti-dumping laws led the U.S. government to block importation, and defendant failed to deliver. Plaintiff sued, seeking specific performance. Defendant moved to dismiss the claim for that remedy. In response, the court stated:

> Plaintiff seeks specific performance based upon Defendant's alleged breaches of the Contracts. Plaintiff alleges that it has no adequate remedy at law because it cannot purchase the subject honey at such prices and in such quantities given the nature of the market.

> Specific performance is an equitable remedy that may be awarded where the legal remedy of damages is impracticable. Under section 2–716 of the UCC, specific performance is granted where the goods are unique or in other proper circumstances. [Official Comment 2] explains that uniqueness may arise from market conditions:

>> Specific performance is no longer limited to goods which are already specific or ascertained at the time of contracting. The test of uniqueness under this section must be made in terms of the total situation which characterizes the contract. Output and requirements contracts involving a particular or peculiarly available source or market present today the typical commercial specific performance situation, as contrasted with contracts for the sale of heirlooms or priceless works of art which were usually involved in the older cases. However, uniqueness is not the sole basis of the remedy under this section for the relief may also be granted "in other proper circumstances" and inability to cover is strong evidence of "other proper circumstances"

> Plaintiff has stated a claim for specific performance. Defendant contends that it cannot purchase this type of honey at the prices and quantities demanded under the Contracts. Essentially, Defendant alleges that it is unable to cover. As set forth above, a claimant's inability to cover may justify a decree of specific performance.

> While courts do not grant specific performance where the defendant simply cannot perform, Geist v. Lehmann, 19 Ill.App.3d

557, 563–64, 312 N.E.2d 42 (1974) (explaining rule that specific performance is not available where the subject property has been destroyed), this does appear to be case in the present action. As alleged, Plaintiff ordered Korean and Indian honey. Instead of attempting to import Korean or Indian honey into the United States, Defendant allegedly imported Chinese honey. As a result, the U.S. Department of Homeland Security refused to allow the honey into the United States because it was subject to anti-dumping duties. Therefore, Defendant perhaps could have performed the Contracts by attempting to import Korean and Indian honey rather than Chinese honey.

. . .

For the reasons stated, the Court . . . DENIES Defendant's motion to dismiss Plaintiff's claim for specific performance. . . .

Is this case distinguishable from *Hilmor*? If plaintiff is unable to cover by procuring Korean and Indian honey, will defendant be able to comply with an order compelling specific performance?

3.   Replevin. Section 2–716 also provides that a buyer has a right of replevin for goods identified to the contract when substitute goods are not available ("unable to effect cover") or if the "goods have been shipped under reservation and satisfaction of the security interest in them has been made or tendered." As amended in 1999 in connection with the comprehensive revision of Article 9, subsection (3) gives consumer buyers a broader right of replevin, which has some importance in cases in which a creditor of the seller claims an interest in goods that have not yet been delivered to the buyer.

In most states the plaintiff in a replevin (or claim and delivery) action gets possession of the goods pending suit by posting a bond and having the sheriff seize them. In nearly all states, however, the defendant can retake the property pending final determination of rights by posting its own bond. The effect is to convert the replevin action into an action for either damages or the property, whichever the defendant chooses. But recovery of damages is exactly what the plaintiff does not want in a replevin action: the plaintiff wants the goods. It is not clear whether the courts will conclude that 2–716 modifies the replevin statute in accordance with the purpose of 2–716.

4.   Contracted-for specific performance. Historically the courts have refused to enforce provisions in a contract stipulating that one of the parties is entitled to an award of specific performance if the other party breaches. They have reasoned that an award of specific performance, as with all equitable remedies, rests within the sound discretion of the court, and the parties by their agreement cannot bind the court. Many law-and-economics scholars challenge this proposition and argue that courts should enforce agreements that provide for specific performance in the event of breach. E.g., Kronman, Specific Performance, 45 U.Chi.L.Rev. 351, 170 (1978); Schwartz, The Case for Specific Performance, 89 Yale L.J. 271, 278 (1979); Ulen, The Efficiency of Specific Performance: Toward a Unified Theory of Contract Remedies, 83 Mich.L.Rev. 341, 346 (1984). In Martin v. Sheffer, page 551 infra, the court agreed, relying on 2–719(1), and awarded specific performance to a seller. Ordinarily, of course, we think of specific performance as a buyer's remedy.

5. **CISG.** In civil law countries, the law generally provides that the buyer is entitled to specific performance by the seller. The Convention on Contracts for the International Sale of Goods follows that tradition by providing in Article 46(1), "The buyer may require performance by the seller of his obligations unless the buyer has resorted to a remedy which is inconsistent with this requirement." In recognition of the variant common law position, however, and the strength of attachment of common law lawyers to their tradition, Article 28 provides: "If, in accordance with the provisions of this Convention, one party is entitled to require performance of any obligation by the other party, a court is not bound to enter a judgment for specific performance unless the court would do so under its own law in respect of similar contracts of sale not governed by this Convention."

The buyer's right to specific performance generated strong feelings on both sides of the issue during the drafting of Convention. After noting that specific performance will almost never be sought in either international or domestic sales situations if replacement goods are available, Professor Honnold commented:

> It is not easy to understand the intractability of the opposing views on the scope of specific performance. In preparing the Convention issues of practical importance have usually yielded to reconciliation or compromise. But on this issue one bred in the common law remains puzzled at the civil lawyer's insistence on a remedy that rarely is useful, while a scion of the civil law must be dismayed by an attitude that seems to subvert the sanctity of obligations.

J. Honnold, Uniform Law for International Sales Under the 1980 United Nations Convention 286 (2d ed.1991).

In accordance with the Convention's preference for specific performance, if the lack of conformity of the original goods constitutes a fundamental breach of contract, Article 46(2) authorizes the buyer to compel delivery of substitute goods. Whether or not the nonconformity amounts to a fundamental breach, Article 46(3) authorizes the buyer to "require the seller to remedy the lack of conformity by repair, unless this is unreasonable having regard to all the circumstances." If the nonconformity does not constitute a fundamental breach, the buyer may ask for "repair" but may not reject the goods.

2. THE RIGHT TO DAMAGES

Section 2–711 sets out a roadmap for damages when a seller breaches a sales contract. It addresses the various remedies available to the buyer who does not have the goods, either because the seller did not tender them or because the buyer has properly rejected or revoked acceptance of the goods. It is not a complete roadmap, however, because it does not address the remedies of a buyer who accepts and keeps nonconforming goods. Please read 2–711 now.

1.   Problem. WoodWorks, in Indianapolis, contracted to buy 18,000 board-feet of clear red oak from Lumberco, which is located in St. Marys, Pennsylvania. The contract price was $3 per board-foot (or $54,000), FOB St. Marys. The goods were to be loaded on June 1 and shipped by rail to Indianapolis. On June 7th the goods arrived in Indianapolis, where WoodWorks inspected them, determined that they did not qualify as "clear," and properly rejected them. The market price of 18,000 board-feet of clear red oak in St. Marys on the 7th was $54,000. In Indianapolis the market price was $72,000. The cost of transportation from St. Marys to Indianapolis was $5,400. What are WoodWorks' damages under 2–713?

If Lumberco had repudiated the contract and therefore had not shipped the lumber, to what damages would WoodWorks be entitled?

2.   Problem. Gasco is a distributor of gasoline to independent service stations and needs approximately 50,000 gallons of premium gas per month in order to meet the demands of its business. Shell contracted to sell Gasco 10,000 gallons of premium unleaded gas at $2.60 per gallon, delivery on May 1. Shell failed to deliver. On May 1 Gasco was buying premium unleaded gas for $2.90 and selling it to its customers for $3.10 per gallon. Gasco claims damages under 2–713, of $.50 per gallon. What result?

3.   Problem. In September 2020 Maynard Imports contracted to sell Kelley a new moonlight blue 2020 Porsche Cayenne for $97,000, delivery in two days. When Kelley returned to pick it up, Maynard informed her that he sold the car to someone else. Kelley attempted to find another moonlight blue Cayenne, but the 2021 models were out, and she could not find a moonlight blue 2020 Cayenne. She was, however, able to find a jet black 2020 Cayenne, which she purchased for $102,000. She now sues Maynard Imports to recover $5,000. Is she entitled to it?

What if she could not find any 2020 Cayennes (even colors other than moonlight blue), so she purchased a blue 2020 Ferrari Portofino for $197,000. Can she recover the excess of that over the price of the Porsche Cayenne?

What if she could not find any 2020 Cayennes, so she purchased a new 2021 moonlight blue Cayenne, for $100,000, plus $1,200 to ship it to her location. What damages can she recover?

––––––––

Valley Die Cast Corp. v. A.C.W. Inc.

Michigan Court of Appeals, 1970.
25 Mich.App. 321, 181 N.W.2d 303.

■ HOLBROOK, JUDGE.

. . .

In 1965, Paul Stafford became interested in the car wash business as an investment. In January 1966, after learning that plaintiff was the manufacturer of [the Thrift-I-Matic pressure] car wash system, Stafford arranged to talk with William Alkire, sales manager of plaintiff corporation. He was shown a working model of a car wash system which was allegedly different from and inferior to the newer stationary model he subsequently purchased. The sales brochure which he was given explained the operation of the new system, emphasized its dependability and profitability as an investment, and represented that it would wash cars "sparkling clean."

During preliminary sales conversations, Stafford [told] Alkire that he knew nothing about the car wash business. Stafford, his father, and his uncle invested in the purchase from plaintiff of its car wash system and, together with their wives, organized the defendant corporation. A purchase agreement was executed by Stafford, president of the corporation, on January 18, 1966, as a part of which a deposit of $1,000 was made to plaintiff by certified check. The purchase agreement included a stationary car wash system for $16,950, a rinse unit for $1,950, and a blower-dryer for $4,800, with a total price of $24,448. Because plaintiff was unable to deliver a blower-dryer as ordered, defendant secured one from another source. The price of plaintiff's blower-dryer was deducted from the total price of the sale. A building was constructed to accommodate plaintiff's system, built pursuant to plans prepared by plaintiff, costing defendant $26,000.

On July 13, 1966, defendant executed a note for $15,802.80, the balance of the purchase price, and a security agreement, providing for payment on September 1, 1966, and every month thereafter, of $263.38 until the full sum was paid. At the time suit was commenced, defendant had made 5 payments pursuant to the note, through January 1967 and was not in default.

The equipment was delivered to defendant's completed building on July 15, 1966. Several of plaintiff's employees assisted the building contractor in installing its system, together with the blower-dryer and an additional wax tower, purchased elsewhere. Defendant gave a certified check for $6,500, representing the balance of the down payment.

Installation of the equipment was completed on July 30, 1966. Plaintiff's employees checked and tested the equipment, following which defendant opened for business in early September 1966.

Stafford and his father testified that the equipment never ran right, and that by October 1966 it became necessary to wash cars by hand, forcing defendant to employ extra help. . . .

On November 30 and December 30, 1966, defendant, per Paul Stafford, forwarded to plaintiff the December 1966 and January 1967 payments, respectively, on its note, with accompanying letters advising that the equipment did not work properly and that payment was not intended as a waiver of defendant's legal rights.

On January 10, 1967, defendant notified plaintiff by letter of its rejection of the auto wash equipment, claiming breach of warranties, demanding that plaintiff remove its equipment and pay to defendant $11,943.90 ($8,816.90 in payments under the contract, and $3,127 installation cost) in discharge of defendant's security interest in the equipment, and giving notice of defendant's intention to resell the equipment should plaintiff fail to remove the same and discharge defendant's security interest therein by 5:00 p.m. January 20, 1967.

Stafford continued to use plaintiff's system until brush equipment, ordered from another source, was delivered on May 16, 1967, and also continued to request and receive necessary service from plaintiff on its equipment. On May 12, 1967, defendant wrote plaintiff that it was in the process of acquiring new auto wash equipment and removing and storing that of plaintiff's with the exception of a boiler, pump and sign which defendant was able to retain and use.

[Plaintiff sued for the balance of the price, and defendants counterclaimed for breach of warranty and fraud. The trial court entered judgment on a jury verdict for defendants for $9,000. Both parties appealed.]

I.

Plaintiff contends that defendant did not rescind but, rather, accepted plaintiff's system as a matter of law, and, in this regard, refers to certain acts of defendant which it claims were inconsistent with plaintiff's ownership of the equipment, viz.: defendant's continued use of all of the equipment after January 10, 1967, until May 12, 1967; its use thereafter of a part of a "commercial unit" up to the trial of the case and its request for service after January 10, 1967; and defendant's act of taking depreciation on the equipment through August 31, 1967. In support of its position, plaintiff cites section 2606 of the uniform commercial code, M.C.L.A. § 440.2606. . . .

It is defendant's position that utilization of plaintiff's equipment before replacement machinery was secured, and utilization of the useable units of the system after replacement, was necessary to mitigate damages, and was limited to "commercial units." . . .

Defendant's assertion that that portion of plaintiff's system which it utilized prior to acquisition of, and in conjunction with, the replacement brush system, could be found by a jury to be a "commercial unit," refers to M.C.L.A. § 440.2601, which allows a buyer to "accept any commercial unit or units and reject the rest." A "commercial unit" is defined in M.C.L.A. § 440.2105 as "a unit of goods as by commercial usage is a single whole for purposes of sale and division of which materially impairs its character or value on the market or in use. A commercial unit may be a single article (as a machine) or a set of articles * * * or a quantity * * * or any other unit treated in use or in the relevant market as a single whole." Testimony revealed that in addition to retaining plaintiff's sign, of a value of $400, which was available from plaintiff as optional equipment, the other items retained by defendant were collectively known as a "power pack" unit, suitable for use with both a brush and pressure system, and which was also available separately as optional equipment.

We conclude that defendant is correct, that the existence of acts tending to show an acceptance or rejection of goods as well as the ultimate fact of acceptance or rejection are, under the facts in this case, for the jury to determine.

Plaintiff claims that the taking of depreciation by defendant upon the value of plaintiff's equipment for the years ending August 31, 1966 and 1967, for tax purposes, considered in conjunction with other actions by defendant in regard to the equipment, amounted to an acceptance by defendant of the equipment as a matter of law. We rule that this contention is [a question for the jury], in view of the uncontradicted testimony by defendant's accountant that the use of depreciation was a proper accounting practice.

. . .

III.

Plaintiff, citing section 2715 of the uniform commercial code, dealing with incidental and consequential damages resulting from a seller's breach, M.C.L.A. § 440.2715, contends that the costs allegedly incurred by defendant in renovating its building to accommodate the substitute brush system, including $1,300.00 as the cost of electrical work to install the brush unit in its building, and $6,519.62 as the amount paid to Center Line Construction Incorporated for renovation of the building, are not recoverable. Plaintiff claims that, there being no special circumstances known to the seller when it entered into the contract which would distinguish the contract here involved from other contracts of the same kind, and no proof of actual damages, recovery of damages includes only such as would result from the natural and usual course of things.

The testimony revealed that the building, as originally built to accommodate plaintiff's equipment, was constructed by Center Line Construction Incorporated for $26,000. Peter Cedroni, president of Center Line Construction Company testified that if he had originally constructed defendant's building to house the brush equipment, he would have done the same work with the exception of replacing the concrete floor. Defendant's proofs included an itemized statement of renovation costs, showing a total cost of $6,519.62.

Defendant asserts that renovation costs were within the contemplation of the parties, inasmuch as plaintiff should have known that if its system failed to perform properly defendant would have to install a system which would wash cars clean, requiring a modification of the building to house a substitute system; that, in any event, the costs of renovation proximately resulted from the failure of performance of the equipment, which plaintiff had reason to know had been purchased for a particular purpose, i.e., that of washing cars clean, citing section 2715 of the uniform commercial code, M.C.L.A., § 440.2715, and American Vitrified Products Company v. Wyer (C.A.6, 1955), 221 F.2d 447. We are convinced that the record contained sufficient proofs to enable the jury to determine whether renovation costs should be included in the award of damages to defendant as a proximate result of the failure of plaintiff's equipment to function properly. There was no substantial error committed by the court in submitting this question of fact to the jury.

IV.

Plaintiff contends that defendant cannot properly claim damages for loss of profits based upon plaintiff's sales brochure, which pointed out that the car wash equipment as sold would wash a car per minute and that by washing the number of cars listed per day and month, the operator could expect to show a profit. Plaintiff relies upon Allis v. McLean (1882), 48 Mich. 428, 12 N.W. 640 and Stevenson v. Brotherhoods Mutual Benefit (1945), 312 Mich. 81, 19 N.W.2d 494, in support of its position that the elements that go to make up a successful car wash business are beyond the control of the manufacturer and are too speculative to allow loss of profits as an element of defendant's damages.

Defendant asserts that the question of profits is one of fact for the jury, and that the law of this State is to the effect that loss of profits is a proper element of damages in contract cases, Atkinson v. Morse (1886), 63 Mich. 276, 29 N.W. 711, and in tort cases, Allison v. Chandler (1863), 11 Mich. 542. Defendant further contends that the proofs in the instant case established loss with reasonable certainty and, although defendant was not required to establish the amount of loss with absolute certainty, Callender v. Myers Regulator Co. (1930), 250 Mich. 298, 230 N.W. 154, there was mathematical certainty in much of defendant's evidence.

In the case of Allis v. McLean, supra, it was stated in 48 Mich. at pp. 431, 432, 12 N.W. at p. 642:

> " * * * But the difficulty in measuring damages by profits is that they are commonly uncertain and speculative, and depend upon so many contingencies that their loss cannot be traced with reasonable certainty to the breach of contract. When that is the case they are said to be too remote; and the damages must be

estimated on a consideration of such elements of injury as are more directly and certainly the result of the failure in performance. *But in some cases profits are the best possible measure of damage, for the very reason that the loss is indisputable, and the amount can be estimated with almost absolute certainty.* * * * " (Emphasis supplied).

The *Atkinson* and *Allison* cases, supra, cited by defendant, approve the recovery of damages for loss of profits where, based upon the factual circumstances of a given case, such profits are not subject to mere speculation. In this regard, the *Atkinson* case states as follows in 63 Mich. 276 at p. 281, 29 N.W. at p. 713:

"Damages for * * * loss of profits are more frequently allowed to be recovered in cases of tort than contract; but when loss of profits arising from a breach of contract can be proved with a reasonable degree of certainty, and [such loss is] directly traceable to the breach of the contract, there is no reason why [such damages] may not be recovered.* * * "

We note that the trial court did instruct the jury against speculation as to damages. Although recovery of damages for loss of profits is a close question, resolution of this question was confined to that measure of damages controlled by the evidence which was reasonably certain and not speculative.

V.

Defendant claims that the trial court's ruling that defendant had not "covered," pursuant to sections 2711 and 2712 of the uniform commercial code, M.C.L.A. §§ 440.2711, 440.2712 by installing a brush wash system in place of plaintiff's pressure system was erroneous and resulted in an insufficient verdict; that the jury should have been allowed to consider evidence of the cost of "cover" which, pursuant to section 2712, consists of the difference between the cost of the defective pressure equipment and the cost of the replacement brush equipment; and that it was for the jury to determine whether, under the circumstances, defendant acted reasonably. Defendant further argues that the uniform commercial code does not limit "cover" to identical goods, but requires only good faith, reasonably prompt action and a reasonable purchase. Defendant concedes that the price of the substituted brush system was $3,328.56 more than that of the pressure system sold by plaintiff, and that the pressure system washed cars while in a stationary position, using high pressure jets of water, while the brush system, using rotating brushes which touched the cars, creating friction, carried cars through the brushes by a conveyor. Defendant states that the important difference was that the brush system washed cars clean, while the pressure system did not.

The trial court, in ruling that defendant had not covered by installing a more expensive brush system, which operated upon a principle entirely different from the pressure system purchased from plaintiff, stated:

> " * * * you put an entirely different system in. If you had gone out and gotten the same system there wouldn't be any question about it."

We rule that the question of admissibility of defendant's offer of evidence of "cover" was one for the court, and that its rejection was not an abuse of discretion but was proper under the facts.

. . .

Affirmed. No costs, neither party having prevailed on its appeal.

QUESTIONS AND NOTES

1. After removing the equipment supplied by plaintiff, defendants replaced it with other equipment that cost $3,300 more than the equipment supplied by plaintiff. In the last section of the opinion, the court upholds the trial court's denial of the $3,300 excess. In reaching that conclusion, what factors does the court consider? Was the court correct? Please read the Official Comments.

What if the evidence showed that the maintenance costs of the jet spray system supplied by plaintiff averaged $5,000 per year, while the maintenance costs of the brush system that defendants later acquired were $3,000 per year. Would those facts be relevant? If so, to what issue?

What if the evidence also showed that the expected life of a spray system is 10 years and the expected life of a brush system is 12 years. To what issue is that relevant? Alternatively, what if the expected life of the brush system is only 8 years. To what issue is that relevant?

2. The court holds (Part III of the opinion) that it was a question for the jury whether the defendants could recover the $6,500 cost of renovating the building and the $1,300 electrical work to accommodate the brush system. What section authorizes recovery of those amounts?

3. In holding that there was sufficient evidence to permit the jury to consider awarding lost profits (Part IV), the court does not cite any section of the Code. Does Article 2 permit a buyer to recover lost profits?

4. Leases. Problem. Agco contracted to acquire and lease a Model 5025 John Deere farm tractor to Nuñez for a two-year period beginning April 1. Rent was $650 per month and Nuñez had the obligation to insure and maintain the tractor and to return it to Agco at the end of the lease term in good condition "reasonable wear and tear excepted."

On April 1 Agco failed to deliver the tractor and notified Nuñez that it would not deliver in the future. On April 15, Nuñez leased the same model tractor from another company for a one-year period beginning immediately, at a monthly rental of $700. The other lease terms are the same as those of the original lease. Can Nuñez can recover as damages the $50 per month excess cost of the replacement lease? See 2A–518, 2A–519(1).

Suppose the new lease had been for three years? Is there any reason to treat the one-year lease and the three-year lease differently?

5.   Problem. Dawson agreed to supply Emory with Emory's requirements of ethanol for three years for $3.00 per gallon. After one year the market price rose dramatically, and Dawson refused to continue performing unless Emory would agree to pay the current market price. You may assume that Dawson's refusal to deliver except at the higher price is a breach. In response, Emory purchased its requirements for the remainder of the three-year period from another supplier, who charged $4.00 per gallon. Emory, which had been charging its customers $3.45 per gallon, increased its price to $4.60 per gallon. At the expiration of the three-year period, Emory sued to recover damages pursuant to 2–712. Dawson claims that Emory's damages should be reduced by the $1.15 that it raised the price to its customers. Is Dawson correct?

6.   Problem. Farmers Co-op contracted to purchase 3,000 tons of fertilizer from Agco at a price of $64 per ton. Agco failed to deliver. The market price at the place for tender when Co-op learned of Agco's breach was $72 per ton. Fifteen days later Co-op purchased 3,000 tons from another supplier for $67 per ton.

   a.   Should Co-op's recovery be based on $72 or $67?

   b.   Suppose that, within the 30-day period following Agco's breach, Co-op purchased 10,000 tons from others at prices ranging from $66 to $74 per ton. Can Co-op claim that the purchases at $74 are cover?

   c.   When Agco breached, Co-op could have purchased fertilizer for $67 per ton but it did not do so. May Co-op recover damages measured by market price less contract price? See 2–715(2).

7.   Problem. Chemco contracted to supply Pharma with its requirements of fluorene for three years for $30 per pound. After one year Chemco wrote Pharma, "The costs of our materials and processing have risen, as has the market price of fluorene. We cannot continue supplying you with the product at a loss. We will not deliver any more fluorene unless you agree to pay $38, which is below the current market price."

Pharma replied, "We need a reliable supplier, one who will stick to a deal. We thought you were that supplier. We have a deal at $30, and we expect you to live up to your word."

Chemco refused to deliver any more fluorene, and Pharma contracted with a supplier who agreed to sell Pharma its requirements for the remaining two years at the then-current market price of $40 per pound.

At the end of the three-year period, Pharma sued Chemco. How should its recovery be measured?

If Pharma had submitted to Chemco's demand, paid $38 per pound for the last two years of the contract, and then sued, could Pharma recover anything? If so, how should its recovery be measured?

Allied Canners & Packers, Inc. v. Victor Packing Co.

California Court of Appeal, 1984.
162 Cal.App.3d 905, 209 Cal.Rptr. 60.

■ ROUSE, J.

[In September 1976 Victor contracted to deliver a large quantity of raisins to Allied in October 1976, at a price of 29.75 cents per pound minus a discount of four percent. Allied contracted to sell the raisins to a Japanese buyer for 29.75 cents per pound. Therefore, Allied's gain from the transactions was to be four percent of the price of 29.75 cents per pound.

The raisin market is subject to the control of the federal government, which divides raisins into various categories, some of which may only be sold to specified buyers and only for resale to exporters. When Victor contracted to sell to Allied, the market price—which Victor would have to pay in order to acquire raisins for delivery to Allied—was 22 cents per pound. After Victor contracted with Allied, but before Victor actually contracted to acquire the raisins from its supplier, a heavy rain damaged the raisin crop, and the government prevented the sale of raisins for export. Victor was unable to acquire raisins and, therefore, failed to deliver to Allied. When Allied sued, Victor conceded that its failure to deliver was a breach of the contract with Allied.]

. . .

Allied did not cover by purchasing raisins on the open market. The earliest that either party could have bought raisins was October 1976, when the price of raisins was in the vicinity of 80 to 87 cents per pound. . . . [Allied's] buyer, Shoei Foods Industrial Co., Ltd. (Shoei), demanded delivery. . . . Allied's contract with Shoei, however, contained a provision holding it harmless from liability caused by strikes, fires, accidents and other developments beyond its control. At trial, Allied conceded that it had not been sued by Shoei for any damages resulting from its failure to deliver raisins to Shoei, but suggested that Shoei would hold off suing it until this action against Victor was concluded. Judgment was entered in this case in July 1981, nearly five years after the transaction occurred. Although the statute of limitations for a breach of contract action had expired (Code Civ.Proc. § 337, subd. 1), Shoei had never brought suit against Allied, and there is no indication that Allied voluntarily paid damages to Shoei.

. . .

Allied contends that pursuant to § 2713, subdivision (1), it is entitled to damages in the amount of $150,281.25, representing the difference between the contract price of 29.75 cents per pound and a market price of 87 cents per pound for 262,500 pounds . . . [of] raisins. The trial court, however, refused to apply § 2713 because it determined, purportedly as a matter of fact, that Allied was a broker, not a buyer, and therefore not subject to the provisions of the Commercial Code governing a buyer's remedies for breach of contract by a seller. The court concluded that Allied was damaged only to the extent of its lost "commission" as a broker in the sum of $4,462.50. Judgment for that amount was entered in Allied's favor.

While we perceive that the trial court was attempting to limit Allied's damages to those actually suffered, and felt that application of the formula set forth in § 2713, subdivision (1), would result in a windfall to Allied, it could not properly do so on the basis that Allied was not a "buyer" within the meaning of the Commercial Code. . . .

. . .

We conclude that Allied was a buyer in its contract with Victor and that it had a "forward contract" to sell the raisins to Shoei. As such, the remedies provided to a buyer by the Commercial Code are applicable to it. Thus, we turn to a consideration of the correct application of such remedies in this case.

. . .

Sections 2–712 and 2–713 of the Uniform Code are sometimes referred to as "cover" and "hypothetical cover," since the former involves an actual entry into the market by the buyer while the latter does not. (See Childres, Buyer's Remedies: The Danger of Section 2–713 (1978) 72 Nw.U.L.Rev. 837, 841 [applying those terms] (hereafter cited as Buyer's Remedies); Peters, Remedies for Breach of Contracts Relating to the Sale of Goods Under the Uniform Commercial Code: A Roadmap For Article Two (1963) 73 Yale L.J. 199, 259 [market under § 2–713 is "purely theoretical"] (hereafter cited as Remedies for Breach of Contracts).) It has been recognized that the use of the market price-contract price formula under § 2–713 does not, absent pure accident, result in a damage award reflecting the buyer's actual loss. (Buyer's Remedies, supra, at pp. 841–842; Remedies for Breach of Contracts, supra, at p. 259; [Simon & Novack, Limiting the Buyer's Market Damages to Lost Profits: A Challenge to the Enforceability of Market Contracts (1979)], 92 Harv.L.Rev. 1395 [hereafter cited as Market Damages]; White & Summers, Uniform Commercial Code 224 [2d ed. 1980].)

For example, in this case it is agreed that Allied's actual lost profit on the transaction was $4,462.50, while application of the market-contract price formula would yield damages of approximately $150,000. In Market Damages, supra, Simon and Novack describe the courts as divided on the issue of whether market damages, even though in excess of the plaintiff's loss, are appropriate for a supplier's breach of his delivery obligations and observe: "Strangely enough, each view has generally tended to disregard the arguments, and even the existence, of the opposing view. These two rival bodies of law, imposing in appearance, have passed each other like silent ships in the night." (92 Harv.L.Rev. 1395, 1397.) In Buyer's Remedies, supra, Professor Childres similarly points out that the courts have generally not undertaken any real analysis of the competing considerations involved in determining the correct measure of damages in such circumstances. (72 Nw.U.L.Rev. 837, 844 et seq.) We will undertake such an analysis.

Professors White and Summers, after noting their belief that "the Code drafters did not by [§ 2–713] intend to put the buyer in the same position as performance would have" (White & Summers, Uniform Commercial Code, supra, at p. 224), advance two possible explanations for the section. First, they suggest that it is simply a historical anomaly:

> "Since cover was not a recognized remedy under pre-Code law, it made sense under that law to say that the contract-market formula put buyer in the same position as performance would have *on the assumption that the buyer would purchase substitute goods.* If things worked right, the market price would approximate the cost of the substitute goods and buyer would be put 'in the same position. . . .' But under the Code, 2–712 does this job with greater precision, and 2–713 reigns over only those cases in which the buyer does not purchase a substitute. Perhaps the drafters retained 2–713 not out of a belief in its appropriateness, but out of fear that they would be dismissed as iconoclasts had they proposed that the court in noncover cases simply award the buyer any economic loss proximately caused by seller's breach." (Ibid.)

They conclude, however, that probably the best explanation for § 2–713 "is that it is a statutory liquidated damage clause, a breach inhibitor the payout of which need bear no close relation to plaintiff's actual loss." (White & Summers, Uniform Commercial Code, supra, at p. 225.) They then observe that this explanation conflicts with the policy set forth in § 1–106 [revised 1–305], which provides in subdivision (1): "The remedies provided by this code shall be liberally administered *to the end that the aggrieved party may be put in as good a position as if the other party had fully performed* but neither consequential or special nor penal damages may be had except as specifically provided in this code or by other rule of law." (Emphasis added.) They find § 2–713 consistent, however, with a belief that plaintiffs recover too little and too infrequently for the law of contracts to be effective, and offer no suggestion for resolution of the conflict. (Ibid.)

In her article Remedies for Breach of Contracts, supra, then-Professor Peters states:

> "Perhaps it is misleading to think of the market-contract formula as a device for the measurement of damages. . . . An alternative way of looking at market-contract is to view this differential as a statutory liquidated damages clause, rather than as an effort to calculate actual losses. If it is useful in every case to hold the party in breach to some baseline liability, in order to encourage faithful adherence to contractual obligations,

perhaps market fluctuations furnish as good a standard as any."
(73 Yale L.J. 199, 259.)

She does not discuss the conflict between the market-contract formula and the "only as good a position as performance" policy embodied in § 1–106 [revised 1–305].

Simon and Novack state:

"While it is generally recognized that the automatic invocation of market damages may sometimes overcompensate the plaintiff, a variety of arguments have been employed by commentators and courts to justify this result: the desirability of maintaining a uniform rule and of facilitating settlements; the public interest in encouraging contract performance and the proper functioning of the market; the prevention of defendant's unjust enrichment; the restoration of the very 'value' promised to plaintiff; and the inherent difficulty and complexity of proving actual economic losses not encompassed within the contract terms." (Fns. omitted; Market Damages supra, 92 Harv.L.Rev. 1395, 1403.)

That a defendant not be unjustly enriched by a bad faith breach is a concern widely shared by commentators and courts. (Id., at p. 1406, fn. 51, and cases there cited.)

Viewing § 2–713 as, in effect, a statutory provision for liquidated damages, it is necessary for us to determine whether a damage award to a buyer who has not covered is ever appropriately limited to the buyer's actual economic loss which is below the damages produced by the market-contract formula, and, if so, whether the present case presents a situation in which the damages should be so limited.

One view is that § 2–713 of the Uniform Code, or a substantively similar statutory provision, establishes the principle that a buyer's resale contract and damage claims made thereunder are irrelevant to an award of damages, and that damages therefore cannot be limited to a plaintiff's actual economic loss. . . . Simon and Novack, while favoring that view, concede that it can be argued that the provision of § 1–106 [revised 1–305] that an aggrieved party be put " 'in as good a position as if the other party had fully performed' " calls for an opposite conclusion. (Market Damages, supra, 92 Harv.L.Rev. 1395, 1412–1413, fn. 71.)

Although we find no cases discussing the interaction of § 1–106 [revised 1–305] and § 2–713, we note that some pre-Uniform Code cases held that a limitation to actual losses should be placed upon the market price-contract price measure of damages under general contract principles. (See, e.g., Foss v. Heineman (1910) 144 Wis. 146 [128 N.W. 881]; Isaacson v. Crean (1917) 165 N.Y.S. 218; Texas Co. v. Pensacola Maritime Corporation (5th Cir.1922) 279 F. 19.) One author on the subject has apparently concluded that such a limitation is appropriate under the Uniform Code when the plaintiff-buyer has a resale contract and the existence of the resale contract is known to the defendant-seller:

> "It may be supposed . . . that the buyer was bound by a contract made before the breach to deliver to a third person the very goods which the buyer expected to obtain from the seller, and the price under the resale contract may be less than the market price at the time of the breach. If the reason generally given for the rule permitting the recovery of additional damage because of an advantageous resale contract existing and known to the defendant when he contracted be applied, namely, that such consequential damages are allowed because the parties supposedly contract for them, it would follow that in every case the damage that the defendant might normally expect to follow from breach of his contract should be recovered even though the plaintiff actually suffered less damage than the difference between the contract price and the market price." (4 Anderson, Uniform Commercial Code (3d ed.1983) § 2–711:15, pp. 430–431.)

. . .

We conclude that in the circumstances of this case—in which the seller knew that the buyer had a resale contract, the buyer has not been able to show that it will be liable in damages to the buyer on its forward contract, and there has been no finding of bad faith on the part of the seller—the policy of § 1106, subdivision (1) [revised 1–305(a)], that the aggrieved party be put in as good a position as if the other party had performed requires that the award of damages to the buyer be limited to its actual loss, the amount it expected to make on the transaction.[8] . . .

We need not determine in this case what degree of bad faith on the part of a breaching seller might warrant the award of market-contract price damages without limitation, in circumstances otherwise similar to those involved here, in order to prevent unjust enrichment to a seller who deliberately breaches in order to take advantage of a rising market. Although Allied implies that Victor was guilty of bad faith here because after its breach it [sold] raisins to which [Allied] was entitled at 36.25 cents per pound, rather than acquiring the raisins and delivering them to Allied, the record is simply not clear on Victor's situation following the rains. It does appear clear, however, that, as the trial court found, the rains caused a severe problem, and Victor made substantial efforts to persuade [the government] to release . . . raisins to it. . . . We do not deem this record one to support an inference that windfall damages must be

---

[8]   Allied suggested at trial that it had suffered additional consequential damages through the loss of its entire account with Shoei. Although it might have been able to establish such damages under § 2715, subdivision (2)(a), little evidence on that issue was presented and Allied has made no contention on appeal that it was entitled to such damages. The view that the true damages it had suffered were $4,462.50 was expressed by its own president when the trial court asked him whether in the event that damages of $150,281 were awarded, he would consider that to be his company's own money. He replied that he would not.

awarded the buyer to prevent unjust enrichment to a deliberately breaching seller. (Compare Sun-Maid Raisin Growers v. Victor Packing Co., supra, 146 Cal.App.3d 787 [where, in a case coincidentally involving Victor, Victor was expressly found by the trial court to have engaged in bad faith by gambling on the market price of raisins in deciding whether to perform its contracts to sell raisins to Sun-Maid].)

The judgment is affirmed. Each party is to bear its own costs on appeal.

———

TexPar Energy Inc. v. Murphy Oil USA, Inc.

United States Court of Appeals, Seventh Circuit, 1995.
45 F.3d 1111.

■ REAVLEY, CIRCUIT JUDGE.

. . .

On May 29, 1992, TexPar contracted to purchase 15,000 tons of asphalt from Murphy at an average price of $53 per ton. On the same day, TexPar contracted to sell the 15,000 tons to Starry Construction Company at an average price of $56 per ton. Hence, TexPar stood to profit by $45,000 if both contracts were performed.

During the first half of 1992, the price of asphalt varied widely. Evidence was presented of prices ranging from $40 to $100 per ton. The wide range of prices reflected volatile market forces. From the supply standpoint, asphalt is one of the end products of petroleum refining, and must be sold or stockpiled to accommodate the production of more valuable petroleum products. Demand depends in large measure on the availability of government funding for highway construction. Weather also affects asphalt supply and demand. The price rose rapidly in June of 1992, and consequently, the sale price of $53 per ton lost its attractiveness to Murphy.

In May and early June TexPar took delivery of 690 tons of asphalt; but, on June 5, Murphy stopped its deliveries and notified TexPar that its sales manager lacked authority to make the contract. By then, the price of asphalt had risen to $80 per ton. Starry insisted that TexPar deliver the full 15,000 tons at $56 per ton as TexPar and Starry had agreed. Ultimately, with TexPar's approval, Starry and Murphy negotiated directly and agreed on a price of $68.50 per ton. This arrangement was reached several weeks after the repudiation by Murphy. By this time the market price had dropped, according to TexPar. TexPar agreed to pay Starry the $12.50 difference between the new price of $68.50 per ton and the original $56 per ton price. TexPar therefore paid Starry approximately $191,000 to cover the price difference.

The jury found that the difference between the market price ($80) and the contract price ($53) of the undelivered asphalt (14,310 tons) on the date of repudiation (June 5), amounted to $386,370. The court entered judgment for this amount. . . .

The district court applied UCC § 2–713. . . .

Murphy does not dispute that if this provision is applied, the damages awarded are proper, since Murphy does not dispute the quantity of goods, the market price or the date of notice of repudiation used by the jury to calculate damages. Instead, Murphy argues that the general measure of damages in a breach of contract case is the amount needed to place the plaintiff in as good a position as he would have been if the contract had been performed. Murphy argues that since TexPar's award—$386,370—far exceeds its out-of-pocket expenses ($191,000) and lost profits ($45,000) occasioned by the repudiation, the court erred in instructing the jury merely to find the difference in market price and entering judgment in that amount.

We cannot quarrel with Murphy that the general measure of damages in contract cases is the expectancy or "benefit of the bargain" measure. The UCC itself embraces such a measure in § 1–106 [revised 1–305], providing that the UCC remedies "shall be liberally administered to the end that the aggrieved party may be put in as good a position as if the other party had fully performed. . . ." Wis.Stat.Ann. § 401.106 (West 1994).

Nevertheless, we do not believe that the district court erred in awarding damages based on a straightforward application of § 402.713. That provision is found in the article on the sale of goods, and specifies a remedy for the circumstances presented here—the seller's nondelivery of goods for which there is a market price at the time of repudiation.

We can see no sound reason for looking to an alternative measure of damages. Murphy argues that TexPar shouldn't be awarded a "windfall" amount in excess of its out-of-pocket damages. Since it depends on the market price on a date after the making of the contract, the remedy under § 402.713 necessarily does not correspond to the buyer's actual losses, barring a coincidence. Our problem with Murphy's suggested measure of damages is that limiting the buyer's damages in cases such as this one to the buyer's out-of-pocket losses could, depending on the market, create a windfall for the seller. If the price of asphalt had fallen back to $56 per ton by the time Starry and Murphy had arranged for replacement asphalt, TexPar's damages would have been zero by this measure,[2] and Murphy could have reaped a windfall by selling at the market price of $80 in early June instead of the $53 price negotiated with TexPar.

Murphy argues that it did not in fact realize a windfall, since its cost of production was $70 per ton and it eventually agreed to sell to Starry for $68.50. We find this argument unpersuasive. Applying the market

---

[2] TexPar would not even have received its lost profits, because Murphy had persuaded the district court that its acknowledgment form effectively precluded the recovery of lost profits. The district court so ruled in granting a partial summary judgment.

value measure of damages under UCC § 2–713, as the district court did, is expressly allowed under the Code. Since § 2–713 addresses the circumstances of a seller's nondelivery of goods with a market price, we see no error in applying this specific provision over the more general remedies provision found at § 1–106 [revised 1–305]. See Tongish v. Thomas, 251 Kan. 728, 840 P.2d 471, 474 (1992) ("[B]ecause it appears impractical to make [§ 1–305] and [§ 2–713] harmonize in this factual situation, [§ 2–713] should prevail as the more specific statute according to statutory rules of construction."). The UCC § 2–713 remedy serves the purpose of discouraging sellers from repudiating their contracts as the market rises, if the buyer should resell as did TexPar, or gambling that the buyer's damages will be small should the market drop. It also has the advantage of promoting uniformity and predictability in commercial transactions, by fixing damages on the date of the breach, rather than allowing the vicissitudes of the market in the future to determine damages. Id. 840 P.2d at 476 ("Damages computed under [§ 2–713] encourage the honoring of contracts and market stability.")

. . .

AFFIRMED.

QUESTIONS AND NOTES

1. Is it relevant in cases like *Allied Canners* and *TexPar* whether the seller knows that the buyer is purchasing for resale? that the buyer already has a resale contract when it contracts with the seller?

2. With which court do you agree? Or are the cases distinguishable, so that you agree with both?

3. Is it relevant to the question whether to use 2–713 or 1–305 that the seller opportunistically used an increase in the market price to make more money by selling to someone else?

4. For a case agreeing with *Allied Canners*, see H-W-H Cattle Co. v. Schroeder, 767 F.2d 437 (8th Cir.1985), another case in which, at the time of contracting with the seller, the buyer had already contracted to resell the goods (cattle). The court did not discuss the question whether the seller knew that the buyer had already made a resale contract. Most courts, however, agree with the result in *TexPar*. E.g., Tongish v. Thomas, 16 Kan.App.2d 809, 829 P.2d 916, aff'd 251 Kan. 728, 840 P.2d 471 (1992), in which the court stated:

> We are not persuaded that the lost profits view under *Allied* should be embraced. It is a minority rule that has received only nominal support. We believe the majority rule or the market damages remedy as contained in [2–713] is more reasoned and should be followed as the preferred measure of damages. While application of the rule may not reflect the actual loss to a buyer, it encourages a more efficient market and discourages the breach of contracts.

The majority rule further permits the parties to measure the expectancy of what might happen if the seller does not perform the contract. The buyer has an option at the beginning of the contract to take actions to protect against an uncertain future. The parties both know that the option is an election that can be exercised by the buyer to protect against future losses. This generates stability in the market by discouraging the seller from breaching the contract when the market fluctuates to his advantage. The rule is further in accord with the rule of statutory construction that a specific statute shall prevail over a conflicting general statute dealing with the same subject matter unless the legislature intended to make the general statute control.

5. CISG. The Convention on Contracts for the International Sale of Goods provides for damages in Articles 74–77. Note the similarity of Articles 75 and 76 to 2–712 and 2–713. If *Allied Canners* were decided under the Convention, what would the result be?

D. REMEDIES WHEN THE BUYER GETS AND KEEPS THE GOODS

1. DAMAGES

The buyer who accepts and keeps goods is obligated to pay for them, and 2–607(1) requires the buyer to pay the price even if the goods do not conform to the contract. The catalog of remedies in 2–711 does not include any remedy for the situation in which the buyer accepts and keeps goods even though the goods or the tender fail to conform and the buyer could have rejected them or revoked acceptance of them. The buyer does, of course, have a remedy in this situation. It appears in 2–714. Please read that section and then consider the following excerpt from Chatlos Systems, Inc. v. National Cash Register Corp., 670 F.2d 1304 (3d Cir.1982), which deals with the application of subsection (2). In a transaction that occurred before the enactment of Article 2A, plaintiff leased a computer system from defendant. Applying the Article 2 rules to the transaction, the trial court held that plaintiff's damages for breach of warranty were $201,826.50, the value the system would have had if it had been as warranted less its actual value, which the court estimated at $6,000. Defendant claimed that trial court should have used the contract price of the computer ($46,020) as the value the computer would have had if it had been as warranted, so that plaintiff's damages were only $40,020. The court responded:

Waiving the opportunity to submit additional evidence as to value on the remand which we directed, appellant chose to rely on the record of the original trial and submitted no expert testimony on the market value of a computer which would have performed the functions NCR had warranted. Notwithstanding our previous holding that contract price was not necessarily the same as market value, 635 F.2d at 1088, appellant faults the district judge for rejecting its contention that the contract price for the NCR 399/656 was the only competent record evidence of the value of the system as warranted. The district court relied instead on the testimony of plaintiff-appellee's expert, Dick Brandon, who, without estimating the value of an NCR model 399/656, presented his estimate of the value of a computer system that would perform all of the functions that the NCR 399/656 had been warranted to perform. Brandon did not limit his estimate to equipment of any one manufacturer; he testified regarding manufacturers who could have made systems that would perform the functions that appellant had warranted the NCR 399/656 could perform. He acknowledged that the systems about which he testified were not in the same price range as the NCR 399/656. Appellant likens this testimony to substituting a Rolls Royce for a Ford, and concludes that the district court's recomputed damage award was therefore clearly contrary to the evidence of fair market value—which in NCR's view is the contract price itself.

Appellee did not order, nor was it promised, merely a specific NCR computer model, but an NCR computer system with specified capabilities. The correct measure of damages, under N.J.Stat.Ann. § 12A:2–714(2), is the difference between the fair market value of the goods accepted and the value they would have had if they had been as warranted. Award of that sum is not confined to instances where there has been an increase in value between date of ordering and date of delivery. It may also include the benefit of a contract price which, for whatever reason quoted, was particularly favorable for the customer. Evidence of the contract price may be relevant to the issue of fair market value, but it is not controlling. [Defendant] limited its fair market value analysis to the contract price of the computer model it actually delivered. [Plaintiff] developed evidence of the worth of a computer with the capabilities promised by NCR, and the trial court properly credited the evidence.

[Plaintiff] was aided, moreover, by the testimony of Frank Hicks, NCR's programmer, who said that he told his company's officials that the "current software was not sufficient in order to deliver the program that the customer (Chatlos) required. They would have to be rewritten or a different system would have to be given to the customer." Hicks recommended that Chatlos be given an NCR 8200 but was told, "that will not be done." . . . [A]nother NCR witness admitted that the 8200 series was two levels above the 399 in sophistication and price. This testimony supported [the testimony of a third witness] that the price of the hardware needed to perform Chatlos' requirements would be in the $100,000 to $150,000 range.

Essentially, then, the trial judge was confronted with the conflicting value estimates submitted by the parties. Chatlos' expert's estimates were corroborated to some extent by NCR's supporters. NCR, on the other hand, chose to rely on contract price. Credibility determinations had to be made by the district judge. Although we might have come to a different conclusion on the value of the equipment as warranted had we been sitting as trial judges, we are not free to make our own credibility and factual findings. . . .

The judgment of the district court will be affirmed.

A dissenting judge thought that plaintiff should have produced evidence of the value the particular system delivered would have had if it had performed as warranted, rather than evidence of what another system that performed all the warranted functions would have cost.

What do you think: did the plaintiff get a larger recovery than it was entitled to? Why do you answer the way you do?

Note that although subsection (2) looks to the value lost as a result of breach of warranty, it permits other ways to measure damages when "special circumstances show proximate damages of a different amount." What circumstances might do that? In Tarter v. Mon-Ark Boat Co., 430 F.Supp. 1290, 1294 (E.D.Mo.1977), plaintiff testified that the custom-built boat that defendant sold him did not conform to the contract and was worth only half of the $160,000 price he paid for it. Holding that plaintiff failed to establish that value, the court held that "the cost of repair, $37,000, provides a stronger measure of the difference between the value of the boat accepted and the value of the boat as warranted." Similarly, in Canterbury Apartment Homes LLC v. Louisiana Pacific Corp., 182 Wash.App. 1032 (2014), the court stated that "the cost of repair or replacement can be used to measure the difference in value as is and as warranted." The court held that the cost of replacing siding was an appropriate remedy when the siding could be repaired only by replacing it.

Both of these courts articulated their conclusions in terms of repair costs as a measure of the difference in values between the goods as warranted and the goods as delivered. In view of the "unless special circumstances" language in 2–714(2), did they need to? Or could special circumstances exist whenever the cost of repairs is less than the difference in values?

———

2.   THE REQUIREMENT OF NOTICE

Section 2–607(3)(a) provides that a buyer who wants to keep the goods but assert a claim for damages "must within a reasonable time after he discovers or should have discovered the breach notify the seller of the breach or be barred from any remedy." Please read Official Comment 4 to 2–607. What is the rationale for the requirement of notice? For another answer see 2–605 and Official Comments 1–2. Do these rationales apply when the seller delivers the goods after the time specified in the contract?

Eastern Air Lines, Inc. v. McDonnell Douglas Corp.

United States Court of Appeals, Fifth Circuit, 1976.
532 F.2d 957.

■ AINSWORTH, C.J.

[Plaintiff contracted to buy 99 jet passenger aircraft from the defendant to be delivered over a period of years. There were substantial delays in delivery of the planes and plaintiff sued to recover the resulting damages. The District Court gave judgment for plaintiff on a jury verdict of just under 25 million dollars. Defendant appealed.]

. . .

During the trial and in final instructions to the jury, the District Court held that Eastern need not prove, as a predicate for recovery in this suit, that it had given McDonnell Douglas reasonable and timely notice of the delivery delays. McDonnell strongly contests the trial judge's rulings for Eastern on this issue and argues either that the airline should, as a matter of law, be barred from any recovery or, alternatively, that the issue of timely notice should have been submitted to the jury.

. . .

McDonnell contends that the trial judge denied it the benefits of [section 2–607(3)(a)], both by ruling that section 2–607 does not apply to late deliveries and by holding in the alternative that Eastern gave adequate notice. Because we are unable to agree with the District Court's ruling on either ground, we hold that the question of timely notice under section 2–607 should have been submitted to the jury.

A.   Applicability of U.C.C. § 2–607(3)(a)

Even though section 2–607, by its very terms, governs "any breach," the trial court found the notice requirement to be inapplicable to delivery delays because a seller necessarily has knowledge of this sort of contract violation. Relying on the case of Jay V. Zimmerman Company v. General Mills, Inc., E.D.Mo., 1971, 327 F.Supp. 1198, 1204, the District Judge concluded that notice is useless where a breach is apparent to both parties.* The trial court apparently was of the view that the sole function of section 2–607 is to inform the seller of hidden defects in his performance. Under this approach, the only purpose of notice is to provide the seller with an opportunity to remedy an otherwise unknown nonconforming tender.

Section 2–607's origins, however, reveal that it has a much broader function. The Code's notice requirement was derived from decisional law in California and several other states which sought to ameliorate the harsh common law rule that acceptance of goods by the buyer waived any and all of his remedies. This approach was codified under section 49 of the Uniform Sales Act which was adopted in California as Civ.Code § 1769.

As Professor Williston, the author of the Sales Act, has noted, section 49 continued the common law rule treating a seller's tender of goods as an offer of them in full satisfaction. 3 S.Williston, Contracts § 714 (rev.ed.1961). The buyer, though, was permitted to accept the offer without waiving any claims if he gave the seller prompt notice to this effect. This approach reconciled the desire to give finality to transactions in which goods were accepted with the need to accommodate a buyer who, for business reasons, had to accept the tendered goods despite unsatisfactory performance by the seller. Pre-U.C.C. decisions in California and elsewhere, therefore, recognized that the primary purpose of notice is to inform the seller that, even though his tender has been accepted by the buyer, his performance is nonetheless considered a breach of contract.

Under section 49 it was irrelevant whether a seller had actual knowledge of a nonconforming tender. Instead, the critical question was whether the seller had been informed that the buyer considered him to be in breach. Consequently, in Professor Williston's words, "the section is applicable not only to defects in quality but to breach of any promise or warranty, as, for instance, *delay in time.*" 5 S.Williston, Contracts § 714 at 409 (3d ed.1961) (emphasis supplied). Pre-U.C.C. decisions, therefore, applied the notice requirement in delivery delay cases. Judge Learned Hand, for example, applied section 49 in a case in which performance had been delayed, noting:

> The plaintiff replies that the buyer is not required to give notice of what the seller already knows, but this confuses two quite different things. The notice "of the breach" required is not of the facts, which the seller presumably knows quite as well as, if not better than, the buyer, but of buyer's claim that they constitute a breach. The purpose of the notice is to advise the seller that

---

*   In *Zimmerman* the court stated, "in any case involving late delivery, both the seller and the buyer are necessarily fully aware *prior* to tender that the seller's contract obligation to timely deliver has not been complied with. It would be an unreasonable, if not absurd, construction of the statute to require a renewed notice of breach *after* acceptance of the goods. . . ."—Eds.

he must meet a claim for damages, as to which, rightly or wrongly, the law requires that he shall have early warning.

American Mfg. Co. v. United States Shipping Board E.F. Corp., 2 Cir., 1925, 7 F.2d 565, 566.

As the drafters of Article 2 acknowledge, section 2–607 continues the basic policies underlying section 49 of the Uniform Sales Act. Indeed, the notice requirement developed in pre-U.C.C. cases is entirely consistent with the Article 2 goals of encouraging compromise and promoting good faith in commercial relations. As Comment 4 to section 2–607 indicates, the purpose of notice is not merely to inform the seller that his tender is nonconforming, but to open the way for settlement through negotiation between the parties. In the words of the California Supreme Court, "the sound commercial rule" codified in section 2–607 also requires that a seller be reasonably protected against stale claims arising out of transactions which a buyer has led him to believe were closed. Pollard v. Saxe & Yolles Development Company, 1974, 12 Cal.3d 374, 115 Cal.Rptr. 648, 525 P.2d 88. Early warning permits the seller to investigate the claim while the facts are fresh, avoid the defect in the future, minimize his damages, or perhaps assert a timely claim of his own against third parties.

Given these undeniable purposes, it is not enough under section 2–607 that a seller has knowledge of the facts constituting a nonconforming tender; he must also be informed that the buyer considers him to be in breach of the contract. The Code's notice requirement, then, is applicable to delivery delays as well as other breaches. Accordingly, we decline to follow the reasoning of the *Zimmerman* decision, and we find that the trial court erred in not applying section 2–607 to the delivery delays at issue in this case.

. . .

QUESTIONS AND NOTES

1. It appears that McDonnell Douglas was not prejudiced in any way by Eastern Air Lines' failure to give notice, yet that failure bars the buyer from all remedies. In view of the clear requirement in 2–607(3), can you think of any rationale for permitting the buyer to recover?

2. At the top of page 485, discussing the *Zimmerman* case, the court seems to acknowledge that one of the purposes of 2–607(3) is to provide the seller with an opportunity to remedy a nonconforming tender. Why do you suppose the court did not rely on this as a justification for the notice requirement? When a buyer notifies a seller that goods do not conform to the contract, must the buyer give the seller an opportunity to cure the nonconformity? What does 2–508 suggest? What else should be considered? How else might the buyer's failure to give prompt notice be relevant to its right to recover damages?

3.   Exactly what must the notice of breach contain? That issue arose in
Peavey Electronics Corp. v. Baan U.S.A., Inc., 10 So.3d 945 (Miss.App.2009),
in which Baan contracted to supply Peavey with computer software and
computer systems to coordinate the operations of Peavey's business,
including ordering, manufacturing, and shipping. Though all the software
was delivered at one time, the system was to be implemented in two phases,
and the parties anticipated that it would take time to adapt the systems to
Peavey's operations. Apparently it took at least two-and-a-half years for the
systems in Phase I to be operating in a usable, albeit imperfect, manner.
Because of the difficulties, Peavey decided not to proceed with Phase II.
Several years later, Peavey sued. The trial court entered summary judgment
for Baan, the seller, in part because Peavey failed to give notice of the breach
within a reasonable time, as required by 2–607(3). Sitting en banc, the
Mississippi Court of Appeals stated:

> Citing the official comment to section 2–607 of the UCC, Peavey
> argues that it was required only to give Baan notice that "the
> transaction is still troublesome and must be watched." Baan cites
> a subsequent sentence from the same comment, arguing that the
> notification must "be such as informs the seller that the transaction
> is claimed to involve a breach, and thus opens the way for normal
> settlement through negotiation." The conflict between these two
> interpretations has been acknowledged by other courts. As one
> court noted:

>> Section [2–607(3)(a)] does not prescribe any form for the
>> required notification. Courts have thus developed their own
>> guidelines for determining what constitutes adequate notice.
>> Some courts have held that virtually any complaint about the
>> transaction will satisfy the requirement. *E.g.* Northern States
>> Power Co. v. ITT Meyer Indus., 777 F.2d 405 (8th Cir.1985);
>> Boeing Airplane Co. v. O'Malley, 329 F.2d 585 (8th Cir.1964).
>> Under this "lenient standard of notification," the buyer must
>> merely let the seller know that the transaction is troublesome.
>> Other courts require the buyer to notify the seller that the buyer
>> considers the seller to be legally in breach. *E.g.* Eastern Air
>> Lines v. McDonnell Douglas Corp., 532 F.2d 957 (5th Cir.1976).
>> The standard adopted by these courts is known as the "strict
>> standard of notification."

United States ex rel. Conroy v. S. Contracting, 862 F.Supp. 107,
111 (D.S.C.1994). By all accounts, the "strict standard" is required
by the majority of courts.

> The notice requirement exists to prevent commercial bad faith,
> promote mitigation and cure, enable the seller to collect evidence
> while still fresh, and promote settlement. . . . Elaborating on how
> to apply the notice requirement, the Fifth Circuit reasoned:

>> *[F]or merchant buyers* § 2–607(3)(a) requires something
>> more than the minimal notification. . . . [T]he dual policies of
>> "encouraging compromise" and "promoting good faith in

commercial relations" . . . underlay the notice requirement. . . .
Notice consequently must fulfill those policies; merely
indicating that the transaction is still troublesome is not
enough. One way in which the policies are fulfilled is by notice
informing the seller that the buyer regards the contract as
breached by the seller, though specific legal rights need not be
invoked.

T.J. Stevenson & Co., Inc., v. 81,193 Bags of Flour, 629 F.2d 338,
360 (5th Cir.1980) (emphasis added) (citations omitted).

We are not aware of any authority requiring this Court to apply
one standard or the other. Nonetheless, after careful study we find
that only the "strict standard of notification" applied by the Fifth
Circuit can be justly applied where both parties are merchants
under the UCC. Peavey is without question a sophisticated
merchant buyer with an experienced IT staff that undertook to
make extensive modifications to the source code of the BAAN
software. On appeal, Baan points out that nearly all of Peavey's
staff with personal knowledge of the project were no longer
employed at Peavey. Likewise, Baan has not retained many of the
documents related to the Peavey project, and it no longer employs
anyone involved with the project. Peavey asserts that it has lost
tens of millions of dollars over a period of more than four years
because of defective software. Under the circumstances of this case,
we hold that Peavey was required to meet the "strict" standard of
notice described by the Fifth Circuit in *Eastern Air Lines*—to give
reasonable and timely notice that it considered Baan to be in breach
of the agreement and to provide Baan with an opportunity to cure
or mitigate Peavey's continuing damages.

As to the notice required, the Fifth Circuit elaborated that "the
adequacy and timeliness of notice under section 2–607 typically
depend upon the reasonableness of the buyer's efforts to
communicate his dissatisfaction." T.J. Stevenson, 629 F.2d at 359
n.41. As such, "[w]here more than one inference may be drawn from
undisputed facts, or the facts are disputed, the timeliness and
sufficiency of a notice of breach . . . are questions for the jury to
resolve. The question of reasonableness must be determined from
the circumstances in the individual case." *Id.*

Peavey argues that Baan was aware of the problems Peavey
encountered during the [initial attempt to activate the new system
in] July 1999 . . . and that Baan knew of the compatibility issues
between SCS and version IVc2 of the BAAN software used by
Peavey. However, as the Fifth Circuit explained, between
merchants notice that a transaction is merely "troublesome" is not
enough. Instead, Peavey was required to produce evidence from
which a reasonable jury could conclude that Peavey provided Baan
with reasonable and timely notice that it considered Baan to be in
breach of the agreement. We have scoured the record, but we have
been unable to locate evidence of a single communication from

Peavey to Baan where Peavey notified Baan that it considered Baan to be in breach. In fact, none of the communications cited by Peavey even attribute Peavey's problems to Baan. In each of these communications, Peavey either accepted responsibility or simply described problems without attributing fault. Peavey argues that because it made Baan aware Peavey was having problems, Baan would have known Baan was responsible. This is simply not sufficient notice under the standard for merchant buyers as described by the Fifth Circuit.

The only evidence Peavey cites that might demonstrate sufficient (if perhaps untimely) notice is an October 22, 2002, letter from Robin Long Harshbarger, Peavey's ERP project manager, to Baan. In the letter, Harshbarger states:

> Thank you for the opportunity to discuss Peavey's issues with the Baan Enterprise Resource Planning implementation project. I am encouraged that Baan will be considering financial concessions that one would expect from a strong, long-term business partner.
>
> . . .
>
> I feel the starting point for consideration of financial concessions should begin with the value of the unused licenses and maintenance fees. Based on my analysis this amount is $3.9 million.

Attached to the letter were charts and graphs detailing the portion of the initial licensing fees and continuing license maintenance fees Peavey had paid for software it asserted it had never used.

On appeal, Peavey characterizes this letter as a "written complaint" over Peavey's "issues" that includes a "demand for at least $3.9 million in 'concessions.'" Peavey's arguments, however, are not evidence. The document itself does not support this characterization, and Peavey cites to no context in the record supporting its arguments. Instead, it is evident from the document and the other evidence that the "issues" Peavey cited were not problems with the software, but the mere fact that Peavey had not been using some of the software it had been paying for. Harshbarger, who left Peavey in 2004, explained:

> As part of these discussions with Baan, I negotiated concessions for Peavey on Baan's offered pricing and fees for additional software and services. As part of this effort, I explained to Baan that Peavey had paid for licenses and maintenance on a variety of software that Peavey, due to Peavey's own decision to stop Phase II of the project, had not used in live production. This included user seats for the Baan IV manufacturing modules and the Baan SCS software and other Phase II parts of the project which Peavey had put on hold in the Fall of 1999 and had never completed.

During these discussions with Baan, I never told Baan or any of its representatives that any of Baan's software was defective. . . . I was instead trying to negotiate for Peavey a better price from Baan for future software and services.

It is evident from the record that Baan shared this understanding of the letter,[10] and Peavey has simply produced no evidence that would allow a jury to accept its characterizations and arguments. Indeed, the record contains no evidence from which a jury could find that Peavey provided Baan with reasonable and timely notice that it considered Baan to be in breach of their agreement. Mississippi Code Annotated section 75–2–607(3) therefore bars Peavey from any remedy on the Software Agreement. Accordingly, the trial court did not err in dismissing Peavey's contract and warranty claims stemming from the Software Agreement. . . .

E. CONTRACTUAL LIMITATIONS OF REMEDIES

It may surprise you to learn that almost all of the provisions in Part 7 of Article 2 are merely gap-fillers, for 2–718 and 2–719 specifically authorize the parties to displace those provisions by agreement. Section 2–718 authorizes the parties to stipulate the damages that will be available in the event of breach. Section 2–719 authorizes them to modify or exclude the remedies that would be available in the absence of their agreement on remedies. The latter section is related to 2–316, which authorizes warranty disclaimers, but it is conceptually very different, and that difference is extremely important to understand. If a seller disclaims warranties, that means there are no warranties and the seller is not in breach just because the goods do not function as one would expect. If, on the other hand, a seller limits damages, a defect in the goods may amount to a breach of the contract but the buyer cannot recover full compensation for the loss caused by that breach. See 2–316(4). Please read 2–719(1) now.

QUESTIONS

1.   Subsection (1) refers to two possible remedies that the parties might place in their contract: refund of the price and repair or replacement of nonconforming goods or parts. No doubt you have encountered each of these

---

[10] For example, the record contains an internal Baan e-mail where a Baan employee discusses the letter:

Here's a little analogy—If I buy a castle and use only 4 of the 20 rooms, whose problem is it, the realtor or the buyer? If I choose to heat the other 16 rooms that I don't use for 3 or 4 years, can I go to the utility company and say give me the money back for the energy I used to heat those 16 rooms because I never received any warmth since I never went into those rooms? . . . If Peavey bought more licenses than they needed, it's their problem. If they paid maintenance on more licenses than they used it's also their problem.

in your own purchases. Can you think of other remedies the parties might place in their contract?

2.   Problem. Goldson purchased a non-stick fry pan. Accompanying the pan was a statement:

> GlideFree Cookware is warranted to be free from defects in material and workmanship under normal household use for a period of 10 years. This pan will continue to release food for a full 10 years when our care and use instructions are followed. We will repair or replace (at our option) any defective part or item during the guarantee period. Should you have a problem with your pan, please return it to us at 136 Woodlawn Rd., Waterloo, IA.
>
> This warranty does not cover damage caused by overheating, accident, misuse, or abuse. Incidental or consequential damages are expressly excluded by this warranty.

After three years food no longer glides out of the pan without sticking. May Goldson recover damages for this breach of warranty?

1.   REFUND OF THE PRICE

An exclusive remedy frequently found in commercial transactions is replacement of nonconforming goods or refund of the contract price. Under what circumstances might that remedy fail of its essential purpose?

Problem. Arco, an oil refiner, delivered petroleum to Chemco, a chemical company that produces resins that it sells to manufacturers of floor tile, shoe soles, paint, and other products. The contract stated that the seller's liability was limited to return of the purchase price and required the buyer to inform the seller of any nonconformity within ten days after delivery. The petroleum was contaminated with a substance that caused the floor tile and other end products to emit a foul odor, rendering them unsaleable. Did the exclusive remedy fail of its essential purpose?

———

Tokyo Ohka Kogyo America, Inc. v. Huntsman Propylene Oxide LLC

United States District Court, District of Oregon, 2014.
35 F.Supp.3d 1316.

[Plaintiff, Tokyo Ohka Kogyo (TOK) contacted defendant, Huntsman, about purchasing propylene glycol. Before agreeing to sell to TOK, Huntsman required TOK to complete a credit application. Attached to the credit application was a separate document, titled "General Terms," which included a provision that limited Huntsman's liability to the purchase price of the goods and excluded consequential damages. At the time of the credit application, no attention was drawn or paid to the General Terms.

After Huntsman approved the credit application, the parties began exploring the actual purchase transaction. TOK intended to mix the propylene glycol (PG) with other chemicals and sell the resulting mixture to a customer that would use the mixture to make semiconductors. This customer's needs were precise and demanding, and over a two-year period TOK purchased small amounts of PG to subject it to testing. When TOK finally concluded that the product was satisfactory, the parties agreed on a "Procurement Specification," which by itself was not a contract. This document contained a provision requiring Huntsman to notify TOK 12 months in advance of any change in Huntsman's manufacturing process so that TOK could verify that the change would not impair the quality of the mixture that TOK was selling to its customer. It also stated that TOK could return unsatisfactory PG to Huntsman for a credit, but that the credit would be limited to the amount that Huntsman received upon sale of the returned product to another purchaser.

Thereafter, TOK purchased large quantities of PG, and for more than a year, all was well. Then TOK discovered that a change in Huntsman's manufacturing process caused a chemical change in the PG, which, when combined with the other chemicals, caused defects in the semiconductors. In breach of the Procurement Specification, Huntsman had not informed TOK of the change in its manufacturing process. At the time of this discovery, TOK had PG on hand, as well as a quantity of chemical mixture containing PG. The unmixed PG was sold, but the chemical mixture was useless. TOK suffered loss consisting of the PG that had been mixed with other chemicals, the wasted chemicals that had been mixed with the PG, and expenses in connection with disposing of the mixture as hazardous waste.

When TOK sued to recover these losses, Huntsman claimed that its liability was limited to refunding the price. Each party filed a motion for partial summary judgment.]

■ SIMON, DISTRICT JUDGE.

Courts struggle with defining what it means for a limited remedy to "fail of its essential purpose." Conceptually, cases invoking Section 2–719(2) are more easily analyzed when they involve a repair-or-replace remedy for a specific product, because it can more readily be determined that the product is not as promised, has not been sufficiently repaired or replaced, and thus the remedy has failed of its purpose. The analysis is more nuanced when a refund remedy is at issue, although courts have found that a refund remedy can also fail of its essential purpose, such as when a seller conceals relevant facts or there is a latent defect.

Comment 1 to Section 2–719 offers guidance on how to analyze whether a remedy limitation fails in its essential purpose.

Understanding that the word "its" refers to the remedy limitation, Comment 1 instructs that when a limitation "fails in its purpose or *operates to deprive either party of the substantial value of the bargain,* it must give way to the general remedy provisions of this Article." (emphasis added). Courts analyzing whether limiting a remedy to a refund of the purchase price fails of its essential purpose generally focus on the requirement that a party should not be deprived of "the substantial value of the bargain" as opposed to otherwise defining what it means for a limitation to fail in its purpose. Additionally, many courts note that if a case involves a latent defect that is not discoverable upon reasonable inspection, then a limitation, including a limitation to a refund of the purchase price, necessarily fails of its essential purpose.

The determination under Section 2–719(2) of whether "circumstances [have] cause[d] an exclusive or limited remedy to fail of its essential purpose" or whether the limitation has "operate[d] to deprive[ ] either party of the substantial benefit of the bargain" requires consideration of the bargain made at the time the contract was entered into and whether, after breach and based on the circumstances of the breach, the limitation is operating to deprive either party of that bargain. A court should attempt to discern the essential purpose of the exclusive or limited remedy when it was first agreed-upon by the parties—the bargain of the parties with respect to their allocation of risks and remedies. . . . The Court should not concern itself, at least under Section 2–719(2), with whether the agreed-upon limitation on remedy was wise, fair, or oppressive at the time of contract formation, but simply ask what was the limitation's essential purpose at that time.

A court must also focus on the circumstances surrounding the alleged breach of contract and resulting harm to discern whether the harm is one caused by novel circumstances not contemplated by the parties and involved a risk not allocated by the parties. . . . Where the circumstances involved were foreseeable by the parties, at least as a possibility, and the risk was allocated, the limitation on remedy properly can be seen to reflect the parties' agreed-upon allocation of anticipated risks. Where the circumstances surrounding the alleged breach of contract and resulting harm were not part of the bargained-for allocation of risk, then one party has been deprived of the substantial value of its bargain, the limitation on remedy fails of its essential purpose, and Section 7–219(2) operates to void that limitation.

This case involves a latent defect that was not discoverable upon reasonable inspection. The mere existence of such a latent defect, however, does not end the Court's analysis. It may be that the parties bargained for an allocation of risk relating to latent defects. Accordingly, the Court looks to the bargain between the parties, including determining the bargained-for allocation of risk and whether it included allocating the risk for the type breach committed by Huntsman and the type of latent defect that occurred.

Huntsman argues that the presence of the boilerplate Limitation Clause in the Huntsman General Terms that was attached to the Credit Application signed by TOK is evidence that the parties intended to allocate all risks to TOK, including the risk of an undiscoverable defect caused by an undisclosed change in the manufacturing process, notwithstanding Huntsman's contractual obligation timely to disclose any such changes. Huntsman's argument is without merit.

The generic Limitation Clause was attached to a Credit Application that was signed more than two years before the parties entered into a significant commercial relationship and signed their first specification contract. The Limitation Clause was not discussed or specifically and expressly bargained-for at the time the Credit Application was signed by TOK. During the two years after TOK's execution of the Credit Application, the parties engaged in extensive negotiations on specifications, five test purchases to ensure the PG would work in TOK's chemical mixture and the Customer's semiconductor manufacturing process, and an approval process with the Customer. TOK also inspected and audited Huntsman's plant and manufacturing process.

After this lengthy process, the parties then signed specification contracts that more specifically defined the parties' obligations and their allocation of risk. Only then did TOK begin to make larger volume purchases. The 2011 Procurement Specification (as amended) expressly allocated the risk of discoverable defects to TOK by providing that if the PG did not meet TOK's specifications then TOK would only be entitled to a refund of the amount, if any, that Huntsman received after reselling the rejected PG. Both the 2010 and 2011 specification contracts also required Huntsman to provide twelve months' notice of any changes in its manufacturing process because a manufacturing change might affect the efficacy of the PG and not otherwise be discoverable by TOK in its inspection and testing.

There is no evidence that in June 2008, when TOK signed the Credit Application, incorporating by reference the Huntsman General Terms, the parties consciously intended that the Limitation Clause would allocate the risk to TOK of an undiscoverable defect caused by Huntsman's breach of its obligation timely to notify TOK of any change in Huntsman's manufacturing process. To the contrary, this type of allocation could not possibly have been intended at that time because Huntsman's obligation to notify TOK of any change in the manufacturing process did not even arise until the 2010 specification contract. Additionally, during the two years that the parties engaged in testing and incremental orders and during the negotiations for the 2010 and 2011 specification contracts, the Limitation Clause was never mentioned. Notably, when Huntsman limited TOK's remedy for nonconforming goods in the 2011 Procurement Specification to only the amount for which Huntsman could resell the PG, thereby amending the Limitation Clause, Huntsman still failed to call TOK's attention to the fact that Huntsman believed the parties' relationship was governed by the Limitation Clause, that the Limitation Clause was being only partially amended, or that Huntsman believed the Limitation Clause remained otherwise in effect for any breach by Huntsman other than selling PG to TOK that did not meet TOK's technical specifications.

. . .

The parties stipulate that they have entered into multiple agreements and that there are multiple documents that relate to the manufacture and sale of the PG by Huntsman to TOK, including the Credit Application, purchase orders sent by TOK, invoices sent by Huntsman, and the 2010 and 2011 technical specification contracts. These documents show that the bargain of the parties included the following allocations of risk: (1) TOK assumes the risk if there is no change in the manufacturing process, the PG complies with TOK's technical specifications, and the Customer's product later fails; (2) TOK assumes the risk if there is no change in the manufacturing process, the PG fails to comply with TOK's technical specifications, TOK still uses the PG in the mixture, and the Customer's product later fails; (3) TOK assumes the risk of losing some of its purchase price if the PG does not comply with TOK's technical specifications and TOK returns the PG to Huntsman, because TOK is only entitled to whatever amount Huntsman obtains in reselling the PG; (4) TOK assumes the risk if Huntsman timely discloses any change in its manufacturing process, TOK uses the PG, and the Customer's product later fails; but (5) TOK does *not* assume the risks created by Huntsman failing timely to disclose a change in its manufacturing process because this information is within the sole knowledge of Huntsman and TOK has no way of discovering any latent defects caused by a change in Huntsman's manufacturing process, thereby rendering the two years of testing useless. Such a breach was a novel circumstance not contemplated by the parties in 2008 when TOK signed the Credit Application.

. . . [S]ome courts have held that a buyer's misbehavior, such as conduct that deprives the seller of the chance to repair or replace a nonconforming product or conduct in which a buyer has made unauthorized modifications to a product before asking the seller to make repair, is relevant to whether a limited remedy fails of its essential purpose. By the same reasoning, it would not be inappropriate to consider a seller's misbehavior in deciding whether a limited remedy fails of its essential purpose. Here, TOK was willing to assume certain inherent risks in accepting Huntsman's PG, and the parties did not agree that Huntsman would be a guarantor for the success of TOK's efforts. There is no indication, however, that TOK was willing to assume the risk of Huntsman's misbehavior, (indeed, Huntsman's arguable "bad faith") in intentionally failing to comply with its contractual obligation timely to inform TOK of changes in Huntsman's manufacturing process, of which only Huntsman could be aware and control.

Because the Court finds that TOK and Huntsman did not allocate to TOK the risk of an unknown, latent defect caused by Huntsman's breach of its obligation timely to notify TOK of a change in manufacturing, the Court also finds persuasive the reasoning of cases that find that refund-only remedies fail of their essential purpose when there are latent defects that were only discovered after the defective product was either integrated into something else or was otherwise put to use in a way that rendered it non-returnable, thus resulting in significantly greater damages than the original purchase price. *See, e.g.,* Viking Yacht Co. v. Composites One, LLC, 2007 WL 2746713, at *6 (D.N.J.2007) (Viking I); Leprino v. Intermountain Brick Co., 759 P.2d 835, 836–37 (Colo.Ct.App.1988). The court in *Viking I* found that because the product at issue, a gel coat, was "combined into a larger product before use" and the purchaser could not "simply re-purchase gel coat from a different company and use it" but must instead engage in expensive remediation measures that were exponentially greater than the purchase price, the refund remedy failed of its essential purpose and provided a severely inadequate remedy.

Similarly, the court in *Leprino* found that a provision limiting the plaintiffs' remedy to the purchase price failed of its essential purpose when the seller's breach was detectable only after the bricks were installed, requiring significant expense in removing and rebuilding the structure they had built with the defective brick. The court found that "[w]hen the parties agreed to limit the buyers' remedy to refund of the purchase price, they contemplated a situation in which the defective bricks would be returned to [the seller] prior to installation and the purchase price would be returned to the plaintiffs." Leprino, 759 P.2d at 837.

Parties may allocate the risk of an unknown latent defect on a buyer and limit damages, even when the limitation results in an inadequate remedy. *See e.g.,* Eddy, On the "Essential" Purposes of Limited Remedies: The Metaphysics of UCC Section 2–719(2), 65 Cal. L.Rev. 28, at 47–48 (1977) (noting that parties should be able to allocate the risk of loss for both discoverable and undiscoverable defects). . . .

As discussed above, in this case there is no evidence that TOK and Huntsman intended to allocate the risk to TOK of a latent defect caused by Huntsman's breach of its obligation timely to notify TOK of any manufacturing process change. The evidence is that TOK was not aware of the Limitation Clause and intended and agreed to the limited remedy of a return of the purchase price, or even less than the purchase price, for nonconforming goods because TOK could test the delivered PG to ensure that it conformed to TOK's technical specifications and return nonconforming goods before using them. TOK attempted to reduce the risk of undetectable defects in the PG by taking two years to ensure that the PG and Huntsman's manufacturing process resulted in a workable chemical mixture and by requiring Huntsman timely to notify TOK of any change in Huntsman's manufacturing process. As in *Viking I* and *Leprino*, the undetectable defect, caused by information solely in Huntsman's possession and avoidable solely by Huntsman, resulted in significantly greater damages than the purchase price of the PG. These damages include transporting the defective PG and defective chemical mixture, the cost of the chemicals that were mixed with the defective PG and rendered unusable, and the cost of the hazardous waste disposal of the defective chemical mixture. Limiting TOK to damages of only the purchase price of the PG does not provide a "fair quantum of remedy" for Huntsman's breach of its obligation timely to notify TOK of any manufacturing change of which only Huntsman would be aware.

     . . .

Under the specific circumstances presented in this case, the Limitation Clause in the Huntsman General Terms fails of its essential purpose and is . . . unenforceable. Accordingly, TOK's motion for partial summary judgment is GRANTED, and Huntsman's motion for partial summary judgment is DENIED.

QUESTIONS AND NOTES

1. Under 2–719(2) the buyer is limited to an exclusive remedy "unless circumstances cause [it] to fail of its essential purpose." The last sentence of Official Comment 1, however, adds, "or operates to deprive either party of the substantial value of the bargain." How much weight should be given to this language in the Comment?

2. Before it was willing to do business with TOK, Huntsman required TOK to demonstrate that it was creditworthy. To that end, it required TOK to submit a credit application. The General Terms accompanying the Credit Application stated:

> LIMITATION OF LIABILITY. Seller's maximum liability for any breach of this Agreement, or any other claim related to the Product, shall be limited to the purchase price of the Product or portion thereof (as such price is set forth on the first page of Seller's invoice) to which such breach or claim pertains. IN NO EVENT SHALL SELLER BE LIABLE FOR ANY CONSEQUENTIAL, INCIDENTAL, SPECIAL OR PUNITIVE DAMAGES, INCLUDING BUT NOT LIMITED TO ANY DAMAGES FOR LOST PROFITS OR BUSINESS OPPORTUNITIES OR DAMAGE TO REPUTATION.

Note that this provision refers to "any breach" of the contract, not just defects in PG. In its entirety, the "LIMITATION OF LIABILITY" seems to place on TOK all risk of Huntsman's failure of performance. How then can the court permit TOK to recover damages beyond refund of the purchase price?

———

2. REPAIR OR REPLACEMENT

Many contracts—both consumer and commercial, even highly negotiated ones—provide that the buyer's *exclusive* remedy is repair or replacement. What reasons might a seller have for wanting this provision? What reasons might a buyer have? Please write down at least two reasons for each.

The adequacy of the remedy to achieve these objectives depends on at least two things: the parties' willingness to attempt repairs (or replacement) and the seller's ability to accomplish it successfully and expeditiously. Occasionally, when a buyer complains about a nonconformity, the seller refuses to take any action, perhaps because the seller does not agree that there is a nonconformity or because the seller thinks that the buyer's misuse of the product caused the problem. If the seller is wrong and in fact the goods do not conform, the seller's refusal leaves the buyer without any remedy. In other instances the seller may attempt to repair the goods—even repeatedly—but simply be unable to make the goods conform. (Obvious examples are motor vehicles properly described as lemons, but the phenomenon occurs with respect to commercial equipment, too.) Here, too, the buyer is left without any remedy. In recognition of these scenarios, subsection (2) provides a remedy. Please read subsection (2) now.

If an exclusive repair-or-replace remedy fails of its essential purpose, the Article 2 remedies are available. To determine whether an exclusive remedy has failed of its essential purpose, the first step is to identify the essential purpose of the remedy. Thus one court stated:

> The purpose of an exclusive remedy of replacement or repair of defective parts, whose presence constitute a breach of an express warranty, is to give the seller an opportunity to make the goods conforming while limiting the risks to which he is subject by excluding direct and consequential damages that might otherwise arise. From the point of view of the buyer, the purpose of the exclusive remedy is to give him goods that conform to the contract within a reasonable time after a defective part is discovered.

Beal v. General Motors Corp., 354 F.Supp. 423, 426 (D.Del.1973).

Assuming that the seller is willing to attempt repairs, the remedy fails of its essential purpose if the seller's attempts are unsuccessful. This may occur in at least two ways: the defect repeatedly manifests itself, as when the seller simply cannot, despite repeated repairs, solve the problem with a car's transmission. It also may occur, however, if notwithstanding the successful repair of a defect, another defect becomes evident. At some point, a succession of defects, even if each (except perhaps the last one) is repaired, justifies a conclusion that the remedy has failed of its essential purpose. As one court stated in connection with a series of attempts to repair a motor home:

It is the position of the defendants that KOA successfully repaired every defect complained of by the Murrays. . . .

Although the Murrays agreed that KOA had never refused to attempt a requested repair, this testimony does not affect their right to revoke acceptance. The limited remedy of repair or replacement of defective parts fails of its essential purpose whenever, despite reasonable opportunity for repair, the goods are not restored to a nondefective condition within a reasonable time, whether or not the failure to do so is willful.

Murray v. Holiday Rambler, Inc., 83 Wis.2d 406, 423, 265 N.W.2d 513, 522 (1978).

Another court stated:

To be effective the repair remedy must be provided within a reasonable time after discovery of the defect. It is not necessary to show negligence or bad faith on the part of the seller. The detriment to the buyer is the same whether the seller diligently but unsuccessfully attempts to honor his promise or acts negligently or in bad faith.

Chatlos Systems, Inc. v. National Cash Register Corp., 635 F.2d 1081, 1085 (3d Cir.1980).

————

It is clear that a seller's refusal or inability to effect repairs, causes an exclusive repair-or-replace remedy fail of its essential purpose. What other circumstances cause it to fail of its essential purpose?

Problem. Bader purchased an SUV, pursuant to a contract that contained an express warranty of no defects and an exclusive repair-or-replace remedy. Six months after purchase, a defective $100 part in the steering mechanism caused Bader to lose control and crash. The vehicle sustained $8,000 of damage, and the new HDTV that he was bringing home from the store was destroyed. Has the exclusive remedy failed of its essential purpose?

Sections 2–712, 2–713, and 2–714 each provides that the buyer may recover consequential damages. But 2–719(3) provides that, whether or not the parties agree on any remedies not found in Article 2, they are free to agree that in the event of the seller's breach, the seller is not liable for consequential damages. Please read subsection (3) now.

Smith v. Navistar International Transportation Corporation

United States Court of Appeals, Seventh Circuit, 1992.
957 F.2d 1439.

■ COFFEY, CIRCUIT JUDGE. . . . In 1984, Smith, an independent owner-operator of long distance trucks, decided to purchase a new truck, and

Smith requested a list of sixteen options and/or components on the truck. After discussing the proposed purchase with several dealers, Smith decided to buy the Navistar semi-tractor truck Model 9370 as specified, from Jones (a Navistar authorized dealership), on November 7, 1984. . . .

Upon delivery of the truck Smith received an Owner's Limited Warranty booklet which in pertinent part read:

"[Navistar] will repair or replace any part of this vehicle which proves defective in material and/or workmanship in normal use and service, with new or ReNewed parts, for the first twelve months from new vehicle delivery date or for 50,000 miles (90,000 Km), whichever occurs first, except as specified under 'What is Not Covered.' "

On the second page of the Owner's Limited Warranty booklet are additional warranty disclaimers:

"NOTE: DISCLAIMER!

THERE ARE NO WARRANTIES WHICH EXTEND BEYOND THE DESCRIPTION ON THE FACE HEREOF. THIS WARRANTY IS IN LIEU OF ALL OTHER WARRANTIES, EXPRESSED OR IMPLIED. THE COMPANY SPECIFICALLY DISCLAIMS WARRANTIES OF *MERCHANTABILITY AND FITNESS FOR A PARTICULAR PURPOSE*, ALL OTHER REPRESENTATIONS TO THE FIRST USER/PURCHASER, AND ALL OTHER OBLIGATIONS OR LIABILITIES. THE COMPANY FURTHER EXCLUDES LIABILITY FOR INCIDENTAL AND CONSEQUENTIAL DAMAGES, ON THE PART OF THE COMPANY OR THE SELLER. No person is authorized to give any other warranties or to assume any liabilities on the Company's behalf unless made or assumed in writing by the seller." (emphasis in original). . . .

Some nine days after Smith's purchase of the truck, he experienced problems with the truck's braking system. On no fewer than ten separate occasions between November 7, 1984 and April 1985, Smith brought the truck to authorized Navistar dealers for repairs. Thus, the truck was out of service for a period of forty-five days.[3] Smith alleges that throughout the period of repair, the defendants were aware that he had a contract with one firm that he relied upon for his business and that if he was unable to operate his truck he would lose the contract. Notwithstanding Smith's dissatisfaction with the number and frequency of the alleged defects, Smith continued to use the truck during the problem time period and eventually ran up some 48,488 miles on it. On June 6, 1985, Smith sent a letter to the three named defendants expressing his intention to revoke his contract based upon his dissatisfaction with the final repair effort. At this same time Smith ceased making installment payments on the truck.

---

[3]   Neither Navistar nor any of its dealers ever refused to work on Smith's truck, and Smith was never charged for any of the repairs undertaken.

[Two years later Smith sued the seller, the manufacturer, and the lender that financed the purchase.] After extensive discovery, the defendants moved for summary judgment, and on January 27, 1989, the district court denied defendants' motion for summary judgment on the issue of liability, but granted defendants' motion as to damages. . . . The practical effect of this order was to limit the amount of damages a jury could award to $19,527.70, the amount Smith had paid for the truck prior to the revocation of his acceptance. [Ultimately, the court entered judgment for Smith for this amount.] Smith appeals.

. . .

Illinois law applies in this diversity action, and the transaction is governed under Article 2 of the Uniform Commercial Code. The plaintiff Smith argues that, because this is a diversity action, the district court was required to determine the applicable law of the State of Illinois when determining whether the plaintiff was entitled to consequential damages. The plaintiff contends that because, "the Illinois Supreme Court has not addressed the issue in question, the district court was required to use the predictive approach and in applying this approach, the district court disregarded the sole Illinois appellate decision on point and chose a resolution having no basis in Illinois law."

Our review of the district court's grant of partial summary judgment in favor of the defendants is de novo: "We must decide whether the record shows that there is no genuine issue of material fact and that the moving party is entitled to judgment as a matter of law." Dribeck Importers v. G. Heileman Brewing Co., 883 F.2d 569, 573 (7th Cir.1989) (citations omitted). In its denial of partial summary judgment, the district court cited two conflicting cases which dealt with the issue of whether consequential damages could be awarded when a limited warranty failed to provide the protection the buyer expected. The first of these cases was a decision of an intermediate appellate court, Adams v. J.I. Case Co., 125 Ill. App. 2d 388, 261 N.E.2d 1 (4th Dist.1970). The second was a decision of this court, AES Technology Systems, Inc. v. Coherent Radiation, 583 F.2d 933 (7th Cir.1978). Smith in essence argues that the district court erred in granting partial summary judgment because it chose to follow *AES* rather than *Adams*. However, federal courts are not bound by the decision of a lower state court unless the state's highest court in the jurisdiction whose law governs the diversity action has ruled on the matter.

Smith's signature on the Retail Order would ordinarily constitute an effective waiver of any right to recover incidental and consequential damages arising from the loss of his single employment contract.[6] However, the U.C.C. provides that "where circumstances cause an exclusive or limited remedy to fail of its essential purpose, remedy may

---

[6] . . . [T]he Retail Order, as well as the owner's manual that Smith received, disclaimed any warranties of merchantability and fitness for a particular purpose and any liability for incidental and consequential damages.

be had as provided in this Act." Ill. Rev. Stat. ch. 26, § 2–719(2). In *Adams*, the Illinois Appellate Court adopted a categorical approach and held that the seller's breach of a limited warranty to repair or replace defective tractor parts automatically exposes the seller to liability for the buyer's consequential damages despite an otherwise enforceable disclaimer:

> "The limitations of remedy and of liability are not separable from the obligations of the warranty. Repudiation of the obligations of the warranty destroyed its benefits. . . . It should be obvious that they cannot at once repudiate their obligation under the warranty and assert its provisions beneficial to them."

Adams, 261 N.E.2d at 7–8.

However, in *AES*, this court rejected the categorical approach enunciated in Adams, and refused to automatically sever a consequential damage disclaimer from a contract merely on the failure of a limited warranty to provide the benefits that the parties bargained for:

> "Some courts have awarded consequential damages, when a remedy failed of its essential purpose, in the face of prohibitions in the contract against consequential damages. However, we reject the contention that failure of the essential purpose of the limited remedy automatically means that a damage award will include consequential damages. An analysis to determine whether consequential damages are warranted must carefully examine the individual factual situation including the type of goods involved, the parties and the precise nature and purpose of the contract. The purpose of the courts in contractual disputes is not to re-write contracts by ignoring parties' intent; rather, it is *to interpret the existing contract as fairly as possible when all events did not occur as planned*."

AES, 583 F.2d at 941 (footnote omitted) (emphasis added).

Other courts have similarly adopted this case-by-case approach. In Chatlos Systems v. National Cash Register Corp., 635 F.2d 1081 (3d Cir.1980), the court held that the failure of the essential purpose of a limited remedy does not automatically mean that a damage award will include consequential damages:

> "New Jersey has not taken a position on this question, so in this diversity case we must predict which view the New Jersey Supreme Court would adopt if the question were presented to it.
>
> It appears to us that the better reasoned approach is to treat the consequential damage disclaimer as an independent provision, valid unless unconscionable. This poses no logical difficulties. A contract may well contain no limitation on breach of warranty damages but specifically exclude consequential damages. Conversely, it is quite conceivable that some

limitation might be placed on a breach of warranty award, but consequential damages would expressly be permitted.

The limited remedy of repair and a consequential damages exclusion are two discrete ways of attempting to limit recovery for breach of warranty. The Code, moreover, tests each by a different standard. The former survives unless it fails of its essential purpose, while the latter is valid unless it is unconscionable. We therefore see no reason to hold, as a general proposition, that the failure of the limited remedy provided in the contract, without more, invalidates a wholly distinct term in the agreement excluding consequential damages. The two are not mutually exclusive."

Id. at 1086 (footnotes and citations omitted).

Similarly, in S.M. Wilson & Co. v. Smith International, Inc., 587 F.2d 1363 (9th Cir.1978) (California law), the court determined that consequential damages were not warranted even though the limited repair warranty failed to achieve its essential purpose:

"The issue remains whether the failure of the limited repair remedy to serve its purpose requires permitting the recovery of consequential damages. . . . We hold it does not. In reaching this conclusion we are influenced heavily by the characteristics of the contract between [seller] and [buyer]. . . . Parties of relatively equal bargaining power negotiated an allocation of their risks of loss. Consequential damages were assigned to the buyer, Wilson. The machine was a complex piece of equipment designed for the buyer's purposes. The seller Smith did not ignore his obligation to repair; he simply was unable to perform it. This is not enough to require that the seller absorb losses the buyer plainly agreed to bear. Risk shifting is socially expensive and should not be undertaken in the absence of a good reason. An even better reason is required when to so shift is contrary to a contract freely negotiated. The default of the seller is not so total and fundamental as to require that its consequential damages limitation be expunged from the contract."

Id. at 1375.

We believe the district court's reliance on *AES* rather than *Adams* was correct. The case-by-case approach adopted by *AES* and the other decisions allows some measure of certainty in that parties of relatively equal bargaining power can allocate all of the risks that may accompany a breach of warranty, and prevents the court from upsetting that allocation upon a breach of contractual duties. Moreover, in those situations where the limited warranty fails to provide the benefits that the buyer expected (i.e., to repair or replace defective parts) and the parties are clearly on unequal terms with respect to relative bargaining power, the case-by-case approach enunciated in *AES* enables the courts to examine "the intent of the parties, as gleaned from the express provisions of the contract and the factual background" to determine whether consequential damages are warranted, rather than automatically exposing the seller to liability for consequential damages despite an otherwise valid disclaimer. AES, 583 F.2d at 941. Thus, we agree with the district court that the rationale underlying *AES* and the other decisions adopting the case-by-case approach is more compelling than the categorical approach enunciated in Adams.

Smith also argues that "even if the district court was correct in the approach that it chose, the case-by-case approach, it misapplied that approach." Smith contends that the district court failed to analyze "all of the attendant objective facts and circumstances, including the language of the agreement, the relative bargaining power of the parties and the commercial context of the transaction" in order to determine which party should bear the risk of consequential damages. In our opinion, this argument is without merit as the district court noted that Smith failed to present any evidence in opposition to the damages awarded in the summary judgment motion. Moreover, our review of the record reveals that at the time Smith purchased the truck he was an experienced operator of long-distance trucks and had visited at least six different truck dealers in Indiana and Illinois, and had drawn up a list of sixteen specifications for the truck that he felt met his specific need. Having refused to accept any truck that did not meet his list of sixteen requirements, Smith presented the necessary components and options to defendant Jones, who offered the plaintiff-appellant the Navistar truck that met his specifications. At the time of purchase, Smith signed a Retail Order specifically excluding liability on the part of the seller for incidental and consequential damages:

> "THIS WARRANTY IS IN LIEU OF ALL OTHER WARRANTIES, EXPRESSED OR IMPLIED, INCLUDING WITHOUT LIMITATION, WARRANTIES OF MERCHANTABILITY AND FITNESS FOR PARTICULAR PURPOSE, ALL OTHER REPRESENTATIONS TO THE FIRST USER PURCHASER, AND ALL OTHER OBLIGATIONS OR LIABILITIES, INCLUDING LIABILITY FOR INCIDENTAL AND CONSEQUENTIAL DAMAGES ON THE PART OF THE COMPANY OR THE SELLER."

Moreover, Smith accepted a warranty which also clearly excluded seller liability for incidental and consequential damages in a section set off with the words, "NOTE: DISCLAIMER"! Smith read the terms and conditions of the warranty and failed to ask any questions regarding the terms of the Retail Order or warranty before signing the same. We have failed to discover evidence in the record that the parties intended that the defendants bear the risk of consequential damages or that the parties' relative bargaining power was so unequal that the disclaimer was unconscionable and we refuse to re-write the contract including the Retail Order's clear exclusion of consequential damages.

. . .

The decision of the district court is AFFIRMED.

QUESTIONS AND NOTES

1.   What warranty did defendants allegedly breach?

2.   Defendants conceded that the exclusive remedy failed of its essential purpose. But they denied liability for consequential damages. Plaintiff argued that if an exclusive remedy fails of its essential purpose, the buyer is entitled to all remedies available under Article 2. The court rejected the conclusion that if the exclusive remedy fails of its essential purpose, the buyer necessarily can recover consequential damages, when the contract contains a separate term specifically excluding liability for consequential damages. Rather, the recoverability of consequential damages must be determined on a case-by-case approach. By what standard is a court to determine whether the buyer may recover consequential damages in the particular case before it? Applying that test, the court in *TOK v. Huntsman*, page 491 supra, permitted recovery of TOK's consequential damages.

3.   In Milgard Tempering, Inc. v. Selas Corp., 902 F.2d 703 (9th Cir.1990), the buyer paid $1.45 million for a furnace for tempering glass. The design of the furnace was complex, and the parties contemplated it would take several months after delivery to get it to work properly. The contract limited the buyer's remedy to repair or replacement and specifically excluded liability for consequential damages. Three years after the scheduled delivery date, the furnace still did not operate as warranted. In the buyer's suit for lost profits, the court held that the exclusive remedy had failed of its essential purpose. As to the buyer's ability to recover lost profits notwithstanding the exclusion of them in the contract, the court stated:

> The task before the district court was to examine the remedy provisions and determine whether Selas' default caused a loss which was not part of the bargained-for allocation of risk. . . . We agree with the district court's decision to lift the cap on consequential damages. Milgard did not agree to pay $1.45 million in order to participate in a science experiment. It agreed to purchase what Selas represented as a cutting-edge glass furnace that would accommodate its needs after two months of debugging. Selas' inability to effect repair despite 2.5 years of intense . . . effort caused Milgard losses not part of the bargained-for allocation of risk. Therefore, the cap on consequential damages is unenforceable.

4.   **Problem.** Carr's Auto Sales delivered an automobile to Bullard, a sales representative for a pharmaceutical company. The contract provided:

> There are no warranties, expressed or implied, made by either the Dealer or the Manufacturer on new Ford Motor Co. motor vehicles, chassis, or parts furnished under this Order except the

Manufacturer's Warranty against defects in material and workmanship set out below:

> Ford Motor Co., as Manufacturer, warrants each new motor vehicle, including all equipment and accessories (except tires and tubes), to be free from defects in material and workmanship under normal use and service; Ford Motor Co.'s obligation under this warranty being limited to repairing or replacing at its option any part or parts thereof that shall, within twenty-four (24) months after delivery of the vehicle to the original retail purchaser, be returned to an authorized Ford Motor Co. Dealer. The repair or replacement of defective parts under this warranty will be made by such Dealer without charge for parts and labor.

The vehicle has defects that Carr's cannot repair within a reasonable time and number of attempts. Is Bullard entitled to resort to the remedies in Article 2? (What remedies might those be?)

Bullard claims that she was unable to make her sales calls on numerous days while Carr's attempted to repair the vehicle and that she lost $16,000 in commissions. Can she recover the $16,000?

5. In the commercial setting, the most commonly occurring example of consequential damages is lost profits. In the consumer context, of course, the buyer cannot incur that kind of loss. Besides personal injuries, what kinds of loss might be within the definition of consequential damages in 2–715(2)?

6. Please look at 2–714. Subsection (2) states the measure of damages for breach of warranty. Subsection (3) states that the buyer may recover incidental and consequential damages "in a proper case." What is "a proper case"? Compare 2–712(2) and 2–713(1).

In Beal v. General Motors Corp., 354 F.Supp. 423 (D.Del.1973), the court addressed this issue:

> Few courts have spoken to the question what is a "proper case" for the award of consequential damages within the contemplation of § 2–714(3). The Pennsylvania Supreme Court in the case of Keystone Diesel Engine Company v. Irwin, 411 Pa. 222, 191 A.2d 376 (1963) relied on pre-Code common law principles in holding that:
>
> > "Special circumstances" entitling the buyer to damages in excess of the difference between the value as warranted and the value as accepted exist where the buyer has communicated to the seller at the time of entering into the contract sufficient facts to make it apparent that the damages subsequently claimed were within the reasonable contemplation of the parties. Wolstenholme, Inc. v. Jos.Randall & Bro., 295 Pa. 131, 144 A. 909 (1929). * * *
>
> In the *Birdsboro* case this test was construed as requiring a tacit agreement that consequential damage would be recoverable:
>
> > * * * Under Pennsylvania interpretation of the general Code provisions dealing with damages, therefore, the plaintiff, in

order to collect damages in excess of the difference between the value of the goods as warranted and as accepted, must prove that the seller was on notice of the fact that the plaintiff would hold it responsible for any loss of profit or loss due to "down time" arising from the inability to use the machinery and equipment in question. Jones & McKnight Corp. v. Birdsboro Corporation, 320 F.Supp. 39, 45 (N.D.Ill.1970).

The "tacit agreement" concept has elsewhere been rejected, however. In the Illinois case of Adams v. J.I. Case Co., 125 Ill.App.2d 388, 261 N.E.2d 1 (1970), the court, relying on the statutory language of § 2–715(2) opted for a different test:

> * * * In their Official Comment upon UCC 2–715(2) its framers make it clear that the "tacit agreement" test for the recovery of consequential damages is rejected. The language of that section should not be so narrowly construed as to require a prior understanding or agreement that the seller would be bound for consequential damages in the event of his breach. If that is the holding * * * of Keystone * * * it must be rejected. The Official Comment further states that the older Common Law rule which made the seller liable for all consequential damages of which he had "reason to know" in advance is followed, modified to require reasonable prevention of loss by cover or otherwise. The Code provision and the Official Comment makes it clear that strictures are not to be applied to the plain meaning of the Code by adherence to what the parties may have agreed or contemplated at the time of sale. * * *

> . . . [This court adopts] the test of the *Adams* case. Under that test, the question then is whether the loss for which recovery is sought is one that results from general or particular requirements or needs of which the seller at the time of contracting had reason to know. If it is, then consequential damages are proper provided that those damages could not have been reasonably prevented by action of the buyer.

What is the flaw in this reasoning? What is the proper analysis?

7. Consequential damages. Each of the sections providing for damages states that the buyer may recover consequential damages, which are defined in 2–715(2). Please read that section. The most commonly sought consequential loss is lost profits, but other losses may fall within this definition as well. Article 2 retains the common-law limitations of causation, foreseeability, mitigation, and certainty (though Official Comment 4 seeks to relax the requirement of certainty). Do not overlook the requirement of causation. For example, in David's Bridal, Inc. v. Cels Enterprises, Inc., 2015 WL 13651382 (E.D.Pa.2015), a buyer of shoes failed to inspect the shoes at the time of delivery and did not notify the seller of the breach until customers returned them. The court held that the proximate cause of the buyer's loss of profits was the delay in inspection, not the defects in the shoes.

8.   Lemon laws. Every state has enacted a so-called lemon law to provide relief to purchasers of defective motor vehicles. The impetus to these laws was a shortcoming of 2–719. Granted, subsection (2) provides that if an exclusive remedy fails of its essential purpose, the buyer may pursue all Article 2 remedies. But it does not provide any standard for when an exclusive remedy fails of its essential purpose. The historic attitude of the automobile manufacturers was to offer repeated repairs, no matter how many prior attempts they had made and no matter how long a vehicle may have been out of service for repairs.

One great innovation of the lemon laws is to establish a bright-line test, typically an alternative test of either four attempts to repair a single defect or the vehicle's being out of service for more than 30 days during the first year after its purchase. There is considerable variation among the states concerning the precise details of this standard. For example, some have specified the number of repair attempts as three or five; some have extended the one-year period to 18 or 24 months.

The other great innovation of the lemon laws is to eliminate the bar of privity and enable the buyer in effect to revoke acceptance as against the remote manufacturer.

9.   Express warranty or remedial promise? To repeat Question 1 on page 505 above, what warranty did the seller in *Smith v. Navistar* breach? Whether or not it is possible to identify a warranty, the seller undoubtedly made a promise to repair or replace. That promise traditionally has been viewed as a part of the warranty obligation of the seller. Therefore, some courts have applied the warranty statute of limitations to enforcement of repair-or-replacement promises. Under 2–725 the statute of limitations starts running when the breach occurs, and breach of warranty occurs when tender of delivery is made. This means that the statute of limitations might have run before the seller failed to perform its repair or replacement promise, especially since the parties may agree to "reduce the period of limitations to not less than one year." Please read 2–725(1)–(2).

Note that subsection (2) modifies the above rule when the warranty explicitly extends to future performance of the goods. The following excerpt, from Trans-Spec Truck Service, Inc. v. Caterpillar Inc., 524 F.3d 315 (1st Cir.2008), illustrates and describes the competing analyses of the question whether the statute starts to run when the goods are tendered or when the seller fails to perform its remedial promise. Trans-Spec purchased 22 heavy-duty, custom-built trucks powered by Caterpillar engines. Almost five years later, after many of the engines failed, Trans-Spec sued. The trial court dismissed the warranty claim because the statute of limitations had expired. The Court of Appeals wrote:

> The Uniform Commercial Code ("U.C.C."), as adopted in Massachusetts, provides that an action for breach of warranty must be commenced within four years of the date when the cause of action accrues. . . . Thus, the default rule in § 2–725(2) is that the cause of action for breach of warranty is time-barred if brought more than four years after tender of delivery. However, if the

warranty explicitly extends to future performance, "the four-year clock begins to tick when the breach is discovered or should have been discovered, or when the explicit time period expires, whichever occurs first." Barkley Clark & Christopher Smith, The Law of Product Warranties § 11:4 (2006).

Trans-Spec's complaint stated that Trans-Spec accepted delivery of the trucks containing Caterpillar's allegedly defective flywheel housing in December 1999 and January 2000. Trans-Spec filed suit for breach of warranty in August 2004. Thus, on its face, Trans-Spec's complaint is not timely unless the warranty on which its claims are based is one that "explicitly extend[s] to future performance of the goods" and the circumstances are such that the " 'discovery of the breach must await' " the time of the promised future performance.

   . . .

To determine whether a warranty is one of future performance, we must look to the language of the warranty itself to determine whether it *explicitly* guarantees the future performance of the goods. For example, if a warranty states that the product "would be free from defects in materials and workmanship for a period of five years," it explicitly extends to the future performance of the goods. If, on the other hand, the warranty states "we promise to repair the product if it malfunctions within the first five years," it does not explicitly guarantee the future performance of the goods. This type of repair promise warrants the future performance of the warrantor, not the goods. The warrantor has not guaranteed that the goods will not malfunction in the future, but rather that the warrantor will remedy any problems that arise in a particular way for a limited period of time. *See, e.g.,* Flagg Energy Dev. Corp. v. General Motors Corp., 244 Conn. 126, 709 A.2d 1075, 1086 (1998) (repair or replacement clause provides buyer only the relief expressly promised and is not a promise of future performance of the goods); Tittle v. Steel City Oldsmobile GMC Truck, Inc., 544 So.2d 883, 889–91 (Ala.1989) (repair or replace language does not guarantee that goods will perform free of defects; rather it anticipates that defects will occur).

The only warranty language properly before us in considering Caterpillar's motion to dismiss is contained in the "On-Highway Vehicle Engine Extended Service Coverage" ("ESC") document, which was appended to Trans-Spec's complaint. The ESC states: "This service contract . . . provides full components and labor coverage for covered components failures due to defects in Caterpillar materials or workmanship under normal use."[6] The

---

[6]   The ESC also states that "it runs concurrently with the Caterpillar On-Highway Vehicle Engine Warranty." This sentence almost certainly refers to the "Limited Warranty" document. Although Trans-Spec refers to this document as the "two-year warranty," it actually contains language that could reasonably be construed as a five-year warranty of future performance on certain parts, including the flywheel housings: "These parts are warranted against defects in

ESC guarantees that "Caterpillar will pay 100% of the components and labor charges for covered failures, with no deductible charges" for failures occurring within the first 60 months or 500,000 miles. It specifies Caterpillar's responsibility to "restore the engine to its operating condition prior to failure by repairing/replacing only the defective components and consequential damaged components necessary to remove/repair/install the defective components."

The ESC thus never guaranteed that Caterpillar's engines would not fail; it merely warranted that Caterpillar would pay to repair them if they did fail. As such, the warranty provided in the ESC is not a warranty that explicitly extends to the future performance of the goods, and the later accrual date specified in § 2–725(2) does not apply. Thus, Trans-Spec's claims are time-barred by the four-year statute of limitations that began to run on the date of delivery of the trucks.

In reaching this conclusion, we note that some courts have interpreted a vehicle manufacturer's promise to repair or replace defective parts as capable of being breached, not at tender of delivery, but only in the event that the promised repairs are refused or unsuccessful. *See, e.g.,* Mydlach v. DaimlerChrysler Corp., 226 Ill.2d 307, 314 Ill.Dec. 760, 875 N.E.2d 1047, 1059–60 (2007) (holding that a promise to repair is not an "express warranty" and thus accrual for breach of a repair promise is not governed by § 2–725(2), which applies only to breach of warranty). These courts have held that the cause of action for breach of a repair promise accrues when the promisor fails to or refuses to repair the defects. However, this view does not prevail in Massachusetts.[7] In New England Power Co. v. Riley Stoker Corp., 20 Mass.App.Ct. 25, 477 N.E.2d 1054 (1985), the Appeals Court of Massachusetts rejected the position that a promise to repair or replace should be viewed as an independent or separate warranty. Instead, the court said that such promises "are generally viewed as specifications of a remedy" and that if the promise to repair "is not fulfilled, then the cause of action is the underlying breach of warranty." The court describes as "a fallacy" the argument that "by failing to remedy its first breach, the defendant committed a second breach, giving rise to a brand new cause of action and starting anew the limitations period." Thus, the court held that the promise to repair had no

---

material and workmanship for 60 months or 500,000 miles or 10,000 operating hours, whichever occurs first after date of delivery to the first user." Trans-Spec perhaps could have argued that this language was incorporated by reference as a result of this sentence in the ESC referring to the "Limited Warranty" document and was, as a result, integral to the complaint. However, Trans-Spec did not make such an argument and does not even point out the cross-reference in its appellate brief. Consequently, we will not consider it.

[7]   Moreover, Trans-Spec argues that the repair promise contained in the ESC constitutes a "remedy of first resort" for breach of an express warranty of future performance. Trans-Spec does not argue that the repair promise is separately enforceable. Thus, the argument has been waived.

effect on the statute of limitations for the breach of warranty. *See* id. at 1058–59.

    The ESC appears to be framed as a separate "service contract," rather than a limitation of remedy on a warranty, and could perhaps be treated as such. However, Trans-Spec styled its complaint as a claim for breach of warranty under the U.C.C., not for breach of a service contract.[8] As such, Trans-Spec's claim is subject to analysis under § 2–725(2), the U.C.C.'s statutory provision regarding the accrual of a claim for breach of warranty. Because Trans-Spec does not allege or even argue that the ESC is a separate service contract, rather than a U.C.C. express warranty, we will not treat it as such for the purposes of our analysis. *Cf.* Cosman v. Ford Motor Co., 285 Ill.App.3d 250, 220 Ill.Dec. 790, 674 N.E.2d 61, 68 (1996) (dismissing a count framed in U.C.C. terms, but sustaining claim for breach of a promise to repair brought under the Magnuson-Moss Act because such a claim "cannot ripen until the promise is broken and has nothing to do with the inherent quality of the goods or their future performance").[9] As a result, any breach of which Trans-Spec is complaining must stem from an underlying U.C.C. warranty on the engines themselves. Trans-Spec has not identified, within the record properly before us, any underlying warranty guaranteeing the future performance of the goods themselves. The claim for breach therefore accrued on the date of delivery of the goods and Trans-Spec's suit, which was filed more than four years after delivery of the trucks, is time-barred.

In the penultimate paragraph of the excerpt, the court acknowledges that some courts measure the limitations period from the time the seller breaches the promise to repair rather than the time of delivery of the goods. Why does the court refuse to adopt that approach here? Is the refusal consistent with the court's reasoning on why the exception in 2–725(2) does not apply? What warranty did Caterpillar breach?

---

[8]   Service contracts, because they are not primarily concerned with the sale of goods, would fall outside the purview of the U.C.C.'s statutory scheme and would be governed by the general six-year statute of limitations and the common law contract principle that the cause of action accrues at the time the promise is breached. *See* Mass. Gen. Laws ch. 106, § 2–102 ("[T]his Article applies to transactions in goods. . . .").

[9]   Trans-Spec's complaint also alleges breach of the Magnuson-Moss Act. *See* 15 U.S.C. § 2304(a). However, that federal provision only applies to consumer goods. The Caterpillar engines in Trans-Spec's trucks are not consumer goods, and the claim was therefore dismissed below.

CHAPTER 8

SELLER'S REMEDIES FOR BREACH BY THE BUYER

A. INTRODUCTION

A buyer may breach, among other ways, by not making a payment when it is due, by repudiating the contract, or by wrongfully rejecting the goods or revoking acceptance of them. Section 2–703 is a catalog of the seller's remedies if one of these events occurs. Subsections (d) and (e) specify the principal damages remedies of the seller: resale (analogous to the buyer's cover remedy under 2–712), the contract-market differential (analogous to the buyer's damages remedy under 2–713), and the action for the price. Please read 2–703 and 2–709.

B. REMEDIES ON WRONGFUL REJECTION OR REPUDIATION

1. ACTION FOR THE PRICE

Industrial Molded Plastic Products, Inc. v. J. Gross & Son, Inc.

Pennsylvania Superior Court, 1979.
263 Pa.Super. 515, 398 A.2d 695.

■ HOFFMAN, JUDGE. This is a breach of contract action brought by Industrial Molded Plastic Products, Inc. (Industrial) against J. Gross & Son, Inc. (Gross). In a non-jury trial below, the court awarded Industrial $2,494.52 damages representing lost profits. Industrial now contends that the proper measure of damages was the contract price of the goods. Gross has cross-appealed on the issue of liability, contending that the salesman who signed the contract lacked the authority to bind the corporate entity.

Industrial is in the business of manufacturing custom injection molded plastics by specification for various manufacturers. Industrial also manufactures various "fill-in" items during slack periods, such as electronic parts, industrial components, mirror clips, and plastic clothing clips. Industrial manufactured plastic clothing clips only for its house accounts of H. Daroff & Sons and Joseph H. Cohen & Sons. Gross is a wholesaler to the retail clothing industry, selling mostly sewing thread, but also other items such as zippers, snaps, and clips. Gross sold only a small amount of plastic clothing clips, never having more than $100–$200 worth of clips in inventory at any one time.

Sometime in the fall of 1970, Mr. Stanley Waxman (Gross' President and sole stockholder) and his son Peter (a 22 year old salesman for Gross) appeared at the offices of Industrial's President, Mr. Judson T. Ulansey. They suggested to him that they might be able to market Industrial's plastic clothing clips in the retail clothing industry, in which they had an established sales force. At this initial meeting, there was no discussion of Peter Waxman's authority or lack thereof in the company. After this meeting, Stanley authorized Peter to purchase a "trial" amount of clips (not further specified) to test the market, but neither this authorization nor its limitation was communicated to Ulansey. All subsequent negotiations were between Ulansey and Peter Waxman only. Deceiving both his father and Ulansey, Peter held himself out as Vice-President of Gross, and on December 10, 1970, signed an agreement obligating Gross to purchase from Industrial five million plastic clothing clips during the calendar year of 1971, at a price of $7.50 per thousand units, delivery at Industrial's plant in Blooming Glen, Pennsylvania. Gross was granted an exclusive distributorship in the clips for the same time, excepting Industrial's two house accounts mentioned above. Before the execution of this agreement, Ulansey telephoned Stanley Waxman, who told Ulansey that Peter could act on behalf of Gross. There was no discussion of the specific terms of the agreement, such as the quantity purchased.

Industrial immediately began production of the five million clips during "fill-in" time. As they were manufactured, they were warehoused in Industrial's plant as per the contract. In February, 1971, Peter Waxman picked up and paid for 772,000 clips. Stanley Waxman, who had to sign Gross' check for payment, thought that this was the "trial amount" he had authorized Peter to buy. These were the only clips which Gross ever took into its possession. On numerous occasions during the year Ulansey urged Peter to pick up more of the clips, which were taking up more and more storage space at Industrial's plant as they were being manufactured. Peter told Ulansey that he was having difficulty selling the clips and that Gross had no warehousing capacity for the inventory that was being accumulated. At no time, however, did Peter repudiate the contract or request Industrial to halt production. By the end of 1971, production was completed and Industrial was warehousing 4,228,000 clips at its plant.

On January 19, 1972, Industrial sent Gross an invoice for the remaining clips of $31,710, less credit of $203.55, for a balance due of $31,506.45. However, Gross did not honor the invoice or pick up any more of the clips. Ulansey wrote to Stanley Waxman on February 7, 1972, requesting him to pick up the clips. Receiving no response, Ulansey wrote to Stanley Waxman again on February 23, 1972, threatening legal action if shipping instructions were not received by March 1, 1972. Finally, on March 30, 1972, Peter Waxman responded with a letter to Ulansey, which stated that Gross' failure to move the clips was due to a substantial decline in the clothing industry in 1971 and competition with new lower-cost methods of hanging and shipping clothes. The letter asked for Industrial's patience and predicted that it would take at least the rest of the year to market the clips successfully. At this point, Industrial initiated legal action. Stanley Waxman learned of the five million clip contract for the first time when informed by his lawyer of the impending lawsuit. Industrial filed its complaint in August of 1972, and at the same time Peter began an extended (four years) leave of absence from Gross.

Ulansey testified that Industrial was unable to resell any of the 4.2 million clips because of a lack of market generally. Additionally, Industrial lost its two house accounts for plastic clothing clips because Daroff went bankrupt and Cohen refused to do further business with Industrial, citing a close personal relationship with Stanley Waxman. Industrial, being a manufacturer, had no sales force to find new customers. However, Industrial did receive a small quantity of new orders from 1972 to 1976, for which new clips were manufactured.

. . .

Industrial contends that the court below erred in entering judgment based upon its lost profits, on the grounds that the proper measure of damages was the unpaid balance of the contract price. The court below limited damages to lost profits because it found in fact that Industrial "did not make a good faith or reasonable effort to resell the goods * * * nor did he demonstrate the futility of any resale attempt."

It is true that in order to maintain an action for the contract price of goods which are merely *identified,* the seller must mitigate damages or show that such effort would be unavailing. Uniform Commercial Code, 12A PS § 2–709(1)(b). However, a seller of goods is also entitled to recover the contract price due for goods *accepted* by the buyer. 12A PS § 2–709(1)(a). Under the Code, a buyer's acceptance of goods occurs, inter alia, when, after a reasonable opportunity to inspect the goods, the buyer fails to make an effective rejection of them. 12A PS § 2–606(1)(b). To preserve his rights, the seller is only obligated to tender the goods in accordance with the terms of the contract. 12A PS § 2–507(1). The seller is under no obligation to resell accepted goods in order to maintain his action for price. 12A PS § 2–709(1)(a). See generally Unlaub Co., Inc. v. Sexton, 568 F.2d 72, 76–77 (8th Cir.1977).

Here, Industrial wholly performed its obligations under the contract, manufacturing five million clips and delivering them to its plant in Blooming Glen, Pennsylvania. For over a year, Industrial entreated Gross to take possession of the growing pile of clips. Thus, Gross had ample opportunity to inspect, but never rejected the goods. In fact, even as late as March 30, 1972, Gross still indicated that it intended to market the clips, but would need more time to do so. As such, Gross accepted the clips and breached its contract by failure to pay for them. Since the goods were accepted, Industrial is entitled to the full unpaid balance of the contract price, notwithstanding its failure to attempt to resell the clips.

The order below is reversed and the court below is directed to enter judgment in favor of Industrial against Gross for $31,506.45, plus interest from January 19, 1972.

QUESTIONS AND NOTES

1. By failing to reject the clips for more than ten months, the buyer accepted them and was liable for the price. A similar result may occur even if the delay in the buyer's action is much shorter than ten months. Consider N. Bloom & Son (Antiques) Limited v. Skelly, 673 F.Supp. 1260 (S.D.N.Y.1987). In August 1985 Skelly purchased two candelabras and a centerpiece from Bloom in London, England, for $45,000, delivery at Skelly's home in Newport, R.I. Bloom's carrier, Artworld, made several attempts to deliver the goods in September but Skelly was not at home, did not authorize anyone to receive the goods on her behalf, and did not respond to Artworld's written notices of its attempts to deliver. On October 1st Skelly instructed Artworld to return the goods to Bloom. Two weeks later she informed Bloom that she was rejecting the items because an appraiser had looked at photographs of them and had informed her that they were not worth the price she had agreed to pay. Bloom sued Skelly for the price. Upholding the seller's claim, the court stated:

> Skelly contends that she never accepted the candelabras and centerpiece, and that instead she rejected them. This distinction affects the measure of damages. The measure of damages in a case of non-acceptance is the difference between the contract price and the market price at the time and place of tender, or lost profits. N.Y.U.C.C. § 2–708. In a case in which goods are accepted but not paid for, the seller may bring an action for the full contract price. N.Y.U.C.C. § 2–709(1)(a).

> N.Y.U.C.C. § 2–507(1) provides:

>> Tender of delivery is a condition to the buyer's duty to accept the goods and, unless otherwise agreed, to his duty to pay for them. *Tender entitles the seller to acceptance of the goods and to payment according to the contract.* [emphasis added]

> The requirements for an effective tender are set forth in § 2–503(1):

>> Tender of delivery requires that the seller put and hold conforming goods at the buyer's disposition and give the buyer any notification reasonably necessary to enable him to take delivery. The manner, time and place for tender are determined by the agreement and this Article, and in particular

>>> (a) tender must be at a reasonable hour, and if it is of goods they must be kept available for the period reasonably necessary to enable the buyer to take possession. . . .

Bloom, through Artworld, attempted on several occasions to deliver the candelabras and centerpiece to Skelly's home in Newport, as the parties had agreed. Although Skelly herself was not present when tender was made, she could have authorized someone else to accept delivery on her behalf. She could also have responded to the notices left by Artworld, in order to arrange a time for delivery when she would be present. She did neither because she had decided not to accept delivery. Since Bloom made proper tender of the goods pursuant to § 2–503(1), it is entitled to acceptance pursuant to § 2–507(1).

Acceptance is also governed by § 2–606(1), which provides:

> Acceptance of goods occurs when the buyer . . .

> (b) fails to make an effective rejection (subsection (1) of Section 2–602), but such acceptance does not occur until the buyer has had a reasonable opportunity to inspect them. . . .

Section 2–602(1) mandates that "[r]ejection of goods must be within a reasonable time after their . . . tender." The determination of what constitutes a reasonable time period depends on the particular circumstances of each case and is generally a question of fact. In this case, Skelly, after being informed of Artworld's attempts to deliver the candelabras and centerpiece throughout September 1985, did not take any active steps to reject them until October 1. Under the circumstances, this was not within a "reasonable time" after tender under § 2–602(1). During the month of September 1985, Skelly did have a "reasonable opportunity to inspect" the goods under § 2–606(1). Skelly proffered no good reason for her repeated failure to take delivery of the goods. Had she done so, an inspection could have been accomplished in a matter of minutes.

Skelly's argument that she cannot be held to have accepted the goods because she did not inspect them, as she has a right to do under N.Y.U.C.C. § 2–513, is untenable. Section 2–513(1), like the N.Y.U.C.C. provisions discussed above, provides a right of inspection "at any reasonable place and time and in any reasonable manner." This provision does not mean that if a buyer chooses not to inspect the goods, she thereby acquires a defense of non-inspection. By refusing to respond to Artworld's repeated attempts at delivery, Skelly gave up her right of inspection, and thus accepted the goods. Under N.Y.U.C.C. § 2–709(1)(a), the amount Bloom may recover is therefore the full contract price of $45,000.

2.   If the buyer has received conforming goods and refuses or fails to pay for them, it makes sense for 2–709 to give the seller an action for the price. But in neither *Industrial Molded Plastic Products* nor *N. Bloom & Son* did the buyer have the goods or want the goods. Granted, the buyers breached, and the sellers are entitled to damages to place them in their expectancy positions. But they still have the goods and presumably can resell them to other buyers. What, then, is the sense in saying that they can recover the price?

3. What could the buyers in these cases have done to avoid being held liable for the price?

4.   Problem. Roseanne contracted with Furrier for a natural, alabaster-colored mink coat to be specially made for her in an extra large size and with an unusually large flare, for $7,500. After the coat was completed, she announced that she no longer desired it. Furrier made no effort to resell the coat, but sued for the price. Is he entitled to it?

5.   Problem. Samuels Manufacturing Co., of Denver, Colorado, contracted to sell 5,000 electric knives to Brandt, a large retailer located in Phoenix, at a price of $50,000. A half hour after delivery at Brandt's warehouse in Phoenix, Brandt sent Samuels an e-mail stating that the knives were being rejected because the handles were not the proper color. In fact, the knives conformed to the contract in every respect. May Samuels recover the price of the knives from Brandt? Are 2–401(2) and (4) relevant?

6.   Problem. Assume that Brandt's trademark had been molded into the handles of the knives. Would 2–709(1)(b) enable Samuels to recover the price?

(In connection with this question, consider McCoy v. Mitsuboshi Cutlery, Inc., 67 F.3d 917 (Fed.Cir.1995). The holder of a patent on a shrimp knife contracted for a manufacturer to fabricate and deliver 150,000 of the knives. When the buyer refused to accept delivery of the knives or pay for them, the seller resold them to another. In rejecting the buyer's claim that the seller had violated its patent, the court held that the seller had an implied license to sell and was not liable for violating the buyer's patent. How does this case affect Samuels' right to recover the price?)

Would it help Brandt to point to 2–608? See 2–709(3).

7.   Problem. Cooper Construction purchased a John Deere backhoe from Foley Equipment Sales for $90,000, paying $9,000 at the time of contract formation and agreeing to pay the balance 30 days after delivery. Cooper painted its name on the side of the backhoe and began using it. Three weeks later the stabilizer arms—which extend perpendicular to the sides of the backhoe to keep it from rocking—ceased working. This made operation of the backhoe very dangerous. Cooper informed Foley of the problem and demanded a new backhoe. Foley refused to take it back, pointed to the exclusive repair-or-replace remedy in their contract, and told Cooper to contact the manufacturer. Cooper replied that it did not want a repaired backhoe, it wanted a new replacement. Foley refused to accept return of the backhoe and demanded payment of the balance of the price. Cooper ceased using the backhoe and refused to pay the balance. Foley sued for $81,000, and Cooper counterclaimed for refund of its down payment. Who wins? See 2–709, Official Comment 5. Of what relevance, if any, is 2–709(3)? 2–608?

8.   Leases. Problem. Equipment Rentals leased to World Paving a road-grading machine for 24 months at a rental of $2,000 per month. The contract provided, "If Lessee fails to make any monthly payment within 30 days of the date it is due, Lessor has the option to treat the transaction as a sale of the machine to Lessee for $84,000" (which was the price that Equipment Rentals had paid to acquire the machine). After nine months, World Paving defaulted, and Equipment Rentals now sues. If Equipment Rentals does not assert any rights under the treat-as-a-sale provision, what is its remedy? See 2A–529.

If Equipment Rentals does assert rights under that provision, what is its remedy? Is the contract provision enforceable? See 2A–503, 2A–504, 2A–523, 2A–528, 2A–529.

Suppose Equipment Rentals argues that the provision is enforceable, that World Paving cannot rightfully reject the goods after nine months, and that, therefore, Equipment Rentals is entitled to the price. What is its remedy? See 2A–529.

Suppose Equipment Rentals argues that the provision is enforceable but agrees that it will take back the machine and sue for its damages as seller. Is the clause enforceable? See 2A–503, 2A–504, 2A–523.

9.   CISG. Article 62 of the Convention on Contracts for the International Sale of Goods provides "The seller may require the buyer to pay the price, take delivery or perform his other obligations, unless the seller has resorted to a remedy which is inconsistent with this requirement." Therefore, the basic rule of CISG is the direct opposite of the Article 2 rule. (See Official Comment 6 to 2–709.) As noted earlier, however, CISG Article 28 provides that a state does not have to grant specific performance of the contract if it would not do so under similar circumstances under its own law. See also Articles 85 and 88. It may be doubted whether in practice there are any significant number of cases in which international sellers would try to force goods on buyers if the buyer repudiates before the goods have been shipped. If the goods have been shipped, the widespread use of letters of credit moots the issue. A letter of credit represents an irrevocable commitment of a third party to pay the seller upon presentation of documents showing shipment of goods. Hence, buyers in international transactions cannot avoid paying the price by rejecting the goods. Chapter 12 provides an introduction to letters of credit.

2.   ACTION FOR DAMAGES

As the problems in the preceding section indicate, the seller has only a very limited right to recover the price from a reluctant buyer who does not have the goods. Notice, by the way, that passage of title has nothing to do with the seller's right to recover the price, as 2–401 provides, "Each provision of this Article with regard to the rights, obligations and remedies of the seller, the buyer, purchasers or other third parties applies irrespective of title to the goods except where the provision refers to such title." Therefore, even if title already has passed to the buyer, the seller can recover the price and force the goods on the buyer only in the situations described in 2–709.

The seller's basic remedy, then, for a buyer's unjustified rejection of goods is recovery of damages (as distinguished from recovery of the price), and in recovering damages, the seller typically has the choice of two measures:

> (1) the contract price less the market price at the time and place for tender, under 2–708(1), or

> (2) upon resale of the goods to another buyer, the contract price less the resale price, under 2–706.

Alternatively, in some circumstances the seller is entitled to recover the lost profit on the transaction, under 2–708(2). What are those circumstances? Please read 2–708.

QUESTIONS

1. Problem. On February 1 of last year, Pants, a manufacturer of clothing, contracted to purchase 60,000 yards of gabardine fabric from Semke Mills, a fabric mill, for $3.00 per yard. Semke agreed to deliver 10,000 yards of the material every six months, on April 1 and October 1, commencing April 1 of last year. Pants agreed to pay for each installment no later than 30 days after delivery. On April 1 Semke delivered and in due course Pants paid for 10,000 yards. On October 1 Semke delivered another 10,000 yards, which Pants accepted. Two weeks later, on October 15, Pants informed Semke that it had decided to cease manufacturing gabardine pants and would not take any more of the fabric. On March 1 of the current year, Semke sued.

a. The market price of gabardine fabric varied over time, as follows:

February 1: $2.95 per yard

April 1: $2.90

October 1: $2.85

October 15: $2.65

March 1: $2.75.

How should Seller's damages be measured?

b. When Pants repudiated the contract, Semke ceased manufacturing gabardine. Assume that Pants can prove that if Semke had completed manufacturing the gabardine for Buyer, its costs of production would have been $2.80 per yard. Should Seller recover $.20 per yard for the fabric that was never delivered? What arguments would you make on behalf of each party?

c. In 2–713(1) how does the phrase, "less expenses saved in consequence of the buyer's breach," affect the answer to Problem a?

2. Problem. On November 20 Vijay contracted to purchase a new Toyota Avalon from Tran's Toyotas for $36,000, delivery on December 1st, the day after he was to receive his annual bonus. On November 26th Vijay decided he would rather have a Buick and therefore failed to return to Tran's lot on December 1st. When Tran phoned him, he explained that he no longer wanted the car. Tran insisted that he complete the purchase, but Vijay was adamant. Tran informed him, "I'm holding you responsible for the car, and if you don't pick it up and pay me by December 7th, I'll sell it to someone else and hold you responsible for my damages." On January 20th Tran sold the car at an auction attended by dealers from a four-state region. The successful bidder paid $28,000, of which the auction company retained $300 for its services in selling the car. How should Tran's Toyotas' recovery be measured?

3.   Problem. Barkley's Bar & Grill contracted to purchase a large-screen TV from TV Barn, for $2,600. When the seller's delivery truck arrived with the TV, Barkley stated that he had found a better TV at a lower price, and he refused to accept the TV. The truck driver took the TV back to the store. Without further communicating with Barkley's, TV Barn sold the TV during its semiannual clearance sale, for $2,000. How should TV Barn's damages be measured?

4. Proof of the market price at the relevant time may be difficult. For long-term contracts 2–723 helps to ease the difficulties of proof. Alternatively, the seller may avoid the problem by reselling the goods under 2–706 and recovering damages based on the resale price rather than the market price. Notice the specific requirements for that resale, especially the requirement that the seller notify the breaching buyer of the anticipated sale.

5.   Problem. Chemco has a contract to purchase its requirements of gasoline additive for $400 per ton. Chemco contracted to sell Chevron 1,000 tons of the gasoline additive for $450 per ton. Before Chemco delivered any of the additive to Chevron, the market price dropped to $350 per ton and Chevron repudiated the contract. If Chemco sues, how should its damages be measured?

Peace River Seed Co-Operative, Ltd. v.
Proseeds Marketing, Inc.
Oregon Supreme Court, 2014.
355 Or.44, 322 P.3d 531.

■ BALMER, C.J.

. . .

The facts material to our discussion are mostly undisputed. Peace River Seed Co-Operative ("plaintiff") is a Canadian company that buys grass seed from and sells grass seed for grass seed producers. Proseeds Marketing ("defendant") is an Oregon corporation that purchases grass seed from various sources to resell to end users. A broker prepared and the parties agreed to multiple contracts for defendant to purchase from plaintiff the total production of grass seed from a certain number of acres for a fixed price over a period of two years. The contracts incorporated the NORAMSEED Rules for the Trade of Seeds for Planting, which have been adopted by the American and Canadian Seed Trade Associations to govern the trade of seed. The NORAMSEED Rules provide that the UCC applies to transactions within the United States, and both parties have litigated this case under the UCC.

Under the contracts, defendant was to provide shipping and delivery instructions to plaintiff. During the contract period, however, the price of grass seed fell dramatically. Although defendant initially provided shipping instructions and plaintiff shipped conforming seed, defendant eventually refused to provide shipping instructions for delivery of additional seed under the contracts. After multiple requests for shipping instructions, and defendant's continued refusal to provide them, plaintiff cancelled the contracts. Over the next three years, plaintiff was able to sell at least some of the seed that defendant had agreed to purchase to other buyers.

. . . In [a] bench trial, the court concluded that defendant had breached the contracts and that plaintiff had been entitled to cancel the contracts and seek damages. When the trial court awarded plaintiff its damages, the court noted that the parties had entered into fixed price contracts, "regardless of the market price at the time of harvest and shipment," and the court explained that "[e]ach party takes certain risks and hopes for certain benefits in this type of a contract." Nonetheless, the court concluded that plaintiff had an "obligation to mitigate damages" and was "not entitled to recover damages in an amount greater than actually incurred." Accordingly, the trial court awarded plaintiff the lesser of two measures of damages: the difference between the unpaid contract price and the market price (the measure under ORS 72.7080(1)) or the difference between the contract price and the resale price (the measure under ORS 72.7060). The trial court directed [the parties] to submit calculations of each measure of damages.

. . .

Each party's calculation of damages for one of the breached contracts, contract 1874, illustrates the implications of using the market price or the resale price to calculate damages. The evidence at trial showed that the contract price for contract 1874 was $0.72 per pound. Plaintiff sought damages of $3,736.00 for that contract, apparently based on a market price of $0.64 per pound, resulting in a contract price minus market price differential of $0.08 per pound for 46,700 pounds of seed not accepted by defendant. Defendant argued, however, that plaintiff had resold at least some of that seed for $0.75 per pound, $0.03 per pound above the contract price and $0.11 per pound above plaintiff's market price calculation. Thus, according to defendant, plaintiff did not have any damages for that resold seed because plaintiff had resold for more than the contract price. If plaintiff recovered $0.08 per pound in market price damages, in addition to the $0.75 per pound that plaintiff allegedly had received on the resale, plaintiff ultimately would recover $0.83 per pound, which was $0.11 more than the contract price.[2]

---

[2] Even if plaintiff could not recover its market price damages, plaintiff would have received $0.03 per pound more than the contract price because plaintiff allegedly resold for more than the contract price. That is a result, however, that the UCC explicitly allows. *See* ORS 72.7060(6) ("The seller is not accountable to the buyer for any profit made on any resale.").

For that same contract, however, where the contract price was $0.72 per pound, defendant noted that some of the seed had been resold for $0.60 per pound. That meant that the resale price damages would be $0.12 per pound. That is, for at least some of the resold seed from contract 1874, plaintiff's resale price damages of $0.12 per pound would exceed plaintiff's claimed market price damages of $0.08 per pound. In sum, the parties' calculations of damages for contract 1874 showed that, with regard to some seed, the market price damage calculation would lead to a larger award, but that, with regard to other seed, the resale price damage calculation would lead to a larger award. On the whole, however, defendant calculated that plaintiff would receive a smaller amount of damages using the resale price measure of damages than plaintiff calculated that it would receive using the market price measure of damages.

The trial court awarded plaintiff damages using the resale price measure of damages as calculated by defendant. . . . Plaintiff appealed. . . .

The Court of Appeals reversed and remanded. . . . [T]he court noted that, at least on its face, the UCC allows a seller to recover damages as calculated under either ORS 72.7060 (contract price less resale price) or ORS 72.7080(1) (contract price less market price). After reviewing the relevant statutory provisions, the court went on to conclude that, "[i]n the absence of a restriction within the UCC that precludes an aggrieved seller from seeking its remedy pursuant to ORS 72.7080 if the seller has resold, we would decline to impose such a restriction." In support of that conclusion, the court explained that, once the buyer breaches, the buyer loses any right to control the goods or to "insist upon a different measure of damages." . . . Defendant sought review and now urges this court to reverse the Court of Appeals and affirm the trial court . . . .

AN AGGRIEVED SELLER'S REMEDIES UNDER THE UCC

The UCC provides a variety of remedies to an aggrieved seller. *See* ORS 72.7030 (providing an index of a seller's remedies). As noted, the issue in this case is whether an aggrieved seller who has resold goods can recover the difference between the unpaid contract price and the market price under ORS 72.7080(1), even when market price damages would exceed resale price damages under ORS 72.7060.

Commentators and courts have taken two different approaches to this issue. Relying on the text and context of the sellers' remedies provisions, some commentators have argued that the drafters of the UCC intended for sellers to be able to recover either market price damages or resale price damages, even if the seller resold the goods for more than the market price. *See, e.g.,* Henry Gabriel, *The Seller's Election of Remedies Under the Uniform Commercial Code: An Expectation Theory,* 23 Wake Forest L Rev 429, 429 (1988) (arguing that an aggrieved seller "should be allowed to elect between the two remedies regardless of the seller's good faith post-breach activities concerning the non-accepted goods"); Ellen A.

Peters, *Remedies for Breach of Contracts Relating to the Sale of Goods Under the Uniform Commercial Code: A Roadmap for Article Two,* 73 Yale LJ 199, 260 (1963) (arguing for a "non-restrictive reading of the various remedies sections to preserve full options to use or to ignore substitute transactions as a measure of damages"). On the other hand, Professors White and Summers, whose view has been adopted by a number of courts, have argued that the UCC's general policy is that damages should put a seller only in "as good a position as if the other party had fully performed," ORS 71.3050(1), meaning a seller who has resold should not be allowed to recover more in market price damages than it could recover in resale price damages. James J. White, Robert S. Summers and Robert A. Hillman, 1 *Uniform Commercial Code* § 8:13, 689 (6th ed 2012) (so stating). We agree with those commentators who have observed that the drafters did not clearly resolve this issue. *See, e.g., id.* at 691 (noting that the UCC and the comments are "equivocal" about whether a seller can recover more under section 2–708(1) than it could recover under section 2–706); Gabriel, 23 Wake Forest L Rev at 430 (noting "the failure of the drafters to clearly resolve the problem of election between sections 2–706 and 2–708(1)"). Nonetheless, we conclude that the text, context, and legislative history of the sellers' remedies provisions support a seller's right to recover either market price damages or resale price damages, even if market price damages lead to a larger recovery.

We analyze the relevant statutory provisions using the framework described in *State v. Gaines,* 346 Or. 160, 171–72, 206 P.3d 1042 (2009). We begin by examining the statute's text and context to determine the legislature's intent regarding a seller's remedies under the UCC. Because the relevant statutes are part of the UCC, we also consider the official UCC comments as an indication of the legislature's intent. *Security Bank v. Chiapuzio,* 304 Or. 438, 445 n. 6, 747 P.2d 335 (1987) (noting that the Oregon legislature took note of the official comments of the UCC, which are "statements of the purpose of each section"). In addition, "the legislative intent to make the UCC a uniform code makes relevant the decisions of other courts that have examined these questions and the discussions of the questions by scholars in the field, especially those scholars who participated in drafting the UCC." *Id.* We also examine legislative history. The Oregon legislature enacted the UCC in 1961 "with little debate or discussion of the legislative intent," but the UCC was proposed so that Oregon could "obtain the same advantages that other states had gained from the adoption of a uniform and comprehensive set of commercial statutes." *Id.* Given "the legislative intent to make the UCC a uniform code," *id.,* we consider prior drafts of the UCC, as drafted by the National Conference of Commissioners on Uniform State Laws (NCCUSL), as part of the legislative history. *Cf. Datt v. Hill,* 347 Or. 672, 680, 227 P.3d 714 (2010) (examining history of uniform act in interpreting Oregon statute taken from that act).

Before examining the statutory scheme, however, we briefly review the law as it existed prior to the enactment of the UCC in Oregon. At common law, an aggrieved seller

"ha[d] the election of three remedies: (1) To hold the property for the purchaser, and to recover of him the entire purchase money; (2) to sell it, after notice to the purchaser, as his agent for that purpose, and recover the difference between the contract price and that realized on the sale; (3) to retain it as his own, and recover the difference between the contract and market prices at the time and place of delivery[.]"

Krebs Hop Co. v. Livesley, 59 Or. 574, 588, 118 P. 165 (1911). *Krebs Hop Co.* suggests that, before Oregon adopted the UCC, an aggrieved seller had to elect between remedies, and if the seller resold the goods, it had elected its remedy and could recover only resale price damages, but not market price damages. *See* Gabriel, 23 Wake Forest L Rev at 446 (explaining that, under pre-UCC law, an aggrieved seller who resold the goods was assumed to have elected the resale remedy and was barred from using an inconsistent remedy, such as market price damages). Although the UCC retained some aspect of each of the remedies available at common law, as explained below, it specifically rejected the doctrine of election of remedies. *See* Legislative Comment 1 to ORS 72.7030, *reprinted in* Legislative Counsel Committee, *Oregon's Uniform Commercial Code with Comments and Index and Tables* 101 (1962) (noting that the UCC chapter on sales "reject[s] any doctrine of election of remedy as a fundamental policy"); Peters, 73 Yale LJ at 204 n 16 (noting that many sections of the UCC were "designed to mitigate the effect of prior law insofar as it forced a choice of remedy on the party aggrieved without regard to the adequacy of compensation"). . . .

[ORS 72.7030] lists the seller's remedies, which, as relevant here, include resale price damages, ORS 72.7060, and market price damages, ORS 72.7080. Moreover, it lists those remedies without any limiting conjunction, such as "or," that might suggest that the remedies are mutually exclusive. In contrast, a similar index of a buyer's remedies after a seller's breach provides that the buyer may "(a) 'Cover' and have damages * * * *or* (b) Recover damages for nondelivery." ORS 72.7110(1) (emphasis added.) Thus, although the buyer's index of remedies suggests that a buyer who covers may be precluded from seeking market price damages, the seller's index of remedies does not contain a similar limitation if the seller chooses to resell. It follows that the text of ORS 72.7030 supports plaintiff's argument that a seller who has resold is not necessarily limited to its resale price damages under ORS 72.7060, but has the option of seeking to recover market price damages under ORS 72.7080.

The UCC comments to the statute describing a seller's remedies confirm that interpretation. Although the comments acknowledge that, in a particular case, the pursuit of one remedy may prevent a seller from

526 OF BREACH BY THE BUYER

obtaining certain damages, the comments also state that the UCC chapter on sales "reject[s] any doctrine of election of remedy as a fundamental policy and thus the remedies are essentially cumulative in nature and include all of the available remedies for breach." Legislative Comment 1 to ORS 72.7030 at 101; *id.* ("Whether the pursuit of one remedy bars another depends entirely on the facts of the individual case."). In contrast, the comments to the statute describing a buyer's market price remedy explain that that remedy "is completely alternative to 'cover' under ORS 72.7120 and applies *only when and to the extent that the buyer has not covered.*" Legislative Comment 5 to ORS 72.7130 at 110 (emphasis added). Thus, while the comments to the statute describing a seller's remedies expressly reject the doctrine of election of remedies, the comments to the statute describing a buyer's market price remedy appear to adopt that doctrine. Those comments further indicate that a seller who resells goods after a buyer's breach would not be considered to have "elected" the resale remedy and thus would not be precluded from seeking a larger damage recovery using the market price measure of damages.

The text of ORS 72.7060, which sets forth the seller's resale remedy, similarly suggests that a seller who resells goods is not necessarily precluded from using the market price measure of damages, even if it leads to a larger recovery. ORS 72.7060(1) states that "the seller *may* resell the goods concerned or the undelivered balance thereof," which suggests that an aggrieved seller is not required to resell. (Emphasis added.) . . . Similarly, the text of ORS 72.7060 indicates that a seller who resells is not required to seek damages using the resale remedy. *See* ORS 72.7060(1) ("Where the resale is made in good faith and in a commercially reasonable manner the seller *may* recover the difference between the resale price and the contract price * * *." (Emphasis added.)). In fact, the unqualified text of ORS 72.7080(1) seems to suggest that market price is in fact the default measure of damages. *See* ORS 72.7080(1) ("Subject to * * * the provisions of ORS 72.7230 with respect to proof of market price, *the* measure of damages for nonacceptance or repudiation by the buyer is the difference between the market price at the time and place for tender and the unpaid contract price * * *." (Emphasis added.)). Thus, the text of the remedy provisions does not limit a seller who resells to its resale price damages.

As defendant notes, however, one of the comments to ORS 72.7060 does indicate that the drafters intended ORS 72.7060 to be a seller's primary remedy, and did not intend to allow a seller to recover more under the market price remedy. Comment 2 to ORS 72.7060 explains that "[f]ailure to act properly under ORS 72.7060 *deprives* the seller of the measure of damages there provided and *relegates* him to that provided in ORS 72.7080 [market price damages]." Legislative Comment 2 to ORS 72.7060 at 104 (emphasis added). That language suggests that the comment drafters viewed market price damages as less favorable, but it does not indicate *why* they viewed them that way. The pejorative language used in the comments does not necessarily lead to the conclusion that a seller who resells cannot use the market price remedy or must use the resale price remedy if it would yield the same or a smaller amount of damages than the market price remedy. That language instead could indicate that market price damages are considered less favorable because market price is often hard to prove, as many commentators have noted. . . . As a result, that comment language is not dispositive, particularly in light of the text of the remedy provisions.

Turning to legislative history, prior drafts of the UCC provide additional insight into the drafters' intent to allow a seller to recover its market price damages, even if the seller has resold. In particular, in an earlier draft of the section describing the resale price remedy, section 2–706, one of the comments stated that that section provided

> " 'the *exclusive* measure of the seller's damages where the resale has been made in accordance with the requirements of this section. Evidence of market or current prices at any particular time or place is relevant *only* on the question of whether the seller acted with commercially reasonable care and judgment in making the resale.' "

See Gabriel, 23 Wake Forest L Rev at 436 (quoting UCC § 2–706 cmt 3 (May 1949 Draft) (emphasis added)). Under that version of the UCC, a seller who had met the resale requirements would be required to use the resale price measure of damages. That comment later was revised, however, and when Oregon adopted the UCC, the comment included language that also had been in the 1949 draft comment, but the mandatory language had been removed, leaving only the permissive wording: "If the seller complies with the prescribed standard of duty in making the resale, he *may* recover from the buyer the damages provided for in subsection (1)." Legislative Comment 3 to ORS 72.7060 at 104 (emphasis added). That shift, from resale as the exclusive remedy to resale as a permissible remedy, indicates that the drafters intended for a seller to be able to choose to recover market price damages, even after reselling under ORS 72.7060.

Defendant argues, however, that even if a seller who resells can recover market price damages under ORS 72.7080(1), those damages cannot exceed the seller's resale price damages. Defendant primarily relies on the general policy statement set forth in ORS 71.3050 to support its argument. ORS 71.3050(1) provides,

> "The remedies provided by the Uniform Commercial Code must be liberally administered to the end that the aggrieved party may be put *in as good a position as if the other party had fully performed* but consequential damages, special damages or penal damages may not be had except as specifically provided in the Uniform Commercial Code or by other rule of law."

(Emphasis added.) Defendant reasons that the reference in ORS 71.3050(1) to putting an aggrieved party "in as good a position as if the other party had fully performed" acts as a limit on the damages that a party can receive. Commentators and courts likewise have relied on that provision in concluding that a seller's market price damages should be limited to the actual loss suffered, by taking into account any goods that have been resold. *See, e.g.,* White, Summers and Hillman, 1 *Uniform Commercial Code* § 8:13 at 689 ("We conclude that a seller should not be permitted to recover more under 2–708(1) [market price damages] than under 2–706 [resale price damages] * * *. Section 1–305 indicates that a seller who has resold may not invoke 2–708(1).").

The text of ORS 71.3050(1) indicates that the drafters of the UCC intended a seller's remedies to be compensatory. *See* Legislative Comment 1 to *former* ORS 71.1060 at 6 (1963), *amended and renumbered as* ORS 71.3050 (2009) (noting that statute is intended to "make it clear that compensatory damages are limited to compensation"). The text of that section, however, also provides that the remedies in the UCC are to be "liberally administered." ORS 71.3050(1); *see also* Legislative Comment 4 to ORS 72.7030 at 101 ("It should also be noted that the Uniform Commercial Code requires its remedies to be liberally administered * * *."). Nonetheless, we agree with defendant that the general policy of compensation provided in ORS 71.3050(1) must be taken into account.

We do not agree, however, that that policy necessarily limits an aggrieved seller who has resold to its resale price damages. Defendant argues that if it had fully performed, plaintiff could expect to recover only the contract price, and that limiting plaintiff to the difference between the contract price and the resale price therefore gives it the benefit of its bargain. As Professor Gabriel notes, however, limiting a seller to its resale price damages does not account fully for either party's expectations upon entering into the contract. He explains that a seller expects to be able to recover the difference between the contract price and the market price because it is the "logical and expected measure of damages," and because the ability to recover market price damages "is the natural assumption the seller makes in return for the risk inherent in the contract that the sale may not turn out to be economically beneficial to the seller. That the seller then resells the goods in no way diminishes this expectancy regarding the first contract." *Gabriel,* 23 Wake Forest L Rev at 449, 453. From the buyer's perspective, he argues that "the [buyer] has specific obligations and will suffer the consequences of the failure to perform these obligations because this is the [buyer's] expectation." *Id.* at 450. In other words, contrary to defendant's argument, an aggrieved seller expects to be able to recover market price damages under the contract, and a breaching buyer expects to have to fulfill its obligation to the seller—even if a seller resells and recovers market price damages, "the buyer's obligation is no more than the right the buyer originally conferred upon the seller." *Id.* at 449.

Moreover, limiting an aggrieved seller to its resale price damages ignores the risk for which the parties bargained. When parties bargain for fixed price contracts, each party assumes the risk of market price fluctuations. The parties are willing to take that risk because of the benefits that they might receive: if the market price decreases, the seller benefits, and if the market price increases, the buyer benefits. In a fixed price contract, therefore, market price damages represent the risk for which both parties bargained. *Cf. id.* ("The logical and expected measure of damages is the contract price-market price differential. *This measure of damages is the risk the buyer assumed by entering into the contract;* it is the right conferred upon the seller by the buyer." (Emphasis added.)).[8] For those reasons, we conclude that a seller can recover market price damages, even if the seller resells some of the goods at above the market price at the time and place for tender.

. . .

In sum, when viewed in light of the bargained-for market risks and the UCC's rejection of the doctrine of election of remedies, the text, context, and legislative history of the sellers' remedy provisions demonstrate that an aggrieved seller can seek damages under either ORS 72.7080(1) or ORS 72.7060. That means that an aggrieved seller can seek damages under ORS 72.7080(1) even if the seller has resold the goods and market price damages exceed resale price damages.

Returning to the facts of this case, the trial court limited plaintiff's damages to resale price damages under ORS 72.7060. We have determined that plaintiff is entitled to market price damages under ORS 72.7080(1). . . . [Therefore,] on remand, the trial court should award plaintiff its market price damages . . . .

QUESTIONS AND NOTES

1. To be entitled to recover under 2–706, a seller must comply with the procedural requirements of subsections (2)–(4): the seller must give proper notice to the buyer and must identify the sale as relating to the buyer's goods. There is no indication in *Peace River* that the seller complied with the

---

[8] Professor Gabriel's explanation also responds to the argument that to permit a seller to recover market price damages when it has resold some or all of the goods confers an improper "windfall" on the seller. If a seller is limited to its resale price damages, it is just as accurate to say that the breaching buyer has received a "windfall," because the seller's success in reselling reduces the damages that the buyer must pay—and not because of anything the buyer did, but only because of the seller's successful efforts. As discussed in the text, the UCC imposes no obligation on the seller to resell, and the buyer's expectation, at the time the buyer entered into the contract, was that it might have to pay market price damages if it breached the contract. The point is not that one party or the other gets an undeserved "windfall," but rather that the provisions of the UCC, as we have interpreted them here, determine the rights and obligations of each party and therefore what is expected of each party and what each may expect of the other, as well as the consequences of either party's breach. The result we reach here is consistent with those expectations. *See generally Gabriel,* 23 Wake Forest L Rev at 453.

procedural requirements of 2–706. Would it not have been much simpler (and shorter) for the court to have rested its decision on the seller's failure to comply with these requirements? Why do you suppose it did not?

2.   The court carefully contrasts the language of 2–703, which catalogs the seller's remedies, with the language of 2–711, which catalogs the buyer's remedies. It states that 2–711 gives the buyer two alternatives, only one of which is available in any given case; it contrasts this with 2–703, which lists several alternatives for the seller without any indication that the seller is limited to only one (and indeed, with Official Comment 1 explicitly rejecting any doctrine of election of remedies). This may not be an appropriate comparison, however, because the structure of the two sections is slightly different. Section 2–703, lists the various triggers to the seller's remedies and then lists all the remedies, some of which may be resorted to simultaneously. Section 2–711, however, includes some of the buyer's remedies in the same passage as the list of triggers, viz., cancellation and recovery of any part of the price already paid. Hence, the buyer is not foreclosed from one remedy, e.g., market-contract damages, even though it has chosen to cancel the contract and/or sought recovery of a down payment. The buyer's remedies, too, are "essentially cumulative in nature," to quote the Official Comment to 2–703.

Similarly, the court notes that the language of 2–706 is permissive: the seller may resell . . . and may recover the difference between the resale price and contract price." But the language of 2–712 is equally permissive, "the buyer may 'cover' [and] may recover . . . the difference between the cost of cover and the contract price." Thus, neither party is required to engage in a substitute transaction when the other party breaches. The question is how to measure damages if the aggrieved party actually does form a substitute transaction. How should that question be answered?

3.   Official Comment 2 to 2–706 states that if the seller resells but fails to comply with the procedural requirements of that section the seller is "relegate[d]" to damages under 2–708. What does this reveal about the drafters' intention?

4.   Problem 5, page 521, is based on Nobs Chemical, U.S.A., Inc. v. Koppers Co., Inc., 616 F.2d 212 (5th Cir.1980), in which the seller had a fixed-price contract to obtain its supply of the goods that it contracted to sell to the buyer. The market price plunged below the price that the seller had with its supplier (and therefore much below the contract price with the buyer). The buyer breached, and the seller did not need to acquire the goods from its supplier. The seller sued to recover under 2–708(1) for the contract-market differential, and the buyer sought to limit the seller's recovery to its lost profits, the excess of the contract price over the price at which it would have acquired the goods from its supplier. The court, agreed, holding that the seller could recover only its lost profit, not the larger contract-market differential.

5.   Professor Gabriel (last paragraph on page 528) refers to the expectations of the parties and asserts that the seller's expectation is to be able to recover the excess of the contract price over the market price and this "is the natural

assumption the seller makes" in return for the inherent risk that the market price at the time of tender will be higher than the contract price. To similar effect is the opinion of the court in Trans World Metals, Inc. v. Southwire Co., 769 F.2d 902, 908–09 (2d Cir.1985), where the facts were similar to *Nobs Chemical*, in that the seller did not resell any goods after the buyer breached, but different in that the seller's costs of performance were not fixed by a contract with a third party.

> The contract at issue in this case is an aluminum supply contract entered into eight months prior to the initial deliveries called for by its terms. The last of the anticipated deliveries of aluminum would not have been completed until a full twenty months after the negotiations took place. It simply could not have escaped these parties that they were betting on which way aluminum prices would move. Trans World took the risk that the price would rise; Southwire took the risk that the price would fall. Under these circumstances, Trans World should not be denied the benefit of its bargain, as reflected by the contract/market price differential. . . . [T]he benefit of the bargain under a completed contract would have been affected by the fall in aluminum prices. Because Trans World accepted the risk that prices would rise, it is entitled to benefit from their fall.

Professor Gabriel and the *Trans World* court emphasize the parties' expectations and the risks allocated by the contract. Be that as it may, what is the objective of the courts when they are called upon to intervene and assign a remedy to redress the aggrieved party's injury?

6.   Leases. Section 2A–528, the analog of 2–708, contains the same ambiguity concerning the relationship between a recovery based on resale and a recovery of lost profits, but Official Comment 4 to 2A–501 tilts Article 2A away from the result in *Peace River*. Subsection (4), on which that Comment is based, provides: "Except as otherwise provided in Section 1–305(a) or this Article or the lease agreement, the rights and remedies referred to in subsections (2) and (3) are cumulative." Section 1–305(a) provides that the remedies provided by Code are to be "liberally administered to the end that the aggrieved party may be put in as good a position as if the other party had fully performed. . . ." Official Comment 4 interprets the reference to 1–305(a) as denying a party the right to cumulation of, or selection among, remedies if the result would be to place the aggrieved party in a better position than it would have been in had there been full performance. Of course, it could be argued that 1–305(a) says only that an aggrieved party should never recover less than the amount that is necessary to put that aggrieved party in as good a position as if the other party had performed, and does not address the issue whether the aggrieved party might ever recover more than the amount necessary to attain expectancy.

7.   CISG. Article 75 of the Convention on Contracts for the International Sale of Goods provides a much simpler substitute-transaction based remedy. It merely provides that if, "in a reasonable manner and within a reasonable time . . . the buyer has bought goods in replacement or the seller has resold the goods, the party claiming damages may recover the difference between the contract price and the price in the substitute transaction as well as any further damages recoverable under Article 74." If there has not been a substitute transaction, Article 76 provides that the aggrieved party may measure damages by the difference between the contract price and the "current" price. In either case, the aggrieved party may also recover other damages, such as lost profit, limited by rules dealing with foreseeability (Article 74) and mitigation of damages (Article 77).

8.　Problem 4, page 518 revisited. What if Roseanne repudiated the contract for the mink coat before Furrier had completed making it? Indeed, assume that the repudiation occurred after Furrier had taken all the appropriate measurements and made a pattern for the coat, but before he had acquired the materials needed to make it. Is Furrier entitled to the price under 2–709? Why or why not? If not, what is Furrier's remedy?

Neri v. Retail Marine Corp.

New York Court of Appeals, 1972.
30 N.Y.2d 393, 334 N.Y.S.2d 165, 285 N.E.2d 311.

■ GIBSON, JUDGE. . . .

　　The plaintiffs contracted to purchase from defendant a new boat of a specified model for the price of $12,587.40, against which they made a deposit of $40. They shortly increased the deposit to $4,250 in consideration of the defendant dealer's agreement to arrange with the manufacturer for immediate delivery on the basis of "a firm sale," instead of the delivery within approximately four to six weeks originally specified. Some six days after the date of the contract plaintiffs' lawyer sent to defendant a letter rescinding the sales contract for the reason that plaintiff Neri was about to undergo hospitalization and surgery, in consequence of which, according to the letter, it would be "impossible for Mr. Neri to make any payments." The boat had already been ordered from the manufacturer and was delivered to defendant at or before the time the attorney's letter was received. Defendant declined to refund plaintiffs' deposit and this action to recover it was commenced. Defendant counterclaimed, alleging plaintiffs' breach of the contract and defendant's resultant damage in the amount of $4,250, for which sum defendant demanded judgment. Upon motion, defendant had summary judgment on the issue of liability tendered by its counterclaim; and Special Term directed an assessment of damages, upon which it would be determined whether plaintiffs were entitled to the return of any portion of their down payment.

　　Upon the trial so directed, it was shown that the boat ordered and received by defendant in accordance with plaintiffs' contract of purchase was sold some four months later to another buyer for the same price as that negotiated with plaintiffs. From this proof the plaintiffs argue that defendant's loss on its contract was recouped, while defendant argues that but for plaintiffs' default, it would have sold two boats and have earned two profits instead of one. Defendant proved, without contradiction, that its profit on the sale under the contract in suit would have been $2,579 and that during the period the boat remained unsold incidental expenses aggregating $674 for storage, upkeep, finance charges and insurance were incurred. Additionally, defendant proved and sought to recover attorneys' fees of $1,250.

The trial court found "untenable" defendant's claim for loss of profit, inasmuch as the boat was later sold for the same price that plaintiffs had contracted to pay; found, too, that defendant had failed to prove any incidental damages; further found "that the terms of section 2–718, subsection 2(b), of the Uniform Commercial Code are applicable and same make adequate and fair provision to place the sellers in as good a position as performance would have done" and, in accordance with paragraph (b) of subsection (2) thus relied upon, awarded defendant $500 upon its counterclaim and directed that plaintiffs recover the balance of their deposit, amounting to $3,750. The ensuing judgment was affirmed, without opinion, at the Appellate Division, and defendant's appeal to this court was taken by our leave.

The issue is governed in the first instance by section 2–718 of the Uniform Commercial Code which provides, among other things, that the buyer, despite his breach, may have restitution of the amount by which his payment exceeds: (a) reasonable liquidated damages stipulated by the contract or (b) absent such stipulation, 20% of the value of the buyer's total performance or $500, whichever is smaller (§ 2–718, subsection [2], pars. [a], [b]). As above noted, the trial court awarded defendant an offset in the amount of $500 under paragraph (b) and directed restitution to plaintiffs of the balance. Section 2–718, however, establishes, in paragraph (a) of subsection (3), an alternative right of offset in favor of the seller, as follows: "(3) The buyer's right to restitution under subsection (2) is subject to offset to the extent that the seller establishes (a) a right to recover damages under the provisions of this Article other than subsection (1)."

Among "the provisions of this Article other than subsection (1)" are those to be found in section 2–708, which the courts below did not apply. . . . [Subsection (2) of that section provides,] "If the measure of damages provided in subsection (1) is inadequate to put the seller in as good a position as performance would have done then the measure of damages is the profit (including reasonable overhead) which the seller would have made from full performance by the buyer, together with any incidental damages provided in this Article (Section 2–710), due allowance for costs reasonably incurred and due credit for payments of proceeds of resale."

. . .

Prior to the Code, the New York cases "applied the 'profit' test, contract price less cost of manufacture, only in cases where the seller

[was] a manufacturer or an agent for a manufacturer" (1955 Report of N.Y.Law Rev.Comm., vol. 1, p. 693). Its extension to retail sales was "designed to eliminate the unfair and economically wasteful results arising under the older law when fixed price articles were involved. This section permits the recovery of lost profits in all appropriate cases, which would include all standard priced goods." (Official Comment 2, McKinney's Cons.Laws of N.Y., Book 62–1/2, Part 1, p. 605, under Uniform Commercial Code, § 2–708.) Additionally, and "[i]n all cases the seller may recover incidental damages" (id., Comment 3). The buyer's right to restitution was established at Special Term upon the motion for summary judgment, as was the seller's right to proper offsets, in each case pursuant to section 2–718; and, as the parties concede, the only question before us, following the assessment of damages at Special Term, is that as to the proper measure of damage to be applied. The conclusion is clear from the record—indeed with mathematical certainty—that "the measure of damages provided in subsection (1) is inadequate to put the seller in as good a position as performance would have done" (Uniform Commercial Code, § 2–708, subsection [2]) and hence—again under subsection (2)—that the seller is entitled to its "profit (including reasonable overhead) * * * together with any incidental damages * * *, due allowance for costs reasonably incurred and due credit for payments or proceeds of resale."

It is evident, first, that this retail seller is entitled to its profit and, second, that the last sentence of subsection (2), as hereinbefore quoted, referring to "due credit for payments or proceeds of resale" is inapplicable to this retail sales contract.[2] Closely parallel to the factual situation now before us is that hypothesized by Dean Hawkland as illustrative of the operation of the rules: "Thus, if a private party agrees to sell his automobile to a buyer for $2,000, a breach by the buyer would cause the seller no loss (except incidental damages, i.e., expense of a new sale) if the seller was able to sell the automobile to another buyer for $2,000. But the situation is different with dealers having an unlimited supply of standard-priced goods. Thus, if an automobile dealer agrees to sell a car to a buyer at the standard price of $2,000, a breach by the buyer injures the dealer, even though he is able to sell the automobile to another for $2,000. If the dealer has an inexhaustible supply of cars, the resale to replace the breaching buyer costs the dealer a sale, because, had the breaching buyer performed, the dealer would have made two sales instead of one. The buyer's breach, in such a case, depletes the dealer's

---

[2]   The concluding clause, "due credit for payments or proceeds of resale," is intended to refer to "the privilege of the seller to realize junk value when it is manifestly useless to complete the operation of manufacture" (Supp. No. 1 to the 1952 Official Draft of Text and Comments of the Uniform Commercial Code, as Amended by the Action of the American Law Institute of the National Conference of Commissioners on Uniform Laws [1954], p. 14). The commentators who have considered the language have uniformly concluded that "the reference is to a resale as scrap under * * * Section 2–704." Another writer, reaching the same conclusion, after detailing the history of the clause, says that " 'proceeds of resale' previously meant the resale value of the goods in finished form; now it means the resale value of the components on hand at the time plaintiff learns of breach" (Harris, Seller's Damages, 18 Stan.L.Rev. 66, 104).

sales to the extent of one, and the measure of damages should be the dealer's profit on one sale. Section 2–708 recognizes this, and it rejects the rule developed under the Uniform Sales Act by many courts that the profit cannot be recovered in this case." (Hawkland, Sales and Bulk Sales [1958 ed.], pp. 153–154.)

The record which in this case establishes defendant's entitlement to damages in the amount of its prospective profit, at the same time confirms defendant's cognate right to "any incidental damages provided in this Article (Section 2–710)" (Uniform Commercial Code, § 2–708, subsection [2]). From the language employed it is too clear to require discussion that the seller's right to recover loss of profits is not exclusive and that he may recoup his "incidental" expenses as well. Although the trial court's denial of incidental damages in the uncontroverted amount of $674 was made in the context of its erroneous conclusion that paragraph (b) of subsection (2) of section 2–718 was applicable and was "adequate * * * to place the sellers in as good a position as performance would have done," the denial seems not to have rested entirely on the court's mistaken application of the law, as there was an explicit finding "that defendant completely failed to show that it suffered any incidental damages." We find no basis for the court's conclusion with respect to a deficiency of proof inasmuch as the proper items of the $674 expenses (being for storage, upkeep, finance charges and insurance for the period between the date performance was due and the time of the resale) were proven without objection and were in no way controverted, impeached or otherwise challenged, at the trial or on appeal. Thus the court's finding of a failure of proof cannot be supported upon the record and, therefore, and contrary to plaintiffs' contention, the affirmance at the Appellate Division was ineffective to save it.

The trial court correctly denied defendant's claim for recovery of attorney's fees incurred by it in this action. Attorney's fees incurred in an action such as this are not in the nature of the protective expenses contemplated by the statute (Uniform Commercial Code, § 1–106, subd. [1] [revised 1–305(a)]; § 2–710; § 2–708, subsection [2] . . .).

It follows that plaintiffs are entitled to restitution of the sum of $4,250 paid by them on account of the contract price less an offset to defendant in the amount of $3,253 on account of its lost profit of $2,579 and its incidental damages of $674.

The order of the Appellate Division should be modified, with costs in all courts, in accordance with this opinion, and, as so modified, affirmed.

QUESTIONS AND NOTES

1. Section 2–708(2) does not use the permissive, "the seller may recover"; rather, it states, "the measure of damages *is* the profit . . . which the seller would have made from full performance." Does that language support or undermine the decision in *Peace River*, where the court emphasized that the language of 2–708(1) is permissive?

2. In *Neri*, what section authorizes the seller's recovery of incidental damages?

3. Did the court correctly conclude that the $674 in charges for storage and upkeep, insurance premiums, and interest payments were recoverable as incidental damages?

Was the sale of the boat facilitated by the fact that it was available for viewing at the seller's place of business? Why is this question relevant to the recoverability of the $674?

4. Assume that in *Neri* Retail Marine's contract with the manufacturer of the boat in question provided that if Retail Marine sold a specified number of those boats in that calendar year, the manufacturer would pay Retail Marine a bonus of $5,000. If the Neris' breach caused Retail Marine to fall one sale short of that number, would they be liable for the $5,000?

5. In R.E. Davis Chemical Corp. v. Diasonics, Inc., 826 F.2d 678 (7th Cir.1987), Davis contracted to buy medical diagnostic equipment from Diasonics, making a down payment of $300,000. When Davis refused to take delivery, Diasonics sold the same equipment to another buyer for the same price that Davis had agreed to pay. Davis sued for return of its down payment, and Diasonics claimed that it was entitled to deduct its lost profit before returning any of the $300,000. The trial court held that when a seller has resold, it is limited to recovery of the excess of the contract price over the resale price under 2–706. The Court of Appeals reversed. After stating that lost-volume sellers are entitled to recover lost profits, it continued:

> However, we disagree with the definition of "lost volume seller" adopted by other courts. Courts awarding lost profits to a lost volume seller have focused on whether the seller had the capacity to supply the breached units in addition to what it actually sold. In reality, however, the relevant questions include, not only whether the seller could have produced the breached units in addition to its actual volume, but also whether it would have been profitable for the seller to produce both units. Goetz & Scott, Measuring Sellers' Damages: The Lost-Profits Puzzle, 31 Stan.L.Rev. 323, 332–33, 346–47 (1979). As one commentator has noted, under
>
> > "the economic law of diminishing returns or increasing marginal costs[,] . . . as a seller's volume increases, then a point will inevitably be reached where the cost of selling each additional item diminishes the incremental return to the seller and eventually makes it entirely unprofitable to conclude the next sale."
>
> Shanker, [The Case for a Literal Reading of UCC Section 2–708(2), 24 Case W.Res.L.Rev. 697, 705 (1973)]. Thus, under some conditions, awarding a lost volume seller its presumed lost profit will result in overcompensating the seller, and § 2–708(2) would not take effect because the damage formula provided in § 2–708(1) does place the seller in as good a position as if the buyer had performed. Therefore, on remand, Diasonics must establish, not only that it had the capacity to produce the breached unit in addition to the

unit resold, but also that it would have been profitable for it to have produced and sold both. Diasonics carries the burden of establishing these facts because the burden of proof is generally on the party claiming injury to establish the amount of its damages; especially in a case such as this, the plaintiff has easiest access to the relevant data.

. . .

We therefore reverse the grant of summary judgment in favor of Davis and remand with instructions that the district court calculate Diasonics' damages under § 2–708(2) if Diasonics can establish, not only that it had the capacity to make the sale to Davis as well as the sale to the resale buyer, but also that it would have been profitable for it to make both sales. Of course, Diasonics, in addition, must show that it probably would have made the second sale absent the breach.

On remand, the trial court awarded Diasonics lost profit of $453,050. On appeal (924 F.2d 709 (7th Cir.1991)), that award was affirmed. The court held that it was clearly established on remand that Diasonics had the capacity to manufacture one more machine and that it was searching for all possible buyers. Therefore, it was a lost-volume seller. The buyer argued on appeal that Diasonics had not proven its profit on the lost sale because it had used average costs rather than actual costs. Presumably the argument is that Diasonics should have had to show the actual marginal cost of producing an additional unit. In any event, the court approved the use of average cost data, saying that Diasonics only had to prove its damages with reasonable certainty, not with mathematical precision.

Davis also argued that the seller had to identify the particular buyer of the rejected machine and show that the buyer would have bought another machine if it had not been able to receive the machine originally intended for Davis. The court also rejected that argument. It stated that the Diasonic units were interchangeable and that it was not necessary for Diasonics to "trace the exact resale buyer for that unit."

6.   "Including reasonable overhead." The parenthetical in 2–708(2), "including reasonable overhead," means that the seller is entitled to be repaid for the overhead allocable to the breached contract. Compensation for the out-of-pocket expenses that the seller incurred before the breach is provided by the phrase at the end of the subsection, "due allowance for costs incurred." The allowance for reasonable overhead, therefore, refers to the portion of the seller's fixed overhead that is allocable to the breached contract. These are the costs the seller incurs regardless of whether it ever formed the contract with the buyer. They include rent, salaries, insurance, and all the other expenses that are to be paid regardless of the existence of the contract in question. To see why this is so, consider the following example.

Bulldozers, Inc., has succeeded in securing contracts this year for the sale of 10 bulldozers at a price of $300,000 each. Therefore, if all 10 contracts are performed, gross income for the year will be $3,000,000. Bulldozers' costs for the year are:

10 Bulldozers @ $200,000	$2,000,000
Rent	100,000
Secretary	100,000
Utilities and office expense	100,000
Insurance	50,000
Sales rep's commission ($10,000 per bulldozer)	100,000
Total Cost	$2,450,000

The total costs are $2,450,000, leaving a net profit of $550,000 ($3,000,000–$2,450,000), or $55,000 per bulldozer.

Now suppose one of the buyers repudiates its agreement to buy a bulldozer. What are the damages? The above numbers change. Gross income (prior to any award for damages for the breach) will be $2,700,000 (rather than $3,000,000 as it would have been but for the breach). Now costs will be:

9 Bulldozers @ $20,000	$1,800,000
Rent	100,000
Secretary	100,000
Utilities and office expenses	100,000
Insurance	50,000
Sales rep's commission ($10,000 per bulldozer)	90,000
Total Cost	$2,240,000

The total costs are $2,240,000, and the net profit is $460,000 ($2,700,000–$2,240,000).

If we allow only the per-unit $55,000 as damages for the lost sale, the seller's net profit for the year will be $460,000 plus $55,000, or $515,000, not the $550,000 it would have had the buyer not repudiated.

On the other hand, if we compute lost profit by deducting only the expenses that were saved as a result of the breach (the $200,000 cost of the bulldozer plus the $10,000 commission) from the breaching buyer's purchase price of $300,000, seller's damages will be $90,000. If we add $90,000 to the $460,000 profit made on the other nine sales occurring the year, we get total profit for the year of $550,000. Therefore, the $90,000 recovery puts the seller in the position that it would have been in if the contract had been performed. The expenses saved sometimes are referred to as variable costs, as contrasted with the fixed costs of running the business. The lost profit is determined by starting with the contract price and deducting the variable costs that the seller has not incurred. The remainder, which is lost profit, therefore includes a portion of the fixed costs. This portion of the fixed costs is the "reasonable overhead" to which 2–708(2) refers.

7. "Due credit for payments and proceeds of resale." A primary application of 2–708(2) is to the "lost-volume seller." This is the seller who has sufficient supply to handle the entire demand for its goods. When a buyer breaches, there is no way for the seller to recoup the loss by making a second sale. Another buyer may take the goods, but as this second buyer would presumably have bought from the seller anyway, the seller has irretrievably lost the volume of the breached contract. The only way to make the seller whole, then, is to allow lost profit on the breached contract.

What, then, is the effect of the last phrase of 2–708(2), "due credit for . . . proceeds of resale"? Since the seller in the typical lost-volume case resells the goods for approximately the same price the breaching buyer had promised, allowing credit for proceeds of resale in the lost-volume case normally will result in little or no recovery under 2–708(2). Therefore, the prevailing view is that the directive to deduct "proceeds of resale" applies only to (1) a seller who is manufacturing goods for a breaching buyer and who sells unfinished goods for salvage; and (2) a seller who is a middleman, as in Problem 5 on page 521 and who acquires goods before the buyer breaches. This is the view of the court in *Neri*.

Even with this qualification, there is room for doubt whether 2–708(2) accurately captures the actual loss of the lost-volume seller. In a case like *Neri*, for example, it is hard, if not impossible, to know whether the second sale would have been made even if the Neris had not breached. Also, it is difficult to know whether the second sale, if it would have been made anyway, would have been at a higher cost to Retail Marine (or at a lower price) if the Neris had not breached. On the other hand, it is practically certain that Retail Marine could have acquired a second boat from the manufacturer at about the same price it paid for the one that the Neris had contracted to buy. Therefore, the better policy choice may be to allow sellers to recover lost profits once they show ability to supply all reasonably expectable buyers, with the burden on the breaching buyer to show, if it can, that the seller's loss was less than the claimed lost profits.

8. In Lee Oldsmobile, Inc. v. Kaiden, 32 Md.App. 556, 363 A.2d 270 (1976), the buyer contracted to purchase a Rolls-Royce for $29,500. When the buyer repudiated, the seller resold the automobile for $26,500. It claimed as damages the following:

Contract price of $29,500 less resale price of $26,500	$3,000
Commission to salesman on second sale	600
Commission to broker on second sale	1,000
Floor plan interest on cost of car, 52 days	335
Transportation expenses	140
Total	$5,075

The court held that since the seller had not given notice of intention to resell, it was not entitled, under 2–706, to the excess of the contract price over the resale price of the automobile. The court, however, did allow recovery of the other claimed items of damage.

    a.   Can you think of any basis for awarding the $3,000?

    b.   Is it appropriate to give as damages the expenses of a sale not meeting the requirements of 2–706? If so, under what section?

    c.   Was the seller's attorney guilty of malpractice in bringing a suit claiming 2–706 damages, rather than seeking to recover lost profits under 2–708(2)?

9. Problem 4, page 518 revisited again. In the contract for the unusual fur coat, what if Roseanne repudiated the contract after Furrier had taken measurements, made a pattern, and acquired and cut the pelts, but had not yet begun assembling and sewing them: can Furrier complete the coat and recover the price?

10. Problem. Tables R Us contracted with Modern Furnishings, a furniture retailer, to manufacture and deliver 4,000 wooden end tables of a specified design, for $250 per table, or $1,000,000. Six weeks later Tables calls to tell you that Modern repudiated. At that time, Tables had acquired all the materials it needed and had cut the tops and legs for the tables. The cost of the materials was $200,000, and the cost of the labor to cut the wood was $100,000. The salvage value of the materials is about $30,000. Tables estimates that the total additional cost of finishing the 4,000 tables would be $500,000 and that they would sell for a total of $900,000 on the market. Tables asks what to do. What would you advise, and why?

---

3. CONTRACTED-FOR REMEDIES

Chapter 7 considered contractual remedies but the focus was on the seller's attempt to limit the remedies of the buyer. Now the focus is on the seller's attempt to expand the remedies available to it in the event of a breach by the buyer. These remedies include liquidated damages, take-or-pay, and specific performance.

a. LIQUIDATED DAMAGES

Kvassay v. Murray
Kansas Court of Appeals, 1991.
15 Kan.App.2d 426, 808 P.2d 896.

■ WALKER, D.J.

Plaintiff Michael Kvassay, d/b/a Kvassay Exotic Food, appeals the trial court's finding that a liquidated damages clause was unenforceable and from the court's finding that damages for lost profits were not recoverable. Kvassay contends these damages occurred when Great American Foods, Inc., (Great American) breached a contract for the purchase of baklava. . . .

On February 22, 1984, Kvassay, who had been an independent insurance adjuster, contracted to sell 24,000 cases of baklava to Great American at $19.00 per case. Under the contract, the sales were to occur over a one-year period and Great American was to be Kvassay's only customer. The contract included a clause which provided: "If Buyer refuses to accept or repudiates delivery of the goods sold to him, under this Agreement, Seller shall be entitled to damages, at the rate of $5.00 per case, for each case remaining to be delivered under this Contract."

. . . After producing approximately 3,000 cases, Kvassay stopped producing the baklava because [Great American] refused to purchase any more of the product.

. . .

In April 1985, Kvassay filed suit for damages arising from the collapse of his baklava baking business. . . . The trial court ruled that liquidated damages could not be recovered and . . . "as a matter of law" that Kvassay would not be able to recover damages for lost profits in the action because they were too "speculative and conjectural." . . .

Kvassay first attacks the trial court's ruling that the amount of liquidated damages sought by him was unreasonable and therefore the liquidated damages clause was unenforceable.

Kvassay claimed $105,000 in losses under the liquidated damages clause of the contract, representing $5 per case for the approximately 21,000 cases of baklava which he was not able to deliver. The trial court determined that Kvassay's use of expected profits to formulate liquidated damages was improper because the business enterprise lacked duration, permanency, and recognition. The court then compared Kvassay's previous yearly income (about $20,000) with the claim for liquidated damages ($105,000) and found "the disparity becomes so great as to make the clause unenforceable."

Since the contract involved the sale of goods between merchants, the Uniform Commercial Code governs. See K.S.A. 84–2–102. "The Code does not change the pre-Code rule that the question of the propriety of liquidated damages is a question of law for the court." 4 Anderson, Uniform Commercial Code § 2–718:6, p. 572 (3d ed. 1983). Thus, this court's scope of review of the trial court's ruling is unlimited.

Liquidated damages clauses in sales contracts are governed by K.S.A. 84–2–718. . . .

[Under the common law] a "stipulation for damages upon a future breach of contract is valid as a liquidated damages clause if the set amount is determined to be reasonable and the amount of damages is difficult to ascertain." This is clearly a two-step test: damages must be reasonable and they must be difficult to ascertain. Under the UCC, however, reasonableness is the only test. K.S.A. 84–2–718 provides three criteria by which to measure reasonableness of liquidated damages clauses: (1) anticipated or actual harm caused by breach; (2) difficulty of proving loss; and (3) difficulty of obtaining an adequate remedy.

In its ruling, the trial court found the liquidated damages clause was unreasonable in light of Kvassay's income before he entered into the manufacturing contract with Great American. There is no basis in 84–2–718 for contrasting income under a previous unrelated employment arrangement with liquidated damages sought under a manufacturing contract. Indeed, the traditional goal of the law in cases where a buyer breaches a manufacturing contract is to place the seller "in the same position he would have occupied if the vendee had performed his contract." Outcault Adv. Co. v. Citizens Nat'l Bank, 118 Kan. 328, 330–31, 234 Pac. 988 (1925). Thus, liquidated damages under the contract in this case must be measured against the anticipated or actual loss under the baklava contract as required by 84–2–718. The trial court erred in using Kvassay's previous income as a yardstick.

. . .

Kvassay produced evidence of anticipated damages at the bench trial showing that, before the contract was signed between Kvassay and Great American, Kvassay's accountant had calculated the baklava production costs. The resulting figure showed that, if each case sold for $19, Kvassay would earn a net profit of $3.55 per case after paying himself for time and labor. If he did not pay himself, the projected profit was $4.29 per case. Nevertheless, the parties set the liquidated damages figure at $5 per case. In comparing the anticipated damages of $3.55 per case in lost net profit with the liquidated damages of $5 per case, it is evident that Kvassay would collect $1.45 per case or about 41 percent over projected profits if Great American breached the contract. If the $4.29 profit figure is used, a $5 liquidated damages award would allow Kvassay to collect 71 cents per case or about 16–1/2 percent over projected profits if Great American breached the contract.

An examination of these pre-contract comparisons alone might well lead to the conclusion that the $5 liquidated damages clause is unreasonable because enforcing it would result in a windfall for Kvassay and serve as a penalty for Great American. A term fixing unreasonably large liquidated damages is void as a penalty under 84–2–718.

A better measure of the validity of the liquidated damages clause in this case would be obtained if the actual lost profits caused by the breach were compared to the $5 per case amount set by the clause. . . . Given the trial court's ruling that lost profits were not recoverable and could not be presented to the jury, it is questionable whether the court would have permitted evidence concerning lost profits at the bench trial.

The trial court utilized an impermissible factor to issue its ruling on the liquidated damages clause and the correct statutory factors were not directly addressed. We reverse the trial court on this issue and remand for further consideration of the reasonableness of the liquidated damages clause in light of the three criteria set out in 84–2–718. . . .

Given the quantity of evidence offered to prove the profitability of Kvassay's business, it is clear the trial court was premature in ruling, as a matter of law, that lost profits could not be proved. Kvassay should have been permitted to offer his evidence and meet his burden of proof on damages. . . .

QUESTIONS AND NOTES

1. Section 2–718 validates the use of a liquidated damages clause, but only if it stipulates damages "at an amount which is reasonable in light of the anticipated or actual harm caused by the breach, the difficulties of proof of loss, and the inconvenience or nonfeasibility of otherwise obtaining an adequate remedy." Does the damages clause in *Kvassay* meet this standard?

2. During the initial proceedings, Kvassay attempted to introduce proof of his actual lost profits. The trial court erred in excluding this evidence and on remand must consider it. If Kvassay proves what his profits were on the 3,000 cases he produced, one could project the profits lost on the 21,000 cases not produced. What rationale would justify awarding him the liquidated damages of $105,000 rather than the amount so projected?

3. When a contract calls for the buyer to make a down payment, it often states that in the event of a breach by the buyer, the seller may retain the down payment as liquidated damages. Should this provision be enforceable? Applying the standard articulated in *Kvassay*, the court in Rodriguez v. Learjet, Inc., 946 P.2d 1010 (Kan.App.1997), the court held yes.

———

b. TAKE-OR-PAY

Take-or-pay provisions originated in the natural gas industry, in which pipelines formed long-term, fixed-price contracts with owners of gas wells. They were concerned that if the market price dropped below the contract price either they would have to take delivery of gas that they could sell only at a loss or they would have to transport and store gas at considerable expense. The parties worked out an arrangement in which the pipelines either would take delivery at the time agreed or would pay for the gas at that time but leave it in the well while retaining the right to take delivery at a much later time, when market conditions were more favorable to them. That is, they could take gas now and pay for it now, or they could pay for it now and take it later. This is known as "take-or-pay."

> The purpose of the take-or-pay clause is to apportion the risks of natural gas production and sales between the buyer and seller. The seller bears the risk of production. To compensate the seller for that risk, the buyer agrees to take, or pay for if not taken, a minimum quantity of gas. The buyer bears the risk of

market demand. The take-or-pay clause insures that if the demand for gas goes down, seller will still receive the price for the Contract Quantity delivered each year.

[Universal Resources Corp. v. Panhandle Eastern Pipe Line Co., 813 F.2d 77, 80 (5th Cir.1987)]. And they are enforced primarily on the basis that what the buyer is actually paying for is not so much a "product"—gas—as the process by which the gas is made available. The payment is intended to compensate the producer for the costs associated with production and to ensure a steady source of income so that he may continue production.

Superfos Investments Limited v. FirstMiss Fertilizer, Inc., 821 F.Supp. 432 (S.D.Miss.1993).

Exemplary of enforcement of a take-or-pay clause in a contract for the purchase of natural gas is Sabine Corp. v. ONG Western, Inc., 725 F.Supp. 1157, 1184–85 (W.D.Okla.1989). Defendant failed to take the specified minimum amount and plaintiff sued to recover the price due under the take-or-pay clause. Defendant asserted that the take-or-pay provision was not an enforceable liquidated damages clause. The court responded:

VI. Penalty or Liquidated Damages

The essence of defendant ONG's fourth affirmative defense, on which plaintiff seeks summary judgment, is that because ONG will not, due to market conditions, be able by later takes to make up payment for gas previously not taken, Sabine will remain free to resell such gas paid for but not taken by ONG, resulting in a windfall to Sabine and demonstrating that Sabine "has not suffered damage to the full extent of the contract price for the gas not taken by the buyer." Therefore, ONG alleges, the take-or-pay provisions operate as a penalty or liquidated damages provision and are unenforceable pursuant to Okla.Stat. title 12A, § 2–718(1) and Okla.Stat. title 15, § 214 because the amount of the deficiency sought by plaintiff bears no reasonable relationship to plaintiff's actual damages and the amount of actual damages is not impracticable or extremely difficult to determine.

Sabine asserts that the payment obligation under a take-or-pay contract is a promise or obligation, not a punishment for breach, and that payment pursuant to such contract provision constitutes performance thereof, not payment for breach of the contract of an amount stipulated as damages. Thus, plaintiff asserts that the payment obligation is neither a penalty or a liquidated damages provision, citing Resources Investment Corp. v. Enron Corp., 669 F.Supp. 1038 (D.Colo.1987) and Universal Resources Corp. v. Panhandle Eastern Pipe Line Co.,

No. CA3–85–0723–R, slip op. (N.D.Tex. April 1, 1986), aff'd 813 F.2d 77 (5th Cir.1987).

ONG ... makes a minimal response, asserting on the basis of the Hughes Affidavit that material issues of fact exist as to whether ONG will be able to recoup take-or-pay payments made to Sabine and as to whether the amount of take-or-pay payments demanded by Sabine bears any reasonable relationship to any actual and potential damages of Sabine due to ONG's alleged breach. . . .

Whether or not ONG will be able to recoup take-or-pay payments is not material. An assumption that ONG cannot recoup such payments does not render the take-or-pay provisions or the payment obligation under the contract a penalty or a liquidated damages provision. The court agrees with plaintiff and with the United States District Court for the Northern District of Texas that "[t]he take-or-pay provision . . . specifies a contractual obligation rather than dictates damages upon breach." Accordingly, the take-or-pay provision, or more particularly the payment provision, cannot constitute a penalty for failure to perform or a liquidated damages provision specifying damages for breach of the "take" obligation. . . . See also International Minerals & Chemical Corp. v. Llano, Inc., 770 F.2d 879, 885 (10th Cir.1985), cert. denied, 475 U.S. 1015 (1986) (take-or-pay contracts impose alternative obligations); Comment b, Restatement (Second) of Contracts § 361 (1981) (distinguishing provision for alternative performance from liquidated damages provision).

———

Although the take-or-pay provision originated in the volatile natural gas market of the 1970s, it has been modified and employed in other industries.

Hemlock Semiconductor Corporation
v. Kyocera Corporation

United States Court of Appeals, Sixth Circuit, 2018.
747 Fed.Appx. 285.

■ THAPAR, CIRCUIT JUDGE.

Kyocera Corporation is locked in a long-running bout with Hemlock Semiconductor Corporation and Hemlock Semiconductor, LLC, which supply Kyocera with polysilicon that it uses to make solar panels. Kyocera is fighting to get out of certain obligations under the parties' contracts. . . .

I.

In the mid-2000s, the market for solar panels was taking off. Kyocera needed a steady supply of quality polysilicon. So it entered into four contracts with Hemlock, in which Kyocera promised to purchase specified amounts of polysilicon from Hemlock at specified prices over the course of the next ten years or so.

Those contracts contain so-called "take-or-pay" provisions. Under these provisions, the contracts require Kyocera to "take" a specified quantity of polysilicon from Hemlock each year. But if Kyocera does not want to take the polysilicon in a given year, Kyocera still has to "pay" full price for it. This means that Kyocera is on the hook for a certain quantity of polysilicon annually, whether it takes the polysilicon or not.

The contracts also contain so-called "acceleration" provisions. If Kyocera defaults under the contracts, these provisions accelerate the amount it owes Hemlock, such that Hemlock can demand *all* remaining sums owed. For these acceleration provisions to take effect, Kyocera must default, Hemlock must serve notice of default, and Hemlock must give Kyocera 180 days to cure its default. But if Kyocera does not cure, Hemlock can elect to terminate, at which point Kyocera becomes liable for all remaining payments due—effectively, the sum of the take-or-pay provisions.

Several years into Kyocera and Hemlock's deal, the Chinese government disrupted the solar-panel market by subsidizing Chinese solar-panel companies. This intervention reduced the market price of polysilicon such that the price Kyocera agreed to pay Hemlock was far greater than the going rate. And so Kyocera sought to renegotiate. Initially, the parties came to a compromise, temporarily lowering the price of polysilicon under the parties' deal. But eventually, Hemlock signaled that it would begin insisting that Kyocera take or pay for polysilicon at the original (and now inflated) price.

This litigation ensued. Hemlock sought a declaratory judgment that Kyocera had repudiated the parties' contracts by indicating that it would not take or pay at the original price. In response, Kyocera counterclaimed, seeking a declaratory judgment that the "pay" portion of the take-or-pay provisions is an unlawful penalty, and thus that the acceleration provisions are too. Kyocera also counterclaimed for breach of contract, alleging that three of the parties' contracts obligated Hemlock to expand certain production facilities, which Hemlock had not done. Hemlock moved to dismiss Kyocera's counterclaims, and the district court agreed. Kyocera now appeals.

II.

Kyocera first appeals the dismissal of its challenge to the take-or-pay provisions. We review the district court's decision de novo. In doing so, we accept Kyocera's well-pled allegations as true and ask whether Hemlock is nevertheless "clearly entitled to judgment. We view the facts as alleged in the light most favorable to Kyocera and draw all reasonable inferences in its favor. Our task is to determine whether Kyocera raises a plausible claim for relief. And Kyocera's claim is plausible if, assuming the truth of Kyocera's allegations, a reasonable factfinder could rule in its favor.

In assessing Kyocera's claim, we apply Michigan law—the law of the forum state and that designated in the parties' contracts. As it happens, Michigan's courts provide little guidance here. The thrust of Kyocera's claim is that the take-or-pay provisions are unlawful penalties in disguise. But there is no case in which a Michigan court has considered such a claim. . . .

With no Michigan authority on point, we must look elsewhere to attempt to discern what path the Michigan Supreme Court might take. Under the approach followed in other jurisdictions, the key question is whether the take-or-pay provisions offer Kyocera two viable performance options, on the one hand, or one performance option coupled with a liquidated damages provision, on the other. *See, e.g.,* . . . 11–59 *Corbin on Contracts* § 59.10 (2017); 14 *Williston on Contracts* § 42:10 (4th ed.). If the former, the take-or-pay provisions are enforceable as written. If the latter, the question becomes whether the "pay" option quantifies lawful liquidated damages or an unlawful penalty. If the payment obligation is a penalty, it is unenforceable—regardless of what the parties' contract labels it. And at least on this point, Michigan law certainly agrees. So if the provisions here are penalties, it is doubtful that Michigan courts would let them fly by night under the guise of take-or-pay provisions.

Alternative Performance v. Liquidated Damages. First, we ask whether the take-or-pay provisions offer Kyocera two viable performance options, or one option coupled with liquidated damages. To make this call, courts consider whether, at the time of contracting, it appears that the parties intended that the "pay" option present a relatively equivalent (and thus desirable) mode of performance—and not, as Kyocera claims, a measure to coerce compliance with the "take" option. And at the outset, common sense points to coercion: Why would Kyocera opt to pay for polysilicon and get nothing in return?

Hemlock offers three suggestions. First, Hemlock reasons that Kyocera must have seen the pay option as a viable alternative, because Kyocera is a big, smart corporation and would never have agreed to the deal otherwise. But the fact that a sophisticated entity has agreed to pay a sum does not necessarily mean that the law will always enforce its promise, and Hemlock points to no Michigan authority holding otherwise. Kyocera's sophistication at the bargaining table may later become relevant, but in this posture, it does not doom Kyocera's claim as a matter of law. So Hemlock's first argument swings and misses. Second, Hemlock hypothesizes that Kyocera might have thought that in certain circumstances it would be willing to pay for polysilicon one year (but not take it) as a way to keep the contract alive in the event it still wanted polysilicon in the future. But if Kyocera wanted to keep the contract alive, it could simply purchase polysilicon *and take delivery*. It would not need to pay and get nothing in return. So here again, Hemlock swings and misses.

Hemlock saves its best swing for last. Moving and storing polysilicon is not free. And so Hemlock theorizes that, if the price of polysilicon tanks (as it did here), it might make sense for Kyocera to pay for polysilicon without taking it in order to avoid transportation and storage costs. If the math is right, and the parties intended for the "pay" provision to account for this possibility, Hemlock may have a point. But nothing in the pleadings suggests that this math influenced the parties' negotiations. In fact, Kyocera alleges that there were no such negotiations. Nor do the pleadings suggest that the price of polysilicon has fallen so much that transportation and storage costs would justify paying for polysilicon without taking it. At this stage, we consider only Kyocera's allegations, viewed in a light most favorable to Kyocera, construing all reasonable inferences in Kyocera's favor. Accepting Hemlock's transportation-and-storage argument at this juncture would disregard those precepts. So we are left with the common-sense conclusion that paying a lot of money for nothing in return is not a real performance option under a contract. To be sure, if discovery bears out Hemlock's point, Kyocera's claim may later fail. But for now, Hemlock goes down swinging.

Moreover, two additional allegations further support the conclusion that paying something for nothing is not a valid performance option. Both have to do with the kind of provisions that normally appear in lawful take-or-pay contracts. First, the take-or-pay provisions do not contain "make-up rights" that would credit any money advanced under the "pay" option to Kyocera's purchase of polysilicon in future years. Make-up-rights are common in enforceable take-or-pay arrangements. Although the absence of make-up rights may not be dispositive, their absence nevertheless pushes Kyocera's claim further into the realm of plausibility. Second, while lawful take-or-pay arrangements often involve the *seller* (here, Hemlock) bearing construction costs and associated risks at the outset of a contract, the contracts at issue required *Kyocera* to front Hemlock money for construction and expansion.[a] So Kyocera—not Hemlock—bore these costs and risks from the start. True, the contracts do require Hemlock to repay this money to Kyocera over time, as a credit against purchases of polysilicon—meaning that eventually, Hemlock internalizes these costs. But it is far from clear that the parties envisioned that the pay option would compensate Hemlock for these costs this late in the duration of the contracts, when construction and expansion are long over and Hemlock has been

---

[a] Historically, producers of natural gas were reluctant to bear the cost of production if they were not assured that they would be receiving regular payments regardless of any fluctuation in the market price of gas.—Eds.

providing Kyocera with polysilicon for over a decade. Thus, these allegations further belie any conceivable purpose for the pay option other than to liquidate damages.

Liquidated Damages v. Penalty. The fact that the pay option might not be a valid mode of performance is not the end of the inquiry. If the pay option is a lawful measure of liquidated damages, then it is nevertheless enforceable. But if not, it is a penalty, and Hemlock can seek only its actual damages.

Under Michigan law, damages can be liquidated, "but only at an amount which is reasonable in the light of the anticipated or actual harm caused by the breach, the difficulties of proof of loss, and the inconvenience or nonfeasibility of otherwise obtaining an adequate remedy." Mich. Comp. Laws § 440.2718(1). Otherwise, the clause is "void as a penalty." *Id.* Demanding full price for nothing in return seems unreasonable for one of two reasons. First, if Hemlock has already produced Kyocera's polysilicon, requiring Kyocera to pay the full contract price fails to account for Hemlock's ability to resell the polysilicon elsewhere. Or, if Hemlock can avoid producing the polysilicon at all—as Kyocera alleges happened here—requiring Kyocera to pay full price fails to account for any costs Hemlock would save. Here again, common-sense points to a problem: Under the pay option, Hemlock can get all the money promised under the contract but do nothing, thereby making a *greater* profit than if the parties performed as envisioned.[2]

Our court's decision in *Hemlock Semiconductor Operations, LLC v. SolarWorld Indus. Sachsen GmbH*, 867 F.3d 692 (6th Cir. 2017), does not solve this problem. There, in a dispute between Hemlock and another buyer, our court affirmed a ruling for Hemlock *on summary judgment* that the *acceleration provisions* in those parties' contracts were not penalties. *Id.* at 696–97, 705–08. Those two pieces of context—the procedural posture and the contractual provisions at issue—are crucial to understanding why *Solarworld* is of no help to Hemlock here.

First, *Solarworld* involved a dispute over acceleration provisions. Those provisions, just like those in Kyocera and Hemlock's contracts, required the buyer to satisfy the remainder of the contract in the event of default, i.e., the sum of the remaining take-or-pay provisions. But unlike in this case, the buyer in *Solarworld conceded* the validity of the take-or-pay provisions. *See id.* at 707. So when the buyer tried to argue that the acceleration provisions failed to account for Hemlock's cost savings (as Kyocera does here), the court rejected the argument. "Although such cost savings might factor into an ordinary breach-of-contract claim," the court observed, the acceleration provisions were

---

[2]   Hemlock points out that a seller has the option to sue for damages under Michigan law even without reselling its goods. *See id.* § 440.2703. But in that circumstance, Michigan law only affords "the difference between the market price at the time and place for tender and unpaid contract price . . . but less expenses saved in consequence of the buyer's breach." *Id.* § 440.2708(1). Thus, Michigan law would not permit recovery of the full contract price.

merely the sum of the unchallenged take-or-pay provisions. *Id.* Thus, in *Solarworld*, the buyer's cost-savings argument fell flat, but only because the buyer chose not to challenge the take-or-pay provisions. Had the buyer elected to do so, that challenge would have been important, just as in the "ordinary" case.

Second, *Solarworld* reviewed a summary-judgment ruling in favor of Hemlock. And the summary-judgment record contained facts that we do not have here. As an initial matter, expert testimony reflected that the buyer had saved (and Hemlock had lost) a large amount of money early in the contract due to Hemlock pricing the polysilicon well below market. So the acceleration provisions were something of a fair deal, given that Hemlock was only making up for what it had lost before. In addition, a forty-one-page expert report established that calculating Hemlock's lost profits would have been difficult at the time of contracting. And finally, the *Solarworld* court was able to conclude the acceleration provisions were meant to account for Hemlock's construction costs. *Id.* at 708. Here, by contrast, the district court dismissed Kyocera's claim at the pleading stage—without the benefit of expert testimony or other record information that might justify the amount owing under the pay provisions. So in this posture, we cannot say that requiring Kyocera to pay full price for nothing is a reasonable measure of damages. This is particularly so in light of Kyocera's allegations that Hemlock could have adjusted the amount due under the "pay" option to account for cost savings at the time of contracting, but did not. Down the road, the record may develop in this case such that Kyocera's claim falters like the buyer's in *Solarworld*. But for now, Kyocera's claim passes muster, and the district court erred by dismissing it on the pleadings. . . .

We . . . remand for further proceedings consistent with this opinion.

QUESTIONS AND NOTES

1. In what respects, if any, does the contract in *Hemlock* differ from the archetypal take-or-pay contract in the natural gas industry?

2. Does the take-or-pay clause in the introductory case, *Sabine v. ONG*, meet the standards of 2–718 for enforcement of a liquidated damages clause?

3. The court in *Hemlock* recognizes that a contract may obligate a party to render either of two alternative performances, whichever that party chooses. It is easy to cast a penalty clause into the form of an alternative performance. Hence the court states that it must consider whether the parties intended the pay option to be approximately as desirable as the other option. Exactly what should Hemlock have to prove to prevail on its argument that paying for the polysilicon without taking it would be a relatively equivalent mode of performance to taking the polysilicon? What relationship among the contract price, the market price, and the cost of transportation and storage would sustain the argument that the pay alternative is relatively equivalent to the take alternative?

4. The contract in *Hemlock* contained an acceleration clause, which provided that if Kyocera defaulted and, upon demand, failed to cure its default, Hemlock could accelerate the amount Kyocera owed, making the full amount to be paid over the entire contract due at once. This provision cannot be justified as an alternative performance. Can it be justified as a liquidated damages clause, i.e. stipulating an amount that is reasonable in light of anticipated or actual harm, the difficulty of proving loss, or the inconvenience or nonfeasibility of obtaining an adequate remedy (2–718(1))?

———

c.   SPECIFIC PERFORMANCE

Martin v. Sheffer

North Carolina Court of Appeals, 1991.
102 N.C.App. 802, 403 S.E.2d 555.

■ LEWIS, JUDGE.

In December of 1987 Daniel Martin and John Duke contracted with J & S Distributors, Inc. to purchase a KIS Magnum Speed printer for $17,000. The parties agreed that Martin and Duke would send one half of the money as a deposit and would pay the balance upon delivery. On 28 December 1987 the KIS machine arrived in Georgia but Duke and Martin refused to accept it, stating that the delivery was five days late and they had purchased a substitute machine elsewhere. The plaintiffs requested return of their deposit and were refused.

. . . Duke and Martin sued Jeff Sheffer and J & S Distributors for breach of contract, fraud, breach of good faith and unfair and deceptive trade practices. Defendants answered and counterclaimed for full performance of the contract pursuant to a clause in the contract which provides:

7.   In the event of non-payment of the balance of the purchase price reflected herein on due date and in the manner recorded or on such extended date which may be caused by late delivery on the part of DIS, the Customer shall be liable for

7.1 immediate payment of the full balance recorded herein; and

7.2 payment of interest at the rate of 12% per annum calculated on the balance due, when due, together with any attorney's fees, collection charges and other necessary expenses incurred by DIS.

. . . [D]efendants moved for summary judgment on their counterclaim. The trial court granted this motion and ordered specific performance of the contract, costs and attorney's fees.

Appellants argue that the trial court erred in ordering them to accept delivery of the KIS machine and pay the entire balance of the contract. They contend that the determination of seller's damages is controlled by

U.C.C. § 2–708 and is limited to lost profits. N.C.G.S. § 25–2–708. Appellants fail to take note of N.C.G.S. § 25–1–102(3) and (4) [revised 1–302(a)–(c)] which provide:

> (3) The effect of provisions of this chapter may be varied by agreement except as otherwise provided in this chapter and except that the obligations of good faith, diligence, reasonableness and care prescribed by this chapter may not be disclaimed by agreement . . .

> (4) The presence in certain provisions of this chapter of the words "unless otherwise agreed" or words of similar import does not imply that the effect of other provisions may not be varied by agreement under subsection (3).

The official comment to Subsection 25–1–102(4) [revised 1–302, Official Comment 1] expressly states the general rule that all provisions of the UCC may be varied by contract. Finally, N.C.G.S. § 25–2–719(1)(a) provides that a contract for sale of goods "may provide for remedies in addition to or in substitution for those provided in this article and may limit or alter the measure of damages recoverable under this article. . . ." *Id.* The official comment to this subsection states that "parties are free to shape their remedies to their particular requirements and reasonable agreements limiting or modifying remedies are given effect." Official Comment to N.C.G.S. § 25–2–719.

A contractual provision expanding seller's damages upon breach of the buyer will therefore be upheld where the contractual provision is reasonable and in good faith. N.C.G.S. § 25–1–102 [revised 1–302]. Appellants have signed a contract agreeing to a specific performance clause upon breach. Appellants do not argue in their brief that they were fraudulently induced into signing the contract, that the clause authorizing specific enforcement is ambiguous or a mistake, or that the seller breached the contract by failing to deliver at the time promised.

The appellants argue that the clause should be struck as an "unconscionable and oppressive" liquidated damages clause pursuant to N.C.G.S. § 25–2–718. A contractual clause authorizing specific performance is different in kind from a liquidated damages clause. Even were this not the case, enforcement of the price the appellant freely agreed to pay for the KIS machine cannot be considered unreasonable or a penalty.

Neither do we find this contractual clause to be otherwise unreasonable or contrary to public policy. N.C.G.S. § 25–1–102(3) [revised 1–302(b)]. To find unconscionability there must be an absence of meaningful choice on part of one of the parties together with contract terms which are unreasonably favorable to the other. Appellant does not argue that he lacked meaningful choice in negotiating the terms of the contract. As a merchant, appellant is presumed to be familiar with the terms and practices of contracts for the purchase of the tools of his trade;

as such "it is rare that a limitation of remedy will be held unconscionable in a commercial setting since the relationship between business parties is usually not so one-sided as to force an unconscionable limitation on a party." Byrd Motor Lines v. Dunlop Tire and Rubber Corp., 63 N.C.App. 292, 296, 304 S.E.2d 773, 776 (1983). The contractual clause authorizing specific performance does not undermine the essential purpose of the contract.

While this is a case of first impression in this jurisdiction, cases from other jurisdictions serve as guidance and explanation as to the purpose of the Uniform Commercial Code, which is "to make uniform the law among the various jurisdictions." Accordingly, in Frank LeRoux v. Burns, 4 Wash.App. 165, 480 P.2d 213 (1971), the Washington Court of Appeals upheld a similar clause which gave the seller the option of demanding the balance of payments on the contract in the case of any delinquent payment for the goods. The Court held that the parties were free to shape their remedies according to their particular needs, and that an expansion of the seller's remedies beyond those specified in the Uniform Commercial Code to include specific performance is neither unreasonable nor unconscionable. *Id.* The same rationale applies to the case before us.

. . .

Affirmed.

QUESTIONS AND NOTES

1. How is *Sheffer* different from a dispute in which the buyer breaches a contract in which the seller promises to deliver a printer to the buyer and the buyer promises to pay the seller $17,000?

2. How is the litigation in *Sheffer* different from a seller's action for the price? Under 2–709, is the seller entitled to the price? Is Official Comment 6 to that section relevant to the dispute in *Sheffer*?

3. The court's reasoning emphasizes 1–102 [revised 1–302] and 2–719, both empowering the parties to stipulate the remedies in the event of breach. Please consider the soundness of this proposition: an agreement that specific performance is the remedy for breach is not within the contemplation of those sections.

4. **Interest charges as liquidated damages.** It is common for contracts to provide that if the buyer fails to pay when payment is due, the seller is entitled to a finance charge or default charge of a specified amount or rate. Are these provisions enforceable? In N. Bloom & Son (Antiques) Ltd. v. Skelly, 673 F.Supp. 1260 (S.D.N.Y.1987) (excerpted in Note 1, page 516 supra), the buyer contracted to purchase two candelabras and a centerpiece for $45,000. The contract called for an interest charge of 24 percent per year on contract balances not paid according to the contract terms. The prevailing interest rate when the contract was made was 13 percent, and the court held that the 11 percent premium above the base rate was not reasonably related to the actual damages (viz., collection costs) that the seller would suffer from delayed payment. It held the provision to be an unenforceable penalty under 2–718.

5. Leases. It is very common for leases of goods to stipulate a formula for calculating the lessor's damages in the event of breach by the lessee. These formulas can be quite intimidating. For example, in Northwest Acceptance Corp. v. Hesco Construction, Inc., 26 Wash.App. 823, 828–31, 614 P.2d 1302, 1306–08 (1980), a construction company defaulted on a four-year lease of a backhoe. The lessor repossessed and sued to enforce a clause of the lease contract that provided:

Lessor and lessee agree, for the purpose of this lease, that:

(A) The cost to the lessor of the equipment hereby leased was $55,544.50.

(B) The fair market value of the equipment hereby leased, at the end of the term of this lease shall be $8,331.67.

(C) At any time during the period of this lease, the present value of rent contracted to be paid in the future (said present value to be computed on the basis of a 5 per cent per annum yield) shall be computed as if the monthly rental was a monthly annuity for the number of future months the rent is promised to be paid.

(D) The total depreciation of the leased equipment during the term of the lease shall be the cost of the equipment to the lessor (Item 'A' above) less its residual value at the end of the lease (Item 'B' above).

(E) For the purpose of this section, the depreciated value of the leased equipment at any particular time during the term of this lease shall be the cost of the leased equipment to the lessor, as above set forth, less the depreciation thereon to such time computed on an accelerating depreciation basis, said computation to be made by dividing the term of the lease into semi-annual periods and spreading the total depreciation over such periods under the sum of the digits method. The sum of the digits computation shall be accomplished by numbering the last semi-annual period with the digit '1'; the next prior to the last period with the digit '2', and so on back, until the first semi-annual period is numbered, and then forming a fraction with a denominator equal to the sum of all the digits used and a numerator equal to the digit of the semi-annual period containing the day to which depreciation is being computed, plus the digits for all prior semi-annual periods. The fraction thus formed shall be used to multiply the total depreciation of the leased equipment during the term of the lease established in paragraph (D) above, and the result shall be the depreciation of the leased equipment to the day selected.

(F) In the event the lessee during the term of the lease elects to reject the lease or defaults in performance thereof and surrenders the leased equipment to the lessor or such equipment otherwise comes into the possession of the lessor, the damage to the lessor because of the lessee's default or breach of the lease exclusive of costs enumerated herein above shall be established as follows: The amount of all rent due and unpaid at the time of the computation of such damage shall be added to the present value of all rent contracted to be paid in the future (item C above) and the sum shall be Item 1 of this computation. If the equipment has been surrendered to the lessor or the lessor has otherwise come into the possession of it, there shall be subtracted from the depreciated value of the equipment at the time it came into the possession of the lessor (established pursuant to paragraph 'E' above), the residual value of the chattel at the end of the term of the lease (item 'B' above) and the difference which is Item 2 shall be subtracted from Item 1. The result, when added to the costs herein provided for, plus 5 per cent interest thereon from the date of computation to date of payment, or if judgment is entered for such damages, to date of judgment, shall be the amount of the damages suffered and costs expended by the lessor because of the lessee's breach of the lease. Interest after judgment shall be at the highest lawful rate permitted by law.

In the event the lessee during the term of the lease elects to reject it or defaults in performance thereof, but the leased equipment does not come into the possession of the lessor, the amount of damages suffered and costs expended by the lessor shall be Item 1 above plus the residual value of the chattels at the end of the term of the lease, which is item B above, plus interest at the rate of 5 per cent per annum from the date of computation to the date of payment, or if judgment is entered for such damages, to the date of judgment, plus the costs expended.

The court applied this formula as follows:

1. The aggregate of rental payments in arrears ($6,640.00) is added to the present value of all future rentals contracted to be paid over the unexpired term of the lease ($34,090.64), which is discounted at the agreed rate of 5 percent, to $32,754.75, for a total of $39,394.75.

2. That total is reduced by the difference between (a) the current depreciated value of the equipment at the time of repossession by the lessor ($21,169.59), and (b) the agreed fair market or residual value of the equipment upon its return at the end of the lease ($8,331.67), or $12,837.92. The total damages under this formula are $39,394.75 minus $12,837.92, or $26,556.83.

It agreed with the trial court that "The liquidated damages are reasonably related to anticipation of possible problems with the leased equipment, the condition it would be in upon its return to the plaintiff and the value of the lease agreement to the plaintiff if the defendants had fully performed said lease." The appellate court stated:

The hydraulic backhoe is a specialized piece of construction equipment, the marketability of which is dependent upon many factors including a fluctuating economy, the state of the construction industry, and the demand for used equipment. Because this was a lease agreement, Hesco is not entitled to a credit for the resale price of the equipment following repossession. But, two features of this formula make it a fair liquidated damages provision—(1) the lessor's expectation for future rentals under the lease were reduced to the present value; and (2) the lessee was given a credit for depreciation savings because the equipment was returned to the lessor before the end of the lease.

There is no basis for a finding of unconscionability. We have here two contracting parties, both with extensive experience in construction equipment. Contrary to assertions by Hesco, the damage formula is not impossible to understand. Mr. Schimmels complains that Northwest did not volunteer an explanation of the formula, but he also admitted that he never bothered to read the contract, and did not ask for an explanation. His son, who was serving as Hesco's secretary-treasurer at the time, is a certified public accountant. Given these circumstances, the trial court properly refused to find the lease unconscionable.

There is no reason why persons, competent and free to contract, may not agree upon this subject (liquidated damages) as fully as upon any other, or why their agreement when fairly and understandingly entered into with a view to just compensation for the anticipated loss, should not be enforced.

6.   Liquidated damages clauses of the type used in *Hesco Construction* are common. If the calculation of damages is tied to the time of the breach, the clause is likely to be sustained. Several elements of the formula might, however, be attacked, depending upon the facts of a particular case.

(1)   The present discounted value of future rents varies inversely with the discount rate: the lower the discount rate, the higher the value of future rents. The five-percent discount rate used in *Hesco Construction* was below the market rate of interest in the late 1970s by a substantial amount. The market rate was probably around ten percent. It might be possible to attack the discount rate as being unreasonably low and therefore overcompensating the lessor.

(2)   The   sum-of-the-digits   depreciation   method   might   assume unrealistically high loss of value in the leased goods during the early part of the lease and, again, overcompensate the lessor. For example, in a four-year lease, the sum-of-the-digits depreciation method leads to about 50% depreciation in the first year. (The sum of the digits 1 through 48 is 1168. The sum of the digits 37 through 48 is 547, so the first year depreciation is 547/1168, or 46.83%, of the total depreciation over the four years.)

(3)   The value of the leased property at the end of the lease (the "residual value") might be set lower than the lessor actually or reasonably expects it to be at the end of the lease.

Section 2A–103(u) of the UCC, which defines present value, states that in determining present value the contracted-for discount rate will be used if it was not manifestly unreasonable at the time the transaction was entered into; "otherwise," the discount is determined by a commercially reasonable rate that takes into account the facts and circumstances of each case at the time the transaction was entered into. See 2A–503 and 2A–504 as to contracted-for remedies and liquidated-damages clauses in lease contracts. Note the differences between 2–718(1) and 2A–504(1), which omits reference to actual harm, difficulties of proof, nonfeasibility of obtaining an adequate remedy, and unreasonably large damages. See 2A–504, Official Comment (penultimate paragraph).

CHAPTER 9

REPUDIATION AND THE PROSPECT OF BREACH

A. INTRODUCTION

A party to a sales contract may breach that contract in any number of different ways. Perhaps the most extreme and dramatic of them is by renouncing the obligations of the contract. The law refers to this as a repudiation, and if the renunciation occurs in advance of the time for performance, it is known as an anticipatory repudiation. Under 2–610(b) a repudiation operates as a material breach. And 2–703 provides that a repudiation by the buyer triggers the seller's right to all of the remedies specified in that section. Similarly, 2–711(1) provides that a repudiation by the seller triggers the buyer's right to all the remedies specified there and in 2–711(2) and 2–714.

Repudiation, then, is a very serious matter. But what exactly is a repudiation? Although the statute is silent, Official Comment 1 to 2–610 states, "anticipatory repudiation centers upon an overt communication of intention or an action which renders performance impossible or demonstrates a clear determination not to continue with performance." If any of these occurs, there is a repudiation, and the other party may invoke the appropriate remedies of Article 2. But the party who invokes one of those remedies may be taking a large risk, because a judge or jury reviewing the situation after the fact may conclude that the other party's conduct or statements do not amount to a repudiation. If this happens, then the party who resorted to the Article 2 remedies is the party in breach. This, then, poses a dilemma for a party who has significant doubt about whether the other party will perform as promised: "should I continue to perform even though I may not get what I bargained for, or should I refuse to perform and be liable for breach if I'm wrong"?

Fortunately, Article 2 provides a way out of this dilemma, a mechanism by which an insecure party may suspend performance until the insecurity is resolved. The first sentence of subsection (1) of 2–609 states the important proposition that a "contract for sale imposes an obligation on each party that the other's reasonable expectation of receiving due performance will not be impaired." The second sentence states the prerequisites for suspending performance. Please read all of 2–609.

———

B. THE PROSPECT OF BREACH

Clem Perrin Marine Towing, Inc.
v. Panama Canal Co.

United States Court of Appeals, Fifth Circuit, 1984.
730 F.2d 186.

■ PATRICK E. HIGGINBOTHAM, CIRCUIT JUDGE. Defendant Panama Canal Company [hereinafter PCC] appeals from an adverse judgment for breach of a lease-purchase of a tugboat. . . .

I

Effective March 15, 1974, PCC and [Clem Perrin Marine Towing, Inc., (hereinafter CPMT)] agreed to a "Bareboat Charter Party," providing for a three-year bareboat charter of a tug at a cost of $344,880.* The agreement called for payments in seven installments, the last five of which were to be paid in advance [of each of the last five] six-month periods. Article XIX of the agreement gave PCC an "option" to purchase the tug during the final ninety days of the three-year period for $26,400, well below CPMT's claimed market value of $190,000. CPMT agreed to provide merchantable title upon exercise of the option. . . .

During August 1976, PCC received information that CPMT was not making its payments on the tug's first mortgage. It also claims it learned for the first time during August that CPMT had encumbered the tug with a third mortgage in addition to the two mortgages outstanding against the tug when the contract was signed. The final installment of $49,480 was due on September 15, 1976, to cover the six-month period from that date until March 15, 1977. On August 27, 1976, PCC wrote to CPMT that "[i]t has come to our attention that one of the outstanding mortgages on this boat has fallen into default and the Panama Canal Company therefore considers that reasonable grounds exist for requiring assurance that clear title to the boat will be perfected on or before December 15, 1976," the date the option to purchase became exercisable. Further, PCC stated that it would not forward the payment due September 15 until it received assurance.

CPMT's only response was to file this suit [on September 17,] two days after PCC withheld payment. On December 20, after the purchase option matured, PCC tendered the final charter-hire installment along with the option payment. Delivery was made subject to the condition that CPMT furnish merchantable title. CPMT did not reply.

On April 13, 1977, the companies holding the first and second mortgages on the tug gave notice to PCC that they planned to foreclose and seize the vessel. On June 2, 1977, PCC bought those mortgages for

---

* Under a bareboat charter, the charterer (here, PCC) takes control of the vessel for the period of the charter as though it owns the vessel, with the obligation of returning it to the owner (here, CPMT) at the end of that period.—Eds.

$111,897. In its countersuit . . . , PCC contends that CPMT breached its agreement to provide merchantable title and seeks damages plus interest, in addition to its request for title to the tug.

After discovery and after the denial of several motions for summary judgment filed by both parties, trial in the case was set for May 8, 1978. On March 28, 1978, however, Clem and Marie Perrin filed Chapter XI bankruptcy petitions, and this case was stayed. On January 9, 1979, CPMT was declared bankrupt. The trustee in bankruptcy obtained an order allowing further prosecution of this suit on October 17, 1979, and PCC says it became aware the stay had been lifted when the trustee commenced new discovery proceedings on March 16, 1981.

. . .

IV

UCC § 2–609 provides that when reasonable grounds for insecurity arise, a party may in writing demand assurance and, if commercially reasonable, suspend performance for which he has not already received the agreed return. A ground for insecurity need not arise from or be directly related to the contract under which a party suspends performance. UCC § 2–609, Comment 3. Here PCC had not already received the return for the performance it suspended; the payment was to be made at the beginning of the last six-month lease-period and title to the vessel had not yet been transferred. Under this standard, PCC need only prove it had reasonable doubt that CPMT would provide merchantable title, and need not prove, for example, that CPMT was insolvent, so long as the doubt is otherwise reasonable. See UCC § 2–609, Comment 4. If PCC further can carry its related burden of proving that it was commercially reasonable to suspend performance in light of that doubt, then its case will be made under the UCC standard. . . .

VI

CPMT claims it was not reasonable for PCC to ask for assurance because CPMT was actually in good financial shape at the time PCC suspended performance and could have provided merchantable title, and further that PCC did not adequately investigate CPMT's financial situation before asking for assurance. The district court made no distinct finding on the reasonableness of PCC's suspension of performance, but did hold that PCC had failed to use "due diligence" in investigating CPMT's financial situation. Whether a buyer has reasonable grounds for insecurity is a question of fact. To the extent CPMT is correct in saying this finding of a lack of "due diligence" may be interpreted to be a finding that PCC was not reasonable in its suspension of performance and request for assurance, we hold that the finding was clearly erroneous.

What prompted PCC's concern was a phone call from Mr. H.J. Lopez of the George Engine Company to the PCC informing PCC that CPMT was not making its mortgage payments on the vessel and that George Engine Company was making them instead. CPMT argues that PCC should have inquired more deeply to determine the extent of any financial difficulty, because in reality CPMT was in no danger of defaulting on its mortgages. CPMT further argues it was unreasonable to suspend performance because PCC was aware that CPMT was relying on the payment to pay off the mortgages. CPMT's argument about the extent of PCC's inquiry misses the point, however. If CPMT was in the fine financial shape it argues it was in, all CPMT had to do in response to PCC's request for assurance was to explain the situation. It was certainly not unreasonable for PCC to become alarmed at Lopez' call, enough so for the call in itself to constitute a reasonable ground for insecurity. Lopez had played a major role in brokering the deal between PCC and CPMT and could reasonably have been considered to have good information about CPMT's financial status. Cf. UCC § 2–609, Comment 3 ("[A] report from an apparently trustworthy source that the seller had shipped defective goods * * * would normally give the buyer reasonable grounds for insecurity.") The standard is one of reasonable insecurity, not absolute certainty. See UCC § 2–609, Comment 4, citing Corn Products Refining Co. v. Fasola, 94 NJL 181, 109 A. 505 (1920). Here PCC's suspicion was reasonable, as was their action in asking for assurance. Further, in the face of CPMT's silence after the demand for assurance, it was obviously reasonable for PCC to protect itself by withholding payment, notwithstanding that it was aware that doing so would probably hurt CPMT. That suspending performance might hurt CPMT was not reasonably PCC's concern.

VII

We therefore reverse the district court's finding that PCC breached the contract. Instead, we hold that CPMT breached its agreement to provide merchantable title and is liable for the damages PCC incurred in buying the mortgages on the vessel. Of course, CPMT is still owed the last payment of charter hire and the option payment. We therefore remand the case to the district court for the purpose of offsetting the amounts owed and then awarding PCC the remaining amount. The district court is further directed to award PCC prejudgment interest, see Com. Standard Ins. Co. v. Bryce St. Apts., Ltd., 703 F.2d 904 (5th Cir. 1983), and to enter an order for specific performance compelling CPMT to deliver clear title to the vessel to PCC. Finally, since the parties did not brief the issue on appeal of whether the third-party defendants may be reached by piercing the corporate veil, we remand that issue to the district court for its consideration.

Reversed and remanded.

QUESTIONS AND NOTES

1.   An omitted portion of the opinion reveals that the contract contained a provision that allowed CPMT to cancel the contract if PCC defaulted in payment. In view of the existence of this provision, did the court err in holding for PCC?

2.   Problem. Tophat Company contracted to sell Warren Construction Company a large construction crane for $250,000, delivery on June 1st. The contract called for payment of 50% of the price on delivery and the balance in two annual payments, with Tophat taking a security interest in the crane to secure those two payments. On May 10th, Teri Toroian, president of Tophat Company, was having coffee with Laurie Liu, an attorney friend. Liu remarked that she had heard that Warren was losing a lot of money on a large apartment building it was building. When Toroian got back to the office she phoned Warren and asked whether Warren's financial position was impaired by losses on the apartment building. Warren's treasurer said, "It's not true that we have lost money. In fact, we are fine, and we don't appreciate your asking." With that the conversation ended.

Toroian, however, then sent a letter to Warren Construction relating the statements she had heard and asking whether there was any truth to the assertion. Warren again responded, this time in writing, "we are not losing money, we are fine"; "keep your nose out of our business"; and "why are you so worried, you're fully secured for the amount we owe you after the crane is delivered."

On May 29th Toroian asks you whether she can safely withhold delivery because, she says, she is afraid that Warren Construction is overextended and may get into trouble. She also asks how, if she may indeed withhold delivery, she should proceed, both before and after June 1st. How do you respond?

Would your answer to the above problem change if Toroian told you that she also had heard the same rumors from persons other than Liu before she had made the contract with Warren?

3.   Problem. Husky, Inc., has contracted to deliver over a 12-month period 100 gasoline pumps at Gas-n-Go's chain of convenience stores. The contract calls for Husky to install them, get them operating properly, and service them for 90 days after delivery. It specifies that payment is due 30 days after installation. Of the first 20 pumps that Husky delivered and installed, 12 do not operate as they are supposed to.

a.   May Gas-n-Go properly send Husky a letter refusing to permit it to install any more pumps until it provides satisfactory proof that they will operate as warranted?

b.   May Gas-n-Go withhold payment for the 12 nonconforming pumps? for the other eight?

c.   With respect to the defective pumps, may Gas-n-Go demand an extension of the 90-day repair period provided in the contract?

4.   Note that 2–609(1) speaks of a *written* demand for adequate assurance. Does an oral demand suffice to trigger the other party's obligation to respond? Several cases have held that, on the facts of the case, an oral demand for assurances was effective under 2–609. E.g., Diskmakers, Inc. v. DeWitt Equipment Corp., 555 F.2d 1177 (3d Cir.1977); ARB, Inc. v. E-Systems, Inc., 663 F.2d 189 (D.C.Cir.1980).

5. The financial condition of a business may change significantly over a relatively short period of time. A change in the financial condition of the seller may affect the seller's ability to deliver the goods, and the buyer may invoke 2–609 to demand assurances that the seller will perform as agreed. Similarly, a change in the financial condition of the buyer may affect the buyer's ability to pay for the goods, and the seller may demand adequate assurance. For this particular cause of insecurity, however, Article 2 has two other provisions to alleviate the seller's insecurity. Under the conditions specified in 2–702, the seller may convert a credit transaction into a cash transaction. Under the conditions specified in 2–705, the seller may withhold delivery of the goods. Please read those sections.

6. Problem. Noflat Tire Company contracted to ship a carload of tires to TBA Stores, Inc. The shipment was to be F.O.B. Noflat's plant and was on open account on 90-day payment terms. While the carload was in transit, Noflat's credit department received a report that TBA was running four months or more behind in paying bills. Noflat calls you and asks whether there is anything it can do to protect itself against the possibility that TBA will pay very late or not at all. The shipment was under a straight bill of lading naming TBA as consignee. (Under a straight bill, the carrier will deliver to the named consignee without requiring payment or the surrender of any document or other evidence of ownership.)

    a. What do you advise?

    b. May Noflat direct the carrier to stop the train?

    c. If Noflat decides to stop the shipment, does it have to notify TBA of that action and the reasons for it?

7. Problem. Global Controls contracted to deliver certain instruments to MissileCo for use in a missile system that MissileCo was installing. The contract called for payment to be made monthly for deliveries made the previous month. Final inspection and acceptance of the goods were to take place at the various missile sites (which were not the place of delivery). About six weeks before making the first delivery, Global began to receive unfavorable credit reports on MissileCo. About three weeks before the first delivery Global secured a Dun & Bradstreet credit report that showed a reduction in MissileCo's credit rating from A1 to A1-1/2 and delays in payment to its suppliers. Global then contacted some individual suppliers, who reported substantial delays in payment. Instead of shipping the goods under a straight bill of lading, Global sent the first order under a sight-draft-with-order bill of lading. (Under that document the carrier will not deliver the goods to the buyer until the price is paid. It permits the buyer to inspect the goods in the hands of the carrier, but requires payment of the price before the buyer is entitled to possession of the goods.) MissileCo refused to pay against the sight draft and the goods were returned to Global Controls. When Global Controls sued, MissileCo filed a counterclaim. Which party has breached? See 2–702, 2–310, 2–505, 2–513.

8. In a contract that calls for payment 30 days after delivery, what if the seller learns of the buyer's insolvency before the seller has shipped the goods: may the seller cancel the contract without offering the goods for cash?

9. Subsection (1) of 2–702 provides that if the seller discovers the buyer to be insolvent, the seller may (a) refuse to deliver except for cash, and (b) stop delivery under 2–705. If a seller learns of a buyer's insolvency after the seller has shipped the goods, may the seller exercise the second alternative in 2–702 independently of the first: may a seller stop delivery of the goods without offering to deliver them for cash?

C. REPUDIATION

1. DEFINITION

The preceding section explores the rights of one party to a sales contract when the words or conduct of the other party have created insecurity about whether that other party will perform in accordance with the contract. If that other party's words or conduct amount to a repudiation of the contract, the aggrieved party need not go through the procedures of 2–609 but instead may treat the repudiation as a breach. See 2–610(b). Alternatively, the aggrieved party may refuse to treat the repudiation as a breach and may continue to await performance by the repudiating party. See 2–610(a). Conversely, 2–611 recognizes that the repudiating party may have a change of heart and want to retract the repudiation. The first question is determining whether the words or conduct amount to a repudiation.

1.   Problem. Assume that there are only five remaining operable U.S. Army amphibious vehicles of World War Two vintage (Ducks) in the entire world. One of these is owned by Motts Motor Car Museum, which restores and displays vintage cars, in Pittsburgh, Pennsylvania; two are owned by Motion Picture Props in Long Beach, California; one is owned by Eduardo Robles of Atlanta, Georgia; and one is owned by Sharon Wahlmut, of Bentonville, Arkansas. On May 1st Robles contracted to sell his Duck to Motion Picture Props for $25,000, delivery in Atlanta on June 2nd.

On May 15th Motion Picture Props learned that Robles had just agreed to sell his Duck to Motts Motor Car Museum. Props understands that Wahlmut is trying to sell her Duck for $35,000. Afraid that Wahlmut may sell the Duck at any moment, Props' chief operating officer asks you whether Props can buy Wahlmut's Duck immediately and charge Robles with the increased cost. What do you advise?

2.   Problem. Specialty Foods formed six separate contracts with Pickle Palace. The contracts call for Pickle Palace to deliver of 100 cases of kosher dill pickles on the first day of each month, April through September. The price of each delivery is $10,000, and payment is due 10 days after delivery. Pickle Palace delivered on the first of April, May, June, and July. Specialty Foods paid for the April delivery on April 12th, for the May delivery on May 20th, but did not pay for the deliveries in June and July. On July 25th, Pickle Palace informed Specialty Foods that it would not deliver the pickles on the August and September contracts unless it received payment on the two earlier contracts on which it had not been paid. Specialty Foods immediately purchased pickles elsewhere for $11,500 per month and sued Pickle Palace. Is Pickle Palace liable?

3.   Problem. Dynamic Auto Detailing contracted to purchase automobile paint from Potter Paints for a period of six years. To help finance Dynamic's operations, Potter periodically paid a rebate on quantities to be purchased in the future. These were characterized as "pre-bates." Shortly into the six-year period, the owner of Potter Paints decided to retire. After considering several alternative ways to dispose of the business, he decided to sell it to his daughter, Corey, who had been working there for several years. He sent the following email to Potter:

> I have decided to sell Dynamic Auto Detailing to my daughter, Corey. My wife and I feel this is the safest exit strategy and allows Corey the opportunity of a lifetime. We have negotiated a fair price and expect to close by the end of the month.

> While reviewing our various contracts, I discussed the current state of our agreement with you. Corey said that she did not benefit from the past pre-bates and therefore will be looking for a proposal that will benefit and make sense to her. I understand there will be pre-bate money owed back to Potter Paints if in fact Corey chooses to go another direction, and my attorney will need to figure out who and how that gets accomplished. I will tell you, I shared with Corey the two proposals I received from your competition a few months ago, and I am certain she will be reaching out to them. I want to encourage you to set up a meeting with Corey as soon as you possibly can.

Granted that this email gives Porter reasonable grounds for insecurity concerning Dynamic's future performance, does it go beyond that and amount to a repudiation?

4.   Consider the following excerpt from Ewanchuk v. Mitchell, 154 S.W.3d 476 (Mo.App.2005):

> Ewanchuk and Mitchell are both in the business of breeding and raising registered Boston terriers. Ewanchuk has been licensed in this business for twelve years and resides in Alberta, Canada. Mitchell has been licensed in this business for three years and operates a kennel in Cabool, Missouri. Mitchell sold only puppies, and she mainly marketed her animals to brokers that purchased animals for resale to pet stores.

> On January 20, 2003, one of Mitchell's breeding females whelped two male Boston terrier puppies ("the puppies"). Rather than being the black and white color normally found in Boston terriers, the puppies were red and white in color. This made them very unique and desirable animals.

On February 20, 2003, Mitchell offered to sell the puppies by placing an ad on the internet. That same day, Ewanchuk responded to the ad by leaving a message on Mitchell's answering machine. In the message, Ewanchuk expressed her interest in purchasing the puppies. She asked Mitchell to return the call, which Mitchell did. Ewanchuk and Mitchell had several more telephone conversations about the puppies, and Mitchell sent photographs of them to Ewanchuk. During these conversations, Ewanchuk did not commit to purchasing the puppies because they were still too young.

On [Friday,] March 21, 2003, Mitchell called Ewanchuk to inform her that the puppies were eight weeks old and were going to be sold to a broker the following Monday unless Ewanchuk agreed to buy them. The timing of the sale was very important to Mitchell because pet stores would not purchase puppies older than nine weeks of age, so she had to get them to a broker immediately if Ewanchuk did not buy them. Otherwise, the value of the puppies would decline because Mitchell would no longer be able to sell them to a broker or a pet store.

Mitchell initially priced the puppies at $350 each, but she agreed to sell the puppies for a total of $600 because Ewanchuk wanted to buy both of them. Ewanchuk provided Mitchell with a credit card number which was used to charge the $600 payment.

Although Ewanchuk and Mitchell were able to agree on the puppies' price, they were unable to agree on when and how the puppies would be delivered to Ewanchuk. . . . Mitchell, however, insisted that Ewanchuk accept delivery by April 15, 2003.

. . . On [April 15] Ewanchuk telephoned Mitchell to discuss shipping arrangements. In this telephone call, Ewanchuk insisted Mitchell ship the puppies together in one crate. Ewanchuk testified that "I wanted the two puppies shipped together in one kennel, and they [Mitchell and her husband] refused to do that." Mitchell would not ship the three-month-old puppies together because she believed they "would fight and that it was not safe for the puppies to be in the same crate at that age." Mitchell was willing to send one puppy in one crate, but Ewanchuk wanted both delivered together. Ewanchuk testified that Mitchell "repudiated" the contract during that call and said she would refund Ewanchuk's money.

After April 15, 2003, Ewanchuk made no further arrangements to have the puppies delivered to her and had no further direct contact with Mitchell. Ewanchuk later hired an attorney, who filed suit on her behalf on May 16, 2003, seeking specific performance of the oral agreement and injunctive relief to prevent Mitchell from selling the puppies to someone else. . . .

. . . [T]he trial court entered judgment for Mitchell. . . . The trial court found for Mitchell, in pertinent part, for the following reason:

> There was no meeting of the minds as to one of the essential terms of the contract, namely when the puppies would be shipped to the Plaintiff in Canada, and how the shipment would be arranged. . . . Further, a dispute arose as to whether the puppies should be shipped in one crate or two crates. Therefore, the Court finds that all of the essential terms of the contract were not agreed upon and that the Agreement lacked a definiteness necessary for its enforcement.

Ewanchuk appealed.

. . . The oral agreement between Ewanchuk and Mitchell was a contract for the sale of goods within the meaning of Missouri's version of the Uniform Commercial Code ("UCC.") See § 400.2–105(1). Therefore, this transaction in goods is governed by the law of sales found in Article 2 of the UCC, which is codified in § 400.2–101 through § 400.2–725.

. . .

The trial court misapplied the law by concluding that the parties' agreement "lacked a definiteness necessary for its enforcement." On appeal, however, we are "primarily concerned with the correctness of the trial court's result, not the route taken by the trial court to reach that result." Business Men's Assur. Co. of America v. Graham, 984 S.W.2d 501, 506 (Mo. banc 1999). "The judgment will be affirmed if cognizable under any theory, regardless of whether the reasons advanced by the trial court are wrong or not sufficient." Id.

The second prong of Ewanchuk's argument is that Mitchell breached the contract by refusing to deliver the puppies. We reject this aspect of Ewanchuk's argument. The trial court entered judgment for Mitchell after concluding the contract was unenforceable. This conclusion is correct, but for a different reason than the one upon which the trial court relied.

. . . Ewanchuk insisted the puppies be shipped to her in one crate, and Mitchell refused. Mitchell offered to ship one dog in one crate, but Ewanchuk was adamant that she wanted the puppies shipped together. At that point, Mitchell cancelled the contract and said she would refund Ewanchuk's money. Thereafter, Ewanchuk made no further arrangements to have the puppies delivered to her, and she never contacted Mitchell directly again.

As noted above, the parties failed to reach an agreement upon the manner and place of delivery during their negotiation.

Therefore, the UCC supplied that term of the agreement by requiring Ewanchuk to pick up the puppies at Mitchell's place of business in Cabool. Ewanchuk did not pick up the puppies by April 15, 2003. Instead, on the date delivery was due to occur, Ewanchuk insisted that Mitchell ship both puppies by air in one crate to Alberta, Canada. It was this demand which caused Mitchell's refusal to deliver the puppies and consequent cancellation of the contract. Absent Mitchell's agreement, the UCC did not give Ewanchuk the right to receive delivery of the puppies in this fashion.

Both by decisional law and statute, Missouri recognizes the doctrine of anticipatory repudiation. Missouri Public Service Co. v. Peabody Coal Co., 583 S.W.2d 721, 724 (Mo.App.1979); § 400.2–610. A party repudiates a contract by manifesting a positive intention not to perform by words or conduct. Gateway Aviation, Inc. v. Cessna Aircraft Co., 577 S.W.2d 860, 862 (Mo.App.1978). Section 400.2–610 states in pertinent part that, "when either party repudiates the contract with respect to a performance not yet due the loss of which will substantially impair the value of the contract to the other, the aggrieved party may . . . (b) resort to any remedy for breach (section 400.2–703 or section 400.2–711). . . ." Upon a buyer's repudiation of the contract, in whole or in part, one of the seller's available remedies is cancellation of the contract. § 400.2–703(f).

Here, Ewanchuk's own testimony demonstrated that she insisted upon a mode of delivery (both puppies in one crate) and a place of delivery (Alberta, Canada, via air transportation) to which Mitchell had not agreed and to which Ewanchuk was not entitled under the UCC. After making this impermissible demand, Ewanchuk also testified that she never contacted Mitchell directly again and made no further arrangements to have the puppies delivered to her.

Thus, Ewanchuk's trial testimony, by which she was bound, proved that she repudiated the contract on April 15, 2003. Since the puppies were then 12 weeks old, Ewanchuk's repudiation impaired the value of the contract to Mitchell because she could no longer sell the puppies to a broker or pet store. Based on this repudiation, Mitchell was authorized to cancel the contract, which she did.

In conclusion, the trial court properly denied Ewanchuk's request for specific performance and other relief because the contract was unenforceable. The reason the contract was unenforceable, however, was because it had been cancelled by Mitchell after repudiation by Ewanchuk. Although the trial court did not rely on the doctrine of repudiation as the basis for its decision, we may do so to uphold the judgment based on the record before us. The judgment of the trial court is affirmed.

5.   Problem. Please reread the facts of Problem 1, page 565 (the contract for the sale of the Duck). Assume now that Props did not know of Robles' agreement with Motts. Since delivery of the Duck was to be made in Atlanta, Props had arranged for one of its large tractor-trailers to leave Long Beach for Atlanta on May 25th. On May 23rd Props received an e-mail from Robles saying that he decided to sell his Duck to Motts, "so I won't be delivering it to you." Props e-mailed back, "We expect you to perform," and sent the truck on its way. The truck arrived in Atlanta on June 2nd, at which time the driver tendered the purchase price and demanded delivery. Robles refused. May Props recover as an element of damages the expense of sending the truck to Atlanta? What arguments would you make on behalf of Motion Picture Props? on behalf of Eduardo Robles?

6.   Problem. Scott Kim contracted to sell Meredith Hendon three holographic-image-making machines for a total price of $50,000, delivery on February 1. On January 15 Kim called Hendon and notified her that he would be unable to supply the machines except at a price of $60,000. Hendon replied, "What! Our contract clearly calls for a price of $50,000. You can't get away with this. I'll see you in court"! Taken aback by her vehemence, Kim retreated, "All right, never mind. I'll perform on the original terms." Hendon said, "No, I'm through with you."

Kim tendered the machines on February 1, and Hendon refused to accept them. Who breached?

————

2.   DAMAGES

Once the court concludes that a party has repudiated the contract, the problem of assessing damages remains. If a buyer repudiates, 2–703 permits the seller to recover under 2–706 (contract price less resale price) or under 2–708 (either contract price less market price or lost profits).

1.   Problem. On January 3 Petra Petroleum contracted to sell 1,000,000 gallons of oil to Oriental Oil. The price was $1.50 per gallon, and delivery was to be August 31. On June 1 Oriental repudiated. The market price per gallon of this quantity of oil fluctuated as follows:

January 3	$1.50
June 1	$1.20
July 1	$1.15
August 1	$1.25
August 31	$1.30

To what damages is Petra Petroleum entitled?

2.   Problem. When Oriental Oil in Problem 1 repudiated, Petra Petroleum sold the oil on June 21 for $1.15 per gallon to another oil company. To what damages is Petra entitled? If the resale were for $1.40 per gallon, what would be the damages award?

————

The preceding problems consider the remedy when the buyer repudiates. If it is the seller who repudiates, 2–711 permits the buyer to recover under 2–712 (cover price less contract price) or under 2–713 (market price less contract price). Unlike the apparent ease of determining the seller's damages in the case of repudiation by the buyer, however, it is considerably more difficult to determine the buyer's damages when the seller repudiates.

Problem. As in the preceding problems, Petra Petroleum and Oriental Oil formed a contract on January 3 for the sale of 1,000,000 gallons of oil for $1.50 per gallon, delivery on August 31. On June 1 Petra (rather than Oriental) repudiated the contract. The market price for August 31 delivery of that quantity of oil fluctuated as follows:

January 3	$1.50
May 1	$1.80
June 1	$1.70
July 1	$1.65
August 1	$1.65
August 31	$1.60

a.   If Oriental purchased 1,000,000 gallons of oil elsewhere on August 15 for $1.65 per gallon, to what damages is it entitled?

b.   If Oriental did not replace the oil, to what damages is it entitled?

Hess Energy, Inc. v. Lightning Oil Co., Ltd.

United States Court of Appeals, Fourth Circuit, 2003.
338 F.3d 357.

[Beginning in 1999 Lightning Oil entered seven contracts with Hess Energy to supply Hess with natural gas at fixed prices at specified dates in the future. In mid-2000 Lightning claimed that Hess had materially breached the contracts and announced that it would not deliver the gas required by these contracts. Hess sued, ultimately establishing that it had not breached and that Lightning's refusal to perform was a material breach. The jury returned a verdict of slightly more than $3 million, which represented the excess of the market price over the contract price on the several dates of delivery. Lightning appealed.]

■ NIEMEYER, CIRCUIT JUDGE:

. . .

For its principal argument on appeal, Lightning contends that the district court erred in instructing the jury that the proper measure of damages under Virginia law was the difference between the contract price and the market price *at the time and place of delivery*. Lightning argues that under the Virginia Uniform Commercial Code § 8.2–713, "[t]he proper measure of damages in this case is the difference between the contract price and the market price *at the time Hess learned that Lightning would not perform*." (Emphasis added). . . .

It is undisputed in this case that the [contracts] were subject to the provisions of Virginia's Uniform Commercial Code. The core dispute between the parties concerns *when* the market price of the undelivered natural gas should be measured for purposes of calculating damages and to what degree Hess' damages may be limited by an asserted duty to cover. While this case presents an archetypal anticipatory repudiation, . . . measuring a buyer's damages in such circumstances "presents one of the most impenetrable interpretive problems in the entire [Uniform Commercial] Code." 1 James J. White & Robert S. Summers, *Uniform Commercial Code* § 6–7, at 337 (4th ed.1995).

We begin the analysis by pointing out that the overarching principle given by the district court's instruction to the jury—"the remedy for breach of contract is intended to put the injured party in the same position in which it would have been had the contract been performed"—conforms to the governing principle for damages under the Virginia Uniform Commercial Code. *See* Va.Code § 8.1–106 [now § 8.1–305(a)] (stating that the Code's remedies "shall be liberally administered to the end that the aggrieved party may be put in as good a position as if the other party had fully performed").

Under the specific provisions for damages, the Virginia Uniform Commercial Code provides that when a seller repudiates a contract, the buyer is given several alternatives, none of which operates to penalize the buyer as a victim of the seller's repudiation. *See* Va. Code § 8.2–610. One option provided by § 8.2–610 is for the buyer to "resort to any remedy for breach (§ 8.2–703 or 8.2–711), even though [the buyer] has notified the repudiating [seller] that he would await the latter's performance and has urged retraction." *Id.* § 8.2–610(b). Section 8.2–711, in turn, allows a buyer either to " 'cover' and have damages under the next section [§ 8.2–712] as to all the goods affected" or to "recover damages for nondelivery as provided in this title (§ 8.2–713)." In this case, Hess chose not to cover, opting instead to recover damages for nondelivery under § 8.2–713.

Section 8.2–713 provides:

[T]he measure of damages for nondelivery or repudiation by the seller is the difference between the market price *at the time when the buyer learned of the breach* and the contract price together with any incidental and consequential damages provided in this title (§ 8.2–715), but less expenses saved in consequence of the seller's breach (emphasis added).

Lightning would have us equate "the time when the buyer learned of the *breach* " with the time when the buyer learned of the *repudiation* and require calculating damages using the market price of the contracted-for natural gas at the time Hess learned that Lightning would not perform. Hess contends, on the other hand, that the time when it learned of the breach for purposes of § 8.2–713 did not occur "until each time [Lightning] failed to deliver natural gas as promised in its contract," rather than at the time Lightning communicated its intent not to perform.

These diverse positions reduce to the core question of whether "breach" as used in "when the buyer learned of the breach" means "repudiation," or whether "breach" refers to the date of actual performance when it could be determined that a breach occurred—in this case, the date of delivery.

While § 8.2–713 might be susceptible to multiple interpretations, *see* White & Summers, *supra,* § 6–7, at 337 (articulating at least three possibilities), we conclude that the drafters of the Uniform Commercial Code made a deliberate distinction between the terms "repudiation" and "breach," and to blur these two words by equating them would render several related provisions of the Uniform Commercial Code meaningless. This is best illustrated by reference to § 8.2–610. In that provision, an aggrieved buyer can wait "a commercially reasonable time" after learning of the seller's repudiation to allow the seller to change its mind and perform. Va.Code § 8.2–610(a). If Lightning's interpretation of § 8.2–713 were the correct one—that the damages should be calculated based on the market price on the date of repudiation—then the buyer would be deprived of his right under § 8.2–610 to await a reasonable time for seller's possible post-repudiation performance. . . .

In another example, if the date of the seller's repudiation is equated with the time when the buyer learns of the seller's breach as used in § 8.2–713, then § 8.2–723(1) would become meaningless. Section 8.2–723(1) provides:

If an action based on anticipatory repudiation comes to trial before the time for performance with respect to some or all of the goods, any damages based on market price (§ 8.2–708 or § 8.2–713) shall be determined according to the price of such goods prevailing at the time when the aggrieved party learned of the repudiation.

This section moves the date that the seller learned of the *breach* under § 8.2–713 to the date that the seller learned of the *repudiation* in circumstances where the case has come to trial before the performance date. To give meaning to § 8.2–723(1), when the case does *not* come to trial before the performance date, as here, damages are *not* measured when the aggrieved party learned of the repudiation. *See* White & Summers, *supra,* § 6–7, at 341 (. . . concluding that the drafters "must have thought 'learned of the repudiation' had a different meaning than 'learned of the breach' ").

Thus, we conclude that the better reading of § 8.2–713 is that an aggrieved buyer's damages against a repudiating seller are based on the market price on the date of performance—i.e., the date of delivery. This reading also harmonizes the remedies available to aggrieved buyers and aggrieved sellers when faced with a repudiating counterparty. Faced with a repudiating buyer, an aggrieved seller is entitled to "recover damages for nonacceptance" under § 8.2–708. Under § 8.2–708, "the measure of damages for nonacceptance or repudiation by the buyer is the difference between the market price *at the time and place for tender* and the unpaid contract price together with any incidental damages." *Id.* § 8.2–708 (emphasis added). There is nothing in the Uniform Commercial Code to suggest that the remedies available to aggrieved buyers and sellers in the anticipatory repudiation context were meant to be asymmetrical. Indeed, the lead-in clause to § 8.2–610, relating to anticipatory repudiation, addresses both parties: "When either party repudiates the contract with respect to a performance not yet due . . . ."

Because our interpretation of § 8.2–713 avoids rendering other sections of the Uniform Commercial Code meaningless or superfluous and harmonizes the remedies available to buyers and sellers, we are persuaded that in this case "the time when the buyer learned of the breach" was the scheduled date of performance on the contract, i.e., the agreed-upon date for the delivery of the natural gas, not the date that the seller informed the buyer that it was repudiating the contract.

This reading is also consistent with Virginia's pre-UCC general common law rule that "the measure of damages is the difference between the contract price and the market price at the time and place of delivery." *See Nottingham Coal & Ice Co. v. Preas,* 102 Va. 820, 47 S.E. 823, 824 (1904). . . . [I]f the drafters of the Uniform Commercial Code had meant to "upset such uniform and firmly entrenched doctrine," the Code would contain explicit statutory language making such a departure clear.

In reaching this conclusion, we point out that Lightning's view would unacceptably shift the risks undertaken by the parties in their contract. Under Lightning's view, an aggrieved buyer facing a repudiating seller has two choices: (1) to cover within a commercially reasonable time and receive damages based on the cover price or (2) to forego the opportunity to cover and simply await the date of performance. Lightning contends that if the buyer opts for the second option and the market price then falls, the buyer's savings must be shared with the seller. "[B]ut if it rises, the aggrieved party cannot recover the higher amount that resulted from his voluntarily undertaking of that risk." This policy argument would penalize an aggrieved buyer for inaction and therefore cannot be valid, particularly when the repudiating seller is in a position to fix his damages on the contract by entering into hedge transactions on the date of his repudiation. As one well-respected commentary explains:

> When the seller of goods has promised delivery at a future time and prior thereto repudiates his contract, the buyer is not required to go into the market at once and make another contract for future delivery merely because there is reason to expect a rise in the market price. If his forecast is incorrect and the price falls, his second contract on a high market increases the loss. If his forecast is correct and the price rises, his second contract avoids a loss and operates as a saving to the repudiator. But the risk of this rise or fall is exactly the risk that the repudiating seller contracted to carry. If at the time of repudiation he thinks that the price will rise, so that his performance will become more costly, he can make his own second contract transferring the risk to a third party and thus hedge against his first risky contract.

11 Arthur Linton Corbin, Corbin on Contracts § 1053, at 273 (Interim ed. 2002). Thus, if Lightning wished to avoid the risk that it undertook in entering into the contract and fix its damages on the date of repudiation, it could have done so by entering into hedge transactions in the futures market. But its repudiation of the contract cannot shift to Hess the very market risk that Hess had sought to avoid by entering into contracts for the future delivery of gas in the first place.

At bottom, we conclude that the district court complied with Virginia Code § 8.2–713 when it instructed the jury in this case that it could calculate damages using the market price on the date of performance, in this case the date of delivery of the natural gas. . . .

Accordingly, we affirm the judgment of the district court.

QUESTIONS AND NOTES

1.   To measure a buyer's damages, 2–713 says to look to the time when the buyer learns of the breach. This is in contrast with the section governing a seller's damages, where 2–708(1) says to look to the time for tender. The Code gives no explanation for this difference. What explanation(s) are there? If the objective is to put the buyer in its expectancy position, under what circumstances might it not be appropriate to measure the buyer's damages as of the date of tender?

2.   In the repudiation context, when does a buyer learn of the breach? Is repudiation a breach? What section(s) are relevant to determining the answer to this question?

3.   In the middle of page 573, the court refers to three possibilities for when to measure damages when a seller repudiates. Two of those possibilities are the time of repudiation and the time for tender. What is the third possibility?

4. The common law determined damages in the case of a seller's repudiation by looking to the market price on the date of delivery, not the date of repudiation. E.g., Reliance Cooperage Corp. v. Treat, 195 F.2d 977 (8th Cir.1952). Even though the buyer could have avoided loss by engaging in a substitute transaction when the seller repudiated, the courts looked to the date of delivery for determining damages. Moreover, this was true even if the buyer did purchase substitute goods at a price that turned out to be higher than the market price at the time of delivery. The buyer was denied recovery based on the substitute purchase and recovered only an amount based on the lower market price. Section 2–712 changes this if the buyer chooses to cover, and it measures damages by looking to the price of the goods in that substitute transaction. But subsection (3) makes it clear that cover is optional. This dovetails with 2–610, which authorizes the buyer to await performance. The buyer need not pursue a remedy—cover or otherwise— immediately upon learning of a repudiation. How long may the buyer await performance by a seller who has announced an intention not to perform? Is the court's holding consistent with 2–610? What does 2–610 suggest about the time for determining damages when a seller repudiates?

5.   CISG. The Convention on Contracts for the International Sale of Goods takes a different approach than Article 2 to the issues of insecurity and suspension of performance. Article 71 provides that a party may suspend performance if it becomes apparent that the other party will not perform a substantial part of his obligations as a result of a serious deficiency in his ability to perform, his creditworthiness, or his conduct in preparing to perform or performing the contract. The party suspending performance, however, must immediately give notice of suspension and continue with performance if the other party provides adequate assurance of his performance.

Article 72 provides that if "it is clear that one of the parties will commit a fundamental breach of contract, the other party may declare the contract avoided," but, unless the other party has declared that he will not perform, the party declaring the contract avoided must, "if time allows," give reasonable notice to the other party so that it may provide adequate assurance of performance.

The difference between the events that trigger rights under Article 71 and the events that trigger the greater rights under Article 72 seems very slight and possibly non-existent. Presumably, however, the ambiguity in the sections will encourage an insecure party to be cautious about declaring the contract at an end. Is that good or bad?

Note that the Convention provides no right to demand assurances unless there is a right to suspend performance, and the right to suspend does not arise unless "it becomes apparent that the other party will not perform a substantial part of his obligations. . . ." Therefore, the right to demand assurances is more limited than the right under UCC 2–609.

As for the measurement of damages when a party repudiates, Article 76 provides that a party who has not entered into a substitute transaction can recover the difference between the contract price and the "current" price at the time of avoidance. To what date does "current" refer? Article 72 permits a party to declare the contract avoided if it is clear that the other party will commit a fundamental breach, but it does not say that the contract is avoided, or that there is a present breach by repudiation. It merely states that the aggrieved party may avoid the contract. Does this mean that the aggrieved party is in control of the time for measuring contract-market damages in the repudiation case by deciding whether and when to declare the contract avoided?

In connection with that question, Articles 49 and 64, which relate to fundamental breach by seller and buyer respectively, state that the aggrieved party "may declare the contract avoided." It seems very unlikely that CISG would be interpreted to allow the aggrieved party to choose the time for measuring damages by delaying a declaration that the contract is avoided in the case, for example, where the seller fails to deliver the goods, or the buyer wrongfully rejects the goods. But, in the case of repudiation, since there is a strong argument for allowing the injured party to measure damages at the time set for performance of the other party, courts might, indeed, give the aggrieved party the power to choose the time to determine contract-market damages by choosing the time to announce avoidance.

CHAPTER 10

DISCHARGE BY IMPRACTICABILITY

Occasionally unanticipated events occur that either impair the ability of the parties to perform or destroy the utility of the performance for which they have contracted. To deal with these situations, the courts of England developed the doctrines of impossibility of performance and frustration of purpose. Taylor v. Caldwell, 3 Best & S. 826 (K.B.1863); Krell v. Henry, 2 K.B. 740 (Ct.App.1903). American courts have embraced these doctrines, excusing the parties from their contractual obligations when an unforeseen, supervening event makes the performance of one of them impossible or frustrates the purpose for which they formed the contract. In 2–613 through 2–616, Article 2 adopts these doctrines for sales contracts, although it abandons the common-law terminology in favor of the term "impracticability."

United States v. Wegematic Corp.

United States Court of Appeals, Second Circuit, 1966.
360 F.2d 674.

■ FRIENDLY, CIRCUIT JUDGE. The facts developed at trial in the District Court for the Southern District of New York, fully set forth in a memorandum by Judge Graven, can be briefly summarized: In June 1956 the Federal Reserve Board invited five electronics manufacturers to submit proposals for an intermediate-type, general-purpose electronic digital computing system or systems; the invitation stressed the importance of early delivery as a consideration in determining the Board's choice. Defendant, a relative newcomer in the field, which had enjoyed considerable success with a smaller computer known as the ALWAC III-E, submitted a detailed proposal for the sale or lease of a new computer designated as the ALWAC 800. It characterized the machine as "a truly revolutionary system utilizing all of the latest technical advances," and featured that "maintenance problems are minimized by the use of highly reliable magnetic cores for not only the high speed memory but also logical elements and registers." Delivery was offered nine months from the date the contract or purchase order was received. In September the Board acted favorably on the defendant's proposal, ordering components of the ALWAC 800 with an aggregate cost of $231,800. Delivery was to be made on June 30, 1957, with liquidated damages of $100 per day for delay. The order also provided that in the event the defendant failed to comply "with any provision" of the agreement, "the Board may procure the services described in the contract from other sources and hold the Contractor responsible for any excess cost occasioned thereby." Defendant accepted the order with enthusiasm.

The first storm warning was a suggestion by the defendant in March 1957 that the delivery date be postponed. In April it informed the Board by letter that delivery would be made on or before October 30 rather than as agreed, the delay being due to the necessity of "a redesign which we feel has greatly improved this equipment"; waiver of the stipulated damages for delay was requested. The Board took the request under advisement. On August 30 defendant wrote that delivery would be delayed "possibly into 1959"; it suggested use of ALWAC III-E equipment in the interim and waiver of the $100 per day "penalty." The Board also took this request under advisement but made clear it was waiving no rights. In mid-October defendant announced that "due to engineering difficulties it has become impracticable to deliver the ALWAC 800 Computing System at this time"; it requested cancellation of the contract without damages. The Board set about procuring comparable equipment from another manufacturer; on October 6, 1958, International Business Machines Corporation delivered an IBM 650 computer, serving substantially the same purpose as the ALWAC 800, at a rental of $102,000 a year with an option to purchase for $410,450.

In July 1958 the Board advised defendant of its intention to press its claim for damages; this suit followed. The court awarded the United States $46,300 for delay under the liquidated damages clause, $179,450 for the excess cost of the IBM equipment, and $10,056 for preparatory expenses useless in operating the IBM system—a total of $235,806, with 6% interest from October 6, 1958.

The principal point of the defense, which is the sole ground of this appeal, is that delivery was made impossible by "basic engineering difficulties" whose correction would have taken between one and two years and would have cost a million to a million and a half dollars, with success likely but not certain. Although the record does not give an entirely clear notion what the difficulties were, two experts suggested that they may have stemmed from the magnetic cores, used instead of transistors to achieve a solid state machine, which did not have sufficient uniformity at this stage of their development. Defendant contends that under federal law, which both parties concede to govern, the "practical impossibility" of completing the contract excused its defaults in performance.

. . .

We find persuasive the defendant's suggestion of looking to the Uniform Commercial Code as a source for the "federal" law of sales. The Code has been adopted by Congress for the District of Columbia, 77 Stat. 630 (1963), has been enacted in over forty states, and is thus well on its way to becoming a truly national law of commerce. . . . When the states have gone so far in achieving the desirable goal of a uniform law governing commercial transactions, it would be a distinct disservice to insist on a different one for the segment of commerce, important but still small in relation to the total, consisting of transactions with the United States.

Section 2–615 of the UCC, entitled "Excuse by failure of presupposed conditions," provides that:

> "Except so far as a seller may have assumed a greater obligation * * * delay in delivery or non-delivery * * * is not a breach of his duty under a contract for sale if performance as agreed has been made impracticable by the occurrence of a contingency the non-occurrence of which was a basic assumption on which the contract was made.* * * "

The latter part of the test seems a somewhat complicated way of putting Professor Corbin's question of how much risk the promisor assumed. Recent Developments in the Law of Contracts, 50 Harv.L.Rev. 449, 465–66 (1937); 2 Corbin, Contracts § 1333, at 371. We see no basis for thinking that when an electronics system is promoted by its manufacturer as a revolutionary breakthrough, the risk of the revolution's occurrence falls on the purchaser; the reasonable supposition is that it has already occurred or, at least, that the manufacturer is assuring the purchaser that it will be found to have when the machine is assembled. As Judge Graven said: "The Board in its invitation for bids did not request invitations to conduct a development program for it. The Board requested invitations from manufacturers for the furnishing of a computer machine." Acceptance of defendant's argument would mean that though a purchaser makes his choice because of the attractiveness of a manufacturer's representation and will be bound by it, the manufacturer is free to express what are only aspirations and gamble on mere probabilities of fulfillment without any risk of liability. In fields of developing technology, the manufacturer would thus enjoy a wide degree of latitude with respect to performance while holding an option to compel the buyer to pay if the gamble should pan out. We do not think this the common understanding—above all as to a contract where the manufacturer expressly agreed to liquidated damages for delay and authorized the purchaser to resort to other sources in the event of non-delivery. If a manufacturer wishes to be relieved of the risk that what looks good on paper may not prove so good in hardware, the appropriate exculpatory language is well known and often used.

Beyond this the evidence of true impracticability was far from compelling. The large sums predicted by defendant's witnesses must be appraised in relation not to the single computer ordered by the Federal Reserve Board, evidently for a bargain price, but to the entire ALWAC 800 program as originally contemplated. Although the record gives no idea what this was, even twenty-five machines would gross $10,000,000 if priced at the level of the comparable IBM equipment. While the unanticipated need for expending $1,000,000 or $1,500,000 on redesign might have made such a venture unattractive, as defendant's management evidently decided, the sums are thus not so clearly prohibitive as it would have them appear. What seemingly did become impossible was on-time performance; the issue whether if defendant had offered prompt rectification of the design, the Government could have refused to give it a chance and still recover not merely damages for delay but also the higher cost of replacement equipment, is not before us.

Affirmed.

QUESTIONS AND NOTES

1.   In *Wegematic,* Judge Friendly says: "If a manufacturer wishes to be relieved of the risk that what looks good on paper may not prove so good in hardware, the appropriate exculpatory language is well known and often used." It is not clear whether he had in mind a special clause for contracts for the sale of new technology machines or the more usual "force majeure" clause. In any event, sales contracts frequently contain a clause reading something like the following (from 5A-2 Bender's Forms and Procedures Under the UCC ¶ 24.22(1)):

> *Force majeure.* Neither party shall be held responsible if fulfillment of any terms or provisions of this contract are delayed or prevented by revolutions or other disorders, wars, acts of enemies, strikes, fires, floods, acts of God, by any other cause not within the control of the party whose performance is interfered with, and which by the exercise of reasonable diligence, the party is unable to prevent, whether of the class of causes above enumerated or not.

These clauses typically excuse one or both parties from performing in situations in which 2–615 would not provide an excuse. Absent such defenses as duress or unconscionability, are these clauses enforceable? Note that 2–615 opens with the language: "Except so far as a seller may have assumed a greater obligation. . . ." Does this mean that 2–615 renders unenforceable a contract clause under which a seller assumes a *lesser* obligation in relation to performing notwithstanding the occurrence of uncertain events?

The drafting history of 2–615 reveals that the introductory language was intended to make it clear that a seller might assume greater liability by implication as well as by express agreement. That language apparently was used without any thought that it might restrict a seller's ability to contract for discharge in the event of occurrences that would not operate as a discharge under 2–615. See Hawkland, The Energy Crisis and Section 2–615 of the Uniform Commercial Code, 79 Comm.L.J. 75 (1974).

2.   **Problem.** Sullivan, a farmer, contracted in April to deliver 20,000 bushels of soybeans to Black Hawk Elevator between October 1 and October 31, for $2.15 per bushel. As a result of drought, Sullivan's land yielded only 12,000 bushels, which she delivered to Black Hawk. Perhaps because of the draught, perhaps not, the market price at that time was $3.50 per bushel. Black Hawk purchased 8,000 bushels at that price from someone else and sued Sullivan for $10,800, the excess of $3.50 per bushel over $2.15 per bushel times 8,000 bushels. Is she liable?

Would it matter if the soybeans had already been planted when the parties formed the contract?

3.   Problem. During a visit to the Carr's Imports showroom, Jessie contracted to purchase a new Hyundai Santa Fe XL for $39,000. As part of the contract, Carr's agreed to upgrade the sound system, and Jessie was to return the next day to take delivery. That night the car was stolen, and it was never recovered. It was the end of the model year, and Carr's had no more of that model. Though Carr's might have been able to find one at another dealership, Carr's did not offer to do so. Instead, it attempted to sell Jessie the next year's model. Unable to afford that, she declined and has come to you to see if she can recover the excess of the market value, which she can establish to be $42,000, over the contract price, or $3,000. What do you advise: is Carr's Imports liable?

———

Chase Precast Corporation v. John J. Paonessa Company, Inc.

Massachusetts Supreme Judicial Court, 1991.
409 Mass. 371, 566 N.E.2d 603.

■ LYNCH, JUSTICE.

This appeal raises the question whether the doctrine of frustration of purpose may be a defense in a breach of contract action in Massachusetts, and, if so, whether it excuses the defendant John J. Paonessa Company, Inc. (Paonessa), from performance.

. . .

The pertinent facts are as follows. In 1982, the Commonwealth, through the Department of Public Works (department), entered into two contracts with Paonessa for resurfacing and improvements to two stretches of Route 128.* Part of each contract called for replacing a grass median strip between the north and southbound lanes with concrete surfacing and precast concrete median barriers. Paonessa entered into two contracts with Chase under which Chase was to supply, in the aggregate, 25,800 linear feet of concrete median barriers according to the specifications of the department for highway construction. The quantity and type of barriers to be supplied were specified in two purchase orders prepared by Chase.

The highway reconstruction began in the spring of 1983. By late May, the department was receiving protests from angry residents who objected to use of the concrete median barriers and removal of the grass median strip. Paonessa and Chase became aware of the protest around June 1. On June 6, a group of about 100 citizens filed an action in the Superior Court to stop installation of the concrete median barriers and other aspects of the work. On June 7, anticipating modification by the

———

*   A road that rings Boston.—Eds.

department, Paonessa notified Chase by letter to stop producing concrete barriers for the projects. Chase did so upon receipt of the letter the following day. On June 17, the department and the citizens' group entered into a settlement which provided, in part, that no additional concrete median barriers would be installed. On June 23, the department deleted the permanent concrete median barriers item from its contracts with Paonessa.

Before stopping production on June 8, Chase had produced approximately one-half of the concrete median barriers called for by its contracts with Paonessa, and had delivered most of them to the construction sites. Paonessa paid Chase for all that it had produced, at the contract price. Chase suffered no out-of-pocket expense as a result of cancellation of the remaining portion of barriers. [But Chase lost the profit it would have generated from producing the remaining portion of the barriers. Chase sued to recover this profit, but the trial court held that Paonessa was excused from its obligations on the basis of impossibility of performance. An intermediate appellate court affirmed, but rested its decision on the excuse of frustration of purpose. Chase appealed.]

This court has long recognized and applied the doctrine of impossibility as a defense to an action for breach of contract. See, e.g., Butterfield v. Byron, 153 Mass. 517, 27 N.E. 667 (1891). Under that doctrine, "where from the nature of the contract it appears that the parties must from the beginning have contemplated the continued existence of some particular specified thing as the foundation of what was to be done, then, in the absence of any warranty that the thing shall exist . . . the parties shall be excused . . . [when] performance becomes impossible from the accidental perishing of the thing without the fault of either party." Boston Plate & Window Glass Co. v. John Bowen Co., 335 Mass. 697, at 700, 141 N.E.2d 715 (1957).

On the other hand, although we have referred to the doctrine of frustration of purpose in a few decisions, we have never clearly defined it. Other jurisdictions have explained the doctrine as follows: when an event neither anticipated nor caused by either party, the risk of which was not allocated by the contract, destroys the object or purpose of the contract, thus destroying the value of performance, the parties are excused from further performance.

In Mishara Construction Co. v. Transit-Mixed Concrete Corp., 365 Mass. 122, at 129, 310 N.E.2d 363 (1974), we called frustration of purpose a "companion rule" to the doctrine of impossibility. Both doctrines concern the effect of supervening circumstances upon the rights and duties of the parties. The difference lies in the effect of the supervening event. Under frustration, "[p]erformance remains possible but the expected value of performance to the party seeking to be excused has been destroyed by [the] fortuitous event. . . ."³ Lloyd v. Murphy, 25 Cal.2d 48, at 53, 153 P.2d 47 (1944). The principal question in both kinds of cases remains "whether an unanticipated circumstance, the risk of which should not fairly be thrown on the promisor, has made performance vitally different from what was reasonably to be expected." See Lloyd, supra, at 54, 153 P.2d 47 (frustration); Mishara Constr. Co., supra, 365 Mass. at 129, 310 N.E.2d 363 (impossibility).

Since the two doctrines differ only in the effect of the fortuitous supervening event, it is appropriate to look to our cases dealing with impossibility for guidance in treating the issues that are the same in a frustration of purpose case.⁴ The trial judge's findings with regard to those issues are no less pertinent to application of the frustration defense because they were considered relevant to the defense of impossibility.

Another definition of frustration of purpose is found in the Restatement (Second) of Contracts § 265 (1981):

"Where, after a contract is made, a party's principal purpose is substantially frustrated without his fault by the occurrence of an event the non-occurrence of which was a basic assumption on which the contract was made, his remaining duties to render performance are discharged, unless the language or the circumstances indicate the contrary."

This definition is nearly identical to the defense of "commercial impracticability," found in the Uniform Commercial Code, G.L. c. 106, § 2–615 (1988 ed.), which this court, in *Mishara Constr. Co., supra* at 127–128, 310 N.E.2d 363, held to be consistent with the common law of contracts regarding impossibility of performance. It follows, therefore, that the Restatement's formulation of the doctrine is consistent with this court's previous treatment of impossibility of performance and frustration of purpose.

Paonessa bore no responsibility for the department's elimination of the median barriers from the projects. Therefore, whether it can rely on the defense of frustration turns on whether elimination of the barriers was a risk allocated by the contracts to Paonessa. *Mishara Constr. Co.* articulates the relevant test:

"The question is, given the commercial circumstances in which the parties dealt: Was the contingency which developed one which the parties could reasonably be thought to have foreseen as a real possibility which could affect performance? Was it one of that variety of risks which the parties were tacitly assigning to the promisor by their failure to provide

---

³ Clearly frustration of purpose is a more accurate label for the defense argued in this case than impossibility of performance, since, as the Appeals Court pointed out, "[p]erformance was not literally impossible. Nothing prevented Paonessa from honoring its contract to purchase the remaining sections of median barrier, whether or not the [department] would approve their use in the road construction." 28 Mass.App.Ct. 639, 644 n.5, 554 N.E.2d 868 (1990).

⁴ Those issues include the foreseeability of the supervening event, allocation of the risk of occurrence of the event, and the degree of hardship to the promisor.

for it explicitly? If it was, performance will be required. If it could not be so considered, performance is excused." This is a question for the trier of fact.

Paonessa's contracts with the department contained a standard provision allowing the department to eliminate items or portions of work found unnecessary.[6] The purchase order agreements between Chase and Paonessa do not contain a similar provision. This difference in the contracts does not mandate the conclusion that Paonessa assumed the risk of reduction in the quantity of the barriers. It is implicit in the judge's findings that Chase knew the barriers were for department projects. The record supports the conclusion that Chase was aware of the department's power to decrease quantities of contract items. The judge found that Chase had been a supplier of median barriers to the department in the past. The provision giving the department the power to eliminate items or portions thereof was standard in its contracts. See Standard Specifications for Highways and Bridges, Commonwealth of Massachusetts Department of Public Works § 4.06 (1973). The judge found that Chase had furnished materials under and was familiar with the so-called "Unit Price Philosophy" in the construction industry, whereby contract items are paid for at the contract unit price for the quantity of work actually accepted. Finally, the judge's finding that "[a]ll parties were well aware that lost profits were not an element of damage in either of the public works projects in issue" further supports the conclusion that Chase was aware of the department's power to decrease quantities, since the term prohibiting claims for anticipated profit is part of the same sentence in the standard provision as that allowing the engineer to eliminate items or portions of work.

In *Mishara Constr. Co.* we held that, although labor disputes in general cannot be considered extraordinary, whether the parties in a particular case intended performance to be carried out, even in the face of a labor difficulty, depends on the facts known to the parties at the time of contracting with respect to the history of and prospects for labor difficulties. In this case, even if the parties were aware generally of the department's power to eliminate contract items, the judge could reasonably have concluded that they did not contemplate the cancellation

---

[6] The contracts contained the following provision:

"4.06   Increased or Decreased Contract Quantities.

"When the accepted quantities of work vary from the quantities in the bid schedule, the Contractor shall accept as payment in full, so far as contract items are concerned, payment at the original contract unit prices for the accepted quantities of work done.

"The Engineer may order omitted from the work any items or portions of work found unnecessary to the improvement and such omission shall not operate as a waiver of any condition of the Contract nor invalidate any of the provisions thereof, nor shall the Contractor have any claim for anticipated profit.

"No allowance will be made for any increased expenses, loss of expected reimbursement therefor or from any other cause."

for a major portion of the project of such a widely used item as concrete median barriers, and did not allocate the risk of such cancellation.[7]

. . .

Judgment affirmed.

QUESTIONS

1. The court states the issue as whether the doctrine of frustration of purpose may be a defense, but 2–615 does not mention frustration of purpose. Was it proper for the court to analyze the case in terms of frustration of purpose?

2. The court barely mentions 2–615 and does not seem to apply it to determine whether the parties were excused from their obligations to perform. Was this proper?

———

Waldinger Corp. v. CRS Group Engineers, Inc.

United States Court of Appeals, Seventh Circuit, 1985.
775 F.2d 781.

■ WOOD, CIRCUIT JUDGE.

In 1977, the Urbana and Champaign Sanitary District was engaged in planning two waste water treatment facilities. CRS Group Engineers, Inc., Clark Dietz Division ("Dietz,") as engineer for the Sanitary District, prepared the specifications for these facilities. Among the equipment necessary for the facilities were belt filter presses.[1] The specifications for these presses detailed two types of requirements—performance capabilities and mechanical components. The Waldinger Corporation ("Waldinger,") a mechanical contractor, preparing to bid on the mechanical portions of the projects, received quotations for sludge dewatering equipment from four belt press manufacturers, including Ashbrook-Simon-Hartley, Inc. ("Ashbrook.") Waldinger successfully bid on the projects and became the mechanical subcontractor; Ashbrook was successful in its bid to be the supplier of the sludge dewatering equipment. Ashbrook, however, was unable to supply the equipment

---

[7] The judge did not explicitly find that cancellation of the barriers was not contemplated and that the risk of their elimination was not allocated by the contracts. However, the judge's decision imports every finding essential to sustain it if there is evidence to support it. Mailer v. Mailer, 390 Mass. 371, 373, 455 N.E.2d 1211 (1983).

[1] The function of a belt filter press is to remove waste solids from the waste water. The district court explained the manner in which it accomplishes this goal:

"Sewage enters the belt filter press as a slurry of solids and water. The slurry is mixed with polymers, organic compounds which cause the solids in the slurry to floculate. The floculated sludge is deposited in a section of the machine where gravity dewatering takes place and excess water drains off from the floculated sludge. The floculated sludge is then fed into a shear press section of the machine where more water is extracted by shear pressure and the sludge emerges from the filter press as a friable, cake solid."

Waldinger v. Ashbrook-Simon-Hartley, Inc., 564 F.Supp. 970, 973 (C.D.Ill.1983).

described in the specifications set forth in its contract with Waldinger, and Waldinger obtained the equipment from The Ralph B. Carter Company ("Carter.")

Waldinger then sued Ashbrook for breach of contract. Ashbrook, in defense, claimed impracticability of performance due to Dietz's intentional or negligent drafting of restrictive specifications. Waldinger also sued Dietz, claiming that Dietz intentionally interfered with the contract between Ashbrook and Waldinger and, alternatively, that Dietz negligently failed to draft proper specifications for the sludge dewatering equipment.

Following a bench trial, the district court found that Dietz intentionally prepared exclusionary specifications, and insisted without justification that Ashbrook comply literally with those specifications. The court also found that Ashbrook did not bid with the realization that it could not comply with the specifications. The court concluded as a matter of law that Dietz intentionally interfered with the contract between Ashbrook and Waldinger and that Ashbrook was excused from performing its contract with Waldinger because performance was impracticable. Waldinger v. Ashbrook-Simon-Hartley, Inc., 564 F.Supp. 970 (C.D.Ill.1983).

I.

The district court made the following factual findings, none of which is clearly erroneous. In the summer of 1977, Dietz decided to use equipment manufactured by Carter as the model for the sludge dewatering equipment to be used on the projects, though Dietz had never seen the Carter 15-31 machine perform.[2] Carter supplied the data and performance descriptions which were incorporated in the specifications drawn by Dietz. Dietz took the Carter performance claims at face value, making no independent study of them. Dietz knew that no manufacturer but Carter recycled the belt wash water used in the machine but nevertheless specified that subsystem.[3] Dietz had no data proving that such recycling would increase solid removal or reduce polymer consumption in the sludge dewatering process. Indeed, the evidence adduced at trial showed that recycling had no positive effect on a filter press' production capacities, but likely had a negative effect. Dietz had no scientific basis for including in the specifications other features of the Carter machine, specifically, the 540 square foot dewatering area and the stainless steel clad rollers. The structure designed to house the filter presses was sized to fit the Carter 15-31 machine.

In November and December of 1977, Ashbrook contacted Dietz concerning the sludge dewatering equipment to be used in the facilities. Ashbrook subsequently asked Dietz to approve its size 1-V Winkelpress

---

[2] At the time the specifications were drafted, Carter had no 15-31 machine in operation.

[3] Carter has since returned to its pre-1975 flat belt press design and no longer manufactures a machine that recycles belt wash water.

for use on the projects. The evidence established that as early as January, 1978, Dietz had decided to reject the Ashbrook machine. Ashbrook, believing it could meet the performance requirements of the specifications and relying on its experience that specific mechanical subsystems were ordinarily waived by an owner's engineer if a supplier could show that its equipment met performance specifications, bid to supply the sludge dewatering equipment in March, 1978. A March 10, 1978, evaluation prepared by a member of the Dietz design team concluded that Ashbrook's equipment did indeed meet the performance specifications.

Subsequently, on April 5, 1978, Dietz retreated from that conclusion, stating that the size 1-V Winkelpress did not have the performance capacity required by the specifications because the machine did not recycle belt wash water. Dietz also questioned the limitation on maintenance space created by the use of an Ashbrook machine in a building designed to house a Carter machine. Dietz stated that it would not approve the machine for use on the projects based upon the information then in its possession. Ashbrook replied that it would provide actual operation data to confirm the machine's capacity and that it would supply equipment that would comply with the specifications.

On May 1, 1978, Waldinger issued, and on May 22, 1978, Ashbrook executed, purchase orders under which Ashbrook agreed to furnish the sludge dewatering equipment "in complete accordance with plans and specifications § 11140—sludge dewatering system. . . ." The purchase orders further provided that the equipment furnished by Ashbrook would require the approval of Dietz. Ashbrook, in executing the purchase orders, agreed to furnish the required submittal data for approval by Dietz. General Condition No. 10 of the purchase orders provided as follows:

"All material and equipment furnished under this Purchase Order shall be subject to the approval of the Owner, architect [or] engineer . . . , and Seller shall furnish the required submittal data . . . for said approval. In the event such approval is not obtained, this Purchase Order shall be deemed to be cancelled, with no liability on the part of either Purchaser or Seller, *unless* this Purchase Order is placed with the requirement that the material [or] equipment . . . is to be supplied of the type and in such a manner as to meet requirements of plans and specifications. In the latter case the material [or] equipment . . . furnished hereunder shall be in strict accordance with plans [and] specifications . . . , and Seller shall be bound thereby. In the event the material [or] equipment . . . does not meet the foregoing requirements, Seller shall, upon receipt of notice, immediately replace same, or remedy any deficiency, without expense to the Purchaser, and further, Seller shall pay to Purchaser all loss or damage resulting therefrom."

At the beginning of the relationship between Ashbrook and Dietz, Dietz requested only performance data on the 1-V machine. Ashbrook set about meeting the production test requirements laid down by Dietz. In August of 1978, Dietz concluded that the 1-V machine met the performance requirements of the specifications. Dietz then demanded performance data on the machine's dewatering capacity with alum sludge. Throughout the testing period, Dietz rejected Ashbrook's performance data as insufficient even though it had no data from Carter. Dietz ultimately rejected the 1-V machine because it did not have proven dewatering capacity with alum sludge; the Carter machine, to the knowledge of Dietz, had never been tested on alum sludge.[4] On November 16, 1978, Dietz discussed with Ashbrook for the first time the mechanical aspects of the Winkelpress, stating that Ashbrook must strictly comply with the mechanical specifications. When Ashbrook notified Dietz that it could not guarantee the machine's performance if built according to Dietz's mechanical specifications, Dietz told Ashbrook not to submit the size 1-V machine again.

. . . Ashbrook notified Waldinger that it was unable to supply the equipment described in the specifications. Waldinger then terminated the purchase orders and obtained the equipment from Carter.[5]

The district court found that no manufacturer but Carter could have literally complied with the specifications for the sludge dewatering equipment; that Dietz intended to use Carter equipment on the projects to the exclusion of other manufacturers; that Dietz's decision to use Carter equipment was conscious and in deliberate disregard of the EPA regulation requiring free and open competition, 40 C.F.R. § 35.936–3 (1976); and that there was no scientific or empirical basis for Dietz's insistence on strict compliance with the specifications. The district court further found that Ashbrook did not bid the project with the realization that it could not meet the specifications; rather, relying upon the EPA requirements that specifications foster competition and that specifications not be exclusionary or discriminatory and upon its experience that specific mechanical subsystems are ordinarily waived if a supplier can demonstrate that its equipment meets performance specifications, Ashbrook bid the project believing it could perform. Ashbrook, the district court found, could not have known that Dietz would interpret its specifications in such a way as to require Ashbrook to manufacture a Carter machine.

---

[4] In the interim between the letting of the bids and the rejection of the Ashbrook machine, Dietz was reassuring Carter that Dietz would insist on rigid adherence to the specifications. Carter expressed the hope that the "successful manufacturer" would be required to meet all process requirements.

[5] Carter ceased manufacturing the 15-31 machine in February, 1978 and began manufacturing instead the 15-32 model. This machine, which Waldinger was required to install, was too large for the structure designed to house the 15-31 machine. The building had to be redesigned to accommodate the 15-32 machine.

II.

Waldinger challenges the district court's conclusion that Ashbrook was excused from performing its contract with Waldinger on the ground of commercial impracticability. Ill.Rev.Stat. ch. 26, § 2–615. Assuming the seller has not assumed the greater obligation under the agreement, three conditions must be satisfied before performance is excused: (1) a contingency has occurred; (2) the contingency has made performance impracticable; and (3) the nonoccurrence of that contingency was a basic assumption upon which the contract was made. . . . The rationale for the defense of commercial impracticability is that the circumstance causing the breach has rendered performance "so vitally different from what was anticipated that the contract cannot be reasonably thought to govern." Eastern Air Lines, Inc. v. McDonnell Douglas Corp., 532 F.2d 957, 991 (5th Cir.1976). Because the purpose of a contract is to place the reasonable risk of performance upon the promisor, however, it is presumed to have agreed to bear any loss occasioned by an event that was foreseeable at the time of contracting.

The applicability of the defense of commercial impracticability, then, turns largely on foreseeability. The relevant inquiry is whether the risk of the occurrence of the contingency was so unusual or unforeseen and the consequences of the occurrence of the contingency so severe that to require performance is to grant the buyer an advantage he did not bargain for in the contract. If the risk of the occurrence of the contingency was unforeseeable, the seller cannot be said to have assumed that risk. If the risk of the occurrence of the contingency was foreseeable, that risk is tacitly assigned to the seller. The seller's failure to provide a contractual excuse against the occurrence of a foreseeable contingency may be deemed to be an assumption of an unconditional obligation to perform. Phrased somewhat differently, if a contingency is foreseeable, the § 2–615 defense is unavailable because the party disadvantaged by the fruition of the contingency might have contractually protected itself.

This analysis assumes, of course, that the parties have not restricted the excusing contingencies or eliminated the protection of § 2–615 by imposing upon the seller an absolute contractual duty to deliver. If a particular contingency is contemplated and the risk of its occurrence specifically assigned to the seller, foreseeability is not an issue. The parties will be held to their bargain.

The district court found that a basic assumption of the contract between Waldinger and Ashbrook was that Ashbrook equipment was competitive and would comply with the specifications drafted by Dietz. That assumption was based upon the belief that Dietz would interpret its specifications in a competitive and nonrestrictive manner. Because Dietz did not do so, performance by Ashbrook was rendered impracticable.

Waldinger contends that Ashbrook assumed a greater obligation to it under their agreement, an issue not specifically addressed by the district court; specifically, Waldinger argues that Ashbrook unconditionally obligated itself to supply whatever equipment was necessary to meet the specification requirements to the satisfaction of Dietz. In support, Waldinger cites the purchase order in which Ashbrook agreed to furnish equipment "in strict accordance with plans, specifications and general conditions applicable to the contract of Purchaser with the Owner or other contractor." Waldinger further points out that Ashbrook failed to indicate, in the space provided on the purchase order, any specific exceptions to the terms and conditions of the purchase order. Thus, although Ashbrook could have attempted to contractually protect itself by making its obligation to supply the equipment contingent upon Dietz's approval, it did not, and now, according to Waldinger, must be held accountable for its breach.

Ashbrook contends that Waldinger views too broadly the scope of the obligation it assumed. Ashbrook argues that it cannot be deemed to have assumed the obligation to meet all mechanical specifications—that is, to build a Carter machine—because Dietz was required, under EPA regulations incorporated in all sub-agreements on EPA projects, 40 C.F.R. §§ 35.9361(b); 35.937–9(a); 35.938–4(c)(5) (1976), to draft and interpret its specifications in a non-proprietary, non-restrictive manner. There is, Ashbrook contends, an "irreconcilable conflict" between the language of General Condition No. 10 which required it to provide equipment in "strict accordance" with the specifications and the EPA regulations prohibiting specifications drawn to only one manufacturer. Ashbrook apparently argues that it obligated itself to supply equipment that would meet the specifications only insofar as Dietz, in accordance with EPA regulations, drafted and interpreted those specifications in a non-proprietary, non-restrictive manner.

Pursuant to the terms of General Condition No. 10 of the purchase orders, the risk of non-approval by Dietz was specifically allocated to Ashbrook. Under those terms, Ashbrook assumed the obligation of providing equipment that strictly complied with the specifications. Although the § 2–615 defense would be unavailable to Ashbrook if this contractual provision stood alone, we are presented with EPA regulations that Ashbrook contends narrow the scope of its otherwise broad contractual obligation to Waldinger. We believe, in light of the express contractual terms prohibiting exclusionary specifications, that Ashbrook obligated itself to provide equipment that would satisfy the specifications when interpreted in a competitive, non-restrictive manner. Ashbrook assumed the risk that it could not supply a machine that satisfied specifications so interpreted, but it did not assume the risk that it could not manufacture a Carter machine. To hold otherwise is to read out of the contract the EPA regulations in which the federal public policy of free and open competition is incorporated. 40 C.F.R. § 35.936–3 (1976). We decline to do so.

The district court found that it was not foreseeable at the time of contracting that Dietz would require strict compliance with all specifications. A district court's factual findings may not be overturned unless they are clearly erroneous. Fed.R.Civ.P. 52. . . . Waldinger has not persuaded us that this finding is clearly erroneous. True, Ashbrook knew that Dietz's approval was required and that at the time it signed the purchase orders Dietz had not expressly approved its 1-V machine. The refusal of an engineer to waive certain mechanical specifications is foreseeable, and a supplier normally assumes the risk of non-approval. But these general principles cannot be deemed to apply where an engineer's insistence on literal compliance with exclusionary specifications has no scientific or rational basis. Given industry practice on waiver of mechanical specifications and the EPA regulations prohibiting exclusionary specifications upon which Ashbrook could rightly rely, Ashbrook could not have foreseen the possibility that Dietz would require it to build a Carter machine even if its machine met the performance specifications. The § 2–615 defense is therefore available to Ashbrook if performance was rendered commercially impracticable by Dietz's insistence upon compliance with the exclusionary specifications.

Ashbrook based its claim that performance was commercially impracticable on the evidence that it could not have supplied a filter press that met both the mechanical and performance specifications. Waldinger argues that performance was not commercially impracticable because Ashbrook could have built and supplied a filter press that met Dietz's mechanical specifications. According to Waldinger, Ashbrook's evaluation that the machine would not meet performance standards did not render performance of the contract impracticable because an owner impliedly warrants that the mechanical specifications it furnishes will, if strictly adhered to, permit the contractor to achieve the desired result; the owner, not the contractor, assumes this risk. Bates & Rogers Construction Corp. v. North Shore Sanitary District, 92 Ill.App.3d 90, 94, 414 N.E.2d 1274, 1278 (2d Dist.1980).

Initially, we note that if the record contains evidence that Ashbrook could have supplied a machine that met both the mechanical and the performance specifications, Waldinger has not pointed to it. Ashbrook produced evidence that it could not have supplied such a machine. Because Carter had no 15-31 machine in operation and because Dietz made no independent study of Carter's performance claims, Dietz apparently could offer no concrete evidence that the mechanical filter press it demanded would satisfy the performance standards.

Secondly, an owner's implied warranty that its specifications are not defective, the effect of which is to shield the contractor from liability when the machine it builds according to the specifications does not serve the intended purpose, yields to a contrary express contractual provision. Specification 11140 provided that the supplier of the sludge dewatering system was responsible for meeting certain performance standards; if it did not, the owner had the options of reducing the contract price, requiring the supplier to replace the equipment, or waiving the penalty.

Under the contract documents, then, Ashbrook was required to guarantee performance. This, the evidence shows, it could not do if required to build its filter press according to Dietz's mechanical specifications. We conclude that Ashbrook's inability to supply a filter press that would both satisfy Dietz's mechanical specifications and perform as required is sufficient to establish that performance of its contract with Waldinger was commercially impracticable.

. . .

In conclusion, we affirm the district court's determination that Ashbrook was excused from performing its contract with Waldinger on the ground of commercial impracticability. . . .

■ PELL, SENIOR CIRCUIT JUDGE, concurring in part and dissenting in part.

. . . I respectfully dissent from that portion of the opinion [affirming the district court's determination that Ashbrook was excused from contractual performance on the ground of commercial impracticability].

In final analysis this is simply a case where a subcontractor apparently anxious to secure a contract, although knowing that he could not meet all of the requirements of that contract, nevertheless was willing to take a chance that it could vary the terms. In this case the effort was not successful and Ashbrook should also be responsible for damages to Waldinger.

The majority opinion accepts the district court's findings of fact as being not clearly erroneous. I cannot agree. Thus a finding that Ashbrook did not bid the project with the realization it could not meet the specifications simply is not supported by the record. Further, it is not clear to me whether there was any evidence in the trial that Ashbrook relied upon the EPA's requirements that specifications foster competition or whether this is merely a post hoc argument advanced by Ashbrook after it found itself in a trial. Ashbrook may have relied upon its experience that specific mechanical subsystems are ordinarily waived if a supplier can demonstrate that its equipment can meet performance specifications but here Ashbrook had no basis for calling that experience into play. There was nothing in the specifications authorizing an "equal" substitute. I am at a loss to find support for the district court's finding that Ashbrook could not have known that Dietz would interpret its specification in such a way as to require Ashbrook to manufacture a Carter machine.

On the reverse side of the purchase orders, at the top of the page in capital letters, Ashbrook was admonished that "SELLER MUST INDICATE IN WRITING THE SPECIFIC EXCEPTIONS, IF ANY, TO THE TERMS AND CONDITIONS OF THIS PURCHASE ORDER." Ashbrook executed the purchase order as written. No exceptions to the purchase order were taken by Ashbrook. I fail to comprehend why Ashbrook did not here assume a "greater obligation." The plain situation was that there was an unconditional obligation to Waldinger, under the circumstances and the contract documents, to provide the materials necessary to satisfy the specification requirements to the approval of the engineer. Ashbrook knew at the time it signed the Purchase Orders that the engineer had expressly not approved acceptability of its 1-V machine to satisfy the performance specifications and knew its subsystem parts were sufficiently different that a waiver of the specifications by the engineer on six separate items would be required. Ashbrook admittedly made the business decision to bid the project under those circumstances, without exculpatory language in the contract. Its decision to do so under those known contingencies was not in accord with custom in the industry, which according to the evidence would be to submit a bid identifying your equipment as an "or equal."

While I regard § 2–615 as not being applicable, even in the event it were, a person seeking its shelter must establish that performance was "impracticable." In Neal-Cooper Grain Co. v. Texas Gulf Sulphur Co., 508 F.2d 283 (7th Cir.1974), this court stated in denying a defense of commercial impracticability:

> "The fact that performance has become economically burdensome or unattractive is not sufficient for performance to be excused." Id. at 293.

> "We will not allow a party to a contract to escape a bad bargain merely because it is burdensome. After one party has entered a contract for supply, he ceases to look for other sources and does not enter other contracts." Id. at 294.

Further, Ashbrook has completely failed to prove that its loss if it had complied with the specification would have been excessive or unreasonable. The district court properly did not find this to be the case. In applying § 2–615 to the circumstances of a case, the courts have uniformly held that the specific contingency which occurred need not have been contemplated but only that the occurrence be in some degree foreseeable.

In the present case, refusal of the engineer to agree to waive all or part of the mechanical specifications in interpreting compliance with the project specifications, could have been foreseen as a distinct possibility that would affect performance.

Ashbrook contends it is excused from performance because it did not obtain the expected performance from the engineer. Ashbrook, however, was aware of the fact that its desired performance of the contract would be possible only to the extent that it was able to obtain the consent or cooperation of the engineer. An agreement which cannot be performed without the consent or cooperation of a third party is not excused by reason of the inability of the promisor to obtain such consent or cooperation.

Waldinger bargained with Ashbrook to receive sludge dewatering equipment which would meet the specifications and receive the Engineer's approval, without restriction or limitation as to source of supply. Whether the necessary equipment was manufactured by Ashbrook in whole or in part or by other suppliers was of no consequence to Waldinger. It offered that contract in the form of two purchase orders to Ashbrook. Ashbrook accepted the contract on those terms without reservation or exception.

Ashbrook contends performance was impossible because the equipment required by the engineer in satisfaction of the specifications could not (in Ashbrook's opinion) have performed and, therefore, Ashbrook would have become subject to those provisions of the contract which required Ashbrook to repair or replace equipment which did not satisfy the performance specifications. The law of Illinois is clearly to the contrary. If Ashbrook had supplied the equipment under its approved drawings, and that equipment did not satisfy the performance specifications by reason of the fact that the approved and specified equipment being supplied could not meet the performance specifications, as contended by Ashbrook, then Ashbrook would be excused from operation of the penalty provisions. Bates & Rogers Const. Corp. v. North Shore Sanitary Dist., 92 Ill.App.3d 90, 94, 414 N.E.2d 1274, 1278 (1980). . . .

Regardless of the ultimate allocation of responsibility between Ashbrook and Dietz, Ashbrook, in my opinion, should be held accountable to Waldinger under the terms of its contract with Waldinger.

QUESTIONS AND NOTES

1.   As between Waldinger and Ashbrook, which of them was likely to have greater knowledge of the risk that Dietz would reject Ashbrook's equipment? Is this question relevant?

2.   As between Waldinger and Ashbrook, which of them should bear the extra expense resulting from Dietz's insistence upon Carter equipment?

3.   How relevant is it that Ashbrook did not anticipate that Dietz would insist not only on compliance with performance specifications but also with exact design specifications? It is common in construction bidding to specify the use of specific equipment, identified by manufacturer and model number. But the specifications usually add, "or equal," to give bidders the chance to base their bid on competing equipment if it can be shown to be equivalent to the specified item. What is the significance, if any, of the absence of this language in the specifications here?

4.   A number of commentators have pointed out that the frequently stated requirement that the discharging event be "unforeseeable" or "unforeseen" (repeated in Official Comment 1 to 2–615) is not workable or accurate. A

good, short statement is the following from Joskow, Commercial Impossibility, The Uranium Market and the Westinghouse Case, 6 J. Legal Stud. 119, 157 (1977):

> The foreseeability doctrine appears to raise a number of difficulties. To some extent every occurrence is foreseeable. There is always some probability that a fire will destroy the anticipated source of supply, that a key person will die, that various acts of God—like floods—will occur, that there will be an embargo or war, etc. In an objective sense, virtually nothing is truly unforeseeable to the extent that theoretically every possible state of the world could be enumerated and some probability assigned to its occurrence.
>
> The foreseeability requirement may only make sense if we introduce the concept of "bounded rationality." . . . [T]he concept of bounded rationality recognizes that human beings cannot evaluate all possible states of the world or all available information that might affect a particular situation. One way of thinking about the foreseeability doctrine is as delineating the boundary between those contingencies that are reasonably part of the decisionmaking process and those that are not. This recognizes that most contracts . . . commonly [include] only some subset of all possible occurrences as a reasonable basis for decisionmaking and appropriately included either explicitly or implicitly in the terms of the contract.

To similar effect is this passage from Specialty Tires of America, Inc. v. CIT Group/Equipment Financing, Inc., 82 F.Supp.2d 434, 438–39 (W.D.Pa.2000):

> The principal inquiry in an impracticability analysis, then, is whether there was a contingency the non-occurrence of which was a basic assumption underlying the contract. It is often said that this question turns on whether the contingency was "foreseeable," on the rationale that if it was, the promisor could have sought to negotiate explicit contractual protection. *See Waldinger Corp. v. CRS Group Eng'rs, Inc.,* 775 F.2d 781, 786 (7th Cir.1985); . . . . This, however, is an incomplete and sometimes misleading test. Anyone can foresee, in some general sense, a whole variety of potential calamities, but that does not mean that he or she will deem them worth bargaining over. The risk may be too remote, the party may not have sufficient bargaining power, or neither party may have any superior ability to avoid the harm. As my late colleague Judge Teitelbaum recited two decades ago in a famous case of impracticability:
>
> > Foreseeability or even recognition of a risk does not necessarily prove its allocation. Parties to a contract are not always able to provide for all the possibilities of which they are aware, sometimes because they cannot agree, often because they are too busy. Moreover, that some abnormal risk was contemplated is probative but does not necessarily establish

an allocation of the risk of the contingency which actually occurs.

Aluminum Co. of Am. v. Essex Group, Inc., 499 F.Supp. 53, 76 (W.D.Pa.1980) (applying Indiana law). So, while the risk of an unforeseeable event can safely be deemed not to have been assumed by the promisor, the converse is not necessarily true. Properly seen, then, foreseeability, while perhaps the most important factor,

> is at best one fact to be considered in resolving, first, how likely the occurrence of the event in question was and, second, whether its occurrence, based on past experience, was of such reasonable likelihood that the obligor should not merely foresee the risk but, because of the degree of its likelihood, the obligor should have guarded against it or provided for non-liability against the risk.

Opera Co. v. Wolf Trap Found., 817 F.2d 1094, 1102–03 (4th Cir.1987).

For an argument that, in applying impossibility and frustration rules, courts should, and largely do, put the risk of the unexpected contingency on the party able at least cost to assess and bear the risk, see Posner & Rosenfield, Impossibility and Related Doctrines in Contract Law: An Economic Analysis, 6 J. Legal Stud. 83 (1977). For a rejection of this argument and a proposal urging adoption of different criteria, see Eisenberg, Impossibility, Impracticability, and Frustration, 1 J.Leg.Analysis 207 (2009); see also Trebilcock, The Role of Insurance Considerations in the Choice of Efficient Civil Liability Rules, 4 J.L. Econ. & Org. 243 (1988).

5.   Problem. PlayTime contracted to manufacture, deliver, and install 50 swing sets at Somerset School District's elementary schools. The contract, which did not contain a force majeure clause, called for delivery and installation during the third week of August. As it completed the swing sets, PlayTime was to store them in its warehouse until they were delivered. On August 10, when PlayTime had 80 swing sets in its warehouse, a fire destroyed 40 of them.

a.   Is PlayTime excused from performing?

b.   Assume that PlayTime also had a contract with Happy Day Care for 15 swing sets. After the fire, if PlayTime delivers 15 swing sets to Happy Day Care, must Somerset School District accept delivery of the other 25?

c.   If Somerset accepts delivery of the 25, can it insist on later delivery of the other 25 swing sets for which it contracted? If so, is it entitled to compensation for the delay?

6.   Problem. Donald contracted to purchase a coat custom-made of an exotic fur by Furrier, for $6,500. He paid $2,500 down and agreed to return in six months to be measured for the coat and to approve the pelts. Before he returned, Congress passed legislation to protect that species of animal by prohibiting the use of its fur for any purpose. Under 2–615(a) Furrier's failure to deliver is not a breach. But is Donald entitled to the return of his $2,500 down payment? See 2–616. Subsection (1)(a) provides that in the event of impracticability under 2–615, the buyer may terminate the contract. But it does not specifically address whether the buyer may recover back a down payment. Is Furrier liable for the $2,500?

Now assume that the government did not ban the use of the fur specified for Donald's coat, but that Donald became concerned about preservation of that species and informed Furrier that he did not want the coat after all and would not take it or pay for it. If this communication occurred before Furrier has incurred any expenses, is Donald entitled to the return of his down payment?

7.   Leases. Article 2A contains rules similar to the rules of Article 2. See 2A–221, 2A–405, 2A–406.

8.   CISG. Article 79 of the Convention on Contracts for the International Sale of Goods relieves a party from liability for failure to perform if "he proves that the failure was due to an impediment beyond his control and that he could not reasonably be expected to have taken the impediment into account at the time of the conclusion of the contract or to have avoided or overcome it or its consequences." The "impediment" language of Article 79 seems to describe impossibility rather than frustration of purpose. In contrast, it is at least arguable that frustration of purpose may be a defense under UCC 2–615. See Official Comment 3 to 2–615. Note that Article 79 applies both to sellers and to buyers, while 2–615 by its terms applies only to sellers. In a proper case, however, it is likely that courts applying Article 2 would apply similar rules to buyers. See Northern Indiana Public Service Co. v. Carbon County Coal Co., 799 F.2d 265 (7th Cir.1986).

Article 79, like UCC 2–615, avoids using "unforeseen" to describe the kind of event that will discharge the parties. Compare the CISG language, "could not reasonably be expected to have taken into account," with the somewhat circuitous language of 2–615, "the occurrence of a contingency the non-occurrence of which was a basic assumption on which the contract was made."

Note also that Article 79(2) requires that if the claimed impediment is the inability of a third party to perform, both the third party and the person claiming discharge must meet the "impediment" test stated above. If Article 79(2) governed the dispute in *Chase Precast* (page 583 supra), what result?

Problem. A seller in North Carolina contracted to sell 10,000 pounds of chicken parts to a buyer in Germany, with delivery to a specified location in the Czech Republic. After formation of the contract and before the delivery date, the Czech government banned the importation of chicken unless the chicken was certified by the International Poultry Association. The seller could not obtain certification in time to meet the contractual delivery date. Upon learning this, the buyer directed the seller to deliver the chicken parts to a specified location in Slovakia, but the seller did not do so. When the buyer sued, the seller claimed that "an impediment beyond his control" excused his performance. What result?

If the transaction were entirely domestic, subject to Article 2, what result?

CHAPTER 11

RIGHTS AND LIABILITIES OF THIRD PARTIES

A. TITLE

For purposes of Article 2, title is irrelevant to the determination of the rights of the buyer and the seller against each other. Article 2 allocates risk of loss according to the rules of 2–509 and 2–510 rather than according to who has title. The right of a buyer to get contracted-for goods from a seller who refuses to deliver is determined by 2–716 and 2–502, and it does not suffice under those sections that the buyer has title. (If the buyer has title but is unable to obtain possession of the goods under 2–716 or 2–502, title revests in the seller. Compare 2–401(4).)

Section 2–401 states that the buyer acquires, by identification of goods to the contract, a "special property." This "special property" is, however, no more than the right to exercise rights under 2–716 and 2–502, the right to insure (2–501), and the right to sue third parties for injury to the goods (2–722).

While rights between buyer and seller do not turn on title, 2–401 does state rules from which one may determine when title passes to the buyer. Official Comment 1 indicates that these rules are necessary in connection with implementing "public regulation" that depends on title. This public regulation includes such things as *ad valorem* taxes that are assessed against the person who has title to goods on a particular date. Title also may be important in determining which of the parties, buyer or seller, has tort liability to third parties.

———

Home Indemnity Co. v. Twin City Fire Insurance Co.

United States Court of Appeals, Seventh Circuit, 1973.
474 F.2d 1081.

■ HASTINGS, SENIOR CIRCUIT JUDGE. [Parker G.M.C. Truck Sales, Inc., contracted to sell a new G.M.C. semi-tractor to Bodge Lines, Inc., a trucking business. As part of the price, Bodge was to trade in a used Mack semi-tractor. The certificate of title to the trade-in vehicle was held by a lender, and Parker Truck promised Bodge that it would to pay the lender the balance due on the trade-in. The parties also agreed that Bodge could remove some new tires on the trade-in and replace them with used tires. Sometime after Bodge took possession of the new tractor, two of Parker Truck's employees went to Bodge's premises to pick up the trade-in.

Bodge's mechanic, Rex Imlay, informed them that he had not yet swapped out the tires and would himself drive the trade-in to Parker Truck's premises after he completed the exchange of the tires.

Later that afternoon, while driving the trade-in to Parker Truck's premises, Imlay was involved in an accident, injuring two persons as well as the trade-in vehicle. The vehicle was towed to the premises of Parker Truck, which repaired it, paid off the lender, and sold it. In a separate proceeding, the two persons injured in the accident sued. In this proceeding, Bodge's insurer, Home Indemnity Co., filed a declaratory judgment action against Parker Truck's insurer, Twin City Fire Insurance Co., to determine which of them is liable.] This question, in turn, is answered by determining who owned the Mack truck at the time of the accident.

. . .

The instant cause was submitted to the trial court upon a joint stipulation. . . . The stipulation further provided:

> " * * * the sole issue for determination is whether said plaintiff or said defendant insures one Rex Imlay for his liability, if any, arising out of an accident which occurred on March 24, 1968 and out of which said accident claims have been presented. . . .

> " * * * there is a single issue of fact which will be determinative of this question, to wit: Was the vehicle driven by said Rex Imlay, at the time of the accident in question, 'owned' by Bodge Lines, Inc. (insured by The Home Indemnity Company), or by Parker GMC Truck Sales, Inc. (insured by Twin City Fire Insurance Company)?"

. . .

The trial court, upon consideration of the record as stipulated and briefs by the parties in lieu of oral argument, . . . found that the trade-in Mack tractor was owned at the time of the collision by Parker Truck and that ownership was acquired at the time of the execution of the contract the morning of March 24, 1969, as a partial payment by Bodge for the new G.M.C. truck. The court further found that the arrangement [for Imlay to deliver] the Mack tractor was made at a time when the vehicle was owned by Parker Truck and was not authorized by Bodge. The court finally concluded that Imlay was not insured by Home but rather was insured by Twin City, and it rendered judgment favorable to Home and adverse to Twin City.

Twin City and Parker Truck alone have appealed. We affirm.

The burden of appellants' appeal is their contention that the trial court erred as a matter of law in finding that the title to the trade-in vehicle had passed from Bodge to Parker Truck before the vehicle left the premises of Bodge. They rely upon certain sections of the Uniform Commercial Code as authority for their claim.

Whether this challenged action of the trial court was a conclusion of law, a finding of fact or a mixed question of law and fact is not determinative of this appeal, and we shall not fashion a label for it. . . .

It is undisputed that the purchase and sale of a motor vehicle is a transaction involving goods governed by Article 2 of the Uniform Commercial Code, Ind.Code § 26–1–2–101, et seq. (1971). We are concerned here with the sale of the new G.M.C. truck by Parker Truck to Bodge and the trade-in of the Mack tractor by Bodge to Parker Truck. Each party to the transaction is the "seller" of the goods it is to deliver. U.C.C. § 2–304(1) provides: "The price can be made payable in money or otherwise. If it is payable in whole or in part in goods each party is a seller of the goods which he is to transfer." Hence, both parties agree that Bodge is the "seller" of the trade-in vehicle.

Again, the parties agree that the place for delivery of the trade-in vehicle is governed by U.C.C. § 2–308, which provides, in relevant part: "Unless otherwise agreed * * * the place for delivery of goods is the seller's place of business or if he has none his residence * * *." Hence, "unless otherwise agreed," the place for delivery of the trade-in vehicle was Bodge's place of business.

Concerning the passage of title, U.C.C. § 2–401(2) provides: "Unless otherwise explicitly agreed title passes to the buyer [Parker Truck] at the time and place [Bodge's place of business] at which the seller [Bodge] completes his performance with reference to the physical delivery of the goods, despite any reservation of a security interest and even though a document of title is to be delivered at a different time or place * * *."

Relevant to the tender of delivery of the trade-in vehicle, appellants cite U.C.C. § 2–503(1), which states, in relevant part: "Tender of delivery requires that the seller put and hold conforming goods at the buyer's disposition and give the buyer any notification reasonably necessary to enable him to take delivery."

Based upon the foregoing sections of the Uniform Commercial Code, appellants advance the following line of reasoning. When Parker Truck sought delivery of the trade-in vehicle at Bodge's place of business, the trade-in unit was not prepared for tender of delivery because the substitution of the used tires for the new tires had not been accomplished. At that time the parties orally agreed through their respective employees . . . to change the place of delivery from Bodge's place of business to Parker Truck's. Since Bodge was unwilling to tender the trade-in vehicle at that time the "otherwise" agreement of § 2–308 was made. Finally, appellants argue, since Bodge had not completed the physical delivery of the vehicle at the time of the accident, and since the accident occurred while the tractor was being operated by an employee of Bodge en route to Parker Truck's premises, in performance of the changed agreement as to delivery, title had not passed to the buyer but remained in the seller. Hence, appellants conclude, Home was obligated to defendant and pay on behalf of Imlay any liability found against him. We disagree.

The trial court found as a fact that when [Parker Truck] called at Bodge's for the trade-in vehicle to take delivery and transport it to the premises of Parker Truck, they were told by Imlay that he had not completed the tire exchange; that [Parker Truck's representative] said he could not return that day; that Imlay then *volunteered* to drive it for them when it was ready; and that [Parker Truck's representative] said that would be all right. We cannot fault this finding of fact. Imlay was driving as a volunteer to accommodate [Parker Truck], rather than as a Bodge employee under a new agreement as to place of delivery which would have affected ownership of the vehicle. Further, our reading of [the deposition of Bodge's president] indicates that he never authorized Imlay or any other employee to make delivery of a truck at any place other than Bodge's premises.

As earlier set out, the trial court found as undisputed facts that, after the accident in question, the damaged trade-in vehicle was removed to the premises of Parker Truck; it was repaired by Parker Truck at its own expense; Parker Truck paid the balance owing on it to the lien holder and later resold the repaired tractor; and no adjustment was made to the contract between the parties because of the damage sustained by that vehicle. . . .

It seems clear to us, as it was to the trial court, that Parker Truck by its own course of conduct placed its mark of approval on the meaning of the agreement of the parties by completing its performance in a manner consistent with the transfer of ownership to it prior to the accident in question.

. . .

Affirmed.

QUESTIONS

1.   If Parker Truck had not repaired and sold the damaged trade-in, would the result change? Why or why not?

2.   If Parker Truck had sought to reduce the trade-in allowance (or recover for the reduced value of the damaged trade-in), would the result change? Why or why not?

B. SITUATIONS IN WHICH THE BUYER GETS BETTER TITLE THAN THE SELLER HAD

1. RIGHTS OF THE BUYER AGAINST A SECURED CREDITOR OF THE SELLER

A seller of goods often grants a security interest in some (or all) of its inventory to secure a debt owed to a lender or supplier. That security interest gives the lender or supplier (the creditor) the right to seize and sell the goods to satisfy the debt if the seller does not pay the debt. If the seller sells goods that are subject to a security interest, the question arises whether the buyer takes free of the security interest. That issue is dealt with in substantial detail in Article 9 of the Uniform Commercial Code and in the law school course that covers secured transactions. This note and the next two cases provide a brief introduction.

To protect its security interest in a seller's goods against the claims of third parties, a creditor (known as a "secured party") must "perfect" its interest, usually by filing a document (a "financing statement") in the relevant state's secretary of state's office showing the existence of the security interest. (A security interest in a motor vehicle, other than one given by a debtor who is a dealer in motor vehicles, must be perfected by notation on the vehicle's certificate of title. A security interest given by a dealer in motor vehicles is perfected by filing a financing statement, rather than by notation on the certificate of title.)

Perfection of a security interest gives the secured party rights superior to the purchaser even if the purchaser has bought the goods in good faith and has taken possession of them without knowledge of the security interest. If the debtor defaults, the secured party can repossess the goods. If the security interest is not perfected, a good-faith purchaser is protected, unless the purchaser knew of the security interest when it took possession of the goods.

When a dealer in goods borrows money to finance its business and grants a security interest in the goods it holds for sale, its lender expects it to sell those goods. This, of course, enables the seller to pay the debt owed to the lender. Persons who purchase goods from a dealer do not expect that they need to search in the secretary of state's office to determine whether the dealer has granted a security interest in the goods they are buying. (For example, did it ever occur to you to ask whether the electronics dealer from whom you purchased your television or computer had granted its lender a security interest in it?) Section 9–320(a) protects this expectation of the typical buyer:

> . . . a buyer in ordinary course of business, other than a person buying farm products from a person engaged in farming operations, takes free of a security interest created by the buyer's seller, even if the security interest is perfected and the buyer knows of its existence.

The requirements necessary to achieve the status of "buyer in ordinary course" are set out in 1–201(b)(9):

> "Buyer in ordinary course of business" means a person that buys goods in good faith, without knowledge that the sale violates the rights of another person in the goods, and in the ordinary course from a person, other than a pawnbroker, in the business of selling goods of that kind. . . .

If the grantor of a security interest is not a merchant who deals in goods of the kind, a purchaser from that person cannot be a buyer in ordinary course of business.

The following cases and problems explore some of the rules briefly summarized above. Article 9 was revised in 1999, and all states have now adopted the 1999 version. The next case cites sections in the pre-1999 version, but nothing in the revised version would affect the outcome of the case.

Snap-On Tools Corporation v. Rice
Arizona Court of Appeals, 1989.
162 Ariz. 99, 781 P.2d 76.

■ ROLL, PRESIDING JUDGE.

. . .

FACTS

Snap-On sold tools to Larry Neal, who operated a tire business in Benson, Arizona. The goods included an air compressor and wheel balancer and were sold pursuant to purchase money security agreements. Snap-On did not perfect its interest in these tools because it is a Snap-On policy not to record financing statements for contracts involving less than $7,500.

In March 1987, Rice entered into a contract with Neal to purchase the tire business, including some tools which constituted collateral covered by the security agreements. Rice had worked for Neal for approximately one and one-half years prior to the purchase.

In July 1987, Rice applied for credit from Snap-On with the intent of taking over Neal's outstanding tool account. The credit application was denied. Snap-On told Rice that it "would not be able to do business with [Rice] and in his name." Based on Snap-On's refusal to extend Rice credit to take over the tool account, Rice and Neal modified the purchase contract. The price was reduced to $4,000 and Neal kept most of the tools that had been part of the original contract for the sale of the business. Neal did purport to sell the air compressor and wheel balancer to Rice. Neal then moved to Kansas and shortly thereafter filed bankruptcy. After the purchase of the business, Rice made no payments to Snap-On. Thereafter, Snap-On attempted to recover the air compressor and wheel balancer from Rice.

PROCEDURAL BACKGROUND

Snap-On filed a complaint and application for provisional remedy of replevin without notice. An order was issued directing the sheriff to replevy the collateral. Rice was served with the summons, complaint, and an application for provisional remedy. Rice filed a request for hearing pursuant to A.R.S. § 12–2402. After the hearing, the court quashed the provisional remedy, ordered the return of the collateral, and awarded Rice his costs and attorneys' fees. Snap-On appeals from this order.

ISSUES

. . .

Snap-On's Right to Replevin

Snap-On argues that its unperfected purchase money security interest in the air compressor and wheel balancer is superior to Rice's interest. A.R.S. § 47–9301(A) provides in part:

A.   Except as otherwise provided in subsection B of this section, an unperfected security interest is subordinate to the rights of:

* * *

3.   In the case of goods . . . a person who is not a secured party and who is a . . . buyer not in ordinary course of business, to the extent that he gives value and receives delivery of the collateral *without knowledge of the security interest.* . . . [Emphasis added]

Snap-On does not deny that goods are involved, that Rice was a buyer not in the ordinary course of business, or that Rice received delivery of the collateral. Snap-On does contend that Rice had knowledge of Snap-On's security interest and that Rice did not give value for the air compressor and wheel balancer. These are questions of fact which the trial court resolved in favor of Rice. Our standard of review is limited to a determination as to whether substantial evidence exists to support the decision of the trial court.

a.   *Knowledge*

For purposes of the Uniform Commercial Code, the definition of knowledge is set forth in A.R.S. § 47–1201(25)(c) [revised 1–202(b)], which states: "[A] person 'knows' or has 'knowledge' of a fact when he has actual knowledge of it." A.R.S. § 47–9301 [revised 9–317(b)] does not mandate good faith; it only requires that delivery be taken without actual knowledge of Snap-On's security interest. Southland Corp. v. Emerald Oil Co., 789 F.2d 1441, 1446 (9th Cir.1986) (interpreting UCC § 9–301 under California law). Actual knowledge does not include a reason to know of the security interest. The purchaser must have actual knowledge that the security interest exists at the time the collateral is purchased.

The code does not require an inquiry into whether a security interest exists. In Clark Oil and Refining Co. v. Liddicoat, 65 Wis.2d 612, 622–23, 223 N.W.2d 530, 536 (1974), the court stated:

By this definition [of knowledge], it is apparent that the framers of the Code required proof of actual knowledge on the part of the lien creditor if he is to be subordinated to the holder of an unfiled security interest. Whether the judgment creditor had reason to know, or might have been alerted to, circumstances that should reasonably have impelled him to check beyond the filed record is irrelevant under the Code.

Snap-On argues that Rice had actual knowledge of the security interest of Snap-On in the wheel balancer and air compressor because Rice worked at the store for a year and a half prior to that purchase, Rice made payments to Snap-On on behalf of Neal, Rice made a credit application to assume the obligation of the tool account, Rice was told of Snap-On's interest in the collateral, and Snap-On demanded that Rice turn over the collateral to Snap-On. Snap-On contends that Scott Garvin's testimony proved that Rice was told of Snap-On's interest in the collateral. Garvin, who was Snap-On's credit manager, testified: "I told Mr. Rice we would not be able to do business with him and we needed to pick up the tools."

Rice testified that when he entered into the contract to purchase the business from Mr. Neal in March 1987, he had no knowledge that Snap-On claimed a lien or held an unfiled purchase money security interest in the air compressor and wheel balancer. Rice did admit that although Neal had indicated that the wheel balancer was not "free and clear," Rice believed Neal was to pay off the balancer.

The judge found that "there may be knowledge on the part of the defendant that a contract exists between the person from whom he purchased his business and your client" and that "he may have some knowledge of the existence of an agreement." However, the judge did not find that Rice had actual knowledge of a security interest. We agree that the fact that Rice knew that Neal owed money to Snap-On does not prove that Rice knew of Snap-On's security interest in the air compressor and wheel balancer. Substantial evidence exists to support the trial court's decision that Rice did not acquire the compressor and balancer with actual knowledge of Snap-On's interest.

b. *Value*

Snap-On also maintains that Rice did not give value for the air compressor and wheel balancer as required by A.R.S. § 47–9301(A)(3) [revised 9–317(b)]because Rice did not pay the full value of the items. Value is defined in A.R.S. § 47–1201(44) [revised 1–204].

[A] person gives "value" for rights if he acquires them:

* * *

(d) Generally, in return for any consideration sufficient to support a simple contract.

The only testimony presented regarding the value of the two items came from Rice, who stated that the air compressor and wheel balancer had a combined value of $2,500. The $4,000 Rice paid for the business was for good will, some used tires, the compressor, and the balancer. Ample evidence existed to support the trial court's conclusion that Rice gave value for the two items in question. That Snap-On's lien on the compressor and the balancer exceeded $4,000 does not prove that these two items had a value equal to the lien. Once again, substantial evidence exists to support the trial court's conclusion that Rice gave value for the compressor and balancer.

. . . We affirm the trial court's granting of Rice's motion to quash provisional remedy and remand this matter for further proceedings.

QUESTIONS AND NOTES

1. The rule applied in *Snap-On Tools* now appears in 9–317(b), which provides in pertinent part: a buyer of goods takes free of a security interest if the buyer gives value and receives delivery of the goods without knowledge of the security interest and before it is perfected. Please read that section. Observe that to prevail against a secured party with an unperfected security interest, the buyer must both give value and receive delivery of the goods without knowledge of the security interest. Therefore, if the buyer pays the price, but acquires knowledge of the unperfected security interest before receiving delivery, the buyer will lose. The buyer also loses if the secured party perfects its security interest (generally by filing) before the buyer obtains possession, even if the buyer has given value before the secured party perfects. On the other hand, the giving of value does not mean that the price actually must be paid. Since 1–204(4) defines "value" as "any consideration sufficient to support a simple contract," a contractually binding promise is value. Therefore, if a buyer takes possession of goods pursuant to a contract that calls for deferred payment, the buyer will prevail over the holder of an unperfected security interest even if the buyer learns of it before paying for the goods. That buyer will prevail also over the holder of a security interest that the secured party perfects before the buyer pays for the goods.

2. Was the fair market value of the goods bought by Rice relevant to whether Rice took free of Snap-On Tools' unperfected security interest?

3. The court states (penultimate paragraph on page 607) that 9–301 (revised 9–317(b)) "does not mandate good faith." In light of 1–304, is the court correct?

4. Rice was not a buyer in ordinary course because Neal, from whom he bought, was not a dealer in air compressors or wheel balancers. Neal may have been a dealer in tires and other goods, but Rice could have been a buyer in ordinary course only if Neal was in the business of selling the particular items that Rice bought. Nevertheless, even though Rice was not a buyer in ordinary course, he took free of Snap-On Tools' security interest. If, however, Snap-On Tools had filed a proper financing statement, its interest would have been superior to Rice's interest.

5. Former Article 9 called a person like Rice, who did not buy from a person in the business of selling goods of the kind, a "buyer not in ordinary course" just to make it clear that there was a different rule for buyers in ordinary course. Revised 9–317(b) drops the "buyer not in ordinary course" language but does not change the rule. The next case involves a buyer in ordinary course of business.

————

Fordyce Bank & Trust Co. v. Bean Timberland, Inc.

Supreme Court of Arkansas, 2007.
369 Ark. 90, 251 S.W.3d 267.

■Tom Glaze, Justice.

This appeal requires our court to determine whether appellees Potlatch Corp. ("Potlatch") and Idaho Timber Corp. ("Idaho") are buyers in the ordinary course of business under the Uniform Commercial Code (UCC). *See* Ark.Code Ann. § 4–9–320.

The appellant in this case, Fordyce Bank & Trust Co. ("Fordyce" or "the Bank"), issued several loans to appellee Bean Timberland ("Bean") so that Bean could purchase timber from various landowners. Bean gave the bank security interests in the purchased timber, and the proceeds from the sale of the timber were intended to repay the loans the Bank had made to Bean. The Bank, intending to perfect its security interests, filed its UCC Financing Statements with the Secretary of State's Office. However, when Bean sold the timber to the various lumber mills with which it did business, including Potlatch and Idaho, Bean failed to remit the sales proceeds to the Bank.

The Bank filed suit against Bean, Potlatch, and Idaho on February 19, 2004. In its complaint, the Bank alleged that Bean had known that the Bank had a valid first lien on the timber covered by the security interests. In addition, the Bank alleged that Potlatch and Idaho had both "negligently entered into contracts" with Bean for the purchase of timber and had "failed to exercise good faith" in those transactions. The Bank further contended that Potlatch and Idaho had been "negligent in failing to request a lien search of the UCC records [from] the Arkansas Secretary of State's Office." Had Potlatch and Idaho conducted a lien search, the Bank argued, they would have discovered the Bank's "properly recorded and perfected financing statement and security agreement granting [the Bank] a valid first lien[.]"

The case was tried at a bench trial in the Dallas County Circuit Court.[1] . . . [The court] found that Potlatch and Idaho were buyers in the ordinary course of business, and thus they were not required to perform a lien search on the timber purchased from Bean. The trial court dismissed the Bank's complaint, and the Bank filed a timely notice of appeal. . . .

[The Bank] contends that the trial court erred in granting Potlatch's and Idaho's directed-verdict motions because there was sufficient

---

[1] Bean, which went into bankruptcy at some point prior to the filing of the lawsuit, filed an answer in which it . . . admitted that it had defaulted on the notes and that the Bank should be "entitled to proceed with liquidation of any collateral which is security for debt owed by Bean Timberlands, Inc." Bean has not filed a brief in this appeal; the issues on appeal are solely related to the Bank's claims against Potlatch and Idaho.

evidence of negligence. Under Arkansas law, in order to prevail on a claim of negligence, the plaintiff must prove that the defendant owed a duty to the plaintiff, that the defendant breached the duty, and that the breach was the proximate cause of the plaintiff's injuries. In its complaint, the Bank asserted that Potlatch and Idaho were negligent in failing to request a lien search of the UCC records in the Arkansas Secretary of State's Office. . . . [T]he Bank asserts that the trial court improperly granted Potlatch's and Idaho's motions [to dismiss] despite testimony that Potlatch and Idaho should have known that their timber purchases from Bean were secured by financing, which would give rise to a duty to check for liens with the Secretary of State. Thus, to answer the question raised on appeal, this court must determine whether Potlatch and Idaho had a duty to perform a lien search; in turn, the answer to this question depends on whether Potlatch and Idaho were buyers in the ordinary course of business.

A buyer in the ordinary course of business is defined in Ark.Code Ann. § 4–1–201(9), in pertinent part, as follows:

> "Buyer in ordinary course of business" means a person that buys goods in good faith, without knowledge that the sale violates the rights of another person in the goods, and in the ordinary course from a person, other than a pawnbroker, in the business of selling goods of that kind. *A person buys goods in the ordinary course if the sale to the person comports with the usual or customary practices in the kind of business in which the seller is engaged or with the seller's own usual or customary practices.* . . . (Emphasis added.)

Under Ark.Code Ann. § 4–9–320(a), a buyer in the ordinary course of business "takes free of a security interest created by the buyer's seller, even if the security interest is perfected and the buyer knows of its existence." Thus, if Potlatch and Idaho were buyers in the ordinary course of business, they would be under no duty to perform a lien search, because even if they knew of a lien and had performed a lien search, they could nonetheless take free of the Bank's security interest.

To determine whether Potlatch and Idaho were buyers in the ordinary course of business, the court must look to see whether the sale to them "comport[ed] with the usual or customary practices in the kind of business in which the seller is engaged or with the seller's own usual or customary practices." *See* § 4–9–320(a). Evidence presented at trial clearly showed that Potlatch and Idaho's practices were "usual or customary" in the timber business.

Bean sold timber to various mills as "gatewood." Gatewood is severed timber that is brought to a lumber mill's front gate by a logger; the wood is weighed and inventoried, and if the timber meets the mill's specifications, the mill will purchase it. If the wood does not meet specifications, the mill will not buy it. Numerous witnesses testified that purchases of gatewood are common in the Arkansas logging industry. For example, Robert Frey, the raw material procurement and marketing manager for Weyerhauser in Arkansas and Oklahoma, testified that the "basic way" the timber industry does business is for a mill to have written contracts with loggers or timber producers; those contracts would have specifications that set the mill's requirements for timber that it would accept.

Frey testified that lumber mills, such as Weyerhauser, would not typically go out and look at growing timber before it was cut, but would instead purchase it at the mill gates based on specifications. The gatewood system, according to Frey, was a "common way of doing business in the timber industry in Arkansas," and most companies that he knew about conduct business in this manner. Further, Frey testified that Weyerhauser does not perform title searches for liens and ownership on any gatewood timber. Frey also noted that, if Bean "delivers all of his product as gatewood, that is normal if that is how he does business. There is nothing wrong with that."

Frey testified that Weyerhauser does not conduct title searches at the county courthouse or at the Secretary of State's office on gatewood; however, it would do a title search and obtain a legal description of the tract for standing timber (as opposed to the cut timber of the type Bean sold) in order to make sure that the supplier was bringing the timber that the mill had contracted for.

[Four other persons with extensive experience in the Arkansas lumber mill business offered similar testimony. One of them stated that "if mills were required to perform a lien check every time a load of gatewood came in, the mills would not take gatewood: 'If lien searches were required . . . , if we had that hanging over our head every time a truckload crossed the scale, we would not let it come in.' "]

In sum, the trial court had before it abundant evidence that purchasing gatewood without performing a lien search was the standard practice in the timber industry. Clearly, Bean's sales to Potlatch and Idaho, and Potlatch's and Idaho's practice of not conducting lien searches, "comport[ed] with the usual or customary practices in the kind of business in which the seller is engaged or with the seller's own usual or customary practices." *See* § 4–9–320(a). As such, the trial court correctly determined that Potlatch and Idaho were buyers in the ordinary course of business. Further, because the mills were buyers in the ordinary course of business, they owed the Bank no duty to conduct a lien search. With no duty, there could be no breach of any duty. Therefore, the trial court properly [dismissed] the Bank's negligence claims.

Nonetheless, the Bank contends in its third point on appeal that Potlatch and Idaho could not have been buyers in the ordinary course of business because the wood they purchased from Bean was not "inventory." The Bank urges that the trial court erroneously concluded that the cut timber was "the type of inventory" covered by the buyer-in-the-ordinary-course-of-business protection. The Bank states that the

UCC provides such protection in this case only if the goods can be classified as inventory.

Under the UCC, "a security agreement is effective according to its terms between the parties, against purchasers of the collateral, and against creditors." Ark.Code Ann. § 4–9–201(a). In this case, the security agreement is between the Bank and Bean. That security agreement between the Bank and Bean, filed in the Secretary of State's office, was intended to secure the payment and performance of Bean's debts, liabilities, or obligations to the Bank, and it gave the Bank a security interest in cut timber.

The Bank concedes that the timber, once cut, becomes ordinary goods. *See* Comment to Ark.Code Ann. § 4–9–501 ("Once cut, however, . . . [t]*he timber then becomes ordinary goods.*") (emphasis added). However, the Bank urges that the cut timber, which is "goods," is not "inventory." This distinction is important to the Bank because the Commentary to Ark.Code Ann. § 4–9–320(a) states that the protection afforded to buyers in the ordinary course of business "applies primarily to inventory collateral." *See* Comment to Ark.Code Ann. § 4–9–320.

All parties to this case agree that the cut timber is "goods." According to the Commentary to Ark.Code Ann. § 4–9–102, there are "four mutually-exclusive 'types' of collateral that consist of goods: 'consumer goods,' 'equipment,' 'farm products,' and 'inventory.'" The Commentary continues as follows:

> The classes of goods are mutually exclusive. For example, the same property cannot simultaneously be both equipment and inventory. . . .

> Goods are inventory if they are leased by a lessor or held by a person for sale or lease. . . . Goods to be furnished or furnished under a service contract, raw materials, and work in process also are inventory. Implicit in the definition is the criterion that the sales or leases are or will be in the ordinary course of business. . . .

Comment to Ark.Code Ann. § 4–9–102. If cut timber constitutes "goods," it must be inventory if it is not consumer goods, equipment, or farm products.

Consumer goods are goods "that are used or bought for use primarily for personal, family, or household purposes." Ark.Code Ann. § 4–9–102(23). Clearly, cut timber would not fall into this category. Equipment means "goods other than inventory, farm products, or consumer goods." Ark.Code Ann. § 4–9–102(33). The Commentary notes that, generally speaking, "goods used in a business are equipment if they are fixed assets or have, as identifiable units, a relatively long period of use." *See* Comment to Ark.Code Ann. § 4–9–102. This obviously does not describe cut timber. Finally, farm products are defined in § 4–9–102(34), as follows:

"Farm products" means goods, other than standing timber, with respect to which the debtor is engaged in a farming operation and which are:

    (A) crops grown, growing, or to be grown, including:

        (i) crops produced on trees, vines, and bushes; and

        (ii) aquatic goods produced in aquacultural operations;

    (B) livestock, born or unborn, including aquatic goods produced in aquacultural operations;

    (C) supplies used or produced in a farming operation; or

    (D) products of crops or livestock in their unmanufactured states.

Again, cut timber does not fall within any of these descriptions. Because timber is "goods," but it is not consumer goods, equipment, or farm products, then logically it must be inventory. Inventory means "goods, other than farm products, which . . . are held by a person for sale or lease or to be furnished under a contract of service [or] consist of raw materials, work in process, or materials used or consumed in a business." Ark.Code Ann. § 4–9–102(48)(B) & (D). The cut timber at issue in this case was held by Bean for sale to Potlatch and Idaho; therefore, the timber certainly meets the definition of inventory.

. . . Accordingly, we hold that the trial court correctly concluded that the cut timber at issue in this case is "inventory," and Potlatch and Idaho are buyers in the ordinary course of business. . . .

Affirmed.

QUESTIONS AND NOTES

1. In footnote 1 we are told that the seller admitted that it had defaulted on its contract with Fordyce Bank and that the bank was entitled to the collateral (or the proceeds from sale of the collateral). Why does the court not give this concession any weight?

2. *Snap-On Tools* and *Fordyce Bank* are similar in that in both cases the major fact issue is the buyer's knowledge with respect to the prior security interest. The rules applicable to the two cases, however, are different. For example, 9–317(b) (addressing the buyer who takes possession of goods before a security interest in the goods is perfected) does not specifically state that the buyer must be in good faith to take free of the prior unperfected interest. On the other hand, a buyer in ordinary course under 9–320 (addressing the buyer who purchases goods subject to a perfected security interest) must "buy in good faith." In addition, the buyer must be "without knowledge that the sale violates the rights of another person in the goods." Did not the buyers from Bean Timberland have reason to know that Bean had given a security interest to Fordyce bank?

3.   Under 9–317(b), for a buyer not in ordinary course to prevail over the secured party, the buyer must get possession of the goods without knowledge of the security interest and before it is perfected. In 9–320(a), which covers purchasers from a dealer, there is no statement that the buyer must obtain possession of the goods in order to prevail over the secured party. This raises the question whether a buyer may have the protection of 9–320 if the secured party repossesses the goods from the seller after the sales contract is formed, but before the goods have been delivered to the buyer: can a buyer who does not obtain possession of the goods at the time of sale be a buyer in ordinary course and get the goods from the possession of the secured party free of the security interest?

Please read 1–201(b)(9), 2–502, and 2–716, and consider the following problems.

4.   **Problem.** Quincy entered into a contract for the purchase of a new car, for use as the family vehicle, and made a deposit of $100 toward the total purchase price of $25,000. The contract obligated Quincy to pay the balance of the purchase price in equal monthly payments over five years at an interest rate of 8% per year. Hentsen Ford, the seller, wrote the vehicle identification number (VIN) on the contract. Before the automobile was delivered to Quincy, Hentsen's lender, which had a security interest in dealer's inventory, seized the automobile. Can Quincy get the automobile from the lender free of the lender's security interest? That question seems easy, right? But what about the payment: must Quincy pay the entire unpaid balance of the price to the lender immediately, or must the lender comply with the credit terms of the sales contract?

5.   **Problem.** In which of the following variations of Problem 4 does Quincy have the same rights as above?

    a.   Hentsen did not write the VIN on the contract but directed its service employees to begin to prepare a particular car for delivery to Quincy, and the employees had done so.

    b.   Hentsen directed its service employees to begin to prepare a particular car for delivery to Quincy, but the employees had not yet begun to prepare the car when it was seized by the lender.

    c.   Hentsen had only one car that would satisfy the contract and intended to deliver that car to Quincy, but had not so indicated by either notation of a specific VIN number or by directing its employees to begin preparing it for delivery.

    d.   Hentsen had two identical cars on hand, either of which would satisfy the contract, but had taken no steps to indicate which car would be delivered.

6.   A buyer for personal, family, or household use may recover the goods from the seller's secured creditor under either 2–502 or 2–716. The latter section reads:

> "(3) The buyer has a right of replevin for goods identified to the contract if after reasonable effort he is unable to effect cover for such goods or the circumstances reasonably indicate that such

cover will be unavailing or if the goods have been shipped under reservation and satisfaction of the security interest in them has been made or tendered. *In the case of goods bought for personal, family or household purposes, the buyer's right of replevin vests upon acquisition of a special property, even if the seller had not then repudiated or failed to deliver.*" [emphasis added]

Does 2–716(3) state for the consumer buyer essentially the same rule as 2–502 but without the requirement that the buyer have paid part of the price?

A buyer acquires a special property in goods when they are identified to the contract. Therefore, the second sentence of 2–716(3) really says the same thing as the first sentence with respect to the time when a consumer buyer's right to replevy the goods arises. What the second sentence does not repeat is the requirement that the buyer be unable to cover (or, if the goods have been shipped under reservation, pay the price). May a consumer buyer, therefore, replevy goods even if he or she could purchase identical goods from another source? If so, the rule is like that of 2–502, except that the buyer need not have paid any part of the price. See Official Comment 3 to 2–716, which notes the distinction between non-consumer buyers and consumer buyers under 2–716(3).

7.   A buyer who has made a down payment of only $100, as in Problems 4 and 5, is not likely to go through the hassle of trying to get an automobile away from the secured party unless the price is an exceptionally good price. It will often be better just to forget the $100 or try to get the money back from the dealer. If, however, the buyer has paid a substantial part, or all, of the price, the ability to get the automobile free of the lender's security interest can be important. If the buyer does not recover the goods, the buyer becomes a general unsecured creditor of the dealer.

Notice how limited the commercial buyer's right is under 2–502. Even if the full price of the goods has been paid, the buyer can get the goods from the secured party only if the seller becomes insolvent within 10 days after the receipt of the *first* installment on their price. It is very unlikely that the buyer can prove that the seller became insolvent within that period. A commercial buyer who is otherwise a buyer in ordinary course might seek specific performance or replevin under 2–716 as a means of taking property free of the security interest of a repossessing secured party.

8.   **Problem.** Anderson purchased a Toyota Tundra from Tommy's Toyota, financing the purchase by a loan from Toyota Credit Corp., to which Anderson gave a security interest in the Tundra. A few months later Anderson sold the Tundra to Shade Tree Motors, a used car dealer. Anderson thereupon stopped making payments to Toyota Credit. In due course, Shade Tree sold the vehicle to Beyer, who paid cash. When Toyota Credit discovered that Beyer had possession of the Tundra, it demanded that Beyer relinquish possession and threatened to repossess the vehicle if Beyer failed to surrender it. Who has superior rights to the Tundra, Beyer or Toyota Credit?

2. RIGHTS OF THE BUYER WHEN THE SELLER DOES NOT OWN THE GOODS: ENTRUSTMENT

What happens when a person purchases goods from a seller who does not own the goods? This may occur when the seller has goods that the owner has delivered for purposes of sale (e.g., to a consignment shop), goods that the owner has delivered for purposes of repair, or goods that have been stolen from the owner. In none of these situations does the seller have title to the goods. What rights does the buyer acquire? Are they superior to the rights of the owner? In the consignment example, presumably the answer should be "yes," because that is the whole purpose of delivering the goods to the consignment shop in the first place. But how about the other examples, in which the owner delivers the goods for purposes of repair or in which the goods are stolen from the owner?

At common law, one could convey only such title as he himself possessed. Thus no one could obtain good title from a thief, no matter how innocent the circumstances of his acquisition.

The harshness of this rule with respect to innocent purchasers who had paid their money in perfect good faith without any indication of anything amiss in the transaction led to statutory modifications of the common law rule, so that where the title owner had conveyed a voidable title he would not be permitted to revoke it as against a bona fide purchaser for value. Personal Property Law § 105. Innocence would thus transmute the imperfect title into a state of perfection and impregnability. Impeccable virtue would receive its just reward, and title would pass from a swindler, if not from a thief. Stanton Motor Corp. v. Rosetti, 11 A.D.2d 296, 203 N.Y.S.2d 273.

The protection of the innocent was further developed to cover situations where the title owner had not conveyed even a voidable title, but had so clothed the transferor with apparent vestiges of authority and indicia of title that equitable principles of estoppel were invoked to preclude the title owner from asserting his title. This would cover such circumstances as the delivery of goods to a retail merchant on consignment, or other situations in which the transferor was permitted to retain and sell inventory, with title retained purely as a security device. Personal Property Law, § 104. Zendman v. Harry Winston, Inc., 305 N.Y. 180, 111 N.E.2d 871. Possession alone by the transferor was not enough; he must have been authorized to sell the goods. Barnard v. Campbell, 55 N.Y. 456. Thus where the goods had been obtained by false representations the true owner was not estopped. Hentz v. Miller, 94 N.Y. 64.

The Uniform Commercial Code has expanded the rights of a third person who has purchased the property in all innocence, even from a thief, or from a person who has been entrusted with possession, even if not authorized to sell. UCC § 2–403. Under the Code, title ordinarily passes when goods are delivered, unless otherwise explicitly agreed. UCC § 2–401(2). If passage of title is dependent upon the performance of some condition subsequent, this is a voidable title which can be transferred to a bona fide purchaser for value even if the transferor was deceived as to the identity of the purchaser, the delivery was in exchange for a check later dishonored, or procured through a fraud punishable as larcenous under the criminal law. Thus what was formerly ambiguous has been made explicit. UCC § 2–403(1).

Atlas Auto Rental Corp. v. Weisberg, 54 Misc.2d 168, 169–70, 281 N.Y.S.2d 400, 403–04 (N.Y. City Civ.Ct.1967).

Best Signs, Inc. v. King

Court of Appeals of Tennessee, 2009.
358 S.W.3d 226.

■ J. STEVEN STAFFORD, J.

. . .

Chris and Donna Sandefur are the owners of Best Signs, Inc. ("Appellant"). Best Signs manufactures and installs on-site ID signs for commercial and residential customers. In May of 2005, the Sandefurs were in the market for a truck to use in their business. Through a business acquaintance, the Sandefurs were put in contact with Appellee Bobby King, who is a dealer in the type of equipment the Sandefurs wished to purchase. Mr. Sandefur informed Mr. King that he was looking for a truck with a square-tube crane, and a two-man basket, which had a 2.5 ton lifting capacity. Mr. King informed Mr. Sandefur that he would contact him if he located a truck that met the specifications. Within a week of their initial conversation, Mr. King notified the Sandefurs that he had found a truck and emailed photos and specifications to the Sandefurs. After reviewing this information, Mr. Sandefur concluded that the truck met Best Signs' requirements except that it was slightly larger than was needed, and appeared to have a lot of salt damage and rust. Mr. Sandefur determined that Best Signs could repair the truck in-house, and notified Mr. King that he wished to proceed with the purchase. [The agreed purchase price of the truck was $65,000.00.]

Mr. King brought the truck to Best Signs within a week of receiving the initial deposit check of $4,000.00. Mr. Sandefur then took the truck to a repair and service shop for the purpose of inspection. The inspection revealed that the switchbox for the two-man basket was damaged and the main boom had a hydraulic leak, which would require it to be rebuilt. Best Signs decided to proceed with the purchase on the condition that Mr. King would repair the switchbox and hydraulic leak. . . . The purchase was evidenced by a Bill of Sale executed by Mr. King and Mr. Sandefur on May 24, 2005 and by [an invoice reflecting that the two repairs were to be made to the truck]. . . .

Best Signs took possession of the truck on May 24, 2005, with the understanding that it would be returned to Mr. King for repairs when the parts arrived. Mr. King executed a title and gave it to the Sandefurs upon delivery of the truck. Best Signs also obtained insurance on the truck. Best Signs began making its own repairs/modifications prior to returning the truck to Mr. King for the major repairs. . . .

In February of 2006, Mr. King notified Best Signs that he had received the ordered parts and was ready to make the agreed upon repairs. Mr. King came to Best Signs and picked up the truck and gave Best Signs a loaner truck for use while its truck was being repaired. During the time that Mr. King had the truck, the Sandefurs contacted him regularly to check the status, and eventually to inquire about the delays. Mr. King made numerous excuses for the delays. Mr. Sandefur testified that he became concerned about the continuous delays in the completion of the repairs.

. . . [Ultimately], the Sandefurs contacted Mr. King who informed them that Design Team [a sign company located in Savannah, Tennessee] had ordered a truck from him, which had not arrived. Mr. King told the Sandefurs that he had "loaned" their truck to Design Team, pending arrival of its truck. Upon further investigation, the Sandefurs learned that, while Mr. King had possession of their truck for repairs, he had actually sold it to Design Team [for $75,000].

. . .

After Mr. King delivered the truck to Design Team, it was never able to obtain title to the truck. . . . Mr. King was ultimately jailed.[2] At the time of the filing of this appeal, the truck was in the possession of the Savannah, Tennessee police department.

On September 28, 2006, Best Signs filed a complaint to recover personal property . . . [and] judgment was entered in favor of Design Team. Best Signs appeals and raises one issue for review as stated in its brief: Whether the trial court erred in its determination as to the rightful owner of the 1997 International truck and crane at issue. . . .

[After quoting 2–403 and 1–201(b)(9) (defining "buyer in ordinary course of business"), the court continued:]

From the record, it is clear that both Best Signs and Design Team were the victims of a scheme orchestrated by Mr. King. Although the equities may dictate another conclusion, we are bound by the mandates of the UCC. Here, the trial court specifically found that Design Team was a buyer in the ordinary course of business, and was a bona fide purchaser. Despite Best Signs' argument on appeal, we find that the trial court's

---

[2] The facts of Mr. King's incarceration are not part of the appellate record.

finding is supported by the record. The facts indicate that Design Team purchased the truck from Mr. King without knowledge that this transaction violated Best Signs' rights. Moreover, it is undisputed that Mr. King was a "a merchant who deals in goods of that kind"—a fact that both Best Signs and Design Team acknowledge. Under the statutory definition set out above, Design Team is a buyer in the ordinary course of business. The record also reveals that neither Best Signs nor Design Team was able to receive a Certificate of Title from Mr. King at the time of purchase. In fact, Best Signs did not obtain a valid title until September 2006, which was approximately sixteen months after it purchased the truck, and approximately seven months after Design Team purchased the truck.

The gravamen of this case rests on the question of whether Best Signs "entrusted" the truck to Mr. King, a "merchant who deal[t] in goods of that kind," for repairs. As set out in the statute, entrusting includes "any delivery and any acquiescence in retention of possession *regardless of any condition expressed between the parties*. . . ." Tenn.Code Ann. § 47–2–403(3). According to the statute, such entrustment on the part of Best Signs would give Mr. King "power to transfer all rights of the entruster (i.e., Best Signs) to a buyer (i.e., Design Team) in ordinary course of business." Tenn.Code Ann. § 47–2–403(2).

Best Sign relies upon the case of Ballard v. Wetzel, 1997 WL 650878 (Tenn.App.1997) to support its argument for ownership of the disputed truck. We find Best Signs' reliance upon this case to be misplaced. In *Ballard,* the Court's decision was based, *inter alia,* upon a finding that the goods at issue were "stolen or otherwise obtained against the will of the owner." In this case, Best Signs voluntarily relinquished possession of the truck to Mr. King. As stated in the UCC, entrustment to a merchant who deals in goods of that kind gives that merchant power to transfer all rights of the entruster to a buyer in ordinary course of business "regardless of any condition expressed between the parties to the delivery or acquiescence and regardless of whether the procurement of the entrusting or the possessor's disposition of the goods have been such as to be larcenous under the criminal law." Tenn.Code Ann. § 47–2–403. Although the actions of Mr. King appear to rise to the level of larceny under the criminal law, this fact does not negate the power that was conferred on him by the Sandefurs' act of voluntarily entrusting him with the truck. Under the applicable statute, once the entrustment was made, Mr. King was vested with the authority to transfer ownership of the truck to Design Team, a bona fide purchaser and buyer in the ordinary course of business, *see supra.*

For the foregoing reasons, we affirm the order of the trial court. . . .

QUESTIONS AND NOTES

1.   In cases like *Best Sign*, the issue comes down to which of two innocent parties will bear the loss. In *Best Signs*, for example, both plaintiff and

defendant had paid the full purchase price to King, but only one of them is going to wind up with the truck. The other would no doubt have a good claim against King, but he was in jail and presumably was judgment proof.

Why does the court suggest (in the last paragraph on page 619) that the equities favor Best Signs?

In *Best Signs* the court held that the loss falls on the first purchaser. In Ballard v. Wetzel, cited in the last paragraph of the opinion, the loss fell on the *last* purchaser. In both cases the purchaser bought the goods from a seller who dealt in goods of the kind. What basis is there for protecting the ultimate purchaser when the seller obtains possession of the goods for purposes of repair but not when the seller obtains possession from a thief? Is not the position of the two buyers identical? What is the effect of 2–403(3)?

2. To prevail under 2–403(1), a buyer of consigned goods must be a buyer in ordinary course of business, which means that the buyer must have purchased in good faith. The definition of "good faith" requires that the buyer must have observed reasonable commercial standards of fair dealing. Consequently, the circumstances surrounding the purchase of consigned goods are important. The existence of warning signs, or red flags, that the seller may not own the goods, may prevent the purchaser who ignores the red flags from being a buyer in ordinary course of business. See Davis v. Carroll, 937 F.Supp.2d 390, 427 (S.D.N.Y.2013), in which the owner of paintings entrusted them to a gallery which sold them to another gallery:

> New York law provides that a heightened duty of due diligence attaches where a purchaser is presented with reason to suspect foul play in a sale. This objective inquiry focuses on whether a sale was transacted in the shadow of red flags that should have put the purchaser on notice of potential illegality. Here, [the owner] identifies a number of such warning signs, including evidence of [the seller's] financial difficulties, evidence that [the seller] was dealing in fakes, mixed signals regarding [the seller's] right to convey valid title to the Eight Disputed Works, [the buyer's] use of special documentation, and bargain basement pricing. Even read in the light most favorable to [the buyer], the record evidence in this case dictates a finding of numerous red flags.

The court held that the buyer was not a buyer in ordinary course of business and the owner was entitled to possession of the paintings.

3. While 2–403(2) deals with the special case of entrusting goods to a person who deals in goods of that kind, subsection (1) deals more broadly with the rights of purchasers who purchase goods from one other than the owner of the goods. Please read 2–403(1).

Problem. Pritchard purchased a used boat from Big River Marine, paying for it with a check. A week later Pritchard sold the boat to Coffman, who used it for a month and then decided he wanted a larger boat, so he traded it in to Lakeshore Boats. Unfortunately, Pritchard had paid Big River with a check drawn on an account that Pritchard closed before the check cleared. Big River now sues Lakeshore to obtain possession of the boat. What result?

In Pine Meadow Autoflex, LLC v. Taylor, 104 Ark. App. 262, 290 S.W.3d 626, 629–30 (2009), defendant car dealer sold a Jeep to Cates, taking a security interest to secure Cates' payment of the price. A year later Cates applied to the state for a duplicate title certificate, falsely representing to the state that the security interest had been satisfied and released. This misrepresentation occurred on a form on which Cates forged a signature of behalf of defendant. The state issued a clean title certificate, and Cates sold the car to Asher, who sold it to a used-car dealer, who sold it to plaintiff. Plaintiff obtained a new title certificate, license plates, and insurance, and she made extensive repairs. Having received no payments from Cates, defendant located and repossessed the Jeep from plaintiff, and plaintiff sued to recover possession. The trial court held for plaintiff, defendant appealed, and the appellate court affirmed:

> The crucial question is whether Cates, at the time of the sale of the vehicle to Walt Asher, had title that was void or instead title that was voidable. The controlling case is Midway Auto Sales v. Clarkson, [29 S.W.3d 788 (Ark.App.2000)], where we held that one who obtains property by fraud acquires voidable title and therefore has power to transfer good title to a good-faith purchaser for value; even where delivery is procured through criminal fraud, voidable title passes. Here, it is likely that Cates obtained the duplicate title by criminal fraud but, even so, the sale to Asher gave Asher voidable title, and the subsequent purchasers therefore were empowered to transfer good title pursuant to Ark. Code Ann. § 4–2–403(1)(d) (Repl. 2001).

> Appellant attempts to characterize the forgery and subsequent sale of the auto as theft,[1] but all instances of obtaining property through criminal fraud could be so characterized. Appellant also cites cases from the courts of New York and Texas holding that a title document procured through fraud can pass only void title to subsequent purchasers, and asks us to adopt this rule on public policy grounds. We decline to do so. Appellant, and used-car dealers in general, are beneficiaries of the provision in section § 4–2–403(1) allowing good-faith purchasers to pass good title even when they have been defrauded in obtaining the goods that they sell. The assurance that the purchaser of second-hand goods will not be subject to potential claims by those in the chain of title that may have been victims of fraud gives buyers of used vehicles confidence that the transaction will be binding and secure, thereby increasing both the value of the individual vehicle and volume of used-vehicle sales in general. We think that confidence in documents of title issued by the State likewise benefits the business interests of used-car dealers. As beneficiaries of these assurances to buyers, and as the parties best equipped to investigate title irregularities, we think that the risk of forged title documents can and should be borne by dealers rather than purchasers.

---

[1] Absent exigent circumstances, one who purchases from a thief acquires no title as against the true owner.

A concurring judge wrote:

I join the majority in affirming the trial judge for correctly applying current law to undisputed facts. However, I disagree with the majority's dicta regarding which party is best equipped to investigate title irregularities and to bear the risk of forged title documents. Here, the basic facts were stipulated. Though this case involves the sale and the multiple resale of one used vehicle, it centers on the handling by the Department of Finance and Administration (DFA) of a forged "State of Arkansas Official Release of Lien or Permission to Issue a Replacement Title." Before us, the parties are the initial seller, a used-car dealership, and after two intermediate sales, the final buyer. At trial, neither side alleged wrongdoing by the other.

This case involves an interplay between the sale of goods under our Uniform Commercial Code and the perfection of liens under our uniform motor vehicle act (the "act"). Our interpretation of Arkansas law, although correct, begs for legislative review of Ark. Code Ann. § 27–14–805. This writer finds there is a gap within the Uniform Motor Vehicle Administration, Certificate of Title, and Antitheft Act, Ark. Code Ann. § 27–14–101 *et seq.*, specifically the interaction between section 27–14–909, "Release of lien by lienholder—Disclosure of Information" subsection (b)(2) and section 27–14–805, "Constructive notice." This case turns on the constructive-notice provision, section 805.

Here, the initial seller, the dealer, followed the act and protected the financed balance owed to it by properly perfecting its lien on the title. (§ 27–14–802–804). Before the initial seller received final payment and satisfied its lien (§ 27–14–909(a)), a forged "official" release of lien was presented to DFA, resulting in a new certificate of title showing no lien being issued by DFA pursuant to section 805. That action on the part of a single DFA employee [constituted constructive notice to defendant under section 805 that its lien had been released].

It is contemplated under the act that local DFA revenue-office employees are to serve the gatekeeper function to protect or release otherwise valid liens against vehicle titles on file with that agency. In this case, the forged "official" release of lien that was presented to the DFA revenue-office employee bore an unknown, unverified signature by an imposter who did not even indicate above his signature that he was acting in an agency or representative capacity of the dealer whose name and address also appeared at the top of the one-page "official" document offered. At the least, if constructive notice, instead of actual notice, is all that is required to be given to the lienholder when his valid lien is released, the constructive notice . . . should be bolstered by the requirement of more elaborate verification of identification, authority, and representation. Sellers and buyers are entitled to equal confidence in the documents of title. Sellers include new-car dealers, used-car dealers, financial institutions and individuals, all of whom are also likely, lenders with perfected liens. The buyer's confidence in the validity of the certificate of title (issued through a local revenue office) should not exceed the seller's confidence in the security afforded by a perfected lien against the title (also filed at a local revenue office). Even "lawyers and used-car dealers" need protection on occasion. The task of equally protecting legitimate interests of both buyer and sellers of used motor vehicles is a legislative function.

In footnote 1 the court signals that if the car had been stolen from defendant, the thief would acquire no title whatever and would not have the power to transfer title to a subsequent purchaser. Since Cates acquired voidable title, however, he had the power to transfer clear title to his subsequent purchaser.

4.   Problem. Martin purchased a new car from Emporio Motors. In connection with this transaction, he traded in a Bentley, on which he still owed $60,000 and which was subject to a security interest in favor of Toyota Credit. The $60,000 debt was rolled into the financing for the new vehicle, and Emporio agreed to pay Toyota Credit the $60,000 still owed to it. Shortly thereafter, Emporio Motors sold the Bentley to Focarino, who paid the agreed price. Focarino completed a title application, which Emporio was to submit to the Department of Motor Vehicles. A month later, when Focarino still had not received title from the DMV, he contacted Emporio Motors, which told him that there were some problems with the title. Focarino demanded the return of his money, but Emporio refused. When Focarino contacted the DMV, he learned for the first time that Emporio had not paid the $60,000 to Toyota Credit, that title to the car was still subject to Toyota Credit's security interest, and that no new title could be issued until Toyota's lien was satisfied. Martin reported the Bentley as stolen and submitted a claim to his insurer, Fidelity Insurance. Fidelity paid $60,000 to Toyota Credit and succeeded to Toyota Credit's interest in the Bentley. Focarino sued Fidelity for a restraining order prohibiting it from repossessing the car to enforce the lien and seeking an order that Fidelity release the lien and deliver the certificate of title so that he could obtain title in his name. Who has superior rights in the Bentley, Focarino or Fidelity Insurance?

These were the facts in Focarino v. Travelers Personal Insurance Co., 2017 WL 1456967 (N.J.Super.Ct.App.Div.2017). The court stated:

> [Section 2–403(1)] is "applicable to a person taking by any form of 'purchase' as defined by this Act." *N.J.S.A.* 12A:2–403, comment 1. "[S]ubsection (1) provides specifically for the protection of the good faith purchaser for value in a number of specific situations which have been troublesome under prior law." *Ibid. N.J.S.A.* 12A:2–403(1) "provides that the sale to a good faith purchaser for value cures the defects in the seller's voidable title." *Touch of Class Leasing v. Mercedes-Benz Credit of Can., Inc.,* 248 *N.J. Super.* 426, 437 (App. Div.), *certif. denied,* 126 *N.J.* 390 (1991). That is not the case where title is void. The sale to a good faith purchaser for value "cannot cure void title." *Ibid.*

In distinguishing a void title from a voidable title, a comparison is drawn "between a thief, who wrongfully takes goods against the will of the owner and has void title, and a swindler, who fraudulently induces the owner to deliver goods voluntarily and has voidable title." *NXCESS Motor Cars, Inc. v. JPMorgan Chase Bank, N.A.*, 317 *S.W.*3d 462, 468 (Tex. App. 2010). Generally,

> voidable title passes to those who lie in the middle of the spectrum that runs from best-faith buyer at one end to robber at the other. These are buyers who commit fraud, or are otherwise guilty of naughty acts (bounced checks), but who conform to the appearance of a voluntary transaction . . . .

[1 James J. White, et al., *Uniform Commercial Code*, § 4:33 at 381 (6th ed. 2012).]

In *O'Keeffe v. Snyder*, 83 *N.J.* 478 (1980), involving an allegation that artwork had been stolen, the Court recognized the distinction. "[T]he U.C.C. permits a person with voidable title to transfer good title to a good faith purchaser for value in certain circumstances." However, a "thief acquired no title and could not transfer good title to others regardless of their good faith and ignorance of the theft."

For a person with voidable title to goods to transfer good title to a good faith purchaser for value, the goods, even though delivered through fraud, must be delivered under a transaction of purchase. *N.J.S.A.* 12A:2–403(1)(d); *see Touch of Class, supra*, 248 *N.J. Super.* at 438 ("For the seller to acquire even voidable title, he must obtain delivery of the goods through 'a transaction of purchase.' "). We have explained that the phrase transaction of purchase "is generally limited to those situations in which a third party delivers goods to a subsequent seller, intending for the subsequent seller to become the owner of the goods." Where the goods have been obtained through a transaction of purchase and thus, the subsequent seller has voidable title, the title defects can be cured "through the sale to a good faith purchaser for value[, which] gives the good faith purchaser clear title, free from any claims of third parties."

Here, the trial court found, and no one has disputed, that Focarino was not aware of the lien held by Toyota when he purchased the Bentley from Emporio. At oral argument . . . counsel for Fidelity referred to Focarino as an "innocent purchaser." Fidelity has not disputed on appeal that Focarino is a good faith purchaser for value under the U.C.C.

We agree with [the trial court] that Emporio obtained voidable title to the Bentley through its transaction with Martin because that was a transaction of purchase. As we said in *Touch of Class, supra*, 248 *N.J. Super.* at 438, it is the intent of the original seller, Martin, to enter into a valid transaction that determines whether a "transaction of purchase" has occurred and not the intention of the subsequent seller, in this case Emporio. Martin intended Emporio to own the Bentley in exchange for his new vehicle, conditioned on the payment of the lien held by Toyota.

The security interest held by Toyota in the Bentley did not change the transaction of purchase. There can be "more than one 'owner' of a vehicle." "[T]he true owner is the person who maintains 'possession and control of the automobile.'" When Martin, who indisputably possessed and controlled the Bentley, delivered it to Emporio, he intended Emporio to become the owner subject to paying the lien. He was not prohibited from transferring his ownership because of Toyota's lien.

Fidelity focuses on the fraud committed by Emporio, contending that the Bentley was stolen, but the U.C.C. expressly contemplated the situation where "delivery was procured through fraud punishable under the criminal law." *N.J.S.A.* 12A:2–403(1)(d). This is not a situation such as *O'Keeffe* where paintings were purloined. In that case, the thief had no title to pass even to innocent buyers. Here, Emporio did not forcibly coerce Martin into transferring possession of the Bentley, but rather fraudulently induced the transfer by falsely promising that it would pay off the lien on the Bentley and provide Martin with good title on his new vehicle.

Nor is this a case factually similar to *Touch of Class* where a lessee, who subsequently tried to sell the vehicle he leased, did not obtain the vehicle by a transaction of purchase. We held that this lease was a "true" lease and not a lease for security. Because the lease was not a transaction of purchase, the lessee "did not even possess voidable title at the time of the sale to [the good faith purchaser]."

We are satisfied that a "transaction of purchase" occurred when Martin entered into what was believed to be a valid transaction with Emporio. Fidelity has referred to this as a "good faith sale from [Martin]." Although Martin had the right to rescind the transaction with Emporio, that right expired upon the sale of the vehicle to Focarino, who was a good faith purchaser for value.

Therefore, . . . Emporio acquired the Bentley from Martin through a "transaction of purchase" because Martin wanted Emporio to own the vehicle subject to paying off the lien. The transaction of purchase gave Emporio a voidable title. The voidable title allowed Emporio, despite its alleged fraud, to sell the vehicle to a good faith purchaser for value, Focarino. Focarino then took the vehicle free and clear of any claims by third parties, including Fidelity, which had paid Toyota's lien under its policy of insurance with Martin. Thus, Focarino is the "rightful and legal owner" of the Bentley.

5. The court in *Focarino* relies on 2–403. We learned in *Fordyce Bank*, page 610, that under 9–302(a) a buyer in ordinary course of business who purchases goods subject to a security interest takes the goods free of the security interest. Focarino was a buyer in ordinary course. Why does the court not rely on 9–302(a)?

6. Subsection (1) of 2–403 provides that a person with voidable title has power to transfer good title to a good faith purchaser for value. Subsection (2) provides that a merchant who deals in goods of the kind has the power to transfer good title to a buyer in the ordinary course of business. What are the policy justifications for protecting a broader range of purchasers under subsection (1) (voidable title cases) than under subsection (2) (entrusting-to-merchant cases)?

7.   Problem. Beau, a well-known, wealthy real estate developer, examined several rings at Star Diamond, a retail jewelry store. His eye was drawn to a flawless 3-carat cushion-cut ring, priced at $380,000. He told Star's manager that he would like to buy it but that he wanted to present it to his girlfriend to make sure that she liked it before he completed the purchase. Star was willing to allow him to do this, but required him to give Star a check for the price and also give his credit-card number. Beau gave both and left with the ring. Instead of presenting it to his girlfriend, however, Beau presented it to 3-Balls, a pawnshop, which loaned him $40,000, taking possession of the ring as collateral for repayment of the loan. When Beau failed to return to Star Diamond as agreed, Star's manager discovered that the check was phony and the credit card was insufficient to cover the price of the ring. With the help of the police, Star located the ring at 3-Balls, which refused to return it unless Star paid the $40,000 (plus interest). Star Diamond sued for possession. Who should win?*

8.   Problem. Murphy leased a road grader from Ross Implements, Inc. for a period of six months at a rental of $500 per month. Four months into the lease Murphy sold the grader to Jacobi, who paid value and took in good faith. Does Jacobi take free of Ross Implements' rights? Was Murphy a purchaser? Could he transfer greater rights than Ross intended to give to him? See 2A–305(1)–(2).

9.   Problem. Owens Construction delivered two front-end loaders to Trico, a dealer in front-end loaders, for repair. Without authority, an employee of Trico transferred the two machines to a corporation she had set up, and that corporation sold the machines to Bayer, a buyer in ordinary course. Does Bayer take free of Owens' interest?

10. Problem. Owens Construction contracted to sell one of its front-end loaders to Pecci, who paid for it in full and was to pick it up in two days. Owens then sold the loader to Kang, who paid in full and took possession. Owens Construction is insolvent. As between Pecci and Kang, who is entitled to the loader? See 2–401(2)–(3).

---

* Truth is stranger than fiction. See http://www.chicagobusiness.com/article/20111103/BLOGS03/111109913/after-losing-diamond-on-a-handshake-graff-jewelers-sues-pawn-shop-to-get-it-back.

C. SITUATIONS IN WHICH THE BUYER GETS WORSE TITLE THAN THE SELLER HAD

1. FRAUDULENT CONVEYANCES

No debtor should be free to conceal or dispose of his property with a view to preventing his creditors from satisfying their legal claims. He must be just to his creditors before he can rightfully be generous with his property for the benefit of others. These basic principles are, in Anglo-American law, associated with the Statute of 13 Elizabeth, c. 5, which declared conveyances with intent to delay, hinder or defraud creditors utterly void, frustrate and of no effect against the persons so hindered, delayed or defrauded.

J. MacLachlan, Bankruptcy 253 (1956).

The clearest example of a fraudulent conveyance is a gift of assets to a family member for the purpose of putting the assets beyond the reach of the donor's creditors. The law of fraudulent conveyances, however, extends far beyond this archetype. The original Statute of 13 Elizabeth invalidated conveyances made with the actual intent to hinder creditors, and over time the courts identified indicia of that intent. Known as "badges of fraud," these indicia created a presumption of fraudulent conveyance when one of them was present. Something of these badges of fraud remain, and the current law of fraudulent conveyances is found in the Uniform Fraudulent Transfer Act (or its predecessor the Uniform Fraudulent Conveyances Act), the Bankruptcy Code, the UCC, and the common law.

Fraudulent conveyance law employs an extraordinary notion—that a transfer of title, valid between the parties, is invalid as to creditors of the transferor. Since creditors protected by the rule do not have to be secured, a fraudulent conveyance of unencumbered goods may be set aside. This means, in effect, that the transferee gets less than a complete interest in fraudulently conveyed goods, even if the transferor had a perfect, unencumbered title. The law is designed to protect creditors, within limits, by enabling them to rely on the property of their debtors. The protection is given at the expense, at least initially, of the transferee.

While a debtor should not be able to frustrate his creditors by fraudulently conveying goods, the interest of the innocent transferee must be considered. Normally, therefore, fraudulent conveyance law is limited by the principle that a transfer will not be upset unless some guilt or fault can be assigned to the transferee.

a. SELLER'S RETENTION OF POSSESSION AFTER THE SALE

Three main classes of cases constitute the great bulk of fraudulent conveyances. The first is "fraudulent retention," in which the seller continues in possession of goods after selling them. Creditors of the seller may be misled by the seller's ostensible ownership. The buyer's failure to take possession causes the ambiguous situation, but the question remains, does the buyer's "guilt" necessarily justify a creditor to disregard the conveyance and seize the property conveyed? Should it matter why the buyer did not take possession?

Lefever v. Mires

Illinois Supreme Court, 1876.
81 Ill. 456.

■ MR. JUSTICE SCHOLFIELD. The contest here is between appellant, as purchaser, and appellee, as judgment creditor, in regard to which has the prior right to certain hay and corn, and a cow.

The property originally belonged to one Brewer, against whom appellee's judgment was obtained, who was tenant of a farm of appellant for the year 1874.

Appellant claims that Brewer sold the property to him on the 21st of October, 1874, which was before the levy of appellee's execution. The corn and hay were raised on the farm of appellant, of which Brewer was tenant, and the hay was in stack and the corn cut up and in shocks on the land where grown, at the time of the alleged sale, and the cow was also then on the same farm.

The evidence fails to show other than a contract of sale. The property remained where it was before the sale—Brewer still being in possession of the farm—until the levy of the execution; and there is no proof of even a symbolical delivery to appellant.

It is argued that the court erred in instructing the jury that, to make the sale valid as against appellee, it was essential the proof should show that there was an actual delivery of possession to the appellant.

The rule undoubtedly is, as contended by appellant, where the goods are ponderous or bulky, or can not be conveniently delivered manually, there may be a symbolical delivery; but we are unable to see why there could not have been an actual delivery of, at least, the cow, here, even if it shall be conceded the shocks of corn and hay were too ponderous for manual delivery. But what act tending to show symbolical delivery can be claimed to have been proven? We have been unable to find evidence of any. It does not appear that the property was present when the contract for sale was made, or that anything else was done between the parties than merely to make the agreement to sell. The property remained in the possession, and, so far as the entire world could see, was still owned by Brewer, after as well as before the sale. This, as against creditors, in our opinion, was insufficient to pass the title.

. . .

The judgment is affirmed.

Questions

1. The rationale for viewing a seller's retention of possession as fraud against the seller's creditors is that the seller's apparent ownership of the goods may mislead the creditors. How was the creditor misled in *Lefever*?

2. The court suggests that if Brewer had handed the purchaser a handful of hay, a stalk of corn, and the bell that hung around the neck of the cow, the result would be different. Presumably, of course, the creditor's perception of Brewer's continued ownership would not have been any different than it was in the case. Why would a different result be justified?

Blumenstein v. Phillips Insurance Center, Inc.

Alaska Supreme Court, 1971.
490 P.2d 1213.

■ Connor, Justice. . . .

The background of this case is connected with a recurrence of gold fever which for a short time struck the community of Nome, Alaska. In the mid-1960's a venture was launched to recover gold from submerged deposits in the ocean offshore from the town. Lucrative dreams of a bygone era were revived briefly by the prospect of recovering this wealth through new dredging technology. But in 1967 the vision faded into the chill reality of economic failure. On the beach at Nome a converted landing craft, the Mermaid I, stands vigil as a tangible but lonely witness to the vanished hopes of a modern day gold stampede. However, it is only with the fate of the Mermaid I as a means of satisfying indebtedness that this appeal is concerned.

On May 14, 1966, appellant, Bernard Blumenstein, conveyed the landing craft Mermaid I to Martin Dredging, Inc. The transaction entered into between Blumenstein and Martin Dredging was labeled a "Conditional Sale Agreement." Although it was apparently intended to leave Blumenstein with a security interest in the Mermaid I, the agreement was never recorded.

The conditional sale agreement called for an initial down payment by Martin Dredging to Blumenstein of 4,000 shares of its stock. At that time the stock was selling for about a dollar a share. A balance of $11,000 was to be paid in installments. Two installments of $1,250 each were due in the summer of 1966. Further payment was then to be deferred until July 15 of the following year, at which time installments were to resume at a monthly rate of $2,500 until the balance had been paid. The terms of the sale also provided for alteration of the boat by Martin Dredging to suit its purposes. Martin Dredging was at the time embarking on the project to mine underwater gold deposits in the offshore area near Nome, and wanted the Mermaid I for test dredging to prove the theory that gold could profitably be retrieved from the underwater deposits. The vessel was converted as planned and was used during the summer of 1966 for mining operations, which initially proved to be successful. With the onset of winter, the Mermaid I was beached near Nome; the boat has not been used since that time, and it remains, to this date, at the location where it was left in the fall of 1966.

In the spring of 1967 Martin Dredging drastically increased the scope of its undertaking by purchasing and outfitting a surplus minesweeper, subsequently named the Mermaid II. Appellee [Phillips Insurance Center, Inc.] was called upon to provide insurance for the Mermaid II. After summoning an underwriter to examine Martin Dredging's operation, Phillips contracted to provide insurance to the company.

The operation of the Mermaid II during the summer months of 1967 proved to be the undoing of Martin Dredging. Through a combination of unfortunate circumstances, the mining operation met with little success, while Martin Dredging incurred inordinately heavy expenses. By late summer it was generally known that the Mermaid II had proved to be a colossal failure. By that time Martin Dredging had been rendered insolvent, with no substantial assets besides the Mermaids I and II, and no funds with which it could pay outstanding obligations.

The financial collapse of Martin Dredging and the failure of the Mermaid II precipitated the events which culminated in this appeal. On July 15, 1967, the day upon which Martin Dredging was to resume monthly installments for the Mermaid I, Blumenstein failed to receive payment; he contacted the company and was assured that the money would be forthcoming within 30 days. However, by August 15, the date set for the second monthly payment of 1967, it became apparent that he would receive neither the delinquent July payment nor the August payment.

Blumenstein made several formal requests for payment at this time and contacted individual members of Martin Dredging's board of directors persistently. Finally, through the efforts of his attorney, Blumenstein persuaded the members of the board to call a special meeting concerning payment of the amounts due on the Mermaid I. In the course of this meeting, which was held on September 7, 1967, Blumenstein apparently proposed that Martin Dredging quitclaim its interest in the Mermaid I to him, in return for which Blumenstein would relinquish any claim for payment which he might have against the company. The members of the board ultimately acquiesced to this arrangement, and the Mermaid I was thus quit-claimed back to Blumenstein.

Testimony adduced below shows that shortly after this reconveyance of the Mermaid I, Blumenstein boarded the vessel and removed several items. A few days later he returned with a workman and spent several hours removing some more equipment and preparing the boat for the onset of winter. Some welding equipment which belonged to the boat was also retrieved from the Martin Dredging shop. Blumenstein took no further measures in reasserting his possession of the Mermaid I.

During this same period of time, Phillips ran into trouble collecting premiums on the insurance which it had procured for the operations of the Mermaid II. On August 19, 1967, Phillips sent Martin Dredging a notice of cancellation, giving the Mermaid II 30 days to repair to a safe port. Nome was not considered a safe port, and at some time around the end of August the Mermaid II was taken to Seward, where she was later sold to satisfy a judgment for unpaid seamen's wages. In the first week of September 1967 Phillips filed suit against Martin Dredging to recover $7,931.25 in unpaid premiums. On September 15, about a week after Martin Dredging had quit-claimed the Mermaid I to Blumenstein, Phillips attached the boat.

At first Blumenstein did nothing about the attachment papers affixed to the Mermaid I. Not until it became evident that Phillips might actually sell the boat did he act. Accordingly, on September 3, 1968, almost a full year after issuance of the quitclaim deed by Martin Dredging, Blumenstein first filed a complaint in intervention against Phillips, alleging that the Mermaid I was his by virtue of the quitclaim deed. Phillips answered, denying the validity of the quitclaim transaction and affirmatively asserting that the conveyance to Blumenstein amounted to an attempt to defraud creditors.

On December 22, 1969, Blumenstein's claim came on for trial in the superior court at Anchorage, and on January 15, 1970, the court entered findings of fact and conclusions of law in favor of Phillips. Specifically, the court found that Blumenstein either knew or should have known of Martin Dredging's insolvency at the time he procured the quitclaim deed, "and that the transfer amounted to a preference of the creditor Blumenstein over the Plaintiff creditor of Martin Dredging Incorporated." The court further held that Blumenstein's conduct was not sufficient to reassert possession of the Mermaid I in a manner which would give public notice of his interest in the boat, and that the quitclaim transaction consequently fell within the presumption of fraud created by AS 09.25.060.[2] It was the court's conclusion that Blumenstein had failed to overcome the statutory presumption.

On appeal, Blumenstein asserts that the trial court erred in deciding that he had failed to properly retake possession of the Mermaid I. It is thus argued that the statutory presumption of fraud should not have been held applicable in the circumstances of this case, and that the quitclaim deed from Martin Dredging to Blumenstein constituted a valid conveyance of the vessel. Phillips rebuts Blumenstein's arguments on

---

[2]   AS 09.25.060 provides in relevant part:

"Every sale or assignment of personal property unless accompanied by the immediate delivery and the actual and continued change of possession of the thing sold or assigned is presumed prima facie to be a fraud against the creditors of the vendor or assignor * * *."

appeal, maintaining that the trial court correctly invalidated as fraudulent the conveyance in question. Phillips points out that the essential concern in determining whether possession over an object has been established should be whether the conduct of the party claiming possession would have sufficiently given notice to the general public of the party's interest in the property possessed. It is urged that Blumenstein's actions in the present case were insufficient under this criterion. Phillips additionally points to various badges of fraud in the transaction between Blumenstein and Martin Dredging, which, it is claimed, support the conclusion that this conveyance was made with intent to defraud creditors.

Although the primary focus of the controversy on appeal has been upon the adequacy of the possession which Blumenstein established over the Mermaid I, we have concluded that the trial court's decision would require reversal regardless of the proper disposition of this issue. Thus, in our consideration of this matter, we may assume that the trial court was correct in finding that Blumenstein's conduct was insufficient as a retaking of possession of the Mermaid I. We will further assume that the trial court properly held that Blumenstein was aware of Martin Dredging's impending insolvency.

Given these assumptions, it is apparent that Blumenstein, under the conditional sale agreement, did not perfect a security interest in the Mermaid I which would give him priority over Phillips' attachment lien. . . .

Though Blumenstein could not prevail on the basis of his intended security interest, he also has a claim as a grantee for valuable consideration. We turn next to the question whether the quitclaim deed delivered to Blumenstein by Martin Dredging should properly have been invalidated under Alaska's law governing fraudulent conveyances.[6] AS 34.40.010 provides that a conveyance of goods made with intent to hinder, delay or defraud creditors is invalid. This statute provides Alaska's basic prohibition against transactions in fraud of creditors. AS 34.40.090 complements the basic prohibition by providing that the existence of fraudulent intent is a question of fact. Thus, under normal circumstances, fraud will not be presumed.

However, AS 09.25.060 qualifies the provisions of AS 34.40.010 and AS 34.40.090, by erecting a prima facie presumption of fraud in cases where a sale of personal property is not "accompanied by the immediate delivery and the actual and continued change of possession" by the vendee. Since we have accepted as valid the finding that Blumenstein did

---

[6] Given our conclusion that no security interest in the Mermaid I was perfected by Blumenstein, and assuming that Blumenstein did not adequately retake possession of the Mermaid I following reconveyance to him by Martin Dredging, it is evident that the provisions of the Uniform Commercial Code do not govern this transaction. Except in cases involving retention by a merchant seller in the course of trade, the code specifically leaves the validity of sales where the seller retains possession of goods sold to determination under existing state laws. See AS 45.05.128(b) [2–402(2)].

not sufficiently retake possession of the Mermaid I after receiving the quitclaim deed from Martin Dredging, the conclusion seems inescapable that the statutory presumption of fraud created by AS 09.25.060 was correctly held to apply to the circumstances of the present case by the trial court. Yet by no means does it follow that the result reached by the lower court was correct.

We must emphasize initially that AS 09.25.060 establishes only a prima facie presumption. This presumption is rebuttable. It serves merely to shift to the vendee the burden of proving that a conveyance was made without fraudulent intent. Under AS 09.25.060, if a vendee has failed to establish immediate and continued possession over personalty which he has purchased, and if he makes no effort to show that the transaction was entered into in good faith, then a finding of fraud will be compelled. Where, on the other hand, the grantee introduces evidence tending to show that the conveyance in question was transacted in good faith, then the presumption will be dispelled, and it will be incumbent upon the finder of fact to determine whether there was actually an intent to defraud creditors.

In ruling upon the circumstances of the present case, the trial court stopped short of reaching the issue of actual intent to defraud. Instead, its decision was confined to the finding that Blumenstein had failed to overcome the presumption erected by AS 09.25.060. In our view, the court's exclusive reliance on the AS 09.25.060 presumption was unwarranted. Ample and convincing evidence was introduced by Blumenstein to show that the conveyance of the Mermaid I by Martin Dredging was undertaken in good faith.

It is significant that Blumenstein furnished a plausible, and, indeed, entirely believable explanation for his failure to take more positive steps in establishing possession of the Mermaid I after receiving the quitclaim deed from Martin Dredging. At the time of the conveyance, the Mermaid I had been beached for approximately one year. The boat was beached at the same location where it had usually been kept by Blumenstein prior to its conveyance to Martin Dredging. With winter impending, refloating of the boat would have been difficult and impracticable. It should further be noted that many indicia of ownership—such as the ship's Coast Guard number and its radio license—which might normally be expected to change with transfer of a boat, had remained unaltered since Blumenstein's original possession. Moreover, it must be considered that, while Blumenstein might not have actively and openly asserted his repossession of the boat, neither can it be said that the Mermaid I was, in any practical sense, retained by Martin Dredging. All of these factors, taken together, tend to explain Blumenstein's failure to retake possession of the Mermaid I, and thereby substantially weaken any inference of fraud which might be drawn.[7]

---

[7] It is relevant to note that even in jurisdictions where legislation provides that failure of a vendee to take possession of purchased goods must conclusively be presumed to be fraudulent,

Even more significant than the facts surrounding Blumenstein's failure to take possession of the Mermaid I is the showing that the quitclaim deed to the Mermaid I was given in consideration for the discharge of a valid debt owed by Martin Dredging to Blumenstein.[8] The validity of Martin Dredging's obligation to Blumenstein under the terms of the original conditional sale agreement is not contested, and, in fact, seems to be assumed in the findings of the trial court. Similarly uncontested is the fact that Blumenstein discharged the debt owed to him by Martin Dredging in return for the quitclaim deed to the Mermaid I. It has previously been held that such a showing tends strongly, if not conclusively, to overcome the type of presumption created by AS 09.25.060. For example, in Scruggs v. Blackshear Manufacturing Company, 45 Ga.App. 855, 166 S.E. 249, 251 (1932), under circumstances not unlike those of the present case, the court reversed a finding of fraud by the lower court, holding that while retention of possession by a vendor gives rise to a prima facie presumption of fraud, "[p]roof of payment of valuable consideration for the property rebuts the presumption * * *."[9]

Because Blumenstein offered a satisfactory explanation for his failure to take more overt steps in attempting to reestablish possession of the Mermaid I, and because he further showed that the quitclaim deed

---

the nature of the purchased goods and the circumstances surrounding the failure to take immediate possession may warrant exceptions to the rule. For example, in California it has been held that "[w]here a movable is bulky and not readily transferable by manual delivery the rule of that section [section conclusively presuming fraud] is relaxed by reason of the impracticability of actual delivery by ordinary means and methods." Shepherd v. Gamble, 95 Cal.App.2d 890, 214 P.2d 403, 405 (1950).

   [8]   Phillips has argued that the consideration paid by Blumenstein for the quitclaim of the boat was inadequate. At the time of the conveyance, a balance of approximately $8,500 remained to be paid on the original conditional sale agreement; Phillips contends that this amount was insufficient consideration for a vessel which had originally been sold for $15,000, and subsequently re-equipped with costly machinery. However, it must be remembered that Martin Dredging, at the time of the quitclaim transaction, was insolvent and had no funds available to meet its current obligations. The company was already two installments in arrears, and apparently Blumenstein was making persistent demands for payment. Moreover, under the terms of the conditional sale agreement, if Martin Dredging had insisted on removing, prior to returning the boat to Blumenstein, the equipment which it had installed, then it would have been obligated to restore the vessel to the condition in which it had been at the time of the purchase in 1966.

The adequacy of consideration in any given instance cannot be viewed apart from the particular circumstances in which the parties find themselves. Any sale conducted under the pressure of economic necessity is bound to produce less than an optimal consideration; however, this fact will not affect the adequacy of consideration. Thus, for the purpose of determining whether fraud is indicated in a transaction, adequacy of consideration is usually judged by broad standards. As the court held in White v. Nollmeyer, 151 Mont. 387, 443 P.2d 873, 883 (1968), in order to determine whether a fair consideration had been paid,

> "the test to be applied is whether the disparity between the true value * * * and the price paid is so great as to shock the conscience and strike the understanding at once with the conviction that such transfer never could have been made in good faith."

Applying this standard, we are unable to conclude in the present situation that the consideration paid by Blumenstein for the return of the Mermaid I was inadequate.

   [9]   See also Andrews v. Lorraine Dance Studios, Inc., 189 A.2d 802, 804–805 (R.I.1963), where the court states that "a showing that there was adequate consideration for the sale of property retained by a vendor tends to rebut the presumption of fraud that arises from its retention."

delivered by Martin Dredging was issued in exchange for valuable consideration, we think that the trial court was unjustified in relying on the statutory presumption to invalidate as fraudulent the conveyance in question. Under these circumstances, the trial court should have considered the validity of the transaction as a question of fact pursuant to AS 34.40.010 and AS 34.40.090. Accordingly, the court should have ruled on the issue whether, in the conveyance of the Mermaid I to Blumenstein, there was an actual, as opposed to a presumed intent to hinder, delay or defraud creditors.

Under normal circumstances a remand to the superior court might be appropriate in order to allow the lower court the opportunity to rule upon the question of actual fraudulent intent. However, in the present case we feel that the necessity for a remand is obviated, since, in our view, the findings of fact rendered below preclude a conclusion of fraud.

In its fourth finding of fact, the trial court ruled that Blumenstein

"reasonably knew or should have known the corporation [Martin Dredging] was insolvent and that the transfer amounted to a preference of the creditor Blumenstein over the Plaintiff creditor of Martin Dredging Incorporated."

Both the tenor of the court's language and the context within which it is placed leave an indelible impression that the court believed that a preferential payment to one of several creditors by an insolvent debtor is in itself an unlawful or fraudulent act. Indeed, this appears to be a notion shared by the parties on appeal.

Yet the rule is settled that in the absence of bankruptcy laws or express statutory prohibition, an insolvent debtor may convey property to one creditor, even if it means that the debtor's assets will thereby be depleted, and that the claims of other creditors will be defeated. . . . As Corbin states in his treatise on contracts:

"At common law it was not illegal for a debtor to pay one of his creditors in full even though he did not have enough left to pay his other creditors in full or even in part. Such a payment was not, and is not now, a fraudulent conveyance. The payment is merely the performance of an existing legal duty. Nor is it illegal for the debtor to transfer property as security for an existing debt; the value of the property in excess of the debt remains available to other creditors. The conveyance of property to a creditor in satisfaction of an existing debt is a fraudulent conveyance only in case its value is in excess of the debt and the purpose of the debtor is to keep that excess out of the hands of his other creditors."[10]

---

[10] 6A A. Corbin, Contracts § 1467, at 566 (1962) (Footnote omitted). 1 G. Glenn, Fraudulent Conveyances and Preferences §§ 289 & 289a (rev.ed.1940), is in accord with Corbin:

The rational underpinning of the rule which allows preferential transfers is not difficult to perceive, and has been aptly stated by the court in Irving Trust Company v. Kaminsky, 19 F.Supp. 816, 818 (S.D.N.Y.1937):

> "[T]he rule against fraudulent conveyances may be availed of by a single creditor. To allow such a creditor, acting in his own interest alone, to set aside a preferential transfer as one in fraud of creditors would amount to substituting that creditor as the person preferred in place of the creditor chosen by the debtor."

Thus, numerous courts hold that a bona fide preference of one creditor over others will be upheld even where the debtor is or will be rendered insolvent, or where other creditors are threatening suit, or where the preferred creditor is aware of the debtor's insolvency. Some courts have held that even if the debtor's intent is fraudulent, and even if the preferred creditor is aware of that intent, a preferential transaction will not be set aside so long as the preferred creditor, by accepting the conveyance from the debtor, is only protecting his own interests as a creditor. Accordingly, it is the rule that a bona fide preference by an insolvent debtor does not, in itself, constitute evidence of fraud.

. . . Here, both Blumenstein and Phillips were found to be creditors of Martin Dredging at the time of the challenged conveyance. In quitclaiming the Mermaid I to Blumenstein, Martin Dredging chose to prefer his claim over that of Phillips. To invalidate this transfer now would accomplish nothing more than the substitution of Phillips for Blumenstein as the preferred creditor of Martin Dredging. This we refuse to do.

. . .

The judgment of the superior court is reversed and this matter is remanded for entry of judgment in favor of the appellant.

QUESTIONS AND NOTES

1.   If a debtor sells one of its assets for the fair value of that asset, the asset is replaced by the price the debtor receives. Because the value of the debtor's assets remains unchanged, creditors of the debtor have no legitimate complaint. But this is not necessarily true if the debtor transfers an asset in exchange for cancellation of debt. Although the debtor's balance sheet shows the same amount of (in)solvency as before the transfer, there are fewer assets for the creditors to reach. Nevertheless, as *Blumenstein* reveals, transfer of goods for extinguishment of an equivalent amount of debt is not a fraudulent conveyance. Whether Martin Dredging received fair value for the vessel is, of course, another matter altogether.

"If there is in our law one point which is more ungrudgingly accepted than others, it is that the preferential transfer does not constitute a fraudulent conveyance." Id. § 289, at 488.

2.   Presumption of fraud: conclusive or rebuttable. Article 2 preserves the various statutory and decisional rules on whether a seller's retention of sold goods is fraudulent as against the seller's creditors, but it limits those rules by stating that "retention of possession in good faith and current course of trade by a merchant-seller for a commercially reasonable time after a sale or identification is not fraudulent" (2–402(2)).

As *Lefever* indicates, in some states retention of possession by the seller after sale is "conclusive fraud." That is just another way of saying that seller's creditors can reach the goods if they are not delivered to the buyer with some promptness. *Blumenstein* illustrates that in other states, retention of goods after sale creates a presumption of fraud, but this presumption may be rebutted by showing that the transaction was bona fide.

There are several somewhat different underlying reasons for the retention-of-possession rules. Most important, perhaps, is the fact that a debtor in financial difficulty may try to put his goods beyond the reach of creditors by entering into a sham sale, and a claimed sale without change of possession is some indication that the transfer is a sham. That is, the purported sale may actually be a fraudulent transfer, one intended to "delay, hinder, or defraud creditors."

Second, creditors may rely on the fact that the debtor apparently owns goods in making the decision to extend credit. It is clear that the likelihood of creditor reliance on appearances was a substantial factor in the early common-law development. See Twyne's Case, 3 Co.Rep. 806, 76 Eng.Rep. 809 (1601). (Today, however, unsecured creditors ordinarily rely not on a debtor's apparent ownership of particular tangible goods, but rather on the debtor's anticipated future income stream, which is estimated from financial reports and other sources.)

Third, creditors who have a judgment against the debtor will rely on debtor's apparent ownership of particular goods by levying on them and foregoing a search for, or levy on, other goods.

These different justifications for the fraudulent-retention-of-possession rules suggest the reasons for the fact that some states treat retention as conclusively fraudulent while others treat it as only presumptively fraudulent. They also explain the rather curious fact that, in a number of states, once the buyer has taken possession of the goods, the goods no longer can be reached by seller's levying creditors, no matter how long possession was left with seller after sale. If retention is prima facie evidence of actual fraud, and is not rebutted, then, as in any actual fraud case, the levying creditor should be able to reach the goods even after their ultimate delivery to the buyer. Similarly, the same result should obtain if the rationale for the fraudulent-retention rules is that creditors will extend credit relying on the seller's ownership of the goods in question. If the rule is based upon the levying creditor's change of position in levying on particular goods, however, the rule that once the goods are delivered to the buyer they are no longer subject to claims of seller's creditors, makes perfectly good sense. As you might surmise, in states in which retention is said to be conclusively fraudulent, there is a strong chance that, once the goods are delivered to the buyer, the seller's creditors can no longer reach them. (Even if such a state bases its rule also on the creditor's reliance in extending credit, the courts may suggest that, since the levying creditor would have lost to another creditor who levied first, it is appropriate to conclude that the levying creditor also loses to a buyer who took possession before the levy.) On the other hand, in a state where retention is only presumptively fraudulent and the presumption is not rebutted, the levying creditor is likely to be able to reach the goods in the buyer's hands.

See generally, G. Glenn, Fraudulent Conveyances §§ 344–363 (1940); S. Williston, Sales ch. 15 (Rev.Ed.1948) (state-by-state summary of the applicable rules). And see P. Alces, The Law of Fraudulent Transactions § 308 (1989).

3.   Problem. On January 3rd Bill Lawton purchased a new sound system from Hi-Tech Electronics for $1,000 during a special sale. Since he was going to be moving into a new apartment on February 1st, he asked Hi-Tech if he might leave the unit in the store until then. Hi-Tech agreed.

a.   On January 4th Hi-Tech sold the system to Tami Konuk, who had no knowledge of Lawton's interest. Did she take free of his interest?

b.   On January 2nd Hi-Tech gave its lender a security interest in its inventory. Does Lawton take free of this security interest? See 9–320(a).

c.   On January 4th a creditor with a judgment against Hi-Tech Electronics levied on the sound system. Is the creditor's interest superior to Lawton's interest? Or does the stereo belong to Lawton, so that it cannot be reached by Hi-Tech's creditors?

———

b.   SALES MADE WITH ACTUAL INTENT TO DEFRAUD CREDITORS

There are two main types of fraudulent transfers other than those involving seller's retention of possession. One is a transfer that is in fact fraudulent—transfers made with actual intent to hinder, delay, or defraud creditors. The other is a transfer at less than fair value which leaves the transferor insolvent or with insufficient assets to reasonably continue a business. In 1918 the National Conference of Commissioners on Uniform State Laws promulgated the Uniform Fraudulent Conveyances Act (UFCA) to deal with these types of fraudulent transfers. In 1984 this Act was revised and replaced by the Uniform Fraudulent Transfer Act (UFTA). Thirty years later, in 2014, the UFTA was revised and renamed the Uniform Voidable Transfer Act (UVTA). Forty-four states (and the District of Columbia) enacted the 1984 UFTA, and more than half of these jurisdictions have replaced it with the 2014 UVTA.

The transferor's actual intent to hinder, delay, or defraud creditors is not necessarily enough to defeat a transfer made to implement that intent. The transfer cannot be set aside as against a transferee who took in good faith and for reasonably equivalent value.[1] The Act does not

---

[1]   U.V.T.A. § 8(a).

define "good faith" and it is, therefore, unclear exactly what the term means. Section 548 of the Bankruptcy Code also permits the avoidance of fraudulent conveyances. It, too, insulates a transfer—even if made with actual intent to hinder creditors—to the extent that the transferee took in good faith and for value.[2] Like the UVTA, the Bankruptcy Code does not contain a definition of "good faith," and courts in the bankruptcy context have resisted a single definition, saying that the content of the requirement depends on the circumstances of the particular case.[3] If the transferee was in good faith but gave less than equivalent value, the transfer can be set aside, but the transferee is entitled to the return of the value actually given.[4]

The actual-intent rules are relatively unimportant for sales law purposes, because transfers made in exchange for consideration are usually purchases in good faith. Occasionally, it is possible to prove that the buyer dealt with the seller for the express purpose of hindering, delaying or defrauding the latter's creditors. In these cases, there is a fraudulent conveyance even though the transferee has paid fair consideration. Many of these cases involve family transactions, such as sales to a spouse.[5]

c. SALES FOR LESS THAN FAIR VALUE BY SELLERS WHO ARE INSOLVENT OR WHO ARE LEFT WITH INSUFFICIENT CAPITAL

The second type of fraudulent transfer—transfers made for less than fair consideration by a transferor who is either insolvent, thereby rendered insolvent, or left with unreasonably small assets for the business in which the transferor is engaged—does have importance for sales law. The applicable rules are in sections 4 and 5 of UVTA. If the transfer is for less than "reasonably equivalent value," the transfer is assailable irrespective of the good faith of the transferee, although a good faith transferee is entitled to a return of the consideration paid. Since the statutory test is fair or reasonably equivalent value, it would seem to follow that a buyer who innocently gets a very good bargain from an insolvent seller runs the risk of participating in a fraudulent conveyance. This has not necessarily been the case. In the application of the "fair equivalence" rule of the 1918 Act in the seller-buyer situation, the courts usually have not resolved the matter solely by determining the value of the thing sold and comparing it to the price paid. Rather they have taken into account all the surrounding circumstances attending the sale, and declare the conveyance fraudulent only when the consideration paid by the buyer is so short of the real value of the property conveyed "as to

---

[2]   11 U.S.C.A. § 548(c).

[3]   E.g., In re Hannover Corp., 310 F.3d 796 (5th Cir.2002); In re Financial Federated Title & Trust, 309 F.3d 1325 (11th Cir.2002).

[4]   Bankruptcy Code § 548(c), 11 U.S.C.A. § 548(c); UFTA § 8(a), (d).

[5]   E.g., Winter v. Welker, 174 F.Supp. 836 (E.D.Pa.1959); see also, Farrell v. Paulus, 309 Mich. 441, 15 N.W.2d 700 (1944).

startle a correct mind."[6] The same rule may be applied under the revised Act, but a Seventh Circuit case has rejected that test, holding instead that under the "fair equivalent value" test in section 8(a) of the Act, if the net effect of the transfer is to diminish the transferor's estate, any difference in value between the property transferred and the price paid for it could be recovered by the creditors of the transferor.[7]

If a conveyance is found to be fraudulent, protected creditors may set it aside to the extent necessary to satisfy their claims, or disregard it and attach and levy execution on the property conveyed. See section 7, which makes it clear that a fraudulent conveyance is not "utterly void, frustrate and of no effect," to quote the Statute of 13 Elizabeth c. 5, but is merely voidable. It follows from this that a bona fide purchaser from a fraudulent grantee is protected against the rights of the creditors of the fraudulent transferor.[8]

2. BULK SALES

The rules regarding fraudulent conveyances protect creditors of a seller by allowing them to subject the transferred goods to their claims if the transferee has participated in a scheme to hinder or defraud them, has taken with notice of such a scheme, or has taken as a donee or for less than fair consideration. These fraudulent-conveyance rules do not protect creditors of transferors who, at one stroke, sell their entire assets for fair value to a person who has no intention of defrauding anyone. Yet such bulk sales enable fraudulent debtors to convert their inventories into cash and to disappear with the proceeds before their creditors learn of the transaction.

Around 1890 it became common in America for unethical debtors to defeat their creditors in this way. In response, the National Association of Credit Men drafted the first bulk-sales statute, and by 1950 all states had some form of bulk-transfer legislation. There were marked differences in the laws of the various states, however, and creditors involved in interstate transactions sometimes were injured by their ignorance of the scope and operation of the bulk-sales laws in other states.

When the UCC was being drafted in the 1940s and 1950s, the drafters decided to include a bulk sales law as Article 6 of the Code. That law requires the buyer of a major part of a seller's inventory in certain situations to notify creditors of the seller of the impending sale. In some states the buyer also is obligated to make payment directly to certain creditors of the seller. If the buyer fails in its obligations under the bulk sales law, the transfer of goods to the buyer is ineffective as to the seller's

---

6   Neal v. Clark, 75 Ariz. 91, 251 P.2d 903 (1952).

7   Scholes v. Lehmann, 56 F.3d 750 (7th Cir.1995). The case involved a Ponzi scheme, and the excess value received by the transferee was clear. It is unclear whether the court would have imposed such a burden on a good faith buyer in a different context.

8   Section 8(a) expressly protects a subsequent bona fide purchaser.

creditors. Therefore, a buyer who has in good faith paid full value to the seller may lose the goods to a creditor (or have to pay a second time to be able to retain the goods). To avoid this, the buyer must get a list of creditors from the seller and notify those creditors of the impending sale. Compliance with this requirement can be a major burden, particularly in transactions involving the acquisition of a major business with hundreds or thousands of creditors. When it applies, the bulk sales law, in effect, makes the buyer an uncompensated policeman for the seller's creditors.

From the beginning Article 6 was controversial. Some thought it bad policy to require good faith buyers to incur the expense and delay necessary to assure that creditors of a seller were paid or had an opportunity to protect their right to be paid. Contrarily, others thought that Article 6 should be expanded and strengthened to provide even greater protection for creditors of the seller when the seller engaged in a bulk sale.

In the 1970s, therefore, the American Bar Association appointed a committee to study Article 6 and make recommendations. The members of that committee were split between those who believed that bulk-sales legislation should be repealed altogether and those who thought it should be strengthened. After due deliberation, the committee recommended revision of Article 6, largely to make it less onerous for buyers, but also to provide some additional protection to the seller's creditors.

Based on the recommendations of the ABA committee, the National Conference of Commissioners on Uniform State Laws appointed a drafting committee to redraft Article 6. The drafting committee ultimately presented alternative recommendations: the first alternative was repeal of Article 6; the second, adoption of a revised version of Article 6 (which the committee had prepared). In 1987 NCCUSL and ALI (co-sponsor of the UCC) chose the first alternative but straddled the fence: they recommended that the states repeal Article 6 but also approved a revised Article 6 as an alternative for states that might choose not to repeal it.

Most states have opted for repeal: 47 (as well as the District of Columbia, Puerto Rico, and the U.S. Virgin Islands) have repealed Article 6; one (California) has adopted revised Article 6; and two (Alaska and Maryland) still have original Article 6.

a.   TRANSACTIONS COVERED

Article 6 applies to a sale not in the ordinary course of the seller's business of "more than half in value" of a seller's inventory (6–102(1)(c)). It applies only to sales by sellers whose principal business is the sale of inventory from stock (6–103(1)(a)). Official Comment 2 to 6–102 of original Article 6 states that the provisions of Article 6 are aimed primarily at businesses to whom unsecured credit normally is advanced on the faith of their stock in trade:

The businesses covered are defined in subsection (3). Notice that they do not include farming nor contracting nor professional services, nor such things as cleaning shops, barber shops, pool halls, hotels, restaurants, and the like whose principal business is the sale not of merchandise but of services. While some bulk sales risk exists in the excluded businesses, they have in common the fact that unsecured credit is not commonly extended on the faith of a stock of merchandise.

The comments to current Article 6 do not repeat this language, but the intent is unchanged in this respect. See 6–103, Official Comment 1.

b. TRANSFERS EXCEPTED

Before enactment of the UCC, transfers in the ordinary course of business were not regarded as falling within the proscription of bulk transfer statutes. Article 6 preserves this point of view by exempting from the scope of Article 6 all bulk transfers in the ordinary course of business (6–102(1)(c)). This exemption excludes routine transfers from the operation of the statute. In addition, 6–103(3) excludes from coverage the creation of security interests, sales under judicial process or in foreclosure of security interests, and sales by a general assignee for the benefit of creditors. It also excludes (a) sales in which the transferee assumes all the debts of the seller and is not insolvent after the transfer; and (b) sales in which the buyer gets from the seller a list of all known creditors and agrees to pay those creditors. Finally, it excludes from coverage very small transactions and very large ones: sales of assets having a net value of less than $10,000 or more than $25,000,000. Official Comment 7 states that the potential loss to creditors in small transactions does not justify the costs of compliance and the publicity that usually attends large transactions obviates the creditors' need for notification from the buyer to alert them to protect their interests.

c. COMPLIANCE WITH THE ACT

(1) Compliance Procedures

The buyer must obtain from the seller a verified list of "claimants" (defined in 6–102(1)(e)), prepare a schedule of distribution of the price being paid, and give all claimants notice of the sale and the planned distribution of the price. If there are more than 200 claimants, however, instead of sending notice to individual claimants, the buyer can file a notice of the bulk sale in the office of the secretary of state. The notice must be sent (or the filing made) at least 45 days before the buyer pays more than 10% of the price or takes delivery of the goods, whichever occurs first. The requirement of a schedule of distribution does not mean that the buyer must make a distribution to creditors. The plan of distribution could merely state that the entire price will be paid to the seller. If, however, the schedule of distribution lists amounts to be paid to creditors, the buyer is liable to creditors who do not receive the amounts on that schedule (6–106(3), 6–107(1)).

(2) Effect of Failure to Comply

A failure by the buyer to comply with the provisions of Article 6 does not make the transfer ineffective. Rather, the buyer is liable for damages caused individual creditors (6–107). Those damages are measured by the amount the seller owes the creditor minus the amount that the creditor would not have realized had the buyer complied with the statute. The buyer has the burden of proving the amount that the creditor would not have realized.

Defenses to the buyer's liability include (a) the buyer's good faith and commercially reasonable belief that the sale was not subject to Article 6; and (b) the buyer's good faith and commercially reasonable effort to comply with the statute. Unless the buyer has concealed the fact of sale, any action by a creditor against a buyer must be brought within one year of the sale.

This overview of the Article 6 is an extreme oversimplification. The statute contains substantial detail and must be read carefully by a lawyer handling a bulk sales transaction.

D. RIGHT OF THE SELLER, AS AGAINST CREDITORS OF THE BUYER, TO RECOVER GOODS FROM A BUYER WHO IS INSOLVENT

The preceding materials have considered the rights of a seller's creditors against a person who has purchased goods from the seller. There remains for consideration the rights of the *buyer's* creditors against the person who sold goods to the buyer when the buyer has not yet paid the seller and cannot pay both the seller and the creditors: do the goods (or their value) go to the seller or to the creditors of the buyer? Please read 2–702.

1. RIGHTS AGAINST LIEN CREDITORS AND THE TRUSTEE IN BANKRUPTCY

A creditor that obtains judgment against a buyer may obtain a lien on the buyer's real and personal property. As to personal property, the creditor (known as a judgment creditor) obtains the lien either by levying on the goods or by filing a notice of the judgment in the public office specified in the statute recognizing judgment liens. If an insolvent buyer purchases goods on credit but has not paid for them and a creditor of the buyer obtains a judgment against that buyer, who has superior rights to those goods, the seller or the creditor of the buyer? If the judgment creditor does not have a lien, the answer is clear: the seller wins, pursuant to 2–702(2), but only if the seller was unaware of the insolvency when the contract was formed. Please read that subsection.

If the creditor has obtained a judgment lien, then 2–702(3) may seem to come into play. That subsection subordinates the seller's right of reclamation to "the rights of a buyer in ordinary course or other good faith purchaser." A lien creditor is neither a buyer in ordinary course of business nor a good faith purchaser. As originally enacted, however, 2–702(3) expressly subordinated the seller's right also to the rights of a lien creditor. This was confusing because in 2–403, which deals with owners who do not have perfect title, subsection (4) states that the rights of lien creditors are governed not by that section, but by Article 9. That Article, however, addresses the priority of a lien creditor vis-à-vis various kinds of secured creditors, not sellers. If the seller who seeks to reclaim goods has not retained a security interest in the goods, nothing in Article 9 speaks to whether the reclaiming seller or the judgment creditor has superior rights to the goods. Courts invoke 1–103 and look to common law. The predominant common-law view is that the seller prevails. Otherwise, the buyer who defrauded the seller, actually or presumptively (by concealing his insolvency), would benefit from the fraud by having the fraudulently acquired goods used to satisfy the debt to the judgment creditor. (Concerning the presumptive fraud, see 2–702, Official Comment 2.)

The issue often arises in the context of a buyer's bankruptcy proceedings, because section 544 of the Bankruptcy Code gives the trustee the rights of a creditor with a judgment lien, permitting the trustee to avoid the interests of competing claims. In addition, section 545 permits the trustee to avoid certain statutory liens. But section 546(c) specifically preserves a seller's right of reclamation of goods sold not more than 45 days before the buyer enters bankruptcy proceedings. Remaining issues concern primarily whether the seller has met the timing requirements specified in 2–702 and in the Bankruptcy Code.

————

2. RIGHTS AGAINST SECURED CREDITORS

A seller asserting a right to reclaim under 2–702 must be concerned about two classes of competing parties other than lien creditors and the trustee in bankruptcy: subsequent buyers and secured parties. The rights of subsequent buyers are dealt with in 2–403(1) and (2), and there seems little doubt that good faith buyers for value under 2–403(1) and buyers in ordinary course of business under 2–403(2) take priority over the seller's reclamation rights. In those cases, of course, the goods are in the hands of the buyer who purchased from the seller, and the subsequent buyer presumably relies on that possession in making the purchase.

A secured creditor who takes a security interest in the goods after they are delivered also relies on the fact that the buyer has possession of the goods. Often, however, creditors take security interests not only in property then in the possession of the debtor, but also in property to be acquired in the future (known as after-acquired property). A secured party whose security interest arises under a general after-acquired-property clause in a security agreement that was taken prior to the sale in question typically does not extend credit in reliance upon having a security interest in the particular goods that the seller seeks to reclaim. Therefore, it has been suggested that a seller's reclamation right ought to take priority over an interest of a secured party which arises under an after-acquired-property clause.

In Lavonia Manufacturing Co. v. Emery Corp., 52 B.R. 944 (E.D.Pa.1985), the United States District Court rejected that suggestion. Lavonia had delivered $10,490 of yarn to Emery on credit. Two days later Emery filed a petition for reorganization under Chapter 11 of the Bankruptcy Code. Lavonia promptly demanded return of the yarn. Sometime prior to the sale of the yarn three creditors had extended credit to Emery, in connection with which they each had taken a security interest in Emery's current and after-acquired property. The court had to decide whether Lavonia's right of reclamation under 2–702 was superior to the secured creditors' rights in the yarn. The court reasoned as follows:

II.

Section 2–702 of the UCC governs the reclamation rights of credit sellers. To reclaim goods under § 2–702, the seller must establish that the debtor was insolvent and that the seller made a timely demand for return of the delivered goods. The parties here do not dispute that Lavonia has met these requirements; Emery was insolvent when the goods were received and acknowledges receipt of the reclamation demand within the required ten day period. Subsection (c) of § 2–702, however, specifically subordinates a seller's reclamation right to the rights of a "good faith purchaser."

The bankruptcy court found that Emery's creditors were not "good faith purchasers" capable of subordinating Lavonia's right to reclamation. The court declined to apply the UCC's broad definitions of "purchase" and "purchaser" for purposes of § 2–702. Instead, the court held that "the term 'purchaser' in § 2–702(c) includes a secured creditor only to the extent that such creditor gives value to the debtor and receives a security interest thereon after the delivery of the goods and prior to the demand for reclamation." In reaching this conclusion, the court first interpreted § 2–403 of the UCC to mean that, because a debtor has voidable title in goods received from a seller, the seller can divest the debtor of the voidable title after delivery by giving notice under § 2–702(b). Therefore, a good faith purchaser must take some action to prevent the seller of delivered goods from divesting the debtor of his § 2–403 right to transfer good title to the good faith purchaser. The court concluded that "[t]he only reasonable triggering event which could occur after delivery . . . is the issuance of credit and the receipt of a security interest."

III.

Section 2–403 grants a person with voidable title and possession of goods the "power to transfer good title to a good faith purchaser for value." 13 Pa.C.S.A. § 2403(a). See Independent News Co. v. Williams, 293 F.2d 510, 512 (3d Cir.1961) ("any entrusting of possession of goods to a merchant who deals in goods of that kind gives him power to transfer all rights of the entrustor"); In re Holiday Meat Packing, Inc., 30 B.R. 737, 740 (Bkrtcy.W.D.Pa.1983) ("a purchaser of goods from a dealer therein takes good title thereto under 13 Pa.C.S.A. § 2403.") I am unaware, however, of any authority supporting the view that § 2–403 gives a seller the right to divest the debtor of title and reclaim goods unless the creditor gives new value, thereby defeating a prior secured creditor's interest in after-acquired property. To the contrary, numerous courts have held that a perfected secured creditor with an interest in after-acquired property is a good faith purchaser within the meaning of § 2–403. A review of the applicable Code sections leads me to concur in this view.

First, the statutory definitions of the UCC are persuasive on the point. Section 1–201 of the Code defines purchaser as "a person who takes by purchase." Purchase, also defined in § 1–201, includes "taking by sale, discount, negotiation, mortgage, pledge, lien, issue or reissue, gift or any voluntary transaction creating an interest in property." A security interest in after-acquired property certainly falls within the broad boundaries set by the above definition. Moreover, the inclusiveness of the definition, particularly of the final phase, suggests that the Code's drafters intended "purchaser" to encompass holders of valid security interests of all types, including interests in after-acquired property. Second, Emery's creditors clearly gave "value" under § 1–201 of the Code, which provides that a "person gives 'value' for rights if he acquires them . . . as security for or in total or partial satisfaction of a preexisting debt." At the time of Lavonia's delivery, Emery owed the three creditors in excess of $10,490.24. The secured creditors gave value when they took an after-acquired interest in the yarn in exchange for this preexisting debt. The Code imposes no demand that a secured creditor give "new" value to maintain a perfected interest in after-acquired property. I find that Emery's three perfected creditors were good faith purchasers under § 2–702, whose rights are superior to Lavonia's rights to reclaim.

. . .

Any seeming unfairness to Lavonia in this result is dispelled by recognition of the fact that the seller could have protected its interest by complying with the UCC's purchase money provisions. As the United States Court of Appeals for the Fifth Circuit noted in Stowers v. Mahon ("Samuels & Co."), 526 F.2d 1238 (5th Cir.) (en banc), cert. denied, 429 U.S. 834 (1976), the Code seeks to encourage specific types of commercial behavior, most importantly, the notice filing of security interests. Specifically, the UCC "limits the seller's ability to reserve title once he has voluntarily surrendered possession to the buyer," Id. at 1246, by requiring that the seller perfect a security interest in the delivered goods to become superior to any prior perfected security interests. Under § 9–107, a seller may take a purchase money security interest ("PMSI") in goods delivered to a debtor. A PMSI in inventory offers a seller unusually good priority. In fact, a PMSI grants a seller of goods the power to defeat a prior perfected secured creditor with an interest in after-acquired inventory. See § 9–312(c) [revised 9–324(b)]. This favored status is the Code's way of mitigating the potential inequity of security interests in after-acquired property.

The various sections and Articles of the UCC work together as an integrated whole. As part of the Code's overall scheme favoring notice filing of nonpossessory security interests in goods, a perfected security interest unquestionably holds a superior position to an unperfected interest. Excusing Lavonia's failure to perfect would frustrate the Code's purpose. Lavonia neglected to take advantage of the Code-provided means for gaining priority over the creditors here, and cannot now contest the loss of its interest.

For the reasons stated above, I will reverse the decision of the Bankruptcy Court. . . .

The result reached in a case like this may be affected by special legislation addressing specific kinds of transactions. For example, the Packers and Stockyards Act, 7 U.S.C.A. § 196 creates a trust for the benefit of sellers of livestock, to ensure they are paid even if a secured creditor has a security interest in the livestock pursuant to an after-acquired property clause. Therefore, it is necessary to be aware of legislation outside the UCC.

CHAPTER 12

DOCUMENTARY TRANSACTIONS

A. INTRODUCTION

The issues dealt with in this chapter generally arise when the seller and the buyer are separated by substantial distances. In these transactions the parties typically use common carriers to transport the goods to the buyer, and the seller extends credit to the buyer for 30, 60, or 90 days after the goods arrive. Credit sales offer substantial advantages to both parties: for the seller, they cut down costs because the seller does not have to engage in the special techniques that are necessary to assure that the buyer does not receive the goods before paying for them. For the buyer, credit sales permit the processing of payments on an orderly, routine basis rather than having to take the special steps necessary to pay before receipt of the goods. In credit sales, of course, the buyer also has the use of additional capital and has the ability to withhold payment if the buyer believes that the seller has breached the contract. The seller's pricing, however, presumably takes account of the fact that the seller loses the use of capital, bears the risk of the buyer's failure to pay, and is in an unfavorable position as to disputes during the credit period.

Credit selling is widespread in this country because there are reliable credit reporting agencies that provide accurate information about the financial position of businesses and because most businesses have sufficient financial strength that the risks involved in selling to them on credit are negligible. Also, the legal systems in the various states are similar and familiar so that, if the buyer does not pay, collection efforts can be made in a relatively efficient manner. In spite of the fact that credit selling is the norm rather than the exception, 2–310 says that "unless otherwise agreed, payment is due at the time and place at which the buyer is to receive the goods. . . ." Therefore, if the contract (including implied terms incorporated by virtue of trade usage or course of dealing) does not provide credit terms, the buyer must pay when the goods arrive.

Sometimes, however, either because insufficient information is available or because the available information shows a weak financial position, sellers refuse to extend credit. In these cases there are standardized mechanisms by which a seller can use the services of the shipping and banking industries to assure that a distant buyer pays the price on or before receipt of the goods.

Sales on credit are also common in foreign transactions, but there are considerations not present in domestic transactions. In addition to the problem of acquiring reliable information as to the credit standing of foreign buyers, there are problems of unfamiliar legal systems, governmental impediments to removal of currency from the buyer's country, and so on, which make credit selling riskier than it is in domestic sales. Indeed, the risks in foreign sales are such that sellers may refuse to sell unless they have the guarantee (in the form of a letter of credit) of a bank in the seller's country that it will pay the price of the goods upon submission to the bank of documents indicating that the goods have been shipped.

The reasons for use of the letter of credit are compelling. Even if a seller has shipped goods to a foreign buyer in such a way that the buyer cannot get possession of the goods before paying for them, the seller may be in a very unsatisfactory position if the buyer does not pay. To be sure, the seller still has control of the goods, but they are in another country, which may be far away. There may be a limited market for the goods in question in that country, and the seller may have little knowledge about the market and may have few business contacts there. Thus even though the seller still has control of the goods, it may be difficult and expensive to sell or re-ship them. Sellers may avoid these risks by requiring bank payment against documents showing shipment of the goods. Similarly, while a bank is perhaps more likely than a buyer to honor its commitments, the possible expense and loss if a foreign bank fails to honor its commitments leads sellers to want a promise from a bank in their own country.

This chapter provides an introduction to the obligations of carriers concerning the goods they carry, the various mechanisms used by sellers to assure payment when they do not extend credit, and letters of credit.

B. OBLIGATIONS OF CARRIERS

Carriers in practically all cases issue bills of lading* covering goods accepted for shipment. Bills of lading have three functions: (1) receipt for the goods, (2) statement of the terms of the shipment agreement, and (3) evidence of ownership of the goods. (As we shall see, "evidence" may be too weak a word in the case of negotiable bills of lading.) "Bill of lading" is defined in 1–201(b)(6). As evidence of ownership, a bill of lading is a document of title, as is a "warehouse receipt" (1–201(b)(42)). Bills of lading and warehouse receipts are the two most common documents of title.

A bill of lading is either negotiable (sometimes called an "order" bill of lading) or non-negotiable (also called a "straight" bill of lading). A straight bill states that the goods are consigned to a named person, and the carrier will deliver the goods *straight* to the named consignee without requiring surrender of any copy of the bill. A negotiable bill, on the other hand, states that the goods are consigned *to the order of* a named person,

---

*   "Lade" appears to have been the Middle English word preferred for what we would now call "load"—hence bill of lading rather than bill of loading—"the bills of lading do declare what goods are laden. . . ." Malyn, Lex Mercatoria 97 (1636).

and the carrier will deliver the goods only upon the surrender of the bill of lading. Therefore, in the case of a negotiable bill, the seller can control the delivery of the goods by controlling the bill of lading. Negotiable bills are transferable by proper indorsement and have many of the characteristics of negotiable money instruments, such as checks and promissory notes. Examples of a non-negotiable bill of lading may be found at http://www.alaskatraffic.com/docs/BillofLading.pdf and https://my.yrc.com/national/pdf/gbol.pdf. The front side of the form is to be filled in with the appropriate information; the back side ("Terms and Conditions") is boilerplate.

There are several sources of law governing bills of lading. For interstate carriers, the basic law is the Federal Bills of Lading Act (Pomerene Act), 49 U.S.C.A. §§ 80101–80166. For intrastate shipments, UCC Article 7 controls. Overseas shipments may be subject to the Carriage of Goods by Sea Act (46 U.S.C.A. § 1300ff), or to the provisions of various treaties, or, of course, to the law of other nations. The Federal Bills of Lading Act, adopted in 1916 and recodified without substantive change in 1994, is practically identical with the Uniform Bills of Lading Act, which was promulgated in 1909 and ultimately adopted in most states. That Act was replaced by UCC Article 7, which deals with both bills of lading and warehouse receipts. Article 7 was revised in 2003, and the revision has been enacted in almost every state. Under the Supremacy Clause of the United States Constitution, of course, the Federal Bills of Lading Act displaces Article 7.

In the typical sale on credit, the seller obtains a straight bill and sends it to the buyer. Upon arrival at the buyer's location, the carrier delivers the goods. But what if the goods do not conform to the contract?

Fine Foliage of Florida, Inc. v. Bowman Transportation, Inc.

United States Court of Appeals, Eleventh Circuit, 1990.
901 F.2d 1034.

■ KRAVITCH, CIRCUIT JUDGE:

This case involves an appeal by a common carrier, Bowman Transportation, Inc. ("Bowman") from the district court's order finding it liable to Fine Foliage of Florida, Inc. ("Fine Foliage") for the value of ferns damaged due to an incorrect temperature setting on a refrigerated container unit. Bowman contends that the lower court erred in finding that Fine Foliage established a prima facie case under the Carmack Amendment, 49 U.S.C. § 11707.* . . . Because we find that the district court ruled correctly . . . , we affirm.

-----

* Now recodified as 49 U.S.C.A. 11706 for rail carriers and as 49 U.S.C.A. 14706 for motor carriers.—Eds.

I. Background

Fine Foliage, a Florida corporation located in DeLeon Springs, Florida, is a grower and international shipper of decorative ferns used in floral arrangements. Bowman is an interstate trucking company that was employed for the inland transportation of the ferns from DeLeon Springs, Florida to Savannah, Georgia.

In April of 1987, Fine Foliage, through its freight forwarder, Wilk Forwarding Company ("Wilk") arranged for the shipment of 939 cartons of leatherleaf fern from DeLeon Springs, Florida to Tokyo, Japan. Wilk arranged to have Bowman undertake the inland transportation from DeLeon Springs to Jacksonville, Florida and then arranged for sea passage with Mitsui Lines ("Mitsui"). Mitsui arranged through its agent, Strachan Shipping, to have the ferns transported by Bowman from a terminal in Jacksonville to its port in Savannah.

The bill of lading covering the DeLeon Springs to Jacksonville portion of the trip specified that the ferns were to be transported by Bowman at a temperature of 39 Fahrenheit. The bill also had printed on it the words "PERISHABLE Keep From Heat or Frost." Leonard Davis, Bowman's driver, testified that he signed the bill of lading without reading it. Testimony at trial established, however, that it is common knowledge among fern growers and truck drivers who transport ferns that the plant must be shipped at temperatures between 38 and 40 Fahrenheit. Davis testified that he knew that ferns should be shipped between 38 and 40.

. . .

[The refrigeration control in the transportation trailer was set for 0 F. When the truck arrived in Savannah, Georgia, the zero temperature in the trailer was discovered by a Savannah marine surveyor who noted that ice appeared on some of the containers holding the ferns. A visual examination of the ferns at that time did not show damage from freezing. They were loaded on a ship for Japan, but the bill of lading issued by the ocean carrier noted "EXCEPTION: CONTAINER RECEIVED BY CARRIER SET AT ZERO DEGREES FAHRENHEIT CARRIER NOT RESPONSIBLE FOR POSSIBLE DAMAGE TO CARGO DUE TO INCORRECT TEMP." When the ferns arrived in Tokyo, they were found to be a "total loss."]

II. The Carmack Amendment

. . .

The Carmack Amendment provides that a common carrier is liable for the actual loss or injury to goods in an interstate commerce shipment. It states in part that:

> A common carrier providing transportation or service subject to the jurisdiction of the Interstate Commerce Commission . . . and a freight forwarder shall issue a receipt or bill of lading for

property it receives for transportation under this subtitle. That carrier or freight forwarder and any other common carrier that delivers the property and is providing transportation or service subject to the jurisdiction of the Commission . . . are liable to the person entitled to recover under the receipt or bill of lading. . . . Failure to issue a receipt or bill of lading does not affect the liability of a carrier or freight forwarder.

The purpose of the Carmack Amendment is to protect shippers against the negligence of interstate carriers and "to relieve shippers of the burden of searching out a particular negligent carrier from among the often numerous carriers handling an interstate shipment of goods." Reider v. Thompson, 339 U.S. 113, 119, 70 S.Ct. 499, 502, 94 L.Ed. 698 (1950). Once liability is established, the defendant carrier may then seek to recover damages from the connecting carrier which had possession of the goods when loss was sustained.

A. *Fine Foliage's Prima Facie Case*

A shipper establishes a prima facie case of the carrier's negligence and liability under the Carmack Amendment by evincing proof by a preponderance of the evidence that the goods "1) were delivered to the carrier in good condition, 2) arrived in damaged condition, and 3) resulted in the specified amount of damage." Offshore Aviation v. Transcon Lines, Inc., 831 F.2d 1013, 1014 (11th Cir.1987) (per curiam).

At trial Fine Foliage put forth evidence in support of each of these elements, and the district court found that Fine Foliage succeeded in establishing a prima facie case. First, it found that "the subject fern was in good condition when loaded by the plaintiff's employees into the reefer* for transportation by the defendant on the morning of April 29, 1987." Second, the district court found that "the subject fern was ruined upon arrival in Savannah, although the total loss of the shipment was not declared until arrival and inspection in Tokyo." Finally, it found that the "plaintiff had substantiated its damages attributed to the loss of the subject fern at $21,035.60."

Bowman claims that Fine Foliage's testimony at trial was insufficient to establish a prima facie case against the carrier and that the district court erred in failing to grant Bowman's motion for involuntary dismissal under Fed.R.Civ.P. 41(b). As the trial judge's ruling on Fine Foliage's prima facie case was based on his findings of fact, we review his conclusions under the clearly erroneous standard.

Bowman argues that the court erred in finding that the ferns were initially in good condition, when the only evidence as to the condition of the ferns when they left Fine Foliage was a Department of Agriculture certificate which showed lack of insect infestation. It argues that prior decisions of this and other courts have required that the condition of the contents of a container be established by eyewitness or other direct

---

*   A reefer is a refrigerated container.—Eds.

reliable testimony. In support of that assertion, Bowman points to Highlands Insurance Company v. Strachan Shipping Company, 772 F.2d 1520 (11th Cir.1985); Pillsbury Co. v. Illinois Central Gulf Railroad, 687 F.2d 241 (8th Cir.1982); and D.P. Apparel Corp. v. Roadway Express, Inc., 736 F.2d 1 (1st Cir.1984).

We find that Bowman's reliance on these cases is misplaced. *Highlands* involved a situation in which there was no proof, other than a bill of lading, that TV sets, reported stolen, had actually been placed in a sealed seagoing container. It stands only for the proposition that evidence "such as the testimony of an eyewitness to the loading of the container is necessary to confirm the contents." Highlands, 772 F.2d at 1521. Here, there is no dispute that the ferns were loaded into the container. In *Pillsbury,* the court held that where goods are shipped under seal, a bill of lading does not establish a prima facie case for the shipper that the goods were in good order. Instead, the shipper must "present[ ] additional evidence sufficient to establish by preponderance of all the evidence the condition of the goods upon delivery." 687 F.2d at 244. The *Pillsbury* court relied on circumstantial evidence to find that the plaintiff had demonstrated that the cars, when loaded, were free of insect infestation. In *D.P. Apparel,* the court found that the plaintiff failed to establish a prima facie case by relying primarily on the bill of lading for the proposition that the goods were delivered to the carrier in good condition. 736 F.2d at 4.

In the instant case, neither the plaintiff nor the trial judge relied on the bill of lading to establish delivery of the goods to Bowman in good condition. Instead, the trial court based its finding regarding the original condition of the ferns on "the approval of the fern by the Department of Agriculture; the testimony as to the care and temperature control of the fern after its harvest; and the fact that other fern, packaged in the identical manner and stored in the same cooler as the subject fern, arrived at overseas destinations in acceptable condition." We find no support for Bowman's assertion that a judge may not rely on circumstantial evidence to establish the original condition of goods when that evidence is substantial and reliable.[3] In light of the evidence in the instant case, we find that the judge did not err in holding that Fine Foliage had established the first prong of its prima facie case.

Bowman further contends that the court erred in finding that the ferns arrived at their destination in a damaged condition. The court based this finding "upon the 0 Fahrenheit temperature setting in the container as evidenced by the temperature chart and the credible testimony regarding the consequent detriment to fern caused by freezing temperatures." Bowman argues that Fine Foliage did not establish the

---

[3] Indeed, the evidence relied on in *Pillsbury* was similar to that presented in the instant case. Pillsbury produced evidence of its preloading inspection and cleaning procedures and also showed that a test car switched through the defendant carrier's yard became infested while one switched to another carrier's yard did not. Pillsbury, 687 F.2d at 245.

accuracy of the particular Ryan recorder used to record the temperature in the container. We note, however, that there was substantial evidence introduced at trial that the temperature setting on the container was at 0: the Mitsui equipment interchange receipt lists a temperature setting of 0, and the marine surveyor in Savannah found both that the temperature had been set at zero and that there was a layer of ice on the ferns. Fine Foliage also presented sufficient testimony to establish that ferns that are subjected to such temperatures for a period of hours cannot possibly remain unharmed. In sum, our review of the record indicates that there was ample evidence presented at trial from which the trial judge could conclude that the ferns were destroyed while in Bowman's possession and we cannot say that the judge erred in finding that Bowman established this prong of the prima facie case.

. . . Because Fine Foliage established each prong of its prima facie case, the district judge did not abuse his discretion in failing to dismiss the case.

B.   *Defenses to a Prima Facie Case under the Carmack Amendment*

Once a plaintiff has established a prima facie case under the Carmack Amendment, the burden of proof shifts to the carrier to show that it was free from negligence and the damage was caused solely by "(a) the act of God; (b) the public enemy; (c) the act of the shipper himself; (d) public authority; (e) or the inherent vice or nature of the goods." Missouri Pacific R. Co. v. Elmore & Stahl, 377 U.S. 134, 137, 84 S.Ct. 1142, 1144, 12 L.Ed.2d 194 (1964); Frosty Land Foods v. Refrigerated Transport, 613 F.2d 1344, 1346–47 (5th Cir.1980).

The district court found that Bowman was negligent in failing to notice and correct the temperature setting on the reefer containing the ferns. It found that there was no reason that Davis should not have noted the incorrect temperature setting of the container prior to loading the ferns, particularly in light of Davis's knowledge of the correct temperature. In finding that Bowman failed to rebut Fine Foliage's prima facie case, the court relied on the fact that the 39 temperature was noted on the bill of lading signed by Davis. It also took note of Bowman's course of dealing with Fine Foliage, Bowman's knowledge of the proper temperature, and Davis' knowledge that the cooling system had malfunctioned. The court stressed that it would have been logical and reasonable for Davis, who had some knowledge of the time required for cooling a container, to check the temperature setting of the container prior to or during the loading of the ferns in order to determine whether the reefer had adequately pre-cooled. The court found that even if Davis was not able to adjust the temperature setting, he could have called the improper setting to the attention of one of the Fine Foliage employees. There is ample support in the testimony introduced at trial for the district court's finding of negligence. We also find no error in the district court's finding that even if Bowman was not negligent, it had not established any of the accepted defenses to Fine Foliage's prima facie case.

. . .

For the foregoing reasons, the opinion of the district court is affirmed. . . .

NOTES

1. The Carmack Amendment is a codification of the common law rule on the liability of common carriers. (The language of the Amendment, 49 U.S.C.A. § 14706, has been modified from that quoted on pages 652–653, to reflect the abolition of the Interstate Commerce Commission.) The Amendment applies to interstate transportation by railroads, highway common carriers, and some freight forwarders. The Amendment does not apply to contract carriers or to intrastate shipments. Common carriers are carriers that hold themselves out as available to the general public for the carriage of goods. Contract carriers, in contrast, are carriers who contract with one or more individual shippers for carriage but who do not hold themselves out as being available to carry for everyone.

While rail and truck carriers are almost strictly liable, the damages allowed a shipper are limited by the classification and tariffs in effect on the day the carrier issues a bill of lading. For intrastate shipments not governed by the federal law, 7–309(b) recognizes limited-liability tariffs.

The carrier-liability rules, the rate charges, and the limitations on the dollar amount of the carrier's liability may bind the carrier and shipper even if no bill of lading is issued. Consequently, it seems correct to say that the rights and duties of the parties do not flow from contract but rather from positive law.

The liability of contract carriers and of common carriers as to intrastate shipments is determined by the law of each state. To determine the law of any particular state it is necessary to examine (1) state statutes for any possible statutory change of the common law rules or any statutory limitation upon the ability of carriers to contract out of those rules, (2) the regulations of any state agency regulating intrastate carriers and (3) the state decisional law to determine the extent to which local decisions have modified the traditional common law rules or permit carriers to contract out of their common law liability. Section 7–309(a) provides that a carrier that issues a bill of lading "shall exercise the degree of care in relation to the goods which a reasonably careful person would exercise under similar circumstances," but then states that the section "does not affect any statute, regulation, or rule of law that imposes liability on a common carrier for damages not caused by its negligence." The Code itself, therefore, does not affect existing liability rules.

2. **Ocean carriers.** The liability of ocean carriers is prescribed by the Carriage of Goods by Sea Act, enacted in 1936. 46 U.S.C.A. §§ 1300–1315. The Act is based on the Brussels Convention of 1924, which was signed by many leading commercial countries. Under the Act and the Convention, the

liability of ocean carriers is considerably lighter than that imposed on rail, truck, and air carriers. The current version appears at 46 U.S.C.A. § 30706 and provides that if the carrier has exercised due diligence to make the vessel seaworthy and to properly staff and equip it, the carrier is not liable for loss resulting from error in navigation or management of the vessel, from dangers of the sea, or from a series of other enumerated causes.

3. Air carriers. Liability of domestic carriers is controlled by tariffs published by the airline. Those tariffs generally exclude liability except for loss caused by the carrier's negligence and also contain provisions limiting the dollar amount of liability unless the shipper states a higher value and pays a higher charge.

The liability of international air carriers is governed by a treaty, the Warsaw Convention, since 1934 adhered to by over 90 countries, including the United States. One authority summarizes liability under the treaty as follows:

> The international air carrier is exempted from liability if it proves that all steps necessary to avoid the damage were taken or that it was impossible to take such measures; if such steps were taken in all other respects but the damage was occasioned by an error in piloting, handling of the aircraft or navigation; or if it proves that the damage is a result of contributory negligence, provided the doctrine is recognized in the forum in which the action is pending. If the international air carrier is liable at all for damage to goods, its liability is limited to approximately $9.07 per pound unless the consignor, at the time the package is delivered to the carrier, has made a declaration of value and paid a supplementary sum, if required, in which case the carrier is liable for the actual value or the declared sum, whichever is less.

S. Sorkin, 1 Goods in Transit § 1.21[2] (2010).

4. Risk of the seller or buyer vs. risk of the carrier. It sometimes happens that goods are totally destroyed while in the possession of a carrier en route from the seller to the buyer under a contract in which the delivery term is "f.o.b. Seller's plant." Under that delivery term the buyer usually has the risk of loss (2–509(1)(a)), but if the goods do not conform to the contract, 2–510(1) provides that the risk remains on the seller. If the goods have been damaged but not destroyed, it may be easy to prove whether or not they conformed to the contract. If they are destroyed, however, proof of this matter is difficult, and the outcome of the case may turn on which party has the burden of proof.

At common law and under the Uniform Sales Act, the burden of proving that the goods conformed to the contract was on the seller, but evidence that the seller delivered goods to the carrier which he claimed conformed to the contract made out a prima facie case. The burden of going forward with the evidence was then on the buyer, but "if the goods had been destroyed while in the carrier's hands this proof would of course be difficult to make and it is probable that the seller's prima facie proof would remain unrebutted." J. Waite, Sales 54 (1921); see Levy v. Radkay, 233 Mass. 29, 123 N.E. 97 (1919);

Skinner v. James Griffiths & Sons, 80 Wash. 291, 141 P. 693 (1914). Nothing in Article 2 changes this.

In *Fine Foliage* the court states that under the Carmack Amendment, to shift the risk of loss to the carrier, the shipper (i.e. the seller) must prove that the goods were in good condition at the time of delivery to the carrier. If the seller proves that the goods conformed to the sales contract, then the risk of loss, as between the seller and the buyer, is on the buyer. Depending on the nonconformity, of course, the goods may be in good condition for purposes of the Carmack Amendment but nonconforming for purposes of 2–509 and 2–510 (e.g., a latent breach of warranty).

G.A.C. Commercial Corp. v. Wilson

United States District Court, Southern District of New York, 1967.
271 F.Supp. 242.

■ FREDERICK VAN PELT BRYAN, DISTRICT JUDGE. Plaintiff G.A.C. Commercial Corporation (G.A.C.), a Delaware corporation, brings this action sounding in . . . negligence against a New York corporation, Norwood & St. Lawrence Railroad Co. (Norwood), a rail carrier in interstate commerce. Defendant Norwood now moves . . . for summary judgment under Rule 56, F.R.Civ.P.

. . . [O]n October 17, 1963, plaintiff G.A.C. entered into an accounts receivable financing agreement with St. Lawrence Pulp & Paper Corp. (St. Lawrence), a New York corporation. Under the terms of the agreement G.A.C. was to make advances to St. Lawrence, which agreed to "pledge, assign and transfer to G.A.C. all the [b]orrower's right, title and interest in and to accounts receivable * * * then owing" to St. Lawrence.

Pursuant to the agreement St. Lawrence forwarded copies of its invoices together with copies of bills of lading to G.A.C., which, upon receipt, advanced the monies to St. Lawrence at the agreed discount. . . . G.A.C. ultimately advanced $356,883.57 under the financing agreement, no part of which has been repaid. St. Lawrence is now a bankrupt.

. . .

[G.A.C. alleged that some of the invoices were fraudulent, in that they purported to represent sales that never occurred and therefore did not represent real transactions for which St. Lawrence would receive payment. G.A.C. claimed that Norwood facilitated this fraud because] the fraudulent accounts receivable described were "upon the form of bill of lading" of defendant Norwood "and were countersigned by its agent." Norwood is charged with negligence in failing to require any inspection of the quantity of goods shipped before verifying the bills of lading and in permitting a situation to occur in which the fraudulent and nonexistent accounts could be forwarded to G.A.C.

Norwood's answer alleges failure to state a claim on which relief can be granted and contributory negligence. By way of separate defense it denies any knowledge or information as to the falsity of the bills of lading or with respect to the financing agreement between St. Lawrence and G.A.C. The answer also alleges that the bills of lading involved are "uniform straight bill[s] of lading—not negotiable," as in fact they are, under Section 2 of the Federal Bills of Lading Act. 49 U.S.C.A. § 82 [now codified, as modified, at 49 U.S.C.A. § 80103].

The controversy here concerns 62 invoices and accompanying straight bills of lading forwarded to G.A.C. by St. Lawrence during 1964. Sixty of these bills concern interstate shipments of paper from St. Lawrence in Norfolk, New York, to Mohegan Converters in Hillside, New Jersey, and involve advances of $245,811.19. Each of the sixty interstate bills was on Norwood's bill of lading, and it is conceded for purposes of this motion, though denied in the answer, that the bills were signed by one of Norwood's agents.

. . .

The method by which the alleged fraudulent scheme was carried out appears for purposes of this motion to be as follows: the bankrupt St. Lawrence, as part of its facilities in Norfolk, New York, maintained a railroad siding connected with the lines of defendant carrier which had a freight office approximately 1/8th of a mile from the siding. St. Lawrence was permitted to load freight at its spur track in preparation for shipments on defendant's line. The railroad cars were sealed by St. Lawrence with seals provided by the railroad. St. Lawrence also prepared the bills of lading on blanks furnished in quadruplicate by defendant Norwood. The bills thus prepared were then presented to Norwood's agent who signed the original and one copy without inspecting the contents of the cars. No notation such as "contents of packages unknown" or "shipper's weight, load and count" was written on the bills. The signed copies were returned to St. Lawrence and forwarded with the invoices to G.A.C. which made advances on the goods described, which, as it turned out, had not been shipped.

Since sixty of the bills of lading were issued by a common carrier for the transportation of goods in interstate commerce, the issues as to these bills are controlled by the provisions of the Federal Bills of Lading Act. 49 U.S.C.A. § 81. This statute stands as "a clear expression of the determination of Congress to take the whole subject matter of such bills of lading within its control." 2 S.Williston, Sales § 406a, at 535 (rev.ed.1948); see Adams Express Co. v. Croninger, 226 U.S. 491, 33 S.Ct. 148, 57 L.Ed. 314 (1913). As such, it squarely bars the fourth claim asserted against defendant Norwood on the sixty bills representing interstate shipments.

Prior to the passage of the Federal Bills of Lading Act "the United States courts held that a carrier was not liable for the act of its agent in issuing a bill of lading for goods where no goods had in fact been received." Josephy v. Panhandle & S.F. Ry., 235 N.Y. 306, 310, 139 N.E. 277, 278 (1923); see, e.g., Clark v. Clyde S.S. Co., 148 F. 243 (S.D.N.Y.1906). The liability of carriers for acts of their agents was expanded, but not drastically, by the passage of the federal legislation which draws a sharp distinction between order bills of lading and straight bills where in fact the goods are never received for shipment by the carrier. Under § 22 of the Act, 49 U.S.C.A. § 102 [rephrased and now codified at 49 U.S.C.A. § 80113(a)], "[i]f a bill of lading has been issued by a carrier or on his behalf by an agent or employee * * *, the carrier shall be liable to * * * the holder of an order bill, who has given value in good faith, relying upon the description therein of the goods, * * * for damages caused by the nonreceipt by the carrier of all or part of the goods upon or prior to the date therein shown." However, the liability of the carrier for nonreceipt extends only to "the owner of goods covered by a straight bill,"[1] provided, of course, he also gives value in good faith in reliance upon the description of goods contained in the bill.

It is clear that a party in the position of Norwood is not included within the narrow category of those liable on a straight bill under the federal legislation. In the first place there is no question that the straight bills of lading here involved are nonnegotiable. * * * As a consequence plaintiff G.A.C., as apparent transferee of these bills and invoices representing accounts receivable under the agreement with St. Lawrence, upon notification to the carrier of the transfer, could only "become the direct obligee of whatever obligations the carrier owed to the transferor of the bill immediately before the notification." 49 U.S.C.A. § 112 [now codified at 49 U.S.C.A. § 80106(c)]; see id. § 109. Norwood obviously owed St. Lawrence nothing because no goods in fact were received. There was therefore no outstanding obligation to G.A.C. . . .

By no stretch of the imagination does G.A.C. qualify as an "owner of goods covered by a straight bill" who can sue the carrier under § 22 of the Federal Bills of Lading Act, 49 U.S.C.A. § 102, for representing that goods in fact had been received. The reason for this is that it is completely illusory to attempt to assign an "owner" to nonexistent goods. R. Braucher, Documents of Title 23 (1958); 2 S.Williston, Sales § 419a, at 576–77 (rev.ed.1948). While the consignee is generally deemed to have title to goods shipped under a straight bill of lading, even he cannot sue

---

[1]   Section 22 of the Act, 49 U.S.C.A. § 102 [as modified, now § 80113(a)], in its complete form, reads as follows:

§ 102. Liability for Nonreceipt or Misdescription of Goods

If a bill of lading has been issued by a carrier or on his behalf by an agent or employee the scope of whose actual or apparent authority includes the receiving of goods and issuing bills of lading therefor for transportation in commerce among the several States and with foreign nations, the carrier shall be liable to (a) the owner of goods covered by a straight bill subject to existing right of stoppage in transitu or (b) the holder of an order bill, who has given value in good faith, relying upon the description therein of the goods, or upon the shipment being made upon the date therein shown, for damages caused by the nonreceipt by the carrier of all or part of the goods upon or prior to the date therein shown, or their failure to correspond with the description thereof in the bill at the time of its issue.

the carrier for representing in a straight bill that non-existent goods had in fact been received. Martin Jessee Motors v. Reading Co., 87 F.Supp. 318 (E.D.Pa.), aff'd, 181 F.2d 766 (3d Cir.1950). The rationale applied in *Martin Jessee Motors*—that the consignee can prevail against the carrier "only by proving its title to specific property," 181 F.2d at 767—applies *a fortiori* to bar the claim of G.A.C. Plaintiff's interest in the "aggregate face value of the accounts receivable pledged as security" under no conceivable reading of the statute can be deemed an "[ownership] of goods covered by a straight bill." G.A.C. is not one of the favored few who can recover under the Federal Bills of Lading Act.

Plaintiff G.A.C. fares no better with respect to the two bills of lading representing intrastate shipments in New York. Of decisive importance, of course, are the facts that these shipments were not on Norwood's forms and were not signed by Norwood's agents. Even if they were, the carrier would escape liability. Although the awkward term "owner" in 49 U.S.C.A. § 102 [now codified at 49 U.S.C.A. § 80113(a)] has been replaced by the word "consignee" in the Uniform Commercial Code § 7–301 and the Uniform Bills of Lading Act § 23, each of which would govern the issues of liability on one of the bills of lading representing an intrastate shipment. The change is immaterial for purposes of this case. Plaintiff, perhaps an assignee, transferee or pledgee of the non-negotiable bills, though it claims not to be, is certainly not a "consignee," which is the only party protected. 2 Anderson, Uniform Commercial Code 261 n. 9 (1961); see R. Braucher, Documents of Title 23–24 (1958). Contrast U.C.C. § 7–203. Thus, as with the sixty interstate bills, G.A.C. cannot successfully sue on the two intrastate bills.

G.A.C. cannot avoid the results dictated by the statute by casting its claim for relief in terms of common law negligence. G.A.C. was sent sixty straight interstate bills of lading by St. Lawrence. The alleged negligence consists of Norwood's permitting a situation to develop in which St. Lawrence could make untrue representations that goods had in fact been shipped under the straight bills. G.A.C. claims that it relied to its detriment upon certain statements contained in the bills. The action is based on the bills not on Norwood's negligence. "[T]he negligent or reckless language on which * * * the action is founded, language certifying the receipt of the goods, is the language of the bills—were the bills ignored, there would be nothing on which to base the action, since no representation was made apart from them." Chesapeake & Ohio R. Co. v. State Nat'l Bank, 280 Ky. 444, 450, 133 S.W.2d 511, 514 (1939). A holding to the contrary would permit any party to circumvent the restrictions of the Federal Bills of Lading Act through the insertion of a talismanic characterization of its claim as one for "negligence." It is quite plain, however, that the declaration in 49 U.S.C.A. § 81—"bills of lading issued by any common carrier for the transportation of goods" between the states "shall be governed by this chapter"—must be taken to preclude alternative and supplementary liability under state law. The substance of the rule cannot be avoided by the form of the complaint.

. . .

It is true that the result dictated by the federal legislation may lead to some inequities. A straight bill under the Federal Bills of Lading Act is obviously not a good security risk. The fraud of the shipper by failing to deliver goods to the carrier can result, as it did here, in misleading statements on the bills of lading, which operate to the detriment of banks and other commercial financiers making advances on the basis of the bills. Moreover, the carrier can readily prevent such a situation from arising by inserting "in the bill of lading the words, 'Shipper's weight, load, and count,' or other words of like purport" to "indicate that the goods were loaded by the shipper and the description of them made by him." 49 U.S.C.A. § 101 [now codified, as modified, at 49 U.S.C.A. § 80113(b)].

But the overriding policy considerations in the Act look the other way on the issue of liability. First, "[t]here is nothing in the statute to indicate that the mere omission of the words 'Shipper's weight, load, and count' in and of itself makes the carrier liable for damages to goods improperly loaded. The omission of the statutory words merely serves to shift upon the carrier the burden of proving that the goods were improperly loaded by the shipper, and that the damage ensued from that cause." Modern Tool Corp. v. Pennsylvania R. Co., 100 F.Supp. 595, 596–597 (D.N.J.1951); see U.C.C. § 7–301(4). According to the allegations the true culprits in this case were the shipper and its agents; there is no reason to saddle defendant Norwood with liability simply because it did not insert the "Shipper's weight, load, and count" language in the bills. In addition, practicality demands loading arrangements such as those here, where the shipper places his goods aboard and seals the railroad car which the carrier has provided. Section 21 of the Act, 49 U.S.C.A. § 101 [§ 80113(b)], anticipates that shippers are expected to do much of the counting and loading on their own sidings or spur tracks. The rapid flow of commerce might well be hindered if the carrier in every instance were charged with ascertaining whether in fact there were goods behind every one of its straight bills.

Moreover, denying security value to a straight bill of lading does not work a hardship upon banks and other commercial institutions. G.A.C., as a knowledgeable lender, is fully aware of the risks inherent in straight bills, and could well have required order bills to protect itself. It nevertheless chose to rely upon straight bills to lend money to the now bankrupt St. Lawrence at a profitable rate of interest. Wiser now, G.A.C. seeks to shift its loss to Norwood, an undoubtedly solvent defendant. The Federal Bills of Lading Act protects against this type of hindsight by requiring the lender to accept this kind of security subject to the defenses between the carrier and the shipper.

The motion of defendant Norwood . . . for summary judgment is granted. . . .

QUESTIONS AND NOTES

1. The court notes that under the language of the statute, even if the plaintiff had been a buyer who, relying on the bills of lading, paid the seller, it would not have been able to recover since the Act protects only "owners" in the case of straight bills. Should a court read "owner" as including a person who would have been owner if goods actually had been loaded?

2. Should the statute be amended to protect persons in the position of G.A.C.? See UCC 7–301(a) for the position of the Code.

3. The court refers to the fact that the shipper could have avoided the problem by inserting in the bill of lading the phrase "shipper's weight, load, and count. . . ."

The section from which this language is taken, now codified at 49 U.S.C.A. § 80113, reads as follows:

> 80113.   Liability for nonreceipt, misdescription, and improper loading
>
> (a) Liability for nonreceipt and misdescription. Except as provided in this section, a common carrier issuing a bill of lading is liable for damages caused by nonreceipt by the carrier of any part of the goods by the date shown in the bill or by failure of the goods to correspond with the description contained in the bill. The carrier is liable to the owner of goods transported under a nonnegotiable bill (subject to the right of stoppage in transit) or to the holder of a negotiable bill if the owner or holder gave value in good faith relying on the description of the goods in the bill or on the shipment being made on the date shown in the bill.
>
> (b) Nonliability of carriers. A common carrier issuing a bill of lading is not liable under subsection (a) of this section
>
>> (1)   when the goods are loaded by the shipper;
>>
>> (2)   when the bill
>>
>>> (A)   describes the goods in terms of marks or labels, or in a statement about kind, quantity, or condition; or
>>>
>>> (B)   is qualified by "contents or condition of contents of packages unknown," "said to contain," "shipper's weight, load, and count," or words of the same meaning; and
>>
>> (3)   to the extent the carrier does not know whether any part of the goods were received or conform to the description.
>
> (c)   Liability for improper loading. A common carrier issuing a bill of lading is not liable for damages caused by improper loading if
>
>> (1)   the shipper loads the goods; and
>>
>> (2)   the bill contains the words "shipper's weight, load, and count," or words of the same meaning indicating the shipper loaded the goods.
>
> (d)   Carrier's duty to determine kind, quantity, and number. (1) When bulk freight is loaded by a shipper that makes available to

the common carrier adequate facilities for weighing the freight, the carrier must determine the kind and quantity of the freight within a reasonable time after receiving the written request of the shipper to make the determination. In that situation, inserting the words "shipper's weight" or words of the same meaning in the bill of lading has no effect.

(2) When goods are loaded by a common carrier, the carrier must count the packages of goods, if package freight, and determine the kind and quantity, if bulk freight. In that situation, inserting in the bill of lading or in a notice, receipt, contract, rule, or tariff, the words "shipper's weight, load, and count" or words indicating that the shipper described and loaded the goods, has no effect except for freight concealed by packages.

UCC 7–301 contains a similar provision.

————

Rountree v. Lydick-Barmann Co.

Texas Court of Civil Appeals, 1941.
150 S.W.2d 173.

. . .

■ SPEER, JUSTICE.

[Plaintiff, Lydick-Barmann, contracted with defendant, Rountree, for the transportation of goods from plaintiff's location in Fort Worth, Texas, to the location of Crone Co., its customer in Louisiana City, Arkansas. Defendant received the goods and issued a non-negotiable (straight) bill of lading, showing that the goods were] "consigned to Lydick-Barmann Company, destination 616 street, Louisiana City, Little Rock County, Ark. State. Notify Crone Company." The bill of lading described the merchandise, was signed by both plaintiff and defendant, acting through their respective agents, and was endorsed in blank by plaintiff. The undisputed evidence further shows that plaintiff has no office or agent at the street address in Little Rock, as given in the bill of lading. The merchandise was delivered to Crone Company. Because of this delivery by defendant, the plaintiff lost the value of its goods. . . .

We do not believe that plaintiff's right of recovery is dependent upon whether or not the bill of lading under which the shipment moved was a shipper's order billing.* It is clear that if it was a shipper's order contract, which would obligate the defendant (the carrier) not to deliver the merchandise until the endorsed bill of lading was produced and delivered to him, and delivery was made as in this case, without obtaining the bill, there would be liability. As we view it, we need not determine whether or not it was a shipper's order contract, although under one count in plaintiff's pleadings, it is claimed to be such. . . .

———————

* I.e., a negotiable bill of lading.—Eds.

The undisputed facts in this case entitled plaintiff to recover, as we view the law applicable. The defendant insists that the bill of lading under which the shipment moved was a straight bill. It has all of the elements of such, except that it was on yellow . . . paper, [which is to be used for negotiable bills,] and contains the expression, "Notify Crone Co.[, which is required in negotiable bills.]" These are elements of a [negotiable] bill. They do not destroy the fact that it could be properly classed as a straight bill.

Defendant urges . . . that the term "notify Crone Co." was equivalent to the expression, "Consigned to" a named person "in care of" another, as is often used in straight bills. Our courts have held that when a bill names the consignee "in care of" another person, such other person is held to be the named agent of the consignor for delivery of the merchandise, and that delivery to that person is delivery to the consignee. See City Nat. Bank of El Paso v. El Paso & N.E.R. Co. et al., Tex.Civ.App., 225 S.W. 391, writ of error refused, affirmed by U.S. Supreme Court, as reported in 262 U.S. 695, 43 S.Ct. 640, 67 L.Ed. 1184. We have not been cited to any case, nor from an independent search have we found where any court has construed the two expressions as synonymous. It is perceivable why, if one is directed to deliver an article to another in care of one named, that delivery to the latter would be a compliance with the contract, but the same course of reasoning would not produce the same result when instructions are given to deliver to a certain person, notify another. This conclusion is emphasized by the fact the word "notify" as used in a bill of lading is only required when a [negotiable bill is used]. In formulating the respective requisites of bills of lading, some significance must be given to the requirement that a [negotiable] bill must contain the word "notify."

For purposes of this appeal, we are construing the bill of lading in this case as a straight bill. The goods were consigned by plaintiff to itself, at Little Rock, Ark. 49 U.S.C.A. § 82 [as modified, now codified at 49 U.S.C.A. 80103] provides: "A bill in which it is stated that the goods are consigned or destined to a specified person is a straight bill." When goods are so shipped the carrier is bound by the provisions of Section 88 [§ 80110(a)], which reads: "A carrier in the absence of some lawful excuse, is bound to deliver goods upon a demand made either by the consignee named in the bill for the goods or * * *." The carrier is justified in making delivery, under 49 U.S.C.A. § 89 [§ 80110(b)] to, "(a) A person lawfully entitled to the possession of the goods, or (b) the consignee named in a straight bill for the goods." If delivery is made by the carrier under any other conditions than those provided, and the consignor suffers a loss on account thereof, the carrier is liable. Estherville Produce Co. v. Chicago, R.I. & P.R. Co., 8 Cir., 57 F.2d 50.

It is conceded by defendant that this was a straight bill of lading; that he delivered the goods to Crone Company, named in the bill as the party to be notified. In this way, defendant earnestly insists that he has performed his contract of shipment. In his brief he emphasizes the contention with many concrete, positive assertions, such as: "The contractual obligations of [defendant] in this case were in writing; were introduced in evidence by the [plaintiff], and the record abundantly demonstrates beyond question that the obligations imposed upon the [defendant] by the contract of carriage were faithfully and literally performed. * * * The [defendant] can be held liable only for the performance of the contract which was actually entered into. He may not be called upon to answer for a breach of a contract which he did not execute. He may not called upon to respond in damages because he did not do something which the [plaintiff] desired, but which was not put into the contract. The [plaintiff] must stand upon the contract as written. * * * The fact is that the parties entered into a written contract which has been fully performed." As indicated, the defendant insists that the written contract of shipment (the bill of lading) was binding alike on both the plaintiff and defendant, and since he had fully performed the contract as written, he should not be called upon to respond in damages because of a loss sustained by the plaintiff.

Defendant's contention that he had "literally" and "definitely" carried out the terms of the written contract between the parties is based upon what we believe to be an erroneous hypothesis—that delivery of the shipment to Crone Company, named as the one to be notified, was delivery to the consignee named in the bill of lading, which was the contract of shipment. Lydick-Barmann Co. (plaintiff) was the consignee in the contract. It was likewise the consignor. It was the owner of the merchandise at all times and was entitled to possession at destination. The fact that consignee had no office or place of business at Little Rock, rendering it impossible for defendant to make physical delivery of it then and there, presented no insuperable difficulty. Defendant had consignor's—consignee's—street address at Fort Worth, Texas, and when defendant found that it could not deliver the freight to the consignee, as he had promised to do, immediate notice should have been given to the consignor. It was not sufficient for defendant to choose to deliver the goods to some one else not entitled to possession.

. . .

Finding no error in the record, all assignments of error are overruled, and the judgment is affirmed.

C. SHIPMENTS UNDER RESERVATION

If the transaction does not contemplate the extension of credit, 2–310(a) states that payment is due at the time and place at which the buyer is to receive the goods even if the place of shipment is the place of delivery. This provision continues prior law and the usual trade custom under which payment is due in the buyer's city, not the seller's. The seller may arrange for an employee to travel to the buyer's place of business to receive payment, or—at much less expense—the parties may use the services of the shipping and banking industries. The remaining materials describe the way in which the typical at-a-distance cash transaction is handled.

Stated simply, the seller uses control of the bill of lading to control the goods and arranges things so that the carrier will not deliver the goods to the buyer until the price is paid. One way to do this is to obtain a negotiable bill of lading from the carrier. Under a negotiable bill the carrier will deliver only on surrender of the bill of lading. Usually the carrier will issue a negotiable bill of lading (to the order of the seller), which the seller will indorse and take to the seller's bank, which forwards the bill of lading to a bank in buyer's city. That bank notifies the buyer that it has received the bill of lading and, when the buyer pays the price, gives the bill of lading to the buyer and sends the price through the customary banking channels to the seller's bank, which credits that amount to the seller's account.

The seller may also control the delivery of the goods by shipping them under a straight bill of lading in which the goods are consigned to the seller himself or some trusted agent for the seller in the buyer's city. If a straight bill is used, a delivery order directing the carrier to deliver to the buyer (or an authorization to execute such a delivery order) ordinarily will be forwarded to a bank in the buyer's city with instructions to transfer it to the buyer upon payment.

Whether a negotiable or a straight bill is used, the buyer has, unless contracted away, the right to inspect the goods before paying for them. (See § 2–310(b)). Therefore, it will be necessary for the bank in the buyer's city, on the buyer's request, to arrange for inspection of the goods while they are still in possession of the carrier.

In cases in which the seller uses the banking system to ship goods "under reservation," the seller typically draws a draft on the buyer and forwards the draft along with the bill of lading or delivery order.

The draft may be payable to the seller or to the seller's bank. In either event, it will be indorsed so that the bank in buyer's city is in possession of a draft indorsed to it or in blank. A typical draft form is set out below.

On Sight   August 10, 2020

Pay to the Order of Hometown Bank $5,468.75

Five Thousand Four Hundred and Sixty-eight and 75/100 dollars

To: Buyer

      1203 Northwood Avenue

      Your City, Your State
                                              _____
                                                      Seller

This draft is like a check and is payable immediately when demand is made on the buyer. A draft payable on demand often is called a "sight draft" because it is payable "on sight."

Frequently the seller's bank will lend the seller the face amount of the draft as soon as the bank takes the draft and the attached documents for forwarding and collection. When the draft is paid, the bank is reimbursed.

Several provisions in Article 2 authorize the procedures just outlined. Section 2–310(b) provides that in cash transactions, "if the seller is authorized to send the goods he may ship them under reservation, and may tender the documents of title, but the buyer may inspect the goods after their arrival before payment is due unless such inspection is inconsistent with the terms of the contract (Section 2–513). . . ."

Section 2–505 is titled "Seller's Shipment Under Reservation," but the text of that section does not define "under reservation." Rather, it says that (1) procurement of a negotiable bill of lading by the seller reserves a security interest in him in the goods and (2) procurement of a non-negotiable bill of lading to himself or his nominee (other than the buyer) reserves possession of the goods as security. " 'Security interest' means an interest in personal property or fixtures which secures payment or performance of an obligation." 1–201(b)(35).

The idea is that under the methods of shipment described above and referred to in 2–505, the buyer cannot get possession of the goods before paying and that, therefore, the seller has a security interest in the goods to secure payment of the price. Unlike the remedy of the typical creditor with a security interest, however, the seller's remedy if the buyer doesn't pay is to refuse to deliver the goods and sue the buyer for breach of contract. See 2–507 and 9–110.

Sometimes a sales contract provides that the buyer will pay "C.O.D." or "against documents." This is almost, but not quite, the same as a cash sale so far as documentary transactions go. In a cash sale the buyer is entitled to inspect the goods before payment even if the seller is entitled to ship under reservation. In the case of a C.O.D. or "against documents" transaction, the buyer has agreed to pay when the documents are exhibited, and, therefore, the buyer does not have a right to inspect the goods before paying for them. (2–513) Generally, the documents will arrive some time before the goods themselves. In the documentary cash-sale transaction, the right of inspection means that the buyer does not have to pay until the goods arrive. In an against-documents transaction, however, the buyer is obligated to pay when the documents arrive.

Sometimes sellers use a draft with attached bill of lading in credit transactions. When this is done, the draft will not be a sight draft, but will be drawn payable on some future date, either a future calendar date or a specified period after sight. This draft often is called a "time draft."

When the time draft and attached documents arrive at a bank in the buyer's city, the buyer is asked to accept the draft, and when the buyer does so (by signing the front of it, thereby "accepting" the draft) the bank surrenders the documents to the buyer. By accepting the draft, the buyer agrees to pay it according to its terms. The use of drafts in this context occurs because banks or other credit extenders may be somewhat more willing to lend on the security of an accepted draft than on the security of an open account.

D. LETTERS OF CREDIT

Particularly in international transactions, but in domestic transactions as well, sellers may decline to sell unless they have the promise of a bank to pay the price of the goods when the bank receives documents that indicate that conforming goods have been shipped. Banks provide this service through the issuance of documentary letters of credit.

A documentary letter of credit is a bank's promise to accept drafts or pay money provided there is a presentment to it of whatever documents (e.g., bill of lading, invoice, etc.) are described in the letter. In almost all cases it is written by a bank at the request of the buyer. It is directed to the seller, and it enables the seller to rely on the credit of the bank in addition to the credit of the buyer. In banking parlance the buyer is the "customer" or the "applicant," the bank promising to honor drafts is the "issuer," and the seller is the "beneficiary." The issuing bank will sometimes notify the beneficiary directly that a credit has been opened, but, if the letter is directed to a beneficiary in another country, normally the issuer will call upon a related bank in the beneficiary's country (the correspondent bank) to notify the beneficiary. The notification form is the "letter of credit," and the correspondent bank is the "notifying" or "advising" bank. Frequently the correspondent bank will be asked to "confirm" the credit. When a credit is confirmed, the correspondent bank is the "confirming bank" and its confirmation renders it liable to honor drafts drawn by the beneficiary. Under a confirmed letter of credit, the beneficiary has the right to be paid by either the issuer or the confirming bank. If the confirming bank pays under the letter of credit, it has a right of reimbursement against the issuing bank.

The advantages of letter-of-credit financing are considerable to both buyer and seller. The buyer benefits from the fact that the device is inexpensive and efficient and from the fact that the buyer is dealing with a local (issuing) bank that knows and trusts the buyer (because typically it is a bank with which the buyer regularly does business).

Frequently, the issuing bank does not demand immediate reimbursement for payments made under the credit, but rather extends the buyer credit (which may be secured by the goods covered by the documents). This leaves the buyer's working capital intact and enables the buyer to repay the issuer out of the proceeds derived from the sale of the goods. The requirement that the seller deliver specified documents before receiving payment greatly reduces the risk to the buyer, because the documents assure the buyer that the goods have been shipped and apparently conform to the contract.

The seller likewise benefits from the use of the letter of credit. Most importantly, it greatly reduces the risk of non-payment, for the seller has the promise of one or more banks, not just the promise of the buyer. In addition, a draft backed by a letter of credit is readily discountable, which means that the seller easily is able to obtain payment immediately upon shipment of the goods. Finally, banks have developed methods that permit the beneficiary to transfer the benefits of a letter of credit, and this enables the seller to use the device to finance the production of the goods.

Two legal and economic facts dominate letter-of-credit financing. The first is that the banks that issue, advise, or confirm letters of credit are financial institutions and not merchants. They deal in documents and not in merchandise. The bank's liability to the beneficiary is a direct liability, and the bank is not an agent for the customer in any regard. The matter can be summed up by stating that the letter of credit is a contract independent of the sales contract between the buyer and seller. If the terms of the letter of credit are satisfied, the issuing bank is liable to the beneficiary, notwithstanding that the seller may have breached the underlying sales contract by shipping defective goods. Conversely, nonperformance by the buyer, caused by insolvency or otherwise, does not excuse the issuer or confirming bank from performing the letter of credit contract.

Banks are isolated from the underlying sales contract for the very convincing reason that their function is only to finance the sale and not to otherwise participate in it. Therefore, letters of credit can be written inexpensively. This is the second fundamental fact of letter-of-credit financing. The inexpensiveness of the letter of credit is largely because banks are not called upon to assume any risks with respect to the performance of the sales contract. This permits them to do letter-of-credit business in a standardized, streamlined manner, for their undertaking requires only the receipt, examination, and payment against documents.

The efficiency of the work of the banks with respect to letters of credit would not be possible without universally accepted rules. As put by a leading bank lawyer:

> It is apparent that the business (letter of credit) can only be done if the letter of credit device is standardized, streamlined and made as mechanical as possible. The letter of credit, as presently conceived and used, is not a substitute for the sales contract, nor for an insurance policy, nor for the precautions which a prudent and experienced merchant ought to take. It is plain cheap food, and not a miracle drug. In concept, it could be

made to be a luxury article, but in practice it is a mass production article, and unless it is to be priced out of existence, it must be a mass produced article. Mass production articles need simple, standard parts with very few trimmings. So the vital and vigorous commercial letter of credit business requires simple, standard, easily applicable rules which are internationally understood and accepted.

These rules do exist, but not as rules of law. Most of the commercial nations of the world have accepted a tabulation of customs and practices in the letter-of-credit field which has been compiled by the International Chamber of Commerce. This comprehensive tabulation is called the "Uniform Customs and Practice for Commercial Documentary Credits." American bankers adopted these rules in 1938. The latest revision, known as the UCP 600, became effective in 2007. International Chamber of Commerce Publication No. 600. The UCP 600 has not been adopted by treaty or by local legislation. Nevertheless, it represents a successful effort by bankers to govern themselves and the international field by consensual regulation. As for statutory regulation, UCC Article 5 states the fundamental theories underlying letters of credit, but does not provide comprehensive regulation.

Courtaulds North America, Inc. v. North Carolina National Bank

United States Court of Appeals, Fourth Circuit, 1975.
528 F.2d 802.

■ BRYAN, SENIOR CIRCUIT JUDGE. A letter of credit with the date of March 21, 1973 was issued by the North Carolina National Bank at the request of and for the account of its customer, Adastra Knitting Mills, Inc. It made available upon the drafts of Courtaulds North America, Inc. "up to" $135,000 (later increased by $135,000) at "60 days date" to cover Adastra's purchases of acrylic yarn from Courtaulds. The life of the credit was extended in June to allow the drafts to be "drawn and negotiated on or before August 15, 1973."

Bank refused to honor a draft for $67,346.77 dated August 13, 1973 for yarn sold and delivered to Adastra. Courtaulds brought this action to recover this sum from Bank.

The defendant denied liability chiefly on the assertion that the draft did not agree with the letter's conditions, viz., that the draft be accompanied by a "Commercial invoice in triplicate stating [inter alia] that it covers * * * 100% acrylic yarn"; instead, the accompanying invoices stated that the goods were "Imported Acrylic Yarn."

Upon cross motions for summary judgment on affidavits and a stipulation of facts, the District Court held defendant Bank liable to

Courtaulds for the amount of the draft, interest and costs. It concluded that the draft complied with the letter of credit when each invoice is read together with the packing lists stapled to it, for the lists stated on their faces: "Cartons marked:—100% Acrylic." After considering the insistent rigidity of the law and usage of bank credits and acceptances, we must differ with the District Judge and uphold Bank's position.

The letter of credit prescribed the terms of the drafts as follows:

"Drafts to be dated same as Bills of Lading. Draft(s) to be accompanied by:

"1. Commercial invoice in triplicate stating that it covers 100,000 lbs. 100% Acrylic Yarn, Package Dyed at $1.35 per lb., FOB Buyers Plant, Greensboro, North Carolina Land Duty Paid.

"2. Certificate stating goods will be delivered to buyers plant land duty paid.

"3. Inland Bill of Lading consigned to Adastra Knitting Mills, Inc. evidencing shipment from East Coast Port to Adastra Knitting Mills, Inc., Greensboro, North Carolina."

The shipment (the last) with which this case is concerned was made on or about August 8, 1973. On direction of Courtaulds, bills of lading of that date were prepared for the consignment to Adastra from a bonded warehouse by motor carrier. The yarn was packaged in cartons and a packing list referring to its bill of lading accompanied each carton. After the yarn was delivered to the carrier, each bill of lading with the packing list was sent to Courtaulds. There invoices for the sales were made out, and the invoices and packing lists stapled together. At the same time, Courtaulds wrote up the certificate, credit memorandum and draft called for in the letter of credit. The draft was dated August 13, 1973 and drawn on Bank by Courtaulds payable to itself.

All of these documents—the draft, the invoices and the packing lists—were sent by Courtaulds to its correspondent in Mobile for presentation to Bank and collection of the draft which for the purpose had been endorsed to the correspondent.

This was the procedure pursued on each of the prior drafts and always the draft had been honored by Bank save in the present instance. Here the draft, endorsed to Bank, and the other papers were sent to Bank on August 14. Bank received them on Thursday, August 16. Upon processing, Bank found these discrepancies between the drafts with accompanying documents and the letter of credit: (1) that the invoice did not state "100% Acrylic Yarn" but described it as "Imported Acrylic Yarn," and (2) "Draft not drawn as per terms of [letter of credit], Date [August 13] not same as Bill of Lading [August 8] and not drawn 60 days after date" [but 60 days from Bill of Lading date 8/8/73]. Finding of Fact 24. Since decision of this controversy is put on the first discrepancy we do not discuss the others.

On Monday, August 20, Bank called Adastra and asked if it would waive the discrepancies and thus allow Bank to honor the draft. In response, the president of Adastra informed Bank that it could not waive any discrepancies because a trustee in bankruptcy had been appointed for Adastra and Adastra could not do so alone. Upon word of these circumstances, Courtaulds on August 27 sent amended invoices to Bank which were received by Bank on August 27. They referred to the consignment as "100% Acrylic Yarn," and thus would have conformed to the letter of credit had it not expired. On August 29 Bank wired Courtaulds that the draft remained unaccepted because of the expiration of the letter of credit on August 15. Consequently the draft with all the original documents was returned by Bank.

During the life of the letter of credit some drafts had not been of even dates with the bills of lading, and among the large number of invoices transmitted during this period, several did not describe the goods as "100% Acrylic Yarn." As to all of these deficiencies Bank called Adastra for and received approval before paying the drafts. Every draft save the one in suit was accepted.

CONCLUSION OF LAW

The factual outline related is not in dispute, and the issue becomes one of law. It is well phrased by the District Judge in his "Discussion" in this way:

> "The only issue presented by the facts of this case is whether the documents tendered by the beneficiary to the issuer were in conformity with the terms of the letter of credit."

The letter of credit provided:

> "Except as otherwise expressly stated herein, this credit is subject to the 'Uniform Customs and Practice for Documentary Credits (1962 revision), the International Chamber of Commerce, Brochure No. 222.' " Finding of Fact 6.

Of particular pertinence, with accents added, are these injunctions of the Uniform Customs:

> "*Article 7.* Banks must examine all documents with reasonable care to ascertain that they *appear on their face* to be in accordance with the terms and conditions of the credit.

> "*Article 8.* In documentary credit operations all parties concerned deal in documents and not in goods.

* * *

> "If, upon receipt of the documents, the issuing bank considers that they *appear on their face* not to be in accordance with the terms and conditions of the credit, that bank must determine, on the basis of the documents alone, whether to claim that payment, acceptance or negotiation was not effected in accordance with the terms and conditions of the credit.

* * *

"*Article 9.* Banks * * * do [not] assume any liability or responsibility *for the description,* * * * quality, * * * of the goods represented thereby * * *.

* * *

"The description of the goods in the commercial *invoice* must correspond with the description in the credit. *In the remaining documents the goods may be described in general terms.*"

Also to be looked to are the North Carolina statutes, because in a diversity action, the Federal courts apply the same law as would the courts of the State of adjudication. Here applicable would be the Uniform Commercial Code—Letters of Credit, Chap. 25 G.S.N.C. Especially to be noticed are these sections:

"§ 25–5–109. Issuer's obligation to its customer."

"(1) An issuer's obligation to its customer includes good faith and observance of any general banking usage but unless otherwise agreed does not include liability or responsibility

"(a) for performance of the underlying contract for sale or other transaction between the customer and the beneficiary; or

* * *

"(c) based on knowledge or lack of knowledge of any usage of any particular trade.

"(2) An issuer must examine documents with care so as to ascertain that on their face they appear to comply with the terms of the credit but unless otherwise agreed assumes no liability or responsibility for the genuineness, falsification or effect of any document which appears on such examination to be regular on its face."

In utilizing the rules of construction embodied in the letter of credit—the Uniform Customs and State statute—one must constantly recall that the drawee bank is not to be embroiled in disputes between the buyer and the seller, the beneficiary of the credit. The drawee is involved only with documents, not with merchandise. Its involvement is altogether separate and apart from the transaction between the buyer and seller; its duties and liability are governed exclusively by the terms of the letter, not the terms of the parties' contract with each other. Moreover, as the predominant authorities unequivocally declare, the beneficiary must meet the terms of the credit—and precisely—if it is to exact performance of the issuer. Failing such compliance there can be no recovery from the drawee. That is the specific failure of Courtaulds here.

Free of ineptness in wording, the letter of credit dictated that each invoice express on its face that it covered 100% acrylic yarn. Nothing less is shown to be tolerated in the trade. No substitution and no equivalent, through interpretation or logic, will serve. Harfield, Bank Credits and Acceptances (5th Ed.1974), at p. 73, commends and quotes aptly from an English case: "There is no room for documents which are almost the same, or which will do just as well." Equitable Trust Co. of N.Y. v. Dawson Partners, Ltd., 27 Lloyd's List Law Rpts. 49, 52 (1926). Although no pertinent North Carolina decision has been laid before us, in many cases elsewhere, especially in New York, we find the tenet of Harfield to be unshaken.

At trial Courtaulds prevailed on the contention that the invoices in actuality met the specifications of the letter of credit in that the packing lists attached to the invoices disclosed on their faces that the packages contained "cartons marked:—100% acrylic." On this premise it was urged that the lists were a part of the invoice since they were appended to it, and the invoices should be read as one with the lists, allowing the lists to detail the invoices. But this argument cannot be accepted. In this connection it is well to revert to the distinction made in *Uniform Customs,* supra, between the "invoice" and the "remaining documents," emphasizing that in the latter the description may be in general terms while in the invoice the goods must be described in conformity with the credit letter.

The District Judge's pat statement adeptly puts an end to this contention of Courtaulds:

> "In dealing with letters of credit, it is a custom and practice of the banking trade for a bank to only treat a document as an invoice which clearly is marked on its face as 'invoice.' " Finding of Fact 46.

This is not a pharisaical or doctrinaire persistence in the principle, but is altogether realistic in the environs of this case; it is plainly the fair and equitable measure. (The defect in description was not superficial but occurred in the statement of the *quality* of the yarn, not a frivolous concern.) The obligation of the drawee bank was graven in the credit. Indeed, there could be no departure from its words. Bank was not expected to scrutinize the collateral papers, such as the packing lists. Nor was it permitted to read into the instrument the contemplation or intention of the seller and buyer. Adherence to this rule was not only legally commanded, but it was factually ordered also, as will immediately appear.

Had Bank deviated from the stipulation of the letter and honored the draft, then at once it might have been confronted with the not improbable risk of the bankruptcy trustee's charge of liability for unwarrantably paying the draft moneys to the seller, Courtaulds, and refusal to reimburse Bank for the outlay. Contrarily, it might face a Courtaulds claim that since it had depended upon Bank's assurance of credit in shipping yarn to Adastra, Bank was responsible for the loss. In this situation Bank cannot be condemned for sticking to the letter of the letter.

Nor is this conclusion affected by the amended or substituted invoices which Courtaulds sent to Bank after the refusal of the draft. No precedent is cited to justify retroactive amendment of the invoices or extension of the credit beyond the August 15 expiry of the letter.

Finally, the trial court found that although in its prior practices Bank had pursued a strict-constructionist attitude, it had nevertheless on occasion honored drafts not within the verbatim terms of the credit letter. But it also found that in each of these instances Bank had first procured the authorization of Adastra to overlook the deficiencies. This truth is verified by the District Court in its Findings of Fact:

> "42.   It is a standard practice and procedure of the banking industry and trade for a bank to attempt to obtain a waiver of discrepancies from its customer in a letter of credit transaction. This custom and practice was followed by NCNB in connection with the draft and documents received from Courtaulds.

> "43.   Following this practice, NCNB had checked all previous discrepancies it discovered in Courtaulds' documents with its customer Adastra to see if Adastra would waive those discrepancies noted by NCNB. Except for the transaction in question, Adastra waived all discrepancies noted by NCNB.

> "44.   It is not normal or customary for NCNB, nor is it the custom and practice in the banking trade, for a bank to notify a beneficiary or the presenter of the documents that there were any deficiencies in the draft or documents if they are waived by the customer."

This endeavor had been fruitless on the last draft because of the inability of Adastra to give its consent. Obviously the previous acceptances of truant invoices cannot be construed as a waiver in the present incident.

For these reasons, we must vacate the decision of the trial court, despite the evident close reasoning and research of the District Judge, Courtaulds North America, Inc. v. North Carolina N.B., 387 F.Supp. 92 (M.D.N.C.1975). Entry of judgment in favor of the appellant Bank on its summary motion is necessary.

Reversed and remanded for final judgment.

QUESTIONS AND NOTES

1.   **Problem.** AmericasBank issued a letter of credit that specified, among other things, that the beneficiary present an invoice and a draft that refers to "Credit #53753." In due course the beneficiary presented an invoice, a draft that did not refer to any particular credit, and a letter that specifically stated that the draft was being presented in connection with "Credit 53753." Is AmericasBank obligated to honor the letter of credit?

2. Article 5 was revised in 1995, and the revision has been adopted in every jurisdiction. The rule that formerly appeared in 5–109 has been reworded and now appears in 5–108(a), (f).

United Bank Ltd. v. Cambridge Sporting Goods Corp.

New York Court of Appeals, 1976.
41 N.Y.2d 254, 392 N.Y.S.2d 265, 360 N.E.2d 943.

■ GABRIELLI, JUSTICE. On this appeal, we must decide whether fraud on the part of a seller-beneficiary of an irrevocable letter of credit may be successfully asserted as a defense against holders of drafts drawn by the seller pursuant to the credit. If we conclude that this defense may be interposed by the buyer who procured the letter of credit, we must also determine whether the courts below improperly imposed upon appellant buyer the burden of proving that respondent banks to whom the drafts were made payable by the seller-beneficiary of the letter of credit, were not holders in due course. The issues presented raise important questions concerning the application of the law of letters of credit and the rules governing proof of holder in due course status set forth in Article 3 of the Uniform Commercial Code. . . .

In April 1971 appellant Cambridge Sporting Goods Corporation (Cambridge) entered into a contract for the manufacture and sale of boxing gloves with Duke Sports (Duke), a Pakistani corporation. Duke committed itself to the manufacture of 27,936 pairs of boxing gloves at a sale price of $42,576.80; and arranged with its Pakistani bankers, United Bank Limited (United) and The Muslim Commercial Bank (Muslim), for the financing of the sale. Cambridge was requested by these banks to cover payment of the purchase price by opening an irrevocable letter of credit with its bank in New York, Manufacturers Hanover Trust Company (Manufacturers). Manufacturers issued an irrevocable letter of credit obligating it, upon the receipt of certain documents indicating shipment of the merchandise pursuant to the contract, to accept and pay, 90 days after acceptance, drafts drawn upon Manufacturers for the purchase price of the gloves.

Following confirmation of the opening of the letter of credit, Duke informed Cambridge that it would be impossible to manufacture and deliver the merchandise within the time period required by the contract, and sought an extension of time for performance until September 15, 1971, and a continuation of the letter of credit, which was due to expire on August 11. Cambridge replied on June 18 that it would not agree to a postponement of the manufacture and delivery of the gloves because of its resale commitments and, hence, it promptly advised Duke that the contract was canceled and the letter of credit should be returned. Cambridge simultaneously notified United of the contract cancellation.

Despite the cancellation of the contract, Cambridge was informed on July 17, 1971, that documents had been received at Manufacturers from United purporting to evidence a shipment of the boxing gloves under the terms of the canceled contract. The documents were accompanied by a draft, dated July 16, 1971, drawn by Duke upon Manufacturers and made payable to United, for the amount of $21,288.40, one half of the contract price of the boxing gloves. A second set of documents was received by Manufacturers from Muslim, also accompanied by a draft, dated August 20, and drawn upon Manufacturers by Duke for the remaining amount of the contract price.

An inspection of the shipments upon their arrival revealed that Duke had shipped old, unpadded, ripped and mildewed gloves rather than the new gloves to be manufactured as agreed upon. Cambridge then commenced an action against Duke in Supreme Court, New York County, joining Manufacturers as a party, and obtained a preliminary injunction prohibiting the latter from paying drafts drawn under the letter of credit. . . . Duke ultimately defaulted in the action and judgment against it was entered in the amount of the drafts, in March 1972. The present proceeding was instituted by the Pakistani banks . . . to obtain payment of the drafts on the letter of credit. The banks asserted that they were holders in due course of the drafts which had been made payable to them by Duke and, thus, were entitled to the proceeds thereof irrespective of any defenses which Cambridge had established against their transferor, Duke, in the prior action which had terminated in a default judgment. . . .

The trial court concluded that the burden of proving that the banks were not holders in due course lay with Cambridge, and directed a verdict in favor of the banks on the ground that Cambridge had not met that burden; the court stated that Cambridge failed to demonstrate that the banks themselves had participated in the seller's acts of fraud, proof of which was concededly present in the record. The Appellate Division affirmed, agreeing that while there was proof tending to establish the defenses against the seller, Cambridge had not shown that the seller's acts were "connected to the petitioners [banks] in any manner." . . .

We reverse and hold that it was improper to direct a verdict in favor of the petitioning Pakistani banks. We conclude that the defense of fraud in the transaction was established and in that circumstance the burden shifted to petitioners to prove that they were holders in due course and took the drafts for value, in good faith and without notice of any fraud on the part of Duke (§ 3–302). . . . This case does not come before us in the typical posture of a lawsuit between the bank issuing the letter of credit and presenters of drafts drawn under the credit seeking payment (see, generally, White and Summers, Uniform Commercial Code, § 18–6, pp. 619–628). Because Cambridge obtained an injunction against payment of the drafts, . . . it stands in the same position as the issuer, and, thus, the law of letters of credit governs the liability of Cambridge to the Pakistani banks. Article 5 of the Uniform Commercial Code, dealing with letters of credit, and the Uniform Customs and Practice for Documentary Credits promulgated by the International Chamber of Commerce set forth the duties and obligations of the issuer of a letter of credit.[2] A letter of credit is a commitment on the part of the issuing bank that it will pay a draft presented to it under the terms of the credit, and if it is a documentary draft, upon presentation of the required documents of title (see § 5–103). Banks issuing letters of credit deal in documents and not in goods and are not responsible for any breach of warranty or nonconformity of the goods involved in the underlying sales contract (see § 5–114, subd. [1]; Uniform Customs and Practice, General Provisions and Definitions [c] and article 9. . . . Subdivision (2) of section 5–114, however indicates certain limited circumstances in which an issuer *may* properly refuse to honor a draft drawn under a letter of credit or a customer may enjoin an issuer from honoring such a draft.[3] Thus, where "fraud in the transaction" has been shown and the holder has not taken the draft in circumstances that would make it a holder in due course, the customer may apply to enjoin the issuer from paying drafts drawn under the letter of credit (see 1955 Report of N.Y.Law Rev.Comm., vol. 3, pp. 1654–1559). This rule represents a codification of precode case law most eminently articulated in the landmark case of Sztejn v. Schroder Banking Corp., 177 Misc. 719, 31 N.Y.S.2d 631, Shientag, J., where it

---

[2] It should be noted that the Uniform Customs and Practice controls, in lieu of Article 5 of the Code, where, unless otherwise agreed by the parties, a letter of credit is made subject to the provisions of the Uniform Customs and Practice by its terms or by agreement, course of dealing or usage of trade (§ 5–102, subd. [4]). No proof was offered that there was an agreement that the Uniform Customs and Practice should apply, nor does the credit so state (cf. Oriental Pacific [U.S.A.] v. Toronto Dominion Bank, 78 Misc.2d 819, 357 N.Y.S.2d 957). Neither do the parties otherwise contend that their rights should be resolved under the Uniform Customs and Practice. However, even if the Uniform Customs and Practice were deemed applicable to this case, it would not, in the absence of a conflict, abrogate the precode case law (now codified in § 5–114) and that authority continues to govern even where Article 5 is not controlling (see White and Summers, op. cit., pp. 613–614, 624–625). Moreover, the Uniform Customs and Practice provisions are not in conflict nor do they treat with the subject matter of section 5–114 which is dispositive of the issues presented on this appeal (see Banco Tornquist, S.A. v. American Bank & Trust Co., 71 Misc.2d 874, 875, 337 N.Y.S.2d 489; Intraworld Ind. v. Girard Trust Bank, 461 Pa. 343, 336 A.2d 316, 322; Harfield, Practice Commentary, McKinney's Cons. Laws of N.Y., Book 62½, Uniform Commercial Code, § 5–114, p. 686). Thus, we are of the opinion that the Uniform Customs and Practice, where applicable, does not bar the relief provided for in section 5–114 of the code.

[Eds. Note: 5–102(4), adopted in New York, Alabama, and Missouri, reads as follows:

"(4)   Unless otherwise agreed, this Article 5 does not apply to a letter of credit or a credit if by its terms or by agreement, course of dealing or usage of trade such letter of credit or credit is subject in whole or in part to the Uniform Customs and Practice for Commercial Documentary Credits fixed by the Thirteenth or by any subsequent Congress of the International Chamber of Commerce."]

[3] Subdivision (2) of section 5–114 of the Uniform Commercial Code provides that,

"[u]nless otherwise agreed when documents appear on their face to comply with the terms of a credit but * * * there is fraud in the transaction

(a) the issuer must honor the draft or demand for payment if honor is demanded by a * * * holder of the draft * * * which has taken the draft * * * under the credit and under circumstances which would make it a holder in due course (Section 3–302) * * *; and

(b) in all other cases as against its customer, an issuer acting in good faith may honor the draft * * * despite notification from the customer of fraud, forgery or other defect not apparent on the face of the documents but a court of appropriate jurisdiction may enjoin such honor."

was held that the shipment of cowhair in place of bristles amounted to more than mere breach of warranty but fraud sufficient to constitute grounds for enjoining payment of drafts to one not a holder in due course. Even prior to the *Sztejn* case, forged or fraudulently procured documents were proper grounds for avoidance of payment of drafts drawn under a letter of credit (Finkelstein, Legal Aspects of Commercial Letters of Credit, pp. 231–236–247); and cases decided after the enactment of the code have cited *Sztejn* with approval. . . .

. . . The evidentiary facts are not disputed and we hold upon the facts as established, that the shipment of old, unpadded, ripped and mildewed gloves rather than the new boxing gloves as ordered by Cambridge, constituted fraud in the transaction within the meaning of subdivision (2) of section 5–114. It should be noted that the drafters of section 5–114, in their attempt to codify the *Sztejn* case and in utilizing the term "fraud in the transaction," have eschewed a dogmatic approach and adopted a flexible standard to be applied as the circumstances of a particular situation mandate. It can be difficult to draw a precise line between cases involving breach of warranty (or a difference of opinion as to the quality of goods) and outright fraudulent practice on the part of the seller. To the extent, however, that Cambridge established that Duke was guilty of *fraud* in shipping, not merely nonconforming merchandise, but worthless fragments of boxing gloves, this case is similar to *Sztejn*.

If the petitioning banks are holders in due course they are entitled to recover the proceeds of the drafts but if such status cannot be demonstrated their petition must fail. . . .

In order to qualify as a holder in due course, a holder must have taken the instrument "without notice * * * of any defense against * * * it on the part of any person" (§ 3–302, subd. [1], par. [c]). Pursuant to subdivision (2) of section 5–114 fraud in the transaction is a valid defense to payment of drafts drawn under a letter of credit. Since the defense of fraud in the transaction was shown, the burden shifted to the banks by operation of subdivision (3) of section 3–307 to prove that they were holders in due course and took the drafts without notice of Duke's alleged fraud. . . . It was error for the trial court to direct a verdict in favor of the Pakistani banks because this determination rested upon a misallocation of the burden of proof; and we conclude that the banks have not satisfied the burden of proving that they qualified in all respects as holders in due course, by any affirmative proof. . . .

Accordingly, the order of the Appellate Division should be reversed, with costs, and the petition dismissed.

NOTE

The rule that formerly appeared in 5–114 (see footnote 3 of *Cambridge Sporting Goods*) has been modified and now appears in 5–109.

INDEX

References are to Pages